PRINCIPLES AND PRACTICE OF SEX THERAPY

Third Edition

PRINCIPLES AND PRACTICE OF SEX THERAPY

Third Edition

Edited by

SANDRA R. LEIBLUM
RAYMOND C. ROSEN

THE GUILFORD PRESS
New York   London

© 2000 The Guilford Press
A Division of Guilford Publications, Inc.
72 Spring Street, New York, NY 10012
www.guilford.com

Printed in the United States of America

This book is printed on acid-free paper.

Last digit is print number: 9   8   7   6   5   4   3   2   1

Library of Congress Cataloging-in-Publication Data

Principles and practice of sex therapy / edited by Sandra R. Leiblum and Raymond C.
Rosen.—3rd ed.
     p. cm.
  Includes bibliographical references and index.
  ISBN 1-57230-574-6 (hardcover)
  1. Sex therapy. I. Leiblum, Sandra Risa. II. Rosen, Raymond, 1946–

RC557.P75 2000
616.85′8306-dc21
                                                                00-039302

To Frank and Jake,
the two men I love most in the world
—S. R. L.

To my wife, Linda,
for your generous support through all the years
—R. C. R.

About the Editors

Sandra R. Leiblum, PhD, is Professor of Psychiatry and Obstetrics/Gynecology and Director of the Center for Sexual and Marital Health at the University of Medicine and Dentistry–Robert Wood Johnson Medical School. A leading authority in sex therapy, she has edited or coedited eight books, including the first two editions of *Principles and Practice of Sex Therapy, Sexual Desire Disorders, Erectile Disorders: Assessment and Treatment,* and *Case Studies in Sex Therapy,* as well as over 70 clinical and research articles. In addition to her expertise in sex therapy, she is an authority on the psychological issues associated with infertility and the new assisted-reproduction options. She recently edited *Infertility: Psychological Issues and Counseling Strategies* and is currently working on a book that will provide a timely and thorough overview of the forces shaping female sexuality as well as the newest options for enhancing female sexual response. She is also the North American editor of *Sexual and Relationship Health.*

A past president of the Society of Sex Therapy and Research, Dr. Leiblum is also a fellow of the Society for the Scientific Study of Sex and a member of the "blue ribbon" committee of the American Association for Sex Therapy, Research and Education. In recent years, she has received awards and acknowledgments for excellence in teaching.

Raymond C. Rosen, PhD, is Professor of Psychiatry and Medicine and Director of the Sexual Pharmacology Unit at the University of Medicine and Dentistry–Robert Wood Johnson Medical School. He is also Adjunct Professor of Psychology at the Graduate School of Applied and Professional Psychology, Rutgers University. Dr. Rosen is past president of the International Academy of Sex Research and editor of the *Annual Review of Sex Research.* He has been a major contributor to the research and literature on sexual dysfunction in the past 20 years, as consultant and advisor to the Food and Drug Administration and the pharmaceutical industry in the clinical trials of sildenafil and other new pro-sexual agents, as coauthor (with J. Gayle Beck) of *Patterns of Sexual Arousal: Psychophysiological Processes and Clinical Applications,* and as co-editor (with Sandra R. Leiblum) of *Case Studies in Sex Therapy, Sexual Desire Disorders, Erectile Disorders: Assessment and Treatment,* and the first two editions of *Principles and Practice of Sex Therapy.* He has also published more than 100 articles and book chapters on various aspects of sexuality and sexual dysfunction.

Contributors

Stanley E. Althof, PhD, Department of Psychology, Case Western Reserve University School of Medicine, Cleveland, Ohio; Center for Marital and Sexual Health, Cleveland, Ohio

Bernard Apfelbaum, PhD, Berkeley Sex Therapy Group, Berkeley, California

Barbara Bartlik, MD, Departments of Psychiatry and Obstetrics and Gynecology, Weill Medical College, Cornell University, New York, New York

Sophie Bergeron, PhD, Department of Sexology, University of Quebec, Montreal, Quebec, Canada

Yitzchak M. Binik, PhD, Department of Psychology, McGill University, Montreal, Quebec, Canada; Sex and Couple Therapy Service, Royal Victoria Hospital, Montreal, Quebec, Canada

Richard A. Carroll, PhD, Department of Psychiatry and Behavioral Sciences, Northwestern University Medical School, Center for Sexual Health, Chicago, Illinois

James Goldberg, PhD, Bari/Goldberg Clinic, San Diego, California

Julia R. Heiman, PhD, Department of Psychiatry and Behavioral Sciences, School of Medicine, University of Washington, Seattle, Washington

Martin P. Kafka, MD, Department of Psychiatry, Harvard Medical School and McLean Hospital, Belmont, Massachusetts

Samir Khalifé, MD, Department of Obstetrics and Gynecology, Faculty of Medicine, McGill University, Montreal, Quebec, Canada

Sandra R. Leiblum, PhD, Departments of Psychiatry and Obstetrics/
Gynecology and Center for Sexual and Marital Health, University of
Medicine and Dentistry–Robert Wood Johnson Medical School,
Piscataway, New Jersey

Joseph LoPiccolo, PhD, Department of Psychology, University of Missouri–
Columbia, Columbia, Missouri

Margaret Nichols, PhD, Institute for Personal Growth/Institute for
Behavioral Solutions, Highland Park and Jersey City, New Jersey

Derek C. Polonsky, MD, Department of Psychiatry, Harvard Medical
School, Boston, Massachusetts

Cathryn G. Pridal, PhD, Department of Psychology, Westminster College,
Fulton, Missouri

Raymond C. Rosen, PhD, Department of Psychiatry and Sexual
Pharmacology Unit, University of Medicine and Dentistry–Robert Wood
Johnson Medical School, Piscataway, New Jersey

David Schnarch, PhD, Marriage and Family Health Center, Evergreen,
Colorado

Leslie R. Schover, PhD, Department of Behavioral Science, University of
Texas, M. D. Anderson Cancer Center, Houston, Texas

R. Taylor Segraves, MD, PhD, Department of Psychiatry, Case Western
Reserve University, Cleveland, Ohio; Department of Psychiatry, MetroHealth
Medical Center, Cleveland, Ohio

John P. Wincze, PhD, Department of Psychology and Psychiatry, Brown
University, Providence, Rhode Island

Preface

It has been more than a decade since the publication of the second edition of *Principles and Practice of Sex Therapy*. Since then, major changes have taken place in our understanding of the physiology of sexual response and the management of sexual problems. New treatment options are now available, particularly in the area of oral pharmacological agents such as Viagra (sildenafil) and Uprima (apomorphine). These new drugs have dramatically altered the way in which sexual problems are viewed by both practitioners and the public at large. The advent of new pharmacological treatments has also posed major challenges for the field of sex therapy, which is rapidly evolving in response to these developments. This third edition of our text is intended to reflect the evolution of sex therapy in response to recent medical and societal changes.

In many respects, the introduction of new pharmacological agents has been a positive development for the sex therapy field. It has launched a new wave of interest in male and female sexuality and has stimulated research into both basic and applied aspects. Significant support for research has been made available by the infusion of new pharmaceutical funding. The public has also been alerted that sexual problems continue to take their toll, despite the facade of sexual permissiveness in our society. However, certain negative trends are also apparent. For example, practitioners with little training or sophistication have capitalized on the increasing demand by opening "sexual medicine" clinics (or even websites) for widespread distribution of drugs or other forms of treatment for male sexual dysfunction. Many of these new "sexual medicine" practitioners are champing at the bit to offer similar "quick fixes" for female sexual dysfunction. This trend, along with the lack of adequate reimbursement for psychological services, has led to a "dumbing down" of sex therapy in many quarters. It has also fostered the increasing medicalization of sexuality, in particular, the belief that a simple pill or salve can resolve complex interpersonal problems.

In part, our concerns about the changes in the culture surrounding sexual problems motivated our decision to edit and update this third edition. We are concerned that naive clinicians may believe that sex therapy is a simple and straightforward specialty, requiring only permission and pills for quick success. We are also distressed by the overemphasis on sexual performance, as opposed to sexual intimacy and pleasure. We are concerned that patients may come to believe that there is just one "right" way to enjoy their sensuality, that intercourse is the necessary or only path to physical intimacy, and that pharmacology is the royal road to sexual satisfaction.

The authors who kindly accepted our invitation to contribute chapters to this edition are a remarkable group of individuals. They are highly experienced and talented clinicians who are sensitive to the many nuances of the biopsychosocial model of behavior as well as systemic therapists who appreciate that sexuality occurs in a dyadic context, each partner influencing and being influenced by the other. They are familiar with the newest developments in medical research and practice, although equally aware of potential dangers and limitations. And they are conceptually innovative. Several, in fact, have developed new ways of formulating and treating familiar problems.

While we value the contributions of our authors in earlier editions, we also wanted to provide readers with fresh perspectives and new approaches from other leading authorities in the field. We are delighted with the range and variety of contributors in this volume, who represent an impressive and highly diverse group of practitioners.

The book is significantly longer than the previous editions, which is an indication of the level of activity in the field and the expanding boundaries of sex therapy. Readers familiar with our previous editions will note that we have added new chapters on female arousal disorders, transgender issues, and nonparaphilic sexual compulsivity, as well as an additional chapter on problems of sexual desire.

Overall, we are impressed with the complexity of formulation and treatment in these chapters and by the candidness with which the authors present their cases. As the reader will note, sex therapy today is by no means a province for the unskilled or faint of heart. It requires sophistication, perseverance, and creativity. The couples and individuals we treat are often highly distressed. Many have been misled by the media about what to expect of themselves and their partners, and many have been disappointed or frustrated by ineffective solutions. Unfortunately, sex therapy is all too often the last stop on the road to separation or divorce.

We hope this edition will provide the reader with new ideas and models for assessing and treating the myriad sexual problems that confront us. Taken together, these chapters present the collective wisdom of today's innovators and "thought leaders" in the evolving sex therapy field. We have learned much in the process of editing and hope the reader will learn much as well. We would like to extend warm and heartfelt thanks to many exceptional therapists and colleagues who provided inspiration and feedback over the years: Lonnie Barbach, John Bancroft, David Bullard, Frank Brickle, Eli Coleman, Al Cooper, Marion Dunn, Irwin Goldstein, Marty Klein, Arnold Lazarus, Harold Lief,

Steve Levine, Barry McCarthy, Monica McGoldrick, Richard Milsten, Harin Padma-Nathan, Raul Schiavi, Patricia Schreiner-Engel, Julian Slowinski, Beverly Whipple, Bernie Zilbergeld, and Ken Zucker. We are indebted to our secretaries, Susan Connoly, Amy Hernandez, Christine O'Hagan, and Dorothy Sima.

Finally, we are especially grateful for the support and enthusiasm of Seymour Weingarten, Editor-in-Chief at The Guilford Press, who has provided us with unwavering encouragement and guidance for over two decades.

SANDRA R. LEIBLUM, PhD
RAYMOND C. ROSEN, PhD

Contents

IV. SPECIAL POPULATIONS

1

Introduction
Sex Therapy in the Age of Viagra

SANDRA R. LEIBLUM
RAYMOND C. ROSEN

It has been over a decade since the publication of the second edition of *Principles and Practice of Sex Therapy* and much has changed in the field of sex therapy, as well as in the societal context in which sex therapy is practiced. In many ways, the new developments are reminiscent of the early post-Masters and Johnson period of the 1970s. Sexual dysfunction and complaints about sexual performance have attained a new level of legitimacy, as more serious attention is paid to the prevalence, etiology, and treatment of sexual dysfunction in both professional and popular publications. As Senator Robert Dole talks candidly about his "ED"(erectile dysfunction) on national television, and is seen frequently in earnest advertisements encouraging men to seek treatment for this widespread "health and quality of life" problem, a new "image" for sexual dysfunction is clearly evolving. And although there is presently no female equivalent of Senator Dole setting an example for middle-age women in speaking out about *their* sexual complaints, women are sharing some of the spotlight in this post-Viagra period. It is certainly the case that women are no longer content being silent and subservient sexual partners.

Research surveys have documented the high rate of sexual problems among both women and men and have emphasized the adverse effects of sexual problems on interpersonal relationships and quality of life (Feldman, Goldstein, Hatzichritou, Krane, & McKinlay (1994); Laumann, Paik, & Rosen, 1999). These surveys underscore the need for increased clinical services and availability of practitioners comfortable and knowledgeable about sexual health and sexual therapy.

CHANGING PERSPECTIVES AND PRACTICES

While the specter of AIDS informed sexuality research and practice during the 1980s, the past decade has been dominated by the impact of the new sexual pharmacology. There has been a proliferation of clinical and research interest in drugs that stimulate desire and arousal, as well as increased interest in the potential adverse effects of drugs on the sexual response cycle in men and women. Major advances have taken place in our understanding of the basic neuroanatomy and neurochemistry of penile erection in males, and similar studies have recently been undertaken in women. Progress in sexual physiology has spurred much of the research in sexual pharmacology, which, in turn, has stimulated research in previously neglected populations, such as those with spinal cord injuries, chronic diseases (e.g., cancer and cardiovascular disease) or major surgeries (e.g., prostatectomy and hysterectomy).

The growth of clinical trials in this area has stimulated a need for more refined definitions of sexual dysfunction and better measurement instruments. Several international consensus conferences have been convened in recent years to review the current nosological and classification system (Cape Cod Conference, 1998; Process of Care Consensus Panel, 1999; Jardin et al., in press). Drawing from a wide diversity of disciplines and specialties, these conferences have fostered communication among different disciplines and have identified key areas of agreement and disagreement. For example, much debate took place at a recent International Consensus Development Conference on Female Sexual Dysfunction (Basson et al., 2000) concerning the evidence and rationale for creating a new diagnosis termed "female sexual satisfaction disorder." Despite heated arguments in favor of this proposed entity, no consensus was achieved.

Renewed debate has centered on whether sexual problems should even be considered "dysfunctions" (i.e., medical or psychiatric disorders) and included in the American Psychiatric Association's *Diagnostic and Statistical Manual of Mental Disorders* (DSM) or the World Health Organization's *International Classification of Diseases* (ICD). Tiefer (1995), for example, is an outspoken social constructionist and critic of current diagnostic practices in sex therapy. She argues that inclusion of sexual problems in the DSM "pathologizes" normal variations in sexual response and focuses on an overly narrow conception of sexuality generally. Despite the debate in academic circles, however, the public remains interested and eager for new drugs and interventions to enhance sexual performance and relationships.

Advances in sexual pharmacology have also stimulated the development of new assessment instruments that can be used to measure the effects of therapeutic interventions (e.g., the International Index of Erectile Function [IIEF]; Rosen et al., 1997; the Brief Index of Sexual Function for Women [BISF-W; Taylor, Rosen, & Leiblum, 1994; Mazur, Leiblum, & Rosen, in press]). Although much of the attention was initially directed toward perfecting instruments for assessing erectile function, more recent measures are focusing on other aspects of sexual function in both men and women, including measurements of female sexual arousal and distress (Rosen et al., 2000; Derogatis, 1998). Although developed primarily for use in clinical trials with new pharmaceutical agents, these instruments have broader potential use in clinical outcome trials of sex therapy or other nonpharmacological treatments.

Research on basic mechanisms of male and female sexual response has also been greatly stimulated by the new sexual pharmacology. In part, the presence of new sources of funding in both government and industry has served as a strong stimulus for basic science and clinical research. Although most pharmaceutical industry funding is obviously directed at the development and marketing of innovative therapeutic agents, the industry has also funded research in male and female sexual physiology, as well as sponsoring the development of new instruments and methodologies in sex research. As greater understanding of sexual physiology increases, dramatic growth in these research areas is likely.

THE VIAGRA REVOLUTION

Looking back, we can pinpoint a watershed event that marked the advent of the new era in sexual pharmacology. On March 29, 1998, sildenafil citrate (Viagra) was approved as the first orally active agent for the treatment of erectile dysfunction. The long-awaited approval of sildenafil launched a tidal wave of demand for prescriptions for this revolutionary new medication. Men with long-standing or recent-onset erectile difficulties due to a wide variety of causes hastened to have their prescriptions filled. Both married and single men of all ages (and sometimes their partners) have sought the "little blue pill" from primary care physicians, sexual medicine specialists, and urologists, as well as increasingly through "alternative channels" such as the Internet. A wave of articles appeared in popular and professional journals debating whether sildenafil and its spin-offs would sound the death knoll for sex therapy and other forms of counseling for sexual dysfunction. Would men and their partners rely on pharmacological solutions for psychosexual disorders? In fact, concerns about the professional future of sex therapy appear to be unfounded, as the limitations and drawbacks of pharmacological therapy have become increasingly evident.

As Riley (1998), and others (Lottman, Hendricks, Vruggnink, & Meuleman, 1998; Althof, Chapter 9, this volume) have noted, pharmacological or other medical treatments do not address or resolve relationship problems or intrapsychic conflicts, and these psychological factors are frequently the major source of sexual inhibition or distress. Even in cases in which sildenafil is effective in restoring erectile capacity, failure to address the relationship context in which sex occurs often stymies meaningful and satisfying sexual exchange (Leiblum, 1999). Moreover, sildenafil is not a stimulant for sexual desire, the lack of which is all too often the major barrier in sexually abstinent or unsatisfying relationships. Beginning in mid- to late 1998, therapists began seeing an increasing number of "Viagra failures," as well as partners of men who had received prescriptions for the drug but were unenthusiastic about reentering the sexual arena. In some cases, men even neglected to fill their prescription but carried the pills around as a sort of comforting talisman.

Moreover, therapists were increasingly being contacted by individuals and couples who were suddenly made aware of a new spectrum of resources and personnel for managing their sexual concerns. This trend was reinforced by the wave of workshops and training programs offered to primary care physicians for assessing and treating sexual concerns. These efforts were stimulated (and paid for) by enlightened self-interest on the part of the pharmaceutical industry, but the effect has also been to increase the flow of referrals to clinicians and therapists working from a more relational and psychological perspective. Althof in Chapter 9 describes the treatment of erectile problems from a primarily psychodynamic and interpersonal perspective.

Although early fears about the demise of sex therapy have not been realized, it is certainly the case that the practice of sex therapy has changed dramatically since the pre-Viagra era. In particular, there is a new focus on integration of medical and psychological treatments of sexual dysfunction, and on combining pharmacological with educational and counseling interventions (See Chapter 3 by Pridal and LoPiccolo, which emphasizes the use of a multielement treatment program, Chapter 11 by Polonsky who describes an integrated approach for treating premature ejaculation, and Rosen in Chapter 10 who describes the newest combined approach to treating erectile problems.) As Bancroft (1999) has observed, "we cannot expect to understand human sexuality unless we consider both biology and culture (and it is important to stress culture, not just environment) and the interface between them as it affects the individual, the dyad and the group" (p. 236).

THE CHANGING SOCIAL CLIMATE

Our social milieu has also changed greatly since the 1980s. Sex education in the schools is more widespread and increasingly recognized as a major public health need. Teenagers who were being advised to "just say no" have increasingly turned to oral sex, once considered unnatural, as an alternative to intercourse. Lesbians, who were formerly considered the most sexually inhibited and restricted pair-bonded dyad, have become less "ladylike" and more sexually adventurous and assertive. As Nichols notes in Chapter 12, many men and women—gay and straight—proudly proclaim their interest in "kinky" sex. Books, chat rooms, and specialized websites are cropping up daily with explicit advice and erotica designed to stimulate the interest and increase the options of heterosexual and homosexual women. Teens, too, have an ever-expanding number of websites and peer advisors to address their sexual concerns.

At the other end of the age spectrum, having a 70-something former senator talk frankly about the importance of maintaining sexual intimacy in old age has given "golden-agers" the message that there is no need to retire sexually when social security payments begin. As Schover notes in Chapter 14, there is growing awareness in our society that most physical obstacles or impediments to sexual functioning can be overcome through the right combination of drugs, devices, and desire.

This third edition of *Principles and Practice of Sex Therapy* is intended to update the reader regarding new treatment approaches to old problems, as well as to introduce several new chapters on problems that were not specifically addressed in the previous two editions. Authors who are especially knowledgeable in such areas as gender identity disorders (Carroll, Chapter 13), sexual paraphilias (Kafka, Chapter 17), dyspareunia (Binik, Bergeron, and Khalifé, Chapter 6) and female sexual arousal disorder (Bartlik and Goldberg, Chapter 4) have contributed important new chapters. Several experts from our first two editions have revised and updated their chapters significantly (Leiblum, Chapter 7, vaginismus; Apfelbaum, Chapter 8, retarded ejaculation; Leiblum and Segraves, Chapter 15, sex therapy with aging adults; and Wincze, Chapter 16, atypical sexual behavior). Consequently, the book is noticeably longer, which is a testimony to the important changes that have taken place in the field of sex therapy since the publication of the second edition a decade ago.

CHANGES IN SEX THERAPY

In the introduction to the second edition (Leiblum & Rosen, 1989), we identified four major trends in the practice of sex therapy: (1) a trend toward greater "medicalization," (2) increasing emphasis on pharmacological intervention, (3) greater attention to desire disorders, and (4) more treatment utilizing interpersonal and object-relations theories. The first three trends have had major impacts on the current field, whereas the fourth trend has been less applicable, due partly to reimbursement constraints, in addition to a lack of satisfactory outcome data. In fact, current treatments for sexual problems are characterized increasingly by their brevity and "problem-oriented" focus. To a large extent, this is due to the influence of managed care on the delivery of all medical and mental health services, as well as patient demands for prompt resolution of sexual difficulties.

Three specific trends are especially worth noting, including the continuing effects of developments in sexual pharmacology, evolving conceptions of female sexuality, and the impact of new technologies, such as the Internet, on sexual relationships and the treatment of sexual problems. Let us consider each of these further because they have an impact on the current theory and practice of sex therapy.

The New Sexual Pharmacology

Throughout history, individuals have sought a "quick fix" to sexual problems—a pill or potion that will magically resolve an inhibition or impediment to sexual desire or arousal. Miraculous cures for erectile failure have included everything from crushed monkey testicles to rhinoceros horns. Stimulants to whet sexual desire have been equally as ingenuous, ranging from herbal concoctions to illicit drug cocktails. Until the last several decades, however, none of these remedies was demonstrated to have more than placebo value.

All that began to change about 15 years ago. Beginning in the mid-1980s, the use of self- or physician-administered intracavernosal injections was shown to be a safe and effective method for treating more severe cases of ED. Inspired by these early successes, various intracavernosal and intraurethral systems were developed (e.g., MUSE). But the search for a safe, oral medication—the "holy grail" or magic pill of sexual dysfunction treatments—took several more years to develop. When sildenafil was finally discovered (serendipitously as it turned out, because the drug was initially developed as a potential treatment for coronary angina), it inspired other pharmaceutical companies to extend the range of products and agents being developed in this area. Suddenly, the process of research into a wide array of potential agents for sexual dysfunction was off and running. This trend has had the additional effect of directing attention to previously neglected areas of pharmacological therapy, namely the treatment of sexual problems in women.

An emphasis on sexual pharmacology continues to dominate the field, with a large and growing investment of research funds being allocated toward the development of drugs that might stimulate sexual appetite and arousal, as well as reduce or counteract the effects of other drugs that interfere with sexual response, such as the selective serotonin reuptake inhibitors (SSRIs) and antihypertensives (Rosen, Lane, & Menza, 1999). Currently, drug treatment trials are being undertaken in men with depression and other psychiatric disorders; in patients with cardiac disease, diabetes, spinal cord injury; and in men with prostate cancer, to name only a few of the major areas in which pharmacological treatment approaches are being studied. Research to develop sexual stimulants have been considered, although concerns about specificity and potential medicolegal issues have restricted development in this area.

A new interest in pharmacological treatments for female sexual dysfunction has also emerged, motivated in large part by the huge market success of Viagra and the realization that there is an ever-expanding population of healthy and active peri- and postmenopausal women who want to enjoy continued sexual pleasure (or perhaps discover it for the first time!) Recently, an international consensus panel was convened in October 1998 to reconsider and update the classification of female sexual disorders (Basson et al., 2000). This conference was intended not only to refine diagnosis and nomenclature but also to delineate categories of female sexual dysfunction (FSD) that might be amenable to pharmacological intervention. Although there were few major changes in the actual nomenclature of female sexual disorders, the conference underlined the point that female sexuality and dysfunction must be taken seriously and considered independently and separately from male sexuality (Leiblum, in press).

Female Sexuality

Until the late 1990s, research interest in FSD was minimal. In fact, pharmaceutical companies had avoided testing new products in women for both valid and, at times, prejudicial reasons. On the one hand, there were concerns about studying women who might be pregnant, or whose menstrual cycle variations might obscure or confound the effects of drugs. On the other hand, there appeared to be an unvoiced and at times barely conscious concern about unleashing the power of female sexual libido and stimulating latent female sexuality. Many female physicians complained of a strong double standard in sexual medicine. As Bartlik (1999) noted, the "dearth of scientific and clinical research on women's sexuality springs more from sociological factors than from medical necessity. The obstacles to the pursuit of this research are rooted in prejudices and fears about sexuality, particularly women's sexuality, that permeate our culture" (p. 21). In Chapter 4, Bartlik and Goldberg note the challenges involved in accurately assessing female sexual arousal but also discuss the tremendous strides that have been made in both conceptualization and treatment.

In the past decade, few novel interventions have been developed for the resolution of anorgasmia or female sexual arousal disorder. Permission, education, sensuality training, and various cognitive–behavioral interventions remain the mainstay of most attempts to treat female sexual inhibitions and complaints. In fact, female sexual arousal disorders were so infrequently diagnosed as independent conditions that we did not even include a chapter on it in the last two editions of this book. Rather, the focus was on hypoactive sexual desire and orgasmic difficulties in women. Although women were known to be more vocal about sexual complaints than men, the treatments designed to alleviate these problems had not changed significantly since the publication of Masters and Johnson's *Human Sexual Inadequacy* in 1970. As Schover and Leiblum (1986) noted more than a decade ago, in many respects the field of sex therapy was "stagnant" with few innovations, and this was particularly true with respect to the biological and physiological underpinnings of female sexuality and the treatment of female sexual disorders. Along these lines, Riley (1998) has observed that "our understanding of sexual function and sexual dysfunction in women is probably at a level comparable to where we were with the male more than 10 years ago" (p. 231).

The situation began changing noticeably in the late 1990s. The hypothesis was developed that if vasoactive substances such as sildenafil were effective in relaxing smooth muscle tissue in the male genitalia, these drugs might be equally effective in increasing blood flow or vasocongestion in female genitalia, thereby increasing vaginal and clitoral arousal (Goldstein & Berman, 1998). Given the large population of women with sexual difficulties (Laumann et al., 1999), and the ever-growing population of baby-boomers who are past menopause, the race to discover preparations that might enhance female sexual response was on. Today, many companies are conducting phase I and phase II studies in women, using both vasoactive and androgenically active drugs. The use of testosterone in various forms, including patches, creams, sublingual tablets, and pills appears very promising as a means of treating both desire and arousal problems in oophorectomized women (Sherwin, 1998; Davis 1998; Mazur et al., in press). In fact, there is renewed interest in the use of testosterone therapy for treatment of sexual complaints of premenopausal women with subnormal levels of androgen who also complain of lack of vitality (Davis, 2000).

Several chapters in this volume address new developments in the assessment and treatment of female sexual disorders. As noted earlier, Bartlik and Goldberg discuss current research on female sexual arousal disorder in Chapter 4, and Heiman reviews the plethora of current treatment approaches to female orgasmic problems in Chapter 5. Although the treatment of vaginismus has not changed significantly, Leiblum (Chapter 7) notes that it continues to be a major problem for scores of women and often eludes diagnosis by gynecologists. Despite the early promise of quick success, long-standing cases often require considerable clinical ingenuity

Perhaps the most significant change in the area of female sexual complaints, however, is the reconceptualization of dyspareunia as a pain disorder rather than primarily as a sexual problem. Dyspareunia, which is quite prevalent among both young and mature women, stems from a complex array of biological, psychological, and interpersonal causes, although a large percentage of cases include an organic component. Vulvodynia is a common and serious sexual complaint, although one that has tended to be dismissed or minimized. In the past it was not uncommon for complaints of sexual pain to be viewed as evidence of psychosexual inhibition and conflict, rather than as genuine somatic manifestations. Binik, Bergeron and Khalifé in Chapter 6 review the various conceptualizations of dyspareunia, demonstrating the importance of both medical and nonmedical approaches to the resolution of sexual pain disorders.

Chapter 12 by Nichols on therapy with sexual minorities is particularly enlightening. She identifies a trend toward increased sexual assertiveness and risk taking among women generally and a breaking of sexual taboos among both gay and straight women. Not only are sexual boundaries being challenged but gender prescriptions are as well. So-called gender blending is an ongoing phenomenon, not only for transvestite individuals but for gay men and women as well.

Of course, it is important that female sexuality not be viewed through the same lens as male sexuality. Women are not men with skirts. And several popular authors have attacked the shibboleths that surround female sexuality. Angier

(1999) in particular has challenged the basic assumptions of evolutionary psychology with respect to female sexuality. She argues that the belief that women have innately less sexual desire than men is unfounded and due primarily to cultural and social artifacts. "A woman can't sleep around without risking terrible retribution, to her reputation, to her prospects, to her life. Women are "universally punished if they display evidence to the contrary—if they disobey their "natural inclinations toward a stifled libido" (p. 334) and reveal a robust and by no means trivial sexual drive. Angier (1999) goes on to say that "men have the naturally higher sex drive, yet all the laws, customs, punishments, shame, strictures, mystiques, and anti-mystiques are aimed with full hominid fury at that tepid, sleepy, hypoactive creature, the female libido. How can we know what is 'natural' for us when we are treated as unnatural for wanting our lust, our freedoms, the music of our bodies?" (p. 335).

Technological Changes in Society: Effects of the Internet

Other technological developments are influencing the practice of sex therapy, albeit indirectly. In particular, the increasing reliance on the Internet in all facets of daily life has had a major impact on sexual practices and behavior. The lure of cyberspace for both the undersexed and oversexed, paraphilic and nonparaphilic alike is considerable. In both positive and negative ways, websites, chat rooms, and virtual marketplaces have stimulated sexual appetites and, in some cases, reinforced preexisting sexually deviations or compulsions (Cooper, Scherer, Boies & Gordon, 1999; Leiblum, 1998). As therapists, we are encountering an increasing number of relationships that were initiated, conducted, and consummated via the Internet. We have also consulted with couples who have encountered major challenges in their relationships due to the diversions of cybersex and the various sexual attractions and opportunities available on-line.

Cooper (1998) has noted that anywhere between 9 and 15 million people go on-line daily and that rate is expected to grow by an estimated 25 percent every three months. For many Internet explorers, sex is the topic being sought. Not only is there a wide array of sexual "chat rooms," erotic and pornographic websites, and special interest groups, there is also a virtual treasure-house of sexual paraphernalia and erotica for individuals of every sexual predilection. Increasingly, clinicians are being asked to treat individuals and couples for whom the diversions of cyberspace have proven disruptive or that have negatively impacted their own lives or that of their children and/or partners.

Sex therapists do not routinely see individuals and couples who have benefited from the various relationship opportunities and sexual options afforded by the Internet but often hear about them from clients. There can no longer be any doubt that the Internet has become a significant element in the current sexual landscape. For many individuals who are physically isolated, socially unskilled, or physically compromised, it has provided a viable means of connecting with others who are similar to, or different from themselves. In some cases, it has led to romance and commitment; in others, it provides a distraction from the dilemmas of everyday life. What is increasingly clear, however, is that therapists can not afford to remain ignorant about what is available in cyberspace. In fact, many knowledgeable sex therapists are referring clients to Internet sites that offer support groups and educational information.

More worrisome, however, are individuals, prone to sexually compulsive behavior, who find the lures of cyberspace appealing. Such individuals are liable to become preoccupied or dependent upon the computer for sexual stimulation in much the same way they might previously have been dependent on x-rated videos or telephone sex. In such cases, treatment follows the general lines recommended for sexual addiction, whether this be involvement in a 12-Step program, behavioral therapy, or some combination of pharmacological (e.g., administration of SSRI or antiandrogenic medications) and psychological interventions (Carnes, 1983, 1991; Goodman, 1999). In Chapter 17, Kafka provides a detailed description of current approaches to the assessment and treatment of men with paraphilia and paraphilia-related disorders.

FUTURE CONCERNS AND DIRECTIONS

While it is often foolhardy to make pronouncements about the future, it can be safely predicted that sexual psychopharmacology will continue to flourish in the decades to come. Although many of us are growing older, we are also staying healthier, and, as discussed in Chapter 15, the wish for sexual options and outlets is strong. And it is also likely that the search for new drugs and improved understanding of basic sexual physiology should continue to flourish as well.

Increasingly, there will need to be more active and close collaboration between sex therapists and other health disciplines (e.g., urology, gynecology, and endocrinology), especially since many primary care physicians are prescribing medications for sexual problems without undertaking comprehensive assessment. Moreover, as Schover notes in Chapter 14, it is not only healthy individuals who need our services but those with chronic illnesses. Sex therapists will be expected to offer creative and viable solutions for such patients, as well as for clients who have neither access to nor financial resources for extended face-to-face treatment.

At this time, it is somewhat premature to assess the long-term efficacy of "long-distance" counseling, bibliotherapy approaches, manual-driven treatments or "Internet therapy," but it is certain that an array of treatment "delivery systems" will continue to develop. It is by no means clear that clients need to be seen as often as we typically see them in order to promote therapeutic change. Many sex researchers (Heiman & Meston, 1998; Bancroft, 1999) have noted that, in general, our field has not taken seriously enough the task of demonstrating the efficacy of what we do as clinicians. Given that we do not have a surplus of studies demonstrating the efficacy of our treatments, it is presumptuous to suppose that we have discovered the most effective interventions and treatment formats for our clients. Moreover, as potential patients avail themselves of the increasing variety and accessibility of sources of sexual information, they will become more articulate and outspoken about the kind of treatment they receive.

Although sex therapy continues to play an important and much needed role in this post-Viagra age, there are few academic postgraduate programs or professional training opportunities in this interdisciplinary field, though there is talk of developing some (Reiss, 1999). Nor is there a visible cadre of young, qualified professionals entering the profession. Academic departments are not offering courses or supervising training in sex therapy to any extent. And despite considerable new funding opportunities for pharmacological research, little if any of these funds has been directed toward outcome evaluation studies in sex therapy. Federal funding for sex therapy research has been essentially nonexistent in the past decade. We hope that the increasing awareness of the prevalence and impact of sexual dysfunction will stimulate a renewed interest in our field.

There is a real danger that the field of sex therapy will become still more "medicalized" in the years to come. With the success of new pharmacological agents, there is an inevitable focus on biological causes for sexual dysfunction and a tendency to seek simple medical solutions for more complex individual or couples' problems. This is particularly true of the nonclinicians who are entering our field who may be naïve about the complexities and subtleties of relationship and sexual dynamics.

As illustrated by many of the chapters in this volume, sex therapy is presently, and always has been, inextricably tied to relationship issues and psychological functioning. In this regard, there can be no substitute for a sophisticated, comprehensive, and thorough understanding of individual and couple psychology. It is hoped that this understanding will resurface as the limits of medical therapy become increasingly apparent.

Finally, there is a strong need for new theoretical approaches and "paradigms" in the field of sex therapy but there are some. In his thought-provoking chapter on sexual desire disorders, Schnarch (Chapter 2) discusses his approach as representing the "second-generation" of sex therapy, and he details his Sexual Crucible Approach to assessment and treatment. While most therapists emphasze the fostering of intimacy in their work with couples, Schnarch discusses the importance of differentiation and the need to self-soothe rather than demand relief and comfort from one's partner.

The development of these new theories and conceptualizations of sexual behavior is necessary to keep the field dynamic. Sex therapists face significant challenges in this new millenium in integrating a growing array of medications and devices with both traditional and innovative ways of counseling individuals and couples. From a theoretical perspective, sex therapy has always been highly eclectic, and this trend is likely to continue as is evident from the chapters in this volume. The upcoming decades promise to be a period of great growth and significant change in our field. It is an exciting time, indeed, to be engaged in the practice of sex therapy.

REFERENCES

Angier, N. (1999). *Women: An intimate geography. New York:* Hougton Mifflin.

Bancroft, J. (1999). Sexual Science in the 21st century: Where are we going? A personal note. *Journal of Sex Research, 36,* 226–229.

Bartlik, B. (1999). Recent developments in the evaluation and treatment of sexual disorders in women. *Psychiatric Annals, 29,* 19–21.

Basson, R., Berman, J., Burnett, A., Derogatis, L., Ferguson, D., Fourcroy, J., Goldstein, I., Graziottin, A., Heiman, J., Laan, E., Leiblum, S., Padma-Nathan, H., Rosen, R., Segraves, K., Segraves, R.T., Shabsigh, R., Sipski, M., Wagner, G., & Whipple, B. (2000). Report of the international consensus development conference on female sexual dysfunction: Definitions and classifications. *Journal of Urology, 163,* 888–893.

Cape Cod Conference on Assessment of Sexual Function in Clinical Trials. (1998). *International Journal of Impotence Research, 10,* S1–S143.

Carnes, P. (1983). *Out of the shadows: Understanding sexual addiction.* Minneapolis: CompCare.

Carnes , P. (1991). *Don't call it love: Recovery from sexual addiction.* Bantam Books.

Cooper, A. (1998). Sexuality and the internet: Surfing into the new millennium. *CyberPsychology and Behavior, 1,* 181–187.

Cooper, A., Scherer, C., Boies S., & Gordon, B. (1999). Sexuality on the internet: From sexual exploration to pathological expression. *Professional Psychology: Research and Practice, 30,* 154–164.

Davis, S. (1998). The role of androgens and the menopause in the female sexual response. *International Journal of Impotence Research: Basic and Clinical Studies, 10,* S82–S83.

Davis, S. (2000, January 28). *Natural hormonal changes and loss of sexual desire.* Paper presented at the Second Taskforce on Female Sexuality, New York City.

Derogatis, L. (1998). Psychological assessment measures of human sexual functioning in clinical trials. *International Journal of Impotence Research, 10*(Suppl. 2), S13–S20.

Feldman, H. A., Goldstein, I., Hatzichritou, D., Krane, R., & McKinlay, J. (1994). Impotence and its medical and psychological correlates: Results of the Massachusetts male aging study. *Journal of Urology, 151,* 54–61.

Goldstein, I., & Berman, J. (1998). Vasculogenic female sexual dysfunction: Vaginal engorgment and clitoral erectile insufficiency syndrome. *International Journal of Impotence Research, 10*(Suppl. 2), S84–S90.

Goodman, A. (1999). *Sexual addiction: An intergrated approach.* New York: International Universities Press.

Heiman, J. R., & Meston, C. M. (1999). Empirically validated treatment for sexual dysfunction. *Annual Review of Sex Research, 6,* 148–194.

Jardin, A., Wagner, G., Khoury, S., Giuliano, F., Goldstein, I., Padma-Nathan, H., & Rosen, R. (in press). *Recommendations of the first international consultation on erectile dysfunction.* (World Health Organization Conference)

Laumann, E., Paik, A., & Rosen, R. (1999). Sexual dysfunction in the United States: Prevalence, predictors, and outcomes. *Journal of the American Medical Association, 10,* 537.

Leiblum, S. (1998). Sex and the net: Clinical implications. *Journal of Sex Education and Therapy, 22,* 21–28.

Leiblum, S. (1999, October 22). *A critical overview of the new consensus-based definition and classification of female sexual dysfunction.* Paper presented at the New Perspectives in the Management of Female Sexual Dysfunction Conference, Boston.

Leiblum, S. (in press). After Viagra: Bridging the gap between pharmacologic treatment and an active sexual life. *Journal of Clinical Psychiatry.*

Leiblum, S., & Rosen, R. (1989). Introduction: Sex therapy in the age of AIDS. In S. Leiblum & R. Rosen (Eds.), *Principles and practice of sex therapy* (2nd ed., pp. 1–16). New York: Guilford Press.

Lottman, P. E., Hendricks, J. C., Vruggnink, P. A., & Meuleman, E. J. (1998). The impact of marital satisfaction and psychological counseling on the outcome of ICI treatment in men with ED. *International Journal of Impotence Research, 10,* 83–87.

Mazur, N., Leiblum, S., & Rosen, R. (in press). The Brief Index of Sexual Functioning for Women (BISF-W): A new scoring algorithm and comparison of normative and surgically menopausal population. *Menopause.*

Meana, M., Binik, Y., Khalifé, S., & Cohen, D. (1997). Dyspareunia: Sexual Dysfunction or pain syndrome? *Journal of Nervous and Mental Disease, 185,* 561–569.

Michael, R., Gagnon, J., Laumann, E., & Kolata, G. (1994). *Sex in America: A definitive survey.* Boston: Little, Brown.

Process of Care Consensus Panel. (1999). The process of care model for evaluation and treatment of erectile dysfunction. *International Journal of Impotence Research, 11,* 59–66.

Riley, A. (1998). Integrated approaches to sex therapy. *Sexual and Marital Therapy, 13,* 229–231.

Rosen, R., Brown, C., Heiman, J., Leiblum, S., Shabsigh, R., Ferguson, D., & D'Agostino, R. (2000). The Female Sexual Function Index: A multidimensional self-report instrument for assessment of female sexual function. *Journal of Sex and Marital Therapy, 26,* 191–208.

Rosen, R., Lane, R., & Menza, M. (1999). Effects of SSRIs on sexual function: A critical review. *Journal of Clinical Psychopharmacology, 19,* 67–85.

Rosen, R. C., Riley, A., Wagner, G., Osterloh, I., Kirkpatrick, J., & Mishra, A. (1997). The International Index of Erectile Function (IIEF): A multidimensional scale for assessment of erectile dysfunction. *Urology, 49,* 822–830.

Schover, L., & Leiblum, S. (1994). The stagnation of sex therapy. *Journal of Psychology and Human Sexuality, 6,* 5–10.

Sherwin, B. (1998). The role of combined estrogen-androgen preparations in the postmenopause: Evidence from clinical studies. *International Journal of Fertility, 43,* 98–103.

Taylor, J., Rosen, R., & Leiblum, S. (1994). Self-report assessment of female sexual function: Psychometric evaluation of the Brief Index of Sexual Functioning for Women. *Archives of Sexual Behavior, 223,* 627–643.

Tiefer, L. (1995). Gender and meaning in the nomenclature of sexual dysfunctions. In *Sex is not a natural act and other essays.* New York: Westview Press.

I

DESIRE DISORDERS

2

Desire Problems
A Systemic Perspective

DAVID SCHNARCH

In proposing a new "paradigm" or treatment model for overcoming sexual desire disorders, David Schnarch takes current theories and approaches to task for not adequately addressing the interpersonal aspects of the problem. While many therapists focus on the task of increasing sexual or emotional intimacy in the relationship, Schnarch argues that the real issue is resolving the need for personal differentiation or "self-validation." It is the tendency to validate oneself emotionally through the reactions of the other that lies at the heart of the problem, according to this perspective. The author further proposes that sexual desire problems are typically indicative of a lack, or loss, of differentiation in the relationship.

In this highly original chapter, Schnarch extends the boundaries of interpersonal approaches to the assessment and treatment of sexual desire disorders. He emphasizes at the outset that "high desire" and "low desire" are systemic positions in every sexual relationship, and that these positions are typically reflective of other (deeper) issues. The emotional and interpersonal consequences for each of the partners is considered as serving specific individual needs (e.g., self-protection from rejection or disappointment). Schnarch notes that the low-desire individual usually controls the frequency and occurrence of sex, an observation that leads to other considerations about the role of couples' dynamics in the regulation of sexual desire.

In his innovative Sexual Crucible™ Approach, the author focuses strongly on differentiation as the "central drive wheel" in interpersonal relationships. His therapeutic goal is directed at maximizing each individual's level of differentiation and setting up new patterns for the couple that permit or facilitate greater intimacy through self-differentiation. A detailed case example illustrates how this process is achieved in actual practice. Schnarch also takes a provocative position on the role of anxiety in treatment, suggesting that the goal should be to develop "anxiety tolerance," rather than anxiety reduction or elimination, as in more traditional sex therapy approaches.

This chapter well illustrates the necessity for an interpersonal perspective in most cases of desire disorders. Studies have suggested that medical or organic factors account for a relatively small proportion of cases. Schnarch has significantly advanced our understanding of the role of specific couples' dynamics, as well as the complex interplay of emotional and sexual needs. This is a major contribution to the field.

David Schnarch, PhD, is the director of the Marriage and Family Health Center of Evergreen, Colorado. He is a widely published author and outstanding lecturer on sexuality and interpersonal relationships. His two books, Constructing the Sexual Crucible *(1991) and* Passionate Marriage *(1997), are major references in the field of marital and sex counseling.*

In the new millennium, the treatment of sexual desire problems—and sex therapy per se—may differ markedly from five decades ago. Research and clinical experience suggests that sexual desire problems are relatively difficult to treat (e.g., DeAmicis, Goldberg, LoPiccolo, Friedman, & Davies, 1985; LoPiccolo, Heiman, Hogan, & Roberts, 1985; Kilmann, Boland, Norton, Davidson, & Caid, 1986). In truth, however, the literature demonstrates that sexual desire problems are difficult to treat *the way clinicians commonly treat them.* How you treat sexual desire problems—and the results you obtain—depends on how you think about sexual desire per se (Schnarch, 1997b).

Like any other physical or emotional difficulty, sexual desire problems can only be known through the "lens" of treatments available to treat them. And, as with all other problems, our picture of sexual phenomena will change as more sophisticated and successful treatments evolve. Just consider how the "faces" of cholera, polio, and sexual dysfunction have changed over the last 1,000 years. Outcome studies reflect the efficacy of the reigning treatment paradigm as much as the nature of the problem itself.

It is hard to remember that contemporary sexual desire treatment is still primarily a first-generation approach. But as recently as 40 years ago, low sexual desire was considered a motivational trait/personality variable by which therapists selected or rejected people for sex therapy treatment of genital performance problems. (Those with low sexual desire were unlikely to complete the sensate focus activities.) Low sexual desire was not even mentioned in the initial contributions from Masters and Johnson (1970) or Kaplan (1974). It was only in 1977 that Lief introduced the concept of *inhibited sexual desire* to refer to a chronic lack of sexual initiation or responsiveness. At approximately the same time, Kaplan (1977) added a desire (initiation) phase to the sexual response cycle originally suggested by Masters and Johnson, giving birth to *desire phase disorders.* Sexual desire problems have gone on to become the most commonly reported sexual complaint of the 1980s and 1990.[1] If the pharmaceutical companies have their way, sexual desire promises to become a major industry in the new millennium (Schnarch, 1999).

For all these apparent changes, and despite the appearance that "postmodern" sex therapy "surpassed" the work of Masters and Johnson (1966, 1970, 1976; Masters, Johnson, & Kolodny, 1986) and Helen Singer Kaplan (1974, 1977, 1979, 1987), sexual desire treatment has remained trapped in the invisible shackles of a first-generation paradigm (Schnarch, 1992a). While clinicians are always potentially "trapped" by the prevailing paradigm (because the limitations of the paradigm are relatively invisible), the traps of a first-generation paradigm are particularly difficult to recognize and avoid. That is because the content and structure of first-generation theories and applications (e.g., understanding and treating sexual desire problems) define the field (e.g., sex therapy) itself. Perhaps more realistically we should ask, "Why *shouldn't* clinicians have difficulty treating sexual desire problems?"[2]

I realize that sex therapy is not monolithic and that therapists like to think they are not cast in a single mold. And yet the history of science demonstrates that entirely new ways of understanding and operating emerge only when basic tenets of a field are challenged and reexamined (Kuhn, 1970). This must be done paradigmatically, which involves making generalizations about "common clinical experience" and characterizations as to "what the literature says." This process risks offending every contributor who holds dear his or her contribution to sexual science and many candidates are people in the field whom I value. And it can seem to homogenize heartfelt differences and ignore critical debates of the time, the same way geology makes a particular culture look trivial. Given that I plan to demonstrate something different from what has come before, the whole venture easily looks as if I am lynching a self-serving strawman.

Almost a decade ago I proposed that contemporary psychotherapy embraced a part–whole error regarding intimacy in committed relationships (Schnarch, 1991, 1993). The "part" in the part–whole error involved confusing *other*-validated intimacy with intimacy per se, thereby ignoring the central importance of *self*-validated intimacy. The distinction between self-validated and other-validated intimacy permitted development of an intimacy-based form of treatment that fundamentally changed my professional and personal life. With intrepidation and respect I propose here that a similar part–whole error exists in how the field of sex therapy has approached sexual desire problems.

Contemporary understanding of sexual desire problems goes back to the earliest professional focus on sexual desire problems in modern times. The first diagnostic criteria for sexual desire problems appeared in the third edition of the *Diagnostic and Statistical Manual of Mental Disorders* (DSM-III; American Psychiatric Association, 1980). It and subsequent revisions (DSM-III-R, 1987; DSM-IV, 1994) largely embodied Kaplan's views. In other words, the current DSM classification of sexual desire problems reflects the paradigm of sexual desire from which it emerged. Today it continues to shape clinical practice, especially for economic and legal purposes, and it continues to reflect the paradigm.

A paradigm is a scientific "world view" by which a body of practitioners of a discipline generally agree to think and operate (e.g., it determines therapy, research topics and methods, licensing exam content, ethics guidelines, and standards of professional practice). A paradigm is a lot more than the way a particular therapist, researcher, or academician conceptualizes what he or she does. Deconstructing the DSM and major texts on sexual desire (e.g., *Disorders of Sexual Desire* [Kaplan, 1979]; *Sexual Desire Disorders* [Leiblum & Rosen, 1988]) provides a useful way of examining what the contemporary paradigm of sex therapy looks like. Having done this extensively in *Constructing the Sexual Crucible* (Schnarch, 1991), I summarize here what I believe to be defining characteristics of first-generation approaches to sexual desire:

1. *"Sex and desire are natural functions."* Following centuries of medical pathologizing and sex-negative cultural attitudes, this treatment stance was much healthier and more enlightened. Unfortunately, this attempt to legitimize sex and desire by proclaiming sex natural backfired (see explanation later).

2. *Sexual desire as biological drive.* From Freud's libido theory to Kaplan's eating disorders model ("sexual anorexia") to hormone replacement therapy, sexual desire has been addressed primarily as a biological drive. Closely related to the "sex is a natural function" philosophy.

3. *Sexual desire implicitly equated with desire for sexual behavior (rather than desire for one's partner).* Few therapists took issue with Kaplan's notion of sex being "friction plus fantasy" and the intimacy-incongruent treatment approach called "bypassing" (Kaplan, 1979).[3]

4. *Desire as initiatory receptivity and aggressiveness.* Subtly narrows clinical thinking of desire as "willingness to get started" (initiatory eagerness) rather than enhancing desire *during* sex. The result is a paradigm that encourages utilitarian sex (e.g., measurable in couples' and research animals' copulatory frequency) and ignores couples' common complaint of boring, meaningless sex devoid of passion, eroticism, and intimacy.

5. *Desire "phase" disorders.* Closely related to item (4). Desire is perceived as an initial stage in sexual encounters, reflecting the initial phase in Kaplan's triphasic model (1974).

6. *Inhibited sexual desire (ISD).* Closely tied to items 1 and 2. ISD presumes a standard of "noninhibited" desire, but from the standpoint of sexual potential (Schnarch, 1991) most people have "inhibited" desire.

7. *Personal characteristics and individual diagnosis.* DSM diagnostic criteria as well as the bulk of the clinical literature predispose clinicians to look "inside the individual" (e.g., unconscious processes, phobic reactions, family-of-origin issues, and job stress) for the source of desire problems.

8. *Inherently pathological emphasis.* "Sex and desire are natural functions" and sex-drive approaches implicitly postulate a pathology or blockage to explain the lack of spontaneous desire/function. People with ISD have long been presumed pathological, and even more so than those with sexual dysfunctions (Kaplan, 1979). Unfortunately, this coincides with many clients' presumption that therapy will reveal they are defective, pathological, or illogical. This creates unbalanced alliances which complicate treatment.

9. *"Blockage" model of therapy.* Treatment involves removing the presumed pathology/inhibition/blockage stifling full expression of the postulated natural drive/ desire/function.

Given the mediocre sex that lies behind common complaints of sexual boredom, low sexual desire often actually reflects good judgment. Rather than automatically focusing on the low-desire partner, clinicians should wonder more about the high-desire partner who often wants more of the usual—often he or she does not know enough about sex or intimacy to realize the sex he or she is having maybe is not worth wanting. This observation—and the resulting shift in clinical stance—is hard to come by in first-generation sexual desire approaches. In this chapter I avoid such terms as "inhibited sexual desire" and desire "disorders" in lieu of a more systemic label: desire "problems."[4]

A SECOND-GENERATION APPROACH

The second-generation approach discussed here involves a paradigm shift from the work of Masters and Johnson and Helen Singer Kaplan and other first-generation approaches. To start with, it differs in three ways: It focuses on (1) desire during sex, rather than just initiatory problems, (2) desire for one's partner rather than desire for sexual behavior, and (3) consciously chosen, freely undertaken desire rather than biological drive or natural function. This approach recognizes human sexual desire as the most complex manifestation of sexual motivation among all living things. Clinical experience with this approach suggests an atypical view of sexual desire problems: Sexual desire problems are no more difficult to treat than most sexual dysfunctions—meaning that they are highly responsive to treatment.

As a consequence of human ontogeny, most people experience "desire out of emptiness." Desire out of emptiness is the neediness, dependency, and deprivation (e.g., horniness, loneliness, contact hunger, and "fears of abandonment") that permeate first-generation clinical views of sexual desire. Desire out of emptiness usually does not contribute to relationship stability or long-term desire, however, especially if people mature and become less dependent.

What people often want (without realizing it) is "desire out of fullness." Desire out of fullness is something that (1) many couples have never experienced, (2) threatens the security of people who need to be needed, (3) lies outside first-generation approaches to sexual desire, and (4) facilitates mutuality and profound sexual desire that can take on spiritual proportions.

Think of desire as wanting. How many people want (or need) to be wanted? Then ask yourself, "Who really wants to *want*?" (Schnarch, 1992b). It makes you stop expecting desire as an automatic "given" and respect those people who dare to want (desire) their partner. It is often easier to want sex than it is to want your partner, and just wanting sex makes you vulnerable. Consider how just openly enjoying and acknowledging sexual pleasure can feel like tempting fate (and your partner) to withhold. Hungering and longing for your partner makes you vulnerable because life offers no guarantee your desires will be fulfilled. Consciously chosen, freely undertaken desire is rooted in courage rather than sexual frustration, deprivation, and loneliness. Intense desire and satisfaction are not safe until people can soothe their own heartaches, disappointments, and fears. Therapists who seek to (re)kindle desire in couples had best respect the personal strength and maturity it takes to *want* a long-term partner.

Beyond resolving emotional blockages, religion-derived inhibitions, and childhood fears (*if* these are necessary at all), people have to grow up to keep sex and intimacy alive in long-term relationships. Struggling through desire problems in ways that enhance personal growth is one way this happens, and when this happens effectively the results are dramatic.

Wanting is an individual *ability* that shapes—and is shaped by—relationship dynamics and personal development. Similarly, desire is an inherently interpersonal (systemic) process that shapes—and is shaped by—relationship dynamics and personal growth. The second-generation approach described here addresses interdependent determination of hard-to-tolerate sexual realities in emotionally committed relationships, particularly as these arise in the form of sexual desire problems. This not only permits conceptualizing sexual desire more broadly but also embraces a level of systemic sophistication missing in first-generation approaches.

A few systemic approaches to sex have emerged in the literature, but none evolved scope and depth in theory and application to approximate a true second-generation approach (e.g., Fish, Fish, & Sprenkle, 1984; Elkaim, 1986; LoPiccolo & Friedman, 1988; Schwartz & Masters, 1988; Verhulst & Heiman, 1988). A truly systemic (ecosystemic) approach involves more than recognizing *multiple* combinations of unidimensional "issues" such as unconscious processes, unresolved family-of-origin issues, physical setting, job pressures, time demands, contemporary family issues, and other social stresses. And it requires more than mounting an eclectic battery of unidimensional interventions such as insight-oriented psychodynamic psychotherapy combined with cognitive–behavioral homework assignments, sensate focus exercises, communication skills/conflict resolution training, "time management," family therapy, and renegotiation of parenting responsibilities. A truly systemic approach recognizes that a sexual desire problem is not simply a symptom of problems elsewhere in the relationship: The sexual desire problem *is* the process of the relationship. Once recognized, sexual desire problems become a way of seeing how relationships *function* rather than seeing them as signs of *dys*function or *dys*regulation in an individual, a relationship, a family, or society.

Numerous changes follow from this shift, including recognizing that sexual desire problems are a form of interpersonal communication. Conventionally, people talk about desire waning because of "inability to communicate." But approaching sexual desire as a form of communication inherent to human relationships (e.g., sexual vibes) helps therapists realize that a desire problem *is* the message (rather than the result of communication difficulties). This permits a sex therapy that recognizes that couples *cannot stop communicating* (the problem is they cannot stand the message). Some couples become celibate in attempts to "stop communicating," but even no sex says a lot.

Moreover, this paradigm shift allows a unified conceptualization/intervention strategy that has multisystemic "isomorphic" clinical impact. An isomorphic intervention has congruent effects on multiple dimensions that potentiate each unidimensional impact as well as overall global impact. Isomorphic interventions give therapy acceleration and momentum. To accomplish this, interventions must be isomorphic with the systemic forces in relationships that control the ebb and flow of sexual desire.

Effective isomorphic intervention requires understanding that emotionally committed relationships operate as a complex system, and that sex—especially sexual desire—is a complex subsystem (part of a larger system but also a system unto itself).[5] In other words, sex in monogamous relationships has rules and processes all its own[6]—processes that often differ from philosophies and strategies of first-generation sex therapy (and many marital therapies). For example, few people have sexual desire for someone with whom they constantly have to listen, validate, and empathize. And many people do not want sex after they have negotiated and compromised about what they want.

SEXUAL DESIRE IS A SYSTEMIC PROCESS

Let us consider two simple systemic principles that immediately illustrate the systemic nature of sexual desire.

Principle 1

High and low (sexual) desire are positions in a system. These positions surface in every committed relationship around every point of contention. Often "high" and "low" desire are not stable personality traits or individual characteristics. For every "individual trait" posited to create desire problems, examples exist having no difficulties (e.g., religious orthodoxy, sexual ignorance, sexual abuse, anger, stress, and problems with intimacy). In other cases, sexual diffi-

culties do not emerge until these traits are triggered by relationship developments.

"Low" desire and "high" desire are always relational, in terms of what is
considered problematic as well as whether someone is the high-desire or low-
desire partner. The same level of sexual desire that makes someone the high-
desire partner in one relationship may make him or her the low-desire partner
in another. Different dynamics in a new relationship can also make the difference—all that is often required, for example, is finding a new partner who is
more dependent than you. Many couples shift sexual desire positions as their
relationship evolves. Moreover, partners repeatedly switch high-desire–low-
desire positions across issues in the relationship: The high-desire partner for
sex may be the low-desire partner for intimacy, living together, having a baby,
spending money, or disciplining the kids.

Approaching high desire and low desire as systemic positions in every
relationship on every issue destigmatizes the low-sexual-desire partner's position and maintains a balanced alliance (differentiated stance) with both partners. This also allows couples to apply their experience dealing with sexual
desire problems to other issues in their relationship. Most important, it permits a fundamental integration of sexual, marital, and individual therapies
that harnesses common forced-choice relationship issues (e.g., sex, intimacy,
money, kids, and in-laws) that require *differentiation* (rather than communication or compromise) for resolution. The result is an effective broad-band approach to marital therapy in general.[7]

How do high-desire–low-desire positions play out sexually? Consider, for
example, the common occurrence in which Partner A defines his or her sexual
adequacy by his or her ability to please his or her partner. (This is known as a
reflected sense of self, a manifestation of low differentiation.) Partner A takes
Partner B's lower (or absent) sexual desire as a negative self-reflection. At the
same time, B is sexually disinterested when he or she feels A is more interested
in "proving him- or herself" than being with B. (B is similarly dependent on a
reflected sense of self, requiring A's unswerving attention to feel important or
"secure.") Partner A is at a loss to explain B's sexual disinterest—until he or
she blames him- or herself or blames it on B or B's past. (That is what people
with a reflected sense of self do.) Either way, the process has a negative impact
on sexual desire in the dyad.

Unfortunately, the system does not stop there. Low desire can predispose
sexual dysfunctions, and likewise, one partner's sexual performance problems
can create sexual boredom and low desire in the dyad: Sexual dysfunctions
frequently destroy intimacy because partners are distracted from each other by
current anxieties or anticipated outcomes. Either partner can develop low desire
as an attempt at self-protection from frustration and disappointment. Notice that
"causation" does not stem from either individual; rather, partners co-create it. The
good news is this same system can be used to increase partners' capacity for desire
and raise their overall personal functioning and the quality of their relationship.

Principle 2

The partner with the least sexual desire always controls sex.[8] The low-desire partner not only controls when sex occurs, he or she often controls the content and style of sex as well. Even when partners trade high-desire/low-desire roles this systemic rule still holds. It also applies most times to other relationship issues that require partners' willing collaboration (e.g., having a baby).

Now, consider one of the millions of poorly differentiated couples: In addition to controlling sex, the low-desire partner controls the adequacy of the high-desire partner as well—whether or not this is wanted, intended, or realized. That is because partners in these relationships depend on each other for a positive reflected sense of self. The high-desire partner complains of feeling controlled and undesired when the low-desire partner declines to have sex. The low-desire partner paradoxically feels inadequate while simultaneously feeling responsible for controlling his or her partner's (and the relationship's) functioning. Oftentimes, the low-desire partner simply wants to feel in control of him- or herself. I have also seen numerous couples in which the low-desire partner has been more sexually active and erotically inclined in other relationships than was the high-desire partner. While the high-desire partner flaunts his or her superior status, the low-desire partner has a very different view of reality. Given the powerful feelings involved, and their inability to see beyond their immediate subjective experience, this natural systemic process creates desire problems for lots of couples.

We are describing normality; no presumption of psychopathology is involved. And from this vantage point, we can explain why couples' spontaneous attempts at resolution often fail: To rescue his or her battered sense of self, the high-desire partner increases efforts to "cure" the low-desire partner and/or attacks the low-desire partner's adequacy—which perpetuates the problem.[9] The low-desire partner has already abdicated his or her sexual competency and has little status left to lose. Improvements are often attributed to the high-desire partner's efforts and used to validate prior claims that the low-desire partner was "defective." The high-desire partner attempts to get more control by becoming more active, while the low-desire partner controls the process (wittingly or not) by doing progressively less. With little to gain and little to lose, the low-desire partner adopts a superficial passive acceptance of inadequacy and appears unmotivated to change, although he or she secretly smolders for years. This further frustrates the high desire partner, who typically escalates by becoming (1) more passively indifferent than the low-desire partner, or (2) more insistent about sexual frequency, or (3) involved in an extramarital affair.

In the field of marriage and family therapy, similar nonsexual interactions have been called *incongruous power hierarchies* (Haley, 1976). Rather than arising out of anger and unconscious resentments, incongruous power hierarchies develop from partners' attempts at self-protection and accommodation to each other's difficulties and weakness. The incongruent power hierarchies which surface around sexual desire problems exemplify the many *inherent paradoxes* in emotionally committed relationships (Schnarch, 1989b, 1991). For example, many of us want to be wanted, but at a more fundamental level we need to be needed. We also fear being exploited by those who need us. As long as we need to be needed we are never free to desire deeply, never sure we are desired for ourselves, and frequently destroy the possibility of being wanted by our partner because we do things to ensure we are needed. Resolving the inherent paradoxes surrounding sexual desire involves more complex (meta-level) solutions, and such solutions typically require personal growth (differentiation). Desire is a systemic process driven and modulated by differentiation that makes relationships the people-growing processes they are.

DIFFERENTIATION:
AN ALTERNATIVE PARADIGM FOR SEX THERAPY

At this point let us consider differentiation more fully, so we can discuss desire as a systemic phenomenon using differentiation as our lens.

With a few notable exceptions, variants of attachment theory, object-relations theory, and psychodynamic/psychoanalytic psychotherapy have dominated sexual desire treatment before and since Kaplan's earliest publications; the same orientation holds sway in many marital therapy approaches as well. The second-generation approach I have been describing is the Sexual Crucible™ Approach. This approach posits *differentiation*[10] as the central drive wheel in human relationships, and especially with regard to sex and intimacy in committed relationships. The Crucible Approach is the first application of differentiation theory (originally proposed by family therapist Murray Bowen, 1975, 1978) to integrated sexual–marital therapy.

Broadly speaking, differentiation involves the ability to distinguish, develop, and balance two fundamental life forces: desire for communion and contact with others and desire to become more uniquely ourselves and to direct our own destiny. Differentiation is crucial to emotionally committed relationships because they involve the intricate entwinement of these two basic human drives: attachment and the refusal to submit to tyranny. Couples constantly experience the struggles of balancing communion with the refusal to submit to tyranny—especially around sexual desire issues—but few recognize this as the process of self-development in action.

Differentiation manifests as an individual characteristic in four distinct ways:

- Maintain a clear sense of self while close (physically and emotionally) to "significant others."
- Regulate one's own anxieties.
- Nonreactivity to others' anxieties.
- Willingness to tolerate discomfort for growth.

But differentiation is an inherently relational concept and process too, applying to couples, families, therapists, and the therapy process itself. Better-differentiated people can tolerate more intimate connection with a highly valued partner before they feel controlled or lose themselves in their relationship (i.e., a more solid sense of self). They can invest themselves in their partner and the relationship without being dependent on either and have greater capacity for intimacy, eroticism, passion, and caring. Well-differentiated individuals can be more considerate of their partner and accept influence from him or her because a solid sense of self is a *permeable* self. People who get their sense of self and emotional regulation from their partner/relationship rarely engage in mutuality because mutuality requires "permeability" and absorbing personal frustrations for the benefit of others.

Differentiation applies to both women and men: Men often sacrifice relationships to maintain their sense of self and women often sacrifice their sense of self to maintain their relationships. Differentiation applies to men and women who differ from these gender stereotypes, including those in homosexual relationships. Many issues that control sexual desire in lesbian and gay couples transcend differences in gender-object choice. Differentiation is about having more of a relationship with yourself *and* more relationship with one's partner. It is having feelings without the feelings having *you*.

It is easy to conceptualize sexual desire problems as resulting from "lack of emotional connection" (e.g., "lack of intimacy" and "fears of abandonment"). But what are often mistakenly viewed as "attachment deficit disorders" are actually *emotional fusion* (lack of differentiation). While greater differentiation permits more profound connection (e.g., intimacy and mutuality), the opposite of differentiation is not lack of connection but, rather, connection without separateness—emotional fusion. A differentiation-based approach facilitates collaborative alliances with clients because lack of differentiation (emotional fusion) is not pathological.[11]

Although there is nothing "wrong" with emotional fusion, it has a drastic impact on sexual desire by promoting *borrowed functioning*. (Borrowed functioning differs from mutuality in that the former suppresses the function of the "donor" while enhancing the function of the "recipient." Mutuality enhances both partners' functioning.) Borrowed functioning commonly plays out sexually—for example, partners feel more attractive when their spouse has desire for them (i.e., a positive reflected sense of self). While borrowed functioning is understandable, common, and feels good at first, it also often creates low sexual desire because the low-sexual-desire partner starts to feel "used" and "sucked dry." One of the strategies of differentiation-based sexual therapy involves reducing emotional fusion.

Returning to the four characteristics of differentiation mentioned earlier, people's willingness and ability to regulate their anxiety and tolerate discomfort for growth largely determine their ability to improve their lot in life. Similarly, self-confrontation, self-validation and self-soothing (i.e., self-regulation) are often more important determinants of long-term sexual desire and relationship stability than are empathy, "communication," and reciprocal validation. That is why resolving couples' sexual desire problems depends more on their willingness to tolerate discomfort for growth than how "screwed up" they are or their willingness to stroke each other emotionally.[12]

This stance toward anxiety is another paradigmatic shift. From its early origins in Masters and Johnson's treatment of sexual dysfunctions, conventional sex therapy has generally focused on anxiety reduction. By focusing on emotional resilience, however, differentiation-based sexual–marital therapy emphasizes anxiety *tolerance*, giving rise to a different set of therapeutic assumptions, goals, interventions, and outcomes. For example, in this approach it is the therapist's explicit responsibility to make every effort to maximize resilience and encourage the best in people to stand up. This process is operationalized by speaking to people's integrity rather than focusing on their fears, anxieties, "wounds" and childhood deprivations.[13] This coincides with a shift from a sensation-based (sensate focus) approach to one fundamentally emphasizing personal growth and intimacy (Schnarch, 1989a).

WHY IS DIFFERENTIATION IMPORTANT IN SEX, DESIRE, AND INTIMACY?

Now, let's return to our discussion of desire and sexual systems using differentiation as our lens: Differentiation is fundamental to sustaining intimacy, eroticism, and sexual desire in long-term relationships. Said differently, the Crucible Approach considers desire problems as natural and inevitable manifestations of—and opportunities for—human evolution on the individual, dyadic, and species level (i.e., differentiation).

Principle 3

Couples' foreplay is a negotiation for the level and kinds of intimacy, eroticism, and meaning of the sex that follows, and resilience is important (Schnarch, 1997). Differentiation (clear sense of self, self-soothing, nonreactivity, accepting discomfort for growth) determines what happens in sex, and what happens during sex has a great effect on sexual desire. Poorly differentiated people get their feelings hurt during foreplay and give up, blame their partner, and withdraw during the sex that follows. They are particularly prone to sexual desire problems because lack of differentiation readily creates other problems, such as lack of intimacy, lack of involvement during sex, and lack of satisfying connection with the partner. The problem for many couples isn't "how to make sex more intimate"—it is that intimacy is much harder to tolerate than it is to create. Enhanced differentiation increases people's *intimacy tolerance*—it helps them stop avoiding intimacy when their reflected sense of self is (inevitably) threatened.

Principle 4

Emotional gridlock is a natural, inevitable, and purposeful development in committed relationships. Sexual desire problems can result from—and cause—a general systemic process called *emotional gridlock* (Schnarch, 1991, 1997a). Gridlock occurs when each partner defines a position on an issue that blocks the preferred position of the mate. When couples are emotionally gridlocked, conflictual issues surface repeatedly. Issues take on monumental importance; positions seem polarized and grow more so every day. Gridlocked partners feel like they are at each other's throat and neither partner can give an inch or apologize. One partner (or both) feels as if his or her integrity, identity, and self-worth are on the line and there is no room left for compromise. Couples often divorce when they do not understand gridlock and do not use the process productively.

Gridlock is not caused by lack of communication, and more communication will not resolve it. Conventional approaches such as "negotiate" and "agree to disagree" do not work because the issues involved require real-world decisions rather than discussing feelings and opinions. Gridlock repeatedly occurs around sex and intimacy, money, kids, and in-laws because these are forced-choice issues couples cannot agree to disagree about and leave it at that (e.g., couples cannot agree to disagree about how and when sex will occur).

Principle 5

Dependence on empathy, validation, understanding, acceptance, and/or accommodation from one's partner creates emotional gridlock (which in turn creates sexual desire problems). Differentiation and gridlock are intricately intertwined in relationship systems. Gridlock (and desire problems) occurs quicker and more intensely among less differentiated people. For example, couples who depend on other-validation as their form of self-regulation readily reach emotional gridlock on intimacy issues *because the partner who wants intimacy the least controls it.* Eventually, the high-desire (for intimacy) partner won't disclose what the low-desire (for intimacy) partner won't validate, especially when the emotional stakes run high. And the low desire partner won't validate the high-desire partner's disclosures because the low-desire partner does not want to listen or disclose in kind. Now combine this with the fact that the low-desire partner (for sex) always controls when sex occurs. It is easy to see why sexual desire problems are couples' most common sexual complaint.

As another example, lack of respect is among the most common and least talked about causes of low desire. Poorly differentiated people often do not respect themselves, and they do not respect their partner (for accommodating their demands). It is also easier for poorly differentiated people to say, "I don't like sex" than it is to say, "I don't like sex with you." Once the false persona is in place, poorly differentiated people have difficulty tolerating the anxiety of setting things straight so their relationship can move forward (i.e,. emotional gridlock). Sexual desire and intimacy typically decline. Discussions about partners' mutual lack of respect is itself an integrity challenge, which is why it so rarely occurs and why it is often so important when it happens.

Principle 6

Anxiety tolerance precedes anxiety reduction in the natural system of sexual development embedded in emotionally committed relationships. Because sexual boredom potentiates sexual desire problems, it is important to consider how normal sexual relationships develop. Systemically speaking, sexual relationships always consist of "leftovers": Each partner gets to rule out what makes him or her nervous and the couple does whatever is left (i.e., tyranny of the lowest common denominator). Said differently, people have sex up to their level of sexual development, and changing the sexual status quo (e.g., frequency, style, and meaning) creates anxiety and challenges partners' reflected sense of self. The Crucible Approach helps clients harness this process to grow themselves up.

Although it sounds unromantic and nonerotic, sexual relationships develop by partners *tolerating* rather than merely *reducing* anxiety, starting with their initial sexual experience and continuing through each addition in sexual behavior, meaning, or style. From its very beginnings, however, and to a large extent today, modern sex therapy (and marital therapy) reinforces couples' beliefs that the process ought to involve "safety and security" (low anxiety) first rather than the other way around.

Many people, especially poorly differentiated individuals, demand stability in their primary relationship (even though when they get it they complain of sexual boredom). When one partner innovates sexually, he or she should not count on validation, empathy, or support from the mate (e.g., "his partner being there for him"). More realistically he or she should count on a defensive response, such as, "Who taught you that?!" Sexual novelty in long-term relationships is always introduced unilaterally and involves tolerating anxiety—which is why differentiation and self-validated intimacy are integral to understanding and resolving sexual desire difficulties, avoiding boredom, and keeping sex alive.

Principle 7

Monogamy in poorly differentiated relationships creates low sexual desire. Monogamy reinforces the togetherness pressure (emotional fusion) in poorly differentiated couples. When one partner manifests low sexual desire in response to feeling "trapped," "controlled," and "pressured," and the other partner responds with heightened neediness in reaction to not feeling wanted, the couple creates a self-perpetuating feedback loop that amplifies desire disparity and hastens gridlock. (If the other partner responds with low desire as well, then celibacy rather than desire disparity results.) Using this gridlock (i.e., sexual desire problem) to enhance differentiation permits an entirely different monogamy dynamic that supports long-term sexual desire, intense intimacy, and robust passion.

Principle 8

Low sexual desire, itself, leads to gridlock in monogamous couples. Low sexual desire surfaces not only as a consequence of emotional gridlock per se. Low desire is a content arena in which gridlock readily arises because of the reality of sexual systems (e.g., the couple cannot agree to disagree) and the nature of low differentiation (e.g., reflected sense of self and anxiety regulation through accommodation).

Principle 9

Emotional gridlock and desire problems prompt "leaps of faith" to self-validation. The resolution of emotional gridlock involves one partner (or both) relinquishing expectations of validation, acceptance, or reciprocity from the other partner and making a "leap of faith" to validating him- or herself when the mate is not accepting or is actively disqualifying. The discomfort of gridlock is, itself, a stimulus for shifting from dependence on other-validation to self-validated intimacy (and greater capacity for intimacy and profound desire, per se). And conversely, the good feeling about oneself that comes from making the "leap of faith" and resolving gridlock is a powerful aphrodisiac.

The leap of faith in sexual desire problems often comes when one partner (1) no longer takes the other's sexual (dis)interest or complaints personally, (2) takes the other's discomfort seriously, (3) dares to see him- or herself as desirable and adequate just as he or she is, and/or (4) refuses to accept (or change) the sexual status quo. It could happen by the high-desire partner refusing to accept the lack or poor quality of sex while also refusing to forever push the other to change. It can also happen by the low-desire partner refusing to have sex he or she does not want or like but not expecting the high-desire partner to automatically go along.

Refusing to have sex—like refusing to be celibate—can represent an attempt to develop an autonomous sense of self in the context of relationship (i.e., differentiation). Likewise, either stance can actually reflect pseudo-differentiation—seeming bold moves that actually stem from emotional fusion and borrowed functioning.[14] Neither the high-desire or low-desire position is inherently "right"—and someone making a differentiating move is not inherently right, either. People can raise their differentiation somewhat even when they are totally wrong about something (they pay the price of being wrong).

Principle 10

Desire problems surface when partners' importance to each other exceeds their level of differentiation. This is the antithesis of conventional wisdom, which suggests low-desire results from indifference, emotional disinvestment, or lack of caring. As one's partner becomes *more* important with the passage of time—even if one does not like the partner—it becomes harder to validate oneself in the face of his or her disconfirmation or inattention. It becomes harder to innovate sexually, expand your sexual repertoire, or introduce deeper levels of eroticism, passion, intimacy—all of which potentiates low sexual desire. When the partner becomes more important than the individual is to him- or herself, the result is often either reduced desire (e.g., fears of loss or being controlled) or compulsive desire (e.g., engulfing the partner). Partners' seeming emotional indifference reflects their attempt to ward off each other's growing influence; their mutual reactivity reveals emotional fusion rather than indifference. This can happen in the earliest relationship stages for poorly differentiated people (e.g., moving in together or getting engaged).

Principle 11

Maintaining sexual desire as relationship duration increases requires continued personal development (differentiation), which is why desire often fades in long-term relationships. When partners' importance to each other exceeds their level of differentiation (their "relationship with themselves"), there are only four possible responses—all of which affect sexual desire in the dyad. They are (1) dominate the partner, (2) "submit" to the partner, (3) withdraw physically or emotionally from the relationship, or (4) become more differentiated. Not coincidentally, these same four choices surface more generally when one partner in an emotionally fused couple starts to differentiate.

For example, the high-desire partner faces these four choices before she makes the "leap of faith." Likewise, once the high-desire partner refuses to accept the sexual status quo (including always "pushing" for sex), the low-desire partner's typical options involve (1) pressuring the high-desire partner to abdicate his or her sexual preferences through tantrums, arguments, and threats of divorce or emotional collapse; (2) "giving in"—which usually leads to "mercy fucking" and passive–aggressive withholding; (3) separate bedrooms, affairs, or overinvolvement with children/parents/job; or (4) doing the necessary self-confrontation, self-soothing, and self-regulation that permits greater desire.

These kinds of forced-choice systemic dilemmas are "crucibles"—severe tests of selfhood and personal integrity built into emotionally committed relationships. Not all relationship crucibles are sexual. But as the following case illustrates,[15] the crucibles that surface around sexual desire problems can be powerful vehicles for personal development and facilitate desire, passion, eroticism, intimacy, and love.

CASE EXAMPLE USING THE SEXUAL CRUCIBLE APPROACH

Mr. and Mrs. B were married for 15 years. He was 50 years old and she was 45. This was her first marriage and his second; his first marriage ended when he discovered his wife was having an affair. They had no children; Mrs. B had difficulty conceiving and Mr. B was not particularly interested in having kids.

At the time they came to see me, Mr. and Mrs. B were on the verge of divorce. Mrs. B was threatening to leave over the lack of sex in their relationship, although neither she nor Mr. B was eager for that. A year ago, Mrs. B discovered that Mr. B was conducting clandestine correspondence with a woman he met on a business trip. The cache of letters she found were romantic and erotic and contained plans to meet for a weekend together. She had a hard time tolerating the lack of sex in her marriage as it was, and the thought of Mr. B having a romance on the side was just too much.

Mrs. B had given her husband the choice of counseling or separation, and he went into individual therapy. He had eventually lost desire for sex with his first wife too. Nine months later there was no change in Mrs. B's sexual relationship. Mrs. B did not think her husband's therapy was helping much, and Mr. B was eager to terminate treatment. After 3 months of trying on their own with no better results, Mrs. B referred herself and her husband to the Marriage and Family Health Center.

Treatment was conducted in an intensive therapy format originally developed for clients who fly in for treatment. This consists of four consecutive days of 3-hour nonstop sessions. Couples use the intervening time to process their reactions. In some cases these sessions are augmented with subsequent meetings (or phone consultations for couples who have flown in for treatment). In many instances the 4-day segment is all the intervention needed. This format is not specific to treating sexual desire problems, but rather, one that works well with a wide range of sexual, relationship, and personal difficulties. Likewise, the clinical approach I describe is a specific application of an integrated sexual–marital therapy that works well with sexual dysfunctions too (including when used in more conventional time frames of weekly or biweekly 1-hour sessions) (Schnarch, in press). However, the intensive therapy format yields results unmatched by briefer and/or less densely spaced sessions, especially with more difficult cases. Although it is only speculation, I (and Mr. and Mrs. B) doubt they would have made the progress they did had they been seen for only 1 hour at a time spaced weeks apart.[16]

Session 1

Mr. B was a successful real estate developer and Mrs. B was a teacher who specialized in working with abused children. Mr. B supported Mrs. B's efforts and after long days at his business, he often spent evenings and weekends raising donations and lobbying for child welfare. Mrs. B was proud of Mr. B's activities, but she felt he was rarely home and invariably exhausted and reclusive when he was.

Mrs. B said she worried when her husband declined to have sex shortly after their wedding. Concern became shock when his sexual disinterest became a stable pattern. Mrs. B described herself sexually as a "late bloomer" who was trying to make up for lost time. She had not had intercourse until she was in her mid-20's and then only with several partners. Mr. B had sex with a number of women before and after his first marriage but never dated any one seriously. Mr. B met Mrs. B through a mutual friend, and he pursued her sexually in spite of her initial hesitancies. Both partners reported sex initially was "great," and Mr. B liked how readily Mrs. B became aroused. Mrs. B anticipated they would have sex nightly once they married—at least for a while—but it was never more than twice a month at best. Throughout their marriage sex often occurred no more than several times a year, and no sex for 6 months at a time was the norm.

Mrs. B hesitantly spoke of her anger over her husband's emotional and physical withdrawal and the frustration of "not being allowed to touch him." Mr. B retorted that he was not as interested in sex as he had been when he was younger, and his numerous commitments left him too tired to be romantic. His own resentments and disappointments about his wife then followed, particularly that she was not a good intellectual partner because she did not like to discuss current events. Mrs. B said she did not like to argue, he always had to win, and she specifically did not enjoy it during foreplay:

When they made plans to have sex, Mr. B often ruined the occasions by finding fault or criticizing her before they started. Mr. B allowed that he was "critical" at times, but denied he was avoiding sex. He was just too tired and "irritable" much of the time. When asked directly, Mr. B acknowledged that he was verbally abusive to his wife. He said he was horrified when he realized in individual therapy he was replaying his father's treatment of his mother. Apparently from past experience in therapy, Mr. B thought his insight and "owning up" would conclude our discussion. I asked how his "horror" allowed him to continue repeating this pattern. Mr. B said he did not have an answer, but both he and Mrs. B sat up and paid more attention to our discussion.

As we continued, I noticed Mrs. B often offered her husband rather cutting remarks with no apparent awareness of doing so. When I referred to her "serrated tongue," Mrs. B was initially shocked to identify this as her own mother's style. She expressed chagrin that she had not seen this sooner. But unlike Mr. B, she chaffed at the realization, made no effort to justify her treatment of her husband, and made efforts to stop it. She invited further discussion whereas her husband avoided it. Throughout the remainder of the session, Mrs. B caught herself as she was "slicing and dicing" her husband, and eventually stopped altogether. Confronting Mrs. B this way not only was of benefit to her but also rebalanced my alliance with Mr. B. It clarified that my prior confrontation of him was not adversarial, nor was I biased against him (i.e., isomorphic intervention). Thereafter Mr. B seemed more collaborative but still wary about what might unfold in therapy.

The Devil's Pact

Mr. and Mrs. B went on to discuss an incident that had happened almost 1 year ago, about which they were still fighting. They had discussed it repeatedly without resolution and Mr. B said they just had to agree to disagree about it and his wife had to let it go. Mrs. B was still furious about what had happened, saying it epitomized their relationship. They described a ubiquitous and ineffective pattern of sexual interaction I call "the devil's pact."

The devil's pact begins by the high-desire partner complaining that the low-desire partner never initiates, to which the low-desire partner offers the defense, "You never give me chance to initiate because you're always initiating!" With varying degrees of rancor, defensiveness, and combativeness, the couple makes a fateful agreement: The high-desire partner will stop initiating sex and the low-desire partner will be more forthcoming. On the surface it makes perfect sense: Create a vacuum and the low-desire partner will fill it because he or she no longer feels pressured by the high-desire partner.

Unfortunately, it does not usually work in practice because it does not fundamentally change the system; in fact, it reinforces the status quo. The low desire partner does not initiate at first because he or she is enjoying not feeling pressured to have sex. Besides, he or she wants sex to be meaningful when they have it rather than just doing it to do it. But with each passing day, the low-desire partner actually feels increasing pressure because he or she is aware of the high-desire partner's expectation and growing exasperation. Because one purpose of the pact is to keep the low-desire partner from feeling pressured, he or she now feels entitled not to initiate because he or she still feels pressure. The high-desire partner's frustration escalates, and the spiral intensifies. The low-desire partner now does not initiate, refusing to capitulate to the high-desire partner who can seemingly pressure for sex by *not* initiating. When the high-desire partner eventually explodes in frustration, the low-desire partner explains that he or she did not initiate because he or she felt pressured to have sex because the high-desire partner still expected it.

Understanding how the devil's pact operates, and why it does not help, reveals the inherent pressures of sexual systems built into committed relationships. The devil's pact is a specific form of emotional gridlock. That is hard to realize if the situation is perceived as a problem of only one person feeling pressured (e.g., Mr. B). Gridlock always involves two people (being pressured). Rampant victimology in psychotherapy today makes the low-desire partner's applications of pressure hard to see, whereas similar moves by the high-desire partner are obvious.[17] Actually, Mr. B trapped Mrs. B every time he backed himself into a corner through his own avoidance. Mrs. B could not take the pressure off him without giving up her own preferences—which is exactly what Mr. B was, in effect, trying to do: pressuring his wife to give up her rightful preference so he would not feel pressured. Mr. B was in a tough spot because his wife's sexual desire, which made him feel pressured, also paradoxically offered him the secret security to *not* want her. It was only safe to *not* want her as long as she wanted him, so Mr. B did things to keep her wanting (e.g., expressing intent to change or having sex occasionally)—which set the stage for feeling pressured again.

The devil's pact is not reducible to partners' unconscious processes or family-of-origin issues (although such issues are often *triggered* by gridlock). It is a systemic dynamic that attracts partners' unresolved differentiation tasks like a magnet, creating a secondary level of gridlock that is unique to the people involved. This process transcends culture, gender, and sexual orientation, but how couples handle it reflects who they are. This is where natural systems and personal dynamics intertwine.

In this case, Mrs. B had grown willing in recent years for Mr. B to make a clear statement that he honestly did not want or care if sex improved; she would make her own choices based on that. But she was stymied by Mr. B's unwillingness to confront his *two-choice dilemmas* (Schnarch, 1997a). One two-choice dilemma involved his unwillingness to risk losing her by openly defining his true position and his unwillingness to confront his own inability to want her. Another was the fact that Mr. B had agreed to monogamy but now he wanted marital celibacy. A third arose because Mr. B wanted to be married to a woman who wanted sex, but he did not want to have sex with her. When Mr. B dodged his two-choice dilemmas by misrepresenting his efforts and his intent, he stole his wife's choice (i.e., borrowed functioning). But rather than see him as a villain, I began to think about what it must be like for Mr. B to live with the constant tensions implicit in his situation and why he might be willing to do so.

Shifting Paradigms

At this point in the session I clarified that I was not automatically aligned with Mrs. B because she was the high-desire partner. Moreover, I told Mr. B that I would not overtly or covertly try to make him more interested in sex. He had a perfect right not to have sex if he did not want to, but he did not have a right to expect his wife to like it or accept it. I made a point of treating Mr. B with respect (including addressing him by surname), and stated that I did not think the low-desire partner was de facto inadequate or pathological. Mr. B relaxed a bit and seemed more willing to discuss his relationship with his wife.

Mrs. B spoke of how remote they were; I commented how they were like "emotional Siamese twins" joined at the hip: Mr. B kept acting as if he had to get away from her and Mrs. B kept taking it personally. Then Mrs. B spoke about how she could not get a response from her husband when she talked to him and how he barely paid attention to her. I pointed out that his attentiveness was evident in the show he made of ignoring her and she clearly "got the message."

Without realizing it, Mrs. B was packaging her subjective experience in the language of "first paradigm" therapy; I was operating from a differentiation framework. Operating clinically as if people are emotionally fused while they are complaining of emotional estrangement may seem illogical at first, but it rapidly defuses arguments and dramatically improves clients' personal and interpersonal functioning. Without much conviction, Mrs. B began considering their interactions from the standpoint she and her husband were "connected" rather than "out of touch."

At one point Mrs. B got upset when Mr. B scowled in response to something she said. Tongue-in-cheek, I proposed her knee-jerk reactivity demonstrated how there was absolutely no connection between them. Mrs. B instantly shifted "world views," recognized their emotional fusion, and went from being "wounded" to bursting in laugher! Mr. B went from being angry at being criticized to anger at being "laughed at" to being piqued that his wife was having "a private joke." From then on Mrs. B held onto her recognition of emotional fusion.

In contrast to their fears that they could not change their situation, Mr. B clearly became anxious when his wife was less reactive to his every move. As is invariably the case when resolving gridlock, one partner (Mr. B) gets nervous when the other (Mrs. B) finally makes the leap of faith to self-confrontation, self-validation, and self-soothing. Said differently, when one partner starts to control him- or herself (i.e., differentiate) within an emotionally fused relationship, the other partner feels controlled. This is what actually brought Mr. B into treatment:

In recent years, Mrs. B was less inclined to take her husband's lack of sexual desire as a negative reflection about herself. Like many women her age she was blossoming, including sexually. She felt better about herself than when she was younger, and more curious to explore what she was made of. When she briefly moved out of their bedroom, Mr. B realized he could no longer contain the situation (or his wife). His only choices were to get divorced or confront himself (or at least appear to do so). He agreed to conjoint therapy only when he sensed their relationship was approaching "critical mass" (Schnarch, 1991, 1997a).

Getting to this point was, itself, a big step for Mrs. B. She had grown up without siblings; two children preceding her had died in infancy from birth defects. Her father was often morose, her mother hopelessly anxious, and her home life unhappy. Mrs. B had been depressed during adolescence and bulimic during her initial years at college. She spent years trying to escape the seductive pull of taking care of her parents' feelings at her own expense.

In contrast, Mr. B presented a classic description of a child who had been "out of connection" during his formative years: He said he was distant with his parents and his two younger siblings now, having had little emotional contact with them while growing up. They never discussed feelings and certainly never talked about sex. Mr. B described his father as an emotionally unavailable workaholic who never attended a single high school athletic event in which Mr. B played. He described his mother as warm, bubbly, and nurturing on the surface but disinterested and unavailable on a deeper level. He was her perfect child who could do no wrong, but he felt she really did not know him.

At the same time, Mr. B's behavior revealed him to be extremely shrewd (if not cunning). He took care not to openly define his thoughts, feelings, and motivations until he scoped out his wife's (and my) reactions. His skill was too highly refined to have developed simply in response to his wife's barbs. I wondered whether this more likely started as a childhood adaptation to what was present (rather than what was absent) in his household. I decided to say nothing at this point.

Further Stage Setting for Treatment

As Mrs. B became less reactive to her husband in session, we created two interlocking crucibles: She focused more on how she took her husband's desire as a negative self-reflection, which took pressure off of him (to want sex) and put more of it on her (to validate or confront herself). On the other hand, this put more pressure on Mr. B to decide whether *he* felt his level of sexual desire was problematic. This, in turn, challenged his differentiation (i.e., his clarity of self, self-soothing, nonreactivity, and tolerating discomfort for growth). Sometimes Mr. B made tentative statements of his position and other times he remained evasive in our session; either way the same four aspects of Mrs. B's differentiation were stretched too. Would he stand pat on their sexual frequency, and would she be forced to choose whether to leave? Would he give in to keep his marriage but continue to be resentful? Would she accept this any longer? Differentiating moves I made with one partner had clinically desirable impacts on the other, creating a very efficient therapy.

As I gathered details of their style of having sex, Mrs. B hesitantly suggested that her husband had difficulty reaching orgasm. Mr. B reluctantly agreed that he sometimes had difficulty and assured me he had discussed this with his individual therapist. They both decided this was not a "sexual problem." It turned out Mr. B had difficulty with delayed ejaculation in almost every sexual encounter: Half the time he was able to eventually reach orgasm by fantasizing about having sex with someone else. Other times he "gave up" and stopped in the middle of intercourse. Often Mr. B would avoid sex out of embarrassment and frustration. The fact that Mrs. B was not taking his difficulty personally any more made him all the more defensive.

In daily life, Mr. B regulated his internal equilibrium by maintaining distance (physically and emotionally) from his wife. Belly to belly during sex, however, the same strategy did not work. Mr. B had difficulty maintaining a clear sense of self and a nonanxious presence in close proximity to those he loved. This limited his capacity for intimacy and intense desire with his wife and predisposed him to sexual performance problems. In other words, Mr. B's ejaculatory problem both reduced his desire for sex and intimacy and was, itself, the end result of limited differentiation.[18]

There were multiple benefits in organizing therapy to facilitate differentiation by resolving their many forms of gridlock (their desire problem, his orgasmic difficulty, both partner's reflected sense of self and emotional reactivity, etc). Their presenting dynamics certainly demanded a well-differentiated therapeutic stance: My clarity of "knowing what I know," my ability to calm myself and not overreact when sessions get tense, and my willingness to go through difficult times with my clients were tested in myriad ways.

Treatment had to be organized so that *if* Mr. B chose to participate in treatment (or in sex), it was clear he was not "submitting" to his wife, to his own fears, or to me. I reiterated my clinical position of not presuming that the low-desire partner was pathological and declined to conduct treatment if the purpose was to make Mr. B have more sex or intimacy with his wife. I proposed our sessions focus on helping both partners "take their own shape" so they could decide what they really wanted to do with each other. I also offered to help Mr. B with his orgasmic difficulty if he wanted, and not as a means to make him want sex with his wife—I articulated the possibility that once his genitals worked better he still might decide to keep them to himself. We briefly discussed things they could do if they were interested in more intimacy (e.g., hugging till relaxed, eyes-open sex; Schnarch, 1991, 1997a) with the explicit caveat that no "homework" assignments (sexual and otherwise) or prohibitions would be given. Mr. and Mrs. B were encouraged to do (or not do) whatever they thought best.

Session 2

Mrs. B opened our next session by asking whether her bulimia and depression were the result of emotional fusion and failed attempts at differentiation. She had spent a large part of the night thinking about herself and her family of origin from the standpoint of fusion rather than alienation, and her new insights helped her understand herself and her past in entirely new light. From there, she moved into serious self-confrontation about using sarcasm and humor to "cut him [her husband] to bits." She had previously thought of her mother's sarcasm as expressions of anger and frustration; now she wondered whether this was actually her mother's way of relating to people.

Mr. B, in contrast, had not a single reflection about his verbal abuse of his wife and expressed no curiosity about it (even when asked)—even though his wife had engaged in serious soul searching on comparable issues moments before. I noted this to myself and waited to see what direction Mr. B wanted to take things. It turned out he wanted to talk about the sex they had in the last 24 hours.

Mr. B had initiated "cuddling" the prior night and it had led to noncoital sex. Mrs. B reported that her husband seemed genuinely energetic and enthusiastic about holding her, and the segue into genital contact seemed comfortable and easy. The next morning Mr. B initiated intercourse directly and had no difficulty reaching orgasm, much to their mutual surprise and delight. Mr. B reported he had been more involved and present than usual during sex.

Refining the Accuracy of the "Lens"

I asked Mr. B how they were able to make such dramatic progress literally overnight. Mr. B glibly said he had no idea and did not care, he was just delighted with their progress. He flippantly proposed, "Maybe it's a miracle." I had the sense Mr. B was trying to "buy me off" with a report of quick success, as if saying, "Thanks a lot Doc, you've been a great help. No need to look further. We're cured."

When I suggested Mr. B might, indeed, want to care why things went so well if he wanted it to happen again, he became more serious. I proposed that the sudden improvement in his sexual interest and sexual functioning was impressive but definitely not a miracle. Mr. B had told me the day before (when asked directly) that he masturbated once or twice a week throughout their marriage although he and Mrs. B had never discussed it. His history also suggested that he had more interest and less orgasmic difficulty when he was not married. Likewise his clandestine correspondence suggested that his interest in sex and romance remained alive and well. Maybe, I proposed, he just did not want to share these with his wife?

My intervention had multiple isomorphic impacts. Mr. B was unmasked, the picture of him as a sexless person was instantaneously revamped, and the meaning of their years of sexual inactivity suddenly changed. Mr. B's clandestine romance came into focus. It was a difficult moment for both spouses.

Rather than his usual bluster and defensiveness, Mr. B did not say anything at first. He was not sure of his wife's reaction, in part, because she was not "slicing him up." He watched a new look of understanding cross her face as she realized he had hidden his sexuality from her and pretended to be asexual.

Who Chose Whom?

Rather than attacking him, Mrs. B launched into a spontaneous reexamination of their early days together. We discussed "who chose whom" as a way to explore the emotional politics of *wanting* in their relationship. In many relationships one partner chooses the other, and the other partner gets married because he or she does not have to choose. But as Mr. and Mrs. B's case revealed, the "pursuing partner" is not necessarily the chooser. Mr. B pursued Mrs. B until she chose him; once this occurred he lost all interest in sex with her.[19] Once this pattern was in place, Mr. B did not want to relinquish the powerful position of being "the undecided chooser." Most of all, Mr. B did not want the vulnerability of really wanting his wife.

This revelation triggered several poignant reactions in session. Tearfully, Mrs. B began to talk about fearing that her husband was a weak man—too weak to love anyone including her. However, she was not "pounding" on Mr. B in her typical fashion. She confronted herself (and her husband) by revealing a difficult truth—She had previously avoided addressing her "serrated tongue" because it would increase the likelihood she would leave the marriage if Mr. B did not deal with his own issues and abusive behavior.

Mrs. B's remarkable display of self-validation, self-confrontation, and self-soothing—her leap of faith—changed everything. Mrs. B sobbed deeply, absorbed in the truth of her own words. She seemed more open and less vulnerable than any time up to that point. Mr. B was speechless. His wife was so solidly grounded at that moment that he did not even try to hook her into an argument.

Mrs. B brightened and functioned better even though the situation was tense. She looked remarkably more relaxed and prettier than the day before. When I asked Mr. B. if he could see the difference in his wife's appearance, he acknowledged that her face looked softer. Because he readily could have denied this—and Mr. B was afraid of her response at the moment—I took his response as an indication that the best in him was coming forward.

Into the Crucible

I took this opportunity to comment on Mr. B's pattern of obfuscation, dodging issues, and inconsistencies in his stories. Mr. B had radar-like ability to "track" other people, which he "cloaked" by acting ignorant and incompetent. I asked him why a man who came from an emotionally distant family would develop such sophisticated ways to keep from being seen, when other people might develop ways to get other people's attention?

Mr. B. talked flatly about how his father was often rageful with everyone in the family—rageful to the point that Mr. B had thought to himself, "He really wants to kill us." Without realizing it, Mr. B drew a picture of someone with more than a bad temper. He described how his father would "come gunning" for him, seeking out whatever was important to Mr. B at the moment and destroying it physically or emotionally. His father would not stop until Mr. B was in tears and demolished in spirit.

In contrast to his earlier picture of wishing his father was more involved in his life, I proposed that Mr. B must have spent a lot of time hoping his father would not come home at all. At the same time, he must have desperately *wanted* his father to be different, and gotten his heart broken in the process. In other words, I shifted the picture of Mr. B's childhood from the absence of a relationship with his father to one colored by the kind of relatedness they did have.

Mr. B was engaging his wife in the form of relatedness he knew best—a sadomasochistic relationship—and he had learned his lessons well: Having been on the receiving end for years, he knew how to corner someone into a dependent position and work that person over emotionally. He had learned that it was more fun to dish it out than it is to take it. And Mr. B lived in a reality in which *somebody* was going to get it. "You know how to tear someone's heart out," I said, and Mr. B begrudgingly nodded in acknowledgement. Normal marital sadism (Schnarch, 1991) often takes the form of mercy fucking, as when Mr. B was stingy with his wife at the same moment he (finally) had sex with her, leaving her no easy recourse.

I framed this discussion as integrity issues in Mr. B's relationship with himself, transcending any decisions about his marriage or his feelings about his wife. Mr. B was stunned by the suggestion that his integrity could be at question at all. But from his descriptions, Mr. B lost some of his integrity in interactions with his father. He was still angry at himself for not having stood up to his dad. And likewise, it sounded as if his father had set out to "break him down," beating him until he sobbed and pleaded for mercy. This created an emotional fusion (rather than "distance") that existed to this day, the image of his father's jaw jutting into Mr. B's face still fresh and vivid in his mind.

I proposed that Mr. B's problem was not as simple as repeatedly acting as if he were still dealing with his father (i.e., playing out the "victim" role). Rather, by playing out the same dynamic from his father's role (i.e., as a "perpetrator"), *he* perpetuated his emotional fusion with his father. If he continued, he might unwittingly convince himself he was unable to "get over it."[20] However, by approaching his current dilemmas in particular ways Mr. B might be able to earn his own self-respect, unhook from his father, and move on with his life (i.e., resolve the past in the present). For instance, Mr. B could stop being verbally abusive because he was afraid his wife would not take it any more, or because he did not want to be like his dad, or because he intentionally wanted to master himself and repair the sense of integrity he had lost on the basement floor groveling at his father's feet.

Mr. B asked for other examples of how personal integrity issues might be surfacing for him. I noted that he was rageful that his wife had read his private mail, but he felt no remorse or guilt that he had been carrying on a romance and made plans to have sex with another woman. As was their typical pattern, Mr. B started to grab the "moral high ground" at that moment and Mrs. B reflexively defended herself. I said it seemed OK with Mr. B if he violated his own integrity and his agreement to monogamy, but he deeply resented his wife violating his privacy. My statement stopped Mr. B dead in his tracks, which had a tremendous impact on Mrs. B as well. He was suddenly confronted with a difficult truth about himself, and she watched him begin to approach it without dodging.

Mr. B sagged. He had been tearful at one point earlier in the session but it seemed superficial and self-indulgent. Now he was deep in anguished self-confrontation and he convulsed in tears. This time he seemed more solid and real.

The Crucial Role of Treatment Paradigm

Instead of asking him to empathize with his wife's plight, I talked to Mr. B about earning his own self-respect and repairing his integrity. I proposed that he had a perfect right not to have sex with his wife regardless of the reason. What he did not have the right to do, however, was to steal his wife's opportunity to make similar decisions about her own life. If he continued to have no desire for sex with his wife, giving her a fair shake might involve advising her to assume he would not change (rather than asking her to be more patient).

Mrs. B went on to discuss three profound realizations she had had in session. First, she saw how what Mr. B and I talked about applied to what she still played out with her mother. She called her mother every weekend without fail although she hated it—and she hated it, in part, because she did not have the courage to call her mother only when she wanted to. Second, realizing that their relationship (e.g., the "devil's pact") was driven by more than their emotional problems or feelings helped her become less reactive. Third, Mrs. B was not sure how she felt about Mr. B's pretending to have no sexual interest altogether. But henceforth she was not going to take Mr. B's "emotional affair" as a negative self-reflection or feel guilty about having briefly moved out of their bedroom. Moreover, she was asking herself why she wanted sex with a man who really did not want her.

This unsettled Mr. B who, to his credit, spoke like an adult realizing that partners often separate when they do not offer each other a fair shake. As always, I offered no behavioral assignments or sexual prescriptions (including sensate focus), created no prohibitions or "bans," and did not teach communication skills, "active listening," or mirroring/validation dialogues. I told Mr. and Mrs. B that I could not wait to find out what they were going to do next.

Session 3

In contrast to his glowing report following our first session, Mr. B announced that the preceding afternoon and evening had been a tearful and somber one for him. He felt bad about himself and more worried about losing his wife. Moreover, he did not feel much desire for sex.

Clearly Mr. B anticipated an adversarial confrontation between us, and he

seemed genuinely surprised when this did not happen. I pointed out that sometimes feeling bad about ourselves is appropriate and healthy, especially if comes
from the best in us. Moreover, I noted that many people do not have sexual
desire when they do not respect themselves—and they have no respect for anyone who wants sex with them. When I did not get defensive or attack Mr. B his
functioning improved and we went on to discuss what else had happened since
our last session.

The previous afternoon, Mrs. B had thought about how much she let
other people's expectations and feelings control her. This led to her making a
sexual overture (because *she* wanted to have sex), which her husband declined.
Mrs. B then decided to carry out her agenda by having sex by herself. Although she didn't expect much going into it, she had a powerful experience
that left her satisfied and self-impressed.

Later that evening, Mr. B initiated sex, in part, to see whether Mrs. B was
angry at him. She was not mad about his prior refusal, but she did get angry
about his timid, obsequious initiation. Mr. B kept saying that she was punishing him for what he did not do earlier; Mrs. B maintained that she was angry
about what he was doing at present. She did not respond initially with her
"serrated tongue." However Mr. B acted as if she was "cutting him up" as she
normally did and Mrs. B started to defend herself. Eventually Mrs. B pulled
out of the argument and calmed down. But Mr. B continued acting as if she
was attacking him and eventually stormed out of the room. He calmed down
in 20 minutes (a record for him) and walked back in to say, "I see how I react
to you like you're my Dad and you're angry at me, and then I act like a little
boy." For long moments they looked eye to eye—and eventually relaxed into a
warm smiling gaze. Mrs. B thanked him for his acknowledgement and reached
out to him sexually shortly thereafter.

Opening the Elicitation Window

When they had intercourse, Mr. B was unable to reach orgasm. We used their
description of sex to create the *elicitation window* (Schnarch, 1991): Couples'
specific patterns of having (and not having) sex are a window into who they
are. Sex is a language and our sexual style is rooted in what is inside us. Couples
act out the story of their lives during sex, and if approached this way even
"dysfunctions" and unsatisfying sexual experiences become useful. Establishing the elicitation window involves tracking sexual patterns and meanings on
current and historical levels. From there, changing sexual styles becomes a
deliberate and purposeful way people can rewrite their stories, make themselves into who they want to be, and create a new future that is not a prisoner
of the past (i.e., "resolve past in the present"). We eventually developed the
following picture from their report:

When Mr. B first realized he was having difficulty ejaculating he did not
say anything about it. As was typical for him, he kept thrusting until he was

exhausted and emotionally distraught. Mr. B had felt particularly inadequate that night because they had already had 2 days of therapy—his sexual "successes" on preceding days only magnified his failure. Locked away in his own anxiety-filled mental world, feeling vulnerable, exposed, desperate, and inadequate, Mr. B had no inkling he had broken all intimate contact with his wife. He felt the fusion—no separateness, no selfhood, and acute anxiety combined with emotional alienation—and as far as he knew this is what it meant to be with somebody. Mr. B's lack of interest in sex was more understandable and rational than he had imagined. The idea he was all alone during sex astonished him. But the life script we extracted from his sexual behavior required no interpretation: "Shut up, perform, don't ask questions, give people what they want, don't expect compassion, and make sure you're a small (or moving) target." (This made Mr. B more open to finding new ways of handling his difficulty even if he could not stop it altogether.)

For her part, Mrs. B usually got nervous when she sensed Mr. B getting anxious about not being able to orgasm. She had her own anticipatory concerns about her own satisfaction too. Having found that Mr. B reacted negatively to any discussion of his difficulty (during sex or afterward), Mrs. B typically conformed by acting as if she was blind to what was happening. She had done the same thing growing up, acting as if the two prior infant deaths, her father's depressions, and her mother's chronic insecurities did not exist. Mrs. B said that seeing this in session made her not only more determined not to replicate the past in bed but even happier about what she had already done.

In contrast to her normal pattern, Mrs. B had spoken up the previous night when Mr. B started having difficulty reaching orgasm. The jackhammer thrusting and his palpable anxiety were all too familiar. This time she encouraged him to stop thrusting and to just lie there with her. Mr. B began making excuses for his "failure" and said she was breaking his concentration. Mrs. B said she was not going to just lie there any more while he "went to war with himself" and, besides, if he was going to concentrate on anything she wanted it to be *her*. Mr. B got off her and they talked briefly before he rolled over to his side of the bed. Mrs. B could tell he was disappointed and frustrated, but he lay looking at the ceiling instead of laying with his back to her as he typically did. Mrs. B took this as his "peace offering" and she accepted it, lying similarly next to him and placing her hand in his. Within moments he turned toward her, racked with wordless moans and tears, and they went to sleep in each other's arms instead of miles apart.

Early the next morning Mr. B apologized for the night before. Mrs. B was pleased with her experience none the less. In response she made the bold move of rapidly arousing her husband with her hand, and he mounted her and quickly came to orgasm without fanfare. Both were pleased, but Mr. B worried that his wife did not have an orgasm; Mrs. B said she was quite satisfied and, in fact, quite happy she did not have one just to relieve his anxiety.

Setting the Stage for Differentiation

Mr. B's positive response in session reinforced what was already a success for his wife. We used this response to set the stage for further work on delayed ejaculation, building on their spontaneous sexual behavior and the meanings being played out in their sex. As long as Mr. B tried desperately to have an orgasm to fend off the response he anticipated, it was as if he was with his father as a little boy. As long as he tried to produce an orgasm to prove he was not inadequate, he reinforced his belief in his own fundamental inadequacy *even* if he succeeded in ejaculating. And as long as he got caught up pushing for orgasm, he was cut off from his wife and as alone and lonely as he had been much of his life.

Correspondingly, we discussed three different meaning realities Mr. B could play with during sex if he chose. First was the question, "Could he let his wife be with him during sex?" This involved switching his emphasis during sex from sensate focus, physical stimulation, and fantasy to emotional connection and intimacy. Rather than encouraging Mr. B to "tell your partner what you want," we discussed "following the connection" (Schnarch, 1991, 1997a)— letting whatever built the sense of intimacy between them determine what to do next. And rather than present this as more relaxing than what they had been doing, we discussed how this was actually more anxiety provoking for Mr. B: He was skittish about letting anybody really know him or be with him.

This led to the second question, "Could Mr. B let anybody *hold* him?" We discussed "hugging till relaxed" (Schnarch, 1997), knowing it would probably make him anxious. Like many people, Mr. B was nervous about relaxing because it felt as if he was dropping his emotional armor and turning off his radar. He also expressed some fear of shifting his body during the hug or letting go before his wife wanted to stop, potentially triggering her anger. When he saw this as the same fear of "standing up" in front of his father, Mr. B recognized the possible benefit in taking new action during "hugging till relaxed" to the face of an old dilemma.

Finally, we talked about the possibility of Mr. B's ceasing to make himself ejaculate and letting his wife *take* him sexually. Rather than present this as a passive stance, we discussed how having the strength and integrity to let himself be held and taken by his wife might make him less afraid of his own healthy sexual aggression. In other words, he might stop trying to "please" his wife and ravish her instead (which she wanted, too). If he intended to remain passive–aggressive and constantly on the defensive, he would have a hard time letting his wife take him.

Each of these three scenarios was presented as requiring anxiety tolerance and self-mastery rather than anxiety reduction: His fears would probably (we hoped) surface in these activities, giving him the chance to observe and master them (i.e., master himself). Mr. B said he liked that I did not present an overly rosy picture of what might be entailed.

Mr. B also began to talk of feeling as if his wife would "win" and he would "lose" if he developed more desire. I responded that as long as he acted as if there was only room for one person to feel competent at any given time, he was, in effect, still living in his father's house. And likewise, although he might willingly act incompetent to make other people feel incompetent, no amount of passive–aggressiveness could help him feel more phallic. He had the choice to give himself up or not, but that did not mean that his wife "got" him—in fact, she got very little of him as long as he did not have much grip on himself. Discussing what happens when people do not hold on to themselves led to talking about the *weakness* behind his father's anger rather than the "power." And this, in turn, led to Mr. B confronting himself about verbally abusing his wife.

Mr. B described a long list of his transgressions in unflattering detail, making no attempt to justify them. Mrs. B helped him out with a few he had forgotten and he did not take offense. Toward the end Mr. B said he felt bad seeing himself act as weak as his father had. I asked him whether his father ever got upset about verbally abusing his family. When he said he did not think so, I proposed that Mr. B might feel good about feeling bad because this was one way he was differentiating from his father's pattern. Mr. B seemed less over-whelmed by his flood of feelings and persevered through a few more difficult acknowledgments about himself.

Although she said little during much of this time, Mrs. B was thinking about how my interaction with Mr. B applied to her. She wondered about her willingness and ability to *take* him, about her own patterns of withholding, and her own difficulties with being held. She also thought about her tendency to be "understanding" when she was bitterly disappointed. She respected Mr. B's self-confrontation about being abusive to her-but she was going to wait and see how much this would actually change. Mr. and Mrs. B left neck-deep in their respective crucibles, wondering what was next. They had new under-standings of the past. Now the real question was, "What they were going to do in the present?"

Session 4

Mr. and Mrs. B returned for their next session more relaxed with themselves and each other, often touching during our meeting. This was hardly the out-come they had expected from the previous afternoon. After the last session Mr. B had teased his wife that maybe she was becoming hooked on sex. When Mrs. B stopped to really think about it, Mr. B taunted her with, "Bet you want it now." Mrs. B felt as if he was playing "power games" with his ability to de-prive her. And she did not like feeling one-down because she *wanted* sex and intimacy.

Mr. B sensed things were going wrong, and after cajoling her not to take things too personally, he made an overture for sex. Mrs. B declined his invita-tion and he became incensed. He felt "wounded," his temper flared, and he launched into his typical verbal battering once again. Mrs. B went from feeling proud of herself to defending herself to refusing to be treated that way all in 2 minutes' time. When she could not get a word in she stood up and quietly walked out.

Mr. B was stunned! At a loss for what to do, he kicked a chair and began ranting to himself about his rotten relationship with his father.[21] Then he started in on his mother, the bubbly woman who was unwilling to confront what was happening in her house, who left him to face the full impact of his father on his own. A torrent of epithets later, his wife was his target again, guilty of numerous torments, frustrations, and demands. Her ultimate indictment was the fact that Mr. B was standing in the room all alone.

The realization of being all alone in the room shattered Mr. B's mental citadel. He felt rageful, mortified, impotent, dependent, and frightened all in that instant. Mrs. B's fear that he was too weak to love anyone returned to mind. He had just been blaming everyone else for his own doing. He could not stand the thought that what she feared was true. Mr. B described it as looking at himself at the bottom of a bottomless pit. In the middle of some pretty dark despair, he thought about the notion that it is sometimes the best in us that feels bad about what we do (and do not do). That helped him turn the corner on his self-pity and self-loathing and see something good in himself. That is when Mr. B first experienced *clean* pain. He hurt like hell but he did not fall apart, and he felt more solid and less self-indulgent. During the time he did not spend thinking about himself that afternoon, he instead wondered about where his wife was and when she would come home. When she returned 4 hours later in good spirits he was greatly relieved.

Mrs. B had gone to one of the open-space parks in Evergreen to take a long walk. She had a lovely afternoon, particularly because she enjoyed herself in spite of what just happened. She was proud of how she handled herself from beginning to end—proud enough that she spent time reexamining her decision not to have sex with Mr. B. She found herself thinking about having sex right there in the park, which triggered more thoughts that maybe she was sex-crazed after all—which led to self-validating her sexual interest all over again.

When she got home Mr. B apologized for his outburst. He complimented her for how she conducted herself even though she really pissed him off. Over dinner they traded stories about their time apart.

Seeing Oneself through Sex

Mr. B then proposed they try "hugging till relaxed," during which he shifted to a more comfortable position although he feared she would criticize him for it. Mrs. B knew he was getting "twitchy" but she focused on herself, calmed herself down, and let her husband take care of himself. Eventually Mr. B relaxed enough to smell the scent of her hair and he rapidly became erect, which surprised and delighted him.

Mr. and Mrs. B used this as an entree into sex, which started by lying down side by side and looking into each other's eyes. Then they took turns holding each other and allowing themselves to be held. Both interactions made Mr. B nervous at first, but he calmed himself down and they enjoyed it. Even Mrs. B had some discomfort to get over. When Mr. B eventually initiated intercourse, Mrs. B declined and offered him oral sex. Mr. B got up on his knees and let his wife *take* him, instead of remaining passive on his back and feeling overwhelmed by her. This interaction was noteworthy because Mr. B often had difficulty reaching orgasm during oral sex and typically declined her offers. Mr. B reached orgasm without difficulty this time, reporting a very solid erection that culminated in an explosive orgasm. Mrs. B echoed his report, saying that he seemed more present both during sex and afterward. Rather than falling asleep as he usually did after orgasm, Mr. B seemed energized and wide awake.

Mr. B said this was the best sex they ever had, and Mrs. B joked that he had more sexual energy than usual: He had tied one of her hands to the leg of their bed with her pantyhose. This allowed Mrs. B to get more involved with him and worry less about him. Mr. B proceeded to give her oral sex during which she was multiply orgasmic. This new style of sex was deeply meaningful to her, a tangible demonstration of something really changing.

This whole intense compact sequence nudged their differentiation forward as individuals (clearer sense of self, better self-regulation, and more willingness and ability to trade comfort for growth) and as a dyad (better balancing of attachment and self-direction). It was why Mr. and Mrs. B were basking in the warmth of their connection in my office. I took this opportunity to further the process by discussing their mutual hatred for each other. This is often important in desire cases given the frustration and anger that has built up (especially when there has been some kind of extramarital affair). In many instances desire problems do not resolve until this happens. The more rapidly, directly, and less gingerly this occurs the better I find that couples handle it.

Mrs. B said she knew her husband often hated her and acknowledged her own hatred of him matter-of-factly. At first Mr. B was floored that his wife actually hated him. He insisted that he did not hate her although he was "very very angry." I proposed he had a gift for understatement and reviewed his many critiques and complaints of his wife. Likewise, I pointed to his tirade the previous afternoon toward his father, mother, and wife. Rather than dodging by claiming that anger versus hate was a semantic issue, Mr. B said he was uncomfortable discussing hate because it sounded so absolute and so antithetical to loving. I said I had no doubt he hated his father—but what twisted him up inside was that he probably loved him too. That last statement caught Mr. B completely by surprise. I suggested that he was living proof someone could love and hate the same person because he felt the same way about his wife too. Mrs. B's nod said she knew this and it did not particularly upset her.

Mr. B settled down and got real quiet. He looked Mrs. B in the eye and acknowledged he hated her. Mrs. B smiled and said, "I know, I hate you too."

Mr. B smiled back. It almost seemed incongruous that they could have such an intimate (and in some ways tender) moment revealing their mutual hatred.

Wrapping Things Up

As much as they enjoyed their new sexual relationship, Mr. and Mrs. B felt the best part was the growing peace and ease they experienced when they were together. They expressed fears that they would lose what they had found when they got home. I reassured them that losing and regaining (at a higher level) advances made in treatment was the only way it is done. The process would teach them to hold onto themselves, not give into their fears and anxieties, and to self-validate the progress they think they have made when the going got rough.[22] Mr. and Mrs. B had come far enough to realize this was the ongoing process of differentiation once again.

As our series of meetings drew to a close, Mr. B said he found several things particularly helpful: One was that I prefaced difficult confrontations by saying I was addressing the best in him. He found my directness surprisingly respectful, and he appreciated that I treated him like an adult—even when he was not acting like one. He also found the notion of emotional gridlock extremely liberating: It made him feel that he and his marriage were not "defective" and that we were not going to reduce everything to his childhood. Given how much we talked about his father in the process of working on his integrity and differentiation, it would have been too much for him had we reduced everything "wrong" in his marriage to that. Mrs. B concurred, adding that my nonpathological viewpoint and the possibility that something good could come of all this helped her hold on during many difficult moments.

CLINICAL COMMENTARY

Because the Crucible Approach is quite confrontational by conventional standards it is important to note that the process and tone are collaborative rather than adversarial. Therapists often worry about confrontation because most therapists confront clients only when the interaction has become adversarial and combative. But when the best in a therapist speaks difficult truths, the best in people often stands up because their integrity demands they acknowledge it. Confronting a client this way is an act of therapeutic empathy, compassion, caring, intimacy, integrity, and, yes, differentiation.

In contrast to "the therapist's office is a safe place" credo, it is important to negotiate an effective level of anxiety and tension (emphasizing anxiety tolerance rather than anxiety reduction) by doing therapy at that level from the outset. And in contrast to a conventional cozy "holding environment," a well-differentiated clinical stance creates therapeutic crucibles by containing existing pressures in the couple's relationship (e.g., pressure to define themselves, mobilize themselves, and validate themselves).[23] Rather than "falling apart" in the face of these pressures (i.e., the realistic pressures of life), however, clients typically demonstrate rapid integration and "brightening" after an acute period of disorganization and self-confrontation.

Poorly differentiated couples do not know the difference between attachment and self-regulation because to them these are one and the same. That is why efforts to create "more attachment" can unwittingly promote *de-differentiation* (i.e., emotional fusion and borrowed functioning). When treating sexual desire problems, many therapists deliberately or unwittingly encourage one partner to subjugate his or her self-direction and self-regulation to the limitations and anxieties of the other (i.e., "the devils' pact," "no exit" commitments, "change requests," and anxiety-reduction-based treatment involving behavior "bans" or "baby-step" increments). My experience as supervisor and consultant to other therapists suggests that it is often why therapists find sexual desire problems difficult to treat.

Suitability for "Difficult" or "Fragile" Cases

Sex therapy for desire problems is usually seen as a narrow-focused symptomatic treatment, one that may be appropriate for highly troubled couples *if and when* they have made progress on the nonsexual aspects of their relationship and are ready to deal with sex. This way of conceptualizing and conducting sex therapy leads to "marital therapy first and sex therapy second" strategies. However, I use the Crucible Approach with poorly differentiated couples having multiple sexual and nonsexual issues from the outset (and through out) because of its powerful integration of sex therapy, couple therapy, and individual therapy.

Although this approach may appear appropriate only for high-functioning couples with good ego strength, experience shows it to be effective with extremely undifferentiated people. This includes highly contentious and combative (gridlocked) couples with significant personality disorders; tumultuous couples who appear "fragile," "primitive," or "explosive"; those on the verge of divorce (or separated); and some who have been celibate for decades. This, I believe, results from the rapid intensive massing of isomorphic interventions which enhance each partner's differentiation and modify their relationship in positive self-perpetuating ways. Speed is also vitally important because it creates *hope*—clients monitor treatment for signs of "how screwed up they are" and the faster they see improvement the more resilient they become.[24] Many poorly differentiated couples cannot tolerate the demands of 1-hour, once-a-week treatment although it looks more comfortable and "supportive" at first glance. Sexual desire issues are one of my preferred presenting problems because the broad-band impact of treatment is so rewarding.

At the other end of the continuum, this approach works well with couples with good relationships who want to improve intimacy and explore their potential for eroticism, passion, and desire. Likewise, couples who do not complain about desire find seeing themselves through their sexuality extremely useful (i.e., the elicitation window), in part because this involves no notion of "problems" or pathology (Schnarch, 1995b).

CONCLUSION

How do I define treatment success? How often do couples succeed? How do I know when we fail? Most times success is easy to recognize because it manifests as increased sexual desire (both partners), more sex, sex with more passion, eroticism and intimacy, increased verbal and physical expressions of caring and loving, and improved relationship satisfaction. Outcomes (and process) like the one in the case described are the norm rather than the exception. Some successful couples maintain the same frequency of sex because the increased quality of sex and intimacy is far more satisfying. But I have seen other couples agree to more frequent sex when one partner or the other refused to self-confront. I considered these cases failures even though the partners stopped complaining about sex: Neither partner got better at self-confrontation and self-soothing or developed more capacity for intimacy and desire (out of fullness). Are such cases failures if couples say they are happy with the results? The scientist in me thinks I need answers for such questions; my pragmatic side is content to leave such debates to others.

I have not resolved some knotty difficulties of defining treatment success, but I have learned a difficult and beautiful truth about relationships that applies to sexual desire problems (principle 12): *Marriage holds your partner's happiness hostage and the ransom price is always your personal growth.* Each of us faces choices between stifling our partner's growth, destroying his or her happiness, or growing ourselves up.

At its essence, true love is desire out of fullness rather than the neediness and grasping of desire out of emptiness (e.g., blueballs, horniness, loneliness, and "fears of abandonment"). Desire out of emptiness never produces compassion or makes room in a marriage for a mate. Sex therapy's focus on desire as a natural function, a biological drive, and initiatory eagerness is a dead end if desire that taps our potential for love, intimacy, and spiritual union is the goal.

Underlying the typical marital agreement ("in sickness and in health, for better and worse") lies the good-faith assumption that partners will work unceasingly to ensure as little "worse" for their mate as possible. However, therapists working with sexual desire problems encounter the most infantile, narcissistic, and sadistic parts of people (high- *and* low-desire partners) who exploit this promise to bludgeon their partner into submission (e.g., "You promised to take me as I am."). If clinicians do not shrink from these kinds of complexities, sex therapy can become the vital tool it has claimed to be (and in many ways failed to become). When that happens more couples will become what they aspire to be too.

NOTES

1. Sexual desire problems are the most common sexual complaint couples bring to therapy. Besides concerns about sexual frequency and desire disparity, couples complain about sexual boredom and passionless mechanical sex devoid of eroticism, intimacy or satisfying meaning. Likewise, sex therapists say they find desire problems the most difficult to treat (Kilmann et al., 1986).

2. In some respects therapists confront 20 centuries of Western culture conducting blatant and subtle wars on sexual desire. De Rougemont (1983) notes that desire and passion have as little association with happiness in European literature and mythology as romance and love have with marriage. Heartache, suffering, irrationality, and self-destruction dominate our basic view of romance, love, and desire.

3. While the intimacy-incongruent aspects of this approach often escape most therapists, Kaplan herself was aware of this. She believed intimacy was not important once the initiatory "desire phase" was completed and sex had begun (Kaplan, personal communication, 1991).

4. Later on I explain how even the notion of "problem" is a misnomer. Desire difficulties are often potential blessings in disguise.

5. Any sophisticated systemic approach preserves the dialectic between the whole system and its "parts." Conventional distinctions between individual and dyadic causes of sexual desire problems are antithetical to a systemic approach. A human being is a complex self-regulating system, and two people form an even more complex system (a relationship). The higher-order system (relationship) is not reducible to its component parts (people), nor reducible to the functions and processes which explain how any particular component (person) operates. For example, a systemic approach takes intrapsychic processes into account but does not reduce the operations of a relationship to this.

6. For another example of people not seeing at first that the rules of a system are "built in," look no further than world ecology. Think of the Crucible Approach as a paradigm shift from "sex is a natural function" to "sex is a natural system."

7. Here and elsewhere I use the term "marriage" to refer to any emotionally committed relationship, including nonmarried couples and gay and lesbian couples, rather than to the legal institution of marriage per se.

8. This hold true in the absence of domestic violence and physical abuse used to coerce sex.

9. Kerr and Bowen (1988) note: "People become overinvolved in trying to fix problems in the name of helping others and on the basis of a belief that what is happening should not be happening. Fixers try to 'correct' the situation and put it on the 'right' track. The fixer's Achilles heel is underestimating the resources of the people he intends to 'help.' In the process he can create a dependence in others that undermines their functioning" (p. 109).

10. Although the term "differentiation" appears in both differentiation theory and attachment theory (i.e., individuation/separation/differentiation), the two approaches produce very different conceptualizations and interventions (Hendrix, Bader, & Schnarch, 1995; Schnarch, 1997c). Jung's notion of "individuation" most closely approximates "differentiation" in differentiation theory. But the real issue is therapy and not theory. While attachment theory literature discusses emotional fusion, attachment-based therapy is often conducted as if partners are "out of connection" rather than hopelessly enmeshed.

11. For example, differentiation theory does not postulate a developmental standard by which all else is considered "developmental arrest" (a pathological condition). Murray Bowen said there was no point to pathologizing the vast majority of humankind.

12. Like Buddhism, differentiation-based therapy proposes that "the undisciplined mind creates reality." People's brains regress when they are confronted with more anxiety and stress than they can "digest." At that point, people's "introjects" pop out, transference storms surface, and they suddenly "realize" they are married to their mother/father. In other words, intrapsychic processes are often shaped by—rather than creators of—the natural sexual crucibles surrounding sexual desire in committed relationships.

13. Some marital therapies embrace a view of infants (and adults) as helpless and dependent that is at odds with the last two decades of infant research. The premise of "infant anticipation of psychic death" (when infants are out of synchrony with their caregiver) does not stand up to psychophysiological research (Tronick, 1989; Gianino & Tronick, 1988).

14. I have witnessed countless leaps of faith in couples resolving desire problems, but they are not reducible to a "prescription." It is possible for someone to exploit either description discussed previously to perpetuate emotional fusion and avoid taking any leap of faith.

15. This case is a composite reflecting common dynamics, events, topics, intensity, speed, and outcomes of treatment. The dialogue, clinical interventions, client reactions, and vignettes of the couple's interactions are taken from actual cases. What is described here emerges repeatedly in live clinical demonstrations involving a wide range of couples with diverse presenting problems (conducted at every Sexual Crucible™ Introductory Workshop).

16. In discussing our respective work, Dr. William Masters and I note we are both strong believers in the benefits of massed intensive intervention, and that we differ in this regard from the way sex therapy is primarily practiced.

17. Many couples make the devil's pact spontaneously. Some therapists mistakenly propose it as part of therapy; it is often a staple of sexual abuse treatment.

18. For conceptualization and treatment strategies for various sexual dysfunctions using the Crucible Approach, see Schnarch (1995a).

19. At that point, his emotional investment exceeded his solid sense of self, his ability to regulate his anxieties, and his willingness to tolerate discomfort for more growth.

20. Although "victim" and "perpetrator" are often value-laden labels, Maddock and Larson (1995) have developed a "victim–perpetrator dialectic" wherein these terms refer to relative positions in a system of interaction (similar to the way high-desire and low-desire positions are used here).

21. Because this behavior is so ineffective, it is often hard to recognize it as an attempt at self-soothing.

22. We observe this same pattern among therapists who attempt to learn the Crucible Approach.

23. At the annual 6-day Sexual Crucible Desire Workshop, attendees experience firsthand how a well-differentiated stance involves corresponding pressures and personal challenges for therapists.

24. The other critical variable seems to be the therapist's level of differentiation, especially willingness to tolerate discomfort for (the clients') growth.

REFERENCES

American Psychiatric Association. (1980). *Diagnostic and statistical manual of mental disorders* (3rd ed.). Washington, DC: Author.

American Psychiatric Association. (1987). *Diagnostic and statistical manual of mental disorders* (3rd ed., rev.). Washington, DC: Author.

American Psychiatric Association. (1994). *Diagnostic and statistical manual of mental disorders* (4th ed.). Washington, DC: Author.

Bowen, M. (1975). Family therapy after twenty years. In S. Arieti (Ed.), *American handbook of psychiatry: Vol. 5. Treatment* (pp. 367–392). New York: Basic Books.

Bowen, M. (1978). *Family therapy in clinical practice.* New York: Jason Aronson.

DeAmicis, L. A., Goldberg, D. C., LoPiccolo, J., Friedman, J., & Davies, L. (1985). Clinical follow-up of couples treated for sexual dysfunction. *Archives of Sexual Behavior, 14,* 467–489.

De Rougemont, D. (1983). *Love in the Western world.* Princeton, NJ: Princeton University Press.

Elkaim, M. (1986). A systemic approach to couple therapy. *Family Process, 25*(1), 35–42.

Fish, L. S., Fish, R. C., & Sprenkle, D. H. (1984). Treating inhibited sexual desire: A marital therapy approach. *American Journal of Family Therapy, 12*(3), 3–12.

Gianino, A., & Tronick, E. Z. (1988). The mutual regulation model: The infant's self and interactive regulation coping and defense. In T. Field, P. McCabe, & N. Schneiderman (Eds.), *Stress and coping* (pp. 47–68). Hillsdale, NJ: Erlbaum.

Haley, J. (1976). *Problem solving therapy: New strategies for effective family therapy.* San Francisco: Jossey-Bass.

Hendrix, H., Bader, E., & Schnarch, D. M. (1995). *Panel discussion on "Empathy and Differentiation."* Recorded at 1995 Milton Erickson Foundation Conference of Intimacy and Sexuality. Phoenix: Milton Erickson Foundation.

Kaplan, H. S. (1974). *The new sex therapy.* New York: Brunner/Mazel.

Kaplan, H. S. (1977). Hypoactive sexual desire. *Journal of Sex and Marital Therapy, 3,* 3–9.

Kaplan, H. S. (1979). *Disorders of sexual desire and other new concepts and techniques in sex therapy.* New York: Brunner/Mazel.

Kaplan, H. S. (1987). *Sexual aversion, sexual phobias and panic disorder.* New York: Brunner/ Mazel.

Kerr, M. E., & Bowen, M. (1988). *Family evaluation.* New York: Norton.

Kilmann, P. R., Boland, J. P., Norton, S. P., Davidson, E., & Caid, C. (1986). Perspectives of sex therapy outcome: A survey of AASECT providers. *Journal of Sex and Marital Therapy, 12,* 116–138.

Kuhn, T. (1970). *The structure of scientific revolution.* Chicago: University of Chicago Press.

Leiblum, S. R., & Rosen, R. C. (Eds.). (1988). *Sexual desire disorders.* New York: Guilford Press.

Lief, H. I. (1977). What's new in sex research? Inhibited sexual desire. *Medical Aspects of Human Sexuality, 11*(7), 94–95.

LoPiccolo, J., & Friedman, J. (1988). Broad-spectrum treatment of low sexual desire: Integration of cognitive, behavioral, and systemic therapy. In S. R. Leiblum & R. C. Rosen (Eds.), *Sexual desire disorders* (pp. 107–144). New York: Guilford Press.

LoPiccolo, J., Heiman, J., Hogan, D., & Roberts, C. (1985). Effectiveness of single therapists versus co-therapy teams in sex therapy. *Journal of Consulting and Clinical Psychology, 53*(3), 287–294.

Maddock, J. W., & Larson, N. R. (1995). *Incestuous families: An ecological approach to understanding and treatment.* New York: Norton.

Masters, W. H., & Johnson V. E. (1966). *Human sexual response.* Boston: Little, Brown.

Masters, W. H., & Johnson, V. E. (1970). *Human sexual inadequacy.* New York: Little, Brown.

Masters, W. H., & Johnson, V. E. (1976). *The pleasure bond: A new look at sexuality and commitment.* New York: Bantam Books.

Masters, W. H., Johnson, V. E., & Kolodny, R. (1986). *Masters and Johnson on sex and human loving.* Boston: Little Brown.

Schnarch, D. M. (1989a). Sexual "systems" in inhibited sexual desire. *The Female Patient.*

Schnarch, D. M. (1989b): The use of inherent paradox in post-modern sexual/marital therapy. In L. M. Ascher (Ed.), *Therapeutic paradox* (pp. 219–243). New York: Guilford Press.

Schnarch, D. M. (1991). *Constructing the sexual crucible: An integration of sexual and marital therapy.* New York: Norton.

Schnarch, D. M. (1992a, February) Sexuality—Time for a paradigm shift! *Family Therapy News.*

Schnarch, D. M. (1992b). Problems of sexual desire: Who wants to *want*? [Audiotape]. Evergreen, CO: Marriage & Family Health Center.

Schnarch, D. M. (1993, March–April). Inside the sexual crucible: The search for intimacy. *Family Therapy Networker,* pp. 40–48.

Schnarch, D. M. (1995a). A family systems approach to sex therapy and intimacy. In R. H. Mikesell, D.-D. Lusterman, & S. H. McDaniel (Eds.), *Integrating family therapy: Handbook of family psychology and systems theory* (pp. 239–257). Washington, DC: American Psychological Association.

Schnarch, D. M. (1995b, June). Sexual–marital therapy with mature couples. *Family Therapy News, 26*(3), 21–22.

Schnarch, D. M. (1997a). *Passionate marriage: Sex, love, and intimacy in emotionally committed relationships.* New York: Norton. [Published in paperback as Schnarch, D. M. (1998). *Passionate marriage: Keeping love and intimacy alive in committed relationships.* New York: Owl Books.]

Schnarch, D. M. (1997b, September–October). Passionate marriage: Forever an oxymoron? *Family Therapy Networker, 21*(5), 42–49.

Schnarch, D. M. (1997c, Winter). Bader, Schnarch, and Hendrix: The authors respond. *Journal of Imago Relationship Therapy, 2.*

Schnarch, D. M. (1999). *Clinical update: Male sexual dysfunction.* Washington, DC: American Association for Marriage and Family Therapy, 1(1), 1–8.

Schnarch, D. M. (in press). Family systems approach to sex therapy: A case study. In D.-D. Lusterman, S. H. McDaniel, & C. Philpot (Eds.), *Integrating family therapy casebook.* Washington, DC: American Psychological Association.

Schwartz, M. F., & Masters, W. H. (1988). Inhibited sexual desire: The Master and Johnson Institute treatment model. In S. R. Leiblum & R. C. Rosen (Eds.), *Sexual desire disorders* (pp. 229–242). New York: Guilford Press.

Tronick, E. Z. (1989, Feburary). Emotions and emotional communication in infants. *American Psychologist,* pp. 112–119.

Verhulst, J., & Heiman, J. R. (1988). A systems perspective on sexual desire. In S. R. Leiblum & R. C. Rosen (Eds.), *Sexual desire disorders* (pp. 243–267). New York: Guilford Press.

3

Multielement Treatment of Desire Disorders

Integration of Cognitive, Behavioral, and Systemic Therapy

CATHRYN G. PRIDAL
JOSEPH LoPICCOLO

Sexual desire disorders are both the most common and the most challenging of the sexual problems confronting clinicians. While such disorders are often associated with women, the gender ratio is close to equal in terms of cases seen in sex therapy clinics. Though such disorders are often associated with sexual performance problems, many individuals lack the motivation to behave sexually, despite having no difficulties in either arousal or orgasm.

Part of the difficulty in assessing desire disorders is the absence of agreed-on norms as to what constitutes "normal" sexual interest in individuals of various ages or lifestyles. Especially for women, desire often manifests itself as receptivity or willingness to be sexually engaged rather than active sexual initiative. Cathryn G. Pridal and Joseph LoPiccolo suggest that some sort of proceptive actions in terms of initiation of either fantasy or behavior are a requisite for the determination of genuine sexual interest.

The authors emphasize the importance of the assessment interview with each partner individually to gather important information as well as to structure subsequent treatment. They note that low desire individuals are often unenthusiastic about beginning treatment, fearing that they will be identified as "the problem" or pressured into behaviors they have little inclination for.

Pridal and LoPiccolo maintain that therapy with low desire clients can be quite successful if the treatment addresses cognitive, affective, behavioral, and systemic elements. Insight and understanding comprise part of their treatment approach as well. The client is encouraged to identify negative feelings associated with sex. Drive induction procedures are offered and the client is encouraged to keep a "desire diary." Finally, relapse prevention is addressed and the couple is asked to identify the indicators of relapse.

Cathryn G. Pridal, PhD, is a member of the Department of Psychology at Westminster College in Fulton, Missouri, while Joseph LoPiccolo, PhD, is at the Department of Psychology at the University of Missouri–Columbia, Missouri. Dr. LoPiccolo is well recognized as being a pioneer in the field of sex therapy, having written, edited, taught, and researched in the field for decades. He has made instructional videotapes as well as written handbooks and guides for both practitioners and patients. Together, Pridal and LoPiccolo are a formidable team with much wisdom to offer in the treatment of sexual disorders.

———

Desire disorders are not discussed as discrete diagnostic entities in the landmark early works on modern treatment of sexual dysfunction. Neither Masters and Johnson (1970) nor Kaplan (1974) presents low sexual desire as a separate diagnostic category with an indicated specific treatment protocol. As clinical experience developed with low desire cases, it became clear that the general sex therapy procedures that are effective with arousal and orgasm disorders often are ineffective with desire disorders. This result led to the development of a wider range of therapeutic procedures aimed specifically at sexual desire disorders (Kaplan, 1979; LoPiccolo, 1980; Zilbergeld & Ellison, 1980).

The interest in treatment of sexual desire disorders has increased, as low sexual desire has come to be called the sexual dysfunction of the 1990s. That is, low desire is now the most common presenting complaint of the clients seen in many sex therapy specialty clinics around the country. This is a marked change from the 1970s and 1980s, when arousal and orgasm complaints were the overwhelming majority of cases. One factor that accounts for this change is the availability of good self-help books on arousal and orgasm problems (e.g., Heiman & LoPiccolo, 1988; Zilbergeld, 1996), so that many people with these problems now do not seek professional help. Another factor is that as our culture has become more accepting of women's sexuality, women married to men with low sexual drive are able to seek therapy with them. In the past, such women were often too embarrassed to raise the issue with their husbands, or if they did, their husbands simply refused to come for therapy and accused them of being "oversexed." Indeed, with the increase in the number of cases seeking treatment for low sexual desire problems has come a change in the sex ratio of such cases. We recently studied our clinic's files and found that of all our low sexual desire cases—more than 70% of those seen in the 1970s were female, whereas of those seen thus far in the 1990s—the sex ratio was equally split between low drive males and low drive females. So although the total number of low desire cases is up, a good bit of this rise comes from the increase in male cases. As noted earlier, much of this increase stems from sociocultural changes resulting in women being empowered enough to bring their men to therapy.

DIAGNOSTIC ISSUES

There are several important diagnostic questions to address in assessment of cases of low sexual drive. One set of distinctions concerns whether the low drive is "lifelong or not lifelong" and "global or situational" (Schover, Friedman, Weiler, Heiman, & LoPiccolo, 1982). Simply put, this means determining whether the client has always experienced low sexual desire, and also whether there is any situation that does bring out a feeling of desire in the client.

Another important distinction concerns differential diagnosis between low sexual desire and aversion to sex. In low sexual desire cases, the client feels little or no sexual interest and may never be aware of any spontaneously occurring sexual desire. However, when this client does have sexual relations with the partner, the experience is not emotionally unpleasant. At worst, they may resent the partner's demands on their time, but there are no negative emotions associated with sex itself. In contrast, the client with sexual aversion disorder experiences negative emotions such as fear, disgust, revulsion, or anger when engaging in sexual activity with the partner or, indeed, even when thinking about sex. This distinction between low desire and aversion is crucial to therapy planning. In particular, aversion cases that are the result of specific traumatic events such as childhood sexual abuse or adult rape experiences absolutely require therapy geared toward resolution of these experiences before any other therapeutic work will be productive.

Yet another important issue is the level of sexual function that occurs when the low desire client does engage in sexual activity with the partner. Some low desire clients are fully sexually functional, with normal arousal and orgasm, when they do engage in sexual activity. These cases show full physiological functioning yet may report no emotional or even physical pleasure from the sexual act. One male client described his orgasm and ejaculation as akin to a sneeze, for all the pleasure it gave him. In another case, a woman was initially unsure whether she was having orgasms, despite describing all the physiological components in exact detail, as she experienced no pleasure from them. Even more puzzling are the individuals who do enjoy sexual activity; have normal arousal, orgasm, and pleasure; but do not have any desire to engage in sexual activity again. One client stated that to her, it was similar to thoughts of getting dressed up and going out for a nice dinner, including a fine wine and dessert. She explained that she enjoyed this experience but would not want to do it too often. Her husband pressed her for how often she *would* like to have sex if he did not push her about it. Her reply was, "Oh, you know, on special occasions. Your birthday, and maybe New Year's Eve."

In contrast, cases in which there is a coexisting sexual dysfunction raise an important question of causality. That is, is the dysfunction caused by the low sexual desire or vice versa? For example, many men with erectile failure develop low sexual desire as a result of their erectile problems. Knowing that attempting to make love is likely to result in another humiliating failure to achieve an erection is often quite sufficient to genuinely suppress sexual desire. However, the causality can also be reversed. If a man has low sexual desire, for whatever reason, and is making love when he really does not feel any desire, he is unlikely to get an erection, and his apparent erectile failure is a symptom of his low sexual desire.

In these cases of coexisting dysfunctions and low desire, the choice of which problem to address in treatment is clearly a crucial one. In the preceding example, the standard erectile dysfunction treatment, which emphasizes reducing performance anxiety, will not help a case in which the erection problem is based on low sexual desire. Similarly, focusing only on the low desire while not addressing the dysfunction may be very difficult for one or both of the members of the client couple.

The diagnosis of desire disorders also raises issues of just what a "normal" level of desire is, and what "oversexed" versus "low desire" is. One could cite the latest large-scale sociological study of frequency of intercourse to give an answer, but such an approach is a mistake in clinical practice. That is, references to an external standard, however derived, are of almost no value in helping the client couple resolve a problem of *genuine* low sexual desire in one member. In addition, in cases where low desire is systemically based in couple relationship issues, comparisons to an external standard will not resolve the conflict. Clinicians must also be aware of the couple who differ somewhat in desired frequency of sexual activity and have marital conflicts centering around power and control. This type of couple may present for therapy to deal with the issue of whether one member has low desire or the other member is "oversexed." The therapist must not accept either of these diagnoses. If a desire diagnosis is given in this type of case the therapist is playing into the power and control conflicts and therapy will not progress satisfactorily until those issues are addressed separately from the desire discrepancy.

A defining characteristic of true low sexual desire cases is a very low level, or total absence of, spontaneously occurring sexual interest. "Interest" here refers not to being *receptive* to the partner's advance but to *proceptive* actions and also to private thoughts and emotional events. On this dimension, most low sexual desire cases are actually *no* sexual desire cases.

The lack of any spontaneous interest in sex is important, as it carries with it a lack of distress on the part of the low sex drive client. That is, these clients are not depressed or anxious about their low drive state; they are not feeling that anything is lacking in their life. The motivation for therapy is usually the distress caused in the relationship by the low sexual desire and conflicts about the frequency of sexual activity. Sometimes, it takes threats of divorce to bring the low drive partner to therapy.

Possible medical causes of low desire should be considered, most particularly in cases of global low desire or when desire has been lost following some illness or surgical procedure. An example is a woman who has lost sexual desire following a hysterectomy with the ovaries also removed, who is not receiving adequate hormonal replacement therapy. If desire level was good prior to surgery, hormone replacement is often all that is needed.

Similarly, a man with lifelong, global low desire should have his testosterone level evaluated. Testosterone levels should not be overinterpreted, however, It has been our experience that low sexual desire men who have testosterone at the lower end of the normal range, and were therefore put on replacement testosterone, do not show a therapeutic response to the testosterone alone.

Loss of sexual interest is also one "symptom" of depression, and this situation should be examined carefully to explore which is the primary issue. That is, is the patient's loss of sexual desire secondary to depression, or is the depression a result of the problems caused by the loss of sexual desire? The real question may be one of whether the patient has a genuine clinical depression that may need therapy and perhaps medication focused on the depression, as well as sex therapy, at the present time. Although such cases are not often seen in those presenting for low sexual desire concerns, careful assessment is always indicated.

THE ASSESSMENT INTERVIEW

The initial interview—or the first session of therapy—can be a productive beginning, or can cripple work with these cases. There are two important tasks that must be accomplished: gathering specific information and defining the structure of therapy.

Information gathering is basic to beginning all psychotherapy, of course, but is likely to be more complicated in couple therapy. In low drive cases, it is even more complicated. Despite the sound principle that one works with both members of a couple when doing couple therapy, in low desire cases it is wise also to see each member of the couple alone during the initial assessment session. The purpose of this private session is to discover any information that might hinder therapeutic progress and that the individual might be uncomfortable or unwilling to share with the partner present. To accomplish this private assessment smoothly, the therapist explains that everyone, in even the happiest relationships, has a few things that they are not comfortable talking about with their partner present. The therapist then gives some "nonthreatening" examples by stating, "These might be things from the past, thoughts on their 'dark days,' self-doubts, or any number of other things." It is explained to the couple that, in order for the therapist to help them, the therapist really needs to know the whole story. Therefore, the therapist would like to meet for a few minutes with each person separately. The ground rule is that anything discussed in these sessions that the person does not want brought to the couple session should be so identified. For any such item, the therapist will either agree to keep the item private or, possibly, suggest that the information is of such a character that it may need to be addressed for the couple to reach their therapeutic goal. This does not mean that the therapist would reveal secrets; rather it might mean that this might not be a good time to begin sex therapy, or that each member of the couple needs to determine how they can become more comfortable with their partner around the issue—and therapy can focus on developing a conducive level of comfort.

This procedure may sound rather strained, but couples are generally quite open to this process when it is presented by the therapist. It has already occurred to the higher drive partner that there may be some secret reason for their low drive partner's lack of interest, and both partners usually find it acceptable to talk privately while knowing that the whole story is being told on both sides of the relationship.

More important, the information that the clinician obtains from this separate interview, which he or she might not have obtained from the standard couples-only format, not infrequently prevents what might have been a clinical disaster. The "secrets" that are revealed prevent major clinical missteps.

The most common secret, not surprisingly, is that the low desire is situational, specific to the spouse. There are a number of causes for this situation. If one member is having an affair it could appear to the other member that his or her spouse had low desire. Another possibility is that one member of the couple no longer finds his or her partner either physically or personally attractive. One low drive male, after checking that the therapist would keep the information confidential from the spouse, admitted that he had high sexual drive for his mistress, with whom he had intercourse three or four times a week. When questioned as to why he was then seeking therapy with his wife, he explained that he feared she was getting suspicious about his lack of concern about his low drive and erectile difficulties with her. He wanted the situation to continue as it was currently; in his opinion he had the best of everything, with his mistress for sex and his wife to mother their children and act as a hostess for his business social events. He indicated that he did not actually want anything from therapy. He just planned to attend one or two sessions to appease his wife.

This case illustrates the downside of obtaining "private" information. In such cases, it seems that the best the therapist can do is to recommend marital therapy to the couple without revealing the specific reason for this recommendation. In this case, the problem was identified as the husband experiencing his relationship as based on kids and social and financial issues rather than on romantic love, and that was underlying the lack of sexual expression. The therapist then suggested that they could benefit from seeing a marital specialist, to try to put love back into their marriage, adjust to this type of marriage, or perhaps consider divorce if their present pattern of marriage was not acceptable to them both. Statements such as these enable the therapist to avoid revealing the secret affair and not to begin what would amount to "sham therapy." There is no ideal solution in this type of situation, but it would be less desirable to begin therapy not knowing about the husband's intact drive for the other woman or to know this and join in his deception of his wife by beginning treatment with them as a couple. Clearly, couple sex therapy would be doomed to failure, and an additional risk is that the wife would learn of the affair and resent the therapist for colluding to conceal it during the course of treatment.

Other difficult secrets may also be revealed during the private session time. For example, one member of the couple may admit a past affair, a sexual fetish, a homosexual orientation, or a history of sexual victimization. Almost none of these issues presents major obstacles to beginning therapy, but they must be addressed in some way during the therapy program.

Occasionally an individual presents for therapy with a self-identified diagnosis of low desire. Careful assessment may reveal that the lack of a desire for sex is actually reality based in the client's current life situation. For example, a 32-year-old woman with not-lifelong, situational low sexual desire requested therapy to restore her sexual desire for her husband. Her low desire began when she learned that her best friend was pregnant by her husband. Through a series of events, this woman was providing daily child care for this child while her friend worked. This woman came by herself for therapy and reported that her husband had no interest in attending therapy with her because it was "her problem." He did, however, threaten her with divorce if she did not regain her sexual desire for him. Instead of agreeing to work on her "desire problem," the therapist asked her what she thought about her lack of desire in this situation. The client's reply was that she did not actually think there was anything wrong with her and even felt it would be a betrayal of her self-respect to continue to passively accept her role *and* further debase herself by agreeing that she had a problem of low sexual desire in the context of their current relationship. The therapist suggested that she should consider individual therapy to address the issues that were keeping her in such an unhappy situation.

LIFE IN A LOW SEXUAL DESIRE RELATIONSHIP

The clinician beginning work in this area can benefit from some background information about the relationship context in which the clinical work will be occurring. These cases of low desire are often considered "treatment resistant" or difficult to treat and sometimes are lost to treatment in the initial assessment session. This is especially true of male low drive cases. In our clinic, one of our therapists coined the phrase, "Men who have low desire for sex have even *lower* desire for sex therapy!"

Couples who come for therapy for low sexual desire are often on the verge of separation or divorce. Although it is certainly true that even the best and most frequent sex is far from sufficient as the basis for a good relationship, a constant struggle over sex is likely to damage an otherwise excellent relationship. In a relationship in which one partner feels constantly sexually deprived and the other constantly sexually pressured, a number of negative results can occur.

One common outcome is that all physical affection between the partners ceases. This happens because affection becomes confused with the initiation of sexual activity. The low drive partner may enjoy simple physical affection (a hug, kiss, pat, or squeeze) but learns never to do anything affectionate for fear that the partner will be turned on by this behavior and want to make love. Similarly, the higher drive partner, tired of asking directly and being refused, often goes through a period of being affectionate as a way of trying to initiate sex without risking a direct "no." The low drive partner soon figures out this pattern and stops responding to any affectionate gesture. Both of these routes lead to the cessation of all physical affection occurring between the couple, with resultant mutual negative feelings and blaming.

Another negative effect of low sexual desire is simply the loss of the positive value of shared sexual experiences. Making love involves sharing physical pleasure and emotional closeness. When this is missing, the normal stresses and strains of married life become more difficult. One of our clients, when asked about the effects of her husband's low sexual desire on her, expressed this very aptly: "Say I go in the bathroom in the morning, and despite the fact I've asked him not to do every one of these things, I trip over his towel on the floor, there's hair in the sink, I can't find the toothpaste, when I finally do find it, he squeezed it in the middle and left the cap off, he didn't flush the toilet and the seat's up. If we made love last night, I just shake my head, and smile— nobody's perfect. But if last night was another "No, can't you just go to sleep!" from him; when I see all that, I get furious!"

THE STRUCTURE OF THERAPY

Beginning with the first assessment session, how the therapist structures the therapy with low drive cases is crucial to achieving success. That is, the low drive client usually enters therapy under duress, motivated by his or her partner's pressure, and by the distress in their relationship, rather than by his or her own intrinsic feelings of wanting to increase interest in sex. This situation is quite different from that of other clients seeking sex therapy, who are typically eager to gain (or regain) their sexual function for their own pleasure. If the therapy remains focused on "curing" the low drive partner, for the benefit of the frustrated, deprived, high drive partner and to save the distressed relationship, therapy is not likely to succeed!

The therapist should restructure the low drive problem with the client couple in three ways. First, the presenting problem should be viewed as a *couple* problem rather than a problem of the low drive individual. Using this joint ownership of the problem means that whatever the origin of the low drive in the client, the partner must be part of the solution. We explain that sometimes during the course of therapy, the partner has to work even harder than the person with the low drive for therapy to succeed, not to say that the low drive person doesn't also work hard indeed.

The second way of redefining the problem is to suggest that the low drive person is not a free agent and is missing out on a fundamental aspect of human nature and human happiness. To support this redefinition, we suggest that all people DO have a sexual nature—a sexual interest or drive—and not being aware of having a sex drive means that something is blocking it. No one makes a choice to lose this aspect of the self, and, as the client is aware, it is a costly loss. The purpose of this restructuring is to enable the low drive person to feel that independent of the partner's wishes, and relationship distress, he or she has something to gain from therapy.

The third change in how the client couple has been viewing their problem concerns the partner of the low drive client. This person often enters therapy feeling sorry for him- or herself and resentful toward the low drive partner. This person seems to feel that he or she has the worst deal in the situation. We suggest that this conceptualization is false and that, in reality, the low drive partner has suffered a costly loss and has no choice in the matter. This person is the one who has the worst end of the situation, and the higher drive partner has a problem that is not too severe and also the freedom of choice. Many people have sex less often than they would prefer to, and some people are even totally celibate for extended periods of time. In addition, the partner can cope with having sex less often than desired by freely choosing to masturbate, or even to leave the relationship. Not ending the relationship indicates that he or she is willing to work on the problem and that therapy can succeed.

DOES THERAPY SUCCEED WITH LOW DESIRE CASES?: ISSUES OF "RESISTANT" PATIENTS

Much of the early sex therapy literature on low sexual desire noted that these patients were resistant to treatment procedures, and that the outcome of sex therapy was often poor. This need not be the case, however. Careful assessment and restructuring of the context of therapy, as discussed previously, sets the stage for successful work with cases of low sexual desire. For a successful outcome, a more broadly focused treatment than was used in the early days of sex therapy is needed. That is, traditional sex therapy, focused mainly on anxiety reduction and sexual skill training procedures, does not address the many other elements involved in the majority of low sexual desire cases.

The treatment model presented here, which was followed in the case that is presented, uses cognitive, systemic, and behavioral therapy procedures. These multiple elements can be conceptualized as occurring in four stages of intervention.

Stage I of Therapy: Affectual Awareness

Many low drive cases, as noted earlier, deny having any negative feelings about sexuality but claim boredom or indifference to it. The negative feelings occur when the individual is pressured to be sexual. To dispute this claim, we suggest that all humans have an innate sexual drive, and that the bland indifference is an "umbrella" which is blocking their awareness of the negative emotions that are masking their sexual nature. Some clients will disagree that sex drive is innate. One can point out the hormonal and evolutionary basis of the sex drive, but supportive remarks about the client's unease about beginning therapy and perhaps discovering a sex drive in him or herself are also indicated in response.

The negative emotions that are under the umbrella are typically anxiety, anger, fear, disgust, or resentment. In trying to bring these negative emotions into awareness, so that they can be addressed therapeutically, clinicians can use a number of tactics.

One useful procedure consists of having both the low drive client and the partner make a set of lists (at least five items per list). One list consists of the personal benefits for each individual of the lower drive partner's coming to have a higher level of sexual desire. A second list consists of the benefits to the couple's relationship, should a higher level of sexual desire occur. These lists might seem sensible and of little therapeutic value. However, the process of producing these lists often allows the client and therapist to become aware of major issues in self-definition and within the relationship. For example, in a recent case of low sexual desire in a woman, the client easily made her list of potential relationship benefits but could not think of even one potential benefit for herself as an individual. She was given this task as a "homework" assignment and after a week still could not think of any possible individual benefits for having sexual desire. When the question was rephrased as "What would you like therapy to do for you?," she replied, "I would like for sex to just stop existing." This woman's low desire was grounded in her identity; she viewed herself as a nonsexual person and would rather not think about sex than change her self-definition. The discussion of possible benefits from being aware and comfortable with one's sexuality can be important to motivating the client's participation in therapy. As long as the client sees no direct positive value for him- or herself, their level of motivation is clearly lower.

After producing the lists of benefits, clients are asked to construct two more lists. One is a list of possible risks or costs to each of them if the lower drive individual gains a sexual drive; the other is a similar list in terms of possible damage to the relationship. We instruct the clients to let their imaginations run wild here; we want to get out all the issues that logically they know are not realistic or true but are lurking anyway. We mention, as a standard example, some of the cultural baggage that most of us are carrying to some extent. For instance, a man raised in our culture is likely to have some thoughts about "nice girls don't," and he wants to be married to a nice girl. Similarly, a woman in our culture might worry about the stereotype that all men desire to "fool around" and wants her husband to remain faithful to her. In either situation, one potential danger of the partner feeling greater sexual desire would be that the stability of their relationship could be threatened. On being asked to make lists of potential costs for feeling more desire, one of our clients asked whether these lists were our way of reminding them of the old proverb, "Be careful about what you wish for—you might get it!"

Actually, the purpose of constructing the "fears" lists is to uncover any potential issues that could result in later sabotage of therapy. We tell our clients that they won't be different people, with different moral values, if they gain sexual desire, but that exploring fears of what it might mean to have a sex drive is very useful. Construction of the "fears" list is sometimes crucial even to beginning the process of therapy. In one case, the low drive wife feared that if she had any sex drive, her husband might not be so nice to her, and do all the household and child-care tasks that he now shared with her. He pointed out to her that it had been more than 3 months since they had last made love. He said that there had been many times that he had been feeling much resentment about his sexual frustration and was sure that he would do even more for her if he were not so sexually deprived. In this case, her sharing of her fears-of-success list was very instrumental in enlisting both his cooperation and her participation in the therapy process.

List construction is a fairly "cognitive" start to the affectual awareness stage of therapy. An advantage of beginning this way is that this procedure is one that does not too directly challenge clients' denial of negative emotions blocking their sexual drive, and so it often can be accomplished during the initial assessment interview. After these lists are completed, some procedures that are more Gestalt therapy–based, and focused on actual emotional experience, are used to explore the emotions involved more deeply.

One of the first procedures involves asking the client to relax, close his/her eyes, and try to visualize and reexperience several types of situations involving sexuality. The client is asked to recall his or her emotional experience when unexpectedly confronted with a sexual scene in a movie, a couple being affectionate in public, an unexpected description of a sexual event in a book he or she is reading, or some similar situation. Another imaginary situation involves clients thinking of having a sexual drive and initiating sex with their partner and describing how that makes them feel. The client can visualize various scenes focused on this theme—involving each member of the pair initiating and either accepting or refusing sexual activity.

In addition to imaginary scenes, role plays may also be valuable. In some cases, the therapist may have the low drive partner role-play having a sex drive, and asking his or her mate to make love and tracking his or her emotional state to see what it feels like to perform this role play. The client couple can also role-play the reverse situation in which the higher drive partner initiates making love, so that the lower drive partner can focus on his or her emotional experience in this situation. These role plays often allow the therapist to facilitate client awareness of negative emotions that have been avoided by not engaging in sexual situations.

Stage II: Insight and Understanding

Through the procedures in Stage I, clients have come to identify negative feelings such as anger, disgust, anxiety, resentment, or fear, that are blocking their sexual drive. Next, an attempt is made to give clients an understanding of the causes of their problem. It is explained that low drive involves multiple causality: there is usually a set of "initiating" causes, and a set of "maintaining" causes. This may seem too academic to be of clinical use. However, it is not. We have seen many cases in which clients have had repeated bitter arguments over the cause of the partner's low sexual desire. For example, a wife might say that her low drive was caused by the way her family or religious values influenced her. Her husband would disagree, because before they were married, he had been with other women raised the same way who did not have low sex drive. In one case the argument was so bitter that the wife replied, "Well, I guess they'd already been with the right guy before they were with you."

In addition to thinking of initiating and maintaining causes, it is also useful to conceptualize causation as individual, couple systemic, or medically based. In today's world of "managed care" brief psychotherapy, detailed sexual history taking at the outset of therapy is very rarely possible. Therefore, at this point in therapy, clients may be asked directly about what they learned in their family of origin, their school, their church, and other childhood/adolescent experiences that may have been "initiating" factors. These factors would be considered "individual"-based initiating causes, because they are specific to the person with low sexual desire.

After exploring past experiences as possible individual initiating causes, the couple is asked about other common individual factors, such as depression, aging concerns, masked sexual deviations, gender identity issues, fear of having children, life-stress issues, fear of loss of control over sexual urges, unresolved childhood sexual abuse, fear of failure secondary to sexual dysfunction, and unresolved grief following the loss of a previous mate.

Couple systemic causes of low sexual desire are complex and multifaceted. We have heard other clinicians, who apparently have seen only a few cases of low sexual desire, make a broad generalization about the pattern of power imbalance in low desire couples. However, there is no consistent pattern of power imbalance. In some cases, the low drive person does seem to have a position of power, as the partner tries to do anything to please him or her, in hopes of being granted sexual access. However, in other cases, the low drive person feels so guilty about his or her partner's sexual deprivation that he or she gives over everything else to the partner and is otherwise entirely powerless in the relationship. In these cases, the low drive person's lack of power is a result of his or her low drive, but in other cases the causality is clearly reversed. That is, the person feels powerless in the relationship and therefore does not feel sexual urges toward the more powerful partner. As one of our clients very clearly stated, "It is difficult to feel romantic towards a steamroller."

Common couple systemic causes of low sexual desire include inability to resolve marital conflict, lack of physical attraction to the partner, poor sexual skills in the partner, inability to fuse feelings of love with feelings of sexual desire (Freud's princess/prostitute syndrome), fear of closeness, vulnerability and trust concerns, personal space concerns, and differences in emotional expressiveness.

In short-term therapy, the therapist often must offer the client an explanation for the low sexual desire that the client often has some difficulty accepting. In more traditional psychodynamic psychotherapy, such an intervention would be considered a "premature interpretation."

Stage III: Cognitive and Systemic Therapy

With the negative individual and couple systemic causes of the low sexual desire identified, therapy now follows established procedures used in other types of therapy. The individual issues can be conceptualized in a model similar to cognitive therapy for depression. For example, clients may be asked to develop lists of the negative thoughts and beliefs that are mediating their negative emotions about sex and thus blocking their sexual drive. Then, they develop a matching list of coping statements, which counter each of those negative items with a positive self-statement. For other clients, we have used a model from Transactional Analysis, that of "tapes." We explain that in regard to sexuality, they seem to be listening to the "frightened child" and the "judgmental parent" tapes, and these scripts are likely to block sexuality. We ask them to write out the content of these tapes. Next, we ask them to develop the content of tapes that would permit and value sexuality—the "playful child" and "adult" tapes.

The other major component of this stage of therapy is systemic therapy for the relationship problems that are suppressing sexual drive. In cases in which the low drive partner's problem results from a clear power imbalance in the relationship, for example, the therapist actually has more ability to help the couple than if there was not coexisting low drive and this was a case of marital distress only. In such cases, the person with the power is often rather unmotivated to change. If sexually frustrated, however, this person may be more willing to reconsider the structure of the relationship.

Stage IV: Behavioral Interventions

As noted previously, by the time low desire couples enter therapy, simple physical affection has generally disappeared. At this point in therapy, methods to increase affectionate behavior are explored and initiation/refusal training is undertaken.

The couple is helped to identify and then begin to engage in a wide range of simple affectionate behaviors that they agree will *not* be ways to initiate any sexual activity. These will be activities that they both can enjoy, knowing that they are not to lead to greater sexual exchange. Such acts might include hugs, pats, brief kisses, holding hands, sitting next to each other while watching TV, taking a walk together arm in arm, and so forth. Most low drive clients really do enjoy these sorts of affectionate behaviors and are happy to be affectionate with their spouse without worry that these behaviors will be misinterpreted as an invitation to having coitus.

The focus of therapy then turns to the initiation of sexual activity. Most of these couples have a very limited understanding of each other's feelings about requests for sex, and misunderstandings often occur. To learn about each partner's preferences and feelings, role plays are used. Role playing begins with the low drive person demonstrating how the partner has, in the past, initiated love making in ways that have negative erotic and emotional value for the low drive person. Low drive clients usually excel at this role play. Next, the role play shifts to the low drive person acting out ways that the partner could initiate love making that would have a positive erotic and emotional value. The therapist should take care to stress that the initiation must be direct and noncoercive.

Training then focuses on the higher drive partner. The partner is asked to role play the low drive client refusing to make love in the hurtful ways this has been done in the past. Again, partners have no difficulty doing this role play. Next, the higher drive partner is asked to role play the low drive spouse declining to make love but in a way that *would* be an acceptable refusal. Often, the first answer is that there is no acceptable turndown, that any refusal is too painful. In response to this type of statement, we explain that even in marriages in which both partners have matching levels of sexual drive, with each of them desiring sex four or five times a week, there will be days on which one of them wants to make love, and one of them does not. Thus, every couple needs to find ways to say "no" and to accept hearing a refusal to an invitation to make love. Right now, any refusal sounds unacceptable to the higher drive partner because of the history of deprivation. The higher drive partner is asked to assume that they are making love more often. Under these conditions, the question of what would be an acceptable refusal is approached again. If the higher drive partner still is unable to suggest ways that his or her partner could decline sex, we suggest some general principles. For most couples, a detailed, specific discussion of the reason one is "not in the mood" is unnecessary, but reassurance about loving the partner, having sexual feelings for the partner, statements about when love making can be expected, and/or what would lead to being "in the mood" are good ideas. These sorts of statements typically make a refusal easier to accept.

A major component of this stage of therapy is a set of procedures that we have labeled "drive induction." The sexual drive is somewhat different from our other biological drives in that we do not have a clear set of bodily sensations associated with it—we do not have "sexual pangs" similar to the hunger pangs that an empty stomach brings us. Rather, our sexual drive is more dependent on external cues and stimuli. Yet, even a more basic biological drive such as hunger sometimes requires stimulation by an external source before we become aware of our internal state of need. Haven't we all had the experience of not being aware we were hungry until we smelled or saw delicious food (or looked at a clock) and only then realized how hungry we were? It is clear that with the sexual drive, the external cues are even more important, and persons with low sexual desire are masters at avoiding awareness of sexually relevant cues. We therefore ask them to begin attending to sexual cues and to keep a "desire diary." They are to note scenes in TV shows and movies that "people who do have a sex drive" would find sexually stimulating, to read books with romantic/erotic content, to note attractive people they see, and so forth. We often ask them to construct their own erotic fantasy—alone and a joint one with their partner. Depending on the case, these fantasies may be written at home or described verbally in the office, with the therapist's assistance if needed.

Just what has the couple been doing in terms of actual sexual behavior until this point in the therapy process? There is no standard answer to this question. The guiding principle is that for the low drive person to recover his or her sexual interest, the low drive person must be free of any coercion from his or her partner or from the therapist to engage in sexual behavior. For some couples, this means that there has been no sexual activity. More commonly, there has been either an arrangement of spontaneous sexual activity, but only at the initiation of the low drive partner, or a scheduled rate of love making, again under the control of the lower drive person.

Of course, if there is any actual sexual dysfunction in terms of arousal or orgasm, this dysfunction would be dealt with at this point in therapy, after the preceding stages have been completed. Even for those clients without a specific dysfunction, the therapist should routinely inquire as to enjoyment experienced in love-making activities and consider trying to help the couple to improve the quality of their love-making sessions, as an aid to increasing sexual desire. After all, one cannot expect a person to have much interest or desire for an unrewarding experience.

At the close of therapy, the couple may be asked to do some *relapse pre-*

vention work. One procedure is to have the couple generate a list of "risk factors and danger signs." This involves the couple identifying the elements in their treatment that they learned were causing their low desire problem and that they now have dealt with but which might emerge again. They are asked to identify what would be some early, small, easily dealt with indications that such problems were perhaps starting to occur again. Then they are asked to problem solve on how they would not let such early warnings either go unheeded or to be overreacted to but would simply discuss them openly.

How well does this treatment approach work? Some years ago, good results were found in treatment research on 72 low desire cases using an earlier, less complete version of this approach (Schover & LoPiccolo, 1982). That publication noted that the treatment program was being modified to emphasize the elements described previously, especially on the issues of helping the client "increase attention to sexual stimuli and to build skill in sexual initiation" (p. 196). Having described the treatment program in terms of principles, what follows is an account of the application of this program to an actual case of low sexual desire. The therapist in this case was the first author.

A CASE OF LOW DESIRE

Beth and George presented for therapy with George's complaint that he felt unloved in their relationship and was thinking about divorce. They had been married for 10 years, Beth was 32 years old and George was 33 years old. Upon further discussion, it became clear that the main problem was Beth's low sexual desire. They were having intercourse once or twice a month and were not affectionate with each other. Beth stated that she did not think about sex at all: She had no fantasies or dreams about sex and only thought about it when George asked her to make love.

Further assessment of their sexual relationship revealed that Beth had never been naked with her husband. Intercourse occurred with her nightgown on, under the covers in the dark. She said that she knew she wasn't "normal" and would like to change the way she felt about sex, but didn't know how to do so. She also stated that she would like to be more affectionate with George but was afraid that he would misinterpret affection as an invitation to be sexual. George indicated that he wished to experiment a little—he would like to see Beth naked and to try love-making positions other than the "missionary" position. George stated that he felt frustrated and thought that Beth did not really love him. He explained that, at the beginning of their marriage, he kind of liked Beth's modesty but had expected that they would become more open with each other as time passed.

The therapist concluded that Beth and George had a limited sexual repertoire. Additional questioning revealed that Beth was inorgasmic. She indicated that she would like to want sex more often and that she would like to become less inhibited. She also stated that she enjoyed the physical pleasure she experienced from their sexual activities and did not feel strongly that she had to become orgasmic.

While giving a sexual history, Beth described negative messages about sex from her parents and threats if she were to become pregnant while unwed. She did not observe any physical affection between her parents, nor were they affectionate toward her. She was raised in a conservative religion and felt that the church supported her parents' position regarding sexuality. George was also raised conservatively but said that the messages he received were slightly different. He was taught that sex before marriage was sinful but after marriage it was one of God's blessings. He also experienced physical affection from his parents and observed frequent affection between them.

Both Beth and George agreed to a "ban" on sexual intercourse as part of entering therapy. The therapist explained that this would allow them to become more affectionate and communicative with each other, without wondering whether these behaviors were leading to sexual intercourse.

Stage I: Affectual Awareness

In the next session, the feelings behind Beth's low desire were explored in more detail. She realized that she actively avoided any mention of sex or exposure to sexual stimuli. As an example, Beth described an interaction that had occurred at the video store she and George own and operate. She was at the store and a customer requested that she order an X-rated video for him. She was so embarrassed that she had to choke back tears and was unable to speak for several minutes. Beth stated that she felt this reaction was extreme and that she did want to become more comfortable with the whole idea of sex, not simply increase her level of desire. Because of her extreme discomfort, Beth requested that she be allowed to meet with the therapist alone for a few sessions and then resume couple therapy when she felt less inhibited. George agreed to this plan because he could see how difficult it was for Beth to talk about sex.

Both members of the couple reported a conservative upbringing and Beth clearly stated that she felt her parents had been overly concerned about any possible sexual behavior on her part. She was aware of some feelings of anger toward her parents for the messages about sex that they conveyed and stated that she was trying not to continue the pattern with her two children. She talked about finding her 4-year-old masturbating in the family room and her reaction: "That feels good, doesn't it? It's nice that you like your body, but touching ourselves there is something that we do in our own rooms. Would you like to go to your room now?" Beth said that she was unsure about how to handle that situation but did not want to "mess up" her child in the same way that she had been.

George indicated that he felt he had been able to overcome any negative messages about sex from his childhood, and Beth agreed that she did not feel inhibited by him or his responses to her when they made love.

Stage II: Insight

During the next few individual sessions with Beth, she explored the emotions and cognitions that were involved with her low desire. She initially identified feeling angry at her parents for the messages that sex was dirty and disgusting. She was unable to move ahead in this area, however, so her relationship with George became the next focus.

Beth stated that she did not want to be dependent on George and was afraid of being sexual with him because he might then think that she needed him. She indicated that she really did not think she respected him very much and she did not trust him to make good business decisions, so she insisted on doing all of the business bookkeeping herself. She realized that being sexually active with George would mean giving up some control in their relationship, and she was afraid of that. It seemed likely that George was aware of Beth's mistrust, and that awareness was contributing to his feelings of being unloved. To explore Beth's mistrust, the Gestalt empty chair technique was used. Beth began by telling "George" (the empty chair) about her concerns with his business acumen. After 5 minutes, Beth was asked to respond to her statements as if she were George. During this process, Beth recalled that George has a bachelor's degree in business and realized that her fears were not based on reality. This realization allowed Beth to identify a fear of closeness that colored all of her interactions with George.

Beth realized that she saw a pattern in her relationships that generally resulted in psychological pain. She recalled being dared by some neighborhood friends to run out to the fence in the backyard, naked, and being caught by her mother. Instead of listening to Beth's explanation, her mother punished her by sending her to her room without supper for the rest of the day, to "think about what a sinner I was." Beth was not allowed to begin dating until she was 18, but she found herself interested in a male classmate when she was nearly 17. They spent time together in school and talked after school and at school functions. After a basketball game, this boy walked home with Beth and they talked for a few minutes before she entered her home. When she went in, her parents were waiting inside the door and began yelling at her. Her father called her a slut and slapped her across the face. Beth stated that she was very confused and hurt by her parents' behavior because she did not understand what she had done wrong. She remembered thinking that the best thing to do was avoid being friendly with people of her own age because she only seemed to get into trouble.

Beth was surprised when the therapist suggested that these memories had something else in common—they both related to Beth's sexuality. In the first memory, she was displaying her body and got in trouble. In the second memory she was attracted to a male and got in trouble. Beth stated that she had never drawn that connection before and speculated that these were not isolated incidents. She guessed that her parents had consistently misunderstood her motives and behaviors and labeled her as being sexual in a negative way. The therapist then suggested that Beth had coped with her parents' disapproval by turning off any awareness of sexual feelings. In that way she could be rightfully innocent and deny further accusations. Beth agreed with this interpretation. She recalled that when she met George she thought that he was "safe" because she did not find him physically attractive and knew it would not be difficult for her to wait until after marriage to be sexually intimate. Upon reflection, Beth decided that she did think George was attractive now, but she had developed a habit of ignoring any thoughts she might have along those lines.

Stage III: Cognitive and Systemic Interventions

Beth realized that the coping strategy that she had developed as an adolescent had now become a hindrance. She wanted to enjoy sex, and to look forward to being intimate with her husband instead of avoiding it. She stated that she was ready to put the past behind her and move forward in her sexual life. With this motivation, Beth was asked to create a set of cards with statements on each card. The statements focused on Beth being in control of her own sexuality (e.g., "My parents can't tell me what to do anymore; I can be sexual for myself and my husband."). She wrote out seven different statements and looked at a different card each morning and then spent the day thinking about the statement as it applied throughout the day. After a week of doing this assignment, Beth reported that she felt stronger and freer than she had ever felt before.

The therapist then suggested that Beth generate a list of at least 20 words that refer to male and female genitalia. For the next week, she was to continue to think about the statements on the cards and also to read her list of words. If she felt any discomfort while reading the words, she was to reword a card statement to help her eliminate the discomfort. For example, she could reword a card statement from "My parents told me that sex was bad, but it's not. Sex can bring great pleasure if I let go and enjoy it." to say to herself "My parents told me that these body parts were bad, but they're not. These parts can bring great pleasure if I let them." At the end of the week, Beth was to read the list of words out loud to herself.

The therapist suggested that she read her list to George each night during the next week and then they could both attend the next session. Beth agreed and suggested that George also make a list to read to her. The session then focused on Beth's relationship with George. She stated that she would like to take some risks with trusting him, but she did not know where to start. The therapist asked Beth about the tasks she was doing at home and at work and wrote them down as Beth described them. After generating this list, Beth was led through a cognitive exercise to identify increasingly catastrophic, and therefore ridiculous, consequences if George did not do any of these tasks correctly.

Beth was then asked what would be the worst thing that could happen if *that* happened, and again what would be the worst thing that could happen if *that* happened. By this point, Beth was laughing at her level of catastrophizing and stated that she was so silly, because George was highly responsible and intelligent and could probably handle some of the tasks better than she could. Beth and the therapist went over the list and picked three tasks that she would ask George to perform during the following week. Beth agreed that she would not tell George how or when to do each of the tasks but would simply notice when and how he did it.

In the next session, Beth shared what she had learned about herself with George. George appreciated Beth's explanation of the origin of her low desire and stated that he wanted to continue to be supportive in whatever way he could. When asked about the lists, George reported that he had enjoyed creating and reading his word list aloud with Beth. Beth stated that she had enjoyed it too and she only had to remind herself once that she was allowed to "behave this way" when she found herself feeling anxious about saying sexual words out loud. Following up on the requests Beth had made, George was asked about how he felt bathing the kids one night, ordering new videos, and placing the new videos on display in the store. He stated that he was surprised that Beth asked him to perform those tasks but was happy to do them. Beth was asked about how she felt giving up those three tasks for the week. She reported that she was impressed with the way that George had handled the video supplier and that the bathroom was neater when he finished bathing the kids than when she did it. She did think that her video displays were more attractive but was pleased that she had time to organize another part of the store while George was doing the displays in the front. She said she felt more connected to George while they were engaged in these cooperative tasks at the store and at home, and George agreed that he felt closer to her as well.

Stage IV: Behavioral Interventions

The therapist suggested that Beth seemed ready to increase her sensual awareness. She was asked to spend at least 20 minutes each day in a sensual activity. For example, she could go through her closet, noticing the different textures of her clothing and determining which felt the best against her face, the back of her hands, and her fingertips. Beth was encouraged to be playful with this assignment, to explore all her senses with special emphasis on her sense of touch. George was to do the same assignment to increase his awareness of his sensuality. The couple was also asked to increase their affectionate behavior. Knowing that there was no possibility of sex, they were to hug and kiss at least five times daily. They were also to spend 20 minutes each day in physical contact—holding hands, legs touching, George's arm around Beth's shoulders, and so on.

These assignments were positive experiences for Beth and George, so additional behavioral tasks were assigned during the next several sessions. Beth was asked to "play" for at least 30 minutes each day, meaning that she should engage in a fun activity with no concern about being productive. She was also asked to purchase a book of sexual fantasies, and the couple was asked to read selected fantasies to each other. They were also asked to each arrange a "date," planned independently with awareness of their partner's preferences. In session they role-played their process of initiation prior to the beginning of therapy and then reverse role-played, in which Beth pretended to be George initiating love making and George pretended to be Beth refusing. They each realized the situation their partner was in with either initiating or refusing. Beth and George then did a third role play in which Beth initiated the way she would like George to ask her to make love and George refusing in the way he would prefer Beth to refuse. Finally, Beth agreed that she was ready for George to see her naked, so they were to dress or undress in front of each other at least three times during the week.

The couple reported that these assignments had gone well, with the exception of undressing together. Beth stated that she felt terrible the first time they undressed together. She felt so bad that she begged George not to do it again until they could discuss her feelings in therapy. Beth was initially unable to explain why she had felt so terrible when undressing with George, but indicated that she felt dirty and ashamed. When asked whether she had any associations to feeling negative about being naked, she said she did not. However, when the therapist suggested that perhaps she was relating to when she had been punished for being naked in her backyard, Beth agreed with the therapist's interpretation.

Beth was frustrated with this situation and expressed her feeling that she would "never get better, never get away from her past." In response, the therapist mentioned all the areas of progress and then suggested an exercise to work on Beth's difficulty with being unclothed. Beth was to close her eyes and imagine that she was in her bedroom, beginning to undress with George at the end of the day. She was to describe her feelings in detail, out loud. The therapist noted that Beth's feelings included shame and feeling that her body was dirty. The therapist suggested that Beth imagine the scene again, but this time try to use some of the self-statements she had developed earlier. Beth did this exercise in the office and stated that she did feel better. Her assignment for the week was to do two things while she was undressing in her bedroom at home. First, she was to imagine that George was there; second, she was to use the self-statements to cope with any negative feelings. Toward the end of the week, if she wanted to, they could try undressing together again.

Beth happily reported that her assignment had gone well and that she and George had undressed together the two nights prior to attending the therapy session. She expressed a desire to move forward, so the therapist suggested that they try a sensual massage several times during the week. The parameters of the assignment were discussed in great detail, and it was agreed that the first massage would involve Beth touching George while they were in bed together. The next massage would be George touching Beth, with her nightgown on, while they were in bed together. The final massage(s) would occur in the shower and would be mutual touching. Breasts and genitals were off limits because the focus of this assignment was continuing to increase sensual awareness and Beth's comfort with being physical with George. Beth liked the shower idea because she anticipated that she would not feel awkward about being naked with George in that situation. The therapist suggested that perhaps this would be a good time to have 2 weeks between therapy sessions, so that they could have ample time to work on this assignment. The couple agreed and committed to having at least two shower massage sessions together, in addition to the individually focused sessions in bed. Beth was asked to call if she experienced any difficulty with this assignment and then a therapy session could be scheduled if needed.

Beth did not call, and when the couple arrived for their next therapy appointment, they were beaming. They explained that they had enjoyed the massage sessions so much that they had done four of them in the shower, and had not been able to resist touching breasts and genitals during the third and fourth massage sessions. During the fourth session, George had become so aroused that he thought he was going to ejaculate, so he suggested Beth stop touching him. She asked why, and when he explained, she laughed and said she would like it if he did. She kept touching George and he did ejaculate. Beth stated that she had actually been curious about what semen looked like and was amazed at the process. She very much enjoyed seeing George aroused and thought she might like to have an orgasm herself someday. They both agreed that they were ready to lift the ban on intercourse, so they could progress from massaging to intercourse if they wished. However, either one was free to decline if he or she did not want to have sex. Beth suggested, with some hesitation, that they consider beginning in the shower because she felt so clean then that she was less inhibited. George agreed that her idea sounded like a good plan and they agreed to return in 2 weeks.

This fifteenth session turned out to be their last session because they described a satisfying 2 weeks. They had had intercourse four times, twice in the shower, once on the bed after showering, and once in bed before going to sleep. Beth described feeling a bit awkward the first time they had intercourse, but she used some of her coping self-statements and was able to enjoy herself. She said she still felt twinges of guilt and embarrassment now and then, but confronted those feelings and reminded herself that she is happily married and sex is permissible for married people. When asked what the most helpful things she had learned in therapy were, Beth listed the coping self-statements and the sensual awareness exercises. She said she knew she could not have progressed without confronting her past and the self-statements were helpful in doing that. However, Beth said that the week when she focused on her senses was the most powerful because it opened a new way of experiencing the world for her. She realized she had been like a robot moving through her life, doing the "right" things but not truly enjoying many of them. Beth also stated that she was now more interested in having an orgasm than she had been when she entered therapy. At that time, she thought having orgasms meant the person was preoccupied with sex, but now she saw that they are one more aspect of enjoying a relationship with someone you love. The therapist told Beth about the book and video, *Becoming Orgasmic*[1] and suggested that she might consider using them at some point in the future after she had consolidated her current gains. Beth replied that she would like to do that but was not ready yet. George said he liked both of the major changes in their relationship—they were more intimate and open with each other and he felt that Beth trusted him more. He felt loved by her, not simply because they were having sexual intercourse but because of their emotional sharing. At the end of the session, the couple agreed that they would contact the therapist if they experienced any further difficulty. It has been several years since this session, and the couple has not sought additional therapy.

There were several features in this case that are quite common in persons with low desire. Most individuals with low desire do have a "reason" for the low drive, but often they are not aware of the connection between past learning and their current feelings about sex. Insight into the reason(s), however, is not enough to produce an increase in desire. The rest of the therapeutic program is critically important to achieve lasting behavior change. In this couple, the wife was the person with low desire, and this has historically been the most common pattern. At this point, as mentioned earlier, our low desire cases seem to be about evenly split between males and females. The treatment issues with males are similar to those illustrated in this case, particularly as they relate to couple interactions. However, men may not have received the negative messages about being sexual from their families of origin. Instead, they often have had personal experiences that have resulted in a reluctance to become emotionally intimate with a partner and this reluctance is expressed as low sexual desire (Pridal, in press). In addition, men with low drive have to cope with the stereotype that males are supposed to be highly sexual; thus some of the cognitive work is aimed at reducing the power of this stereotypical message.

This case was typical of low drive cases in another way: The couple came to therapy at the request of the higher drive partner with divorce looming as a strong possibility. This situation was motivating for the low drive partner, and her motivation to work diligently in therapy was the key to the successful outcome of this case. This treatment program generally produces a positive outcome, but only if the clients are motivated to actually follow the program. Any number of factors can sabotage the treatment program—many of these were mentioned earlier in this chapter. Because this program requires personal exploration that is often psychologically painful, the client's motivation is a critical factor in predicting treatment outcome.

Overall, it seems that sex therapy for low drive cases can be successful if a multielement treatment approach is used. In these days of managed care and short-term therapy, it is tempting to omit some of these elements and focus only on "the problem." However, such a strategy is a mistake because each of the elements is critical to therapeutic success. Low drive does not exist as a separate entity; it is inextricably intertwined with family-of-origin issues, thoughts and feelings about sex and sexuality, personal motivations and self-image, and the actual behaviors involved in being a sexual, sensual person. Ignoring any of these aspects in therapy is likely to produce less than satisfactory results. However, each client is unique and typically requires more focus on one or two areas. Further research to develop an assessment protocol that would identify which element(s) is most critical for each client would be beneficial. With such a protocol, the therapist could tailor a limited number of sessions most efficiently to address all the elements but allow more time on areas of special concern.

In addition, as we move more and more into the computer age, issues of intimacy are likely to be increasingly important for all psychotherapy clients. One can easily imagine a couple who met on the Internet, and got to know each other as printed words on a screen, having serious sexual desire issues in a face-to-face relationship. Likewise, in reverse, couples who engage in "computer sex" may have major performance and desire problems if they attempt to take their relationship into the real world. These issues will have to be researched and additional therapy techniques developed to deal with interpersonally disconnected relationships.

NOTE

1. *Becoming Orgasmic* (Heiman & LoPiccolo, 1988) is a therapist-developed program to guide a women through a series of steps to achieve orgasm. The video is available alone or packaged with the book from the Sinclair Intimacy Institute, 919-929-3797.

REFERENCES

Heiman, J., & LoPiccolo, J. (1988). *Becoming orgasmic* (2nd ed.). Englewood Cliffs, NJ: Prentice Hall.

Kaplan, H. (1974). *The new sex therapy*. New York: Brunner/Mazel.

Kaplan, H. (1979). *Disorders of desire*. New York: Brunner/Mazel.

LoPiccolo, L. (1980). Low sexual desire. In S. Leiblum & L. Pervin (Eds.), *Principles and practice of sex therapy* (pp. 29–64). New York: Guilford Press.

Masters, W., & Johnson, V. (1970). *Human sexual inadequacy*. Boston: Little, Brown.

Pridal, C. (in press). Treating men with sexual dysfunction. In G. Brooks & G. Good (Eds.), *The handbook of counseling and psychotherapy approaches for men*. San Francisco: Jossey-Bass.

Schover, L., Friedman, J., Weiler, S., Heiman, J., & LoPiccolo, J. (1982). Multiaxial problem-oriented system for sexual dysfunctions: An alternative to DSM-III. *Archives of General Psychiatry, 39*, 614–619.

Schover, L., & LoPiccolo, J. (1982). Treatment effectiveness for dysfunctions of sexual desire. *Journal of Sex and Marital Therapy*, 8, 179–197.

Zilbergeld, B. (1996). *The new male sexuality*. New York: Signet.

Zilbergeld, B., & Ellison, C. (1980). Desire discrepancies and arousal problems in sex therapy. In S. Leiblum & L. Pervin (Eds.), *Principles and practice of sex therapy* (pp. 65–104). New York: Guilford Press.

II

FEMALE SEXUAL DISORDERS

4

Female Sexual Arousal Disorder

BARBARA BARTLIK
JAMES GOLDBERG

Until recently, female sexual arousal disorder received little or no attention from clinicians or researchers as a separate, bona fide problem of women. The analogous problem in men, erectile dysfunction, has been the prime subject of investigation and intervention for decades and continues to occupy center stage. Nevertheless, since the widespread success of sildenafil, there has been growing interest in studying female sexual arousal disorder with the hope that what worked well with men might work equally well in women.

Barbara Bartlik and James Goldberg present a comprehensive overview of the factors contributing to arousal disorder and highlight the problems in definition, diagnosis and treatment of this multidimensional sexual difficulty. It is interesting to note that anxiety, which stimulates general sympathetic arousal, may stimulate sexual arousal—in predefined laboratory situations. Whether or not the anxiety has the same effect in more realistic situations remains an open question.

For women even more than men, hormonal contributions are relevant, particularly when treating peri- or postmenopausal women. Estrogen replacement therapy may both facilitate and inhibit sexual arousal, while supplemental testosterone is receiving increasing attention for women showing "androgen deficiency." There are also many medications, which interfere with sexual arousal, particularly the popular selective serotonin reuptake inhibitors, such as fluoxetine.

Bartlik and Goldberg point out that sexual arousal in women tends to be more diffuse and difficult to measure than sexual arousal in men, which tends to focus almost exclusively on the quality of erection. Female sexual arousal is difficult to objectively assess, although new techniques are developing as pharmacological researchers explore this dysfunction with greater urgency. Never-

*theless, the psychological contributions to arousal difficulties cannot be ig-
nored or they will interfere with treatment success, as is illustrated by the case
study presented in this chapter.*

*Bartlik and Goldberg propose an integrated approach to treatment, with
both medical and cognitive behavioral sex therapy interventions. Their treatment approach is both sensible and essential, because female sexual arousal
disorder often represents a complex overlay of physical and psychological
causes.*

*Barbara Bartlik, MD, is a Clinical Assistant Professor of Psychiatry, De-
partments of Psychiatry and Obstetrics and Gynecology, Weill Medical College of Cornell University, New York, New York. James Goldberg, PhD, is a
Clinical Research Psychopharmacologist at the Bari/Goldberg Clinic, San Diego,
California.*

———————

Though its actual prevalence is not known, female sexual arousal disorder
(FSAD) is believed to affect a significant proportion of women in all age groups
(Rosen, Phillips, & Gendrano, 1999). In a 1994 epidemiological survey, 19%
of women between the ages of 18 and 59 reported lubrication difficulties
(Laumann, Gagnon, Michaels, & Michaels, 1994). In postmenopausal women,
the rate of lubrication problems is even higher, reaching 44% in one study
(Rosen, Taylor, Leiblum, & Bachmann, 1993). Of all the sexual disorders that
affect women, FSAD has received the least attention, with most studies
favoring the more readily quantifiable desire and orgasm disorders. However,
owing to the work of a few innovative researchers, as well as the momentum
generated by sildenafil's (Viagra) impact on male erectile disorder, this has
begun to change.

This decade has brought a greater appreciation of the physiological factors that underlie problems of sexual arousal in women. Historically, impaired
female sexual arousal has been viewed as secondary to either estrogen deficiency or psychological inhibitions. Thus, women presenting with arousal difficulties typically have been referred to either a gynecologist for hormone replacement therapy or to a psychotherapist, who might or might not have specific
training in sexual therapy. In contrast, in the last decade men with erectile
disorder, the analogous disorder of the arousal phase of the sexual response
cycle, are generally viewed as having a physical, often hemodynamic problem
and are referred to a urologist, who typically administers a battery of physiological tests before providing one of a host of available pharmacological therapies or other interventions. Aside from estrogen, which has only a weak sexually
enhancing effect, there are no approved or well-researched pharmacological
treatments for sexual disorders in women. Without treatment options, physicians and patients alike are disinclined to raise the issue of impaired female
sexual arousal. Moreover, in comparison to that of the male, the pathophysiology of female sexual arousal disorder is still only minimally understood.

This chapter outlines a conceptualization of female sexual arousal disorder in terms of diagnosis, assessment, and treatment. The chapter concludes with a case study that underscores the importance of a multidimensional approach to FSAD, encompassing physiological, psychological, behavioral, and interpersonal factors.

DEFINITION AND DIAGNOSTIC ISSUES

Female sexual arousal disorder (FSAD) specifically refers to the arousal phase of the sexual response cycle, and the engorgement–lubrication response of sexual excitement in women (American Psychiatric Association, 1994). Table 4.1 lists criteria for FSAD according to the fourth edition of *Diagnostic and Statistical Manual of Mental Disorders* (DSM-IV; American Psychiatric Association, 1994). The essential criteria of a deficient physiological response agree with the *International Classification of Diseases* (ICD-10; World Health Organization, 1992) and with the prior DSM-III criteria (American Psychiatric Association, 1980) criteria; however, they differ from DSM-III-R criteria (American Psychiatric Association, 1987), which included diagnosis by a deficiency of the subjective sense of arousal (Vroege, Gijs, & Hengeveld, 1998). Because physiological tests are extremely sensitive to the nature and variety of arousal stimuli available for laboratory testing (e.g., film, fantasy, and situation), criteria based solely on the lack of a physiological response will inevitably rely on subjective report. The same behavioral sensitization techniques of erotic thought training, sensate focus, heightened physical sexual stimulation, and cognitive therapy will and should continue to be used whether or not a physiological deficiency is established. In a research study, Palace (1995) has shown that psychologically induced autonomic arousal and positive feedback can be used to treat insufficient vaginal arousal in dysfunctional women.

The criterion that the condition causes either "marked distress" or "interpersonal difficulty" confounds the diagnosis because a partner's complaint alone may be sufficient for diagnosis, regardless of whether the woman herself feels distress (American Psychiatric Association, 1994). These qualifying criteria also

---

TABLE 4.1. DSM-IV Criteria for Female Sexual Arousal Disorder

A. Persistent or recurrent inability to attain, or to maintain until completion of the sexual activity, an adequate lubrication-swelling response of sexual excitement.

B. The disturbance causes marked distress or interpersonal difficulty.

C. The sexual dysfunction is not better accounted for by another Axis I disorder (except another sexual dysfunction) and is not due exclusively to the direct physiological effects of a substance (e.g., a drug of abuse, a medication) or a general medical condition.

Note. From American Psychiatric Association (1994, p. 502). Copyright 1994 by the American Psychiatric Association. Reprinted by permission.

confound sexual arousal disorders with sexual desire or aversion disorders. In addition, partner problems or inadequate physical stimulation will frequently be responsible for both sexual arousal and orgasmic deficiencies.

The reference to other Axis I psychiatric disorders or to medical conditions can be difficult to apply in practice (American Psychiatric Association, 1994). Depression, anxiety, panic, phobia, or psychotic disorders are frequently associated with sexual dysfunction. Successful treatment of these conditions often does not mean cure, and the residual force of these disorders may still be sufficient to prevent adequate sexual arousal. In such circumstances, explicit sexual therapy for arousal will be more effective than treatment by a mental health professional untrained in sexual therapy. Furthermore, Axis I psychiatric disorders are typically treated with medications such as selective serotonin reuptake inhibitors (SSRIs), anticonvulsants, and neuroleptics, which themselves can often cause arousal deficiencies. Thus, the specific sexual disorder may be confounded by both another Axis I disorder and by a side effect of a medication. In addition, the overuse or misuse of such medications is not uncommon.

The reference to a general medical condition properly calls for treatment (American Psychiatric Association, 1994). However, sexual dysfunction may be attributed to a medical condition despite the lack of research-based evidence demonstrating a definitive effect of the medical condition on sexual functioning. For example, although it is known that diabetes (Cummings & Alexander, 1999) hypertension (Newman & Marcus, 1985), and cigarette smoking (Hirshkowitz, Karacan, Howell, Arcassey, & Williams, 1992) can directly cause male erectile dysfunction, the information linking these conditions to FSAD is less clear. More baffling is the consideration of menopause or hormone deficiency as causes of dysfunction, as they are frequently confounded by aging.

DSM-IV criteria specification of a physiological response deficiency easily becomes interpreted as a lubrication deficiency routinely treatable with estrogen replacement. The notion and nature of "swelling" in contrast to lubrication has only been studied in laboratory research, which generally has been separated from routine medical practice (Myers & Morokoff, 1986). There is often an assumption that swelling is relevant only to the extent that it generates lubrication. With such an assumption, sensation (throbbing, tension, fullness) and sensory feedback essential to the arousal response are ignored. In fact, investigation of the adequacy of sensation and sensory feedback to arousal has been minimal. Attention to physical sensation in relation to sexual dysfunction is generally limited to orgasm disorders.

Rosen and Leiblum (1995) have discussed the practical issues in the use of the FSAD diagnosis, particularly pointing out that FSAD is rarely diagnosed by itself in clinical practice. In preparation for DSM-IV revisions, Segraves (1996) emphasized that FSAD hardly exists as a distinct entity, and when considered as an entity distinct from desire and orgasm disorders, it should probably be limited to lubrication deficiency. Segraves and Segraves (1991) have reported that only 8 of 527 women treated for sexual dysfunction in their practice had a single diagnosis of FSAD. An obvious example of this specificity problem has been the frequent clinical reports of treatment of SSRI-induced sexual dysfunction, which predominantly consists of desire and orgasm deficiencies, with sildenafil (Hensley, Nurnberg, Laurello, Parker, & Keith, 1999). Sildenafil has been studied and approved by the FDA solely as a treatment for male erectile disorder, a dysfunction of physical arousal (Medical Economics Company, 1999).

The specific FSAD diagnosis has remained undeveloped even though its relevance to female sexual dysfunction has been indicated for more than 20 years. In a *New England Journal of Medicine* report from 1978, Frank, Anderson, and Rubinstein surveyed 100 "normal" couples, finding that 48% of women reported "difficulty getting excited" and 33% reported difficulty "maintaining excitement." However, despite this frequent difficulty in regard to sexual excitement/arousal, 86% of these women rated their sexual relations as "very satisfying" or "moderately satisfying." This discrepancy may be attributed to the fact that intercourse may occur even though a woman is minimally aroused while males require a sufficiently rigid erection for intercourse to occur. In this regard, despite the 48% and 33% of women reporting difficulty getting excited and maintaining excitement, only 15% of the husbands thought their wives had this problem.

Though arousal has typically been considered synonymous with lubrication, research sometimes has shown large discrepancies between measures of vaginal/clitoral arousal responses and lubrication (Myers & Morokoff, 1986; Heiman, 1975). Vaginal response measurement studies as discussed later in this chapter have found serious discrepancies between measures of vasocongestion and subjective evaluations (self-report) of physical sexual arousal. In addition, the focus on vasocongestion and/or lubrication overlooks the role of clitoral arousal, which in the majority of women is the chief source of physical sexual excitement/arousal. A technological imperative not yet met is attention to measurement of the clitoral response both by itself and in relation to vaginal response, equivalent to the medical evaluation of male erectile function and dysfunction.

The diagnosis and treatment of FSAD has been confounded in particular by preemptive attention to the other categories of sexual dysfunction. Hypoactive sexual desire appears, on the surface and in available questionnaires, to be measurable by subjective ratings and summation of the quality of sexual behaviors, including intercourse, masturbation, sex thoughts and fantasies, and satisfaction with sexual activity (Lieblum & Rosen, 1998). However, these peripheral measures are not directly applicable to physical sexual arousal itself. On the other hand, focus on orgasm dysfunction perhaps has been excessively concerned with a limited aspect of physical sexual arousal. Orgasm dysfunction itself is poorly described and inadequately related to its part in the continuum of physical sexual arousal (e.g., the relation of orgasm to the preceding crescendo of arousal). Nevertheless, for the purpose of measurement and testing in women, orgasm can be identified (with questionable accuracy) as a "thing" and an "accomplishment" corresponding to the physical achievement and maintenance of a "firm" enough erection in men.

RELATION OF SEXUAL AROUSAL
TO GENERAL AROUSAL AND ANXIETY

Palace and Gorzalka (1990, 1992; Palace, 1995) have found that sexually dysfunctional women often show less general autonomic sympathetic arousal of the nervous system to sexual stimuli, which could factor into a decreased genital arousal response. On the assumption that sympathetic arousal would reduce genital vasocongestive responses directly through inducing vasoconstriction and indirectly through opposing parasympathetic function underlying the genital response, it would be predicted that preexposure of women to sympathetically arousing stimuli prior to a test for vasocongestive genital response would reduce this response. Instead, she found that sympathetic activation through preexposure to films depicting "impending danger without violent or sexual materials" facilitated the genital arousal response in both functional women and in women with various sexual dysfunctions, including deficient desire, arousal, and/or orgasm.

Similarly, Meston and Heiman (1998) showed that the sympathetic stimulant ephedrine increased genital arousal in sexually functional women, and Meston and Gorzalka (1995) showed that acute exercise-induced sympathetic arousal facilitated genital arousal 15 minutes later in functional women. However, despite increases in measured vasocongestive responses, sympathetic activation had no effect on subjective ratings of sexual arousal by these women.

Palace (1995) suggests that general sympathetic arousal "jump starts" the female genital vasocongestive response. She proposes that increasing the genital response through prior sympathetic activation and other facilitators could be used to show sexually dysfunctional women that they are capable of normal genital arousal, thereby facilitating therapy for FSAD. General sympathetic activation may also partially underlie the therapeutic effect of the stimulants on sexual dysfunctional women (Bartlik, Kaplan, Kaminetsky, Roentsch, & Goldberg, 1999).

Although in real life genuine anxiety and fear would be expected to interfere with sexual arousal, within the safe confines of the laboratory they may actually facilitate arousal through anxiety-induced sympathetic activation. Such findings from direct measurement of female sexual arousal under various circumstances might help clarify the causes of FSAD and lead to innovative treatments uninfluenced by conventional preconceptions of the nature of female sexual arousal.

ANATOMY AND PHYSIOLOGY
OF FEMALE SEXUAL AROUSAL DISORDER

Goldstein and Berman (1998) have provided a radically advanced description of female genital anatomy, vascular function, and arousal, which ideally will allow proper medical and/or urological evaluation and treatment of FSAD equivalent to the current evaluation and treatment of male erectile dysfunction. In answer to Henry Higgins's quandary of why a woman can't be more like a man, these authors would propose that actually a woman is very similar to a man. Goldstein and Berman have labeled female sexual arousal dysfunction targeted by their investigation as "vaginal engorgement and clitoral erectile insufficiency syndromes." The strict urological/gynecological focus of these investigations will allow for welcome medical advances in the treatment of FSAD. However, FSAD is clearly more diffuse and difficult to measure than male erectile dysfunction, which itself should be viewed as only part of the entirety of male sexual arousal disorders.

The key anatomical aspect of female genital arousal is the relationship of the clitoris to the vagina within the genital/pelvic nerve, vascular and muscular matrix. Separate measurement of clitoral and vaginal arousal is confounded by the anatomical fact that the extended base of the clitoris (hidden from view) runs down and through the vaginal structure. The clitoris is divided into three sections: the glans, the body, and the crura (Berman, Berman, & Goldstein, 1998). Taken together, the glans and body, are a total of 2 to 4 cm long, and the crura (or base) are each 5 to 9 cm long. The body of the clitoris contains two parallel corpora cavernosa that are each encompassed by a fibrous envelope. As in the male, each corpus contains erectile tissue which consists of 40 to 45% smooth muscle (Parks, Moreland, Goldstein, Atala, & Traish, 1998). It has been shown through research studies on cadavers that the quantity of smooth muscle mass in the clitoris diminishes with age and with the degree of cardiovascular deterioration (Tarcan, Park, & Goldstein, 1999).

Preliminary studies suggest that as with the male, natural vasodilating substances such as vasoactive intestinal peptide and nitric oxide play a role in female sexual arousal. Nitric oxide is involved in clitoral engorgement in women, just as it is integral to the process of erection in men. Nitric oxide synthetase immunoreactive neurons have been isolated from clitoral tissue (Parks et al., 1998). Clitoral corpus cavernosum smooth muscle cells obtained from women undergoing surgery for adrenal hyperplasia were cultured and treated with either sildenafil or zaprinast cyclic guanosine monophosphate (cGMP) phosphodiesterase inhibitors. The treatment resulted in a threefold increase in cGMP, enhanced smooth muscle relaxation, and vasodilation (Parks et al., 1998).

Alzate (1985) has proposed that the clitoris and outer anterior vaginal wall have the same sensory innervation from the pudendal nerve and have a common physiology of arousal and orgasm. Similarly, Sherfey (1972) has identified the clitoral–labial extension as a single functional unit. Rosen and Beck

(1988) have described the extension of the vascularized spongy tissue of the labia minora (inner lips) up to the clitoris and down to the perineum forming the area, termed the "vestibule," which includes the urethral opening and the introitus. The introitus is bounded by erectile tissue, which becomes engorged during arousal. The labia minora are bounded by the labia majora (outer lips), which also swell during arousal.

It has been estimated that per pound of body weight, women possess as much erectile tissue as do men (Sevely, 1987). However, women's erections are more diffuse, internal, and less obvious than men's. Stimulation of the clitoris, vestibule, and outer third of the anterior vaginal wall has been shown to trigger orgasms involving contractions of the circumvaginal muscles (Kline-Graber, & Graber, 1975); however, neural correlates of orgasm have rarely been measured. In some women, there is also a zone or area popularly identified as the G-spot on the anterior wall of the vagina (Whipple & Komisaruk, 1998). Given the assumed continuum of the clitoris and vagina, the distinction of "clitoral" from "vaginal" or "G-spot" orgasms, though certainly provocative, seems unnecessary. However, persuasive arguments have been made for a different type of orgasm chiefly produced by deep uterovaginal and cervical pressure from penetration. This type of orgasm is characterized as involving global reactions of the body, such as acute apnea, in addition to or instead of circumvaginal muscle contractions (Singer & Singer, 1978; Tordjman, 1980) and may involve alternate neural pathways as described later in this section. These distinctions notwithstanding, attention to momentary orgasm should not be isolated from the extended sensations and features of genital arousal, which precede and are the source of the crescendo leading to orgasm, and which exist even when orgasm does not occur. Individual differences in clitoral and vaginal sensation should exist for arousal as much as for orgasm.

Though neural and spinal components of female sexual arousal anatomy have been examined only in animals and spinal cord–injured patients, a particularly promising neural circuit has been proposed by McKenna and his colleagues (McKenna & Nadelhaft, 1989; Marson & McKenna, 1990; Crenshaw & Goldberg, 1996). These researchers studying female rats have related pelvic muscle reflexes (e.g., the pudendo–pudendal reflex) to the generation of rhythmic nerve activity in the vagina, leading to increased genital arousal. These reflexes pass down the spinal cord in reaction to pressure applied to the area surrounding the urethra. The spinal conduction of these reflexes is facilitated by adrenergic stimulation from the brain and inhibited through serotonergic activity in the brain.

Another potential excitatory effect on female genital sexual arousal through neural circuitry has been proposed to occur through vagus nerve stimulation (Komisaruk & Whipple, 1998). Because this afferent pathway projecting from the genitals to the brain bypasses the spinal cord, genital stimulation through the vagus nerve may allow sexual arousal in spinal cord–injured women and additional sexual arousal in normal women (Whipple & Komisaruk, 1998).

RESEARCH MEASUREMENT OF FEMALE SEXUAL AROUSAL

By its very nature, female sexual arousal is more diffuse and difficult to measure than that of the male. Whereas research on male sexual arousal has focused almost exclusively on quality of erection, specific measurement of female genital arousal developed over the last 25 years chiefly uses changes in vaginal vasocongestion or temperature in vaginal tissue. Clitoral vasocongestion and sensitivity have rarely been measured but should be. Apparently, Berman et al. (1999) are including clitoral blood flow, vaginal pH changes due to lubrication, and doppler ultrasonography among their research measures. They are aggressively applying these measures in testing efficacy of vasodilating drugs such as sildenafil for treatment of FSAD. Lubrication and cervical secretions are reported to raise vaginal pH. Absorbent tissues and tampons have occasionally been used to measure changes in lubrication. Certainly the measurement of lubrication alone is inadequate to assess the degree of physical sexual arousal. The validity and meaning of these lubrication and clitoral measurements have not yet been determined, but their development will be necessary for treatment of menopausal FSAD when conventional vaginal vasocongestion measures may fail to show differential response from normal premenopausal function (Myers & Morokoff, 1986).

Unfortunately, the standard physical measurements of female genital arousal by vaginal photoplethysmography (light reflectance) and thermistors have shown limited or nonsignificant correlation to subjective self-report measures of sexual arousal. There is little proof that these objective measures are the true index of female physical sexual response. Nevertheless, they have been used by some investigators to show that women cannot accurately perceive their sexual response (in contrast to men). While noting that males would always report at least some arousal during full erections, Heiman (1977) reported that among women showing the largest physiological change in vaginal blood volume, 42% claimed to feel no physical response, 54% no vaginal sensations, and 63% no signs of lubrication. Correlations between photoplethysmograph measures and self-reported sexual arousal in female samples range from about 0.4 to 0.7 and are often nonsignificant (Rosen & Beck, 1988; Henson, Rubin, & Henson, 1979).

The vaginal photoplethysmograph is a tampon-sized sensor which, when inserted into the vagina, emits lights into the surrounding vaginal capillary bed. The amount of light reflected back is inversely proportional to blood volume. Gradual change (pooling) in vaginal blood volume (VBV) is measured through a direct current (DC) signal coupling. Phasic changes in vaginal engorgement with each heartbeat are called vaginal pulse amplitude (VPA). VPA is measured through an alternating current (AC) signal coupling. Though VPA has generally been found to correlate better with self-reported sexual arousal (Laan, Everaerd, & Evers, 1995; Rosen & Beck, 1988), VBV continues to be used and often both VPA and VBV are reported. Surprisingly, VBV measurement, but not VPA, has shown clear differences between sexually functional and dysfunctional women (Palace & Gorzalka, 1990).

VPA increases may occur within 10 to 20 seconds of exposure to erotic stimuli, even when the stimuli are negatively evaluated or found to be threatening (Laan & Everaerd, 1998). In addition, VPA increases have been reported to be equal between premenopausal and postmenopausal women, even when the postmenopausal women have not been treated with estrogen supplementation and presumably experience less lubrication (Myers & Morokoff, 1986; Laan & van Lunsen 1997). However, with assessment of vaginal blood flow by a device measuring both thermal change and oxygen diffusion within the vagina, Semmens and Wagner (1982) showed that estrogen replacement given to sexually dysfunctional postmenopausal women suffering vaginal atrophy, "sexual inhibition," and pain during intercourse restored blood flow to levels shown by sexually functional premenopausal controls. Clearly, elaboration and refinement in genital arousal measurements are needed for the diagnosis and treatment of postmenopausal FSAD.

The chief alternative to the photoplethysmograph is measurement of surface temperature change through a thermistor clipped onto the labia minora (Henson et al., 1979). Fisher et al. (1983) used a thermoconductance measure to show that females have nocturnal vaginal arousal similar to male nocturnal penile tumescence (NPT) during rapid eye movement (REM) sleep phases (Fisher et al., 1983). Nocturnal sleep measures of sexual response could be used in the future to diagnose FSAD due to nerve, vascular, or menopausal/hormonal deficiencies. Compared to VBV, labial thermistor measures have shown higher correlations to self-reported arousal comparable to those shown for VPA photoplethysmography measures (Henson et al., 1979). However, thermal measures have been infrequently used and have not been tested to show differences between sexually functional and dysfunctional women.

Perry and Whipple (1982) developed myographic instruments to measure muscle contractions during sexual arousal (Perry & Whipple, 1982). However, these devices have generally been used to measure orgasm rather than the continuum of genital arousal.

CLINICAL ASSESSMENT OF
FEMALE SEXUAL AROUSAL DISORDER

As previously stated, women with impaired physiological response of sexual arousal frequently experience other forms of sexual dysfunction concurrently, such as problems with desire or orgasm and/or genital pain. Therefore, it is necessary to undertake a complete sexual history that assesses all phases of the sexual response cycle, with particular attention to arousal. The evaluation may entail from one to several sessions, depending on the complexity of the problem. In women with physiologically based impaired arousal, it is often preferable to have several sessions with the women alone before bringing her partner in for conjoint sessions. An individual session with her partner is often valuable as well. The model presented here is a modified version of that developed by Kaplan (1983).

Exploration of the Chief Complaint

The clinician obtains information about the evolution of the sexual problem, how it began, whether it developed suddenly or gradually, whether it occurs in all situations or occasionally, and whether there are ameliorating or aggravating factors. Any changes in sexual interest, excitement, behavior, pleasure, anxiety, or overall satisfaction are noted.

The Sexual Status Exam

The clinician obtains a detailed description of the patient's current sexual experience. The patient is asked to describe in detail a typical or recent sexual experience, which gives a clear picture of the problem. This would include the *actions, thoughts,* and *feelings* from start to finish of the sexual encounter. Information both for masturbation and sex with a partner is obtained. Because patients tend to race through and summarize their experience, bypassing important details, the clinician often needs to ask them to go back and explain exactly what they were *doing, thinking,* and *feeling* during each step, as though they were describing a movie: who initiated, how did they communicate, what worked for them and what did not, when and how did a problem arise, was anger or anxiety present and how it was handled, were there any counterproductive behaviors, and what, if anything, caused discomfort or pain.

It is important to know whether the woman has ever had an orgasm and, if so, under what circumstances. Can she bring herself to orgasm on her own? Where and how does she touch herself when she masturbates? Does she use her finger, a vibrator or other means? Does she have fantasies when she masturbates? What thoughts or fantasies does she find most arousing? Does she use these fantasies during sex with her partner? If not, why? Has she shared these with her partner or does she prefer not to? When she is with her partner, what type of stimulation does she receive and for how long? Is it enough or would she like more? Does she experience pleasurable sensations (warmth, tingling, increased sensitivity) in the vagina and clitoris, and if so, from what? Does she experience changes in pulse rate and respiration when aroused? Do her genital tissues swell, become engorged, tense or firm? How well does she lubricate? Does she experience vaginal dryness? Does she use a lubricant? What, if any, sexual activities does she find arousing and how often does she engage in them? How often, if ever, does she achieve orgasm and from what activity? Does she fear letting go? If so, why? Does she have difficulty concentrating during sexual activity? If so, what interferes? Does she focus on upsetting or unpleasant thoughts? What about her partner excites her or turns her off?

Does she find him or her sexually attractive? Does she feel tense or anxious before sex? What goes on in her mind just before making love . . . just after? How frequently does she experience sexual desire, thoughts, or fantasies? How often does she engage in sexual activity, alone or with her partner?

Assessment of Medical Status

The evaluator should inquire about any health problems that could be contributing to the sexual dysfunction. What, if any, illnesses or surgical procedures has the patient had recently or in the past? What medications has she taken recently and in the past? Does she use cigarettes, alcohol, or other substances? Are menses normal and regular? Is she using birth control pills, which can impair arousal? Have there been problems surrounding pregnancy, delivery, or postpartum? In menopausal women or in those with compromised ovarian functioning, the evaluator may want to obtain additional laboratory tests such as free and total testosterone, estradiol, progesterone, prolactin, luteinizing hormone, or follicle-stimulating hormone. Additional tests may include thyroid studies, complete blood count, serum chemistries, blood sugar, or glycohemoglobin A1C. Women with vaginal discomfort or pain should be referred for a gynecological evaluation.

Assessment of Psychiatric Status

It is also necessary to determine whether sexual symptoms are secondary to a psychiatric disorder such as an affective disorder, or an anxiety disorder. A few screening questions that may be helpful are as follows: Has substance abuse or mental illness ever been a problem? Has the woman ever received psychiatric treatment or been hospitalized for psychiatric reasons? Has she ever taken psychiatric medications (including tranquilizers, antidepressants, or sleeping pills)? Has she ever experienced depression, phobias, or panic attacks?

If a psychiatric disorder appears to be present, the diagnosis and treatment should be clarified. It is important to know whether any medications could be contributing to the sexual dysfunction. It is also informative to know which came first, the sexual symptoms or the psychiatric problems, and whether extreme stressors are present. As always, the patient should also be asked about suicidality. Patients with severe psychiatric illnesses may be too fragile to tolerate psychosexual therapy or otherwise unable to benefit from it.

Psychosexual History

The clinician should obtain a developmental sexual history from patients including information about their earliest recollections of sexual feelings, early sexual experiences, age at the start of masturbation, popularity in adolescence, first intercourse, sexual fantasies, sexual trauma, and sex life before, during, and in between marriages, as well as during menopause.

Family History

The patient's family of origin and cultural and religious backgrounds are significant because conflicts originating here profoundly affect sexuality and the development of problems in adulthood. The composition of the family, the quality of parent's relationship with one another and with the patient, family themes, and sexual messages that were conveyed are some of the important areas.

Relationship History

The clinician must assess the quality of the person's past romantic relationships. For example, are there any consistent patterns of attraction or problems with commitment or rejection.

Assessment of the Couple's Relationship

The clinician needs to evaluate the patient's present relationship and determine whether a problem here could be contributing to impaired arousal. Not uncommonly, the origin of the sexual problem lies in the couple's interaction. Common obstacles include poor communication, inadequate sexual technique, unfulfilled expectations, conflict in the relationship, sexual dysfunction in the partner, partner psychopathology, fear of intimacy, incompatible sexual fantasies, familial transferences, unresolved conflict, and power struggles.

Summation and Recommendation

By the conclusion of the evaluation, the clinician should have a working knowledge of the diagnosis and an understanding of whether the problem has primarily an organic or psychogenic basis. The clinician should also be able to identify whether relationship issues, unrealistic expectations, or inadequate technique may be contributing factors. The clinician should offer encouragement whenever possible, without comprising accuracy. Recommendations for treatment should be given, including what to expect with regard to prognosis, time and effort.

TREATMENT OF FEMALE SEXUAL AROUSAL DISORDER

The treatment of FSAD may be carried out individually with the patient alone, or in conjoint sessions with the patient and her partner, or through a combination of the two. Sessions may occur as frequently as once a week or more infrequently, such as once a month, depending on the patient's needs, availability, resources, and degree of commitment.

In patients with impaired sexual arousal, treatment may proceed along medical or counseling sex therapy lines or with both in combination. Medical treatments are rarely considered for premenopausal women. Menopausal patients who are estrogen deficient and have impaired arousal and dysparunia are often given hormone replacement therapy alone without specific counseling. This approach, although it improves lubrication and discomfort, is often inadequate for the treatment of sexual dysfunction. The most effective approach for these cases would be specific sex therapy counseling for arousal deficiency, in addition to hormonal or other medical treatment.

For patients with impaired sexual arousal that is psychogenic, the range of cognitive–behavioral sex therapy techniques may be employed. These techniques are integrated with psychodynamically oriented psychotherapy when deeper emotional issues and resistances to treatment become apparent. A thorough description of the multitude of cognitive maneuvers and behavioral assignments employed in sex therapy is beyond the scope of this chapter. A few of the techniques described by Kaplan (1995) are as follows: increased awareness of counterproductive thoughts, emotions, and behavior; sexual fantasy training; the use of erotica; masturbation assignments; sexual skills training; improved communication; sensate focus exercises; taking turns; and improved intimacy. Some women find intimacy, or the act of sharing feelings with someone special, an essential prelude to arousal. Many sex therapy homework assignments involve exercises that are not sexual in nature, yet they are geared toward improving intimacy (Harrar & Vantine, 1999).

Electric and battery operated vibrators are very effective in enhancing female sexual desire, arousal, and orgasm. The intense stimulation they provide can help to overcome psychological inhibitions and medical causes of inhibited arousal. They may be incorporated into therapeutic exercises performed individually or with the partner (Kaplan, 1983). Vibrators come in various shapes and sizes. In addition to the traditional phallic-shaped vibrators, there are now powerful but small "lipstick"-size models, "palm-of-hand" shaped models designed specifically for clitoral stimulation, and curved wands for "G-spot" stimulation. Many vibrators are now fitted with expandable silicone sleeves for greater comfort and cleanliness.

The addition of a lubricant may be helpful not only for menopausal and postpartum women, but for those with adequate sex hormone levels. Many of the new water-based lubricants have improved in recent years, and are silkier and longer lasting. They are preferable to oil-based lubricants in that they will not damage latex condoms and are less likely to cause infection. Silicon-based lubricants are preferable for sex in water or for particularly vigorous activity; however, they tend to be more expensive. Though they improve safety, lubricants containing the antiviral spermicidal nonoxynol-9 can be irritating to some patients. In general, the fewer the number of additives, the lower the risk of allergic reaction.

MEDICAL THERAPIES
FOR FEMALE SEXUAL AROUSAL DISORDER

Hormones

Estrogen

Women vary considerably in their sexual response to exogenous estrogen. Premarin has been said to cause both increases and decreases in libido and sexual functioning . The sex-positive effect may in part be psychological due to the feminizing effect of estrogen on the skin, breasts, and vagina. Improved self-confidence and mood, which also may occur, can lead to increases in libido indirectly. Certainly, it is essential to correct dyspareunia secondary to estrogen deficiency as this is a powerful inhibitor.

Estrogen may have a direct positive effect on arousal as well in that it may activate oxytocin in the brain and vaginal tissues (McCarthy, 1995). Oxytocin may facilitate physical arousal in females as it stimulates erection in males (Argiolas & Melis, 1995). It also may enhance relaxation with the partner and increases sensitivity to touch (Crenshaw & Goldberg, 1996). In addition, estrogen stimulates nitric oxide production necessary for vasocongestion (Berman et al., 1998). However, estrogen's sexually enhancing effects appear less powerful than those of testosterone.

On the other hand, many women who are given exogenous estrogen (with or without progesterone) report a diminution in desire and arousability. This may be due to the inhibiting effect of medroxyprogesterone or to elevations in blood proteins that bind to the hormones (including testosterone) and inactivate them. Thus, taking exogenous estrogen may actually lead to sexual dysfunction by precipitating a deficiency in free testosterone (Rako, 1996). Estrogen is now available through a number of routes of administration, including oral, transdermal patch, vaginal cream, and an intravaginal ring that remains in place for 3 months.

Testosterone

It has been known for the past 40 years that testosterone is essential for sexual desire and arousal in women. However, this knowledge has not been incorporated into routine medical practice. Testosterone production declines gradually at menopause as ovarian function diminishes, or more precipitously after hysterectomy or certain forms of chemotherapy. A significant proportion of women who undergo hysterectomy or chemotherapy lose some degree of desire or functioning, and they often are not adequately informed of this potential risk.

Many women with testosterone deficiency experience diminished sexual desire and fantasies, and their nipples, vagina, and clitoris become less sensitive to stimulation. In addition, they often lose the capacity to become sexually aroused and achieve orgasm. The sensation of orgasm, if it occurs at all, is often weaker, briefer, less pleasurable, and more localized to the genitals (Rako, 1996). Testosterone deficiency may also cause a diminished sense of vitality and well-being, a loss of muscle tone, and genital atrophy not responsive to estrogen replacement (Rako, 1996).

There is concern that making a woman more masculine by giving her testosterone will render her more susceptible to cardiovascular disease. A slight diminution in high-density (good) cholesterol is known to occur, but this is offset by other cardiovascular advantages. Rako (1998) has proposed that this concern is unfounded and that low dosages of testosterone may actually be cardioprotective for women.

A woman with testosterone deficiency will report loss of responsiveness in all phases of the sexual response cycle—desire, arousal, orgasm, and resolution (Bartlik & Kaplan, 1999). The adverse affect on desire and orgasm may be particularly noticeable. Women with testosterone deficiency can be given replacement therapy. However, the dosages of testosterone for women are far lower than those for men (women's bodies have only one-twentieth as much testosterone as men's). The genital tissue may be unresponsive to oral forms of testosterone at first, perhaps because of atrophy or lack of receptors. Therefore, it is often preferable to begin by applying topical testosterone in a cream base directly to the vulva once a day (Roentsch, personal communication, February 1999). After a week or two, the cream should be applied to the inner thigh or wrist 5 days a week and to the vulva twice a week. Dosages should be kept as low as necessary to restore levels to the physiological range. For women, testosterone dosage of 0.25 to 0.8 mg per day, topically, is usually adequate (Rako, 1999).

Often, patients find it more comfortable to switch to methyltestosterone, which also may be taken orally in dosages of 0.25 to 0.8 mg per day. Methyltestosterone is also preferred for patients at risk for breast cancer because it is not readily converted to estrogen. However, unlike testosterone itself, methyltestosterone confounds the assay for the measurement of blood testosterone levels. Another convenient option is transdermal testosterone via skin patch. Although transdermal systems are only manufactured in dosages suitable for men, women may use them for a fraction of the time that men do (e.g., for only 4 hours per day). Thus, a 5-mg patch would deliver approximately one-sixth the usual daily dose, or 0.8 mg. Adverse side effects of testosterone, which are uncommon in the low dosages prescribed for women, include weight gain, liver damage, reduced levels of high-density (good) cholesterol, enlargement of the clitoris, acne, irritability, and male secondary sexual characteristics such as facial hair, deep voice, and a tendency to baldness. Sometimes the response to testosterone fails after a few weeks or months, possibly because receptors are becoming less sensitive or numerous (Roentsch, personal communication, February 1999). A drug holiday of 2 weeks may then restore the hormone's effectiveness.

In my clinical experience, many women notice heightened libido and arousal half an hour to a few hours after the topical application of testosterone cream to the vulva. Tuiten, Van Honk, and Koppeschaar (2000) set out to determine the response time in women to sublingual testosterone. In a double-blind placebo-controlled crossover study, women experienced a significant increase in genital responsiveness 3 to 4½ hours after a single dose of testosterone. Because testosterone levels peak in 15 to 90 minutes, and responsivity peaks hours later, the lag may be explained on the basis of brain mechanisms responsible for female sexual arousal (Tuiten et al., 2000).

Oxytocin

Oxytocin, the neuropeptide secreted during touching, parturition, and breastfeeding, appears to stimulate sexual arousal in male and female laboratory animals. In male rats, penile erection is facilitated through augmentation of nitric oxide (Argiolas & Melis, 1995). Synthetic oxytocin taken to facilitate milk letdown caused one woman to experience spontaneous orgasm on two occasions (Anderson-Hunt & Dennerstein, 1994). Oxytocin is also activated by estrogen, as mentioned earlier.

Progesterone

Natural progesterone has been reported to stimulate libido (Lee, 1997) and to do the reverse (Crenshaw & Goldberg, 1996) as well. The increase in sex drive that some women experience during the late stages of pregnancy and premenstrually has been said to be linked with elevated progesterone levels at these times (Laux & Conrad, 1997). A topical preparation of natural progesterone and L-arginine is being prescribed as an aphrodisiac and a sexual performance enhancer for women (Roentsch, personal communication, December 1999), though these have not been formally studied and are not approved for this purpose. The preparation is rubbed into the labial tissues approximately half an hour before sexual activity. In addition, a topical preparation of progesterone or pregnanolone, which is converted into progesterone, is being prescribed for both men and women. Anecdotally, it has been observed to increase libido, enhance sexual performance, and improve well-being (Roentsch, personal communication, December 1999) when rubbed into the skin of the neck or under the chin.

Vasodilators

It appears plausible that medications proven to enhance erection in men may possess the same potential to enhance arousal and ease of orgasm in women. In fact, in some ways women may possess the advantage (Bartlik et al., 1999).

The vaginal mucosa is more permeable than the penile skin to topical preparations, and many patients find topical applications preferable to other routes of delivery. Following is a description of some medications that may be sexually enhancing for women (see also Table 4.2) These medications have not been formally studied in women, nor are they approved for these purposes; however, some have been studied in male populations and are approved for men.

• *Sildenafil citrate* (Viagra), theoretically, should enhance the vaginal engorgement/lubrication response in women just as it enhances erection in men, through localized genital vasodilation. In one small uncontrolled study, nine women who took sildenafil an hour before sexual activity experienced a reversal of antidepressant-induced sexual dysfunction (Nurnberg, Hensley, Lauriello, Parker, & Keith, 1999). In another study, which was double-blind and controlled, using doppler ultrasonography and vaginal pH levels, sildenafil appeared to enhance the female sexual response in posthysterectomized or menopausal women (Berman et al., 1999). The authors (Bartlik et al., 1999) have observed several individual cases of heightened sexual responsivity in response to sildenafil among patients with primary anorgasmia, antidepressant-induced delayed orgasm, and posthysterectomy-related sexual dysfunction. In some

TABLE 4.2. Potential Sex-Positive Medications for Women

Hormones	Antidepressants and other medications
Estrogen	Bupropion
Testosterone	Deprenyl
Oxytocin	Apomorphine
Progesterone	Trazodone
	Nefazodone
Vasodilators	Buspirone
Sildenafil citrate	Psychostimulants
Prostaglandin E-1	Methylphenidate
Phentolamine	Adderall
Pentoxifylline	Ephedrine
Aminophylline	
Ergoloid mesylate	Alternative and over-the-counter medications
Isosorbide dinitrate	Caffeine
	Damiana
	Dehydroepiandrosterone (DHEA)
	Dong Quai
	Ginkgo biloba
	Ginseng
	L-Arginine
	Ma huang
	Muira Puama
	ProSensual
	Royal jelly
	Sarsaparilla root
	Yohimbine

instances, sildenafil has resulted in enhanced sexual desire and the desire for repeated sexual experiences following orgasm. In addition to the standard pill form, the authors have found a compounded topical preparation of sildenafil in half the dose of the oral form to be effective. Some women who have objected in principle to the idea of taking a pill to enhance sexual functioning will readily accept a topical cream.

• *Prostaglandin E-1*, a naturally occurring vasodilator, has been used to stimulate penile blood flow through intracavernosal injection and transurethral suppository. It has been applied topically to the female genital with encouraging results in isolated cases (Bartlik et al., 1999). Several pharmaceutical companies are currently investigating prostaglandin E-l creams and gels for topical use in women (Hitt, 2000).

• *Phentolamine.* Another medication used in penile injection therapy, phentolamine, in the form of a vaginal suppository for women, is currently being studied (Hitt, 2000).

• *Pentoxifylline.* Crenshaw and Goldberg (1996) observed that men on pentoxifylline (Trental) not only benefited with respect to their intermittent claudication but had improved erections as well. Pentoxifylline improves circulation by enhancing erythrocyte flexibility. However, it is associated with side effects of nausea, nervousness, flushing, anorexia and dizziness.

Recently, compounding pharmacist George Roentsch (personal communication, January 2000), has found that topical pentoxifylline applied to the clitoris and labia of women with problems of sexual arousal is beneficial and associated with minimal side effects.

• *Other topical vasodilators* (aminophylline, ergoloid mesylate, isosorbide dinitrate). In one Egyptian study, a combination of three vasoactive medications applied topically to the penis in men with erectile disorder was found to be effective in increasing penile blood flow and in improving erection (Gomaa et al., 1996). When applied as a topical cream to the clitoris in women, this combination was found to be effective in one isolated case (Bartlik et al., 1999).

Antidepressant and Other Medications

In recent years, the sexual side effects of antidepressant medications have received a great deal of attention. With the exception of bupropion, mirtazepine, nefazodone, and trazodone, all the antidepressant medications frequently inhibit sexual functioning (Sussman, 1999). Some of the medications that have been reported in individual cases to reverse antidepressant-induced sexual dysfunction include amantadine, cyproheptadine, ginkgo biloba, nefazodone, yohimbine, and low dosages of the psychostimulants, methylphenidate, and dextroamphetamine (Bartlik et al., 1999). There is great interest in whether sildenafil will be proven effective in reversing sexual side effects in patients receiving antidepressants. Because sildenafil specifically affects vasodilation in the arousal/excitement phase, it may not improve diminished desire and delayed orgasm so prominent with SSRIs. In fact, sildenafil may even delay orgasm. Some clinicians have noted that sildenafil is effective for treating premature ejaculation (F. Eid, personal communication, September 1999). To date there have been no double-blind, controlled studies on the use of medications to reverse sexual side effects, and such studies are sorely needed.

Bupropion

(Wellbutrin, Zyban) is an unconventional antidepressant with primary dopamine reuptake and secondary noradrenaline reuptake actions, but without any effect on serotonin reuptake or serotonin receptor activity (Crenshaw, Goldberg, & Stern, 1987; Bartlik et al., 1999). Though a chemical derivative of ephedrine with mild dopaminergic stimulant effects, it is not metabolized to amphetamine, is not a scheduled drug, and has not been found to be abused. It has recently been approved by the Food and Drug Administration (FDA) for smoking cessation under the brand name Zyban.

Prior to its approval as an antidepressant in the late 1980s, bupropion was tested in a 60-patient controlled, double-blind, 32-week trial for the treatment of low sexual desire and other sexual response deficits in nondepressed women and men (30 female, 30 male). Beneficial sexual effects were expected due to bupropion's selective dopamine reuptake action, because dopamine stimulation has been consistently associated with pleasure and sexual stimulation in both male and female animal research studies. Statistically significant sexual improvement was found in over 60% of patients treated with bupropion but in less than 10% treated with placebo (Crenshaw et al., 1987).

The bupropion dose appropriate for women in treatment of sexual dysfunction and/or depression is 225 to 300 mg per day. The sexual studies were conducted with the immediate-release (IR) formulation, but currently a sustained-release (SR) formulation (Wellbutrin SR) is typically prescribed. At this time, the SR formulation is currently being tested in a controlled clinical trial for treatment of hypoactive sexual desire. Problematic side effects due to bupropion's stimulant properties include nervousness, insomnia, tremor, and a rare possibility of seizure. Combinations of SSRIs and bupropion are being prescribed for patients with sexual concerns, however, this area needs further study (Bodkin, Lasser, Wine, Gardner, & Baldessarini, 1998).

Bupropion has chemical actions similar to methylphenidate though with far less noradrenergic potency. Its stimulant potency is less than methylphenidate or amphetamines so that it may not be as potent as stimulants for treatment of sexual dysfunction. Furthermore, there is a delay of at least 10 to 14 days before any therapeutic effect is noted, which is typical with antidepressants.

Other Dopaminergic Drugs

New dopamine stimulants are currently being developed for use in treatment of cocaine abusers, but the only other dopamine activator available is the nonamphetamine deprenyl (Selegiline, Eldepryl), which is prescribed as an adjunct medication to treat Parkinson's disease. Deprenyl has shown strong aphrodisiac actions in old male rats, enabling sexually sluggish rats to copulate and ejaculate with as great a frequency as younger rats (Knoll, Yen, & Dallo, 1983; Crenshaw & Goldberg, 1996) but has not been tested for sexual effects in female animals or humans. The clinical impression is that it may have a mild beneficial sexual effect on female sexual desire but less than that of bupropion. However, it is a safe drug associated with minimal anxiety-producing or sleep-disturbing side effects. Of particular note, much of its chemical action is due to a massive increase in the endogenous body stimulant phenylethylamine (PEA), which has been promoted over the last decade as the "chemistry of love" component causing chocolate to act as an aphrodisiac (without any research or clinical evidence) (Liebowitz, 1983; Bartlik et al., 1999).

An oral (sublingual) form of apomorphine (Uprima), a direct dopamine receptor agonist, currently is in clinical trials for erectile dysfunction treatment. This dopamine agonist can be taken on an as-needed basis shortly prior to sexual activity. Because it apparently has both a local genital vasodilation effect and a central action on areas of the brain inducing sexual response, it may be particularly effective in facilitating female orgasm. However, no research, even of an investigational nature, has been conducted regarding oral apomorphine for women. Although apomorphine is considered solely a dopaminergic agonist, its efficacy in stimulating penile erection has been shown to involve direct stimulation of nitric oxide (Melis, Stancampiano, & Argiolas, 1994). Initial findings of research in progress show a strong synergy among dopamine, nitric oxide, and testosterone. This suggests that the mixtures of sildenafil with dopaminergic agents such as apomorphine and/or testosterone may eventually be used to treat severe female sexual dysfunction (Bartlik et al., 1999).

Serotonergic Drugs

Gartrell (1986) reported an unusual increase in libido in 6 of 13 women treated with trazodone (Desyrel) for depression and presented three case descriptions of this increased sexual arousal. Nefazodone (Serzone) is a newer antidepressant chemically similar to trazodone and has been characterized by a relative lack of negative sexual effects. This may be due to nefazone's antagonism of the 5HT2 receptor, a receptor thought to be involved in SSRI-induced sexual dysfunction. This suggests that nefazodone may be a superior antidepressant for postmenopausal women, particularly those with diminished sexual responsivity secondary to declining levels of endogenous testosterone. The SSRIs may further exacerbate sexual dysfunction in these patients.

Kaplan (1987) has written an entire book detailing the involvement of sexual aversion, phobia, and panic disorder particularly in female sexual dysfunction. She suggests the use of SSRIs to resolve these difficulties that are often unrecognized but crucial factors in female sexual disorders. In addition, SSRIs may be used to decrease aggressive and irritable tendencies, which often disrupt marital harmony and undermine progress in sexual therapy treatment.

Buspirone (Buspar) is a serotonin 5HT1A agonist prescribed for treatment of generalized anxiety disorder. Othmer and Othmer (1987) treated nine patients (six female, three male) with both generalized anxiety and low sexual arousal with an average daily dose of 45 mg a day buspirone for 4 weeks. Eight of the nine patients returned to normal sexual arousal and function while on buspirone, without any evidence of hypersexuality. Further investigation on the sexual effects of buspirone is warranted.

Psychostimulants

In her 1974 book, Kaplan included occasional use of low-dose amphetamines among the drugs that enhance libido and sexual functioning. Hallowell and Ratey (1995) reported on a case of a preorgasmic woman with attention-deficit/hyperactivity disorder (ADHD) who had her first orgasm during a routine sexual experience days after initiating treatment with methylphenidate (Bartlik, Kaplan, & Kocsis, 1995). Though not formally studied, low dosages (5–15 mg) of the psychostimulants, methylphenidate, and dextroamphetamine have been reported in individual cases to alleviate delayed or inhibited orgasm secondary to SSRIs and other antidepressants (Gitlin, 1995; Bartlik, Kaplan, & Kaplan, 1995). In the authors' limited sample of private patients (Bartlik, Kaplan, & Kaplan, 1995), women appear to respond more vigorously than men, which may be due to known heightened sensitivity to dopamine in the female brain (Crenshaw & Goldberg, 1996). In one of her patients, Bartlik (1997) found Adderall (10 mg), a racemic mixture of amphetamine and dextroamphetamine salts, more effective than comparable dosages of both dextroamphetamine and methylphenidate. Though stimulants may ease orgasm, they also have the potential to diminish arousal and excitement secondary to vasoconstrictive and potentially anxiety producing effects. In addition, because psychostimulants are not approved for this use and have the potential to cause arrhythmia, addiction, and other side effects, caution should be exercised when prescribing.

Ephedrine

Sympathetic nervous system activity plays an important role in the female sexual response, particularly during the stages of high arousal when there is generalized sympathetic discharge (Meston & Heiman, 1998). One study has shown that strenuous physical exercise, which causes sympathetic discharge, heightens plethysmographic measures of vaginal blood volume and physiologic arousal (Meston & Gorzalka, 1995).

Ephedrine, an alpha- and beta-adrenergic agonist, facilitates sexual behavior in female rats (Yanase, 1977). Ephedrine has also been found, in double-blind, controlled studies of sexually healthy women, to increase plethysmographic measures of vaginal engorgement during the viewing of erotic video (Meston & Heiman, 1998).

Whether ephedrine or similar medications have the potential to aid women with sexual dysfunction is another area worthy of investigation. Although ephedrine may facilitate sexual arousal and orgasm, its capacity to cause nervousness and vasoconstriction may limit its usefulness in sexual medicine.

Alternative and Over-the-Counter Medications

Increasingly, patients are taking over-the-counter nutritional supplements in efforts to augment sexual desire and performance. However, the evidence in their favor is strictly anecdotal and none have been studied empirically. Furthermore, little is known regarding their safety, particularly during pregnancy. An abbreviated list of some of the nutritional substances purported to have sex positive effects is given below and described more fully elsewhere (Cohen, 1999; Walker, 1994).

• *Caffeine* may enhance sexual functioning through dopaminergic stimulation. It has been reported to heighten sexual functioning in one woman (Bartlik, Kaplan, & Kocsis, 1995) and in older men (Crenshaw & Goldberg, 1996).

• *Damiana* is reputed to enhance libido, increase sperm count, stimulate genital nerve endings, and enhance genital blood flow (Cohen, 1999).

• *Dehydroepiandrosterone (DHEA)* replacement therapy in women with adrenal insufficiency resulted in improved sexual functioning in all phases of the sexual response cycle (Casson et al., 1996). Anecdotally, DHEA (10 mg per day) has been observed to restore libido in menopausal women who were taking it orally, transdermally, or transvaginally for hot flashes. In isolated cases, some men have found DHEA effective in improving sexual desire and performance (Roentsch, personal communication, December 1999).

• *Dong Quai,* which contains phytoestrogens, is reputedly effective as a sexual tonic for both genders and as a treatment for premenstrual and menopausal symptoms.

• *Ginkgo biloba* has been reported to reverse sexual dysfunction caused by antidepressant medications in an open trial (Cohen & Bartlik, 1998). Possible mechanisms of action include enhanced genital blood flow, cholinergic stimulation, inhibition of platelet-activating factor, and augmentation of prostaglandin activity. Caution should be exercised, due to ginkgo's blood-thinning action.

• *Ginseng* contains phytoestrogens and other chemical substances, which may augment sexual functioning in both genders.

- L-*Arginine* is an amino acid precursor to nitric oxide, a principle mediator of penile erection. L-Arginine is contained in many over-the-counter impotence remedies and has been systematically studied in humans and in laboratory animals with encouraging results. In aging male rats, L-arginine stimulates penile erection when given in large oral dosages (Chen et al., 1999). In men with organically based erectile dysfunction, oral L-arginine improves performance, but only when levels of plasma and urinary nitrate and nitrate are low at baseline (Moody, Vermet, Laidlaw, Rajfer, & Gonzalez-Cadavid, 1997). Topical preparations of L-arginine combined with either pentoxifylline or progesterone are being administered topically to women with sexual dysfunction as an off label use. The cream, applied to the vulva approximately 30 minutes prior to sexual activity, has been observed anecdotally to be effective in several women (Roentsch, personal communication, 1999).
- *Ma huang,* a plant from which ephedrine is derived, is another herbal remedy purported to have positive sexual effects, perhaps due to stimulation of the peripheral sympathetic nervous system, as previously discussed.
- *Muira Puama* is used both topically and orally by native Brazilian men and women as a sexual enhancer.
- *ProSensual,* recently marketed as a topical sexual stimulant for women, comprises an assortment of herbs and spices in a soy oil base. The aphrodisiac potential of these herbs and spices was first described in the *Kama Sutra* two thousand years ago. The ingredients include glycine max, cinnamonium cassia, zingiber officinalis, mint, orange, sandalwood, and clove. The product has not been studied empirically and has not been proven safe or effective.
- *Royal jelly* is secreted by worker bees to be eaten exclusively by the queen of the hive. It is purported to have an aphrodisiac effect.
- *Sarsaparilla root* contains precursors of progesterone and testosterone. It has been said to remedy impotence and to cure sexual diseases.
- *Yohimbine* improves penile blood flow and enhances erection in a moderate proportion of men with this problem (Crenshaw & Goldberg, 1996).

CASE STUDY

A 50-year-old woman presented with a 2-year history of the complete loss of sexual functioning following an ovary-sparing hysterectomy. Her symptoms included the loss of libido, the inability to become aroused, lack of lubrication, inhibited orgasm, and total inability to experience sexual pleasure. A year after the operation, she began taking supplemental estrogen for hot flashes, which appeared to make her sexual symptoms worse. Attempts to try to stimulate her desire with activities that used to arouse her, such as massages and erotic films, did not change her situation. She stated that she felt as though she was sexually dead and that she had lost an important part of herself.

The patient had been married for 28 years and was the mother of three grown children. Until the hysterectomy, she had enjoyed sexual relations with her husband approximately once a week. However, she was orgasmic only occasionally and only during intercourse. Furthermore, she could not identify any specific activity that reliably brought her to orgasm. She had always been reluctant to ask her husband for the type of touching and positioning that she enjoyed because of his erectile difficulties. The patient had never masturbated and had no sexual partners other than her husband.

The patient's husband had experienced intermittent erectile problems throughout his life associated with periods of stress. He had been diagnosed with panic disorder and major depression years before and was treated with antidepressant medication; however, he was not currently taking any medication. Urological workups, including nocturnal penile tumescence tests, were within normal limits. His erectile problems grew significantly worse after her hysterectomy and after his wife lost all interest in sexual relations. Increasingly, the couple became less physically affectionate with one another in attempts to avoid situations that would inevitably result in disappointment. However, they were emotionally intimate and loving with one another in other respects.

The patient found her husband attractive and was not turned off by him in any way. She was not clinically depressed or suffering from a psychiatric disorder that could interfere with sexual functioning. She was not on medication that could inhibit sexual functioning, nor did she have a medical illness that could account for her problem. Her liver function tests, cardiolipids, and electrocardiogram were within normal limits.

Testosterone deficiency secondary to diminished ovarian functioning was suspected as the cause of the patient's more recent loss of sexual functioning. Lack of information, inadequate stimulation, and excessive concern about her husband's sexual problem also contributed to her more long-standing orgasmic dysfunction. Total and free testosterone levels were obtained. Free testosterone was zero and total testosterone was in the middle of the normal range. The patient had no cardiac risk factors.

Masturbatory exercises with a water-based lubricant were suggested as a first step. The patient reported that when she stroked her clitoris or labia, it felt no more sensitive than other nonsexual parts of her body, which was typical for her since the surgery. In addition, an educational erotic video that included a discussion of women's sexual anatomy and functioning was recommended. Though the patient appreciated the video for what it was, she did not feel any degree of desire or arousal when she watched it and subsequently did her exercises.

The patient had read a popular book about testosterone and female sexuality and was motivated to try testosterone supplementation. She was asked to write a letter to be included in her chart documenting her reasons for wanting to take testosterone. The letter mentioned the fact that she was aware that the treatment had not been studied adequately, that it was not FDA approved for this purpose, and that she had been informed of the potential risks and side effects, which were listed in detail.

The patient was started on 0.25 mg a day of topical testosterone propionate cream (prepared by compounding pharmacist George Roentsch) applied to the clitoris and labia once a day after bathing. After 2 weeks with minimal response, the dosage was increased to 0.5 mg a day and then to 0.75 mg a day. Two months after starting testosterone, the patient reported a dramatic return of sexual feeling. Spontaneous sexual thoughts and fantasies that had been absent for many years, were back. Moreover, she had progressed to achieving orgasm during masturbation on her own. She experienced no undesirable side effects. In fact, she noted some positive psychological effects in that she was more energetic and found it easier to stick to her exercise routine. However, the couple's attempts at intercourse remained problematic due to the husband's erectile difficulty, and the wife's unwillingness to compromise him further by discussing her sexual needs.

At this point, the husband was invited to come in for both an individual session and conjoint sessions with his wife. During the individual session, the husband revealed that he regularly masturbated to erotic images on the Internet. He had no problem achieving erections and orgasm in this way. He was having strong nocturnal and morning erections. He explained that he had always had erectile difficulty when anxious, as when he was with a new partner or when he was upset about something at work. After his wife's hysterectomy, he could not function because he was anxious about hurting her. Then it became apparent that she was not enjoying herself, which made it impossible for him to maintain an erection. A urologist had recommended sildenafil, but the patient was hesitant to use it because the drug was new and the long-term effects were not known.

The couple continued sex therapy sessions approximately once a month for the next half-year, during which time they addressed long-standing issues about their sexual life. This included her husband's tendency to engage in intercourse as soon as he achieved an erection with minimal conversation, foreplay, and attention to her sexual needs and her tendency to passively wait for him to take the lead in bed rather than show him what she wanted.

At first, sexual intercourse was prohibited and sensate focus exercises were prescribed, which included sensual massage, gradually progressing to sexual massage and eventually to orgasm through manual stimulation. To help the husband learn to overcome his anxiety, he was instructed to deliberately let his erection subside and then to regain it with further manual stimulation. In addition, the couple was instructed to find ways, apart from intercourse, for her to achieve orgasm in the presence of her husband. After enjoying successes in these areas, the couple progressed to intercourse, at first for brief periods and then for increasingly longer periods. The wife was encouraged to provide herself with clitoral assistance during intercourse.

The couple began to have the most satisfying sex they had ever had. The patient reported feeling as though she was on her "second honeymoon" only this time it was "even better than the first." She felt that she had achieved what she wanted out of therapy and wished to terminate. The administration of testosterone was taken over by her gynecologist.

A year later, the patient returned for "a tuneup." She had not filled her testosterone prescription because she thought it might be exacerbating the gradual hair loss that she had experienced since the hysterectomy. Although she was not sure, she thought her hair felt thinner in the temple area. Upon examination, it did exhibit a slight male patterned thinning. The patient was referred to a dermatologist for closer monitoring.

She had fallen back into a rut of not desiring sex at all, yet she felt slightly "less dead" sexually than she had at the time of her initial consultation. She was bothered by her husband's erectile difficulty and reticence about foreplay. They had not made love in 6 months. In addition, she was unable to become aroused or to achieve orgasm on her own during masturbation. She had also made the decision to stop taking estrogen and she was experiencing mild hot flashes. However, for the sake of her marriage, she felt it was necessary to begin taking the testosterone again even at the risk of further hair loss.

Laboratories showed total and free testosterone levels both to be within normal limits—however, on the very low end of the normal range. Treatment with testosterone supplementation was reinitiated; however, only a low dose was prescribed (0.25 mg a day). The lower dosage resulted in a slight resurgence of sexual desire; however, the patient still had difficulty sustaining arousal and achieving orgasm. She was prescribed sildenafil (Viagra) 50 mg, from one to three hours prior to an anticipated sexual experience. Having learned more about the medication, her husband was also motivated at this time to try sildenafil himself. The wife noticed no improvement in her level of arousal an hour after taking sildenafil. However, the following morning she felt highly aroused. Upon manual stimulation, she noted more engorgement, sensation and pleasure, improved lubrication, and the ability to experience orgasm.

The couple continued in sex therapy for several sessions with good results. The husband was able to reduce his dosage of sildenafil from 50 to 25 mg successfully and then to discontinue it almost entirely. He found that he only needed the medication occasionally, during periods of increased stress or marital tension. After engaging in several homework assignments, the couple experienced more varied, more communicative foreplay, which pleased the wife. She found that the oral sildenafil seemed to work best for her when she took it 6 or 8 hours before sex. In addition, she preferred the topical cream preparation of sildenafil (25 mg per application) that was prepared by compounding pharmacist Roentsch, because she experienced a quicker response and less flushing that way. Their sessions tapered down in frequency from once every other week, to once every 6 months.

Discussion

This patient's sexual dysfunction appeared to be partly related to a testosterone deficiency arising from a partial hysterectomy. Even when the ovaries are preserved, hysterectomy can result in a diminution in ovarian functioning due to surgical trauma. However, the patient also had a long-standing primary sexual disorder, namely, female orgasmic disorder, which is best treated with traditional sex therapy techniques. In addition, the husband's erectile disorder, which appeared psychogenic, also contributed to the couples' sexual dysfunction.

Before the orgasm dysfunction could be addressed, it was necessary to first restore testosterone to normal levels. Only then was the patient able to respond to the guided masturbatory and sensate focused exercises that were prescribed.

When the patient returned for another course of treatment the following year, it was necessary to keep the dose of testosterone very low because of the question of hair loss. This time sildenafil was used to augment the effect of topical testosterone, making it possible for the patient to become aroused and orgasmic on very low dosages of testosterone. At that time the patient's free (active) testosterone levels were in the low end of the normal range, compared to unmeasurably low levels (zero) the year before. This may have been due to the effect of the estrogen she was taking the first time and the resulting increased levels of sex hormone binding globulin, which binds to free testosterone.

The fact that the husband was brought in not at the beginning of treatment but in the middle, after the testosterone deficiency was addressed, is noteworthy. This approach is a departure from the usual couple-centered approach in sex therapy, but it is often preferable in cases of testosterone deficiency and female orgasmic disorder, which often require concentration on the female partner initially.

This case demonstrates the need for a comprehensive approach to treating the treatment of sexual dysfunction in menopausal women. Once the patient's testosterone deficiency was corrected, the other more long-standing sexual problems could be addressed with traditional cognitive–behavioral sex therapy techniques. Either the medical or the psychological therapy alone would not have been as successful as both in combination. Had the patient not received supplemental testosterone, she would not have been likely to respond to behavioral approaches. Similarly, without the sex therapeutic interventions, the couple might not have been able to overcome their long-standing sexual difficulties that were exacerbated by the testosterone deficiency.

CONCLUSION AND DIRECTIONS FOR FUTURE RESEARCH

An important area for future research will be the development of medications to help women overcome sexual dysfunction. The vasoactive medications are likely to feature prominently in the treatment of FSAD, as they have with the treatment of the analogous disorder in men, erectile disorder. Though the evidence of testosterone's importance to female sexual functioning is strong, much research remains to be done regarding indications, dosages, routes of delivery, and side effects, particularly long-term side effects. The administration of combinations of vasodilators, hormones and dopamine agonists as a treatment for FSAD appears promising.

Simultaneously, basic groundwork toward understanding female sexual disorders needs to be conducted. Elementary questions on incidence, prevalence, pathophysiology, and etiology still remain unanswered. In addition, instruments for the subjective and objective measurement of sexual arousal need further development and refinement before high-quality treatment research can be conducted.

One of many potential avenues worthy of exploration involves the development of an instrument to measure periodic nocturnal genital arousal during REM sleep in women, as exists for men. Such an instrument could be useful in diagnosing physiological conditions in women such as nerve, vascular, or hormonal abnormalities. Ideally, such technology will integrate measures of clitoral response with vaginal response, orgasm, perceptual sensation, attention/cognition, and even personality type in a comprehensive examination. Such an approach will additionally suggest corrections and improvements to the evaluation of male sexual arousal, which has focused almost exclusively on the presence of a sufficiently rigid erection.

As previously stated by Goldstein and Berman (1998), it is essential to approach female sexual complaints multidimensionally, considering both physiological and psychological factors. This is particularly true with FSAD, which often has, at least in part, a physiological basis. Until recently, however, the role of physiological factors in female sexual dysfunction has been, with the exception of estrogen, largely ignored.

In the future, the medical workup for patients with FSAD may encompass modalities similar to those used to evaluate its male analog, male erectile disorder, including cardiovascular risk assessments, measures of genital blood flow, nocturnal monitoring of clitoral engorgement, nerve conduction studies, assessment of sensory capacity, and hormonal profiles. Similarly, future treatment of FSAD may include a host of pharmacological agents that are currently available for men but not for women. The judicious use of such medications, in combination with existing psychotherapeutic and behavioral techniques, may ultimately prove to be the optimal approach for the treatment of FSAD.

ACKNOWLEDGMENT

We gratefully acknowledge The Mary Putnam Jacobi Fellowship of the Women's Medical Association of New York City for its generous support.

REFERENCES

Alzate, H. (1985). Vaginal eroticism and female orgasm: A current appraisal. *Journal of Sex and Marital Therapy, 11*, 271–284.

American Psychiatric Association. (1980). *Diagnostic and statistical manual of mental disorders* (3rd ed.). Washington, DC: Author.

American Psychiatric Association. (1987). *Diagnostic and statistical manual of mental disorders* (3rd ed., rev.). Washington, DC: Author.

American Psychiatric Association. (1994). *Diagnostic and statistical manual of mental disorders* (4th ed.). Washington, DC: Author.

Anderson-Hunt, M., & Dennerstein, L. (1994). Increased female sexual response after oxytocin [Letter]. *British Medical Journal, 309,* 929.

Argiolas, A., & Melis, M. R. (1995). Oxytocin-induced penile erection: Role of nitric oxide. In R. Ivell & J. Russell (Eds.), *Oxytocin* (pp. 247–255). New York: Plenum.

Bartlik, B. (1997, May). Unpublished data presented at the Research Colloquium for Young Investigators, American Psychiatric Association, San Diego, CA.

Bartlik, B., & Kaplan, P. (1999, December). Testosterone treatment for women. *The Harvard Mental Health Letter, 16,* 4–6.

Bartlik, B., Kaplan, P., Kaminetsky, J., Roentsch, G., & Goldberg, J. (1999, January). Medications with the potential to enhance sexual responsivity in women. *Psychiatric Annals, 28,* 46–52.

Bartlik, B., Kaplan, P., & Kaplan, H. S. (1995). Psychostimulants apparently reverse sexual dysfunction secondary to selective serotonin re-uptake inhibitors. *Journal of Sex and Marital Therapy, 21,* 264–271.

Bartlik, B., Kaplan, P., Kocsis, J. H. (1995). Psychostimulants apparently reverse antidepressant-induced sexual dysfunction [Letter to the editor]. *Primary Psychiatry, 2*(10), 13.

Berman, J. R., Berman, L. A., & Goldstein, I. (1998). Female sexual dysfunction. *The Female Patient, 23,* 45–51.

Berman, J., Goldstein, I., Werbin, T., Wong, J., Jacobs, S., & Chai, T. (1999, April). Double blind placebo controlled study with crossover to assess effect of sildenafil on physiological parameters of the female sexual response. *Journal of Urology, 161*(Suppl. 210).

Bodkin, J., Lasser, R., Wine, J., Gardner, D., & Baldessarini, R. (1998). Combining serotonin reuptake inhibitors and bupropion in partial responders to antidepressant monotherapy. *Clinical Psychiatry, 58,* 137–144.

Casson, P. R., Straughn, A. B., Umstot, E. S., Abraham, G. E., Carson, S. A., & Buster, J. E. (1996). Delivery of dehydroepiandrosterone to premenopausal women: Effects of micronization and nonoral administration. *American Journal of Obstetrics and Gynecology, 174,* 649–653.

Chen, J., Wollman, Y., Chernichovsky, T., Iaina, A., Sofer, M., & Matzkin, H. (1999). Effect of oral administration of high-dose nitric oxide donor L-arginine in men with organic erectile dysfunction: Results of a double-blind, randomized placebo-controlled study. *British Journal of Urology International, 83,* 269–273.

Cohen, A. (1999). *The use of natural products in the treatment of antidepressant-induced sexual dysfunction.* Manuscript submitted for publication.

Cohen, A., & Bartlik, B. (1998, April–June). Gingko biloba for antidepressant-induced sexual dysfunction. *Journal of Sex and Marital Therapy, 24,* 139–143.

Crenshaw, T. L., Goldberg, J. P. (1996). *Sexual pharmacology.* New York: Norton.

Crenshaw, T. L, Goldberg, J. P., Stern, W. C. (1987). Pharmacologic modification of psychosexual dysfunction. *Journal of Sex and Marital Therapy, 13,* 239–252.

Cummings, M. H., & Alexander, W. D. (1999). Erectile dysfunction in patients with diabetes. *Hospital Medicine, 60,* 638–644.

Fisher, C., Cohen, H. D., Schiavi, R. C., Davis, D., Furman, B., Ward, I. T., Edwards, A. T., & Cunningham, I. (1983). Patterns of female sexual arousal during sleep and waking: Vaginal thermoconductance studies. *Archives of Sexual Behavior, 12,* 97–122.

Frank, E., Anderson, C., & Rubinstein, D. (1978). Frequency of sexual dysfunction in "normal" couples. *New England Journal of Medicine, 299,* 111–115.

Gartrell, N. (1986). Increased libido in women receiving trazodone. *American Journal of Psychiatry, 143,* 781–782.

Gitlin, M. J. (1995, March). Letter to the editor. *Journal of Clinical Psychiatry, 56,* 3.

Goldstein, J., & Berman, J. R. (1998). Vasculogenic female sexual dysfunction: Vaginal engorgement and clitoral erectile insufficiency syndromes. *International Journal of Impotence Research, 10*(Suppl. 2), 584–590.

Gomaa, A., Shalaby, M., Osman, M., Eissa, M., Eizat, A., Mahmoud, M., & Mikhail, N. (1996). Topical treatment of erectile dysfunction: Randomized double blind placebo controlled trial of cream containing aminophylline, isosorbide, dinitrate, and co-dergocrine mesylate. *British Medical Journal, 312*, 1512–1515.

Hallowell, E., & Ratey, J. (1995). *Driven to distraction*. New York: Touchstone.

Harrar, S., & Vantine, J. (1999). *Extraordinary togetherness: A woman's guide to love, sex and intimacy*. (B. Bartlik, Medical Advisor). Emmaus, PA: Rodale Press.

Heiman, J. R. (1975). Women's sexual arousal. *Psychology Today, 23*, 91–94.

Heiman, J. R. (1977). A psychophysiological exploration of sexual arousal: Patterns in females and males. *Psychophysiology, 14*, 266–274.

Henson, D. E., Rubin, H. B., & Henson, C. (1979). Women's sexual arousal concurrently assessed by three genital measures. *Archives of Sexual Behavior, 8*, 459–469.

Hensley, P. L., Nurnberg, G., Lauriello, J., Parker, L. M., & Keith, S. J. (1999). *Sildenafil for antidepressant-induced sexual dysfunction in women*. Poster presented at New Clinical Drug Evaluation Unit Program, 39th annual meeting abstracts, Boca Raton, FL.

Hirshkowitz, M., Karacan, I., Howell, J. W., Arcasoy, M. O., & Williams, R. L. (1992). Nocturnal penile tumescence in cigarette smokers with erectile dysfunction. *Urology, 39*, 101–107.

Hitt, J. (2000, February 20). Search for the female Viagara and other tales from the second sexual revolution. *The New York Times Magazine Section*, p. 38.

Kaplan, H. S. (1974). *The new sex therapy: Active treatment of sexual dysfunctions*. Toronto: Random House.

Kaplan, H. S. (1983). *The evaluation of sexual disorders: Psychological and medical aspects*. New York: Brunner/Mazel .

Kaplan, H. S. (1987). *Sexual aversion, sexual phobias, and panic disorder*. New York: Brunner/Mazel.

Kaplan, H. S. (1995). *The sexual desire disorders: Dysfunctional regulation of sexual motivation*. New York: Brunner/Mazel.

Kline-Graber, G. & Graber, B. (1975). *Women's orgasm: A guide to sexual satisfaction*. Indianapolis: Bobbs-Merrill.

Knoll, J., Yen, T., & Dallo, J. (1983). Long-lasting, true aphrodisiac effect of (–)deprenyl in sexually sluggish old male rats. *Modern problems in pharmacopsychiatry, 19*, 135–153.

Komisaruk, B. R., & Whipple, B. (1998). Love as sensory stimulation: Physiological consequences of its deprivation and expression. *Psychoneuroendocrinology, 23*, 927–944.

Laan, E., & Everaerd, W. (1998). Physiological measures of vaginal vasocongestion. *International Journal of Impotence Research, 10*(Suppl. 2), S107–S110.

Laan, E., Everaerd, W., & Evers, A. (1995). Assessment of female sexual arousal: Response specificity and construct validity. *Psychophysiology, 32*, 316-385.

Laan, E., & van Lunsen, R. H. (1997). Hormones and sexuality in postmenopausal women. *Journal of Psychosomatic Obstetrics and Gynecology, 18*, 126–133.

Laumann, E. O., Gagnon, J. H., Michael, R. T., & Michaels, S. (1994). *The social organization of sexuality: Sexual practices in the United States*. Chicago: University of Chicago Press.

Laux, M., & Conrad, C. (1997). *Natural woman, natural menopause*. New York: HarperCollins Publishers.

Lee, J. R. (1997). *Natural progesterone: The Multiple roles of a remarkable hormone*. Sebastopol, CA: BLL.

Liebowitz, M. R. (1983). *The chemistry of love*. Boston: Little Brown.

Marson, L., & McKenna, K. E. (1990). A role for 5-hydroxytryptamine in mediating spinal sexual reflexes. *Society for Neuroscience Abstracts: 20th Meeting, 16*(Pt. 2), 1066.

McCarthy, M. M. (1995). Estrogen modulation of oxytocin and its relation to behavior. In R. Ivell & J. Russell (Eds.), *Oxytocin* (pp. 235–245). New York: Plenum.

McKenna, K. E., & Nadelhaft, I. (1989). The pudendo–pudendal reflex in male and female rats. *Journal of Autonomic Nervous System, 27*, 67–77.

Medical Economics Company. (1999). *Physicians' desk reference* (53rd ed.). Montvale, NJ: Author.

Melis, M. R., Stancampiano, R., & Argiolas, A. (1994). Prevention by NG-nitro-L-arginine methyl ester of apomorphine and oxytocin-induced penile erection and yawning: Site of action in brain. *Pharmacology, Biochemistry and Behavior, 48,* 799–804.

Meston, C. M., & Gorzalka, B. B. (1995). The effects of sympathetic activation following acute exercise on physiological and subjective sexual arousal in women. *Behaviour Research and Therapy, 33,* 651–664.

Meston, C. M., & Heiman, J. R. (1998). Ephedrine and activated physiological sexual arousal in women. *Archives of General Psychiatry, 55,* 652–656.

Moody, J. A., Vermet, D., Laidlaw, S., Rajfer, J., & Gonzalez-Cadavid, N. F. (1997). Effects of long-term oral administration of L-arginine on the rat erectile response. *Journal of Urology, 158*(3, Pt. 1), 942–947.

Myers, L. S., & Morokoff, P. J. (1986). Physiological and subjective sexual arousal in pre and postmenopausal women and postmenopausal women taking replacement therapy. *Psychophysiology, 23,* 283–292.

Newman, H. F., & Marcus, H. (1985). Erectile dysfunction in diabetes and hypertension. *Urology, 26,* 135–137.

Nurnberg, H. G., Hensley, P. L., Lauriello, J., Parker, L. M., & Keith, S. J. (1999, August). Sildenafil for women patients with antidepressant-induced sexual dysfunction. *Psychiatric Services, 312,* 1076–1078.

Othmer, E., & Othmer, S. C. (1987). Effect of buspirone on sexual dysfunction in patients with generalized anxiety disorder. *Journal of Clinical Psychiatry, 48,* 201–203.

Palace, E. M. (1995). Modification of dysfunctional patterns of sexual response through automatic arousal and false physiological feedback. *Journal of Consulting and Physiological Psychology, 63,* 604–615.

Palace, E. M., & Gorzalka, B. B. (1990). The enhancing effects of anxiety on arousal in sexually dysfunctional and functional women. *Journal of Abnormal Psychology, 99,* 403–411.

Palace, E. M., & Gorzalka, B. B. (1992). Differential patterns of arousal in sexually functional and dysfunctional women: Physiological and subjective components of sexual response. *Archives of Sexual Behavior, 21,* 135–159.

Parks, K., Moreland, R., Goldstein, I., Atala, A., & Traish, A. (1998). Sildenafil inhibits phosphodiesterase Type 5 in human clitoral corpus cavernoum smooth muscle. *Biochemical Research Communications, 249,* 612–617.

Perry, T. D., & Whipple, B. (1982). Vaginal myography. In B. Graber (Ed.), *Circumvaginal musculature and sexual function* (pp. 61–73). New York: Karger.

Rako, S. (1996). *The hormone of desire: The truth about sexuality, menopause, and testosterone* (Introduction by B. Bartlik and H. S. Kaplan). New York: Harmony Books.

Rako, S. (1998). Testosterone deficiency: A key factor in the increased cardiovascular risk to women following hysterectomy or with natural aging? *Journal of Women's Health, 7,* 828.

Rako, S. (1999). Testosterone deficiency and supplementation for women: Matters of sexuality and health. *Psychiatric Annals, 29,* 23–26.

Rosen, R. C., & Beck, J. G. (1988). *Patterns of sexual arousal: Psychophysiological processes and clinical applications.* New York: Guilford Press.

Rosen, R. C., & Leiblum, S. R. (1995). Treatment of sexual disorders in the 1990s: An integrated approach. *Journal of Consulting and Clinical Psychology, 63,* 877–890.

Rosen, R. C., & Lieblum, S. R. (1998). Changing perspectives on sexual desire. In S. R. Leiblum & R. C. Rosen (Eds.), *Sexual desire disorders.* New York: Guilford Press.

Rosen, R. C., Phillips, N. A., & Gendrano, N. C. (1999). Oral phentolamine and female sexual arousal disorder: A pilot study. *Journal of Sex and Marital Therapy, 25,* 137–144.

Rosen, R. C., Taylor, J. F., Leiblum, S. R., & Bachmann, G. A. (1993). Prevalence of sexual dysfunction in women: Results of a survey of 329 women in an outpatient gynecological clinic. *Journal of Sex and Marital Therapy, 19,* 171–188.

Segraves, R. T. (1996). Female sexual arousal disorder. In T. A. Widiger, A. J. Frances, H. Pincus, R. Ross, M. First, & W. Davis (Eds.), *DSM-IV sourcebook* (pp. 1103–1108). Washington, DC: American Psychiatric Association.

Segraves, R. T., & Segraves, K. B. (1991). Diagnosis of female arousal disorder. *Sexual and Marital Therapy, 6*, 9–13.

Semmens, J. P., & Wagner, G. (1982). Estrogen deprivation and vaginal function in postmenopausal women. *Journal of the American Medication Association, 248*, 445–448.

Sevely, J. L. (1987). *Eve's secrets: A new theory of female sexuality.* New York: Random House.

Sherfey, M. J. (1972). The nature and evolution of female sexuality. New York: Vintage Books.

Singer, J., & Singer, T. (1978). Types of female orgasm. In J. LoPiccolo & L. LoPiccolo (Eds.), *Handbook of sex therapy* (pp. 179–186). New York: Plenum.

Sussman, N. (1999). The role of antidepressants in sexual dysfunction. *Journal of Clinical Psychiatry Monograph, 17*, 9–14.

Tarcan, T., Park, K., & Goldstein, I. (1999). Histomorphometric analysis of age-related structural changes in human clitoral cavernosal tissue. *Journal of Urology, 161*, 940–944.

Tordjman, G. (1980). New realities in the study of the female's orgasms. *Journal of Sex Education and Therapy, 6*, 22–26.

Tuiten, A., Van Honk, J., & Koppeschaar, H. (2000). Effects of testosterone on sexual arousal in women. *Archives of General Psychiatry, 57*, 149–153.

Vroege, J. A., Gijs, L., & Hengeveld, M. W. (1998). Classification of sexual dysfunctions: Towards DSM-V and ICD-11. *Comprehensive Psychiatry, 39*, 333–337.

Walker, M. (1994). *Sexual nutrition: How to nutritionally improve, enhance, and stimulate your sexual appetite.* Garden City Park, NY: Avery.

Whipple, B., & Komisaruk, B. R. (1998, June). Beyond the G-spot: Recent research on female sexuality. *Medical Aspects of Human Sexuality, 1*(3), 19–23.

World Health Organization. (1992). *The ICD-10 classification of mental and behavioral disorders: Clinical descriptions and diagnostic guidelines.* Geneva, Switzerland: Author.

Yanase, M. (1977). A possible involvement of adrenaline in the facilitation of lordosis behavior in the overiactomized rat. *Endocrinology Japan, 24*, 507–512.

5

Orgasmic Disorders in Women

JULIA R. HEIMAN

While not as prominent a sexual problem as it was in the early days of sex therapy, difficulty achieving orgasm continues to be a significant issue for many women. In the history of sexuality, anorgasmia problems may be considered a relatively new disorder, although in recent surveys orgasmic difficulties are often noted as the second or third most common sexual complaint among women of all ages. The woman who does not regularly experience orgasm often feels deficient, deprived, and sometimes depressed.

Despite the concern about achieving orgasm (historically, there has been much concern about having the right "kind" of orgasm as well), there is no clear agreement on the subjective or objective criteria for orgasm. There are, however, a variety of orgasmic difficulties, ranging from complete lack of orgasm to unreliable or absent orgasms during intercourse. Most investigators agree that the brain plays a central role in the experience of orgasm, and that central or psychological factors are important in most cases.

In her chapter, Julia R. Heiman notes that the ultimate causes of orgasmic dysfunction are uncertain in most cases, although she describes a number of important contributing factors. Anatomic and physical factors, sociocultural and interpersonal factors, and psychological determinants all appear to be involved in the etiology and maintenance of orgasmic problems. Conceptual and therapeutic interventions are similarly varied, and include a range of psychoanalytic, cognitive-behavioral, and systems–interpersonal approaches.

Overall, Heiman favors a cognitive–systemic orientation to the treatment of orgasmic problems, in which a couple learns to recognize that their relationship consists of intricate sexual patterns. The couple automatically engages or constructs these patterns and in turn is constructed by them. Couple interactions occur on symbolic, affect-regulated, and sensory levels. Sometimes functioning occurs independently at each of these levels, although the levels may interact with each other within each individual and between partners. A systems–interpersonal orientation enables therapists to formulate and treat the orgasmic problem in interactional, rather than purely mechanical or behavioral terms. The patient, according to this perspective, is not the anorgasmic woman alone but, rather, the sexual and couple's relationship and all the attendant issues.

Helping couples to understand the function of the symptom at both the individual and interactional level is a central focus of treatment. What does having an orgasm mean to the woman? To her partner? What solution does the problem provide for the couple? Does the woman have a sense of ownership over her body? Does she want to achieve orgasm to satisfy her partner or herself? Can the couple communicate directly about sexual preferences? These and similar issues become the major treatment focus in this approach.

Julia R. Heiman, PhD, is an internationally recognized authority on the research and therapy of male and female sexuality and sexual psychophysiology. She is a professor of psychiatry and behavioral sciences at the University of Washington School of Medicine in Seattle, Washington and the author of several books on sexuality, including the most recent edition of Becoming Orgasmic: A Sexual Growth Program for Women *(with Joseph LoPiccolo).*

HISTORICAL AND CULTURAL CONTEXT

Across the centuries, varied meanings and various levels of importance have been attributed to women's orgasm. At different historical periods, orgasm has been believed to be either good or bad for the woman, for her partner, or for her marriage. Ambivalence about women's orgasm still continues to the present. Currently women's orgasm is more likely to be valued and seen as positive for herself and her relationship. Thus this chapter in a book on sexual disorders, because the lack of female orgasm is seen as a problem that needs clinical attention.

If we look across cultures of Western societies, as is the bias of this chapter, we can notice some interesting patterns. Laqueur (1990) has illustrated an example, in parable form, of the meaning given to orgasm. In late 17th to early 18th century western Europe, it was believed that women needed to feel the pleasure of orgasm to conceive. By the 1830s, beliefs had shifted; conception was believed possible without pleasure, orgasm, or even consciousness. This change emerged not from new scientific information but from a "radical reinterpretation" of the female body. For centuries prior to the 1700s, women's bodies were seen as being on a continuum with men's; by the late 18th century, writers insisted on fundamental differences between men and women. Laqueur (1990) uses this example to show how changes in epistemology and politics, rather than scientific progress per se (though all three interact dynamically), shape the meaning of sex.

From a clinical problem perspective, one of the core factors separating more traditional from more modern views of sexuality is the degree to which sexual problems have been seen as needing control and inhibition as opposed to needing stimulation and facilitation. In the latter half of the 19th century, therapeutic and social control of sexual activity was of great importance whereas inhibited or lost sexual behaviors and feelings have become the therapeutic and social concern of the more prosexual 20th century (see Robinson, 1970, for further discussion of traditionalists vs. modernists). On the cusp of the turn of the century was Sigmund Freud's work. Freud presented a categorization of female orgasm based on personality maturity. His theory viewed clitoral orgasms as superficial and immature whereas vaginal orgasms were authentic and adult. Although controversial, this anatomically based distinction of different types of orgasms represented an important transition from Victorian values. It recognized the presence and power of female orgasm without abandoning the cultural paradigm of procreative sex as the more valued and correct expression.

Contemporaneous with Freud's work was that of Havelock Ellis. Ellis not only suggested that women's responses were equivalent to men's but that women were probably more sexual than men. He saw women's sexuality as the more mysterious and more extensive given that women not only had a clitoris but also a womb, which gave them a large and diffuse sexual anatomy that could respond to sexual stimulation. Ellis said little specifically about female orgasm. He did see women as innately passive beings who required both courtship and the driving interest of men to elicit a sexual response.

A different perspective came from Alfred Kinsey, who prepared the way for a new conceptualization of female orgasms. Kinsey did not distinguish between anatomical types of orgasms in women. He did use orgasms as one of the several markers of human sexuality. An indirect outcome of his survey research was that orgasm frequency became one of the key variables that made up a person's, a group's, and a society's sexual demographics. It was also Kinsey who reported, much to the distress of the readers in the 1950s, that a woman was more likely to be orgasmic during masturbation than during sex with a partner.

Masters and Johnson (1966) interpreted their data on sexual response to mean that all female orgasms were the result of the same neurophysiological process of response and that women's orgasms were more similar than dissimilar to male orgasms. They published their research in 1966, when the atmosphere promoting sexual equality was more outspoken than in the previous decade. Women were claiming reproductive rights with the help of an easily available oral contraceptive method. The "right" to orgasm made sense in this context, and it was Masters and Johnson's *Human Sexual Inadequacy* (1970) that proposed a plan for making orgasms possible to women who never or rarely experienced them. Masters and Johnson offered a nonpathological model for cure: Remove the anxiety and the "natural expression of sexual response" will appear. As modest and atheoretical as this model was, it probably would not have been accepted in 1900. Masters and Johnson required the data of Kinsey's work as well as a different cultural environment to be heard.

It becomes rather obvious as we look across these major contributors to the understanding of sexuality that the simple fact that we recognize and treat orgasmic problems in women is, in part, a cultural accident. One hundred years ago, at least in northern Europe and Victorian England and certainly in the United States, we would not have done so. Thus, we must be cautious about classifying orgasm problems as either purely physical or purely psychological. Although such purity may exist on occasion, such as medication-induced orgasmic dysfunction, a woman's experiences of her history, her relationship, and her culture continuously interact with her neurophysiology.

The purpose of this chapter is to examine the ways in which the complexity of physical, psychological, and sociocultural factors can interact. After reviewing the incidence of orgasmic problems, etiological factors, theoretical treatment approaches, and treatment efficacy, the chapter addresses how to assess psychological, sociocultural, interactional, and physiological factors. I am aware that I am writing this chapter at a time when female sexuality in general is being examined with a heavy emphasis on the physiological factors that affect her functioning. The release of oral medications specifically for men's erections has prompted a new interest in understanding how physical factors may impact female sexuality. This is a positive trend in my opinion. The neurophysiological aspects of female sexual response have been minimally researched. However, if new research proceeds without a simultaneous examination of the subjective data on sexual response and satisfaction of women, it will ultimately not contribute to a broader understanding of sexuality. As readers will see, although we have some knowledge about female sexuality and have treatments for orgasmic dysfunction, in fact we know very little about mechanisms that might contribute to a complex model of female sexual response that encompasses biological and psychosocial factors.

DEFINITIONS AND PREVALENCE OF ORGASMIC PROBLEMS IN WOMEN

Orgasms are usually defined as a combination of both subjective experience and physiological changes in the vagina and pelvic area. Subjective descriptions women use include such words as "reaching a peak," feeling a building tension and then letting go, a feeling of contractions in the genital area, and/or a period of high excitement followed rather suddenly by a release into relaxation. There are no defined requirements for the subjective experience of orgasm; for example, some women report experiencing an orgasm with no accompanying muscular contractions (Levin, 1980, 1983; Levin & Wagner, 1987). Another subjective aspect of orgasm is a sense of the loss of the passage of time. Levin and Wagner (1985a) found that the women they studied in the laboratory setting underestimated the duration of their experience of orgasm by as much as 50% when compared with the physiological measures of the same experience. With respect to the physiological and behavioral indexes of orgasm, Masters and Johnson (1966) were the first researchers to study this in a laboratory setting. They documented that the entire body was in some way involved in the orgasmic experience. Rhythmic contractions occur in the uterus, the vaginal barrel, and the rectal sphincter, beginning at 0.8-second intervals and then diminishing in intensity, regularity, and duration. Facial grimaces, generalized muscle myotonia, carpopedal spasms, and contractions of abdominal and gluteal muscles also occur, though they are not required for the experience of orgasm.

Although there is a general impression that orgasmic problems are common in women, there are few well-controlled studies that have carefully examined the incidence of orgasm. An exception is the National Social and Health Life Survey done in the early 1990s (Laumann, Gagnon, Michael, & Michaels, 1994; Laumann, Paik, & Rosen, 1999). This study was a random probability sample of men and women which included 1,749 U.S. women between the ages of 18 and 59. The women were 75% Caucasian, 12% African American, and 7 to 9% Hispanic, with a range of educational, economic, and religious backgrounds. This study included heterosexual, lesbian, and bisexual individuals. Orgasmic problems were the second most commonly identified problem, with 24% of women reporting that in the past year, for at least several months or more, they had experienced a lack of orgasm.

A Massachusetts population–based, random sample of 349 women, ages 51 to 61, found a lower prevalence: 10.3% reported having difficulty reaching orgasm all or most of the time (Johannes & Avis, 1997). Of a random community sample of 521 British women ages 35 and 59, 16% reported infrequent orgasm (Osborn, Hawton, & Gath, 1988). Using the same sample but including only those women with partners (n = 436), 15.8% had no orgasms and 22.2% had orgasm on less than half the occasions of sexual activity with their partner in the last 3 months (Hawton, Gath, & Day, 1994).

Clinic-based data typically show higher frequencies of dysfunction. In an outpatient gynecological clinic, of a sample of 329 healthy, 18- to 73-year-old women followed for routine care, many reported orgasmic problems (29%), frequent intercourse pain (11%), and anxiety or inhibition during sex (38%) (Rosen, Taylor, Leiblum, & Bachmann, 1993). Of 104 patients attending a U.K. general practice clinic, 23% of women 18 to 65+ (mean age = 45) reported anorgasmia (Read, King, & Watson, 1997).

A common distinction made about orgasmic dysfunction is whether a woman has primary or secondary anorgasmia. Primary anorgasmia refers to never having had an orgasm; secondary anorgasmia refers to orgasmic infrequency or restricted conditions for being orgasmic (e.g., masturbation only). This chapter emphasizes secondary orgasmic problems because they are more common and typically more difficult to treat (Arentewicz & Schmidt, 1983; Heiman & LoPiccolo, 1983; Kaplan, 1974; Masters & Johnson, 1970). Clinical or epidemiological studies have not examined the distinction between primary and secondary anorgasmia. Kinsey's work, now 50 years old, reported that 10% of women remain incapable of orgasm (Kinsey, Pomeroy, Martin, & Gebhard, 1953). In addition, there are no distinctions made between women with *both* orgasmic and arousal disorders versus women with *only* orgasmic disorder. It is important to note that orgasmic problems do not always cause sexual distress or marital unhappiness for women. A nonrandom sample of couples found that 63% of the women reported arousal and orgasm problems although they were happily married, and 85% reported that they were satisfied with their sexual relationship (Frank, Anderson, & Rubinstein, 1978).

ETIOLOGICAL FACTORS INFLUENCING ORGASM IN WOMEN

A woman's capacity to experience orgasm appears to be influenced by a number of factors. These include neuroanatomic, physiological, psychological, sociocultural, and interactional factors. However, none of these influences on orgasm has been confirmed as being primary or absolute. Difficulties in studying orgasm include the lack of (1) an objective measure to document when orgasm is occurring for those who are studying the neurophysiological aspects of orgasm and (2) an agreed-on subjective definition of orgasm. This latter point is extremely important for a therapist to keep in mind. If one listens carefully to patients with sexual problems, some of them will report experiencing orgasm though it later becomes apparent that they were not, and other women will not identify orgasms when they are indeed occurring.

Neurophysiological Factors

Several anatomical areas are important for the experience of orgasm. Those most frequently mentioned are the clitoris and the vagina. The areas of the body that seem to be most sensitive to touch are the labia, the introitus to the vagina, and the clitoris. These areas, particularly the clitoris, are highly innervated and also have vasocongestive capacity. The vagina is relatively insensitive to touch, though strong deep pressure may act as a sensory stimulus. This is believed to be true partly because of the pubococcygeal (PC) muscle located at the 4 and 8 o'clock positions of the vagina, which itself is well supplied with proprioceptive nerve endings and has been found to generate pleasurable feelings when stimulated by pressure stroking (Graber & Kline-Graber, 1979; Kegel, 1952; Semmens & Semmens, 1978). Thus the strength and tone of the PC muscle have been proposed as a contributing factor to orgasmic capacity (Kline-Graber & Graber, 1978). However, correlations between PC muscle tone and orgasmicity are low and probably PC tone is idiosyncratically related to orgasm in women. Further evidence suggestive for the role of vaginal stimulation is that researchers have found that vaginal stimulation can increase the threshold for pain in women (Whipple & Komisaruk, 1985, 1988).

A few centimeters from the vaginal introitus on the anterior vaginal wall, an area about 1 cm in diameter has been identified as the Grafenberg (1950), or the "G-spot." The exact nature of this area has not been completely confirmed, but for some women, stimulation of this area has been shown to produce a fluid that is expelled at orgasm. It remains controversial whether this substance is really distinct from urine. Stimulation of this area has been found to consistently result in more sexual excitement than does stimulation to the posterior wall (Levin, 1992). It has been theorized that G-spot stimulation will help women reach orgasm (Richards, 1982, 1983). However, this has not been carefully documented in other than a few clinical subjects.

The brain is also an important source of sexual arousal and orgasm in women. Though research documentation is almost nonexistent for human females, there is evidence that individuals can have orgasm with no direct stimulation to the genitals. This evidence comes from the phantom orgasms experienced by paraplegics (Money, 1960), from orgasms induced hypnotically, from orgasms stimulated by fantasy alone, and from orgasms by stimulation of brain areas. In addition, there have been reports of orgasm from women who have had clitoral and labial excision and vaginal reconstruction. One research project has studied 10 volunteers who reportedly were able to experience orgasm from fantasy alone (Whipple, Ogden, & Komisaruk, 1992). Orgasm resulting from either self-induced imagery or genital self-stimulation was associated with the same physical correlates. This evidence is suggestive but points to the importance of including the brain as part of the sexual anatomical requirement for orgasmic experience. Whipple and colleagues have proposed several different nerve pathways involved in sexual response: the pudendal nerve for clitoral stimulation, the hypogastric plexis and pelvic nerve for vaginal stimulation, and possibly the vagus nerve directly from the cervix to the brain (Whipple & McGreer, 1997).

Little is known about the pertinent neuroanatomy and neurophysiology necessary for female sexual response. Many of the statements currently available in literature are based on extrapolations from male neurophysiology. Nevertheless, some important basic information is that the innervation of the female genital tract is mediated by the somatic and autonomic nervous system. The somatic innervation is conducted through the branches of the pudendal nerve, derived from sacral spinal segments 2 through 4 and travels laterally through the pelvis. Disruption, injury, or disease that affects this process could likely have an impact on orgasmic ability. The autonomic innervation consists of fibers from both sympathetic and parasympathetic nervous systems. The sympathetic fibers are derived from spinal segments $T^{10}-L^2$ and the parasympathetic fibers from S^2-S^4, though these data are based primarily on men. One controlled study of found that 52% of women with spinal cord injury at or above T^{10} were orgasmic compared to 100% of able-bodied women (Sipski, Alexander, & Rosen, 1995).

Sexual stimulation results in pelvic vasocongestion, vaginal lubrication, vaginal lengthening and tonic contractions, labial size increase, uterine elevation, and clitoral retraction (Masters & Johnson, 1966). Whereas both the physiological and subjective responses of orgasm are important, they are not always well correlated. Similar to sexual arousal experiences (Heiman, 1998; Laan, Everaerd, & Evers, 1995), correlations between respiration rate, heart rate, or average pelvic contractions with reported subjective intensity or satisfaction of orgasm have not been found (Bohlen, Held, & Sanderson, 1983). In addition, Levin and Wagner (1985a) found no correlation between increases in vaginal blood flow, orgasm latency, or duration of orgasm with the intensity of orgasm. However, they did find a correlation between orgasm intensity and change in heart rate (Levin & Wagner, 1985b).

Recently, vasculogenic insufficiency of the genitals has been proposed as one possible cause of female sexual arousal disorder and potentially orgasmic disorder (Goldstein & Berman, 1998). Parallel to male erectile dysfunction, atherosclerotic vascular disease is a common etiology. To date there are few data supporting this position in women but research is currently exploring this possibility.

The innervation of female genitalia is known to include cholinergic and adrenergic nerves. In addition, a number of peptides have been found to be involved in neurotransmitter or neuromodulator roles and have been located in female genital tissue (Ottesen, Wegner, & Fahrenkrug, 1988). Three of these peptides have been found to have roles in the sexual arousal processes of the female human genitalia and have been reviewed elsewhere (Levin, 1992). Further work on the neuropeptides as well as neurotransmitter substances is expected to take place over the next decade. Meanwhile, it is clear from the impact of medications on female sexuality, an important example being selective serotonic reuptake inhibitors (SSRIs), that serotonergic factors play an important role in arousal, in orgasm latency, and potentially in sexual desire. Typically increased availability of serotonin and decreased dopamine have a negative impact on sexual response, although the mechanisms are incompletely understood (Meston & Gorzalka, 1992; Steele & Howell, 1986). In addition, adrenergic blockade or anticholinergic activity peripherally may delay or inhibit orgasm.

Psychosocial Factors

In spite of assumptions about the impact of religion, education, age, social class, and other sociocultural factors, few supporting data are available. Laumann et al. (1999) analyzed their data on sexual dysfunctions from the perspective of the demographic characteristics that might differentiate by dysfunction as well as risk factors that might predict who is more likely to experience a sexual dysfunction. The only significant demographic factors that were related to women being unable to achieve orgasm in the past year were education, marital status, and age. Women more likely to experience difficulties with orgasm were younger, currently unmarried, and of lower education levels. In assessing risk factors that might have an impact on sexual dysfunction, a Sexual Arousal Disorder category, derived using latent class analysis included high loadings on orgasmic complaints, low sexual desire, nonpleasurable sex, and trouble lubricating (categorical information from Laumann & Paik, personal communication, 1999). Predictors of this Arousal Disorder category included a decrease in household income, infrequent sex, infrequent thoughts about sex, a history of sexual harassment, being sexually touched before puberty, and being sexually forced by a man. An important distinction is that being sexually touched before puberty was significant for the Arousal Disorder category but not significant for Low Desire or Sexual Pain categories. Health and lifestyle issues, including ever having a sexually transmitted disease, ever having had urinary tract symptoms, being in less good health, and having emotional problems or stress, were also quite important predictors of Arousal Disorder. Most of these factors were also important for Pain and Desire Disorders. In earlier work on this data set by Laumann et al. (1994), they analyzed the impact of religion on female orgasm in sexual relationships and found that women without religious affiliation were the least likely to report always having an orgasm with their primary partner. Having a religious affiliation was associated with higher rates of orgasm for women. This is contrary to the typical clinical experience and may reflect differences in populations as to who comes in for therapy versus who does not.

Other studies have found several interesting correlates of sexual dysfunction. In the randomly selected community sample of 436 British women with partners noted earlier, predictors of orgasm included younger age, better general marital adjustment, and a shorter duration of relationship (Hawton et al., 1994). Current psychiatric status was also associated with the lack of orgasm. Women's satisfaction with their sexual relationship was closely related to marital adjustment and bore no relationship to age. Another study that assessed historical and current factors discriminating sexually functional from dysfunctional married couples compared 110 nonclinical and 94 clinical couples from a volunteer community sample (Heiman, Gladue, Roberts, & LoPiccolo, 1986). Compared to the dysfunctional women, sexually functional women reported greater frequency of orgasm during partner sex, less emotional involvement and a shorter duration relationship with their first intercourse partner, more arousal and more pleasure during and greater sexual interest following the first coitus, and more positive reactions to their partner's body.

Psychological factors that can have impact on orgasmic ease are difficult to confirm. Depression is often accompanied by hypoactive sexual desire and thus can contribute indirectly to orgasmic problems. Sexual abuse does not necessarily produce orgasm difficulties although such problems have been reported to be higher in abused than non-abused women (Tsai, Feldman-Summers, & Edgar, 1979; Norris & Feldman-Summers, 1981). Decreased sexual responsiveness (Walker et al., 1999) and decreased sexual arousal (Wenninger & Heiman, 1998) has also been reported in women with a sexual abuse history. One of the more extensive studies of personality and background variables and women's orgasm was Fisher's (1973). The most consistent finding was that anorgasmic women often had experienced their early love objects, especially fathers, as undependable and tended to experience later love objects similarly. These women had both an increased need to control situations involving high arousal and the potential for loss of control. Certainly, there is clinical evidence of early abandonment by an important male figure. However, there is no further confirming or disconfirming research on this point since Fisher.

If one looks to earlier work by sex therapists (Kaplan, 1974; Masters & Johnson, 1970), anxiety in various forms is often seen as the culprit of adequate sexual functioning, including orgasmic disorder. However, there are different types of anxiety and often distinctions are not made as to the different ways researchers and clinicians use this term. Women who get aroused but cannot experience orgasm except with a vibrator may have a different "anxiety" process than do women who never get aroused or who are never orgasmic.

In addition, to the extent that anxiety includes some sympathetic nervous system activity, the latter has been shown to enhance sexual arousal in laboratory settings. When women are shown frightening films (Palace & Gorzalka, 1990), asked to exercise just before a sexual stimulus (Meston & Gorzalka, 1995), or given a drug such as ephedrine, which increases sympathetic nervous system activity (Meston & Heiman, 1998), then vaginal response to sexually explicit films increases beyond what it did during control conditions. However, a later study by Meston and Gorzalka (1996) found that this effect only applied to women with no sexual dysfunction or with low sexual desire, not to women with anorgasmia. General arousal itself may have a negative impact on some women with orgasmic problems, especially those who report feeling uneasy with the experience of sexual arousal. Further exploration is needed regarding the role of physical or psychological general excitation and its impact on arousal and orgasm. For the present, we can say that sexual arousal requires enough "relaxation" to take in sexual stimulation and enough "tension" to respond with arousal and orgasm.

In addition to historical relationship factors regarding family-of-origin and prior relationship experience, the current quality of the marital interaction does contribute to orgasmic response, but other than the obvious points of providing adequate stimulation and being a sexually arousing partner, there really is little clarification on what relationship factors are important. The earlier cited Hawton et al. (1994) study found that the frequency of orgasm was positively related to marital adjustment. This by no means suggests that a satisfying marital relationship is required for women to be orgasmic. It is clear that women are able to respond under a wide range of conditions with partners who treat them well or treat them badly, in situations that make them uncomfortable or comfortable, and with either a great deal of foreplay or almost none at all. Thus, if one is studying married couples and examining group means, some of the previously discussed correlations between marital satisfaction and orgasm will apply. But if one is studying individual women, the possible different relationship arrangements that can accompany experiencing orgasm and sex are very broad.

In summary, there are no consistent empirical findings that support a constellation of factors separating orgasmic from nonorgasmic women. One reason for this is that the labels "orgasmic," "nonorgasmic," or "situationally orgasmic" are in themselves too global and unlikely to ever yield reliably discriminant factors. We might find more satisfying results if patterns of orgasmicity and nonorgasmicity were developed based on early history factors, personal (physiological and psychological) factors, and relationship factors.

TREATMENT APPROACHES: THEORY AND APPLICATIONS

The following section provides a brief overview of salient features of three major theoretical treatment approaches to inhibited female orgasm: Psychoanalytic, cognitive–behavioral, and systems theory. Readers should look elsewhere for more in-depth discussions of theoretical approaches. It should be noted that only cognitive–behavioral approaches have a substantial body of research support (see Heiman & Meston, 1997), though other approaches may assist in conceptualization and interpretation.

Psychoanalytic Approaches

Traditionally sexual dysfunction has been viewed as a symptom that expresses a pathological process in personality development; a developmental arrest is thought to result from castration fantasies, guilt over wishes for gratification with father, and unconscious fears (e.g., Bergler, 1944 and Fenichel, 1948, cited in Faulk, 1973). More recently, "maturity" from clitoral to vaginal orgasm is no longer seen as a goal; the focus has shifted from the debate about physiological origins of arousal to the experienced psychological differentiation between vaginal and clitoral orgasm. The implications are that the capability to experience orgasm and pleasure during sexual intercourse is intrinsically related to the woman's capacity to relate intimately to another person.

From the perspective of object-relations theory, an individual's capacity to relate to another is innate, begins at birth, and is partly determined by an ability to form an internal representation of the other. Later both negative and positive attributes of the caretaker are internalized, and these engender the capability for relatedness in later life. Tolerance of the ambivalence brought about by recognizing a loved one's faults contributes to a person's ability to maintain interest and intimacy with another. Newer formulations about female psychological development have emphasized the relationship with the mother as critical to adult heterosexual functioning (Jordan, 1985; Stiver, 1984; Surrey, 1983). Rather than being a pathological dependent syndrome as it often has been labeled, the reliance of a woman on relationships is considered a normal part of self-definition (Stiver, 1984).

The pitfalls of reliance on relationships for self-definition in terms of adult sexual functioning are that intimate relationships may be threatening because they recreate a feeling of merging with the mother similar to the preverbal, undifferentiated experience between the infant and mother. Sexually intimate relationships may re-create the demand of having to meet another's emotional needs, previously the mother's, currently the sexual partner's. Clear boundaries with an internal sense of separateness are necessary to enable one to tolerate intimacy; conflicts with closeness may result in hostility, anger, an inability to trust, and inhibited orgasm. A woman needs to feel secure enough in her self-identity to experience pleasure in the physical "taking in" of the other without fears of merging with a partner or loosing herself.

Several defenses, the ego's unconscious means of coping with anxiety, are pertinent to orgasm dysfunction (Kernberg, 1987; Scharff & Scharff, 1987). Denial may be expressed in the minimization of physical sensation. Repression, the removal from consciousness of an experienced feeling, allows an individual to continue life when events are too stressful to tolerate. Trauma, such as childhood physical or sexual abuse, can be a precursor of some forms of repression. Projective identification, unconsciously projecting one's feelings onto a significant other, is another way of dealing with unacceptable feelings or impulses. For example, a nonorgasmic woman who feels uncomfortable with her own desire to control others may see and interact with her husband in a way that identifies whatever he does as controlling. In psychoanalytic psychotherapy the emphasis is not on symptom removal but on working through conflicts that are believed to lead to the symptom. The symbolic content and functional utility of the symptom are explored (Cohen, 1978). Other common features include examining and reclaiming the memories of early childhood experience in relationships, interpreting and working through the resistance to change in therapy, and attending to the transference and countertransference aspects of the therapeutic relationship. Therapy focuses on the patient–therapist dyad using longer and more frequent sessions than with other approaches. Variations from traditional psychoanalytic treatment have combined individual and couple treatment with additional sex therapy (Kaplan, 1974; Levay, Weissberg & Blaustein, 1976; Segraves, 1986). However, sex therapy has caused concern because it requires an alternation of the therapist's neutrality to investment in the patient's recovery of sexual function (Rosen, 1982). Outcome data on psychoanalytic therapy are extremely sparse and restricted primarily to clinical reports. Dynamic therapy combined with symptom removal is thought (but not documented) to contribute to long-term recovery of sexual functioning (Obler, 1982; Frances & Kaplan, 1983).

Cognitive–Behavioral Approaches

Cognitive–behavioral therapists depend on theories of learning and cognitive processing to help explain the origins of orgasmic problems. Anxiety that has been associated with sexual experiences may interfere with relaxation, prevent arousal and inhibit orgasmic response (cf. Barlow, 1986). Similarly, the lack of association between sexual thoughts and behaviors and positive feelings can lead to the avoidance of behaviors that might be likely to result in arousal and orgasm. Anorgasmia in clinical samples has been correlated with poor self-image, feeling "different" from others, and feeling incapable of communicating sexual desires (Kuriansky & Sharpe, 1981; Cotten-Huston & Wheeler, 1983). The latter may be caused by a lack of assertiveness or limited communication skills (Kuriansky, Sharpe, & O'Connor, 1982).

The goals of cognitive–behavioral therapy are to promote cognitive change, attitude shifts, reduced anxiety, increased orgasmic frequency and increased connections between positive feelings and sexual behavior (Ellis, 1975; Fichten, Libman & Brender, 1986; LoPiccolo & LoPiccolo, 1978). Variables such as sex of the therapist, single therapist versus a co-therapist team, and spacing of sessions have been demonstrated not to influence sexual and marital outcome measures (Ersner-Hershfield & Kopel, 1979; Heiman & LoPiccolo, 1983; LoPiccolo, Heiman, Hogan, & Roberts, 1985). The hallmark of cognitive–behavioral therapy is the prescriptions of privately enacted behavioral exercises, the results of these "debriefed" and new exercises tailored to meet the client's needs. Treatment is generally brief, averaging 15 to 20 sessions, although with more complex cases it can take longer.

Directed masturbation (DM) is most frequently used with primary anorgasmic women (Andersen, 1983; Heiman & Meston, 1997). The procedures include a period of education and information followed by visual and kinesthetic self-exploration of the woman's body. DM has been successful in a variety of modalities, including minimal therapist contact of four sessions at monthly intervals and the viewing of a film and reading matter (Morokoff & LoPiccolo, 1986) and in group, individual, and couple therapy. Most studies report high success rates, with greater than 80% of women being able to experience masturbatory orgasm and a lower percentage, 20–60%, able to have orgasm with their partner. Most women report increased enjoyment and satisfaction of coital activities, a more relaxed attitude to sex and life, and increased acceptance of their bodies (Ersner-Hershfield & Kopel, 1979; Leiblum & Ersner-Hershfield, 1977; Nairne & Hemsley, 1983; Riley & Riley, 1978; Wallace & Barbach, 1974).

Group treatment helps normalize each woman's perception of her condition (Mills & Kilmann, 1982). Groups emphasize sharing, assertiveness, self-touch, and masturbation (Barbach, 1974; Kuriansky & Sharpe, 1981) as well as education, relaxation, reading, and prescribed sexual activity (Mills & Kilmann, 1982). The group format has been criticized for using DM because of its emphasis on autoerotic technique and response (Barbach, 1974; Wakefield, 1987) and because these experiences may not transfer into partner-related activities (Wakefield, 1987; Kuriansky & Sharpe, 1981). Wallace and Barbach (1974) reported that 87% of 22 women did transfer treatment gains to partner sex. Schneidman and McGuire (1976) found 80% of women under 35 years to be orgasmic with partners at 6-month follow-up compared to 60% of the older women. Other studies have found lower success rates for orgasms with partners, ranging from 30% (Spence, 1985) to 66% (Weiss & Meadow, 1983). Coital orgasm does not always improve significantly from pre- to posttreatment (Libman et al., 1984; Fichten et al., 1986; Kilmann, Mills, et al., 1986). Couples need to be educated that additional stimulation is normal for many women to experience orgasm during coitus (Hoch, Safir, Peres, & Sopher, 1981; Kaplan, 1974; LoPiccolo & Stock, 1986).

Another controversy has been the effectiveness of Kegel exercises (contraction of the PC muscle) in producing orgasm. Roughan and Kunst (1981) found no difference in orgasmic frequency among groups whose members used Kegel exercises, relaxation training, or attention control, although the PC group had increased muscle tone. These findings have since been supported by Trudel and Saint-Laurent (1983) and Chambless et al. (1984). Tensing the vaginal musculature has been found to be less arousing than using fantasy on both physiological and subjective measures of arousal; however, tensing plus fantasy was most arousing (Messen & Geer, 1985). Kegel exercises thus may have arousal enhancement value, but it is also possible that they facilitate orgasm by increasing women's awareness and comfort with their genitals.

Whether anorgasmia is primary or secondary is important to treatment planning. Directed masturbation is most effective in treating primary anorgasmia, and the success rate is at least 80 to 90% (Riley & Riley, 1978; LoPiccolo & Stock, 1986). The success rate of secondary anorgasmia treatment ranges from 10 to 75% (Fichten et al., 1986; Kilmann, Boland, Sjortus, Davidson, & Caid, 1986; Kilmann, Mills, et al., 1986; Kuriansky et al., 1982; Mills & Kilmann, 1982). Younger, emotionally healthier, and more happily married women have a higher probability of success (Schneidman & McGuire, 1976; Libman et al., 1984; LoPiccolo & Stock, 1986). In some studies an increase in sexual and relationship satisfaction occurred without a significant improvement in the presenting sexual symptom (Everaerd & Dekker, 1982; DeAmicis, Goldberg, LoPiccolo, Friedman, & Davies, 1986; Heiman & LoPiccolo, 1983, LoPiccolo et al., 1985).

Systems Theory Approaches

General systems theory claims to offer a paradigm to account for multifactoral phenomena. In medicine, it has been applied primarily to those illnesses, psychosomatic conditions, for example, for which the traditional linear–causal model of disease is inadequate (Brody, 1973; Engel, 1980). In psychotherapy, a systems approach has been primarily developed within family and marital therapy.

Systems theory has been applied to general dysfunctions or inhibited sexual desire rather than orgasmic problems per se (Heiman, 1986; Verhulst & Heiman, 1979, 1988; Schnarch, 1991; Weeks, 1987). Systems theorists themselves tend to view symptoms such as anorgasmia rather suspiciously, even as a smokescreen produced by a distressed dyad in order to divert all parties from more essential marital problems (Whitaker & Keith, 1981). Sexuality is a sensitive subject for family therapists, many of whom broke away from psychoanalytic positions where sexuality was conceptualized as part of the core structure of individual development (cf. Weeks & Hof, 1987).

Masters and Johnson have been described as taking a systems perspective. However, in spite of seeing the couple as "the patient" and using the couple to treat the sexual problems, the conceptualization of sexual disorders was focused on individualistic etiological factors. Their program's effectiveness was based on a treatment that worked well for most symptomatic, nonphysically based sexual problems. One could call it a "universal prescription" (cf. Selvini-Palazzoli & Viaro, 1988).

Whereas family therapists have eschewed sexual dysfunctions, sex therapists have typically ignored family issues. Reasons for this go beyond the scope of this chapter, although one issue to keep in mind is the relative youth of each specialty. Family therapy was initially too infused with psychoanalytic rebels to consider sex as only a symptom. Sex therapists, in their own reaction against the past and affirmation of the cultural and reproductive freedom of the 1960s, aligned with "sex for pleasure" rather than "sex for reproduction." At times, this position became almost imperious and may have contributed to their continued isolation from family therapists who often treated the consequences of reproductive sex by adults or acting-out teenagers.

Work stressing the integration of sex and marital therapy has been compiled (Weeks & Hof, 1987). Interestingly, one book on this topic makes no mention of orgasm, erection, or ejaculation in the index, nor could any references to these be located in case examples. Verhulst and Heiman (1979, 1988) have outlined a systemic approach to sexual dysfunction, with particular attention to sexual desire problems. Schnarch (1991) has also proposed an integration of sex and marital therapy, using systemic thinking and generally eschewing a "symptom" approach.

There are several systems concepts that are important in considering its application to sexuality. Living systems are composed of mutually interacting components. They have boundaries, yet they are open and constantly interchanging information with their environment (von Bertalanffy, 1968; Miller, 1978). Each person is a system and is a part of subsystems within a family; the family is embedded in a sociocultural context, yet another system.

The systems principle of *emergent qualities* states simply that a system, such as the couple, is more than the sum of its parts. Relationships therefore have properties of their own, beyond the properties that people bring to it. It is helpful to impart this information to couples early in order to get beyond the stance of "one against the other," to decrease the sense that there is one patient and one nonpatient, and to build a general nonjudgmental working alliance. For example, we might suggest to a woman, "Isn't it interesting that you are a competent, assertive person in your relationship with your coworkers, even your boss, but you feel inadequate and dependent around your husband." And to her husband we might suggest, "Others seem to experience you as easygoing and generous, and yet you feel resentful about sharing time with your wife." With periodic examples, couples begin to see that the relationship currently has as much power over them than they have over the relationship.

Other important theoretical elements to consider include *homeostasis*, the system's self-regulating process that maintains stability; *morphogenesis*, the capacity to change and adapt; and *circularity* or circular causality, meaning that a change in one element influences the other elements.

These general principles can be incorporated into a systems perspective of sexual dysfunction. Following is a brief summary of a theoretical model presented in greater detail elsewhere (Verhulst & Heiman, 1988). Different levels of interactions are exchanged between the two people during sex. One level, *symbolic interactions*, refers to the exchange of words, ideas, symbolic gestures, and other representational cognitive features. This symbolic level needs to be considered detached from the affective tone of speech. A simple example is that two people must come from a similar enough cultural background for each to have a similar interpretation of such symbols as presenting flowers, making eye contact, and even use of the word "marriage." These are not issues of agreement but issues of shared understanding of meaning.

A second level, *affect-regulated* interactions, describes the interacting expressions and perceptions of affect, exclusive of the symbolic level just discussed. Affect-regulated interactions are coordinated by the affective states of the participants and are expressed through autonomic responses, movements, postures, facial expressions, gestures, and the affective component of speech. Affect-regulated interactions predominate in sexual interactions because of sexuality's emphasis on desire, arousal, and nonverbal communication. In an earlier paper, Verhulst and Heiman (1979) described four different types of "affect-regulated interactions" that can steer a couple toward or away from a sexual context of meaning: attachment, exploratory, territorial, and ranking-order interactions. Attachment interactions focus on establishing, preserving, and intensifying the affiliative bond between individuals. Exploratory interactions focus on familiarity through sensory contact. Territorial interactions focus on the acquisition, management, and defense of ownership over material and psychological possessions. Ranking-order interactions focus on the acquisition and defense of social position and status, with dominance and submission issues often the visible evidence. Affect regulation patterns can both enhance and detract from sexual interactions.

A third level of interactions are *sensate exchanges*, referring to the sensory pattern, neurophysiological responses, and motor reflexes that each partner elicits from the other. Masters and Johnson's (1970) work was particularly aimed at coordinating the sensate stimulation while decreasing physiological anxiety and the influences of affective and symbolic interactions.

These three levels—symbolic, affective, and sensate—can function somewhat independently but are constantly interacting with each other within each individual. In addition, they comprise subsystems. Each level requires some type of interactional fit between individuals or there will not be a connection on that level.

There is not enough written about the systems approach to treatment of sexual problems to estimate therapy length and success. In general, therapists from this perspective aim toward brief rather than long-term treatment and emphasize the integration of treatment interventions and treatment vacations of several months (e.g., Heiman, 1986; Sanders, 1988).

Other Treatments

Other treatments of orgasm dysfunction have had variable successes. Pharmacotherapy with bupropion hydrochloride has not proven effective in increasing specific sexual responses (Crenshaw, Goldberg, & Stern, 1987). Adding testosterone with sex therapy does not appear helpful (Carney, Bancroft, & Mathews, 1978 versus Mathews, Whitehead, & Kellett, 1983). The only published study (uncontrolled) on sildenafil showed no effect on orgasm or sexual satisfaction for postmenopausal women (Kaplan et al., 1999). Sex education and bibliotherapy have shown positive results. For example, Kilmann et al. (1983) found significant increases in orgasmic frequency and decreases of sexual anxiety in secondary anorgasmia after 4 hours of sex education in 1 week. Jankovich and Miller (1978) reported that 7 of 17 primary anorgasmic females had orgasm in the week following an audiovisual presentation designed to educate health care providers. The content included anatomy and physiology of sexual response and a film on intercourse. Minimal therapist contact appears to be effective in conjunction with self-help manuals (e.g., Barbach, 1975; Heiman & LoPiccolo, 1988) that outline exercises for women to try on their own (Tripet Dodge, Glasgow, & O'Neill, 1982; Morokoff & LoPiccolo, 1986). For a motivated primary anorgasmic woman, reading may be an adequate intervention. Finally, hypnotherapy used adjunctively to sex therapy has been reported to be useful for individuals and couples. Hypnosis can be a vehicle for allowing people to experience themselves differently (Araoz, 1982; Beigel, 1972; Stewart, 1986).

INTEGRATED THEORY AND PRACTICE

When faced with the complaint of lack of orgasm, how does a therapist combine the theoretical and empirical information already discussed? Although no formula exists, there are important elements that require attention during assessment and treatment.

Assessment: Elements and Issues

It is revealing to track closely what happens in the first 15 to 30 minutes of the first visit. Both *content* and *context* are important. In what words does each individual present the initial description of the problem? "I don't like sex," "I find sex humiliating," "My wife doesn't enjoy sex," "He thinks I should have an orgasm," provide useful initial clues as to how the lack of orgasm is experienced by both partners. Their views on the problem's origin, maintenance, and connection to the rest of their lives are important.

The affect surrounding the expression of the problem is also important. Common affects are sadness, self-denigration, anger or irritability, anxiety, and depression. An apparent lack of affect or detachment is common in primary anorgasmic women, who often seem somewhat removed from their search for this unknown entity. The therapist also develops an initial sense of the relationship's emotional climate: tension, frustration, and territorial and ranking-order interactions are common. Nonverbal expressions such as posture, mannerisms, eye contact, verbal–nonverbal contradictions, and the general energy level of the couple can help reveal unspoken conflicts and fears.

The therapist first needs a carefully detailed problem description documenting the level and frequency of desire, arousal, orgasm, genital pain, degree of sexual satisfaction (for further details, see Schover, Friedman, Weiler, Heiman, & LoPiccolo, 1982, and American Psychiatric Association, 1994), and distress about the problem. A woman reporting arousal without orgasm will usually need a different therapeutic intervention than does a woman who is never aroused. As a natural lead-in to more historical material, the therapist should ask whether the sexual symptoms are *global* or *situational* and whether they have been *lifelong* or are intermittent (*acquired*).

Masters and Johnson's (1970) thorough sex histories lasted some 5 hours, a length that is impractical in today's brief therapy climate. Cognitive–behavioral and systems (e.g., strategic family therapy) therapy may focus minimally on historical factors, believing that a current focus is essential if the past is not going to continue invading the present. Masters and Johnson's extensive, evocative history-taking session, culminating in a roundtable discussion with therapists and patients present effectively drew a line between the past (acknowledging the contribution of historical factors) and the present (doing sex-therapy exercises). An alternative form of history taking is the sexual genogram (Bergman & Hof, 1987) in which couples are taught the basics of making a genogram and then sent home to construct one over three generations, with an emphasis on sexual, gender, and intimacy issues across the different generations.

A detailed history taking, although not absolutely essential, has many valuable features, especially with anorgasmic women. It is usually informative to do her history in the presence of her partner—the reactions of both individuals to the material and process cannot be captured in individual interviews. We use assessment sessions to obtain content, develop the therapeutic relationship, and to develop an understanding of the symbolic, affective, and sensory aspects of the problem. The content of the sex history varies (see Masters & Johnson, 1970; LoPiccolo & Heiman, 1978). Areas of special importance include formalized overt and covert treatment of sexuality and affection in the family of origin with special attention to the behavior of the parents toward each other and the children, early sexual experiences, adolescent development, sexual and physical abuse, losses particularly of early male and female figures, affects associated with sexual ideas and experiences, and degree of enjoyment of sensual experiences. Information is obtained concerning the parent's attitude toward sex and the perception of the parental relationship. A straightforward and nonthreatening approach is, "What did you learn about how men and women relate to each other from your parents' relationship?"

The therapist must assess whether the orgasm problem is secondary to a physical or biochemical disorder. Psychotropic medications have been reported to impair orgasmic function (Pohl, 1983; Segraves, 1985). All classes of antidepressants can impair sexual functioning (Aldridge, 1982; Gitlin, 1997; Segraves, 1985). The impact of SSRIs on delayed orgasm and desire range from a few percentage points to 80% with more effects found for women (Rosen, Lane, & Menza, 1999). Cyproheptadine, a serotonergic receptor antagonist, has been used to reverse the inhibiting effects of SSRI antidepressants (Riley & Riley, 1986). Clomipramine, used to treat severe obsessive–compulsive disorders, is also an α-adrenergic blocking agent, preventing the sympathetic nervous system activation required for orgasm (Monteiro, Noshirvani, Marks, & Lelliot, 1987). Quirk and Einarson (1982) effectively switched two clomipramine patients to desipramine and lowered the dose of the third, restoring orgasmic function. Current prescribed and over-the-counter medications, as well as recreational drug and alcohol use, should be checked to see whether their onset coincides with the sexual problem.

Other medical conditions may affect orgasmic response. Back problems or nerve damage should be considered in cases in which the woman has noticed an injury-related change, can tolerate long periods of intensive vibratory stimulation, or has a lack of sensation of any kind in her genital area. Sexual dysfunction has been reported in the early stages of multiple sclerosis, often in conjunction with bladder and bowel problems (Lundberg, 1980), as well as in diabetic women who have peripheral neuropathy (Jensen, 1985). Abdominal surgeries that cut vascular tissue and lymph nodes may interfere with autonomic nervous system functioning and inhibit orgasm (Wise, 1983). Hysterectomy with or without oophorectomy has been reported to inhibit the experience of orgasm in 33 to 46% of women who undergo the procedure (Zussman, Zussman, Sunley, & Bjornson, 1981), but data vary considerably across studies and most are poorly controlled. There is evidence that the retention of the cervix in hysterectomy protects against dyspareunia or loss of orgasmic ease of response (Kilkku, Grönroos, Hirvonen, & Raurumo, 1983). The more common variable studied is sexual desire and frequency, which has been found to decrease postpartum, especially if the mother is nursing (Apt & Hurlbert, 1992; Alder & Bancroft, 1988).

An evaluation of current depression is important. Undiagnosed or subclinical levels of depression may be behind the presenting symptom of infrequent orgasm in a woman, especially if she reports low sexual desire as well.

Seasonal depression may also require diagnosis, although sexual symptoms have rarely been reported with this disorder (Avery, 1997; Rosenthal & Wehr, 1987).

An important task of the clinician is to understand with the clients why the symptom makes sense and what functions it may serve. This step may be critical in determining the therapeutic interventions and managing therapeutic impasses. A natural place to begin is to ask the anorgasmic woman what having orgasms means to her, "What would it mean if you had no more orgasm difficulties?" Reactions to this question vary: "I would feel powerful," "I would be vulnerable," "I would be close to my partner," "Extremely sexual." Usually these meanings are conflicted—desired and feared, sought and avoided—by both the woman and her partner. A couple who believes that the woman's orgasms will make them feel closer may be singing silent praise to the symptom bearer who does them both the service of regulating closeness. A lesbian client responded to the question about her reaction to having the orgasm problem resolved with the comment, "Well, then Paula would be *the* relationship in my life." This was a telling remark from a 39-year-old single woman involved with a female lover 2,000 miles away and for whom being in a committed relationship signaled the beginning of the end of her life. From this woman's perspective, being orgasmic was connected to loss, dependency, or even death.

An assignment we frequently give after the first session, particularly when the problem seems entrenched, is to think about what the problem does for the couple. It is a good sign if the couple can come up with a response. The symptom then stops being the enemy and, instead, opens ideas toward solutions.

The therapist's role is to listen to what the person says, cannot remember, omits, glosses over, or emphasizes in order to help frame or reframe the picture into one that helps explain why the sexual problem exists and may have served a valuable function. To a woman whose view of orgasm is loss of control and whose family background is explosively physically violent and alcoholic, we might begin the therapy by agreeing that it makes sense not to ever have orgasms, especially around others. This hypothesis would be proposed to the couple. A therapeutic issue then becomes whether orgasm can mean something besides loss of control.

The power of past patterns is sometimes more striking when each partner hears the other discuss earlier events. Interactional patterns and themes begin to surface, and therapists can begin to weave an initial systems understanding of the problem with the couple. Our clinic has seen a number of couples in whom the partners experienced childhood and adult sexual abuse. A therapeutic dilemma in certain cases of abuse is whether to see each person individually, which might make it possible to obtain more information but could leave the therapist vulnerable to inclusion in the systemic proclivity to keep sexual secrets or repress them. One solution is to meet partners separately but to tell each person that the purpose of the sessions is to find another way besides secrets and forgetting to protect each of them. Standardized assessment can also be useful. We include formalized assessment routinely: The Spanier Dyadic Adjustment Scale (Spanier, 1976), which examines relationship factors including consensus, satisfaction, cohesion, and affectional expression; a medical history form; the Brief Symptom Inventory (BSI; Derogatis, 1977), which assesses psychiatric symptoms; the Life Experiences Survey—Abridged & Revised (adapted from Sarason, Johnson, & Siegel, 1978); and a sexual history form (Heiman & LoPiccolo, 1983; LoPiccolo et al., 1985), which asks about specific sexual behaviors.

Treatment: Elements and Issues

Initially a decision of format is required: Would this woman or couple benefit most from an individual, couple, or group setting? The outcome data are not very helpful in making this decision. If the woman has an ongoing partner and no current affairs, it is likely she will benefit from couple therapy, especially if her desire is to have orgasms with that partner. Women in tentative relationships, hopeless marriages, or a history of abusive relationships may benefit from individual treatment, at least initially. Women-only groups are valuable if the woman is anorgasmic and without a partner.

Symbolic Issues

The initial symbolic issue to explore is the meaning of the orgasm for the woman and her partner. The might say, "Our sexual relationship would be more complete if my orgasm were part of it," whereas her partner's response might be, "If she has orgasms, our marriage would be perfect." The woman in this situation may find it difficult to begin to change if it means that (1) she is the only obstacle between their current situation and a "perfect" relationship, and (2) he will not acknowledge the problems that she experiences in the relationship after she becomes orgasmic. To understand the couple's images of orgasm, one often asks about images of relationships, sexual behaviors, and having children. This material helps formulate, on a symbolic level, where avenues for and barriers to change might be on a symbolic level.

Affect

Many anorgasmic women do not feel that their body, or its sexual responses, belongs to them. Or, if they do have a sense of ownership, their body image may be so negative that they cannot feel good about being sexual. This issue can take many forms. Women may report that they find their bodies ugly and their genitals disgusting. They may try to make their bodies "look better." However, because appearance standards are derived from social norms, conforming to these norms implies that society is at least co-owner of women's bodies. Alternatively a woman may report feeling nothing when her body, especially her genitals, is touched. These examples of disconnectedness are also examples of historical and current *territorial* themes. The woman may feel that any partner who touches her touches something she does not like, cannot feel, and/or does not own. This gives the partner ownership with a sense of burden and responsibility when sex does not go well. How crucial is a sense of bodily ownership to orgasmic responsivity? No one knows. It depends on what is missing from the woman's sense of self when she is involved in a relationship. Some sense of ownership over her own body does seem to be important for the woman whose orgasm evades her. It seems especially useful for women with histories of abuse because they have had experiences of having their bodies invaded territorially. The masturbation program (LoPiccolo & Lobitz, 1972; Heiman, LoPiccolo, & LoPiccolo, 1976; Heiman & LoPiccolo, 1988) can be used as a means for women to claim their bodies and sexual sensations.

Ranking-order interactions commonly present in the form of "I want to have orgasm for my partner," or "I do everything I can to try to please her so that she will get aroused." One person is in charge of trying to get the interaction to move in a particular direction. Although this pattern is not necessarily a problem, if orgasm is elusive one person's steering the other to obtain orgasm rarely works. A man we were seeing reported that he was constantly trying different forms of stimulation in order to get his wife closer to orgasm. As a result, he was irritated, she was distracted, and each felt inept. Using sensate focus as a medium, the therapist had the couple focus on the touching he enjoyed giving (rather than touching they thought would get her aroused) and on her initiating tender caressing if she felt pressured. Ranking-order interactions were thus corrected with an *exploratory–attachment* interaction that helped to resexualize the couple's experience.

Sensate Exchanges

Women and their partners often have difficulty facilitating arousal and communicating about the stimulation they want during sexual activity. Many women do not know what is arousing or are committed to a restricted arousal pattern. Often partners feel out of tune with each other. For example, the male may ejaculate too quickly. Greater sensate exchange for the woman thus can overstimulate the male, increasing the nonorgasmic woman's sense of being left behind. The interaction will need to be slowed down, perhaps by excluding ejaculation for a while or introducing attachment interaction patterns such as nongenital tender stroking.

There are other sensate patterns, however. Some time ago, we saw a woman who was having an affair for the prior 2 years with a man she had decided not to "commit to" because of a clash in values. Ann was a 34-year-old divorced nurse with one daughter. She has been raised in an authoritarian Calvinist family. Although orgasmic in masturbation, she never had experienced an orgasm with a partner. Her masturbation pattern began as a young girl, when she would urinate as part of her masturbation ritual. She no longer urinated during masturbation, although she did occasionally urinate with her boyfriend during high arousal. For her, urination was connected with "total relaxation." Her sensate exchange pattern was in tune with her boyfriend, even to the point of "letting go." However, orgasm was not the result. She enjoyed sex with her boyfriend more than masturbating. Her experience of the difference between masturbation and partner sex (illustrating an interaction between symbolic and affective levels) was that masturbation connected to what she called her erotic, pornographic, genital center. It was not connected to what she called her "heart center."

The major effort of four sessions of therapy was (1) to appreciate her current pattern, as it allowed her both to enjoy mutual sex and to sequester orgasm, her most private sexual experience, from a relationship of limited commitment potential; and (2) to suggest *Becoming Orgasmic* (Heiman & LoPiccolo, 1988) as preparation for eventual merging of orgasm and partner sex. Ann left therapy feeling good about herself although not orgasmic with her partner. Ann is an example of someone whose sensate exchange pattern reflected conflicts in the symbolic–affective interaction level with respect to sex and her relationship with her boyfriend.

CASE EXAMPLES

My contact with patients occurs exclusively within a university-based medical school clinic, the Reproductive and Sexual Medicine Clinic, which I direct along with a colleague from urology, Dr. Richard Berger. Because of this setting and visibility, we increasingly are asked to see more etiologically complex or previously treated individuals and couples. Thus the following case examples are instructive for these features, but if the reader is looking for the more straightforward approaches to orgasmic disorders, they can be found particularly in the cognitive–behavioral literature as highlighted in the earlier sections. The following cases reflect our current practice—a mixture of brief 1-hour consultations and ongoing treatment. A one-hour consultation interview requires selectivity of focus while attending to a wide array of possible contributing etiological factors. Typically the outcome is to refer for further evaluation or to return recommendations to the referring therapist.

Consultation Cases

Anita: Somatic Focus and Neurophysiological Questions.

Anita, a 39-year-old woman of Finnish background, was referred to me by her primary therapist who was treating her for panic disorder. She complained of lifelong lack of orgasm. She was married 9 years to her second husband. Her first husband had died of cancer 2 years after they married. She had no children.

Anita's *medical and psychiatric history* was significant for several features. She had an atrial septum defect (ASD) causing her to have a stroke and surgery to repair the ASD 2 years prior to the consult. She fully recovered from the stroke. She had been diagnosed with panic disorder, stating that she first noticed occasional symptoms when she was 25 but they had worsened in the last 2 years. She currently experienced heart palpitations, shortness of breath, nausea, and numbness in her extremities. She described her panic symptoms as severe and stressful. She acknowledged no other psychiatric symptom history except for a brief period when her first husband was ill. She reported other symptoms: decreased organization and concentration; sudden fatigue, in spite of adequate sleep, including recently falling asleep while driving; and a job demotion in the prior month after years of receiving excellent performance reviews. She further reported that a gynecologist had diagnosed her with an "immature cervix" and suggested that there was evidence that she was a diethylstilbestrol (DES) baby as her mother had several miscarriages and the patient was born premature. Also, as a child she had fallen "very hard" directly on her groin while riding a boy's bike, resulting in visible bruising. Her current medications included Paxil (paroxetine), Prozac (fluoxetine), Klonopin (clonazepam), and Lotensin (benazepril hydrochloride), all having potential sexual side effects. She reported no recreational drug use, no nicotine, and less than one alcoholic drink per week.

With respect to *sexuality and her current relationship*, Anita noted a decrease in sexual desire within the last 6 months only, adequate sexual arousal and lubrication, and no pain associated with sexual activity. Only her anorgasmia was lifelong and global. She reported no history of sexual or physical abuse or coercion around sexual activity. She stated that she was "very happy" in her current relationship but that the sex issue, including her lack of orgasm and especially her more recent decrease in desire, was causing some problems. During sex, when her husband would try to touch her genitals, especially around her urethral area, she was extremely sensitive and had to ask him to stop. However, this information was probably imprecise, given that at the close of the interview, Anita acknowledged that she was not sure of the location of her clitoris and requested an illustration of female genitalia.

Impression and Recommendations. There were a variety of possible explanations for Anita's lack of orgasm. Contributing factors included (1) neurophysiological including the childhood groin injury, correlates of her cardiovascular health, and possible very long-standing anxiety spectrum disorder; (2) her current medications—the SSRIs were likely to decrease orgasm latency even further and her more recent desire decrease could be influenced by the addition in the last 6 months of Prozac and Lotensin to Paxil; (3) congenital factors as suggested by the diagnosis of immature cervix and possible DES history; and (4) sexual inhibition with respect to discomfort with high arousal and release of tension (her panic disorder symptoms perhaps increasing her discomfort with these experiences).

It was fairly clear from her focus in the interview that she was vigilant about her body's conditions and symptoms. Whether this focus was excessive, meaning it comaintained her anorgasmia, would require further exploration. With her history, she had reason to be vigilant and for thinking something is wrong with her body. Thus it may come as no surprise that when offered the option of further assessment and treatment, she selected the workup for possible pelvic nerve damage over pursuing a behavioral attempt to try increased levels of intense stimulation with a vibrator. The concluding recommendations to her that she accepted were (1) a referral to urology, where a more careful look at pelvic nerve conduction and genital anatomy could be carried out, even though this might produce a diagnosis that contained considerable uncertainty about its functional effects; (2) a photocopied diagram of female genitalia for her to use to identify the exact location of her clitoris and urethral meatus; and (3) the option to return for behavioral treatment, which might include vibrator use, and exploring tolerance for high levels of sexual arousal. The option of changing her medications was discussed briefly but the patient was adamant that she would do nothing to put her in further "danger" of panic attacks and she only recently had stabilized on her current regimen. Also, this did not seem like a first-line approach as her anorgasmia was lifelong and her medication use only spanned the past year.

Carin: Delayed, Weak Orgasm

Carin was referred from her family physician. She was concerned about her sexual arousal and desire and only secondarily her orgasmic response, but for her all were closely related. Carin was 41, divorced for 10 years, with two daughters at home. She worked in a job she liked. She was in a 2-month relationship with someone she found interesting and attractive, who often wanted sex one to two times a day. She was not responding sexually and felt it was her issue rather than the relationship. For the past 2 years, her sexual arousal and desire had decreased. She also experienced "very faint" orgasms that took a long time, about 30 minutes, to occur. This was a different pattern than she had experienced in earlier years. She was currently pretending to respond but felt she did not want to continue pretending as a long-term pattern.

Several issues in Carin's *medical and psychiatric history* required attention. Her family physician had diagnosed her as perimenopausal and she had migraine headaches and a history of depression symptoms. Carin had never received treatment for depression. Her current medications included Inderal (propranolol), Imitrex (sumatryptan), and Zonig (zolmitriptan) for migraine headache and birth control pills for her perimenopausal symptoms. The Inderol was the most likely to affect sexual arousal because it was taken daily, but all the medications were prescribed long after her first sexual symptoms appeared. Carin stated that she drank less than one alcoholic drink a week.

In terms of *relationship and sexual history*, she noted that her ex-husband had "wanted sons" and had moved to Israel (both were Jewish) and not kept up contact with their daughters. During the marriage he was physically aggressive with her and "emotionally abusive," and he sexually forced himself on her after she served him with divorce papers. For much of the marriage her sexual response was adequate. She described her current partner as "very creative," running two businesses and inventing tools. She stated that he was an attentive and responsive lover, very affectionate, and she felt a close connection with him. This made her lack of sexual response even more frustrating. In addition to decreased desire and arousal and weak and delayed orgasm, she reported that her genitals felt "smaller" and less sensitive. She did not report any pain involved during or after sexual activity.

Impression and Recommendations. With a possible contribution of depressive symptoms at the beginning of this decline in sexual functioning, the most likely first hypothesis is that Carin's symptoms were due to early menopause, which may have interacted with her worsening migraine symptoms. She was having frequent vascular disregulation, including hot flashes, and migraines. Given that she also had some concerns about her genital sensitivity and shrinking, I suggested she see a gynecologist whom I knew was willing to take time to do careful genital exams and examine hormone profiles from sexual as well as general women's health perspectives.

Ongoing Treatment Case

Diane and David: A Good but Elusive Interactional Fit

This couple was referred to me by a marital therapist who had seen them for adjustment and conflict issues following David's serious illness. Both were 46, married 16 years, with two children 11 and 13. He owned his own business and she was a homemaker. Two years prior, he had a 6-month viral infection that was life threatening. This caused a number of work and family problems as he was used to being independent and the primary wage earner. His illness had taught him that "time is crucial," and he began making changes that Diane had asked for over the years. Sex had been a problem almost from the beginning of their relationship and his main complaint was that it was not frequent enough (about once a month) and was not pleasure focused. She reported both low desire and infrequent orgasm, some arousal difficulty, but no pain during sex.

At the time we began meeting, only low desire seemed to be the problem as she almost never wanted sex. But by the end of the first session it was clear that there were more symptoms and more interactional issues. His goal was to get sex to be "normal" and to signify their uniqueness as a couple. Her goal was to feel "special" to him and to have more affection expressed outside the bedroom. She had a long history of not speaking up about what bothered her sexually. For example, she refrained from telling him, for many years, that he ejaculated too quickly for her to get satisfaction, and she felt she used sex in order to get him to treat her better. In addition, she had a great deal of trouble refusing sex, so she often engaged in it when she did not want it. His premature ejaculation had improved and was no longer viewed as a problem.

In terms of *medical and psychiatric history* factors, David was currently healthy and able to work full time. His viral illness was not expected to recur and he suffered no long-term sequelae. With the exception of this illness, neither David nor Diane had a history of medical problems, nor was either currently taking any medications. Diane had recently had knee surgery and wore a knee brace for stability which somewhat limited her movements. She was having irregular periods for the last 12 months but no other symptoms that indicated menopause. She and David drank little alcohol, reporting less than one drink (2 oz.) per week.

There were several important features of their *relationship and sexual histories*. In his family of origin, David was usually ignored by his parents, who were extremely hard-working owners of a small food market and did not take much time for their four children. David learned to work hard, fend for, and quietly take care of himself. During his viral illness 2 years earlier, his parents did not visit him in the hospital, though they lived 35 miles away.

Diane was the only girl among four children. She grew up on a ranch in a small community in Montana. She summarized her early family relationship in two phrases: "never getting acknowledged" and "girls work, boys play." These schema remained part of her filter on her current relationship. She reported that her mother was the disciplinarian and was judgmental and hard to please, though Diane continued to try into adulthood. She was more in tune with her father's interests than with her mother's. David said little about his prior sexual relationships except that Diane was the first person he knew he wanted to marry, commenting, "I have always know we were the two." He reported having 10 lifetime sexual partners. Diane said that she had previously been involved with men (10 to 20 lifetime sexual partners) who were very possessive and jealous. This appealed to her because she felt very special and her attention needs were soothed. However, from the beginning of the relationship with David, he was not possessive but instead supportive of her developing her own interests.

The course of treatment consisted of (1) a focus on symbolic and affective (attachment and territorial) interaction patterns and (2) pursuing replacements for past interactional hurts, disappointments, and protective beliefs. When the couple returned for their second session, with no assignment given except that they do what ever they usually do in terms of affection and sex and we would discuss it, they reported two sexual encounters. He reported enjoying them but experienced some performance worries, which in his case were defined as "wondering whether what I was doing was what she wanted." He had reason to be uncertain about this because she had not spoken up for years about her unhappiness with his quick ejaculation and was still not able to say anything about what she wanted. Indeed, though she also felt both experiences were good, she felt "a little pressured about enjoying myself" and was aware of the pressure he felt to perform. She did experience orgasm on one of the occasions. Each was also aware that she preferred sexual intercourse rather than other sexual activities, though she did say she wished for more kissing and hugging outside of sex. After David's illness, he had made an effort to be more physically affectionate (and help with the children more), but he felt she did not really notice and, especially important to him, it made no difference in her sexual interest and involvement.

The suggestions at the end of that session were to develop a "hurt museum" (explained below), initiate sex only if you feel like it, say no to an initiation if you are sure you do not want to, during sex try to get something out of it for yourself, and allow yourself to give feedback that would increase or maintain your own enjoyment. These topics were raised so that each would take responsibility and ownership over their own desire, arousal, and orgasm. Diane's inability to say no to sex combined with her lack of communication about what pleased and displeased her meant increased resentment toward David and disconnection from her own desire and response.

At the next session, Diane reported having negative affect consisting of feeling anxious, upset, irritable, and not finding pleasure in her usual activities. They had had some physical affection and two sexual encounters but she was not really in the mood and had no desire for them and, in spite of the discussion of the prior session, acquiesced anyway. I decided to meet with her individually and gave her the Beck Depression Inventory (BDI) to complete. She scored 24 (moderately depressive range) on the BDI but said she had now felt much better than the day she completed it. In obtaining a family history, it was clear that Diane had never felt accepted, and currently felt like she was "not worth anything to David," because he almost never said to her "Have I told you how much I like you," or "How good you look!" I suggested that they both wanted the same thing: attention and acceptance. I also suggested that she had chosen David rather than the possessive men she had known and that perhaps she did not accept attention well because she was suspicious and even fearful of it because it did not match her world view. She was surprised by this remark but considered it.

The *symbolic interaction* issues with this couple were primarily that they were similarly intelligent, used words sparingly, and were more comfortable with action than language (thus more reactive than reflective). They had a 10-acre small farm and enjoyed horses, skiing, and fishing together. Conversations were less satisfying and they were not particularly careful about how they chose words. Diane would often be a bit extreme, once saying, for example, that she felt forced "like a rape" to have oral sex when in fact she had never simply said she did not want to have oral sex but went along because "he wanted it." This type of word choice would either start David asking questions in a Socratic method or get him to withdraw from the conversation. His use of language was usually tentative and rather vague, and his style of saying "you" when he meant himself was actually confusing and resulted in an in-session request to use "I," which he did after some practice. He was more likely to give Diane gifts as a sign of caring while she preferred verbal appreciation, so there were resentments and disagreements over this symbolic difference.

The *affective patterns* we focused on were attachment, because both wanted to preserve and increase their affiliative bond, and territorial interactions. Diane did not have a clear sense of what the territory of her own desire, arousal, and orgasm was, as she was always going along with David. Repeated assignments around the topic of "Yes means I want it and I need to say no when I do not" were helpful but cost Diane significant effort and required repeated encouragement and discussion.

Probably the most challenging theme in the therapy was Diane's fearful grip on all the past disappointments with David. In each of the early sessions she would bring up examples from past situations or make interpretations based on earlier patterns—all having little to do with what David was actually doing and feeling now. This is a common issue in relationship therapy and can ossify any attempts to change behaviors or interpretations. We discussed this from many perspectives. The "hurt museum" is a technique that allows the person/couple to come up with a list of past hurts, discuss them briefly, and then "enter them" in this museum. It helps if incidents are written down briefly. The point is to use this as a device for remembering but putting aside the past, in a place where it can be reviewed and updated from time to time. This worked minimally in their case. More helpful was challenging Diane's interpretations by asking her whether she was talking about then or now. It was easier to see David in the old ways because if she accepted that he was indeed being attentive and appreciative, she might risk losing this new pattern and be hurt again.

Across 20 sessions and about 9 months, David and Diane made changes. Diane felt more desire, spoke up more about what she did and did not want, and experienced orgasms during about 50% of their contacts. For David, it seemed as if she was enjoying sex with him and he was increasingly able to let go of his worry about how she was doing because he could depend on her to let him know. Diane was also better able to take care of her resentful feelings because she did not let them fester. They did not become more at ease verbally but did develop a pattern of measured, careful, and brief exploration of conflictual issues in the area of affection and sex.

SUMMARY

The value of women's orgasm and the classification of orgasmic disorders are clearly a product of history and culture. This chapter has summarized the prevalence, classification, and treatment effectiveness of treating orgasm disorders as we currently define them. There is evidence that cognitive–behavioral interventions are effective, particularly with primary orgasmic disorder, and that an active approach to treatment is more effective than a purely reflective one. In addition, a systems framework provides a theoretical perspective with which to understand and implement effective treatment modalities. The cases discussed point out the need for broadly based assessments, psychological and physiological knowledge, and strategies for treatment when there are multiple diagnoses. One would expect a number of additions to this topic over the next decade, particularly in the area of increased knowledge of women's sexual arousal, more physiological information, more information on medications for treating sexual arousal, and perhaps orgasm and desire problems. Without question, treatment efficacy data are limited and further testing of psychological and physiological treatments, alone and in combination, would benefit women and their partners.

REFERENCES

Alder, E., & Bancroft, J. (1988). The relationship between breast feeding persistence, sexuality and mood in post-partum women. *Psychological Medicine, 18*, 389–396.

Aldridge, S. A. (1982). Drug induced sexual dysfunction. *Clinical Pharmacy, 1*, 141–147.

American Psychiatric Association. (1994). *Diagnostic and statistical manual of mental disorders* (4th ed.). Washington, DC: American Psychiatric Association.

Andersen, B. L. (1983). Primary orgasmic dysfunction: Diagnostic considerations and review of treatment. *Psychological Bulletin, 93*, 105–136.

Apt, C. V., & Hurlbert, D. F. (1992). Motherhood and female sexuality beyond one year postpartum: a study of military wives. *Journal of Sex Education Therapy, 18*, 389–396.

Araoz, D. L. (1982). *Hypnosis and sex therapy.* New York: Brunner/Mazel.

Arentewicz, G., & Schmidt, G. (1983). *The treatment of sexual disorders.* New York: Basic Books.

Avery, D. H. (1997). Seasonal affective disorder. In D. Dunner (Ed.), *Current psychiatric therapy: II* (pp. 243–247). Philadelphia: Saunders.

Barbach, L. G. (1974). Group treatment of preorgasmic women. *Journal of Sex and Marital Therapy, 1*, 139–145.

Barbach, L. G. (1975). *For yourself.* New York: Doubleday.

Barlow, D. H. (1986). Causes of sexual dysfunction: The role of anxiety and cognitive interference. *Journal of Consulting and Clinical Psychology, 54*, 140–148.

Beigel, H. G. (1972). The use of hypnosis in female sexual anesthesia. *Journal of the American Society of Psychosomatic Dentistry and Medicine, 19*, 4–14.

Bergman, E. M., & Hof, L. (1987). The sexual genogram—assessing family-of-origin factors in the treatment of sexual dysfunction. In G. R. Weeks & L. Hof (Eds.), *Integrating sex and marital therapy* (pp. 37–56). New York: Brunnel/Mazel.

Bohlen, J. G., Held, J. P., & Sanderson, M. O. (1983). Update on sexual physiology research. *Marriage and Family Review, 6*, 21–33.

Brody, H. (1973). The systems view of man: Implications for medicine, science, and ethics. *Perspectives in Biology and Medicine, 17*, 71–92.

Carney, A., Bancroft, J., & Mathews, A. (1978). Combination of hormonal and psychological treatment for female sexual unresponsiveness: A comparative study. *British Journal of Psychiatry, 132*, 339–346.

Chambless, D. L., Sultan, F. E., Stern, T. E., O'Neill, C., Garrison, S., & Jackson, A. (1984). Effect of pubococcygeal exercises on coital orgasm in women. *Journal of Consulting and Clinical Psychology, 52*, 114–118.

Cohen, S. J. (1978). Sexual interviewing, evaluation, and therapy: Psychoanalytic emphasis on the use of sexual fantasy. *Archives of Sexual Behavior, 7,* 229–241.

Cotten-Huston, A. L., & Wheeler, K. A. (1983). Preorgasmic group treatment: Assertiveness, marital adjustment and sexual function in women. *Journal of Sex and Marital Therapy, 9,* 296–302.

Crenshaw, T. L., Goldberg, J. P., & Stern, W. C. (1987). Pharmacologic modification of psychosexual dysfunction. *Journal of Sex and Marital Therapy, 13,* 239–253.

DeAmicis, L. A., Goldberg, D. C., LoPiccolo, J., Friedman, J., & Davies, L. (1986). Three-year follow-up of couples evaluated for sexual dysfunction. *Journal of Sexual and Marital Therapy, 12,* 215–228.

Derogatis, L. (1977). *SCL-90-R: Administration, scoring and procedures manual.* Baltimore: Clinical Psychometrics Research.

Ellis, A. (1975). The rational–emotive approach to sex therapy. *Counseling Psychologist, 5,* 14–21.

Engel, G. L. (1980). The clinical application of the biopsychosocial model. *American Journal of Psychiatry, 137,* 535–544.

Ersner-Hershfield, R., & Kopel, S. (1979). Group treatment of preorgasmic women: Evaluation of partner involvement and spacing of sessions. *Journal of Consulting and Clinical Psychology, 47,* 750–759.

Everaerd, W., & Dekker, J. (1982). Treatment of secondary orgasmic dysfunction: A comparison of systematic desensitization and sex therapy. *Behavior Research and Therapy, 20,* 269–274.

Faulk, M. (1973). "Frigidity": A critical review. *Archives of Sexual Behavior, 2,* 257–265.

Fichten, C. S., Libman, E., & Brender, W. (1986). Measurement of therapy outcome and maintenance of gains in the behavioral treatment of secondary orgasmic dysfunction. *Journal of Sex and Marital Therapy, 12,* 22–34.

Fisher, S. (1973). *The female orgasm.* New York: Basic Books.

Frances, A., & Kaplan, H. S. (1983). A case of inhibited orgasm: Pschodynamic or sex therapy? *Hospital and Community Psychiatry, 34,* 903–917.

Frank, E., Anderson, A., & Rubinstein, D. (1978). Frequency of sexual dysfunction in "normal" couples. *New England Journal of Medicine, 299,* 111–115.

Gitlin, M. J. (1997). Psychotropic medication-induced sexual dysfunction. In D. Dunner (Ed.), *Current psychiatric therapy: II* (pp. 385–391). Philadelphia: Saunders.

Goldstein, I., & Berman, J. R. (1998). Vasculogenic female sexual dysfunction: Vaginal engorgement and clitoral erectile insufficiency syndromes. *International Journal of Impotence Research, 10*(Suppl. 2), S84–S90.

Graber, B., & Kline-Graber, G. (1979). Female orgasm: Role of pubococcygeus muscle. *Journal of Clinical Psychiatry, 40,* 348–351.

Grafenberg, E. (1950). The role of the urethra in female orgasm. *International Journal of Sexology, 3,* 145–148.

Hawton, K., Gath, D., & Day, A. (1994). Sexual function in a community sample of middle-aged women with partners: Effects of age, marital, socioeconomic, psychiatric, gynecological, and menopausal factors. *Archives of Sexual Behavior, 23,* 375–395.

Heiman, J. (1986). Treating sexually distressed marital relationships. In N. S. Jacobson & A. S. Gurman (Eds.), *Clinical handbook of marital therapy* (pp. 361–384). New York: Guilford Press.

Heiman, J. (1998). Psychophysiological models of female sexual response. *International Journal of Impotence Research, 10,* S94–S97.

Heiman, J., Gladue, B. A., Roberts, C. W., & LoPiccolo, J. (1986). Historical and current factors discriminating sexually functional from sexually dysfunctional married couples. *Journal of Marital and Family Therapy, 12,* 163–174.

Heiman, J. R., & LoPiccolo, J. (1983). Clinical outcome of sex therapy: Effects of daily v. weekly treatment. *Archives of General Psychiatry, 30,* 443–449.

Heiman, J. R., & LoPiccolo, J. (1988). *Becoming orgasmic: A sexual and personal growth program for women* (rev. and expanded ed.). New York: Simon & Schuster.

Heiman, J. R., LoPiccolo, L., & LoPiccolo, J. (1976). *Becoming orgasmic: A sexual growth program for women*. Englewood Cliffs, NJ: Prentice-Hall.

Heiman, J., & Meston, M. (1997). Empirically validated treatment for sexual dysfunction. *Annual Review of Sex Research, 8,* 148–194.

Hoch, Z., Safir, M. R., Peres, Y., & Sopher, J. (1981). An evaluation of sexual performance—comparison between sexually dysfunctional and functional couples. *Journal of Sex and Marital Therapy, 7,* 195–206.

Jankovich, R., & Miller, P. R. (1978). Response of women with primary orgasmic dysfunction to audiovisual education. *Journal of Sex and Marital Therapy, 4,* 16–19.

Jensen, S. B. (1985). Sexual dysfunction in younger insulin-treated diabetic females. *Diabetes and Metabolism, 11,* 278–282.

Johannes, C. B., & Avis, N. E. (1997). Gender differences in sexual activity among mid-aged adults in Massachusetts. *Maturitas, 26,* 175–184.

Jordan, J. (1985). *Empathy and self boundaries. Work in progress, 16.* Wellesley, MA: Stone Centers Working Papers Series.

Kaplan, H. S. (1974). *The new sex therapy.* New York: Brunner/Mazel.

Kaplan, S. A. , Reis, R. B., Kohn, I. J., Ikeguchi, E. F., Laor, E., Te, A. E., & Martins, A. C. P. (1999). Safety and efficacy of sildenafil in postmenopausal women with sexual dysfunction. *Urology, 53,* 481–486.

Kegel, A. H. (1952). Sexual functions of the pubococcygeus muscle. *Western Journal of Surgery in Obstetrics and Gynaecology, 60,* 521–524.

Kernberg, O. F. (1987). Projection and projective identification: Developmental and clinical aspects. *Journal of the American Psychoanalytic Association, 35,* 795–819.

Kilkku, P., Grönroos, M., Hirvonen, T., & Rauramo, L. (1983). Supravaginal uterine amputation versus hysterectomy: Effects on libido and orgasm. *Acta Obstetrica et Gynaecologic Scandinavica, 62,* 147–152.

Kilmann, P. R., Boland, J. P., Sjortus, S. P., Davidson, E., & Caid, C. (1986). Perspectives of sex therapy outcome: A survey of AASECT providers. *Journal of Sex and Marital Therapy, 12,* 116–138.

Kilmann, P. R., Mills, K. H., Bella, B., Caid, C., Davidson, E., Drose, G., & Wanlass, R. (1983). The effects of sex education on women with secondary orgasmic dysfunction. *Journal of Sex and Marital Therapy, 9,* 79–87.

Kilmann, P. R., Mills, K. H., Caid, C., Davidson, E., Bella, B., Milan, R., Drose, G., Boland, J., Follingstad, D., Montgomery, B., & Wanlass, R. (1986). Treatment of secondary orgasmic dysfunction: An outcome study. *Archives of Sexual Behavior, 15*(3), 211–229.

Kinsey, A. C., Pomeroy, W., Martin, C., & Gebhard, P. (1953). *Sexual behavior in the human female.* Philadelphia: Saunders.

Kline-Graber, G., & Graber, B. (1978). Diagnosis and treatment procedures of pubococcygeal deficiencies in women. In J. LoPiccolo & L. LoPiccolo (Eds.), *Handbook of sex therapy* (pp. 227–240). New York: Plenum.

Kuriansky, J. B., & Sharpe, L. (1981). Clinical and research implications of the evaluation of women's group therapy of anorgasmia: A review. *Journal of Sex and Marital Therapy, 7,* 268–277.

Kuriansky, J. B., Sharpe, L., & O'Connor, D. (1982). The treatment of anorgasmia: Long-term effectiveness of a short term behavioral group therapy. *Journal of Sex and Marital Therapy, 8,* 29–43.

Laan, E., Everaerd, W., & Evers, A. (1995). Assessment of female sexual arousal: Response specificity and construct validity. *Psychophysiology, 32,* 376–385.

Laqueur, T. (1990). *Making sex: The body and gender from the Greeks to Freud.* Cambridge, MA: Harvard University Press.

Laumann, E. O., Gagnon, J. H., Michael, R. T., & Michaels, S. (1994). *The social organization of sexuality: Sexual practices in the United States.* Chicago: University of Chicago Press.

Laumann, E. O., Paik, A., & Rosen, R. C. (1999). Sexual dysfunction in the United States: Prevalence and predictors. *Journal of the American Medical Association, 281,* 537–544.

Leiblum, S. R., & Ersner-Hershfield, R. (1977). Sexual enhancement group for dysfunctional women: An evaluation. *Journal of Sex and Marital Therapy, 3,* 139–151.

Levay, A., Weissberg, J., & Blaustein, A. (1976). Concurrent sex therapy and psychoanalytic psychotherapy by separate therapists: Effectiveness and implications. *Psychiatry, 39,* 355–363.

Levin, R. J. (1980). The physiology of sexual function in women. *Clinics in Obstetrics and Gynaecology, 7,* 213–252.

Levin, R. J. (1983). Human female sexual arousal—an update. *Nordisk Sexologi, 1,* 138–151.

Levin, R. J. (1992). The mechanisms of human female sexual arousal. *Annual Review of Sex Research, 3,* 1–49.

Levin, R. J., & Wagner, G. (1985a). Heart rate change and subjective intensity of orgasm in women. *IRCS Medical Science, 13,* 885–886.

Levin, R. J., & Wagner, G. (1985b). Orgasm in the laboratory—quantitative studies on duration, intensity, latency and vaginal blood flow. *Archives of Sexual Behavior, 14,* 439–449.

Levin, R. J., & Wagner, G. (1987). Self-reported central sexual arousal without vaginal arousal—duplicity or veracity revealed by objective measurements? *Journal of Sex Research, 23,* 540–544.

Libman, E., Fichten, C. S., Brender, W., Burstein, R., Cohen, J., & Binik, Y. B. (1984). A comparison of three therapeutic formats in the treatment of secondary orgasmic dysfunction. *Journal of Sex and Marital Therapy, 10,* 147–159.

LoPiccolo, L., & Heiman, J. (1978). Sexual assessment and history interview. In J. LoPiccolo & L. LoPiccolo (Eds.), *Handbook of sex therapy* (pp. 103–112). New York: Plenum.

LoPiccolo, J., Heiman, J., Hogan, D., & Roberts, C. (1985). Effectiveness of single therapists versus co-therapy teams in sex therapy. *Journal of Consulting and Clinical Psychology, 53,* 287–294.

LoPiccolo, J., & Lobitz, W. C. (1972). The role of masturbation in the treatment of orgasmic dysfunction. *Archives of Sexual Behavior, 2,* 163–171.

LoPiccolo, J., & LoPiccolo, L. (Eds.). (1978). *Handbook of sex therapy.* New York: Plenum.

LoPiccolo, J., & Stock, W. E. (1986). Treatment of sexual dysfunction. *Journal of Consulting and Clinical Psychology, 54,* 158–167.

Lundberg, P. O. (1980). Sexual dysfunction in female patients with multiple sclerosis. *International Rehabilitation Medicine, 3,* 32–34.

Masters, W., & Johnson, V. (1966). *Human sexual response.* Boston: Little, Brown.

Masters, W., & Johnson, V. (1970). *Human sexual inadequacy.* Boston: Little, Brown.

Mathews, A., Whitehead, A., & Kellett, J. (1983). Psychological and hormonal factors in the treatment of female sexual dysfunction. *Psychological Medicine, 13,* 83–92.

Messen, M. R., & Geer, J. H. (1985). Voluntary vaginal musculature contractions as an enhancer of sexual arousal. *Archives of Sexual Behavior, 14,* 13–28.

Meston, C. M., & Gorzalka, B. B. (1992). Psychoactive drugs and human sexual behavior: The role of serotonergic activity. *Journal of Psychoactive Drugs, 24,* 1–40.

Meston, C. M., & Gorzalka, B. B. (1995). The effects of sympathetic activation following acute exercise on physiological and subjective arousal in women. *Behaviour Research and Therapy, 33,* 651–664.

Meston, C. M., & Gorzalka, B. B. (1996). The effects of immediate, delayed, and residual sympathetic activation on physiological and subjective sexual arousal in women. *Behaviour Research and Therapy, 34,* 143–148.

Meston, C. M., & Heiman, J. R. (1998). Ephedrine-activated physiological sexual arousal in women. *Archives of General Psychiatry, 55,* 652–656.

Miller, J. G. (1978). *Living systems.* New York: McGraw-Hill.

Mills, K. H., & Kilmann, P. R. (1982). Group treatment of sexual dysfunctions: A methodological review of the outcome literature. *Journal of Sex and Marital Therapy, 8,* 259–296.

Money, J. (1960). Phantom orgasm in the dreams of paraplegic men and women. *Archives of General Psychiatry, 3,* 373–382.

Monteiro, W. O., Noshirvani, H. F., Marks, I. M., & Lelliott, P. T. (1987). Anorgasmia from clomipramine in obsessive–compulsive disorder, a controlled trial. *British Journal of Psychiatry, 151,* 105–112.

Morokoff, P. J., & LoPiccolo, J. L. (1986). A comparative evaluation of minimal therapist contact and 15 session treatment for female orgasmic dysfunction. *Journal of Consulting and Clinical Psychology, 54,* 294–300.

Nairne, K. D., & Hemsley, D. R. (1983). The use of directed masturbation training in the treatment of primary anorgasmia. *British Journal of Clinical Psychology, 22,* 283–294.

Norris, J., & Feldman-Summers, S. (1981). Factors related to the psychological impacts of rape on the victim. *Journal of Abnormal Psychology, 90,* 562–567.

Obler, M. (1982). A comparison of hypnoanalytic/behavior modification technique and a cotherapist-type treatment with primary orgasmic dysfunctional females: Some preliminary results. *Journal of Sex Research, 18,* 331–345.

Osborn, M., Hawton, K., & Gath, D. (1988). Sexual dysfunction among middle aged women in the community. *British Medical Journal, 296,* 959–962.

Ottesen, B., Wagner, G., & Fahrenkrug, J. (1988). Peptidergic innervation of sexual organs. In J. M. A. Sitsen (Ed.), *Handbook of sexology: The pharmacology and endocrinology of sexual function* (vol. 6, pp. 66–97). Amsterdam: Elsevier.

Palace, E. M., & Gorzalka, B. B. (1990). The enhancing effects of anxiety on arousal in sexually dysfunctional and functional women. *Journal of Abnormal Psychology, 99,* 403–411.

Pohl, R. (1983). Anorgasmia caused by MAOIs. *American Journal of Psychiatry, 140,* 510.

Quirk, K. D., & Einarson, T. R. (1982). Sexual dysfunction and clomipramine. *Canadian Journal of Psychiatry, 27,* 228–231.

Read, S., King, M., & Watson, J. (1997). Sexual dysfunction in primary medical care: Prevalence, characteristics and detection by the general practitioner. *Journal of Public Health Medicine, 19,* 387–391.

Richards, B. (1982). The Grafenberg spot and female ejaculation: I. *British Journal of Sexual Medicine, 9,* 17–20.

Richards, B. (1983). The Grafenberg spot and female ejaculation: II. *British Journal of Sexual Medicine, 10,* 37.

Riley, A. J., & Riley, E. J. (1978). A controlled study to evaluate directed masturbation in the management of primary orgasmic failure in women. *British Journal of Psychiatry, 135,* 404–409.

Riley, A. J., & Riley, E. J. (1986). Cyproheptadine and antidepressant-induced anorgasmia. *British Journal of Psychiatry, 148,* 217–218.

Robinson, P. (1970). *The modernization of sex.* New York: Harper & Row.

Rosen, I. (1982). The psychoanalytic approach. *British Journal of Psychiatry, 140,* 85–93.

Rosen, R. C., Lane, R. M., & Menza, M. (1999). Effects of SSRIs on sexual function: A critical review. *Journal of Clinical Psychopharmacology, 19,* 67–85.

Rosen, R. C., Taylor J. F., Leiblum S. R., & Bachman, G. A. (1993). Prevalence of sexual dysfunction in women: Results of a survey study of 329 women in an outpatient gynecological clinic. *Journal of Sex and Marital Therapy, 19,* 171–188.

Rosenthal, N. E., & Wehr, T. A. (1987). Seasonal affective disorders. *Psychiatric Annals, 17,* 670-674.

Roughan, P. A., & Kunst, L. (1981). Do pelvic floor exercises really improve orgasmic potential? *Journal of Sex and Marital Therapy, 7,* 223–229.

Sanders, G. (1988). Of cybernetics and sexuality. *Family Therapy Networker, 12,* 38–42.

Sarason, I. G., Johnson, J. H., & Siegel, J. M. (1978). Assessing the impact of life changes: Development of the Life Experiences Survey. *Journal of Consulting and Clinical Psychology, 46,* 932–946.

Scharff, D. E., & Scharff, J. S. (1987). Objects relations theory and family therapy. In D. E. Scharff & J. S. Scharff (Eds.), *Object relations family therapy* (pp. 43–64). Northvale, NJ: Jason Aronson.

Schnarch, D. M. (1991). *Constructing the sexual crucible: An integration of sexual and marital therapy.* New York: Norton.

Schneidman, B., & McGuire, L. (1976). Group therapy for nonorgasmic women: Two age levels. *Archives of Sexual Behavior, 5,* 239–247.

Schover, L. R., Friedman, J. M., Weiler, S. J., Heiman, J. R., & LoPiccolo, J. (1982). Multiaxial problem-oriented system for sexual dysfunctions. *Archives of General Psychiatry, 39,* 614–619.

Segraves, R. T. (1985). Female orgasm and psychiatric drugs. *Journal of Sex Education and Therapy, 11,* 69–71.

Segraves, R. T. (1986). Implications of the behavioral sex therapies for psychoanalytic theory and practice: Intrapsychic sequelae of symptom removal in the patient and spouse. *Journal of the American Academy of Psychoanalysis, 14,* 485–493.

Selvini-Palazzoli, M., & Viaro, M. (1988). The anorectic process in the family: A six-stage model as a guide for individual therapy. *Family Process, 27,* 129–148.

Semmens, J. P., & Semmens, F. J. (1978). Role of vagina in female sexuality. In E. S. E. Hafez & T. N. Evans (Eds.), *The human vagina* (pp. 213–221). Amsterdam: North Holland.

Sipski, M. L., Alexander, C. J., & Rosen, R. C. (1995). Orgasm in women with spinal cord injuries: A laboratory-based assessment. *Archives of Physical Medicine and Rehabilitation, 76,* 1097–1102.

Spanier, G. B. (1976). Measuring dyadic adjustment: New scales for assessing quality of marriage and similar dyads. *Journal of Marriage and Family Therapy, 38,* 15–28.

Spence, S. H. (1985). Group versus individual treatment of primary and secondary female orgasmic dysfunction. *Behavior Research and Therapy, 23,* 539–548.

Steele, T. E., & Howell, E. F. (1986). Cyproheptadine for imipramine-induced sexual anorgasmia. *Journal of Clinical Psychiatry, 6,* 326–327.

Stewart, D. A. (1986). Hypnoanalysis and orgasmic dysfunction. *International Journal of Psychosomatics, 33,* 21–22.

Stiver, I. (1984). The meanings of dependency in female–male relationships. *Work in progress,* 83-07. Wellesley, MA: Stone Center for Developmental Services and Studies.

Surrey, J. (1983). Self-in-relation: A theory of women's development. *Work in progress.* Wellesley, MA: Stone Center Working Papers Series.

Tripet Dodge, L. J., Glasgow, R. E., & O'Neill, H. K. (1982). Bibliotherapy in the treatment of female orgasmic dysfunction. *Journal of Consulting and Clinical Psychology, 50,* 442–443.

Trudel, G., & Saint-Laurent, S. (1983). A comparison between the effects of Kegel's exercises and a combination of sexual awareness, relaxation and breathing on situational orgasmic dysfunction in women. *Journal of Sex and Marital Therapy, 9,* 204–209.

Tsai, M., Feldman-Summers, S., & Edgar, M. (1979). Childhood molestation: Variables related to differential impact on psychosexual functioning in adult women. *Journal of Abnormal Psychology, 88,* 404–414.

Verhulst, J., & Heiman, J. R. (1979). An interactional approach to sexual dysfunction. *American Journal of Family Therapy, 7,* 19–36.

Verhulst, J., & Heiman, J. R. (1988). A systems perspective on sexual desire. In S. R. Leiblum & R. C. Rosen (Eds.), *Sexual desire disorders* (pp. 243–267). New York: Guilford Press.

von Bertalanffy, L. (1968). *General systems theory.* New York: Brazillier.

Wakefield, J. C. (1987). The semantics of success: Do masturbation exercises lead to partner orgasm? *Journal of Sex and Marital Therapy, 13,* 3–14.

Walker, E. A., Gelfand, A., Katon, M. J., Doss, M. P., Von Korff, M., Bernstein, D., & Russo, J. (1999). Adult health status of women HMO members with histories of childhood abuse and neglect. *American Journal of Medicine, 107,* 332–339.

Wallace, D. H., & Barbach, L. G. (1974). Preorgasmic group treatment. *Journal of Sex and Marital Therapy, 1,* 146–154.

Weeks, G. R. (1987). Systematic treatment of inhibited sexual desire. In G. R. Weeks & L. Hof (Eds.), *Integrating sex and marital therapy* (pp. 183–201). New York: Brunner/Mazel.

Weeks, G. R., & Hof, L. (Eds.). (1987). *Integrating sex and marital therapy.* New York: Brunner/Mazel.

Weiss, L., & Meadow, R. (1983). Group treatment for female sexual dysfunction. *Arizona Medicine, 9,* 626–628.

Wenninger, K., & Heiman, J. R. (1998). Relating body image to psychological and sexual functioning in child abuse survivors. *Journal of Traumatic Stress, 11,* 543–562.

Whipple, B., & Komisaruk, B. R. (1985). Elevation of pain threshold by vaginal stimulation in women. *Pain, 21,* 357-367.

Whipple, B., & Komisaruk, B. R. (1988). Analgesia produced in women by genital self-stimulation. *Journal of Sex Research, 24,* 130–140.

Whipple, B., & McGreer, K. B. (1997). Management of female sexual dysfunction. In M. L. Sipski & C. J. Alexander (Eds.), *Sexual function in people with disability and chronic illness* (pp. 511–536). Gathersberg, MD: Aspen.

Whipple, B., Ogden, G., & Komisaruk, B. R. (1992). Physiological correlates of imagery-induced orgasm in women. *Archives of Sexual Behavior, 21,* 121–133.

Whitaker, C. A., & Keith, D. V. (1981). Symbolic experiential family therapy. In A. S. Gurman & D. P. Kniskern (Eds.), *Handbook of family therapy* (pp. 187–225). New York: Brunner/ Mazel.

Wise, T. N. (1983). Sexual dysfunction in the medically ill. *Psychosomatics, 24,* 787–805.

Zussman, L., Zussman, S., Sunley, R., & Bjornson, E. (1981). Sexual response after hysterectomy-oophorectomy: Recent studies and reconsideration of psychogenesis. *American Journal of Obstetrics and Gynecology, 140,* 725–729.

6

Dyspareunia

YITZCHAK M. BINIK
SOPHIE BERGERON
SAMIR KHALIFÉ

The new conceptualization of dyspareunia as a pain disorder *rather than in the traditional category of sexual dysfunction, is a central thesis of Binik, Bergeron, and Khalifé's chapter and related research. They note that most clinicians regard dyspareunia as ascribable to a particular physical pathology or, if a discernible physical cause is not detected, as a reflection of psychosexual conflict. They suggest that this model is both scientifically unsound and disrespectful to the patient. Rather, they suggest, dyspareunia should be assessed and treated like other pain disorders.*

According to the authors' proposed model, assessment of coital pain should include involvement of a multidisciplinary team working together to consider the different aspects of the pain—neurological, muscular, affective and interpersonal—and treatment should be similarly coordinated. Understanding the intrinsic parameters (i.e., location, intensity, and time course) of the pain, as well as the circumstances of its occurrence, are all important, because these facts may legititize the patient's pain complaint, as well as help to guide intervention. Gynecologists should be involved in the assessment process along with clinicians. Determining which subtype of dyspareunia (e.g., vulvar vestibulitis, vaginal atrophy, and mixed pain disorder) may determine the choice of therapy and outcome in most cases.

Yitzchak M. Binik and his coauthors assert that all reports of dyspareunia include both psychogenic and organogenic elements, and that both aspects should be taken seriously. Interestingly, these investigators have determined that women who attribute their pain to psychosocial causes tend to report higher pain scores, higher levels of distress, lower marital adjustment scores,

154

and more sexual problems than do those women ascribing their pain to physical causes. This finding is open, of course, to alternative explanations.

One puzzling aspect of dyspareunia is the observation that some women are able to function reasonably well sexually, despite the report of increased pain, whereas others clearly cannot. Similarly, the rated intensity of pain does not usually correlate with physical findings. Moreover, behavioral disruption cannot be reliably predicted from the gynecological exam or even from past history.

For many women, the pain of dyspareunia cannot be totally eliminated. It is therefore important that coping strategies be reviewed and enhanced as part of the overall treatment package. Active rather than passive coping is encouraged, as well as the avoidance of catastrophizing.

Finally, there are a great variety of treatment options for managing the disorder, including psychological, medical, and surgical treatments. There are not many well-designed outcome studies at this time supporting one treatment intervention over another, although Bergeron and colleagues found that vestibulectomy appears to be quite effective in specific cases. Clearly, there are a large number of women for whom this procedure would clearly not be appropriate.

Binik, Bergeron, and Khalifé have offered a real service to women who experience coital pain by taking their complaints seriously, and by developing a comprehensive assessment and treatment package. Their program includes detailed attention to both relevant psychological and medical issues. More than this, they have championed the view of dyspareunia as a pain disorder rather than as simply a sexual dysfunction. In their prolific research and writings, they have effectively alerted clinicians to a new (and improved) understandings of coital pain.

Yitzchak M. Binik, PhD, is Professor of Psychology at McGill University and director of the Sex and Couple Therapy Service of the Royal Victoria Hospital. Sophie Bergeron, PhD, received her doctorate in clinical psychology from McGill University in 1998 and is currently a postdoctoral fellow in the Department of Sexology at the University of Quebec in Montreal. Samir Khalifé, MD, is an associate professor in the Department of Obstetrics and Gynecology of the Faculty of Medicine of McGill University.

Most acute and recurrent genital or pelvic pains associated with intercourse are classified as dyspareunia. Unfortunately, the diagnosis of dyspareunia is not a useful one. Consider the following brief case summaries: (1) a 40-year-old woman experiences a *dull/aching* pain close to her right ovary during deep penile thrusting; (2) a 21-year-old woman feels a *burning/cutting* pain at the introitus during penile penetration; (3) a 55-year-old postmenopausal woman experiences a *sore/sharp* vaginal pain during penetration and intercourse despite adequate arousal. Most intelligent laypeople would assume that these are quite different problems yet the *Diagnostic and Statistical Manual of Mental Disorders* (DSM-IV; American Psychiatric Association, 1994) and many other nosologies assign them one diagnosis. Implicit in DSM-IV's (American Psychiatric Association, 1994) classification is the notion that sexual problems or conflicts are central to our understanding of women with dyspareunia. Although this may be true some of the time, it is probably not true most of the time because the same pain experienced during intercourse can typically be elicited in nonsexual situations such as gynecological examinations, tampon insertion, and so on.

An interesting analogy may be the problem of back pain and work disability. Although back pain is one of the major causes for work-related disability, no one would seriously suggest that it should be classified as a work disorder even though there is little doubt that for some individuals, conflicts related to work may account for or exacerbate their pain. Clinicians who deal with back pain–related disability carefully and independently examine the pain, the work situation, and the potential relationship between the two. Sometimes the pain and interference with work are closely linked; other times they are not. We believe the same to be true for dyspareunia. What has been missing in our conceptualizations of dyspareunia is a focus on the central phenomenon of the problem, the pain. Our current undifferentiated classifications for dyspareunia have probably resulted from the failure to distinguish between genital pain and the primary activity with which it interferes, sexual intercourse. The implications of this distinction are highly significant for the assessment and treatment of women with pain during intercourse.

BACKGROUND

Traditionally, most clinicians have attempted either to reduce dyspareunia to physical pathology or to understand it as the outcome of psychosexual conflict. These different and often opposing views are the outcome of a 4,000-year history of attempts to describe and treat coital pain (cf. Meana & Binik, 1994). Masters and Johnson (1970) summarized this point in the following way:

> For years, woman's [*sic*] complaint "it hurts when I have intercourse" has been an anathema to the therapist. Even after an adequate pelvic examination, the therapist frequently cannot be sure whether the patient is complaining of definitive but undiagnosed pelvic pathology or whether, as has been true countless thousands of times, a sexually dysfunctional woman is using the symptomatology of pain as a means of escaping completely or at least reducing markedly the number of unwelcome sexual encounters in her marriage. (pp. 266–267)

Early sex therapy monographs dealt with the topic of dyspareunia in a variety of ways. Helen Singer Kaplan's (1974) influential text almost totally ignored the topic. Other important texts reflected Master and Johnson's dualistic view (e.g., Abarbanel, 1978) by limiting their discussion to either "organic" or "psychogenic" (functional) dyspareunia. In general, discussions of dyspareunia were always secondary to those of vaginismus. The prevailing view appeared to be that most instances of dyspareunia could be attributed to organic causes and that the small percentage of remaining cases could be dealt with psychologically. Smith and Buck (1983) summarized this view in the following way:

> A diagnosis of functional dyspareunis [*sic*] is one of exclusion. While it is a more rare condition, it is as incapacitating as organic dyspareunia. It is more likely to find its way into a psychiatric setting or one which deals specifically with sexual disorders after an initial gynecological consultation. In the 10-year history of the Sexual Behaviors Consultation Unit (SBCU) of the Johns Hopkins Medical Institutions, we have evaluated less than 20 cases. (p. 206)

What appears to have developed, in practice, is that women who experience pain during intercourse typically and not unreasonably go to their gynecologist to find out whether there is a "physical" cause for their pain. Many of these women undergo numerous uncomfortable and sometimes invasive tests (e.g., vaginal cultures, ultrasonagraphy, colposcopy, and laparoscopy). Some are treated successfully by standard medical interventions (medication, surgery, etc.), but it is our impression that a large number experience little or only partial relief for their pain. Those women who persist in complaining to their gynecologist are often told that "the pain is in their heads" and that they should see a mental health professional. Although the message behind this statement is often well-intentioned, it typically is not a positive or acceptable one for many women who give up at that point and decide to grit their teeth and bear the pain. Those who do consult mental health professionals often find themselves in the frustrating position of being asked about every aspect of their psychosocial functioning except the pain.

Alternative clinical models are possible. Once again the analogy of low back pain is a useful one. It is rare for the degree of diagnosable physical back pathology to be highly correlated with the experience of low back pain or with the degree of interference with everyday activities. It is equally rare for a single intervention whether medical or psychosocial to cure the problem. Current clinical models emphasize the utility of multidisciplinary teams consisting of physicians, physical therapists, psychologists, social workers, and so on, to concurrently assess the different aspects of the pain (e.g., neurological, muscular, affective, and interpersonal) and to develop a coordinated and comprehensive treatment plan (Melzack & Wall, 1982). Such a biopsychosocial approach should not be foreign to sex therapists as it is being adopted in the area of erectile dysfunction and is used in treating sexual dysfunction resulting from chronic illness (e.g., Schover & Jensen, 1988).

Modern sex therapy has only recently begun to confront the complexity of the phenomena included in the current diagnosis of dyspareunia. More recent texts (e.g., O' Donahue & Geer, 1993; Maurice, 1998) are beginning to integrate sex and pain research and therapy in an attempt to develop a more comprehensive and clinically useful model. This type of approach is at the base of our working model for the assessment and treatment of dyspareunia.

ASSESSMENT

Our psychosocial evaluation of dyspareunia focuses first on a detailed description of the pain and then on the resulting degree of interference with sexuality, relationships, and personal well-being. Our description includes specific information concerning pain location, quality, intensity, elicitors, time course, and meaning. In addition to providing important diagnostic information, the gathering of this information serves the important therapeutic purpose of legitimating the presenting complaint which, in our experience, is often not taken seriously. The evaluation of interference focuses on disruption of the sexual response cycle and sexual frequency, on disruption of nonsexual aspects of intimate or dating relationships, and on an evaluation of pain coping strategies and their effects on personal adjustment. We do not believe that mental health professionals should try to assess dyspareunia alone. A concurrent assessment by an informed and interested gynecologist is crucial; we are also finding it extremely useful to ask for an assessment of the pelvic floor musculature from a physical therapist.

This assessment strategy is based on several assumptions. First, we take the presenting problem, the pain, as the crucial starting point for our assessment. This point of view is similar to the one most sex therapists employ with a presenting sexual problem. Second, we initially assume that any psychosexual conflict, relationship, or personal distress is at least as likely to be the result as the cause of the pain. This view is supported by the available empirical evidence (Van Lankveld, Weijenborg, & Ter Kuile, 1996; Meana, Binik, Khalifé, & Cohen, 1997b) and our clinical experience. Third, we do not believe that we can usefully differentiate between psychogenic and organic dyspareunia. For practical purposes, we always assume that there are interacting psychosocial and biological factors which contribute to the problem (cf. LoPiccolo, 1992, for a similar discussion with respect to erectile dysfunction). These assumptions are in contrast to the current DSM-IV (American Psychiatric Association, 1994) view which considers dyspareunia as any old pain down there which interferes with intercourse and attempts to characterize it as it would characterize other sexual dysfunctions (e.g., psychogenic vs. combined psychogenic and organic etiology).

Pain Description

Location

It is important to ask women with dyspareunia the same question one would ask of anybody complaining of pain: "Where exactly is the pain?" Some dyspareunic women are able to immediately point to a diagram or to their bodies or are able to describe the exact location of the pain. For others, this is not an easy question. An inability to describe the location of the pain may reflect the fact that it is not highly localized or that it may "travel" from one pelvic area to another or that women are not familiar with their pelvic anatomy. Some women with dyspareunia have never been asked the question. We typically ask women whether the pain is "vulvar" (at the opening, or at the external genitalia), vaginal, deep, or some combination of these. If a woman cannot respond to the question of location, we typically ask whether her gynecologist was able to "create" a similar pain during a gynecological examination or whether she would be willing to examine herself with a hand-held mirror to try to determine location(s).

Quality

A second crucial aspect of our assessment of dyspareunic pain is an attempt to characterize the "quality" of the pain. Is it "burning," "sharp," "dull," "shooting," and so on? Clients often lack the vocabulary to do this easily, but clinicians can provide them with lists of pain descriptors from the McGill-Melzack Pain Questionnaire (Melzack & Katz, 1992) or actually administer the inventory. Such pain descriptions have been shown to be useful clinical and research markers of different pain syndrome.

Pain Elicitors and Time Course

Equally important is a characterization of which activities in addition to intercourse elicit the pain and how long the pain lasts once it is elicited. For example, Z is a 30-year-old woman who experienced only minor discomfort during intercourse but a severe burning pain for up to 36 hours afterward. This pain disturbed her sleep and often caused her to miss work or forgo activities the next day. In our experience, it is rare that intercourse is the only stimulus or activity that can elicit the pain. Gynecological examinations, urination, tampons, manual or oral stimulation, friction with clothing, and sports often result in a pain similar to the one felt during intercourse (Bergeron, Binik, Khalifé, Pagidas, & Glazer, 1998b). It is not clear, however, whether describing pain elicitors on the behavioral level of activities is appropriate. For example, the activity of intercourse would typically involve pressure, rubbing, and increased temperature. Which of these stimuli alone or in combination is sufficient to elicit pain is not clear.

Some women report pain during intercourse or other activities but also consistently report the same pain in situations unrelated to intercourse or to any activity that may affect the painful area. Most clinicians and researchers reasonably believe that the distinction between a recurrent acute pain and a chronic one is important, yet there is little relevant data. Characterization of the time course of the pain once it is elicited is also important. Does the pain last for seconds, hours, or days? Does it change over time? What relieves or increases the pain?

Intensity

We also ask women to rate the intensity of the pain during intercourse and at other times if relevant. There are numerous instruments and strategies to do this formally, but two simple 0–10 scales, one for the sensory aspect of the pain ("no pain"–"worst pain I've ever felt") and one for the affective aspect of the pain ("not at all distressing"–"terribly distressing"), are useful clinically. Women with dyspareunia may often systematically and reliably differ in their ratings of these two dimensions. It is also often useful to have women keep relevant pain diaries. We typically ask women to fill out a diary entry after each episode of pain. In addition to rating the pain quantitatively and describing its location and quality, we ask them to describe the situation and activities leading up to the pain; their thoughts and feelings before, during, and after the pain; their attempts, if any, to reduce the pain; and the effectiveness of these attempts. If the situation eliciting the pain is a sexual one, we ask women to record how subjectively and physically (lubricated) aroused they were and how their partner responded to the pain.

Meaning

The meaning of the pain is also important to assess. Most women are willing to give their "personal theory" of the causes or meaning of having pain during intercourse. This personal theory can have important implications for assessment and treatment even if the theory is not well worked out or substantiated by "evidence." We recently assessed a 35-year-old woman who believed that her dyspareunia was caused by a sexually transmitted disease (STD) that her husband had transmitted to her after having an affair. The husband denied the affair and as far as we could determine neither she nor her husband showed any evidence of STDs. Leventhal et al. (1997) hypothesized that there are five major attributes to disease representation, including (1) disease identity and label, (2) time line, (3) consequences, (4) causes, and (5) controllability. These attributes have been shown to greatly affect attempts to cope with symptoms and illness.

Our experience suggests that Leventhal's dimensions are highly relevant to women with dyspareunia. For example, women appear to prefer to conceptualize dyspareunia as a physically based pain syndrome rather than a sexual problem. Attribution of the pain to physical causes may make adherence to psychological interventions more difficult; it may also reduce psychological distress. For example, Meana, Binik, Khalifé, and Cohen (1999) have shown that women who make psychosocial attributions for the cause of their dyspareunia report higher pain scores, higher levels of psychological distress, lower levels of marital adjustment, and more sexual problems than do those who make physical attributions.

Pain Interference

Sexual Response Cycle and Frequency

It is not surprising that many women with dyspareunia experience significant disruption of their sexual responses. It is, perhaps, more surprising that some women do not appear to experience these disruptions despite the pain. Unfortunately, our current ability to predict which women will experience the greatest disruptions of their sex life is quite poor. The rated intensity of pain during standardized gynecological examinations (cf. later section) or nonsexual activities does not correlate highly with the pain intensity experienced during intercourse (Bergeron et al., 1998b). In addition, the relationship between the pain experienced during intercourse and the degree of disruption of desire, arousal, orgasm, and sexual frequency is complex and poorly understood. From a pain syndrome perspective, this is not surprising. Some individuals suffering from tennis elbow often continue playing and enjoying tennis despite significant pain; others do not. We rarely can predict behavioral disruption from the degree of physical pathology, from pain reports, or from previous behavior. For example, we recently assessed a 27-year-old graduate student with an endometriosis and vulval fissures. During our standardized gynecological examination, the student experienced severe pain almost everywhere the physician touched. Despite this, she reported a 2-year relationship during which she had sex an average of twice a week and regularly experienced orgasms during intercourse.

It has been our experience that a significant minority of women who have experienced coital pain for long periods do not report this as a primary problem. Instead, they present for help with complaints of lack of desire or arousal and do not mention the pain until directly asked. The reluctance on the part of some women to report pain during intercourse is not well understood. In some cases these women initially experienced significant arousal or desire with coexisting pain and seem to expect a certain degree of pain with intercourse. They do not perceive a problem until arousal or some other sexual response is affected. This highlights the need to ask all women presenting with sexual problems about whether they experience pain during sexual activities. In an outpatient gynecology setting, Plouffe (1985) has demonstrated that most cases of dyspareunia (and other sexually related problems) will go undetected unless specific questions are asked.

DSM-IV (American Psychiatric Association, 1994) appears to preclude a diagnosis of dyspareunia if there is inadequate lubrication. It seems clear that for some postmenopausal women inadequate lubrication can lead to pain during intercourse, but it also seems clear that pain during intercourse can lead to reduced arousal and lubrication. A detailed history can sometimes help to illuminate the development of the problem, but we are often unable to reach definite conclusions. In a laboratory study, Wouda et al. (1998) failed to demonstrate striking differences in vaginal vasocongestion in response to erotic films between women with dyspareunia and controls. It seems premature, at this point, to assume that inadequate lubrication or arousal is an a priori exclusion criterion for or cause of dyspareunia.

Disruption of Nonsexual Relationships

Women with dyspareunia are legitimately concerned about maintaining or developing intimate relationships. It is important to assess how much this influences the nature of the pain. Meana, Binik, Khalifé, & Cohen (1998) have shown that higher levels of couple adjustment are significantly correlated with lower pain ratings in women with dyspareunia. A significant percentage of the dyspareunic women we have seen, however, do not have a stable partner. Some have chosen to totally avoid heterosexual interactions until they can solve the problem. Others maintain unsatisfactory relationships for fear of not being able to establish another. Such concerns appear diminished but nonetheless important in older women with more established relationships. There is suggestive evidence that the experience of pain can be affected by one's partner's reaction (Flor, Turk, & Rudy, 1989). This should be carefully evaluated.

Pain Coping Strategies

Individual differences in how women cope with their coital pain are dramatic. There is still much controversy on how to describe coping, yet it is clear that many of the proposed dimensions (e.g., passive vs. active, avoidant vs. attentional, emotion vs. problem based) can be easily applied to women with dyspareunia. Understanding how a woman is attempting to cope with dyspareunia is important in designing a treatment. It may take extensive initial therapeutic effort to involve a passive and avoidant coper in a problem-focused behavioral treatment program. One particular coping reaction, "catastrophizing," is well-known to gynecologists who often assume an emotional etiology as a result of a somewhat dramatic or histrionic reaction to an attempted examination. Such reactions may have been termed hysterical in the past and have often focused attention away from the problem and more on the coping reaction. Pilot data (Binik & Koerner, 1998) we have collected suggest a significant positive correlation between catastrophizing as measured by the Pain Catastrophizing Scale (Sullivan, Bishop, & Pivik, 1995) and women's pain reports during a standardized gynecological examination. Catastrophizing cognitions (e.g., "I'm going to have unbearable pain which will never get better") are closely related to others, such as "I am a failure as a woman" or "My partner will leave me" or "I must be tearing inside." These should be carefully assessed.

Although women with dyspareunia may have slightly elevated symptom scores on standard psychopathology inventories, these elevations do not typically approximate clinical levels. Our clinical impression suggests that the disruption of sexual and nonsexual relationships caused by dyspareunia may have important effects on self-esteem, femininity, and perceived well-being. In our view, these effects are best seen as a relatively "normal" reaction to a distressing problem. There is little evidence to suggest that preexisting psychopathology is an important etiological factor in dyspareunia. Nonetheless, anxiety and depression levels should be carefully assessed because they are typically highly correlated with pain reports (Meana, Binik, Khalifé, & Cohen, 1999). Elevated distress levels can also interfere with therapeutic progress or treatment adherence. There is no evidence to suggest that women with dyspareunia have experienced higher levels of sexual or physical abuse or trauma (Meana, Binik, Khalifé, & Cohen, 1997b).

Differential Diagnosis from Vaginismus

DSM-IV (American Psychiatric Association, 1994) and most sex therapists feel that dyspareunia is clearly distinguishable from vaginismus. In principle, the differential diagnosis can only be made by a gynecologist who observes the purported vaginal/pelvic muscle spasm that characterizes vaginismus. In practice, many nongynecological clinicians make this differentiation based on the woman's ability to experience penetration with a penis. There are no published diagnostic studies that have demonstrated that a gynecologist or a mental health professional can reliably diagnose vaginismus, or distinguish vaginismus from dyspareunia. Based on a critical review of the literature, Reissing, Binik, & Khalifé (1999) have questioned the validity of the vaginismus diagnosis. There are several clinical studies that suggest a high degree of comorbidity for dyspareunia and vaginismus and several gynecological reports that question the validity of the distinction (Basson & Riley, 1994; Van Lankveld, Brewaeys, Ter Kuile, & Weijenborg, 1995).

Dyspareunia or Dyspareunias

We predict that the use of the term "dyspareunia" will come to parallel the use of such terms as "headache" and "low back pain." Such terms refer to a group of different pain syndromes which manifest in the same body area. It is unlikely that the different types of headache or back pain share the same etiology or require the same treatment. If our analogy is correct, the same will be true of dyspareunia. Ultimately, it might be more appropriate to adopt a term such as "vulvo/vaginal" or "pelvic" pain.

Currently, we have limited evidence for several subtypes of dyspareunia. Vulvar vestibulitis syndrome is perhaps the most common type of premenopausal dyspareunia. This highly localized "burning" or "cutting" type of pain can be induced by pressure to the vulvar vestibule. Intercourse and particularly penile penetration places pressure on and rubs this area, thus inducing pain. Pressure to other surrounding areas has no such pain-inducing effects. This syndrome can sometimes be inferred from the woman's report of the type, location, and circumstance of pain. It can be reliably diagnosed by a gynecologist via the cotton swab test (cf. later in the chapter). For some women erythema (i.e., reddening of the skin) or inflammation may be associated with the painful areas. However, there is controversy about whether this is typical (Bergeron et al., 1998b; Meana, Binik, Khalifé, & Cohen, 1997a) have provided initial evidence concerning another possible group of premenopausal women who do not have pain localized to the vulvar vestibule. These women report a variety of different locations and qualities of pain and no gynecological abnormalities.

Vulvar or vaginal atrophy is another possible subtype of dyspareunia. This type of dyspareunia is presumed to occur postmenopausally from decreasing estrogen levels which results in vulvo/vaginal atrophy and decreased lubrication during arousal making intercourse uncomfortable and sometimes painful. Although such discomfort and pain is a common report in menopause clinics, no one has demonstrated a direct link between estrogen levels, vulvo/vaginal atrophy, and discomfort/pain during intercourse. In fact, Laan and van Lunsen (1997) showed that vaginal atrophy was related to estrogen level but not to vaginal dryness and dyspareunia.

Women with vulvar vestibulitis and vulvo/vaginal atrophy tend to report pain or discomfort upon penetration or pain located in the vulvar area or anterior portion of the vagina. There is a large group of women who report deeper vaginal or pelvic pain. Little is known about these types of pain except that they are often presumed to be linked to gynecological conditions such as endometriosis, ovarian cysts, pelvic adhesions, inflammatory disease or congestion, and so on. Steege (1998) and Rapkin (1995) have questioned the assumption that such conditions can account for the pain, but there is very little nongynecological clinical experience or research concerning deep dyspareunia. It is quite common in our experience to find women who consistently report more than one type of pain during intercourse. For instance, one third of a group of women reliably diagnosed with vulvar vestibulitis also reported a distinctively different and deeper pain which also occurred during intercourse (Bergeron et al., 1998b).

Gynecological Assessment

Most women reasonably and logically want the potential physical contributors to their pain to be carefully assessed. In our view, the assessment of dyspareunia should always be a multidisciplinary one and should always include a gynecological examination. Such an assessment typically requires specialized knowledge and substantial change from a standard gynecological examination (Steege, 1997). The following special investigations are typically necessary: (1) a cotton swab investigation of the vulvar vestibule to assess vulvar vestibulitis, (2) a careful assessment of the strength and flexibility of the muscles of the pelvic floor, (3) laboratory tests to exclude bacterial or viral infection, and (4) a careful examination for vulvo/vaginal atrophy. Painful or invasive assessment procedures such as colposcopy and laparoscopy are often overused and without adequate preliminary clinical indication.

Most gynecological examinations of women with dyspareunia are uncomfortable for both doctor and patient; as a result, they require a substantial investment of time and energy. It is not surprising that many gynecologists do not wish to be extensively involved. From our perspective, the major requirements for successful gynecological consultation include patience, knowledge of specialized assessment procedures, and a biopsychosocial view of pain and sexuality. In principle, the full participation of a gynecologist in dyspareunia should parallel the role of the urologist in the assessment of erectile dysfunction.

TREATMENT

Background

Recent reviews indicate that a wide variety of psychosocial, medical, and surgical procedures have been used to treat dyspareunia (Meana & Binik, 1994; Bergeron, Binik, Khalifé, & Pagidas, 1996). In the psychosocial realm, treatment interventions have included psychodynamic psychotherapy, cognitive–behavioral interventions for pain, couple therapy, hypnosis, relaxation, biofeedback, and such sex therapy interventions as sensate focus, Kegel exercises, and vaginal dilation. Medical and surgical treatments have included sitz baths, diet, oral medications, topical applications, interferon injections, laser surgery, and vestibulectomy. Overall, it appears that sex therapists and mental health professionals have been relatively inactive as compared with physicians in developing and implementing clinical interventions for dyspareunia. In general, the stated rationales for both the psychosocial and medical/surgical treatments are often not clear and it is our impression that many have been used because they were presumed effective for other related problems (e.g., vaginismus and vaginal infection). Most of the literature consists of case reports or uncontrolled clinical studies. None of the available treatments can be considered empirically validated or efficacious by today's standards (Heiman & Meston, 1997).

As far as we are aware, there is only one therapy outcome study that begins to meet current methodological standards (Heiman & Meston, 1997). This randomized controlled treatment outcome study (Bergeron, Binik, et al.,

1997; Bergeron, Binik, Khalifé, Pagidas, & Glazer, 1998a) compared group cognitive–behavioral therapy (Bergeron & Binik, 1998), surface electromyographic biofeedback (sEMG) (Glazer, Rodke, Swencionis, Hertz, & Young, 1995), and vestibulectomy (Nichols & McGoldrick, 1995; Bergeron, Bouchard, Fortier, Binik, & Khalifé, 1997), in the treatment of dyspareunia resulting from vulvar vestibulitis. The vestibulectomy condition consisted of a minor day surgical procedure involving the excision of the vestibular area. sEMG biofeedback and group cognitive–behavioral therapy both comprised a total of eight sessions over a 12-week period. The biofeedback condition involved practicing a series of muscular contraction/relaxation exercises with a view to increasing proprioception, maintaining stable contractions, and using the pelvic floor muscles exclusively. This treatment also included the use of a portable sEMG trainer for two 20-minute daily home practice sessions. Group cognitive–behavioral therapy included the following: education and information about vulvar vestibulitis and how dyspareunia affects desire, arousal, and orgasm; education concerning a multifactorial view of pain; education about sexual anatomy; relaxation techniques, Kegel exercises, vaginal dilation exercises, and cognitive restructuring exercises (replacing erroneous or irrational beliefs about pain and sexuality by more realistic ones). Avoidance of sexual activities was also actively and regularly addressed.

Subjects were 78 women randomly assigned to one of three treatment conditions and assessed at pretreatment, posttreatment, and 6-month follow-up via gynecological examinations, structured interviews, and standard questionnaires pertaining to pain, sexual function, and psychosocial adjustment. As compared with pretreatment, all treatment groups reported statistically significant reductions on pain measures at posttreatment and 6-month follow-up, although the vestibulectomy group was significantly more successful than the two other groups. Overall, approximately 65% of the vestibulectomy patients could be considered "treatment successes" at the 6-month follow-up as opposed to 30% of the biofeedback and 40% of the cognitive–behavioral group therapy participants. All three groups significantly improved on measures of psychological adjustment and sexual function from pretreatment to 6-month follow-up. A 2½-year follow-up is currently under way. Results of this study suggest that women with dyspareunia can benefit from both medical and behavioral interventions. Unfortunately, our data do not identify which clients are most likely to benefit from which treatment.

Given the almost total lack of psychosocial therapy outcome studies or reported clinical experience for most types of dyspareunia, we will focus the rest of our discussion on vulvar vestibulitis syndrome. There are several additional justifications for this. First, vulvar vestibulitis is thought to be the most common form of premenopausal dyspareunia (Friedrich, 1987). Second, current treatment recommendations from the American College of Obstetrics and Gynecology (ACOG; 1997) more or less ignore psychosocial approaches. Finally, we believe that the general principles underlying our approach will be applicable to other types of dyspareunia.

Therapeutic Principles

Our approach to treatment follows directly from our multidisciplinary pain focused assessment approach. Our treatment team includes gynecologists, clinical psychologist/sex therapists, and physical therapists. We also find it useful to consult closely with basic science pain specialists. In our view, it is unlikely that any simple or unimodal intervention will "cure" most women. What is required is a multidisciplinary and coordinated treatment approach that will deal with the different aspects of the pain and its effects. In general, therapeutic efforts must be directed toward three major goals: (1) reducing or controlling the pain, (2) dealing with the negative consequences of having experienced the pain; and (3) reestablishing a pleasurable sex life.

For some women reducing or controlling the pain will almost automatically lead to dramatic improvements in their sexual relationships and quality of life. For others, pain relief may only bring to the surface pre- or coexisting other problems. Sometimes, dealing with the negative consequences of the problem (e.g., catastrophizing and relationship difficulties) must precede or parallel pain relief efforts. For some women, pain during intercourse is associated with feelings of dependency, loss, abandonment, or the experience of trauma. The use of in-depth psychotherapeutic approaches may be necessary to motivate pain control attempts. We have found that our ability to predict which kinds or which order of intervention will be the most effective rarely exceeds chance. As a result, we typically explain to the client the range of possible interventions and indicate that at our current state of knowledge, we often cannot predict which interventions will be most effective. We usually suggest the least invasive therapeutic options as a first step and leave it to the client to decide which or how many to pursue initially. In the absence of clear guidelines, we find that placing the burden of responsibility for treatment choice on the client is a useful therapeutic strategy. One member of the team typically becomes the main contact person for a particular client and coordinates further treatment interventions should initial ones fail.

Unfortunately, as far as we are aware, multidisciplinary teams currently dealing with dyspareunia are rare. Sex therapists are often consulted after unsuccessful or partially successful treatment by a variety of medical and other professionals who may have given the client conflicting and confusing messages about treatment. The frustration, anxiety, anger, and depression resulting from the referral process and the lack of symptom remission is a common initial problem with which sex therapists will have to deal. Sex therapists may naturally tend to overemphasize the sexual interference. Although this is an important goal, it is always useful to keep a therapeutic focus on the pain whether or not one believes this to be the "true" problem. Many, if not most, women with dyspareunia prefer to consider their problem a pain syndrome rather than a sexual dysfunction. Creating a therapeutic alliance on this issue may be useful in promoting adherence. One disadvantage of the pain label is that many laypeople tend to reduce pain to physical pathology. It is, therefore, often necessary to explain the biopsychosocial nature of pain and why non-medical interventions can be helpful. We often give an explanation something like the following:

"The pain that you experience during intercourse is the result of different causes that develop over time and become connected to each other in a negative feedback loop. For example, one cause involves physical factors related to the nerves of your vulva (vagina, uterus, etc.) which appear to be hypersensitive to touch and friction. This original injury may have been caused by an infection, virus, allergy or any local irritation to the area. Some treatments like surgery are focussed on eliminating these damaged nerves.

"What often happens, however, when you suffer from pain for an extended period of time, is that the muscles surrounding the painful area become contracted and tense in an effort to protect the area. When the pain is short-lived (e.g. a cut), this reaction is helpful; when the pain continues or recurs, like in dyspareunia, then this muscular reaction may actually increase the pain by adding muscle pain to the original pain. This increased muscular tension may make penetration more difficult and may reduce blood flow to the vulva and vagina thus reducing lubrication and feelings of arousal. This is why physical therapy can be helpful.

"As the pain continues and your sex life is affected your reaction to the pain also begins to have important effects. Women will often have thoughts such as "I cannot live with this problem; it's unbearable." These kinds of thoughts are called catastrophizing and individuals who focus on them frequently tend to report higher levels of pain. These thoughts can also provoke unpleasant emotional states such as anxiety, depression, or increased stress. Such emotional states are known to affect the chemical balance in your body and brain which may further increase your pain. Your interest in sex may diminish, which in turn will also affect the pain since you may naturally anticipate the pain and focus more on it, as opposed to focusing on sexual thoughts and sensations. Finally, your partner also reacts to your pain, and his reactions or your worries about his reactions may affect your perception of pain. He may initiate sex less often or become more tentative in touching you which may further decrease your arousal and interest and increase your stress.

"By using sex therapy, pain management and cognitive interventions, we can reduce the negative effect that your thoughts, emotions and interactions with your partner can have on your pain. In fact, these interventions can help maximize the beneficial effects that positive thoughts, a good sex life and a positive relationship can have on reducing or eliminating your pain."

We find that an explanation like this is helpful in informing women about causes of their pain and in motivating them to engage in active coping.

Two additional general therapeutic issues are relevant. First, we have not been able to develop guidelines concerning whether or when individual, couple, or group treatment is ideal. The arguments for and against each option are already familiar to most sex therapists. Because many women with vulvar vestibulitis are very young and do not have established relationships, partner involvement is often not an option. A vulvar vestibulitis or dyspareunia group may then provide a therapeutically supportive and motivating environment. For those women involved in a stable relationship, we typically ask the couple to consider the pros and cons of coming to therapy together and then make a decision. Whatever the decision, we attempt to maintain the flexibility of including or excluding the partner as therapy goals dictate. Second, we often need to emphasize to our clients that the original etiology of the problem may no longer be a clinically relevant issue. For example, many women with vulvar vestibulitis report the onset of their pain to coincide with a vaginal infection. Even when the infection has long passed the pain during intercourse remains. This sequence of events can be explained by some pain models, but the explanations are speculative and certainly not intuitively obvious to clients or many professionals for that matter. We often admit that we are not certain about how the pain started but we may be able to help relieve it without fully understanding the original cause.

CASE STUDIES

The following three case summaries illustrate many of the issues that sex therapists or mental health clinicians will face in treating women with dyspareunia resulting from vulvar vestibulitis syndrome. We have tentatively labeled the cases as "successful," "partially successful," and "unsuccessful."

Case 1: Successful

Assessment

Jane, a 25-year-old university student, had been diagnosed with vulvar vestibulitis 2 years previously at about the same time she had begun her current relationship. At that time, she experienced several yeast infections which responded to medication and have not recurred. However, the pain that was originally associated with the yeast infections did not subside and ultimately developed into a "sharp, tearing" sensation which Jane experienced during penetration. Once penetration was achieved, her pain diminished somewhat but she still described it as "horrible" and experienced no pleasure during intercourse. Jane did not report pain in other situations. She did, however, report that gynecological examinations were "very unpleasant" and she did not use tampons because "it wasn't necessary." Her gynecologist told her that she had "particularly tense vaginal muscles" and it would be useful to consult a sex therapist. Prior to consulting, Jane had been prescribed a topical cortisone application and antibiotics and had undergone laser surgery followed by a "minor vestibulectomy," which occurred 2 weeks before initiating the sex therapy.

Although she and her partner, John, age 26, had not attempted intercourse for approximately 6 months, they were still active sexually using manual and oral stimulation about twice a week. Jane was orgasmic about two thirds of the time, whereas John was always orgasmic. Although she was aware that most of her friends did not agree with her, Jane "did not like masturbation" and saw it as a temporary substitute to intercourse, which she was desperate to resume. Jane reported that her desire and arousal had diminished over the course of their relationship and she attributed this to the pain. She also reported being a successful but somewhat compulsive student who was anxious to succeed. She dealt with her studies and stress in general, by "overcontrolling," and when this did not work tended to catastrophize.

Jane reported that she and John were committed to a long-term relationship and had begun to discuss the possibility of having children. John was working full time while finishing his university degree at night. He was unable to attend any assessment or treatment sessions because of these commitments, but Jane felt that he would be very supportive and help in any way necessary. She reported that although they had very different personalities, their communication was excellent, and they shared a large number of interests and friends. They both maintained separate apartments but slept together several times a week. Both had experienced previous serious relationships which had been successful sexually and interpersonally but had broken up because of a variety of "normal" factors such as a partner moving away, reluctance to commit, and so on. Their family and personal histories were unremarkable.

Treatment

The goals of treatment were to learn to relax vaginal muscles, reduce pain during penetration and intercourse, and increase desire and arousal. The treatment included interventions such as information concerning a biopsychosocial perspective on pain and sexuality, cognitive restructuring, and behavioral exercises such as, self-exploration, relaxation, Kegel exercises, vaginal dilation, and biofeedback with a home trainer. Pain was monitored via a diary of pain experiences. Thirteen therapy sessions occurred over a period of 7 months. Much of the therapy focused on Jane's overcontrolling and catastrophizing coping style.

When Jane was feeling anxious about pain and penetration, she tended to take control of the couple's sexual interactions; this pattern greatly frustrated her partner and typically reduced her pleasure. For example, when John initiated sex, Jane would often insist on practicing her biofeedback exercises first. Although Jane was quite willing to experience penetration in the context of a "dilation exercise," she was hesitant to try it in the context of a "sexual activity." Much of the therapy was thus directed at helping Jane find more constructive ways of diminishing her legitimate anxiety about experiencing more pain. She was encouraged to (1) engage in clearer and more frequent communication with her partner, (2) focus on pleasure rather than performance, (3) put less pressure on herself to "succeed" at intercourse, and (4) view her pain in a less dramatic manner.

Although John was concerned and supportive of Jane in her attempts to overcome the pain, Jane initially refused to discuss anything related to the pain with him. Over the course of therapy, she gradually began to initiate such discussions with John and was reinforced by the fact that he responded positively to these attempts. He independently echoed the therapist's suggestion that sex was an opportunity to relax and share intimacy and pleasure rather than an opportunity to perform and achieve. Midway through therapy, Jane "confessed" to the therapist that much of her anxiety about intercourse was accompanied by recurrent images of her vagina stretching, tearing, and finally ripping while she experienced severe pain. The therapist reassured her concerning this image and provided her with coping self-statements (e.g., "I am feeling some pain now, but I know how to deal with it"; " I can reduce my pain by imagining pleasant scenes") and by encouraging her to replace the unpleasant images with relaxing and sexy ones.

Jane was a highly motivated and compliant patient who did her homework diligently and never missed a session. Despite her initial shyness in discussing sexual matters with a stranger, a strong therapeutic alliance quickly developed; this alliance was probably facilitated by the fact that patient and therapist were similar in age and background. Although John did not attend the sessions, Jane ultimately made significant efforts to involve her partner in the treatment. Her increased attempts to communicate with him were reciprocated on his part by disclosures of his anxieties concerning his ability to succeed in his studies. She responded empathically and began to help him structure and plan his work. By the end of treatment, Jane was experiencing pain-free intercourse about twice a week. She reported increased desire and arousal and had experienced her first orgasm during intercourse.

Comment

Despite the positive outcome of this case, it is hard to infer the source(s) of the pain or the essential therapeutic mechanisms. In addition to the unknown original cause of vulvar vestibulitis, there were at least several other potential sources to Jane's pain including the following: tense pelvic muscles, decreased arousal, an overcontrolling and catastrophizing coping style, a lack of communication with her partner, and a performance-oriented approach to intercourse. A variety of factors potentially contributed to the positive outcome including the vestibulectomy, the psychotherapeutic interventions, a relatively early diagnosis and treatment, the prior experience of pain-free intercourse, a healthy family background, a stable dyadic relationship, the absence of major life stresses, the maintenance of sexual activities other than intercourse, excellent adherence to behavioral assignments, and a good therapeutic alliance with the therapist.

Case 2: Partially Successful

Assessment

Joan, a 28-year-old college professor, had suffered from dyspareunia since her first intercourse attempt at age 18. Her pain, which had a burning and cutting quality, first occurred during penetration, lasted throughout intercourse, and persisted for about a half an hour afterward. She sometimes experienced pain while riding a bicycle or wearing tight clothing and avoided the use of tampons because she didn't "like them." Gynecological examinations were always painful. The intensity of her coital pain varied depending on her sexual partner but had been most intense with her current cohabiting partner of 5 years who was a 36-year-old building supervisor. She also experienced pain during oral or manual stimulation depending on where her partner touched her. In three previous unsuccessful relationships she had experienced intense coital pain. Joan attributed the breakup of these relationships to her pain. She had considered her pain a "normal" part of sex until she read a magazine article and began to seek help. She was referred to us several years later after having received a diagnosis of vulvar vestibulitis and subsequently undergoing a vestibulectomy. The surgery was considered a failure by her gynecologist because her pain intensified afterward. Our gynecologist confirmed the diagnosis of vulvar vestibulitis via the cotton swab test but could find no gynecological pathology other than some "possible minor inflammation" of the vulvar vestibule. A later colposcopic examination revealed nothing.

Joan and Jack were seen in separate initial assessment interviews at their request. She reported low desire for her partner and difficulty becoming aroused during foreplay. She did, however, report significant attraction to male colleagues at work. Jack usually initiated sex but according to Joan he did this in ways that were irritating to her. Joan did not currently masturbate on her own but had masturbated about once a month before the relationship began. In the last year, Jack had greatly reduced the frequency of his initiation, but in an attempt to improve their sex life, the couple had begun to frequently use erotica and a vibrator which helped give Joan a sense of control over the pain. She was reliably orgasmic during masturbation alone or with a partner if painful spots were avoided.

Joan stated that her dyspareunia and concomitant lack of arousal had quite a negative impact on her partner, who took it as a blow to his masculinity. He confirmed this in a separate individual interview and indicated that he had totally lost his sexual desire, which he interpreted as a defense mechanism to protect himself from frustration. Jack reported a series of previous relationships in all of which the women appeared to experience sexual problems. He was quite dubious about the success of therapy and asserted that if it were not a success, he would leave the relationship.

As a couple, Joan and Jack spent a lot of their free time together but did not engage in many outside activities. When they socialized, it was with Joan's friends and family as Jack did not get along well with his family and did not appear to have close friends. Jack was aloof, unemotional, concrete, and generally unmotivated about work or outside interests. Joan was anxious, eager to please, quite psychologically minded, emotional, and a workaholic. They both reported having excellent communication and being good friends, but Jack felt that Joan was too dependent on him financially and psychologically. Jack had been initially reluctant to get involved with Joan because they met when she was a student and he had not felt that she was ready to settle down.

In addition to vulvar vestibulitis, Joan had experienced repeated vaginal infections throughout her relationship with Jack. She also had a variety of vague and recurring somatic complaints and had been diagnosed by one physician as suffering from fibromyalgia. These somatic complaints also interfered with sex. She had experienced one depressive episode upon the breakup of a relationship in graduate school for which she had briefly taken antidepressants and anxiolytics. Jack suffered from mild hypertension and high cholesterol and was taking a variety of medications to control these. He also complained of chronic fatigue.

Treatment

The goals of therapy included decreasing pain during intercourse, increasing arousal and desire, and learning to make more time for pleasure and intimacy. Both Joan and Jack attended most of the 20 therapy sessions which were spaced over a period of 6 months. Initial treatment sessions focused on information concerning vulvar vestibulitis and dealing with the disappointment over the failure of the vestibulectomy. Much session time was spent trying to improve communication about sex in an attempt to improve desire and arousal and increase sensitivity about their respective needs. A variety of behavioral exercises were discussed or suggested, including pain monitoring, sensate focus, Kegel exercises, vaginal dilation, and biofeedback. The couple never showed any enthusiasm for these exercises and consistently failed to implement them. After this pattern became apparent, no further homework assignments were discussed. At the therapist's recommendation, Joan did consult a physical therapist for several sessions.

Joan's fear of abandonment and low self-esteem became an important focus of the therapy. She believed that Jack would leave her if she did not solve "her problem" and Jack initially confirmed this. Her attraction to other men, which she expressed openly to Jack, appeared to be a way of protecting herself from his ultimate abandonment. Her low self-esteem drove her to excel at her academic work, about which she became increasingly obsessive and perfectionist. She found that it became harder to relax and forget about work. Jack, on the other hand, found himself in a dead-end job and felt professionally inferior to Joan. This feeling coupled with his history of unsuccessful relationships also resulted in a low self-esteem and borderline depression. Although he threatened to leave Joan if she did not solve her dyspareunia problem, he was afraid that this relationship, as all his previous ones, would not work out. While Joan worked at home, he did very little except complain that she was working too much, ignoring him, and avoiding sex.

When Joan and Jack realized that they both wanted the relationship to continue, the pattern of their interactions changed. Joan lost interest in men at work and made more time at home to spend with Jack. Jack stopped threatening to leave and became much more active in the therapy and in supporting Joan psychologically. She began to feel desire for Jack and was willing to engage in nonpainful sex. Joan began to initiate sex occasionally but still felt moderate pain during penetration and intercourse. Jack reported that Joan was much more relaxed at home and a pleasure to be with. They began going out together and socializing more frequently with friends.

At the beginning of treatment, Joan appeared highly motivated but Jack would say little. Joan often cried during the sessions and appeared distressed about her pain yet resisted most suggestions made by the therapist. Her high anxiety level often slowed discussion of key issues. When Jack became more active in the sessions, they began to make significant interpersonal progress and diminished their use of avoidant coping styles. When Joan's spring term was over, they planned a long relaxing break at a remote cottage they had rented for the summer. Jack quit his job and registered for an MBA program in the fall. They suggested a break from therapy until the fall. When they returned after the summer, Joan's pain was very much reduced and her desire and arousal had increased dramatically. They had engaged in intercourse several times a week over the summer with great pleasure on both their parts. Jack no longer looked depressed and expressed enthusiasm about returning to school. They felt that they did not need further therapy. Two months later they called the therapist to say that Joan still felt pain during intercourse but was more concerned about her lack of desire and arousal. Once she began teaching and immersing herself in her research, she seemed to lose interest in sex. She hoped to be able to control her obsessive involvement in work and thus reinstate her desire. Jack was very busy and doing well in his MBA course. He was optimistic about their sex life and future together.

Comment

Joan and Jack came to therapy with a lot of accumulated frustration and distress concerning their previously unsuccessful sex lives, the failed vestibulectomy, and their stressful work situations. Neither had any desire for sex and both had medical problems that interfered with their sexual and professional lives. All these factors, in addition to dependency and low self-esteem issues, complicated the problem of painful intercourse. The turning point in therapy appears to have been their mutual discovery that they both wanted a committed relationship with each other. Pain during intercourse was significantly reduced but did not totally disappear. At follow-up, the pain during intercourse had increased slightly but Joan's fluctuating desire became her major concern. She was convinced that this was related to her workaholism, which she was attempting to control. Jack seemed to have become less concerned with sex altogether, perhaps as a result of quitting his job and starting a new career. Both were enjoying their relationship and felt that they were building a future together. The therapist felt that although there had been important progress, therapy termination was premature and that pain, desire, and commitment issues had not been adequately resolved.

Case 3: Unsuccessful

Assessment

Jill, a 37-year-old single administrative assistant for a local company, was referred by her gynecologist for a problem of low desire. She came alone to the assessment. Jill insisted that she experienced no desire for her cohabiting partner of 2 years, Jerry, and had not experienced significant desire for many years. She did report masturbating about once a month to relax and having the occasional sexual dream but said that these were not important indications of desire. Jill was not interested in foreplay or other sexual activities and reported very little, if any, arousal or interest toward sexual stimuli. She maintained that she could easily experience orgasm during appropriate oral or manual stimulation but that it just was not worth the effort. It had been about 8 months since Jill had engaged in any intimate contact with Jerry and she was worried about the future of their relationship. Jill had been to see an endocrinologist, who indicated that her hormonal levels were in the "low normal" range; otherwise, she was in excellent health.

Upon questioning, Jill indicated that she had always experienced pain during intercourse and had accepted this as "just the way she was." She described this pain as "stabbing" during penetration and burning during intercourse. The burning pain lasted for up to 24 hours after intercourse and was particularly painful when she urinated. Jill had experienced pain since her first attempt at intercourse at age 19, which she had described as "excruciatingly painful." After this attempt, she consulted a gynecologist who said she had an imperforate hymen which was subsequently surgically removed. The pain, however, persisted in early sexual relationships even when she did experience significant amounts of arousal and desire. Upon examination by one of the gynecologists on our team, Jill manifested maximal pain ratings limited to the vulvar vestibule during the cotton swab test. There were no other gynecological findings.

Jill reported "not being able to remember most of her childhood," which she nonetheless described as unhappy and restricted as a result of her family's ethnic and religious background. She described her mother as always angry and her father as nonexistent although physically present in the house. She said that she did remember one instance at age 12 when her older brother exposed himself to her. She ran away and nothing else happened.

Jill's initial goals in coming to therapy were to be able to have "enough sex with her partner in order to keep him." She also felt that he was uncommunicative and unromantic but felt that there was a possible future to their relationship and wanted to sort out her feelings about this. She had once before started therapy and had found it useful but was unable to afford it at that point. For the moment she preferred to come alone to therapy but was willing to consider including her partner in treatment. Jerry was aware that she was consulting a therapist and had offered to participate.

Therapy

Over a period of a year, Jill came to therapy for 9 individual sessions, 11 conjoint sessions with Jerry, and 5 additional individual sessions. In the first 9 sessions of therapy, Jill obsessed about whether to pursue her relationship with Jerry. Although she acknowledged that dealing with her own sexual issues was a necessity, she was not willing to spend much time on this. She did not carry out any sexually related homework exercises and as a result these were ultimately dropped. She resisted attempts to talk about her childhood but focused on day-to-day difficulties in her current relationship. She pointed out that Jerry was a very happy-go-lucky guy who took care of immediate household requirements but refused to consider the future. This was in contrast to her perfectionistic long-term planning in which he refused to participate. She was also frustrated by his lack of interest in discussing his feelings. Jill was still "haunted" by an "ideal" relationship that had ended about 15 years earlier because of her sexual difficulties. She was still occasionally in touch with this man who had since married and settled down but maintained that he still loved her. Jerry was unaware of this history, nor was he aware of Jill's feelings.

Without warning at session 10, Jill brought Jerry to therapy announcing that she had decided to work on their relationship. Jerry was an intelligent, 42-year-old factory worker who had been divorced 4 years previously after a 20-year marriage. Jerry's previous marriage had broken up because his wife had lost her job and become depressed and he had been unable to support her when she needed it. She had asked him to come to therapy with her but he refused. She went alone and came to the conclusion that she was better off without him. He came to therapy announcing that he was not going to make the same mistake twice.

Jerry confirmed most of what Jill had previously asserted about their relationship. He stressed that after being an intense worrier and having an ulcer when he was younger, he was never going to worry again. He said he could make problems go away by avoiding them and intended to continue doing that. He said that if Jill wanted to plan and worry, he would go along with whatever she decided but would not participate in the process. This is, in fact, how they solved their budgeting problems after several stormy sessions of discussion. She drew up a budget, collected his check, pooled it with hers, paid the bills, and issued him an allowance. Jerry was very happy with this outcome but had also been happy with their lack of planning and their debts before.

Jerry did bring up one issue about which he was not happy. Jill wanted children and felt that at age 37, this had to happen soon. Jerry was actively disinterested, saying that he had never wanted children and was too old. He did not discount the possibility altogether but kept delaying in making a final decision. At one point, Jill gave him an ultimatum saying that he had to agree to have children or that he would have to move out. He began to look for an apartment and she relented.

Jerry asserted that Jill was too emotional, too perfectionist, and too anxious. He said that she exaggerated all the negative aspects of their relationship and that on a day-to-day basis they got along very well. He acknowledged the difficulty with sex and her pain during intercourse but was optimistic that a solution could be found. He admitted, in a somewhat embarrassed fashion, that he was so horny all the time that on the few occasions that Jill agreed to have intercourse, he barely noticed her pain.

After 11 sessions of conjoint therapy, Jill came to therapy alone. She said that Jerry felt that there was no longer any purpose for therapy together but that if she wanted to come alone, he was not opposed. She returned to focusing on the future of the relationship and her wish to have children. She said that she no longer wanted to force Jerry to reach a solution and was reluctant to do anything to endanger the relationship. Although she acknowledged that her pain during intercourse was a serious problem and was probably closely related to her lack of desire, she was reluctant to open any discussion concerning sexuality or pain and rejected both medical and psychosocial interventions. She had begun to have intercourse with Jerry once a week despite severe pain and hoped that this would make him more amenable to the idea of children. At our last session, she announced that she was tired of struggling and that perhaps Jerry was right that things were not so bad.

Comment

The issue of pain during intercourse was never directly dealt with in this therapy. Jill felt that couple and relationship issues were primary. Although she acknowledged that issues related to sexuality and pain were important, she avoided dealing with them. When the therapist confronted her about this avoidance, she insisted that she was not avoiding but was trying first to deal with what was most important in her current life. At one point the therapist suggested that there was more to the story of her brother exposing himself. She calmly disagreed saying that if she had really felt abused or traumatized, she would be more than happy to discuss it. She felt fortunate that this one instance had not affected her and she did not think she had forgotten any others. Jerry would have probably liked to deal with sexual issues in therapy but did not pursue it.

Overall, there was little progress on any of the individual or couple issues. Neither Jill nor Jerry was highly motivated to change their individual patterns except if it were absolutely necessary to accommodate the other. They each appeared to recognize that their partner's different personality constituted a good counterbalance to their own. They also realized that it would be difficult for the other to change in any basic way. Although it was never explicitly stated, the therapist believed that the couple was reaching the tacit agreement that if Jill would consent to regular intercourse, Jack would agree to having children.

CONCLUDING COMMENTS

Determining the success or failure of therapy is a difficult endeavor. The criterion we used for the previous examples and the one we believe should be used for all cases of dyspareunia is pain reduction because pain is the defining characteristic of the problem. How to assess outcome when the central symptom does not improve but the client makes significant progress on other important and related issues is not an unfamiliar problem to sex therapists. Although we believe that dyspareunia is best conceptualized as a pain problem, this idea remains controversial (Meana, Binik, Khalifé, Bergeron, et al., 1997). Whatever the final conceptualization of dyspareunia, it is important for sex therapists to begin to pay attention to this neglected women's health problem as interference with sexual intercourse is the major motivation for treatment. Once this interference becomes chronic, removal of the original symptom, the pain, may often not be sufficient to allow for the resumption or the development of a satisfying sexual life. This task requires intensive and focused interventions relating to sexual feelings, attitudes, and behaviors. Sex therapists are uniquely suited to carry out this important therapeutic task.

REFERENCES

Abarbanel, A. R. (1978). Diagnosis and treatment of coital discomfort. In J. Lopiccolo & L. LoPiccolo (Eds.), *Handbook of sex therapy* (pp. 241–259). New York: Plenum.

American College of Obstetricians and Gyencolgists. (1997, October). Vulvar nonneoplastic epithelial disorders. *ACOG Educational Bulletin, 241,* 1–7.

American Psychiatric Association. (1994). *Diagnostic and statistical manual of mental disorders* (4th ed.). Washington, DC: Author.

Basson, R., & Riley, A. J. (1994). Vulvar vestibulitis syndrome: A common condition which may present as vaginismus. *Sexual and Marital Therapy, 9,* 221–224.

Bergeron, S., & Binik, Y. M. (1998). *Treatment manual for cognitive–behavioral group therapy with women suffering from vulvar vestibulitis.* Unpublished treatment manual, McGill University, Montreal.

Bergeron, S., Binik, Y. M. Khalifé, S., Meana, M. Berkley, K. J. & Pagidas, K. (1997). The treatment of vulvar vestibulitis syndrome: Toward a multimodal approach. *Sexual and Marital Therapy, 12,* 305–311.

Bergeron, S., Binik, Y. M., Khalifé, S., & Pagidas, K. (1996). Vulvar vestibulitis syndrome: A critical review. *Clinical Journal of Pain, 13,* 27–42.

Bergeron, S., Binik, Y. M., Khalifé, S., Pagidas, K., & Glazer, H. A. (1998a). *A randomized comparison of group cognitive–behavioral therapy, surface electromyographic biofeedback, and vestibulectomy in the treatment of dyspareunia resulting from vulvar vestibulitis.* Manuscript submitted for publication.

Bergeron, S., Binik, Y. M., Khalifé, S., Pagidas, K., & Glazer, H. (1998b). *Reliability and validity of the diagnosis of vulvar vestibulitis syndrome.* Manuscript submitted for publication

Bergeron, S., Bouchard, C., Fortier, M., Binik, Y. M., & Khalifé, S. (1997). The surgical treatment of vulvar vestibulitis syndrome: A follow-up study. *Journal of Sex and Marital Therapy, 23,* 317–325.

Binik, Y. M. & Koerner, N. (1998). [Catastrophizing as a predictor of pain ratings in the cotton swab test]. Unpublished raw data.

Flor, H., Turk, D. C., & Rudy, T. E. (1989). Relationship of pain impact and significant other reinforcement of pain behaviors; the mediating role of gender, marital status and marital satisfaction. *Pain, 38,* 45–50.

Friedrich, E. G. (1987). Vulvar vestibulitis syndrome. *Journal of Reproductive Medicine, 32,* 110–114.

Glazer, H. I., Rodke, G., Swencionis, C., Hertz, R., & Young, A. W. (1995). The treatment of vulvar vestibulitis syndrome by electromyographic biofeedback of pelvic floor musculature. *Journal of Reproductive Medicine, 40,* 283–290.

Heiman, J. R., & Meston, C. M. (1997). Empirically validated treatment for sexual dysfunction. *Annual Review of Sex Research, 8,* 148–194.

Kaplan, H. S. (1974). *The new sex therapy.* New York: Brunner/Mazel.

Laan, E., & van Lunsen, R. H. W. (1997). Hormones and sexuality in postmenopausal women: A psychophysiological study. *Journal of Psychosomatic Obstetrics and Gynecology, 18,* 126–133.

Leventhal, H., Benyamini, Y., Brownlee, S., Diefenbach, M., Leventhal, E. A. Patrick-Miller, L., & Robitaille, C. (1997). Illness representations: Theoretical foundations. In K. J. Petrie & J. A. Weinman (Eds.), *Perception of health and illness* (pp. 19–45). New York: Harwood.

LoPiccolo, J. (1992). Postmodern sex therapy for erectile failure. In R. C. Rosen & S. R. Leiblum (Eds.), *Erectile disorders: Assessment and treatment* (pp. 171–197). New York: Guilford Press.

Masters, W. H., & Johnson, V. E. (1970). *Human sexual inadequacy.* Boston: Little, Brown.

Maurice, W. L. (1998). *Sexual medicine in primary care.* Toronto, Canada: Mosby.

Meana, M., & Binik, Y. M. (1994). Painful coitus: A review of female dyspareunia. *Journal of Nervous and Mental Disease, 182,* 264–272.

Meana, M., Binik, Y. M., Khalifé, S., Bergeron, S. Pagidas, K., & Berkley, K. J. (1997). Dyspareunia: More than bad sex. *Pain, 71,* 211–212.

Meana, M., Binik, Y. M., Khalifé, S., & Cohen, D. (1997a). Dyspareunia: Sexual dysfunction or pain syndrome? *Journal of Nervous and Mental Disease, 185,* 561–569.

Meana, M., Binik, Y. M., Khalifé, S., & Cohen, D. (1997b). Biopsychosocial profile of women with dyspareunia. *Obstetrics and Gynecology, 90,* 4, 583–589.

Meana, M., Binik, Y. M., Khalifé, S., & Cohen, D. (1998). Affect and marital adjustment in women's rating of dyspareunic pain. *Canadian Journal of Psychiatry, 43,* 381–385.

Meana, M., Binik, Y. M., Khalifé, S., & Cohen, D. (1999). Psychosocial correlates of pain attributions in women with dyspareunia. *Psychosomatics, 40,* 497–502.

Melzack, R., & Katz, J. (1992). The McGill Pain Questionnaire: Appraisal and current status. In D. C. Turk & R. Melzack (Eds.), *Handbook of pain assessment* (pp. 152–164). New York: Guilford Press.

Melzack, R., & Wall, P. D. (1982). *The challenge of pain.* New York: Basic Books.

Nichols, D. H., & McGoldrick, K. L. (1995). Minor and ambulatory surgery. In D. H. Nichols & P. J. Sweeny (Eds.), *Ambulatory gynecology* (pp. 407–409). Philadelphia: Lippincott.

O'Donahue, W. O., & Geer, J. H. (1993). *Handbook of sexual dysfunctions.* Boston: Allyn & Bacon.

Plouffe, L. (1985). Screening for sexual problems through a simple questionnaire. *American Journal of Obstetrics and Gynecology, 151,* 166–168.

Rapkin, A. J. (1995). Gynecological pain in the clinic: Is there a link with the basic research? In G. F. Gebhart (Ed.), *Visceral pain, progress in pain research and management* (vol. 5, pp. 469–488). Seattle, WA: International Association for the Study of Pain Press.

Reissing, E., Binik, Y. M. & Khalifé, S. (1999). Does vaginismus exist?: A critical review of the literature. *Journal of Nervous and Mental Disease, 187,* 261–274.

Schover, L. R., & Jensen, S. B. (1988). *Sexuality and chronic illness.* NY: Guilford Press.

Smith, E., & Buck, N. (1983). Dyspareunia. In J. K. Meyer, C. S. Schmidt, & T. N. Wise (Eds.), *Clinical management of sexual disorders* (pp. 205–215). Baltimore, MD: Williams & Wilkins.

Steege, J. F. (1997). Office assessment of chronic pelvic pain, *Clinical Obstetrics and Gynecology, 40,* 554–563.

Steege, J. F. (1998). Scope of the problem. In J. F. Steege, D. A. Metzger, & B. S. Levy (Eds.), *Chronic pelvic pain* (pp. 1–4). Philadelphia: Saunders.

Sullivan, M. J. L., Bishop, S. R., & Pivik, J. (1995). The Pain Catastrophizing Scale: Development and validation, *Psychological Assessment, 7,* 524–532.

Van Lankveld, J. J. D. D. M., Brewaeys, A. M. A., Ter Kuile, M. M., & Weijenborg, P. TH. M. (1995). Difficulties in the differential diagnosis of vaginismus, dyspareunia and mixed sexual pain disorder. *Journal of Psychosomatic Obstetrics and Gynecology, 16,* 201–209.

Van Lankveld, J. J. D. D. M., Weijenborg, P. TH. M., & Ter Kuile, M. M. (1996). Psychologic profiles of and sexual function in women with vulvar vestibulitis and their partners. *Obstetrics and Gynecology, 88,* 65–70.

Wouda, J. C., Hartman, P. M., Bakker, R. M., Bakker, J. O., van de Wiel, H. B. M., & Weijmar Schultz, W. C. M. (1998). Vaginal plethysmography in women with dyspareunia. *Journal of Sex Research, 35,* 141–147.

7

Vaginismus
A Most Perplexing Problem

SANDRA R. LEIBLUM

In recent decades, there has been an outpouring of media materials and self-help literature devoted to female sexual problems. In many respects, sexual education and societal permissiveness in this area are greater than ever. Nevertheless, the incidence of women complaining of vaginismus, the specific difficulty or inability to tolerate genital penetration, has remained essentially unchanged. Although etiological theories have varied, the treatment of vaginismus is still directed at eliminating the spasmodic reflexive contraction of the muscles controlling the vaginal entrance, typically through a series of graduated approximations with the insertion of increasingly larger dilators or fingers.

Although there is increasing appreciation of the role of organic and physical factors that may be contributing to the women's vaginismic difficulty, psychological investigation of the individual woman and her partner relationship is crucial to treatment. This observation holds true even when physical factors might be involved in causing the genital pain, and which are sometimes successfully treated.

What is the motivational issue(s) of the woman seeking treatment for this problem? Often, the desire for a child is as or more intense than the desire to accomplish successful intercourse. Some therapists wonder whether to recommend conception using artificial insemination with the husband's sperm, thereby bypassing the presenting problem of penetration. This may be a welcome suggestion to the woman, but the partner's wishes in this area should be taken into account as well, particularly if the couple's satisfaction is a desired treatment outcome.

Treatment is not always successful, despite the prevailing belief that vaginismus is easily diagnosed and readily treated. Treatment outcome is generally positive with motivated couples in good relationships, but difficulties often accompany cases in which there is persistent pain, little genuine motivation, relationship conflict, and unmotivated or uncooperative partners.

This chapter illustrates two cases, one readily treated, the other more refractory to standard clinical interventions. It is clear that more research is needed into the many physical and psychological determinants of vaginismus, as well as additional outcome studies for determining treatment effectiveness.

Sandra R. Leiblum, PhD, is professor of psychiatry and obstetrics/gynecology, and director of the Center for Sexual and Marital Health at the University of Medicine and Dentistry of New Jersey–Robert Wood Johnson Medical School. She is an authority on female sexual disorders and has published widely in the theory and practice of sex therapy.

Vaginismus is a perplexing and fascinating problem. The woman who experiences the involuntary spasmodic contraction of the puboccygeus and related muscles controlling the vaginal introitus may be unable to tolerate vaginal penetration or have intercourse but may be quite capable of becoming sexually aroused, lubricating and even experiencing multiple orgasms with manual or oral stimulation. In fact, some "virgin" wives and their partners occasionally report a rich sexual repertoire. More commonly, however, women with vaginismus report periods of relative harmony with respect to noncoital sexual exchange followed by outbursts of anger and frustration by partners who are disappointed or humiliated by the absence of intercourse.

It is certainly the case that when a vaginismic woman anticipates or senses that her vagina is going to be "penetrated," she experiences an involuntary spasm of the pelvic muscles surrounding the outer third of her vagina, namely the perineal and levator ani muscles. Her anxiety increases greatly and while the severity of muscular spasm varies, it is often sufficient to prevent penetration of anything from the smallest speculum to the largest phallus. With such a strong fear reaction to vaginal penetration, it is not uncommon for women to have experienced years or even decades of dating and/or marriage without coitus. Many women with this condition have never satisfactorily completed a gynecological examination or used tampons. Consequently, not only is vaginismus a source of considerable personal and relationship frustration, but it thwarts adequate gynecological health care (e.g., Pap smears) and procreation. Often it is either the threat of divorce or the desire to have children that ultimately drives a woman to seek treatment.

Whereas primary vaginismus precludes any sort of vaginal entry, situational vaginismus refers to the woman who can tolerate certain types of penetration, such as that of a tampon or speculum, but who tenses at the anticipation of penile entry. During sexual encounters, the vaginal introitus is reported to be so constricted that it feels impenetrable, like a "wall," and lubrication may be scant. Women with primary vaginismus describe the pain or sensations they experience at the anticipation or attempt of penetration to be "ripping," "tearing," "burning," or "stinging." Not surprisingly, given the women's expression of pain and discomfort at the approach of the penis, over time her partner may have developed erectile problems, or at the very least, may be reluctant to continue attempts at either vaginal or digital penetration.

PREVALENCE

Although figures concerning the incidence of vaginismus vary widely, it is likely that it occurs with greater frequency than is typically acknowledged. Vaginismus rates have been reported as ranging between 12 and 17% of females presenting to sexual therapy clinics (Spector & Carey, 1990). Higher rates have been reported in studies conducted in Canada and Ireland (Lamont, 1978; Barnes, Bowman, & Cullen 1984). The most recent National Health and Sexual Life survey using random sampling and structured interviewing reported that between 10 and 15% of women complained of pain during intercourse during the last 6 months (Laumann, Gagnon, Michael, & Michaels, 1994). However, this study did not differentiate between vaginismus and dyspareunia.

The incidence may vary depending on diagnostic criteria and accuracy, the population studied, and the willingness of women to seek either gynecological or sex therapy treatment. The numbers of women experiencing partial or situational vaginismus without seeking treatment is unknown and may be considerably higher in the general population than in clinic samples.

While primary vaginismus precludes any sort of vaginal entry, situational vaginismus refers to the woman who can tolerate certain types of penetration, such as that of a tampon or speculum, but who panics at the anticipation of intercourse.

HISTORICAL OVERVIEW

Vaginismus was first described in the scientific literature in 1834 by D. K. Huguier, who compared the involuntary spastic constiction of the circumvaginal musculature to the spasms of the anal sphincter as a result of painful fissures The term "vaginismus" was coined by an American gynecologist, J. Marion Sims. In an address to the Obstetrical Society of London in 1862, he said: "From personal observation, I can confidentially assert that I know of no disease capable of producing so much unhappiness to both parties of the marriage contract and I am happy to state that I know of no serious trouble that can be cured so easily so safely and so certainly" (quoted in Drenth, 1988, p. 126).

Sims advocated complete excision of the hymen, a Y-shaped incision of the introitus as far as the perineum, a transection of part of the sphincter muscle, and the use of a glass bougie to be worn for 2 hours twice daily for a few weeks. Today, such treatment is unthinkable. Not only is it ineffective because the fear underlying the symptom is never addressed, but the basic contraction of the circumvaginal muscle will remain.

Nineteenth-century writers assumed that there was a predisposition to the condition. Faure and Sireday (1909) observed that the condition was more common in arranged marriages. First intercourse was often traumatic in these instances and was exacerbated by the woman's ignorance and, perhaps, by her spouse's lack of empathy and adequate foreplay. Although the major cause of the penetration phobia was different for each woman, there was some recognition of the psychosomatic nature of the problem by these early authors (Drenth, 1988).

Early writings about vaginismus also assumed that the disorder was caused by inadequate vaginal size. It is clear, however, that the vagina functions as a potential space which increases in length by approximately 50% during sexual arousal and can accommodate almost any size penis. The vagina itself is composed of smooth muscle with the pubococcygeus muscle surrounding the outer third of the vagina. This muscle is under voluntary control, which is why women are usually successful in learning how to relax and permit vaginal intromission.

THEORETICAL EXPLANATIONS AND APPROACHES TO VAGINISMUS

Psychoanalytical Explanations

Psychoanalytical views have tended to view vaginismus as a rejection of the female role, a resistance against male sexual prerogative, a defense of the woman against her father's real or fantasized incestual threats, and/or a warding off of her own castration images (Drenth, 1988). Musaph (1977), a Dutch physician, suggests that the woman is unconsciously saying to herself, "Now this big, dangerous instrument is going to penetrate me; there will be bleeding wounds; I will suffer unbearable pain and my revenge will be terrible" (quoted in Drenth, 1988, p. 127).

Currently, traditional psychoanalytical therapists advocate an exploration of the unconscious fears and ambivalence underlying the problem. Other psychoanalytic-oriented therapists believe that a more active behavioral approach is needed in addition to unconscious exploration in order to overcome the high anxiety accompanying the symptom. Kaplan (1974), for example, rejects the psychoanalytical view of vaginismus as a conversion symptom expressive of the woman's hostility toward men and her unconscious wish to castrate them in revenge for her own castration. Rather, she suggests a multicausal concept of vaginismus as a conditioned response to any adverse stimulus associated with intercourse or vaginal entry: "vaginismus occurs when a negative contingency becomes associated with the act or fantasy of vaginal penetration" (p. 417) The aim of treatment, then, is the extinction of the conditioned vaginal response, through gradual insertion of rubber or glass catheters until a catheter the size of an erect penis is inserted without pain or discomfort.

Cognitive–Behavioral Explanation and Approaches

Learning theorists generally view vaginismus as a conditioned fear reaction, a learned phobia. Reinforcing the conditioned fear response is the cognitive belief that penetration can only be accomplished with great difficulty as well as pain and discomfort. To overcome the avoidance of intercourse, it is necessary to challenge both the cognitive and the phobic elements.

Masters and Johnson (1970) viewed vaginismus as an involuntary reflex "due to imagined, anticipated, or real attempt at vaginal penetration" (p. 250) They refer to it as a psychosomatic disorder and discuss a variety of etiological factors including a response to male sexual dysfunction, the psychosexually inhibiting influence of religious orthodoxy, prior sexual trauma, a response to homosexual identification, and/or a secondary response to dyspareunia. They also emphasize the importance of acknowledging the contribution of the male partner: "Interestingly, the syndrome has a high percentage of association with primary impotence in the male partner, providing still further clinical evidence to support procedural demand for simultaneous evaluation and treatment of both marital partners" (p. 252). Although the male partner may not initially have had erectile or ejaculatory problems, he may develop them after repeatedly encountering frustration and resistance to vaginal intromission.

A recent case seen at our own center illustrates the importance of treating both partners. The couple, a religiously orthodox Italian–Catholic pair, were raised by "old world" parents. The wife's mother strongly reinforced traditional beliefs. She rebuked her daughter, the patient, if she wore red nail polish—"You look like a whore"—or purchased sheer lingerie. Sex was never discussed and modesty was strictly enforced. The fact that the maternal mother lived with the couple complicated the situation, but neither husband nor wife felt entitled to ask her to leave.

History revealed that both husband and wife were virgins at marriage and had not been successful in accomplishing any sort of penetration during the 5 years of their life together. The wife, a 33-year-old ecologist, initiated the request for treatment only after she had completed her master's degree and felt that the time had finally come to directly address the sexual problems in her marriage. Both she and her husband concurred in assigning the "cause" of their difficulty to the husband's inability to sustain erections. It was only after interviewing the husband alone that it became apparent that his erectile failure had begun only *after* he had made repeated, unsuccessful attempts to penetrate his wife during intercourse on their honeymoon. She had displayed such anxiety and discomfort following the initial intercourse "catastrophe" that they both had avoided all sexual intimacy for the next 6 months. In fact, both husband and wife displayed high degrees of sexual anxiety. He blamed himself for his sexual incompetence and erectile difficulties and she felt inadequate as a woman and as a lover. Neither wanted to expose their perceived inadequacies to a therapist. It was clearly important that they be seen both individually and together if treatment was to be successful.

In their approach to treatment, Masters and Johnson begin with a demonstration of the existence of the involuntary nature of the vaginal spasm or contraction. They consider it important that both partners understand that the response is involuntary and reflexive rather than intentional. Beyond this, the main element of treatment is the use of Hegar dilators in graduated sizes to enable the woman to allow penetration by an object the size of a penis. The use of the dilators is initiated and conducted by the husband with the wife's physical control and verbal direction. Masters and Johnson reported that they had seen 29 cases in 11 years and were successful with each case once the cooperation of the partners in the dilator therapy was obtained. Other therapists have not reported such felicitous results.

Currently, cognitive–behavioral approaches to treatment involve equal attention to the erroneous cognitive beliefs and the conditioned vaginal spasm. The inappropriate cognitions about the size of the vagina—in both its collapsed and aroused state—the size of the penis, and the likelihood of pain are challenged. In a recent case, it was also necessary to explore and confront the patient's feelings about her hymen. She believed that the retention of her hymen signified that she was a "good, pure, and virginal" woman. When she learned that it was likely the case that her hymen had already been broken during her teens when she was an active cyclist, she became more receptive to the anticipation of intercourse, not as a symbolic loss of purity but as a sign of marital commitment. In those instances in which ignorance about sexual anatomy is evident, which almost always exists, the woman may be encouraged to purchase and read *Our Bodies, Ourselves*, as well as other educational books about women and sex, such as *Woman: An Intimate Geography* (Angier, 1999), which provides an enthusiastic and educational introduction to female genitalia.

To reduce the conditioned fear reaction to vaginal penetration, the woman is taught progressive relaxation exercises and is encouraged to begin exploring her vulva in a gentle and deliberate fashion. She may be invited to use a hand mirror to look at her genitals and identify relevant parts. Once she is comfortable with both visual and manual exploration of her external genitals, she is encouraged to begin exploration of her vagina. This is accomplished either with her fingers (beginning with the smallest) or with graduated dilators. The use of external lubricants to promote ease of insertion is recommended, such as Astroglide or K-Y jelly. Throughout the exercises, the woman is reminded that she is in control—she may stop or pause at any time. The rate of progress is determined by the motivation and compliance of the patient with the prescribed assignments.

The Experiential Approach

Drenth (1988), a Dutch sex therapist, suggests that there are women who dislike or fear genital intercourse but who are interested in having a biological child. With these women, traditional treatment with dilators or systematic desensitization is likely to end in failure. In fact, some authors have argued that it may be disrespectful and an unfortunate holdover from a male phallocentric point of view to urge women to overcome their fear of coitus in the face of their antipathy to it. Rather, these authors suggest that it may be useful to explore the womens' thoughts and feelings in greater depth in order to discern the "meaning" of the symptom (Kleinplatz, 1996) and to determine what their body "is trying to tell them" (Keen, 1979, p. 20). The goal of this form of existential–experiential therapy is to promote connection, choice, and embodiment rather than simply vaginal containment. While the goals of this therapeutic approach are appealing, this treatment often ignores or minimizes the dissatisfaction of a male partner who may be quite reluctant to accept or embrace a sexual life that precludes occasional intercourse.

On the other hand, for the couple who agree that intercourse is *not* a requirement of their sexual life together but who want to have children, artificial insemination with the husband's sperm has occasionally provided a route to conception. Although this approach does not resolve the fears about penetration, it does permit the couple to achieve parenthood.

A Reconceptualization of Vaginismus

Reissing, Binik, and Khalifé (1999) and his collaborators have recently suggested that vaginismus is not a useful diagnosis at all and may be better reconceptualized as a genital pain disorder. They note that despite the existence of many etiological theories, none have been supported by controlled empirical studies. In their proposed reconceptualization of vaginismus, Reissing et al. (1999) recommend that vaginismus be considered a type of genital pain disorder with the pain described in terms of quality, intensity, location, and time course. A description of the disorder should detail whether the pain is associated with imagined, attempted, or successful vaginal penetration.

DIFFERENTIAL DIAGNOSIS OF VAGINISMUS AND DYSPAREUNIA

While dyspareunia and vaginismus are distinguished in the fourth edition of *Diagnostic and Statistical Manual of Mental Disorders* (DSM-IV; American Psychiatric Association, 1994), in practice it is sometimes difficult to make the distinction (van Lankveld, Brewaeys, Ter Kuile, & Weijenborg, 1995). The criteria for vaginismus are the "recurrent or persistent involuntary spasm of the musculature of the outer third part of the vagina which prevents sexual intercourse" and is not caused exclusively by physical illness and is not due to another Axis I mental disorder. However, for many patients the report of pain and the vaginismic spasm occur together. In fact, the most immediate cause of superficial dyspareunia is the spasmodic contraction of the vaginal entrance along with inadequate sexual arousal and lubrication. A similar set of etiological factors may lead to either or both dyspareunia and vaginismus, and in such cases the resultant difficulty may be termed "mixed sexual pain disorder." In these instances, it is often the case that even when the physical or biological causes of the pain are treated, the spasmodic vaginal contraction may occur causing partial vaginismus. With *any* complaint of dyspareunia or vaginismus, it is important to assess organic factors that may be causing, contributing to, or maintaining the disorder.

For instance, one important cause of vaginismus is vulvar vestibulitis. Vulvar vestibulitis is discussed in great detail in Chapter 6, on dyspareunia. Suffice it to note that it refers to an inflammatory condition of the vulvar vestibule—the area between the labia minora—which causes exquisite pain when touch—even the most gentle—is applied. Women may complain of great pain during attempts at penetration. A gynecological examination may reveal vulval erythema (excessive redness) of varying degrees around the vestibular gland duct openings, but, otherwise, the woman may not display or report other symptoms. To differentiate this complaint from vaginismus, the physician must apply gentle probing of the vestibule with a cotton swab. If great tenderness or pain is reported, it is likely that the woman is suffering from vulvodynia (chronic vulvar burning), of which vulvar vestibulitis is a particular type. Treatment in these cases may involve a variety of interventions, from antidepressant drugs to surgical excision of the involved areas, as well as sex therapy and vaginal dilation exercises (Basson, 1994).

TREATMENT OUTCOME

Despite the fact that vaginismus is a prevalent female sexual complaint, there have been few controlled treatment comparison studies documenting the relative efficacy of treatment approaches (Heiman & Meston, 1999). Nevertheless, insertion training appears to be quite beneficial in helping the woman accomplish sexual intercourse—if that is her goal. Hawton and Catalan (1986) in an early study reported that sexual education and psychotherapy plus dilator insertion over an average of 15 sessions resulted in an 80% success rate.

CLINICAL OBSERVATIONS ABOUT VAGINISMUS

1. There is considerable variation in the conceptualization of the vaginismic response. It is alternatively described as a psychosomatic disorder, a phobia, a conditioned fear response, or a conversion reaction. More recently, it is has been recognized as a conditioned reaction to recurrent vulvodynia.

2. There are no reliable data concerning the incidence of vaginismus. Although most authors regard it as uncommon, others suggest that it may be

more widespread than we suspect. The incidence is probably higher than might be expected, given that most women seek treatment from gynecologists who may or may not accurately diagnose the problem. Further, many women never get diagnosed at all.

3. A variety of etiological factors, both psychological and physical, can contribute to the symptom, ranging from a specific traumatic event to an underlying psychodynamic conflict. Sexual abuse is *not* the most salient contributing factor, but prior traumatic pelvic examinations and misinformation about pain and bleeding with the rupture of the hymen often exist. In most cases, the vaginismic response is overdetermined and multicausal in nature. Often, the husband or partner's role is important in maintaining, if not causing, the problem.

4. Regardless of the etiological hypothesis, most authors believe that the treatment of choice includes the gradual insertion of objects into the vagina (e.g., fingers, dilators, and tampons) of increasing size under conditions of relaxation and patient control. Systematic desensitization in which the patient and therapist construct a hierarchy of situations involving imaginal vaginal insertion, from the smallest q-tip to the largest penis, can be helpful for particularly phobic patients. For such patients, eye movement desensitization and reprocessing of specific traumatic memories involving vaginal penetration may be helpful. In cases in which the anxiety is extremely high, antianxiety medication may be prescribed as well.

5. Views concerning the husband's participation in treatment vary from recommending full involvement at every stage of treatment to inclusion once the wife has started to make progress to a varied response depending on the particular dynamics of the case.

6. Most authors view the prognosis as good. For the most part, failures tend not to be discussed, although recently Drenth (1988) and Leiblum (1994) have suggested that treatment is not always successful and that, moreover, even though successful penetration may be achieved, the woman may continue to avoid coitus.

To demonstrate the variety of both presenting complaints and treatment outcomes, several case studies are presented. I then discuss some of the patient and treatment characteristics that appear to affect treatment success or failure.

A SUCCESSFUL CASE

The C's, both age 41, had been together for 20 years and married for 16 years in a relationship that outwardly appeared harmonious, although onlookers might have wondered about the absence of children in this rather traditional church-going Catholic couple. In fact, Robin was anxious, dependent, and terrified of many things, but most of all of vaginal penetration. She had guarded her virginity throughout her adolescence and early adulthood because of her wish to preserve premarital virginity, but more significantly because of her

private awareness that she was phobic. Her husband, Robert, was an unasser-
tive and supportive husband who tolerated the absence of intercourse without
complaint for many years. More recently, however, he would explode in anger
periodically, at Robin's failure to resolve "the Problem." He wanted to become
a father at some point in his life, he said, but more immediately, he wanted a
"normal" sexual relationship.

Throughout their marriage, it was Robert who periodically introduced
the demand that Robin seek gynecological consultation and remediation for
her penetration phobia. While she maintained that the problem was physical,
that she was "too small," Robert could not help thinking the problem had
psychological underpinnings. He diligently searched for references or clues as
to what the problem might be, eventually calling the American College of
Obstetrics and Gynecologists. He was told that the problem sounded like
vaginismus and referred to the author (SL) for treatment.

Robert's initial contact was via e-mail (an increasingly common way of
capturing the attention of a professional), describing the problems he and his
wife were having, and asking many questions about the possibility of successful treatment and resolution. I replied to his e-mail and agreed to an initial
consultation if he could persuade his reluctant wife to come in.

After several e-mail exchanges, Robert called for an appointment.

Session 1

Robert and Robin were both visibly anxious throughout the first appointment. Robin, in particular, avoided eye contact and sat tensely poised at the
end of the chair. She emitted a scent of stale cigarettes, having been a pack-a-
day smoker for years, and was dressed in a fashion suitable to a younger woman,
with a long blonde pony tail and short skirt. When she spoke, she punctuated
each sentence with a short, mirthless laugh. Robert was the spokesperson for
the couple and he related the following problem history.

The couple met in college and formed an immediate attachment based on
mutual attraction. Both tall, thin, and socially awkward, they recognized each
other as kindred spirits. Each had been raised in sexually "negative" households with little emotional communication of any kind, let alone sexual education or encouragement.

After dating for a full year, Robin decided to go to the health service for
an examination because she anticipated intercourse would be a problem. The
female physician who examined her was unable to complete the examination,
commenting, "I don't see any blockage or anything wrong with you but your
opening is very, very small." Robin flew out of the office in fear and anxiety,
convinced she would never be able to have intercourse.

She and Robert continued to date, but she refused coitus on the grounds
that she wanted to maintain her virginity until marriage. He agreed, feeling
confident that all problems would be resolved after they got married.

From the start of their relationship, sex was difficult. While Robin enjoyed carresses and nongenital touch, she tensed up at the mere approach of a finger or penis near her genitals. Following several unsuccessful attempts at penetration after their honeymoon, Robin made Robert agree never to bring up intercourse as a topic of conversation or as a sexual alternative and, incredibly, he kept to this promise.

For the most part, sex consisted of manual stimulation and occasional oral stimulation. Robin refused oral sex for herself. Sexual frequency was about once weekly, although for a 6-year period they ceased genital sexual exchange altogether. Robert then became furious and insisted that Robin seek another gynecological opinion to determine the source of the penetration problem.

Robin did as she was told. The new gynecologist concurred with the first one. When he encountered difficulties performing the examination, he asked whether she used tampons. "No," she replied. He then asked if she had ever had intercourse. "No," she replied. "Then, I can't do the examination," he said, "Your opening is too small. You may have a problem because your opening is too small. Try to get aroused first." With that, he ended the visit, without a referral or further suggestions.

The years passed. Finally, at age 39, Robert insisted that Robin consult yet another gynecologist. This new physician recommended a hymenectomy, saying that this procedure would solve the problem. Robin agreed to the outpatient surgery and was told to return in one week, after attempting intercourse. Despite this promise, Robin "freaked out" when Robert attempted to insert his fingers in her vagina after the surgery.

Three more years passed. Finally, after consulting several therapists, Robert was referred to me.

When Robert was queried as to why he had been patient for so long before insisting on more concerted efforts to resolve the problem, he replied, "I know I avoid conflict like the plague." He blamed his passivity on Robin, saying that he did not want to upset her. He behaved somewhat like an indulgent but occasionally exasperated parent in their relationship. For instance, he said that he had to drive her to new places because she was "frightened of getting lost." He did acknowledge, though, that he would periodically erupt in rage at his feelings of frustration and "impotence" regarding their sexual relationship.

Robin sat silently for the most part during this history, occasionally crying. I suggested that it would be helpful if I could speak to her alone during the second session.

Robin's History

Robin was as nervous during the next session as she had been during the first. She described an unhappy childhood and a wish to get away from her family as quickly as possible. She said she was the middle daughter of Irish parents.

Although she had two older sisters she tended to be a loner. Her father was overprotective toward her and considered her his favorite daughter. Her mother was the family disciplinarian who ruled with an iron will and a hand to match, using physical discipline to enforce her points. Robin remembers that her mother would slap her across the face for particularly notable transgressions.

The family was not close. Her older sister was totally estranged from the family, and her name was never mentioned. Her younger sister was divorced. Robin felt unattractive and insecure throughout most of her life. She did not like school and was a mediocre student. She never spoke up in class and tried to make herself invisible most of the time. She was overjoyed to meet Robert in her senior year of college and she quickly became dependent on him. He was gratified by her adoration and attention and respected her wish to remain a virgin until marriage.

Following three sessions of history collection, I established the following treatment plan:

1. Begin a systematic program of self-exploration and dilation for Robin along with encouragement of greater self-assertion and personal autonomy.

2. Support Robert in his attempt to be more directly expressive of his feelings and wishes.

Treatment

Robin demonstrated great resolve in overcoming the problem. She immediately acquiesced to the use of dilators and, in fact, came to the fourth session announcing that she had already inserted the first dilator. Robert was jubilant and she looked pleased.

By the fifth session, she was able to insert the first two dilators without difficulty and was feeling very optimistic. However, as is commonly the case, she had her first disappointment when she tried to insert the third dilator which appeared enormous to her. Nevertheless, she was conscientious in spending 30 minutes each night practicing. She reported that if she "stuck with it," she could, in fact, manage to insert the third. It didn't feel "good" but she could move it around somewhat. She admitted, though, that she continued to feel nervous at the thought that she was getting closer to intercourse, and so time was spent exploring and challenging negative or erroneous thoughts and beliefs.

During one of these sessions, Robin reported a particularly negative memory associated with one of her first sexual encounters. Given the traumatic nature of the memory, I suggested EMDR (eye movement desensitization and reprocessing) as a tactic for reducing the anxiety reactions accompanying genital touch and insertion of the third dilator.

Her negative memory centered on an old boyfriend who, in his enthusiasm to attempt penile penetration, kept jabbing at her vagina with a taut erection. He was unable to find her "entrance" and the penile probing "hurt horribly." She felt mortified at the end of the evening.

After several "passes" with this image, she began to laugh at the thought of her boyfriend's ignorance and incompetence—he was like a blind man looking for a needle in a haystack. Nevertheless, the thought of Robert attempting to insert his finger into her vagina continued to elicit some anxiety. Robin reported feeling better—"lighter"—at the end of the EMDR session.

She was encouraged to become a more active partner in guiding Robert's penis across and around her vagina rather than lying passively on the bed, "like a patient." She was reminded that she was "in control" and could take the lead in "inserting his finger when and if she felt ready."

She returned the next session, thrilled that she had been able to successfully insert the fourth dilator. Although she felt some discomfort, she persevered and even permitted Robert to insert one of his fingers. When alone, she had practiced inserting two of her own fingers and, for the first time, reported feeling confident that she would be able to "conquer the problem, at last."

When she encountered difficulty inserting the fourth dilator, we scheduled another EMDR session in which we "rehearsed—in imagery—doing this with ease and confidence." Again, the EMDR session helped. Following the session, Robin reported no longer feeling panicky. In fact, she said, Robert was more nervous than she at the thought of the upcoming intercourse. He was, she said, worried about "hurting her." She was encouraged to take the lead in reassuring him as she was now in charge of their sex life.

At this time, the couple was invited to screen the video *Treating Vaginismus* (LoPiccolo, 1984) in which a couple is seen dealing with and successfully resolving vaginismus.[1] It was hoped that the video would provide a positive role model for each of them and illustrate comfortable vaginal containment with Robin responsible for guiding Robert's penis into her vagina.

They had a positive reaction to the video. Robin said, more assertively than ever before, "It's no longer a question of 'if' we solve problem, but when." Robert enthusiastically complimented Robin on her perseverance in sticking with the dilation exercises. The positive and optimistic mood of the session evaporated, however, when the issue of birth control was raised. Robert immediately announced that birth control was not necessary—he wanted to have a child, the sooner, the better. Robin looked anxious and, when questioned, expressed ambivalence about becoming a mother. "I'm so old," she said, "and we are doing so well."

Robert became furious, saying that Robin had never indicated ambivalence about motherhood. Robin then equivocated, saying that she was not ruling it out totally, but she enjoyed their lifestyle and did not want to risk losing what they currently enjoyed. The tension between them was palpable and the earlier mood of euphoria vanished. Robert muttered that "we can't negotiate having a child, you either want it or don't and time is running out." When I made the observation that neither of them appeared to have dealt directly with the issue of parenthood, Robert became angry with me and continued to blame Robin for the entire problem.

The following session, they returned. Robert admitted that he had colluded in avoiding the issue of fatherhood, but that he now felt confident about assuming the emotional and financial responsibilities. "I have no choice, though, but to do what she wants," he angrily exclaimed.

He said that he had berated himself all week for "waiting too long" and missing the opportunity to have a family. Robin sat rather passively, defending herself only weakly. She said, "I need time to think about it; it was never a possibility before."

Despite the conflict over parenthood, they made progress. Robin permitted Robert to insert the fourth dilator into her—which he successfully accomplished. She said that she now felt ready for intercourse and was eager to try. Time was spent imaginally rehearsing intercourse along with eye movement desenitization. Robin left the session feeling optimistic. She was reassured that having intercourse in no way obligated her to agree to conception attempts or even to regular intercourse with Robert. Many women fear that once they *can* have intercourse they will never have the option of refusing it. They need to be reassured that being able to have intercourse—when and if they want it—adds another option to their sexual repertoire but is in no way obligatory.

The following week Robin returned announcing gleefully, "I did it—three times!" She reported that she successfully inserted Robert's penis in her vagina the day following our session and again on two occasions the following week. Robert ejaculated inside of her twice. Their success had resulted in renewed feelings of intimacy and closeness between them. Moreover, they were both thrilled: Robin admitted that she felt "relieved" and very, very happy while Robert was jubilant.

Robin said that she did not feel any strong feelings of sexual pleasure but the satisfaction of accomplishing intercourse after so many years of failure overshadowed her disappointment at the lack of arousal with penile thrusting. We spent the remainder of the session discussing various ways of increasing her pleasure and sensations during coitus.

The final session spent with Robin and Robert addressed the issues raised by their successful resolution of the vaginismus. We discussed the implications of having a choice as to whether or not to include coitus as a sexual option—rather than making it an imperative in their sexual relationship and the need to continue an active, forthright discussion as to whether or not to pursue pregnancy in the future. They agreed to focus for the present on becoming more comfortable with their sexual relationship before embarking on new challenges. In this case, a resolution of a problem that had persisted for over 20 years was accomplished in twelve sessions.

Case Discussion

This was a typical case in many respects. Robin and Robert had colluded, as do many couples, in avoiding the problem because of shared fears and misgivings. It was only when the marital and sexual tension had escalated that they were both motivated to pursue treatment actively rather than sporadically. Robin was committed to overcoming her vaginismus after two decades of feeling inadequate, depressed, and sexually avoidant. Accomplishing vaginal penetration became a personal goal and accomplishment, albeit one that was motivated by the threat of losing Robert.

It is noteworthy that in this and similar cases, gynecologists unwittingly reinforce the patient's anxieties by offhand comments concerning the state or condition of either the hymen or the vagina. Women seize on such comments as self-fulfilling prophecies about the pain or problems inherent in vaginal penetration. In treatment, it is often necessary to refer the patient to a gynecologist who can take the time to conduct an educational gynecological examination with sensitivity and patience.

Finally, resolving the vaginismus does not resolve all the relationship and communication problems that accompany the problem. Often, as in this case, new issues emerge and must be dealt with.

A TREATMENT-RESISTANT CASE

Maria and Juan, ages 36 and 43, respectively, were a successful professional Hispanic couple: He was a chief executive officer in a computer company; she was a lawyer. Juan's first marriage had ended unhappily when he discovered that his wife had had an extramarital affair. Maria had never been married; she was distrustful of men and fearful of real intimacy with anyone—man or woman. She had developed an outward demeanor of sophistication and self-possession but admitted that most people saw her as aloof and remote.

Maria had grown up in a traditional, religiously observant Catholic household as the older sister, with a younger brother who subsequently "came out" as homosexual. Her mother was strong willed and deeply antagonistic toward men; her father was physically abusive and frightening.

As a child, Maria had been punished and humiliated for "touching herself." She recalls that as a young child, she liked to sleep with her hands resting on her genitals. When her mother chanced to observe her from the bedroom doorway one night, she startled Maria by screaming, "Get your hands away from your privates!" Maria was humiliated, she did not know what she had done wrong, but she cried herself to sleep and thereafter avoided touching her vagina again.

She felt unattractive as an adolescent—being heavy and clumsy. She felt the need to protect her younger brother, who was teased and abused by her father.

After several months of treatment, Maria recalled one particularly traumatic memory which seemed to reinforce her minimal trust in close relationships. She had grown up in an inner-city neighborhood where she was somewhat friendly with several girls on her block. One day they "turned against me," she recalled. They invited her to a vacant lot and then surrounded her, throwing stones and taunting her, saying that she thought she was better than they. She ran home crying, feeling betrayed and confused by their rancor.

She devoted herself to succeeding academically and professionally, working long hours and advancing in her firm. When an attractive man showed an interest in her, she dated briefly but always ended the relationship before any real sexual intimacy could occur.

Finally, at age 35, she met and subsequently married Juan, a man with similar values and goals. He found her beautiful but remote. Nonetheless, he liked the fact that she was sexually timid, having been disappointed by the more overt sexuality of his former wife. He agreed to wait until marriage to have intercourse.

Marriage, however, did not result in eliminating the sexual timidity and fear of intercourse that had plagued Maria for most of her life. She giggled when Juan touched her, pushed his hands away from her genitals when he attempted to caress her, and avoided sexual intimacy. She did not like to be touched—ever—and rarely initiated physical affection.

After 1 year of marriage, Juan insisted that she get "treatment" or he was leaving. She contacted me and reluctantly attended the first session.

Although Maria answered all questions that were posed to her, and readily agreed with any observations about her past and present behavior, she rarely initiated dialogue and waited passively for me to "direct" the sessions. When homework assignments were suggested, she agreed to them but then failed to comply. She repeatedly canceled appointments and never purchased or read suggested books.

During the year, her husband would periodically attend sessions, complaining bitterly about Maria's lack of commitment or progress. He noted that her behavior during the sex therapy sessions was analogous to her behavior at work and at home. She would avoid new situations, shy away from confrontations, acquiesce to various "action plans" for improving herself or their relationship, and then fail to follow through.

A number of interventions were attempted throughout the first year of therapy, from progressive relaxation to systematic desensitization. She was prescribed propanolol, an antihypertensive medication that helps eliminate the peripheral signs of anxiety. Her husband indicated that when he took it before a talk , it was very effective in extinguishing his anxiety about public speaking, but it did little to relax Maria in bed. She was given a prescription of antianxiety medication, with similar results.

Maria refused to engage in self-exploration or self-stimulation exercises, saying that she could not bring herself to touch herself. When we "uncovered" her earliest memory of punishment associated with touching, we scheduled several EMDR sessions to reduce the traumatic associations involved with the thought or sensations of genital touching. While Maria reported feeling better after these sessions and reported lower SUDS (subjective units of discomfort) ratings, there was no evidence of greater sexual self-comfort at home.

Over the course of the year, progress was achieved in improving the communication between Juan and Maria. Maria became more outspoken about responding to Juan's "self-improvement" lectures to her and challenged his description of her as overly dependent and insecure. Following these sessions, she was able to be more available during sexual encounters and reported feeling aroused and even orgasmic with manual stimulation—something she had been unable to do at the start of treatment. But she still stiffened when he tried to stimulate her external genitals with his penis.

After a several-month hiatus over the summer initiated by Maria, she contacted me in the fall, at Juan's urging, and said that she was ready to go for a gynecological examination—her first in several years. She had avoided seeking gynecological care because of an unpleasant experience with a former gynecologist who had tried to "talk her through" the exam slowly and deliberately rather than "taking charge" in a more directive way. She actually preferred a male physician who was "authoritarian in his approach, rather than the more gentle female gynecologist who tried to be educational and persuasive." I referred her to a male colleague who was willing to take the time to talk with her prior to the exam and discuss her fears in a respectful yet professional way.

Maria successfully completed the visit and returned to treatment more motivated. The new year was approaching and she was determined to accomplish intercourse over the long holiday break.

When I saw Juan and Maria during this interlude, their increased rapport and comfort with each other was apparent. The vacation break had provided time for daily intimacies and each was considerate and loving of the other in a way that had not been apparent in earlier visits. However, they had not had intercourse as planned and had backslided into spending many hours at their respective jobs. While they verbalized the wish for greater time together, they often managed to sabotage "dates." Nevertheless, the time they did spend together was more intimate, warm, and affectionate.

At the time of this writing, Juan and Maria had discovered a new way of transitioning into sex. They each knelt by the side of their bed and prayed together. This was meaningful for both of them—they felt united—and it did help relax Maria. But she remains anxious about the thought of full intercourse, although determined to accomplish it. Her new goal, which is motivated in large part by the fear of Juan's leaving her, is to have intercourse by her second anniversary, which is several months away.[2]

Case Discussion

Why has it been so difficult for Maria to tolerate penile penetration? Several factors appear to conspire to make intercourse an ambivalent goal for Maria. Her earliest memories of genital touching were negative ones—genital touch was strongly associated with physical punishment, humiliation, and dread. These were reinforced by several unpleasant experiences with gynecologists. She left such visits feeling defective, shamed, and inadequate. Her trust in relationships was similarly fraught with conflict. She wanted intimacy, but her experiences had all been negative. Friends abandoned her and colleagues treated her in a formal but distant fashion, taking their cues from her interpersonal style, which was pleasant but remote. Her experience with men had been negative from the start. Her father's physical abuse of her mother and brother had conditioned her to be vigilant and suspicious, and she reacted to the men in her life in a similar fashion. Although she loved Juan, she did not trust him, fearing that he would leave her, as he had left his first wife, if she disappointed him. She believed that if she did not succeed in intercourse by her second wedding anniversary, he would initiate a separation, and, indeed, he had made remarks to this effect.

In therapy, she related to me as a supportive professional, but did not readily or easily confide in me until many months had passed. She admitted that after the first several months, she began to enjoy coming to our sessions because I supported her in her dealings with Juan. At the same time, she saw me as part of the "establishment," someone respected but not completely trusted. Our different ethnic and cultural backgrounds were discussed, although she denied that this was a problem for her. It certainly seemed that maintaining virginity represented "purity" for her, a quality highly valued and in line with her devout religious beliefs. At times, it may have seemed that I was urging her to be more "sexual" than she felt comfortable with.

Medication, relaxation, and EMDR had only modest effects. Masturbation was not an option, because Maria had strong inhibitions and religious beliefs against it. Dilator treatment was similarly rejected, although she purchased the dilators. And, finally, although "insight" was apparently achieved during many sessions it failed to have any demonstrable effect on Maria's sexual anxieties, although it did help in various areas of her personal life. She became more assertive at work and at home and was actively seeking more satisfactory work. Because she was somewhat ambivalent about having a child, the goal of intercourse as a route to parenthood did not provide much of an incentive for Maria (although it often does for women who are motivated to become mothers).

Will Maria succeed in overcoming her vaginismus? I believe she will, eventually, because she wants her marriage to continue and intellectually recognizes that Juan is a sincere and loving partner, not one who will betray or abandon her. But I believe it will take more time and patience. She will probably never become an enthusiastic sexual partner.

DISCUSSION

These cases illustrate both the variety and complexity of sex therapy for women dealing with vaginismus and their partners. In the first case, treatment was brief, effective, and successful. Robin, the vaginismic women, was highly motivated and capable of reliable arousal and orgasm, although she feared vaginal penetration. She readily complied with treatment suggestions, and they worked for her. She trusted her husband and knew that he would never leave her despite his frustration. He had been a loyal friend and partner for over 19 years at the start of treatment.

In the second case, the client, Maria, was generally sexually aversive. She lacked desire and considered sex an obligation rather than a potential joy. She came from a background of physical abuse and humiliation around sexual issues. Sex was "toxic" from her earliest experience of self-touching. Moreover, her strong religious convictions supported her internal ban against premarital sex, even though it meant postponing intercourse until her mid-30s when she married. She was interpersonally distrustful and worried that her husband would eventually leave her the way he had left his first wife. She had fewer resources, either internal or external, for soothing her anxieties about sexual intimacy.

The partners of these women also differed. The first husband was as insecure as his wife. Like her, he had been a virgin at marriage and was tentative and uncertain sexually. His attraction to Robin was based, in part, on feelings of identification and sympathy—they shared insecurities. The second husband had been sexually competent and experienced at the time of marriage. Although he was drawn to his wife physically, he was impatient, and occasionally intolerant of her various anxieties. He wanted a strong, sexual helpmate and he would become periodically frustrated and impatient with her passivity. His threat to leave the marriage was real—he had, indeed, left his first wife. So, although he was usually supportive, he did not provide the "safe" environment that she needed to "let go" and trust the process.

Factors Important in the Etiology of Vaginismus

The etiology of vaginismus remains a perplexing question. The literature reports a wide variety of factors contributing to vaginismus, including past sexual trauma, psychological and social factors in the family of origin, physical pain associated with infection or past gynecological trauma, as well as immediate contributions such as the partner's sexual difficulties (early ejaculation, erectile problems) or the women's distrust of men generally and her partner specifically. Childhood sexual abuse is not often found.

Religious orthodoxy is not always a consistent theme, although the women are often raised in homes that proscribe sex before marriage. The mothers of vaginismic women are often themselves conflicted about sex and transmit negative messages about men and sexual pleasure. These messages are often internalized by the patient and the idea of penile penetration takes on a negative cast. Sex is usually anticipated as being disappointing if not painful.

As one explores the histories of the women in greater detail, it is often possible to identify specific sexual or gynecological experiences that are associated with strongly negative memories. In such instances, EMDR can be helpful. When physical factors contribute to the problem, as they often do because of repeated urinary or vaginal track infections with resultant pain and discomfort, the development of vaginismus is not surprising. However, even when the immediate physical or medical problems are satisfactorily resolved, anticipatory anxiety about vaginal penetration often remains and must be dealt with.

To summarize, it is clear that there are multiple paths to the development of vaginismus and that no single etiological pattern is definitive. Although the etiology is different in each case, it is usually not necessary to determine exact causes in order to help most patients with this sexual disorder.

Factors Influencing the Course of Treatment

While most, if not all, vaginismic women display considerable ambivalence about confronting their problem, significant differences remain across women in their motivation to change. Motivation to change clearly involves both the quality of the relationship with the partner and a more general potential for meaningful interpersonal relationships. Marital satisfaction appears to be associated with more positive and rapid outcome.

Overall sexual comfort appears to be an important prognostic factor as well. Women who enjoy physical affection, sensual touching, and orgasm are more likely to take risks sexually to expand and enhance their already positive sexual repertoire. Women who dislike or fear touch and who have found less pleasure or relief in sensual exchange have little incentive to tolerate the anxiety associated with penetration—their bank account is empty.

Despite the various treatment options available, the mainstay of treatment remains the deconditioning of the reflexive vaginal response. Whether or not dilators are used, some form of gradual vaginal insertion, whether by the woman alone or by her partner, appears to be essential for a successful outcome. Further, the skillful handling of the gynecological examination can often eliminate basic fears and misconceptions about vaginal size and normality and can be a useful adjunct to treatment. Relaxation training as well as imaginal desensitization is often necessary for women who are particularly phobic.

These treatment techniques clearly are important, but they occur in the context of a patient–therapist relationship. All the suggested procedures require the active cooperation of the *patient*. The patient's attitudes toward herself and her difficulty, toward her partner, and toward the therapist become important aspects of the treatment. Transference issues may work for or against rapid progress. The patient must perceive the therapist as a supportive and sympathetic ally—rather than as aligned with the impatient partner. In short-term therapy especially, the therapist relies on the positive feelings of the patient to give weight and credence to the educational and prescriptive program and to overcome minor resistances.

CONCLUSION

Most therapists report good success in treating vaginismus. The woman who has succeeded in overcoming her anxieties feels an affirmation of herself as an adult woman, relief from long-standing feelings of shame, and freedom to decide on motherhood. When the marital or partner relationship is good, both partners feel jubilant that they no longer have a shameful secret that makes them seem different from others. It is the case, however, that sex therapy is not always completely successful in the treatment of vaginismus and that many cases never come to the attention of sex therapists. Sometimes, penile penetration is achieved but is not routinely incorporated into an ongoing sexual relationship. In other cases, once intercourse is accomplished, it becomes a staple of the sexual repertoire. Often, therapists receive joyous announcements of new births following the termination of therapy. When treatment succeeds, it is one of the most gratifying experiences for both the couple and the clinician.

NOTES

1. The video *Treating Vaginismus* illustrates the complete treatment program used with a woman suffering from vaginismus. It may be purchased through The Sinclair Institute in Chapel Hill, North Carolina.

2. Despite her fervent hopes, Maria was not able to relax sufficiently for intercourse to occur by the final editing stage of this chapter, one year after it was written.

REFERENCES

American Psychiatric Association. (1994). *Diagnostic and statistical manual of mental disorders* (4th ed.). Washington, DC: Author.

Angier, N. (1999). *Women: An intimate geography.* New York: Houghton-Mifflin.

Barnes, J., Bowman, E. P., & Cullen, J. (1984). Biofeedback as an adjunct in the treatment of vaginismus. *Biofeedback and Self-Regulation, 9,* 281–289.

Basson, R. (1994). Vulvar vestibulitis syndrome: A common condition which may present as vaginismus. *Sexual and Marital Therapy, 9,* 221–224.

Drenth, J. J. (1988). Vaginismus and the desire for a child. *Journal of Psychosomatic Obstetrics and Gynecology, 9,* 125–138.

Faure, J. L., & Sireday, A. (1909). *Traite de gynecologie* (3rd ed.) Paris: Octave Doin.

Hawton, K., & Catalan, J. (1986). Prognostic factors in sex therapy. *British Journal of Psychiatry, 24,* 377–385.

Heiman, J. R., & Meston, C. M. (1999). Empirically validated treatment for sexual dysfunction. *Annual Review of Sex Research, 6,* 148–194.

Kaplan, H. S. (1974). *The new sex therapy.* New York: Brunner/Mazel.

Keen, S. (1979). Some ludicrous theses about sexuality. *Journal of Humanistic Psychology, 19,* 15–22.

Kleinplatz, P. (1996). *Sex therapy for vaginismus: A review, critique and humanistic perspective.* Unpublished manuscript.

Lamont, J. (1978). Vaginismus. *American Journal of Obstetrics and Gynecology, 131,* 632–636.

Laumann, E. O., Gagnon, J. H., Michael, R. T., & Michaels, S. (1994). *The social organization of sexuality: Sexual practices in the United States.* Chicago: University of Chicago Press.

Leiblum, S. R. (1994). Relinquishing virginity: The treatment of a complex case of vaginismus. In R. C. Rosen & S. R. Leiblum (Eds.), *Case studies in sex therapy.* New York: Guilford Press.

LoPiccolo, J. (1984). Treating vaginismus. [A video]. Chapel Hill, NC: The Sinclair Institute.

Masters, W. H., & Johnson, V. E. (1970). *Human sexual inadequacy.* Boston: Little, Brown.

Musaph, H. (1977). Vaginismus. In H. Musaph & A. A. Haspels (Eds.), *Dyspareunia: Aspects of painful coitus* (pp. 240–255). Utrecht: Bohn.

Reissing, E., Binik, Y., & Khalifé, S. (1999). Does vaginismus exist?: A critical review of the literature. *Journal of Nervous and Mental Disease, 187,* 261–274.

Spector, I., & Carey, M. (1990). Incidence and prevalence of the sexual dysfunctions: A critical review of the empirical literature. *Archives of Sexual Behavior, 19,* 389–396.

van Lankveld, J. J. , Brewaeys, A. M., Ter Kuile, M., & Weijenborg, P. (1995). Difficulties in the differential diagnosis of vaginismus, dyspareunia and mixed sexual pain disorder. *Journal of Psychosomatic Obstetrics and Gynecology, 16,* 201–209.

III

MALE SEXUAL DISORDERS

8

Retarded Ejaculation
A Much Misunderstood Syndrome

BERNARD APFELBAUM

It has been over a decade since Bernard Apfelbaum contributed a chapter on the treatment of retarded ejaculation, and little has changed in the last 10 years in either the conceptualization or clinical approach to this infrequent, though often persistent problem.

In this updated version of his original chapter, Apfelbaum challenges ex-isting clinical accounts of retarded ejaculation as the result of inhibition of coital orgasm in the male and presents instead a reformulation based on the concept of "autosexuality" in the retarded ejaculator. He notes that this disor-der is primarily seen from the partner's point of view rather than the patient's and might, perhaps, be called "partner anorgasmia" because many men can ejaculate when alone.

Noting that retarded ejaculation is a relatively rare clinical phenomenon, Apfelbaum suggests that it is significant in revealing current biases in the field. For example, he points out that coital anorgasmia in the female, which he equates with retarded ejaculation in the male, is commonly treated by focusing on the negative feelings of the woman toward her partner, and by relieving her of performance pressures during intercourse. In contrast, most sex therapy manuals recommend the use of guided stimulation techniques for increasing the level of arousal in the retarded ejaculator. These procedures, according to Apfelbaum, produce enormous performance pressure for the patient and bor-der on sexual coercion.

The account of retarded ejaculation presented in this chapter begins with the author's observation that some males appear able to achieve erections suf-ficient for intercourse despite a relative absence of subjective arousal. These "automatic erections" are taken as evidence by both the male and his partner that he is ready for sex and capable of achieving orgasm. Instead, these individuals frequently experience detachment, performance anxiety, and hostility or resentment toward their partners. Most female partners, in fact, report multiple orgasms during intercourse with these men. This is in marked contrast to the conventional view of the retarded ejaculator as withholding pleasure or satisfaction from his partner. Apfelbaum argues further that retarded ejaculation may represent one end of a continuum, ranging from those who strongly prefer stimulation by a partner to those who, like the retarded ejaculator, are more responsive to their own stimulation. Most of these individuals, he points out, are likely to avoid partner sex altogether and may, thus, never enter treatment.

Given this conceptual framework, not surprisingly, Apfelbaum is highly critical of conventional sex therapy approaches to retarded ejaculation. These typically assume that the ejaculatory reflex in the male is "blocked" or "inhibited," requiring increasing levels of stimulation by the female partner. Most sex therapists treat retarded ejaculation in a manner analogous to vaginismus, he notes, rather than approaching it in a similar fashion to female coital anorgasmia. Rather than increasing the performance demands on the patient, Apfelbaum suggests we consider a counterbypassing strategy. This involves encouraging the male to openly express his lack of arousal and feelings of distance or hostility from his partner rather than denying or bypassing such feelings. The goal of therapy is to focus awareness of the patient's fundamental lack of arousal and to overcome the powerful performance demands these individuals typically experience. It is only then, according to Apfelbaum, that real progress can be made.

Bernard Apfelbaum, PhD, is the director of the Berkeley Sex Therapy Group. He is the author of numerous articles and chapters in the field of sex therapy.

––––––––––

At one time all sexual disorders were thought of as symptoms of severe personality disturbances. Long-term therapy was thought to be indicated and even with extended treatment the prognosis was poor. With the development of the field of sex therapy, this diagnostic assessment has been revised for most of the sexual disorders. The most conspicuous exception is retarded ejaculation (RE).

I propose that the pessimism about treating RE is a consequence of diagnostic and therapeutic misunderstandings of such magnitude and direction as to suggest a pronounced clinical bias. This bias can be seen as intrinsic to both psychoanalytic and behavioral approaches but also is reinforced by easily misunderstood clinical features of RE.

If we correct for this, RE is as treatable in brief sex therapy as are the other sexual disorders. This hypothesis is difficult to confirm with certainty because of the clinical rarity of this condition (1 to 2% of most clinical populations). The actual incidence of RE in all likelihood far exceeds its clinical incidence. Masters and Johnson's (1970) sample of 17 was the largest reported as of the first edition of this volume. Our sample was then 12, with 10 of these being treated cases. Partly as a result of the impact of the first edition, our sample is now 34. Kaplan's (1974) original statement that her sample size was too insignificant to report has not been revised.

Because RE is rare, it is of only limited clinical interest. However, it is of special interest just because of its rarity: The way it is understood and treated is more revealing of underlying clinical assumptions than is the case for the other sexual disorders as these biases are less constrained by data and experience.

To begin with, the generally accepted treatment approach to RE uniquely exposes the limitations of the "dysfunction" conception. This conception leads the clinician to expect that the most rapid treatment results will be gained if performance problems are taken as the therapeutic point of entry. However, it is this focus that has partly been responsible for the difficulty in treating RE because, as I will try to demonstrate, this syndrome is a case of a performance symptom that masks a subtle and specific desire disorder. The radical simplification of diagnosis by dysfunction, that is, by performance symptom, has obscured the key diagnostic signs of RE.

DIAGNOSTIC ISSUES

What Is Retarded Ejaculation?

A clue to diagnostic ambiguities in the standard conception of RE is to be found in the diagnostic label itself. In actual practice, "retarded ejaculation" refers to male coital anorgasmia. All causal conceptions and treatment strategies are directed only at the inability to have specifically coital orgasms. At most treatment facilities retarded ejaculation is seen because his partner wants to be impregnated. Hence the stress is on not ejaculating rather than on not being coitally orgasmic, a clue to one source of bias in the understanding and treatment of RE: This disorder typically is looked at from the partner's point of view rather than the patient's.

Clearly, if this disorder was simply a difficulty in reaching orgasm but orgasm and ejaculation nevertheless did occur, pregnancy would not be an issue. In the typical case, the man will never have experienced a coital orgasm. Yet, the term "retarded ejaculation" equally clearly would seem to refer to a slowness to ejaculate, a meaning even more directly suggested by "delayed ejaculation," an alternate label in use. However, only Kaplan (1974, p. 317) mentions that the term can be used in this sense, and she does not discuss this interpretation of RE further; as is true of all other writers, her discussion is focused exclusively on coital anorgasmia. Interestingly, slowness to ejaculate is not discussed in the literature.

"Partner anorgasmia" might be an apt term for this condition because the retarded ejaculator has difficulty reaching any kind of orgasm with a partner, although it sometimes is possible, with difficulty, to be orgasmic with manual or manual-plus-oral stimulation, as heavy and prolonged friction can be applied in a way that is not possible in coitus.

In addition to the ambiguity of the diagnostic label, there is an ambiguity in the way the label is customarily applied. All men who are unable to have coital orgasms are diagnosed as retarded ejaculators (as long as coital orgasm is not prevented by premature ejaculation or erection problems). This not only includes men whose anorgasmia is specific to coitus. It also includes men who do not have coital orgasms because they have difficulty reaching orgasm in general.

Men who have difficulty reaching orgasm in general are like women with primary anorgasmia. These women do not have coital orgasms because they do not have any kind of orgasm; it would make no sense to include them with women who are easily orgasmic in general and whose anorgasmia is specific to coitus. Yet this is exactly what is done with men, a practice that is all the more puzzling in view of the fact that no one has attempted to justify it; indeed, it has yet to be noted at all.

As we will see, the whole focus of the standard treatment approach is on vaginal containment. The capacity to masturbate to orgasm is simply assumed and, indeed, is essential to the standard behavioral treatment of RE. The question whether the man may also have difficulty masturbating to orgasm is never raised. Men who have difficulty with masturbatory orgasms require quite different treatment than do men who are specifically coitally anorgasmic, but there is as yet no discussion of such cases.

What makes this important is that it is only when masturbatory anorgasmia is removed from consideration that the features of RE, that is, of specifically coital anorgasmia, appear. I propose that the key diagnostic sign of RE is that only the patient's *own* touch is erotically arousing, and his basic sexual orientation is "autosexual" (masturbatory) rather than heterosexual or homosexual. This is the critical differential diagnostic cue. RE patients invariably report enjoying masturbation more than sex with a partner. If a man has had difficulty with masturbation that is not simply episodic, RE should be ruled out.

Thus, diagnosis by dysfunction has grouped together men who are coitally anorgasmic but who enjoy masturbation and for whom it even is their primary sexual orientation with men who are coitally anorgasmic but who masturbate only with difficulty and who, in general, experience little sexual pleasure. The true retarded ejaculator could never develop masturbatory anorgasmia.

Retarded Ejaculation as a Desire Disorder Specific to Partner Sex

Diagnosis by dysfunction has obscured one desire disorder, masturbatory anorgasmia, by classifying it as RE. It also has obscured another desire disorder that is specific to true RE, a desire disorder that appears only when a partner is present but is masked by the presence of facile and sustained erections.

We are accustomed to thinking that any loss of desire or erotic arousal would be reflected by a loss of erection. Not only does the retarded ejaculator not lose his erections, but a hitherto overlooked feature of this condition is the presence of erections that almost suggest priapism. They are sustained far beyond the ordinary range, but, strangely enough, this almost seems to be a consequence of *lack* of erotic arousal rather than of a high level of arousal.

This quasi-priapism helps account for the repeated and rather startling finding that the retarded ejaculator's partners often are coitally multiorgasmic despite his coital anorgasmia. Still more surprising, these sustained erections are present even when the patient admits feeling sexually repelled by or angry at his partner.

I have no adequate explanation for this phenomenon, although it is reminiscent of the rare reports of men who have been successfully raped by women, that is, men who have had sustained erections under stress. It has been speculated that a contributory factor is the total lack of performance anxiety, even of performance intention. In any case, sexual functioning at low levels of arousal or even accompanied by aversion is clinically familiar, if theoretically unaccounted for as yet. It is as if the retarded ejaculator's excitement (erection)-phase functioning is out of phase or out of "sync" with his level of desire and erotic arousal.

Performance Implies Arousal

Perhaps the most striking illustration of the effect on the clinician of the RE patient's sustained erections is the fact that *partner-specific* RE is considered a clinical condition. This is a fully accepted diagnostic practice, even though one might ask why, if a man is coitally anorgasmic with only one partner and not others, it is not assumed that something is going on with this particular partner that is causing the problem rather than that he is suffering from a sexual disorder. This is, in fact, exactly the logic that is applied when a man has an erection problem with one partner but not with any others.

If a patient has erection problems with one particular partner and not with others it is common for the man himself to leap to the conclusion that he has an erection problem, almost invariably then being reassured by the clinician that being functional with other partners rules it out. But if the patient has sustained erections and is merely coitally anorgasmic with one particular partner, more likely than not he will be diagnosed as a retarded ejaculator, especially if he is married and if his wife wishes to be impregnated.

If, as is true of partner-specific erection difficulties, partner-specific RE is not necessarily a disorder, this further clouds the diagnostic picture because a man who experiences RE with only one partner will not show the other critical signs of RE, that is, long-sustained erections and a preference for masturbation.

The clinician may also be influenced by the fact that although "no man can will an erection," in Masters and Johnson's famous phrase, most men (and women) can will orgasms. An orgasm can be produced by heavy and sustained friction despite the total absence of erection or even erotic arousal, a practice common among men who suffer from severe chronic erectile dysfunction.

The Retarded Ejaculator as a Malingerer

Because it is easy to assume that the retarded ejaculator is aroused and should be able to have coital orgasms, he typically is seen as a kind of malingerer. What makes this an almost unavoidable impression is that the retarded ejaculator often *acts* like a malingerer. He may confess, although only privately, that he is unwilling to impregnate his partner or that he is repulsed by his partner and enjoys denying her the satisfaction of seeing him have coital orgasms.

But if he is angry at his partner and wants to reject her, why does the RE patient choose such surreptitious means? Why does he not simply refuse to have intercourse with his partner if he is repulsed by her? If he does not want to impregnate her why has he has entered treatment with her to find a way to conceive? An obvious answer is that he feels guilty about wanting to say no to his partner or is afraid she will get angry or retaliate. If this is the case, shouldn't he be helped to be able to say no directly or to at least express his reluctance?

This alternative is nowhere mentioned in the literature and is not considered in either standard sex therapy or in psychoanalytic therapy, as we will see. Masters and Johnson (1970) even report that of the 14 men suffering from RE who came to treatment with their wives, "three men offered dislike, rejection, open enmity for their wives *as sufficient reason* [italics added] for failure to ejaculate intravaginally" (p. 120). If these men believed they had sufficient reason not to ejaculate, from whose point of view was their not ejaculating a disorder? Clearly, from their wives' point of view and, apparently, from Masters and Johnson's point of view as well. Despite this reluctance, the RE patient is expected to be coitally orgasmic and in standard sex therapy even is so aggressively pushed to perform that I consider it to be reminiscent of sexual abuse.

One of Masters and Johnson's (1970) RE patients was a man "who should not have been seen in therapy, as there really was no specific ejaculatory dysfunction. This was only a case of a man's complete rejection of the woman he married" (p. 134). Here is a man who was so completely rejecting of his wife that Masters and Johnson thought it inappropriate of him to have entered treatment with her, yet when the treatment outcome was that he did not become coitally orgasmic, Masters and Johnson rated the case as a *failure*, and recommended divorce "to the wife" (she did not take the recommendation).

This advice was a significant departure from the position of neutrality (rather than advocacy) that Masters and Johnson, alone among sex therapists, recommend (Apfelbaum, 1985). Aside from the question of whether a therapist is ever in a position to recommend divorce, Masters and Johnson's statement that they recommended divorce not to the couple but to the wife suggests that there is something about the RE patient that causes therapists to lose their neutrality.

This example deserves further consideration. The patient apparently made it clear that he did not want to have coital orgasms with his wife and that, further, it was unlikely that he wanted to have intercourse or perhaps any kind of relationship with her at all. Masters and Johnson (1970) even add that this was a case of partner-specific RE: "He was consistently involved with other women outside of marriage with, of course, no ejaculatory difficulty" (p. 121). Yet it was thought of as a treatment failure if despite this he was not coitally orgasmic with her.

Now, this patient did consent to enter treatment with his wife and did present with the complaint of RE. Therefore, it could be argued that he did want to be coitally orgasmic with her. Although this does raise some question about how "complete" was his rejection of his wife, it looks more as if his willingness to enter treatment was itself the symptom, representing guilt or fear about being more openly rejecting of his wife. If this is true, the treatment objective should not be for him to be coitally orgasmic with his wife but for him to be able to reject her more directly.

What this example seems to indicate is that the clinician takes the wives' point of view that these men should not be so rejecting and should want to be coitally orgasmic. This bias makes not wanting to be coitally orgasmic a "dysfunctional" attitude and can even lead, as we will see, to the interpretation that the RE patient is withholding the correct or "functional" attitude of wanting to be coitally orgasmic with his partner. Hence, he should be more *giving*. This normative bias makes more understandable the typically unempathic treatment of the retarded ejaculator.

TREATMENT ISSUES

The retarded ejaculator is the object of what is by far the most aggressive attack on a symptom to be found in the field of sex therapy. The standard procedure for treating the retarded ejaculator is to use a demand strategy in which he begins to masturbate with his partner, who then takes over and is required to stimulate his penis in an aggressive and forceful way, suddenly switching to intromission near the point of ejaculatory inevitability.

The idea behind this strategy is that the orgasm reflex has been inhibited and that heavy stimulation will break the "spell." No attempt is made to reconcile this reflex conception with the picture of the retarded ejaculator as a kind of malingerer. The patient who, in Masters and Johnson's words, speaks of his "open enmity" and offers it "as sufficient reason" for his lack of coital orgasms can hardly be thought of as suffering from a subcortical inhibition. This makes it appear that the reflex conception serves as justification for a treatment approach that the clinician wants to apply quite independently of whether it in fact fits the case.

Indeed, one must wonder at the *furor therapeuticus* that grips the clinician who employs this coercive strategy with a man who has apparently made it clear that he is repelled by his wife and wants to reject her, or at least does not want to impregnate her. This approach to patient care reveals a normative bias and a potential for coercion inherent in standard sex therapy practices.

The contrast between the way men and women are treated emerges quite sharply in this regard. For example, Masters and Johnson use the high-pressure, performance-demand strategy with RE, that is, with male coital anorgasmia, but with female coital anorgasmia they take special pains to avoid even the slightest hint of coercion and place special stress on the need to avoid all performance demands (Williams, 1977).

Indeed, the treatment for RE that I will be advocating is entirely consistent with Masters and Johnson's treatment of *female* coital anorgasmia. I propose that Masters and Johnson's insights into female coital anorgasmia are especially relevant to the male version in that the RE patient is suffering such an intense performance demand that he must perform regardless of his reluctance.

I am suggesting that the performance pressure felt by the RE patient is overlooked in part because he simply is expected to perform, but I should emphasize that this expectation is strongly reinforced by the man's sustained erections, whereas the clinician is less likely to look with suspicion at the coitally anorgasmic woman's disorder because she does not manifest such a seemingly obvious orgasmic readiness. Therefore, any attempt to correct the clinical bias against the retarded ejaculator must establish that the RE patient's erections are indeed out of "sync" with his level of desire.

BEYOND DYSFUNCTION

Automatic Erections

The automatic erections that I have claimed are pathognomonic of RE are evident from our own cases, but I will begin with case illustrations taken from Masters and Johnson (1970) and Kaplan (1974) to demonstrate that the evidence for this diagnostic cue has been there all along, although its significance has been overlooked.

Masters and Johnson (1970) note in passing that "the incompetent ejaculator [their diagnostic term] can maintain an erection indefinitely during coital sex play, with mounting, and not infrequently for a continuum of 30 to 60 minutes of intravaginal penile containment" (p. 128). They might well have added that he can maintain an erection even under extremely adverse conditions: They report that one patient was married to a woman "whom he found totally objectionable physically." Yet "he was able to perform coitally with his wife from an erective point of view," this despite the fact that "after penetration he was repulsed rather than stimulated by her demanding pelvic thrusting" (p. 120). In the case of the man who was rated a failure and whose wife was advised to divorce him, he "was so physically repulsed by his wife that, *although erections were maintained*, he rarely reached sufficient levels of sexual tension to approach ejaculation [italics added]" (p. 121). (Note Masters and Johnson's recognition that in this case, at least, the man did not reach orgasm because he was not sufficiently aroused.) In both cases, we find what amounts to a prescription for "impotence," but instead we find extraordinary "potency."

I can only surmise that all these clinicians believe that the RE patient's erections are long-sustained simply because they are not terminated by orgasm. This, in fact, is the typical RE patient's own belief. Many retarded ejaculators believe, reasoning from their own experience, that there is nothing unusual about their erections and that any normal erection would continue indefinitely unless terminated by orgasm.

In case readers are still tempted to share this belief, a few striking examples from our own work may be convincing. One of our patients said that he hated the workhorse role but felt that with a sustained full erection he could not gracefully decline to go on to penetration. He seemed to genuinely dread these erections and puzzled over why they were so persistent because he dreaded having them. Another RE patient said that after extended periods of thrusting, his back gave out before his erection did. I (Apfelbaum, 1977) have reported on one RE case in which, during the treatment, the patient learned to urinate through his erect penis. His erection was unaffected.

I should note here that we do not find evidence of automatic functioning in every published case of RE. However, this variable has not been assessed in each case, and the examples given of automatic functioning by retarded ejaculators are among the most dramatic examples of this response style to be found in the literature. Further, almost all the cases treated by us have evidenced this characteristic. There are some published cases in which the patient was also diagnosed as having an erectile dysfunction (Razani, 1977), and Masters and Johnson reported that some of their RE patients eventually did have erection problems. I take these to be mixed conditions.

Case 1: An Automatic Performer

One of the three cases presented by Kaplan (1974, pp. 321–323) provides a striking example of the retarded ejaculator as an automatic performer. This patient had suffered a spinal cord injury that badly impaired the sensitivity of his penile skin. He was afraid his wife would leave him if she knew he could not reach coital orgasms, and so he faked it for the first 4 months of his marriage. Sexual contact left him "very frustrated and upset," ending in his secretly masturbating. "He was frantic in his attempts to overcome his dysfunction and tried to have intercourse at least once every day." Later in the marriage "he had continued to insist compulsively on daily sex." Evidence for his continuing to have sustained erections despite his panic, drivenness, and lack of desire is the fact that in the "system of lovemaking" they had worked out, "they would have intercourse until she climaxed," and then "she would stimulate him to orgasm manually" even though "stimulation was often very prolonged and tedious." Here is a prescription for the inhibition of erection, and again the opposite is the case.

Autosexuality

The case cited previously is of interest because the numbing of this patient's penile skin mimics the condition that I have proposed is present in the intact retarded ejaculator. In other words, here we have a case of demonstrable penile numbness leading to RE. This may also be a case in which the RE patient's autosexuality has been overlooked, making his organic impairment appear to be the sole case of his RE. A close reading of the case report indicates that despite his organic impairment, he may have been a true retarded ejaculator by my definition. His penile numbness may have affected him only when he was with his wife. We are not told whether this patient had equal difficulty masturbating. We only know that "he would wait for her to fall asleep, at which point he would masturbate in the bathroom" (p. 322). This appears to suggest that even this patient could masturbate relatively easily. Only manual stimulation by his wife is described as "often very prolonged and tedious." In other words, it may only have been with his wife that he needed the additional sensitivity he had lost because of his injury.

Case 2: Trying to Include the Partner

The retarded ejaculator is much more responsive to his own hand than to his partner's. This phenomenon deserves more attention than it can be given here. One couple, married 4 years, illustrates what the retarded ejaculator goes through when trying to include a partner. The husband was able to masturbate easily in his wife's presence. He could also reach orgasm, although with some difficulty, through manual stimulation by his wife, but only if he held his testicles himself. In couple sex therapy they were encouraged to see whether he could taper off self-stimulation while increasing his wife's participation. He was unable to reach orgasm unless he used at least three fingers of his own, while the maximum number of his wife's fingers that could be simultaneously included was two. If this ratio were reversed, with her fingers outnumbering his, his erection was unaffected but he was unable to reach orgasm. Unfortunately, our information stops there because this was a failure case (largely a consequence of a conflict between the cotherapists).

The Autosexual Orientation

It is as if this patient's genitals were numb to his wife's touch, though not to his own. In this regard, I think that the retarded ejaculator falls at one end of a continuum. Suppose a survey were to be done and men were asked how they ranked penile stimulation by their partner's hand (heterosexual and/or homosexual) versus their own hand. My prediction is that we would find two relatively distinct groups, each having a clear preference for one hand or the other— and each assuming that all men are like themselves. This prediction is based on the finding that in our body-work therapy (see later), about 35% of all patients say that they prefer manual stimulation by their own hand rather than the body-work therapist's. Of course, we do not often find the rigid exclusiveness characteristic of the retarded ejaculator, but the difference is clear in these men's minds. They will often say, as if it is obvious, "How could anyone else know how to do it better than me? After all, I've been doing it for years."

It is evident that this is what a retarded ejaculator such as the husband just described would say if he could. He cannot because he feels so totally discredited. He just feels that he should enjoy his partner more. The RE patient will rarely say how much he enjoys masturbation in contrast to heterosexuality and/or homosexuality. However, if Women's Lib and Gay Lib were to be followed by Masturbators' Lib, he might go on at length extolling the relative joys of masturbation—how you are completely freed from the hassle of a demanding partner, free to enjoy yourself in any way you want, free to lose yourself totally, as by devoting yourself to your favorite fantasy.

Of course, there is no Masturbators' Lib; there is only the new freedom to masturbate, *not* to prefer masturbation to sex with a partner. And the retarded ejaculator appears to be the least of the liberated in this regard. His position is typically wholly undermined, and he can only doggedly pursue the coital orgasm, or, at best, he can reap whatever rewards are his due as the workhorse of sexual relationships.

His position is so undermined that he has no way to report it to the clinician, and the clinician is not predisposed to recognize a masturbatory sexual orientation. Thus, Masters and Johnson (1970) only note that for 14 of their RE cases, "masturbation had been the major form of sexual tension release" (p. 129). (Apropos of my previous argument, the remaining "three of the 17 men had never been able to masturbate to ejaculation before therapy," thus obscuring the true RE patient's autosexuality.) Kaplan (1974) does not even provide such a summary statement. However, it is clear that in each of her case examples, perhaps even in her one case of organic impairment, the patient at least had no difficulty in masturbation.

To offer a perspective on those with an autosexual orientation, I should note that retarded ejaculators must be only a small part of this group, as many of those whose primary orientation is autosexual will not have automatic erections, whereas others may but probably escape being retarded ejaculators because they have "automatic" orgasms or orgasms with effort as well. Of course, the largest group of autosexuals may be those who make no effort to have an orgasm with a partner, including those who avoid partners altogether to simply pursue their solitary masturbatory ways.

CAUSAL CONCEPTIONS OF RETARDED EJACULATION

My Own View

My own explanation of RE begins with the observation that, for reasons yet unknown, some people are highly reactive genitally even when erotic feeling is minimal or absent. Just as there are men who have automatic erections, there are women who lubricate easily, even copiously, when they have hardly begun to experience passion. There also are those who are bored by orgasms, though they still have them, and even those who are sexually aversive but still respond with erection or lubrication and orgasm.

I think of the retarded ejaculator as being a member of this genitally reactive group. He is inhibited by the touch of a partner, but this is easy to avoid and, like many men, he may turn himself on by handling his penis himself, shutting out the partner mentally, and going on to intromission. However, he cannot continue to stimulate himself and inevitably must experience partner (vaginal) stimulation of his penis during penetration and thrusting. This automatically orients him to his partner, and he experiences a compulsion to satisfy her and a detachment from himself that blocks orgasm. This is exactly what happens to women in coitus who feel compelled to monitor and cater to the male ego.

In the presence of a partner, the retarded ejaculator's penis is relatively insensate or numb because it is out of synch with his level of erotic arousal. If we think of arousal as accelerating over the course of the response cycle (and I am not sure we should), the RE patient's sexual response to a partner does not show this interdependency of erotic and physical reactions. In this sense, he has what might be called "premature" erections. If the standard view is that the retarded ejaculator should have coital orgasms, my view is that he should have an erectile dysfunction.

The retarded ejaculator's erect penis with a partner is like a flaccid one: Because the typically correlated erotic feelings are absent or minimal, his erect penis does not amplify sensation in the usual way. This is why he cannot have coital orgasms. During intromission, he is less able to stimulate himself, and he does not get enough stimulation from his partner. Like a man with a chronic erection problem, he gravitates toward heavy friction in the effort to reach orgasm. His situation is exactly analogous to that of women who, as has recently been recognized, do not necessarily experience adequate physical stimulation during coitus but need focused and reliable manual or oral stimulation.

It is apparently easy to be drawn into the RE patient's scale of values. Although by the RE patient's standard he is depriving and punishing his partner, we should remember that in reality she is likely to be multiorgasmic. After all, what he is depriving her of is his own orgasm. Depriving the partner of his own pleasure must be seen as a rather mild form of "rejection" or "open enmity," *especially considering that this rebellion never includes refusing or even shortening coitus, much less denying the partner her multiple orgasms.* We have to take account of the scale of values by which such a subtle deprivation is considered to be an indication of rejection or open enmity. It seems to me that the retarded ejaculator's exaggerated view of his negative reactions is a measure of the yoke of conscientiousness under which he labors, that is, is evidence of a compulsion to *satisfy* the partner which the patient has no way to recognize on his own.

The necessity to satisfy a partner can be so taken for granted by the patient that he is only aware of the times he inwardly balks. Any hesitation to devote himself to the partner's satisfaction can seem to him like a serious transgression. Thus, his admissions of enmity, repulsion, and wishes to frustrate his partner must be understood as *confessions* of a guiltily experienced aversion generated by feeling trapped, especially in coitus.

It also seems to me that it is this compulsion to please the partner that creates the resentment and impulse toward sexual sabotage that some retarded ejaculators acknowledge. The RE patient's compulsive, genitally focused style can make the partner feel that there is nothing she can do for him. Add to this that he finds her touch unexciting, even oppressive, and it is easy to see how she could fall into a passive role. Because he has no sense of consciously choosing this style, his experience of sex is of a continuous demand for performance. This can create a potential for feeling used, but he typically takes his role so much for granted that he has no way to feel entitled to experience himself as being used. Instead, he has flashes of disgust and/or hatred for his partner.

He also feels disgusted at his own ejaculate, as expressed by his fear of soiling his partner with it. I take this as a sign of his turned-off state. When people are in a sexual situation but not aroused, they often have disgust reactions that disappear when they are aroused.

As for the fear of impregnating the partner, it may be that the reason this fear is featured so prominently in discussions of this syndrome is that RE comes to most clinician's attention only because of the female partner's wish to conceive, another bit of evidence that RE is looked at from the partner's point of view. In any event, I suggest that too much is made of this because RE (in anal intercourse) is found in gay men and may even have a higher incidence in these men.

Depth Explanations

Fenichel (1945, pp. 172–174) offers a one-sentence comment on RE that can still serve to summarize the psychoanalytic view: "It may express unconscious fears about dangers supposed to be connected with the ejaculation (castration, death), or strivings, anal (retaining) or oral (denial of giving) sadistic or masochistic in character." In other words, Fenichel here summarizes two causes of RE: (1) a fear that ejaculation will mean castration or death and (2) an unwillingness to "give" (anal retentiveness, oral sadomasochism).

The first of these two causes is based on the symbolic implications of a coital orgasm. Thus, Ovesey's (1971) conception of RE is as follows:

> [It] results from the patient's misconception of sexual intercourse as an act of masculine aggression in which the penis becomes a weapon of destruction. The patient then fears murderous retaliation from the woman, just as he does from men.
>
> [Retaliation from men is a feared consequence because] successful completion of the act is unconsciously equated with victory over male competitors in which the defeated male is killed, castrated, and homosexually subjugated. (p. 12)

In short, the retarded ejaculator appears to believe that no one wants him to have a coital orgasm. If this is so, why then does he not simply choose to not have coital orgasms? Why, instead, can he not be a thankful *non*ejaculator? Or, better put, why does Ovesey not consider this question?

As I see it, these repressed fantasies are generated by the retarded ejaculator's compulsion to enter into coitus. His penis is, in effect, not his own: He loses it. He has no way to conceptualize this, and so he has highly symbolic fantasies, and even these are repressed. In simple terms, the psychoanalytic view is that the fantasies are the cause of an unconscious aversion to coital orgasms. My view is that these fantasies represent, in exaggerated form, the feelings that the retarded ejaculator is already having. His is the mentality of the trapped: He is already castrated. (It is generally true of classical psychoanalytic explanations that they reverse the causal sequence in this way because they treat fantasies as ultimate explanations rather than symptoms of repressed affect.)

No matter how horrible his unconscious fantasies are, what many analysts are likely to miss is that the retarded ejaculator is unable to have a good reason to dislike sex with a partner. He has no way to feel entitled to complain about feeling turned off by a partner's demands.

Thus, the fantasies Ovesey describes do clearly reveal the guilt-ridden world of the retarded ejaculator, feeling at risk and on trial in sex. However, I think that if Ovesey were familiar with what we might call the *politics* of RE, he might be less convinced of the interpretation that the retarded ejaculator fears punishment for ejaculating and more likely to interpret these fantasies as representing the fear of being punished for not ejaculating.

The second causal conception summarized by Fenichel is that the retarded ejaculator is unwilling to "give." Despite their formidable abstruseness, psychoanalytic formulations are, at bottom, based on the familiar, if superficial, impression that the RE patient wants to deprive his partner and thus is withholding his own orgasm from her. We look in vain for any effort by psychoanalytic theorists to make this explanation plausible. It simply fits the classical psychoanalytic assumption that symptoms are unconsciously gratifying, meaning as applied to the RE patient that he unconsciously wants to be anorgasmic.

Unfortunately, retarded ejaculators are typically accused of not wanting to "give" by their partners, just as premature ejaculators are typically accused by their partners of being inconsiderate. As Masters and Johnson (1970) note of their relatively large sample: "Although only three men constrained their ejaculatory processes to frustrate their wives [Masters and Johnson mean that only three men confessed to this motive], many more were accused of this motivation by their partners" (pp. 192–194). The retarded ejaculator's own belief that he is withholding is widely endorsed, understandably by his partners and, less justifiably, by most therapists.

The RE patient *cannot* be withholding, cannot *stop* giving. In all my cases, the retarded ejaculator is a classic example of the partner who is unable to take, to be selfish, or, as the current jargon has it, to be responsible for his own satisfaction. It is only when he is alone that he can enjoy his own sensations without worrying about the partner's satisfaction. In fact, I am tempted to say on behalf of the retarded ejaculator, "How much *more* can you give?" He is the workhorse of sex, as I put it earlier, doing the work of 10.

This is by far the most damaging and disturbing misunderstanding of RE. The damage done by this misunderstanding is not limited to confounding the patient's conflicts. It also intensifies his guilt-ridden confusion over who his orgasm is for. Sex therapists and most other therapists are especially clear on this point with the anorgasmic woman. They insist that her orgasm is for her. In Barbach's well-known phrase, it is "for yourself." Thus, no one suggests that the anorgasmic woman is withholding her orgasm from her partner and if she does give any indication that she is trying to have an orgasm for him, this attitude is quite likely to be questioned.

However, it appears that no one hesitates to endorse an RE patient's guilty belief that it is his partner who suffers from his not having an orgasm. Those therapists who confront him with the interpretation that he is withholding (see Kaplan, 1987) show no concern about the implication that if not being coitally anorgasmic means that an individual wants to withhold from his or her partner, it must be his or her partner that the orgasm is for.

This is exactly what the RE patient himself believes and is one way of explaining why it is he does not have coital orgasms. Almost all therapists are well aware of the fact that what prevents many women from being orgasmic is their belief that their partner is the one who is deprived if they are not orgasmic. In other words, it indeed is difficult to have an orgasm for someone else.

I would even venture to suggest that because the RE patient believes it is so abusive of him to not have a coital orgasm for his partner, he might even feel it was more abusive of him to have a coital orgasm *for himself*. If he is so unable to be selfish that he feels his is depriving his partner by not having an orgasm, it might well feel even more selfish to have an orgasm just to please himself. This may be the best way to look at Ovesey's interpretation that the retarded ejaculator fears punishment for being coitally orgasmic.

A common rejoinder to this argument has been that the retarded ejaculator's orgasm, or at least his ejaculation, *is* for his partner if she wishes to conceive, and therefore it makes sense to think that by withholding it he is punishing *her*.

This argument implies that a man would not be a retarded ejaculator with an infertile partner or would be cured if his partner became infertile, an absurd possibility on its face. I find this point especially interesting because this willingness to risk absurdity would appear to reveal the general bias against the retarded ejaculator.

I should here consider Kaplan's psychodynamic formulation (her reflex conception is discussed later), because in the revised edition of her *Illustrated Manual of Sex Therapy* (1987) it has been reprinted unchanged. It recapitulates the standard explanations I have just considered:

> Two conflicts do emerge with predictable frequency when treating the retarded ejaculator, namely: fear of involvement with the woman, and related conflicts centering around hostility and sadistic impulses toward women. During the course of treatment with these couples it is often revealed that the man is really "holding back" psychologically as well as physiologically with his orgasm. Frequently also a great deal of hostility to women is evident of which the man is unaware. The patient must often be confronted with this hostility. (p. 151)

First, one wonders on what grounds Kaplan can say that the two conflicts she identifies "emerge with predictable frequency," a statement originally published in 1975, when a year earlier she declined to state the number of RE cases she had treated, only saying that her experience "has been too limited to be statistically significant" (1974, p. 336). Where the two conflicts emerge with predictable frequency is in the literature, a case of persuasion by authoritative repetition rather than by an appeal to clinical data.

The classical psychoanalytic formulation continues to be repeated. In their column of advice to readers, "Keeping Fit in Bed," Shore and Shore (1987) inform the public that retarded ejaculators are "overcontrolled," listing the causes of overcontrol as guilt over sexual activities, fear of pregnancy, "pressure placed on the man to hold off ejaculation for longer and longer periods of time," conflict with a partner, lack of interest in or dislike of a partner, and difficulty in letting go and giving up some control.

The only new contribution in this list is "pressure . . . to hold off ejaculation" (p. 55), the assertion that in trying to delay orgasm the retarded ejaculator somehow overshoots the mark and gets stuck there. This does not explain how he manages to be so successful where legions of men fail. One can only conclude that in explaining RE at least, clinicians are constrained only by the limits of their imagination.

Behavioral Explanations

The chief behavioral explanation of RE is that it is an inhibited reflex and that the causes of this inhibition are irrelevant to its treatment. This interpretation of RE is evident just from the diagnostic labels used by Masters and Johnson and by Kaplan. For Masters and Johnson, it is "ejaculatory incompetence," a label that has not achieved currency probably because only Masters and Johnson can keep in mind what it means—that the reflex and not the person is incompetent. Kaplan heads her chapter in *The Illustrated Manual of Sex Therapy* (1987): "Retarded Ejaculation—Ejaculatory Overcontrol." Kaplan (1974) offers the clearest and most revealing statement of the reflexogenic interpretation of RE:

> Clinical evidence suggests that all the traumatic factors...can result in retarded ejaculation. It may be speculated that the mechanism by which these various factors impair the ejaculatory reflex involves an involuntary, and unconscious, conditioned inhibition. According to learning theory, the ejaculatory response has become inhibited because of its association with a painful contingency. The response is blocked just exactly as though the patient anticipated punishment by an electric shock each time he ejaculated or even had the impulse to ejaculate. (p. 327)

The precise nature of the original painful contingency becomes irrelevant when it is considered in this conceptual context. Kaplan (1974) goes on to propose that RE is similar to "constipation, which results from inhibition of the defecatory reflex, globus hystericus, which is due to an inhibited swallowing reflex, and spastic colitis due to impaired peristalsis" (p. 327). Kaplan has not said how her reflexogenic conception can be reconciled with her psychodynamic one, making it difficult to know how far she takes her parallel between RE and constipation. She undoubtedly does not mean to suggest that constipation is a hostile act in which the retarded defecator deprives someone else by withholding his feces.

Also, Kaplan's diagnostic conception makes no distinction between masturbatory and coital anorgasmia. The true retarded ejaculator's orgasmic "inhibition" is specific to one particular context. Constipation is not. It seems unlikely that this formulation would be put so definitively if Kaplan were to recognize that the retarded ejaculator is easily orgasmic in masturbation.

Kaplan (1987) does not acknowledge the way that her reflexogenic formulation is difficult to reconcile with her psychodynamic one. The idea that the RE patient has associated orgasm with a painful contingency, and hence is afraid of it, is different from the idea that the RE patient has "conflicts centering around hostility and sadistic impulses toward women" (p. 151). The first idea is that he avoids coital orgasm out of a fear of being punished; the second idea is that he avoids coital orgasm as a way of punishing his partner.

Of course, both ideas take as self-evident what is actually an assumption, that in the RE patient, orgasm is blocked rather than that his level of arousal is insufficient.

THE TREATMENT OF RETARDED EJACULATION

The Demand Strategy

The reflex conception treats RE much as if it were a male version of vaginismus. At least that is the metaphor: The idea is that where muscles should be responsive, they are locked in a clonic spasm. This makes it instructive to compare the treatment of vaginismus with the treatment of RE. A major difference from the treatment of vaginismus (Masters & Johnson, 1970, pp. 129–131) is that the spasm is "forced" abruptly in the case of RE rather than gradually as in the case of vaginismus: The female partner is encouraged "to manipulate the penis demandingly" so as "to force ejaculation." Once this has been achieved, she is to manipulate her partner nearly to orgasm and then to execute "rapid intromission." (This is what Kaplan calls the "male bridge maneuver.") If orgasm does not follow, she is to "demandingly" manipulate the penis, "quickly" reinserting.

Masters and Johnson's treatment of *female* "RE," that is, of female coital anorgasmia, is, of course, strikingly different. Their whole point with women is to avoid precisely the demand pressure that they impose on men. Whereas with men, Masters and Johnson (1970) advise a demanding style of pelvic thrusting, in the case of female coital anorgasmia, their advice is just the opposite: Coitus is to be done "without any concept of a demanding thrusting pattern" (p. 304).

With a man, the female partner is advised to force ejaculation. With a woman, the male partner is advised that she should have "the opportunity to express her sexual responsivity *without any concept of demand for an endpoint (orgasmic) goal*," (p. 307, emphasis added) and that a "forceful approach will not contribute to facility of response." With men, the objective is to build up sensation almost before they realize it; with women, Masters and Johnson (1970) warn that if "a high level of biophysical tension is reached before the psychosocial concomitant has been subjectively appreciated, the woman experiences too much sensation too soon and finds it difficult to accept" (p. 309).

Masters and Johnson rarely mention subjective arousal; thus, they nowhere state that the female with "RE" is not aroused, but it is apparent from their treatment strategy that this is how they see it. The nondemand strategy may have been seen by Masters and Johnson as required only when the process of arousal is blocked. What they consider blocked in RE is the orgasm reflex, not the process of erotic arousal. No one has ever suggested that female coital anorgasmia is a case of reflex inhibition. Thus, unlike the treatment of male coital anorgasmia, it makes no sense for the clinician to work in opposition to the patient's responses.

Consistent with their etiological conception (discussed earlier), Shore and Shore (1987), in their advice column, recommend the usual demand strategy. They call it a seven-step program. The steps (slightly abridged) consist of masturbation with partner present, partner stimulates manually to orgasm, then orally, then orally preceded by a period of penetration, then penetration when close to orgasm. If this does not work, they assert that the problem is "deeply ingrained . . . and may require extensive counseling." Shore and Shore do not even raise the possibility that a treatment program employing such direct pressure to perform can create performance pressure.

From my perspective, what we have here is a program presented to the public which is, in effect, designed to create performance pressure and hence likely to fail, with the retarded ejaculator being advised that this failure will mean that his problem is deeply ingrained and may require extensive counseling.

One might expect that given Masters and Johnson's revolutionary insight into the role of performance anxiety (Apfelbaum, 1985), such misguided efforts might be avoided. However, the Shores can hardly be faulted because by turning it into a self-help program, they have only made more graphic the demand strategy that Masters and Johnson themselves employ, thus explaining why the general conclusion has been that RE is deeply ingrained and may require extensive counseling.

Kaplan (1987) introduces a somewhat different note into the treatment of RE. Recall that in discussing what she calls the patient's "holding back," she argues that the motive for this withholding is "a great deal of hostility to women . . . of which the man is unaware" (p. 151). She then adds that "the patient must often be confronted with this hostility" (p. 151).

Those familiar with Kaplan's (1979) treatment of desire problems will recognize her heavy reliance on authoritative persuasion, which she refers to as confrontation. My impression (Apfelbaum, 1988), is that in those cases this approach has an effect that can also be seen in Kaplan's treatment of RE. The patient's guilt is reinforced: There is no way the retarded ejaculator can defend himself against the charge that he wants to withhold and that he is ungiving.

The retarded ejaculator's enslavement to his partner's demands (as he conceives of them) is of heroic proportions. Another way to put this is to say that he is extremely conscience-ridden and thus is unable to be selfish. He chronically experiences himself as not giving enough, and he is all too ready to agree that it is his partner who suffers from his not having coital orgasms.

Any man who was freer to be selfish and thus to be clear about what is in his own interest and what is in his partner's interest would find Kaplan's interpretation baffling at best, as he would have no trouble realizing that he is actually the one who is deprived by his not having orgasms. He would have the ability to remember that in fact his partners were often multiorgasmic (as I noted previously), hardly the picture of sexual deprivation.

On these grounds I cannot avoid the conclusion that Kaplan's confrontations must have the effect of further intensifying the conscientiousness that the retarded ejaculator suffers from. (She does not report success rates with this disorder, as I have indicated. Kaplan [1979, p. xvi] makes only one published reference to outcome rates, reporting a "provisional" combined dropout and failure rate of 30% for all conditions treated at her facility, by far the largest reported in the literature.)

Effects of the Standard Strategy: An Alternative View

My way of understanding how the standard (demand) strategy succeeds with RE, when it does, is to see it as an accommodation to the retarded ejaculator's need for rough, heavy stimulation. Unlike many premature ejaculators whose penises are exquisitely sensitive to touch, the penis of the retarded ejaculator is insensitive. In Kaplan's case, discussed earlier, the patient's penis was seriously numbed by a spinal cord injury. His wife used a rough leather glove to stimulate him manually and he used a towel to masturbate with. Similarly, in the intact retarded ejaculator, penile numbness is overcome by rapid and heavy stimulation.

My explanation does not account for why, at least at other treatment centers, a single experience of coital orgasm or even, as Masters and Johnson report, the experience of some of the ejaculate entering the vagina can result in successively easier coital orgasms. Our cases have not shown this all-or-none responsiveness. The first coital orgasm has not led, by itself, to dramatic changes. (Similarly, Kaplan, 1974, pp. 332–334, reports both "stable" and "unstable" results.) This has also been true of vaginismus in our population: We have only seen cases of intermittent vaginismus, so there was no "spell" to break.

In this treatment model, no distinction is drawn between RE and masturbatory anorgasmia, which makes the results difficult to evaluate. My guess is that "stable" results are more likely with masturbatory anorgasmia, paralleling the prognostic difference between primary and coital female anorgasmia (for a primary anorgasmic woman, to experience one orgasm can mark a qualitative change).

When the treatment of RE *does* have an all-or-none outcome, however, it does look as if a spell has been broken, directly confirming the conception of RE as an inhibited reflex. My alternative interpretation of this treatment effect is that what gets broken is not a spell but a set. The retarded ejaculator's sexual set is to satisfy the partner. In the strategy recommended by Masters and Johnson and by Kaplan, the partner is helped to overcome her feeling that there is no way to do anything for him. She is brought out of her withdrawal and transformed into a singlemindedly aggressive partner, determined to *give* no matter how unreinforcing it is for her. The result is that what I have characterized as the retarded ejaculator's numb response to the partner's touch is overcome, although we cannot tell from published reports of the results of this approach whether coitus and coital orgasms become as exciting as masturbatory orgasms for him and whether the partner's touch comes to rival the patient's own.

A serious drawback of this strategy appears in its effect on the patient for whom it fails. When it succeeds, it undoes the patient's oppressive compulsion to satisfy the partner. When it fails, it seems likely that its effect is to strengthen this compulsion. The patient's own belief that he should be having coital orgasms has now been supported not only by the therapist's authority but by the belief that his partner is now doing everything humanly possible for him. As a result, he would feel even less entitled to feel used, even though he would be all the more convinced that if he were to have a coital orgasm, it would be his partner's and not his own. It would be the prize that she had worked so hard to produce and that he owed her for her efforts.

Although I will not discuss the non–sex therapist's strategy for treating

RE because there is not a strategy specific to RE, from my vantage point there is not much difference between the psychodynamic therapist's approach and the behavior therapist's approach to RE. In effect, the patient is treated as if he must overcome feeling used and resentful. The patient's unconscious aversion to coital orgasm is treated as irrational and groundless.

The Counterbypassing Strategy

As I see it, not only should the retarded ejaculator not have a coital orgasm, he should not have an erection. The functionalist model makes such a formulation sound odd only because the phenomena of functioning with inadequate erotic arousal have been conceptually overlooked although they are familiar to everyone.

The standard sex therapy approach begins with the assumption that the RE patient does not experience performance anxiety. This is because his anxiety is believed to be associated with *having* coital orgasms rather than with *not having* them. If those using the standard approach were to see the retarded ejaculator as not aroused and as driven by a performance compulsion, they would be unlikely to use their present strategy. They would be more likely to use a strategy such as the one Masters and Johnson use to treat female coital anorgasmia.

In the treatment of female coital anorgasmia, Masters and Johnson's goal is to train the woman to be in control of her sexual context. During penetration in the female-astride position, the male partner is to remain passive while she meditatively regulates thrusting movements, learning to attend closely to her own sensations and to not cater to her partner. She learns, in effect, to take possession, not just of her body, as it is sometimes put, but of her sexual relationship. However, this can be difficult to accomplish with couples whose basic rapport is not up to the Masters and Johnson standard. The woman cannot as easily shed her insecurity about ignoring her partner, and the man plays a passive role only in the sense of biding his time. In such a couple, these tensions cannot be bypassed.

Such a couple can still reach the same objective by switching to what I call *counterbypassing*, an expressive technique in which the woman is helped to verbalize her worries about her partner's impatience. However, a merely expressive technique in the style of bioenergetics or Gestalt therapy is of limited value unless the woman's worries are validated, that is, unless she is helped to feel entitled to them by virtue of recognizing that her worries are valid. This is not at all difficult to do because the therapist always has the choice of picking up either her sensitivity (resulting from childhood experience, later trauma, guilt, inhibition of assertiveness, etc.) or the external reasons that her sensitivity is engaged.

In the instance just described in which a woman may be worried about her partner's impatience, the therapist might demonstrate that the partner was, in fact, impatient and that his impatience was the result, perhaps, of a fear of being turned off and losing his erection if he is too passive. Having her reactions validated is a form of endorsement that helps give the woman a way to feel more as if a sexual encounter is for *her*.

Such a counterbypassing strategy raises the specter of precipitating an inconclusive and interminable therapy. However, I would argue that this only happens when an expressive or uncovering approach *has the same objective* as a bypassing approach, that is, to extinguish negative feelings. Thus, RE can be seen as the outcome of "an unconscious refusal to ejaculate" (as an anonymous journal consultant put it in response to a manuscript submitted by one of my colleagues). The implication is that this is an inappropriate response and even that it is repressed because it is inappropriate. However, as I see it, the patient must be helped to make a *conscious* "refusal to ejaculate." It is the attempt to get the patient to give up his refusal that can result in an interminable or at least extensive uncovering therapy.

Case 3: An Illustration of Counterbypassing

It is fortunate that most of our RE cases were treated in individual body-work sex therapy, as this modality makes possible on-the-spot reports by the body-work therapist, who serves as a participant/observer. This creates an unparalleled opportunity to study and experiment with a symptom *in vivo*, which partly accounts for whatever is unique in our explanations of sexual symptoms and our treatment model. It also makes possible a far more detailed case presentation than is possible based on protocols from the treatment of couples.

Unique to our center, it is now rarely used even by us (for reasons external to the therapy itself). It is a revision of Masters and Johnson's surrogate-partner program in which the substitute-partner concept is discarded in favor of the use of paraprofessional staff members who function both as cotherapists in the therapy sessions and as body-work therapists in sessions comparable to those in which couples carry out their assignments (for further procedural details, see Williams, 1978; Apfelbaum, 1984).

The application of this strategy to RE can be quickly illustrated by the case of a Canadian architect, age 36, who requested body-work sex therapy at his second wife's urging. (Although she was a U.S. citizen, an outstanding legal problem made it risky for her to reenter the United States, and she also had concerns about confidentiality that made it difficult for her to obtain couple sex therapy in her area.) In her telephone contact with us, she complained that her husband was turned off, a unique perception in my experience for the partner of an RE. He said that he gradually became turned off while thrusting but went on in the hope of becoming aroused again, although he never did. He described the typical retarded ejaculator's automatic erection, mentioning that once when he was hospitalized after a sports accident, he was tormented by having erections when being washed by the nurses. No matter what stratagem he tried, he was unable to avoid having continuous erections during this process. However, he said that he was otherwise grateful for his constant erections because his partners never had to know how turned off he was.

He had read the first edition of Kaplan's *The Illustrated Manual of Sex Therapy* (1975; second edition, 1987) and had perfected the bridge maneuver with his wife. Using it, he was able to reach coital orgasms about 50% of the time but found it tedious and unrewarding.

Although this patient was only seen for 1 week of body-work therapy, he was quick to learn counterbypassing. He felt liberated with unusual suddenness when he was coached to express the components of his performance anxiety while being stroked by the body-work therapist. He became elated—and this turned into sexual excitement—when he told her how he hated sex, how it was an ordeal, a job, how he had to just put himself through it, measure up, and how afraid he was that the body therapist would feel insulted by his expressing these feelings. This is the kind of turning point we look for. Out of this can come an insight, a body insight as well as a cognitive one, about what has been turning the patient off and what it will take to turn him on.

The insight is that what I (Apfelbaum, 1985) have called the "ego boost" (p. 450) necessary for erotic arousal can be more powerfully generated by partner acceptance of negative feelings than by the standard "sex hype" that has the same goal.

When such a turning point is reached, it is not unusual for the patient and the therapists to feel that the job has been done. In contrast, one *performance* success is much more likely to be experienced as a random event, a fluke, and performance anxiety is intensified.

When the body-work therapist went on to manual stimulation, the patient got turned on by talking about how little he was getting out of it and how frustrating it was going to be for her, as well as by talking about how "the electric feelings" came and went. He enjoyed this so much that he could not wait to try it out on his wife and so returned home before we could go further. The questionnaire follow-up on this case was ambiguous, but I offer this case only as a brief illustration of our strategy before going on to a more extensive case presentation.

Case 4: A Successful Course of Treatment

Background

Frank, 20, a college student, complained of being unable to have a coital orgasm. He was unusually experienced sexually for his age, having had two 2-year relationships and several other briefer ones. He described himself as obsessed with sex and masturbated frequently and easily (two to three times daily), becoming aroused by intricate and extensive fantasies. His principal fantasy was of being a male prostitute (heterosexual) who aggressively "raped" women at their request.

He was concerned enough about not having coital orgasms to have inves- tigated artificial insemination in the event that his problem continued into marriage. However, after several counseling hours it became clear that his pri- mary complaint was that the reality of his sexual experiences never matched his fantasies. Although this is not in itself unusual, it became clear that Frank got very little satisfaction from his sexual encounters. Further, his continuing sense of sexual frustration and ubiquitous sexual fantasies were seriously un- dermining his ability to concentrate, threatening a loss of scholarships and making it necessary for him to consider interrupting the career line he had planned. He was unambivalently devoted to his field and had no history of previous work inhibitions.

Sexual contact with women was a proof of masculinity for him and a way of satisfying them, but masturbation was far more enjoyable. He was able to reach orgasm with a partner through manual stimulation, but only if he could call up his fantasies. However, he found it difficult to maintain a fantasy in the presence of a partner, and when he did reach orgasm by this means, it did not seem worth the effort. He had not experienced fellatio, and his lack of interest in it seemed consistent with his interest in being an aggressive "phallic" part- ner as in his fantasies.

His actual sexual role was, as in his fantasies, the compromised form of passivity represented by being aggressive on demand. A clue to this was his report that his partners were all easily orgasmic. They apparently were asser- tive and freely able to control their sexual contacts with him. His account also suggested that they encouraged rather than disliked the long-sustained coital thrusting toward which Frank was inclined. He shyly admitted that he was regularly told that he was a great lover, and this seemed based solely on his no- frills approach to thrusting and his reliable and sustained erections. He was a partner who could be easily controlled and safely ignored.

His background was white, middle class, stable, suburban, and sexually liberal. Both parents were alcoholics, although this apparently did not inter- fere with their duties and was not out of place in their social circle. He saw himself as the sexual adviser to his 5-years-younger sister, who, he proudly recounted, was already sexually active and experienced.

A self-referral, he had been in once-a-week psychotherapy for a year and reported that although he now had some insight into his problem, nothing had changed. The insight was that he was afraid of losing control and was unable to "give."

Initial Treatment Findings

Frank did not have a current partner and had to make a 400-mile round-trip commute from his campus, which limited partner availability. Although the much higher fees for body-work sex therapy as compared with couple sex therapy put him under pressure to work out an arrangement with a partner, he was unable to accomplish this. We offered to reduce the fee in exchange for his seeing a body-work therapist in training, and he agreed. He was seen in once-a-week sessions, a practice we subsequently discontinued. His was one of the cases that persuaded us that daily sessions could have shortened treatment by perhaps a third from the 18 sessions he was actually seen.

He was frightened of seeing a surrogate but was somewhat reassured when he was told that she would not be a surrogate but a body-work therapist (BT) who worked as a cotherapist with me as the review therapist, and that we worked one session at a time rather than on the basis of a fixed number of sessions. It was apparent from the first body-work session that, as Frank had reported, he had the automatic erections that I have suggested are characteristic of RE. Whereas full erections lasting as long as half an hour are uncommon, Frank's erections would last almost the entire body-work period, which could be as long as 2 hours out of a 2½-hour session. The BT reported that it was not until the 10th session that she saw Frank's penis in a flaccid state.

As Frank had previously reported, his level of arousal was not at all commensurate with his "excitement-phase" functioning. He claimed to feel nothing and said that his penis felt numb. This was corroborated by the way the BT felt: She found herself feeling bored and aimless. Perhaps because this was her first case and it also was early in the development of our treatment model, we let ourselves entertain the possibility of penetration, a relatively infrequent event in any approach to sex therapy with surrogates (Apfelbaum, 1984) and one that not only happens rarely in body-work therapy, but in no other case has been done for more than a few minutes. Further, given our present understanding of RE, it is clear that although the symptom is most noticeable in coitus, this partner-specific desire disorder can only be treated outside coitus, as this case will make apparent.

When the BT felt aroused she decided to take the previously agreed-on option of penetration. As we later realized, she responded as his partners had in that she felt relieved of the stress of Frank's tension, only to discover in the review session that he had not enjoyed it and, further, that he was recriminating himself for not being as aroused as she was. Despite this, thrusting went on for almost 2 hours. The result of such "premature" functioning has typically been the prolongation of treatment (calling into question the widespread belief in the relieving effect of performance successes). This event is another indication that our treatment of this case represents an early model.

The Necessity for a Focus on Level of Arousal

To keep treatment brief, we have found it necessary to monitor closely the patient's level of arousal and to make it the focus of our efforts. It eventually became evident to us that it is easy to do too much body work, that is, to outstrip what the patient can encompass and to move him into functioning relatively autonomous from feeling. Masters and Johnson have already pointed out that this can easily happen with women (see earlier discussion). With this recognition, we have increasingly centered on events that occur early in the body work and, as I have noted, now rarely find it necessary to go on to penetration.

Frank was a clear case in point. We found that when he was involved in coitus, he felt isolated, passive, and helpless. At this point, Frank invoked the interpretations that he had been given in his previous therapy: These ideas were that he needed to learn to lose control and to be more willing to "give." We pointed out that he condemned himself with these interpretations while, in reality, he was being left out by the BT when she withdrew from him into a sexually aroused state. He criticized himself rather than criticizing her.

In the review session with Frank and me following their engaging in coitus, the BT reported being shocked at having lost track of how turned off Frank was. She said that she had just "tripped out" in a way that she had never thought possible for her. She had had this done to her many times by men but had never thought that she could herself be an "oppressor," as she put it. This was a climactic event for Frank, suggesting to him that at least part of his problem was that he "gave" *too* much, and that, in contrast to his partners, he was not *in* control at all.

It began to dawn on Frank that he had no way to withdraw into sensation the way the BT had just done and the way his partners had. I pointed out that this dependency on the partner's response did offer an increased potential for intimacy, but that for this potential to be realized would require him to develop communication skills that others could get by without.

Inappropriateness of the Reflex Model

As I have indicated, the generally accepted strategy with RE in couple sex therapy is to increase sensation in a forceful and goal-directed way. This strategy is even more difficult to apply in body-work sex therapy than it is in couple sex therapy. As in the cases reported by Masters and Johnson and by Kaplan, Frank required his partners to work hard at stimulating him manually for him to reach orgasm. The BT was unwilling to do this. She reported that if she felt more aroused, it might be possible to become more vigorous in stroking Frank, but as it was, it just seemed too dreary. The relationship seemed too tense, and Frank already seemed under too much pressure.

As the three of us investigated her reaction further in review sessions, the BT also realized that as matters then stood, to work on physically arousing Frank would make her feel used. This fascinated Frank, and he questioned her at length about it. He had never felt entitled to feel used, as had just been demonstrated by the climactic incident in which he had been, as we had put it, *taken advantage of* by the BT during coitus. We used this way of describing what she had done for its shock value, as he considered such moral language to be, at best, quaint. However, it communicated with a deep vein of feeling in him. If he had felt anything in his previous sexual contacts, it would have been to feel used, but he had had no cognitive structure to accommodate such a feeling.

This brings up the question whether the partner in couple sex therapy should be encouraged to take the risk of being seen as rejecting, a risk the BT can take because her responses are likely to be seen by the patient as having a clinical rationale. The demand strategy used with couples in the standard approach to RE requires more subordination of the partner's needs than does the treatment of any other sexual disorder. She must aggressively stimulate the patient, either manually or orally, until he comes close to ejaculatory inevitability. This typically requires heavy, prolonged, and uninterrupted application to the task, followed by rapid intromission, also executed by the partner. Thus, it is in Kaplan's (1974) chapter on RE that she raises the problem of the effect on the partner of being required as Kaplan puts it, to "service" her husband. Kaplan warns that this may be a lot to expect of the partner unless the relationship is "good enough":

> If the women is mature enough to withstand temporary frustration without hostility, and if the couple's relationship is good enough to make her generosity psychologically rewarding, treatment can proceed smoothly under these conditions.
>
> However, the wife's intrapsychic conflicts and consequent marital discord may be evoked by the man's progressive improvement and the fact that she is required to "service" her husband. (p. 332)

"Generosity" may not be the most accurate word for the spirit with which the partner carries out her assignment. She can hardly avoid feeling obliged to comply. The alternative is to sacrifice the patient's chance to overcome his symptom. Add to this the fact that the female partner is usually the one who brings the patient into treatment, and we have what amounts to a contractual obligation on her part.

This is not to say that the partner necessarily resents this obligation, at least at first. However, recall that most of the partners in Masters and Johnson's sample experienced "a real concept of personal rejection" and a level of frustration "beyond comprehension." Some were rejected by their husbands as physically unappealing, but probably for most of them it was their husband's unresponsiveness that they took as a rejection. (Unlike the therapist and the patient himself, the partner cannot avoid recognizing that the retarded ejaculator is not aroused by her.)

This treatment strategy depends on the partner being "mature enough," as Kaplan puts it, and on the couple's relationship being "good enough" for the partner to stand further frustration and feelings of rejection. More than that, it depends on the partner's ability not just to tolerate such feelings but not to communicate them unduly by the way she stimulates the patient. It is easy to imagine her being a bit too aggressive—or not aggressive enough.

Further, even when the partner succeeds, she is modeling conscientiousness for the patient, an unfortunate reinforcement of his sex-as-work philosophy.

As for the virtues of a nondemand approach, Masters and Johnson themselves have written the text. Thus, the BT ideally models a resistance rather than a submission to sexual demands, and this would be my objective with the patient's partner as well. She can be helped to have *her* complaints about the patient's unresponsiveness and about his lack of joy. He can then be helped to say his side of it—"But I'm doing it all for you"—something she undoubtedly has never realized and would then insist was not at all what she wanted. This is how their compulsive set would begin to break up.

Psychogenic Arousal

To return to the case, when the BT first said that she found herself reluctant to do manual stimulation, Frank was unbelieving. At first he thought it was a pose or a trick, but when he decided it was a reaction she really was having, he accused *her* of being unwilling to give. This gave him a chance to watch her cope with the same accusation that had been flung at him by one of his partners and put as an interpretation by his previous therapist. To his surprise, the BT responded that she did not know why he wanted her to stroke him so vigorously, even though she could understand it intellectually. To condense this three-way discussion: Frank acknowledged that he did not know that you needed reasons to do things and that he had always just done what he was supposed to do. The BT was able then to say that she found little to respond to in Frank and that if she did not *know* that he was obsessed with sex, she would have thought that he had no interest in it.

This seemed to liberate Frank to be critical of the BT for the first time. He told her that she just did not turn him on, and then he suddenly felt a surge of sexual feeling. This was the turning point in the case. Much like the turning point I noted in Case 3, it was an example of becoming aroused by counterbypassing. At first, Frank was disturbed by it. He reported it to the BT at the time and both of us in the review session with some embarrassment, thinking that it must be abnormal to feel turned on by a complaint, especially by the complaint that he was turned off. We reassured him that this had become a familiar occurrence to us and encouraged him to go further in this direction.

At this point, he reported more sensation in his penis, though this soon disappeared as he reacted with renewed performance anxiety. He then responded with despondency, and we helped him articulate this through our technique of script construction. The patient is instructed to review his experience with the body therapist, and they both construct and shape a list of statements that he can subsequently use to identify and make contact with what he is experiencing. Frank's list included such lines as "I am afraid of feeling hopeless," "I'm afraid there is something really wrong with me," "I'm afraid you're going to give up on me," and, in a different vein, "I just don't know what you want."

In reaction to saying these lines, especially the first one, Frank again experienced sexual feelings (for more detailed examples, see Apfelbaum, 1984). Simultaneously, Frank no longer had his automatic erection, and it rarely appeared in the subsequent sessions. Although he still had erections quickly, they were typically accompanied by erotic feeling, and when his mood shifted, at moments that were usually clearly distinguishable, his degree of erection reflected this shift. For example, whenever Frank lapsed into compliance, he now would lose some, or all, of his erection. These shifts all took place during genital stroking, and the body work was confined to this during the remaining sessions.

Uncovering Residual Performance Anxiety

During this period, signs of pelvic tension were noted that related to what Frank was experiencing. He and the BT also located tension in his pubococcygeus muscle, which then reminded him of past difficulties urinating in public men's rooms.

Although Frank was now noticeably more relaxed, he still had not reached orgasm, our goal for the genital stimulation. He then reported that his masturbatory fantasy had changed: Instead of being paid to "rape" women, they now paid him to do female-superior coitus. It was just as aggressive, but they did most of the moving. He revealed that he had begun trying to fade his fantasy women out of the fantasy and to bring the BT into the fantasy just before orgasm in the hope of associating her with erotic feeling.

A Complaining Assignment

We felt fortunate that in Frank's spontaneous self-assignment of stimulus fading we had stumbled on a clue that he still felt it was up to him to generate erotic feeling. We said that this feeling of responsibility was the last hiding place of his performance anxiety and then gave him a complaining assignment to do during the genital stroking. While it was going on, it was his responsibility not to get turned on but to complain about what the BT was doing. He found himself enjoying saying, "I'm not feeling anything." When the BT jokingly responded, "Well, I'm doing the best I *can*," he felt close to orgasm but only reached it when he said, "This *really* feels mechanical."

This was Frank's only orgasm during the treatment period. Although this might be a minor event if the standard strategy were used, what happened in this instance was a "spontaneous" orgasm, that is, one that occurred without heavy and deliberate stroking, something Frank had not experienced with a partner before. With this experience of orgasm, the whole treatment approach was then reinforced and internalized. Generalization to a partner was to be expected as this orgasm made sense to Frank. He could easily see what was arousing about his exchange with the BT.

In contrast, I would not expect an "accidental" orgasm to generalize. Thus, if Frank had had a coital orgasm during his earlier episode of coitus with the body therapist, I would not expect this to affect his sexual responsiveness with other partners or, for that matter, with the BT herself. Nothing would have happened to change his sexual set. Regardless of the source of stimulation, what is needed is a "spontaneous" orgasm, that is, one that happens as an outcome of peak arousal rather than of prolonged and intense local stimulation. This is what is likely to generalize to coital orgasms, as it did in Frank's case. The coital specificity of RE is not dynamically meaningful; what is dynamically meaningful is the retarded ejaculator's insensitivity to a partner's touch in contrast to his own.

In the next session, Frank tried to repeat the series of events that had led to an orgasm, but, as usually happens, it had become a formula, and, to Frank's disappointment, neither he nor the BT felt aroused.

He then had a sudden financial setback and had to interrupt the treatment. His father's alcoholism had finally cost him his job, and his father had borrowed Frank's savings on a short-term loan to get started in a business venture. It failed, and Frank could not afford further treatment or to return to school.

Treatment Effects

I saw Frank again 5 years later. He was now in his last year of a professional school and reported that although his sexual "obsessions" no longer interfered with his work, his sexual experiences had been only partly satisfying. He reported now being able to have an erection without assuming that it required him to go on to penetration and also being able, at least at times, to stop the action when he felt out of contact. He appeared to retain awareness of his dependency on psychogenic stimulation and reported being able to tell his partner when he was turned off. He claimed to have coital orgasms easily when he felt aroused, although this was not often. It was difficult to evaluate this claim, because Frank knew it was what I wanted to hear, and he was still essentially the same person, someone whose first impulse is to satisfy the other.

For such a person, changing partners can be a solution, and it became clear that Frank had made a truly inspired choice. He apparently had instinctively shied away from the enthusiastic performers who would have reinforced his sexual compulsions and instead had a 3-year relationship with a woman who was not coitally orgasmic. This did help reverse his order of priorities, but he found toward the end of that relationship that he did not *want* to have coital orgasms, although he was somewhat less reluctant about having extravaginal orgasms. He was disturbed about not wanting coital orgasms, and it was for this reason that he wanted to resume body-work therapy. However, I thought what he needed was some reassurance and a redefinition of the problem.

Fear of Being Exploitive

Bearing in mind that what makes a retarded ejaculator is *having* to have coital orgasms, my strategy was to help Frank stay with his reluctance rather than to help him overcome it. True to type, Frank thought that he should not feel this reluctance, seeing it as unmanly to be so squeamish, and foolish as well to feel that he was using his partner if she were not equally orgasmic, as she reassured him that she enjoyed it when he had coital orgasms.

Given our sexual norms, it is all too easy for the clinician to share Frank's concern and to believe that he should be helped to overcome his ambivalence. However, in accordance with my conception of the pathogenesis of RE, my expectation is that an intervention of this kind would have led to a recurrence of Frank's RE.

I congratulated Frank on being able to acknowledge his ambivalence about having coital orgasms, as to experience sex as exploitive could at that time (the present-day awareness of sexual abuse was then lacking) make one feel unenlightened. I told him that I thought RE is created by having to deny and overcome this ambivalence, and that when the feeling of being exploitive returns (from repression), it comes back in concretized form as a fear of soiling or impregnating.

I also suggested that needing his partner to have coital orgasms reflects the retarded ejaculator's inability to "take." I reminded him of the "climactic" incident with the BT in which we said that *we* thought he had been used by her, and I suggested that on this basis, Frank's worry might be at least partly iatrogenic. He agreed but added that this had made him realize how he had always felt used and how he could hardly imagine it otherwise, even in his masturbatory fantasies.

Now that he could have coital orgasms, he worried that his partner would feel used just as he had, although she might not be aware of it, or if she were aware of feeling this way, she might be just as skilled as he had been at concealing it. Frank then realized that this worry resolved into his being afraid that she had to like everything, just as had been true for him. This turned his attention to the possibility of helping her, or a future partner, to be freer to have her dislikes, perhaps by doing a better job of having his own.

TWO FAILURE CASES

Case 5: A Missed Arousal Deficit

Two failure cases are of interest. The first patient was 23, unmarried, and a college dropout who drove a cab in a midwestern city. He was the only retarded ejaculator we have seen who bragged openly about his sustained erections and about how capable this made him as a sex partner. This was a one-week body-work therapy case, a patient who, like other retarded ejaculators, had an erection in the first session could masturbate easily on day 3 but, unlike other retarded ejaculators, in the fifth session reached his first coital orgasm (he was, like Frank, an early case). He then terminated, feeling he could no longer justify the expense of continued treatment.

His coital orgasm might best be thought of as an "accidental" orgasm, in that the therapists saw no evidence that the patient's sexual set had changed in any way. It was a relatively joyless experience, and the therapists believed that he had never really been turned on and that he was relieved to terminate before his turned-off state was exposed. My impression is that such a performance success is experienced by the patient as a fluke that he is afraid he will never be able to repeat. I have not found the "one good experience" to be reassuring unless it is accompanied by an increase in sexual pleasure.

This patient has not returned. We now might treat this case differently, having learned to resist the pressure to go ahead with the body work when the patient is not turned on. However, this can be a difficult determination to make and to be done effectively requires an experienced co-therapy team.

Case 6: A Failure to Relieve Performance Anxiety

The second failure case was a man of 43, never married, and a tutor in the humanities at a British university; he had just completed a 7-year analysis. As in the previous case, he was proud of his sustained erections (although not as openly), advertised in British swinger-style magazines, and maintained current sexual relationships with more than 30 women. He nevertheless found mastur-bation more satisfying and had never come close to a coital orgasm. He had only reached orgasm four times with a partner, all with the same partner, by masturbating and then switching to fellatio only at the point of ejaculatory inevitability.

He was a highly urbane man who made the memorable comment, "Girls just don't have the touch" (the comparison being with himself, not with men). What he seemed most attracted to in women was neatness, cleanliness, quiet-ness, and decorum. He denied that this suggested that he did not see women as sex objects. In the body-work sessions he was cool and impersonal, but our efforts to reflect this back to him were interpreted to him as a sign that the BT was disappointed.

Some work was done with muscle relaxation, which led to somewhat greater responsiveness. He said that he had never enjoyed manual stimulation of his penis before, but he (perhaps correctly) attributed it all to the use of Albolene (our preferred genital lubricant). His defensiveness continued, and he became difficult to control in the body-work sessions. Contrary to our advice, he would keep his eyes closed when stroked and also would make thrusting movements. However, we were able to get him in touch with some of the com-ponents of his sexuality.

He said that it felt like a sacrifice to penetrate a woman, as if he had given her a part of himself, but at the same time it was an honor to be allowed this act of chivalry. He also said that he was afraid that if he reached orgasm, he would be "under a woman's dominion." (I see the presence of this fear as a symptom of his low level of arousal in the face of the pressure he felt to perform; compare vagina dentata fantasies as a reflection of the experience of feeling trapped in coitus, discussed earlier.) He was able to recognize, seemingly for the first time, that he felt no warmth from women and that he wanted to be held more than he wanted to reach orgasm.

Despite his gaining these insights, we lost control of the therapy. The BT felt incapacitated, and this proved difficult to present properly to the patient. He felt at fault and became alarmed when, for the first time, his erections were no longer as firm. When the typical 2-week limit was reached, he was obviously relieved to have a pretext for termination. Although we were only guardedly optimistic, we encouraged him to continue, saying that we thought his case might simply be long term (3 or 4 weeks). He did not continue and, despite his expressed intention to return, probably will not.

I do not think that a more aggressive BT or the use of the standard technique of vigorous manual stimulation and rapid intromission would have been any more effective in this case. He may have been most like the relatively content nonclinical retarded ejaculators who have elaborated their symptom into a lifestyle and, as I speculated earlier, may represent the majority of men with this disorder.

TREATMENT RECOMMENDATIONS

Although RE is reputed to be especially difficult to treat, this appears to be an iatrogenic artifact. It is my impression from informal reports from therapists, as well as from patients, many of whom have contacted me only by phone or letter, that even a reading of the previous edition of this chapter has resulted in symptom relief.

Typically it is possible to establish the basic insights in an hour or two because they are either already familiar to the patient—he has just not seen their relevance—or they are instructive in a way that immediately fits the patient's experience. For example, these patients assume that any man has orgasms most easily and often most enjoyably in masturbation and also that any man is more excited by his own hand than by his partner's.

Of course, this also is a diagnostic cue. If the patient also has difficulty being orgasmic in masturbation, it rules out RE, as does a history of being coitally orgasmic (as I have suggested, male coital anorgasmia makes no more sense as a diagnostic entity when specific to one partner than does partner-specific erectile disorder—just as no one would diagnose partner-specific female coital anorgasmia).

Although some retarded ejaculators know that they have unusually sustained erections because they have had partners who told them so, most think that erections are terminated by orgasms and the only reason other men do not have such sustained erections is that they have partner orgasms more easily. They usually readily agree that their erections are relatively numb. Why orgasm is not forthcoming then makes a new kind of sense to them.

If it is then suggested that sex with a partner is something of a trial for them, especially in contrast to masturbation, they are quick to agree. The next step is for the retarded ejaculators to see how their lack of excitement is only to be expected in view of their proneness to be accommodators and to be givers rather than takers (to have trouble asking for favors, to be self-reliant and excessively conscientious).

For those retarded ejaculators who have been accused of hostile withholding by a partner or have been presented with a similar interpretation by a therapist, it is instantly relieving to be told that they have more than earned their stripes.

It also should be made clear to the patient that working at generating orgasms by heavy friction will quickly get into diminishing returns and that in evaluating his level of responsiveness with a partner he should keep constantly in mind the contrast with his orgasmic experience in masturbation, in which little friction is necessary to reach orgasm.

This means introducing the idea to the RE patient that he is the kind of person who may need to be erotically aroused before he can have a coital orgasm. Although he may protest that he *is* aroused, it should be easy for him to recognize how much more aroused he is in masturbation than he is with a partner, and, of course, he is well aware of how coitus feels like drudgery. He can then be introduced to the next idea, which is that he does not feel entitled to be critical of his partner (this is not hard to demonstrate even to the RE patient who begins by confessing that he is repelled by his partner; after all, what is he doing still trying to be orgasmic with her?).

The therapist can then present the view that anyone might feel left out, ignored, or used when he is getting little out of sex at the same time that his partner is multiorgasmic. Because the patient invariably expects to be treated as if he is abnormal for not having coital orgasms, this insight can be immediately relieving.

It is especially important to introduce the idea that the patient is trying too hard to have an orgasm for his partner. He needs to know that many women have now realized that they cannot have an orgasm for their partners, but that it is a hard lesson for men to learn because everyone simply assumes that men do not need to learn it. This is especially true because most therapists, both sex therapists and non–sex therapists, think of the retarded ejaculator as withholding his orgasm from the partner. We point out that women who have the same problem (i.e., who are coitally anorgasmic) are never thought of as withholding their orgasms from the partner.

The usual behavioral outcome criteria are especially inappropriate as applied to this syndrome. One crucial outcome criterion is relief at having the stigma lifted of being seen as hostile toward women or unwilling to give. Another is relief at feeling entitled to the experience of drudgery in sex. Having the autosexual orientation endorsed is helpful in this regard. For some men, feeling free to not want to have coital orgasms feels like a special privilege, but the more complete liberation comes with recognition that they have a right to expect much more from sex than they have ever gotten. Indeed, in this regard Case 6, a man whose treatment we rated a failure, had what for a retarded ejaculator is a rare and especially revealing insight. This was his recognition in the therapy that he felt no warmth from women and that he wanted to be held more than he wanted to reach orgasm. He said this as if he were confessing a fault, but if we could have convinced him to take this yearning seriously, as an eminently valid wish, and had he been able to act on it, we might well have considered him our most successful case.

In other words, it is difficult to divorce outcome criteria from the whole diagnostic and therapeutic treatment frame. If RE is seen simply as male coital anorgasmia and outcome is measured in coital orgasms, then my own success rate cannot properly be assessed because this is not the treatment goal. If RE is seen as a desire, or even intimacy disorder, then the criterion is less specifiable, although given that criterion, failures are rare, even in the brief counseling that usually is all the typical RE patient is motivated for.

CONCLUSIONS

Retarded ejaculation is thought of as difficult to treat because, uniquely among the sexual disorders, the standard interpretations have not been revised and still reflect early psychodynamic thinking. The retarded ejaculator is thought of hostile and withholding, his inability to have coital orgasms seen as a refusal that must be aggressively overcome in sex therapy.

What should have alerted clinicians to the inadequacy of this interpretation is the well-known fact that the retarded ejaculator does not merely have difficulty reaching orgasms in coitus; his coital anorgasmia is absolute. Even to experience coital orgasm once in the course of treatment constitutes a major breakthrough. It is difficult to imagine a hostile act being carried out so unwaveringly.

In my view, what accounts for this consistency is simply that the retarded ejaculator is never sufficiently aroused to reach orgasm in intercourse. This is the same consistency shown by the woman who is coitally anorgasmic.

However, the absolute lack of male coital orgasm is accounted for in the standard view by offering a second explanation, that RE is a reflex inhibition. Putting these two explanations together, it looks as if the retarded ejaculator refuses to be coitally orgasmic (the dynamic explanation), evidently not realizing that he could not be orgasmic even if he changed his mind (the reflex explanation).

I propose that the two explanations simply exist side by side with no attempt to reconcile them because they both justify aggressively attacking the retarded ejaculator's reluctance. Given the dynamic interpretation that retarded ejaculation represents a *refusal*, the therapist feels justified in aggressively overcoming this refusal rather than helping the retarded ejaculator to feel less self-condemnatory about it, that is, to be able to refuse more directly.

The reflex explanation helps buttress this justification. Sex therapists can think of themselves as trying to break a spell because they would, of course, not want to think of themselves as trying to break the patient's will. In other words, the two standard explanations are a disguised expression of disapproval.

Even sex therapists who are sensitive to the role of performance anxiety, and who recommend a scrupulous avoidance of performance demands in the treatment of coitally anorgasmic women, recommend an intensely demanding regimen in the treatment of coitally anorgasmic men. To explain this discrepancy requires a recognition of hitherto masked features of RE, as well as of a normative bias in the way clinicians react to socially deviant attitudes.

Among those diagnosed as retarded ejaculators (i.e., as suffering from coital anorgasmia) are men who also have difficulty masturbating. This has masked the pronounced autosexual (masturbatory) orientation that emerges as a critical diagnostic cue for RE, once men who have difficulty masturbating are excluded. This autosexual orientation is manifested by masturbatory facility and enjoyment, and a loss of desire in partner sex.

An additional reason why therapists are not disposed to help the retarded ejaculator to refuse to be coitally orgasmic is that, much as once was true for homosexuality, autosexuality is not acceptable as a bona fide orientation.

The loss of desire in partner sex has also been masked by the retarded ejaculator's quasi-priapic erections. Because the retarded ejaculator manifests unusually sustained erections in partner sex, it has been assumed that he must be fully aroused and therefore that his disorder is specific to the orgasm phase. Although the retarded ejaculator's erections are long-sustained, they are insensate to such an extent that the behavioral objective with the retarded ejaculator should not be for him to have coital orgasms but to have enjoyable erections with a partner. The retarded ejaculator is not likely to report his lack of desire with a partner because, just as is true for the coitally anorgasmic woman, he focuses on his partner's enjoyment rather than his own.

Although the cues that reveal the retarded ejaculator's desire disorder are masked, this alone does not account for the standard misinterpretations of RE. Some retarded ejaculators make plain their aversion to the partner, but it is discounted. In effect, the retarded ejaculator is treated as if he should want to have coital orgasms. No consideration is given to the possibility that he needs to be better able to refuse to have coital orgasms and to refuse coitus, and that he may have good reason to do so.

Recognition of the retarded ejaculator's desire disorder specific to partner sex makes it clear that he does in fact have good reason to refuse coitus. He believes that he should be enjoying partner sex and he typically is in full agreement with the clinician that he should be having coital orgasms. The use of a demanding treatment regimen is congruent with the retarded ejaculator's conscientious approach to sex and reinforces the performance pressure he already feels.

The way the retarded ejaculator is disapproved of is reminiscent of the once-popular disapproving interpretation of "frigidity." Most sex therapists now have a secure grasp on the insight that the "frigid" woman is not with-holding and that her problem is quite the opposite, that she is too preoccupied with pleasing the partner. She is told that she needs to learn to please herself. The retarded ejaculator can benefit from the same insight, but he is not likely to be presented with it.

The psychodynamic bias that originally was directed against "frigidity" and all the sexual disorders, and still affects the way retarded ejaculation is thought of, is based on the assumption that symptoms gratify unconscious wishes. Therefore, the patient is not seen as authentically suffering from a symptom. Only those around him or her are seen as suffering. They are the ones that need to be rescued, not the one who is symptomatic.

The possibility that patients are authentically suffering has been granted, at least by behavioral and cognitive therapists and by ego analytically oriented psychodynamic therapists, but this dispensation not yet been extended to the retarded ejaculator. He is still viewed with suspicion. Hence, the standard treatment of retarded ejaculation continues to be unempathic.

REFERENCES

Apfelbaum, B. (1977). Sexual functioning reconsidered. In R. Gemme & C. C. Wheeler (Eds.), *Progress in sexology*. New York: Plenum.

Apfelbaum, B. (1984). The ego-analytic approach to individual body-work sex therapy: Five case examples. *Journal of Sex Research, 20,* 44–70.

Apfelbaum, B. (1985). Masters and Johnson's contribution: A response to "Reflections on sex therapy," an interview with Harold Lief and Arnold Lazarus. *Journal of Sex Education and Therapy, 11,* 5–11.

Apfelbaum, B. (1988). An ego-analytic perspective on desire disorders. In S. Leiblum & R. Rosen (Eds.), *Sexual desire disorders* (pp. 75–104). New York: Guilford Press.

Fenichel, O. (1945). *The psychoanalytic theory of neurosis*. New York: Norton.

Kaplan, H. (1974). *The new sex therapy*. New York: Brunner/Mazel.

Kaplan, H. (1979). *Disorders of sexual desire*. New York: Brunner/Mazel.

Kaplan, H. (1987). *The illustrated manual of sex therapy* (2nd ed.). New York: Brunner/Mazel.

Masters, W. H., & Johnson, V. E. (1970). *Human sexual inadequacy*. Boston: Little, Brown.

Ovesey, L. (1971). Inability to ejaculate in coitus. *Medical Aspects of Human Sexuality, 5,* 121.

Razani, J. (1977). Ejaculatory incompetence treated by reconditioning anxiety. In J. Fischer & H. L. Gochros (Eds.), *Handbook of behavior therapy with sexual problems* (vol. 1). New York: Pergamon.

Shore, D., & Shore C. (1987). Keeping fit in bed. *Penthouse Forum, 17,* 2, 54–56.

Williams, M. H. (1997, March). *An unnoted inconsistency in Masters and Johnson's use of nondemand techniques: Retarded ejaculation*. Unpublished paper presented at the California State Psychological Association Convention, Los Angeles.

Williams, M. H. (1978). Individual sex therapy. In J. LoPiccolo & L. LoPiccolo (Eds.), *Handbook of sex therapy* (pp. 477–483). New York: Plenum.

9

Erectile Dysfunction
Psychotherapy with Men and Couples

STANLEY E. ALTHOF

As Stanley E. Althof notes, cures for impotence have enjoyed widespread and wide-eyed popularity, across cultures and across time. Nevertheless, few treatments, whether pharmacologically sound or not, are likely to succeed without addressing the psychological as well as organic contributions to the problem. In his chapter, Althof presents a treatment approach to cases of primarily psychogenic erectile failure that includes an integration of psychodynamic, object relations, self psychology, and behavioral therapy within a short-term treatment model. The goal is to both clarify the meaning of the erectile problem as well as to understand the context in which it occurs.

For instance, Althof points out that erectile dysfunction can serve a multitude of purposes, as, for example, it may disguise a paraphilic problem, a homosexual orientation, a lack of desire toward one's partner, or even a gender identity disorder. Acknowledging these and other intrapsychic and/or interpersonal issues is critical in resolving the erectile dysfunction. Treatment with men experiencing psychogenic erectile difficulties has many components, including helping the patient to acknowledge buried feeings, developing new solutions to interpersonal problems, improving couple's communication, overcoming barriers to intimacy, and developing more realistic sexual expectations and feelings of sexual confidence.

Althof notes that many men have difficulty revealing aspects of their life about which they feel embarrassed and hiding shameful or embarrassing aspects of themselves, which they may or may not be fully aware of. Uncovering or resolving these issues can move therapy forward in an effective way and help the client to make better sense of his current difficulty.

While every clinician has a unique style or way of conducting psychotherapy with men with erectile dysfunction, Althof notes that presently there are insufficient data supporting specific patient or therapist variables as predictors of outcome; that is, what kind of patient does best with what kind of treatment approach or therapist? Especially in cases of primarily psychogenic erectile dysfunction, long-term data are needed on the role of pharmacological interventions alone, versus either psychotherapy alone or a combination of therapies. Nevertheless, Althof recommends individual rather than couple therapy for the man with lifelong erectile failure. This is frequently required because these cases generally require uncovering early life events and pressing intrapsychic conflicts. In men with viable or good partner relationships, working with both the man and his partner is recommended, primarily because the erectile difficulty may represent the couple's "shared solution to some aspect of their relationship."

At times, pharmacological intervention is useful with men experiencing primarily psychogenic erectile failure. Althof suggests that men with lifelong erectile dysfunction, low sexual confidence and assertiveness, or significant medical factors, in addition to psychological conflict and previous unsuccessful psychotherapy, may be candidates for adjunctive medication. Pharmacological therapies are not always indicated in men who have recent onset erectile difficulties, couples with severe marital discord, or younger males with significant sexual performance concerns or anxiety.

In addition to empathy and dynamic understanding, Athof recommends an exploration of the patient's cognitive beliefs and expectations, an appreciation of transference phenomena, behavioral assignments and exercises, including sensate focus, and relapse prevention work also as part of the therapy process. Throughout his illuminating chapter, Althof offers salient case examples illustrating key points, while demonstrating the blend of art and science that makes up effective psychotherapy.

Stanley E. Althof, PhD, is associate professor of psychology at the Case Western University School of Medicine, and the codirector of the Center for Marital and Sexual Health in Cleveland, Ohio.

INITIAL CLINICAL PRESENTATIONS OF IMPOTENCE

A stylishly dressed, recently divorced, anxious 38-year-old vice president rhetorically asks, "What woman would want to go out with a man who can't get it up?"

Given Viagra by his internist, a 45-year-old depressed male complains that the drug works when he "takes it for a test drive by himself" but mysteriously does not when he tries to make love to his girlfriend.

A distinguished 55-year-old man enters the office, slowly seats himself, and says, "I'm impotent. I've lost my manhood. I'm no good, useless; I can no longer perform. My wife will probably have an affair and leave me." During her interview his wife laments, "He no longer loves me. I'm not attractive anymore. Maybe he's involved with another woman!"

A stooped, sad, tired-looking retired 65-year-old grandfather declares, "My wife sent me to you because we are no longer affectionate." His short, gray-haired 63-year-old wife confides, "I'm very sad. It's ended our sex life. Now he won't even touch me."

AN OLD CONCERN

Man has always been concerned with his sexual prowess. Treatments, rituals, folk remedies, and sex manuals have been discovered among the writings of the ancient Greek physicians, the Islamic and Talmudic scholars, and the Chinese and Hindu practitioners. Cross-cultural rituals to ensure potency run the gamut from elaborate circumcision ceremonies to having pubertal adolescents fellate and swallow sperm of mature warriors. In ancient Greece impotent men were treated in the Temples of Aphrodite by prostitute–priestesses who functioned as religious surrogate therapists (Kaplan, 1974). The venerable Indian text, *The Kama Sutra* (Vatsayana, 1964), offered sage advice and illustrated the varied coital positions.

Even today folk remedies for erectile failure include ginseng, rhinoceros horn, and vitamin E. Promoters of "impotence cures" prey on the desperation of men deprived of their potency. At a recent National Institute of Health meeting, an attorney from the Federal Trade Commission (FTC) gave accounts of Internet health–related fraud schemes, noting that the most common scams involved weight loss products and impotence cures. During the 6 months following the release of Viagra, one company prosecuted by the FTC had acquired sales of more than $19 million.

A BIOPSYCHOSOCIAL UNDERSTANDING OF THE SYMPTOM OF ERECTILE DYSFUNCTION

Pure cases of psychogenic or organic erectile dysfunction are considered the exceptions rather than the rule (Ackerman & Carey, 1995). The National Institute of Health's consensus conference report stated that in the majority of cases, erectile dysfunction results from the additive and interactive nature of various neurological, vascular, pharmacological, hormonal, affective, cognitive, behavioral, lifestyle, and social influences. The biopsychosocial/interactive paradigm captures the ever-changing influences of biology and psychological life on sexual response (Althof & Seftel, 1999; Althof & Levine, 1997; Levine, 1992; LoPicolo, 1992; Schnarf, 1990; Segraves, 1989).

THE CENTER FOR MARITAL AND SEXUAL HEALTH (CMASH) PERSPECTIVE

This chapter describes my method for conducting psychotherapy with individuals or couples who present with primarily psychogenic erectile dysfunction. It represents an integration of psychodynamic, object relations, self psychology, and behavioral theory within a short-term psychotherapy model. The importance of the sexual equilibrium and the contextual elements within individual's/couple's lives is emphasized. This model for treating and understanding sexual problems is an outgrowth of many years of work with my colleagues Stephen Levine, MD, and Candace Risen, MSW.

Such an integrative model risks being misunderstood as a prescription for undisciplined eclecticism. Although techniques from different schools of thought are used, treatment is not an impressionistic mosaic of interventions. Rather, the guiding principles of the treatment model are to clarify the meaning of the symptom and to understand the context in which it occurs.

The model is appropriate for helping single men or couples where the man suffers from primarily psychogenic erectile dysfunction. However, the principles of this chapter can be extended to help men/couples with organic and mixed psychogenic/organic erectile difficulties overcome their psychological resistances to the effective use of medical treatments currently available (Althof, 1999; Althof & Seftel, 1999).

A MODEL FOR UNDERSTANDING SEXUAL LIFE

Figure 9.1 illustrates the CMASH model for understanding sexual life. The six components of this schema include gender identity, object choice, intention, sexual desire, sexual arousal, orgasm, and sexual satisfaction. This dyadic, interpersonal model is an elaboration of Masters and Johnson's two-part model of arousal and orgasm and Kaplan's tripartite model of desire, arousal, and orgasm. The contextual elements of sexual life are symbolized by the blank space between the two individuals who could be of the same or opposite sex. Context is composed of all the interpersonal and social elements that contribute to the couple's relationship (e.g., quality of the relationship, health status,

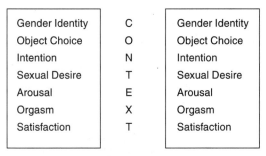

Sexual Equilibrium

FIGURE 9.1. Model for understanding sexual life.

children, job satisfaction, financial worries, retirement issues, and overall mental health). These life events may enhance or interfere with sexual functioning. Context, therefore, is given a major focus in the treatment of erectile problems.

Sexual Equilibrium

Rounding out this model is the notion of the sexual equilibrium which characterizes the ever-shifting dynamics between the couple. The sexual equilibrium is the balance among forces that promote sexual health and initiate or maintain normal sexual functioning as well as problematic sexual behavior. Sexual life operates in a closed system in which change in one partner influences the other. An erectile disturbance affects both partners but serves different psychological functions for each. For instance, the dysfunction may be a passive–aggressive expression of the man's anger. His wife may welcome the erectile problem as it helps her avoid feeling vulnerable and inadequate each time they make love. Sometimes partners sabotage treatment efforts; that is, when given homework assignments they refuse to participate, or push to go too far too quickly. These actions can be recognized as attempts to maintain the status quo, the sexual equilibrium.

Contextual issues influence the equilibrium and, assuming that sexual life operates as a closed system, any change in one partner has an impact on the other. For example, imagine a couple whose sexual life has been dormant for 2 years due to the man's erectile problem. Regaining potency does not necessarily translate into the couple resuming intercourse. The nonsexual equilibrium may be maintained by the partner developing a sexual aversion or by her instigating an argument over their finances.

The power of the sexual equilibrium surprises many therapists. Often couples seem to take one step backward for each step forward. For example, when a man begins to get firmer erections his partner suddenly loses her sexual desire. This trading of symptoms between partners occurs with such frequency that we refer to it as the "hot potato syndrome." Like a sexualized version of Newton's second law of motion, the sexual equilibrium implies that any change in one partner will produce a change in the other.

The experienced clinician anticipates the resistances engendered by the sexual equilibrium and uses them to point out the need for such a symptom in the couple's sexual life. Slowly, each partner's contribution to the initiation and maintenance of the impotence is understood and worked through. The following vignette illustrates the power of the sexual equilibrium:

> The sexual life of a demure, young professional couple who had been married for 2 years had been hampered by John's psychogenic erectile dysfunction. His difficulties began shortly after they were married. Susan felt entitled to a satisfying sexual life and was distressed by John's lack of concern about his continued problem and avoidance of any form of sexual

play. They had not touched one another for 6 months prior to seeking consultation.

Both John and Susan had attended parochial schools; currently, however, he was more invested in Catholicism. Prior to marriage, they dated for 2 years and engaged in premarital intercourse. Unfortunately, Susan had become pregnant and had undergone an abortion. During the evaluation, John said, "It was like dragging her down the sewer. I forced her to have sex with me and look what happened." Susan responded that he had not forced her; she had very much wanted to be sexual and had enjoyed it. She regretted the abortion but thought it was the right decision under the circumstances.

I suggested that treatment focus on their premarital sexual life. They agreed, and John's potency returned during the following week. John seemed pleased, but Susan suddenly lost her desire. As John was talking about "robbing Susan of her virginity," she seemed increasingly uncomfortable. When I asked what was troubling her, she "confessed" that John was not her first sex partner. We then shifted the focus to why she had allowed John to believe she was a virgin. She explained that she felt very guilty about her past behavior and feared John would not love her if she told him about her first intercourse. Although John felt angry and betrayed by Susan's "secret," he also felt relieved that he was not the only one who had done something sexually wrong prior to their marriage. The couple began to appreciate their need for some sexual symptom to alleviate their guilt. Over the next two sessions, Susan's desire returned and John's potency remained intact. At 2-month follow-up the sexual gains had persisted.

Gender and Sexual Identity

Gender identity, object choice and intention comprise the substructure of sexual functioning known as *sexual identity*. Desire, arousal, orgasm, and satisfaction comprise the more visible suprastructures of sexual functioning. *Gender identity* is a person's subjective sense of him- or herself as male or female. The most dramatic form of gender identity disturbance is transsexualism, in which a male patient might describe himself "as a woman trapped in a man's body." More subtle and disguised forms of gender identity disturbance are often seen in cases of primary impotence and paraphilias. Yet, all men struggle with their subjective sense of masculinity (e.g., feelings of competence, adequacy, and power in accomplishing responsibilities of daily life). When masculinity is significantly compromised, erectile failure can result. And the development of the problem is likely to further impair the man's sense of masculinity. The following vignette describes a case of lifelong impotence based on gender identity disturbance:

Ralph, a burly, gruff, 35-year-old electrical engineer dressed in a Cleveland Indians' windbreaker, consulted me because he wished to have a sex change operation. His wife of 2 years, a shy, plain-looking 42-year-old teacher supported his cross-gender aspirations. This couple had met through a church social group; each had limited dating experience. Their marriage was unconsummated because of Ralph's primary erectile dysfunction. She was a virgin with little sexual desire and was tolerant of her husband's cross-dressing. She planned to live with him after he had sex reassignment surgery.

Ralph's childhood was dominated by his father's violent behavior. He recalled episode upon episode of the father's unprovoked violent outbursts. In addition, as punishment for presumed misbehavior, the father would make him wear his sister's clothes and stand in the corner. In school he did well enough academically but felt socially isolated. Although he discovered his homoerotic attraction in adolescence, he still made feeble attempts to date girls and became staunchly homophobic.

He began cross-dressing and having fantasies of himself as a woman being made love to by a man. After high school, he enlisted in the Army and was sent to Vietnam. He stopped cross-dressing out of fear of being caught but drank heavily and attempted unsuccessfully to have intercourse with prostitutes. Upon return to the States, Ralph seldom dated and resumed cross-dressing. He was fired from several jobs because of his inability to get along with others. After 5 years, he married Gladys.

After several years of treatment the patient had settled on a nonsurgical solution to his gender conflict. Soon the couple divorced but remained close friends and Ralph began to cross-dress full-time. Although the patient attempted once to become sexually involved with another male-to-female transsexual, the nature of this attraction was never clear (i.e., male-to-male or female-to-female). He lived and worked full-time as a woman. Over the next 15 years, Ralph occasionally came to see me dressed as a male. Sadly, his life became more marginal and he developed a number of serious health concerns for which he was declared disabled. He then gave up full-time cross-dressing but on weekends worked as a makeup artist for "female impersonators." During his infrequent attempts at sex with his ex-wife or male friends he continued to be impotent.

Object Choice

Object choice describes the multiple sources of one's personal attraction—who or what a person finds sexually arousing. This construct transcends the traditional one-dimensional view of an individual's sexual behavior or subjective erotic life (fantasy) being designated as a point along a heterosexual to homosexual continuum. Object choice extends the gay/straight continuum to consider that individuals can have multiple sources of attractions or behaviors in different realms at the same time. A person's attractions may be based on age rather than gender alone (i.e., to children or adolescents, male or female). Also, one may be attracted to animals or inanimate objects such as shoes or lingerie; in fact, gender may have nothing to do with the source of one's attraction. The following vignette describes a case of acquired erectile dysfunction based on object choice:

Chuck, a 29-year-old married minister entered treatment for lifelong erectile dysfunction. The marriage was essentially unconsumated but the couple now wanted children. Chuck was able to achieve firm long-lasting erections as long as he wore a slip; without lingerie he could not maintain an erection. Fran, his 25-year-old wife of 2 years, could not tolerate his wearing slips to bed.

When he was a youngster his two "good Aunties" dressed him in slips and smothered him with affection. Their kindness stood in stark contrast to his alcoholic father and narcissistic mother.

Fortunately, Chuck also had a minor degree of conventional attraction to Fran. She was a doting wife and Chuck could experience her lovingness. We were able to help him "turn down the volume" on the slips and increase his interest in conventional love making. While in private he continued to masturbate with slips; he also was able to infrequently make love to Fran with an adequate erection.

This next vignette is more typical of object choice based on orientation:

Jim, a 39-year-old corporate executive, was "sent in to be fixed" by his fiancee of 4 months. He had no trouble achieving an erection but would inexplicably lose it during intercourse. Jim believed it had been a mistake to have proposed to Beth and did not want to go through with the wedding.

He had a secret: He was attracted to men but not to women. Jim had waged a lifelong war against this "dark side of himself." As a youngster he had set up an altar in his room and prayed for God to remove these "evil" impulses. He also developed a handwashing compulsion, symbolically trying to rid himself of these urges. On only a few occasions as an adult had he given in to his homosexual impulses and hired young male prostitutes. He had no erectile problems with them.

Jim loved Beth as a friend but had little desire to be sexual with her. He had hoped that marriage would help him contain his homosexual urges. I told him that his lack of desire and impotence helped solve his current life crisis; for example, they provided him with a way out of the marriage and highlighted his struggle about being gay. I asked him how it felt to be less than honest with someone he truly loved. Over six sessions Jim decided to tell Beth his secret, and the wedding plans were canceled. Jim became more accepting of his homosexuality and "came out." He found several gay professionals who invited him to join their support group.

Intention

Intention refers to what one wishes to do with a sexual impulse. Is the aim to share warmth and intimacy or is it to shock, dominate, hurt, or humiliate? Intention disorder is the name we use to characterize paraphilic or perverse behavior. Stoller (1975) observes that all sexual behavior includes some aggression, but that perversion represents an "erotic form of hatred." Alternatively, Money (1989) speaks of paraphilia as turning "tragedy into triumph." He believes that paraphilia is a means of adapting to a childhood trauma (the tragedy) by victoriously enacting it (the triumph) in a sexual context in adult life. Unfortunately, many clinicians remain unaware of their patient's paraphilic ideation either because the patient keeps it secret or because the therapist does not ask. The following vignette describes the treatment of a man with erectile dysfunction and paraphilia.

Paul, a 52-year-old nationally recognized poet, suffers from lifelong erectile dysfunction for which he has been unsuccessfully treated by a series of therapists over the past 25 years. Masochistic impulses to have women dominate, humiliate, and hurt him pervade his erotic life. On occasion he has been able to have intercourse by acting out masochistic scenarios with accommodating women. Masturbation with a firm erection has been possible only by combining masochistic imagery and mild self-inflicted pain. At age 40 he married a "ball-busting" corporate attorney who treated him as badly as he wished, but he came to hate her for the very reasons that allowed him to function sexually. After 2 years of trying unsuccessfully to conceive, they divorced.

When he entered treatment with me Paul was convinced that he was "disabled." Either he could date sadistic women and episodically function sexually or he could be with "interesting but nice" women and not get erections. Angry and dispirited about being "wired this way," he wanted to live a "normal life." Over 3 years in therapy he talked about his narcissistic mother, abusive violent father, and sexualized relationship with his older cousin. At age 7 he recalled desperately wanting to touch his cousin's budding breasts but choosing not to because "it was wrong." In time he understood his masochism represented a condensed compromise package of punishment and pleasure for his guilt over his sexual longings toward his cousin. Paul viewed all women as extensions of his cousin; therefore, sex was fraught with primitive incestual taboos. Although he found these interpretations intellectually and emotionally satisfying, he continued to feel hopeless about being sexual without masochistic fantasy. Convinced he could never transcend this template he sought to terminate treatment. I thought this might be appropriate because he had worked with several other therapists, had been in treatment for more than two decades, and was not actively seeking dating relationships. Ironically, as he was working toward terminating he met a charming and beautiful divorced 50-year-old woman. He was "smitten" by her and she with him. Initially he avoided any sexual encounters, but with encouragement from me, he began to talk to her about his sexual anxieties and eventually confided in her about his masochistic fantasies. She wanted a sexual life with him but had no interest in acting out his fantasies. However, his growing feelings of love for her motivated him to continue treatment, during which he was able to develop a new template essentially free of the ancient incestual sexual paradigm. With her encouragement and support he began to have intercourse successfully without recourse to his masochistic fantasies for arousal. For the past year he has continued to maintain good erections and only occasionally calls upon his masochistic fantasies to achieve orgasm. The couple appear to have a loving and devoted relationship.

THE GOALS OF PSYCHOTHERAPY FOR ERECTILE PROBLEMS

We often tell patients that the three requirements for having a good sexual life are (1) you have to be willing to make love, (2) you have to be relaxed; and (3) you have to concentrate on your sensations. Willingness can be aided by working through conflictual intrapsychic and interpersonal issues; relaxation and concentration on sensation can be learned through behavioral exercises.

Psychotherapy aims to restore men's potency to the optimal level possible, given the limits of physical well-being and life circumstances. Treatment seeks to overcome the psychological barriers that preclude mutual sexual satisfaction. To accomplish this goal, the patient(s) and therapist embark on an intrapsychic and interpersonal journey to discover and demystify the meaning of the impotence. On this journey the psychosomatic symptom of impotence is transformed into cognitive and emotional experiences. The therapist views the patient's symptom of impotence as a metaphor, one that contains a compromised solution to one of life's intrapsychic or interpersonal dilemmas.

Men with erectile dysfunction often feel puzzled, disgraced, weakened, and frightened. They have lost hope and confidence and wonder, "Why me?" Their "failure" may be attributed by them to physical illness, psychological concerns, interpersonal disturbance, or religious retribution. Generally, erectile dysfunction is overcome by understanding their responses to their dilemmas, integrating previously unacknowledged feelings, seeking new solutions to old problems, increasing communication, surmounting barriers to intimacy, developing realistic sexual expectations, and restoring sexual confidence.

AN OVERVIEW OF THE VARIOUS TREATMENT APPROACHES

Historically, the psychoanalytic understanding of symptom formation linked discrete, unresolved, unconscious conflicts occurring during certain developmental periods with specific symptoms. Therefore, identical symptoms were retrospectively traced to a designated constellation of conflicts dating back to childhood. Consistent with this universal pathogenesis theory, Freud (1912/ 1957a) ascribed erectile dysfunction to a man's failure to resolve his Oedipal struggle. He believed impotent men confused their mothers with their lovers. Being sexual with one's lover, now an incestuous love object, was unconsciously taboo. His view persists today as the "deep" explanation for erectile dysfunction held by many analytically trained therapists. In this tradition, men entering psychoanalysis were seen up to five times weekly for several years. Treatment of the couple was not undertaken.

More modern psychodynamic perspectives view erectile dysfunction as the end product of multiple converging past and present influences. Oedipal dynamics sometimes account for the symptom, but not for everyone. Examples of other past influences that might contribute to adult dysfunction include preoedipal separation–individuation conflicts and adolescent masturbatory guilt. The more commonly seen current influences are relationship deterioration, depression, widowhood, health concerns, and aging.

Behavior therapy focuses on eliminating performance anxiety, which is the fear of future sexual failure based on a previous failure—a universal experience for almost all impotent men (LoPiccolo & LoPiccolo, 1978; Obler, 1973). Performance anxiety is seen as the primary mechanism interfering with sexual arousal or erection. Systematic desensitization, the pairing of relaxation with a hierarchy of anxiety-provoking sexual scenes, is the most common behavioral method employed to treat erectile disturbances. Like psychoanalysis, however, behavior therapy concentrates on individual rather than couple treatment..

Cognitive therapy focuses on uncovering the scripts (Gagnon, Rosen, & Leiblum,1982) or irrational beliefs (Ellis, 1980) that interfere with the erectile response. Therapy helps men/couples to shed these beliefs and learn more adaptive cognitive strategies.

Masters and Johnson (1966, 1970) revolutionized the treatment of sexual problems by working with couples to overcome the psychological and behavioral obstacles that impede natural function. They developed a highly structured 2-week treatment model employing male and female cotherapy teams. The multiple facets of their treatment include physical examination, history taking, individual and couple psychotherapy, and prescription of behavioral tasks.

Today treatments for erectile failure have evolved into blends of psychodynamic, behavioral, and cognitive therapies utilizing individual, couples, and group formats (Levine, 1985, 1988, 1992; McCarthy & McCarthy, 1984; Zilbergeld, 1975, 1993). The first integrated approach was developed by Helen Kaplan (1974) and described in her book *The New Sex Therapy*. She incorporated Masters and Johnson's methods with modern-day psychodynamic theory and eliminated the necessity for male and female cotherapy teams. Her method emphasized the intrapsychic and interpersonal aspects of each partner's contribution to the sexual dysfunction.

A more sophisticated approach is Rosen and Leiblum's (1994) cognitive–interpersonal treatment model. The five key elements of this paradigm include (1) psychoeducational remediation, (2) reduction of sexual and performance anxiety, (3) script modification techniques, (4) relationship enhancement and conflict resolution strategies, and (5) relapse prevention procedures.

CURRENT RESEARCH MODELS ON THE TREATMENT OF ERECTILE DYSFUNCTION

Clinicians consider anxiety stemming from any source (intrapsychic, interpersonal, or performance) to be responsible for erectile failure. Barlow (1986) investigated this long-held concept by experimentally manipulating anxiety and cognitive interference in sexually functional and dysfunctional men. He found that, as expected, anxiety decreased arousal/erection in dysfunctional men. It had just the opposite effect, however, in the functional men; it facilitated arousal. From these results, Barlow developed a preliminary working model of psychogenic dysfunction which stated:

> Cognitive interference processes interacting with anxiety are responsible for sexual dysfunction, specifically inhibited sexual excitement in men and women and possibly other related forms of sexual dysfunction. The nature of these cognitive processes in dysfunctional subjects seems to revolve largely around focusing on or attending to task irrelevant contexts. This focus then becomes driven by the physiological aspects of arousal that clinicians more commonly refer to as anxiety which in turn results in further deterioration in sexual performance. On the other hand, sexually functional subjects focus on and process erotic cues without difficulty. Anxiety may enhance this processing (up to a point) and therefore may facilitate sexual arousal. (p. 146)

Alternatively, Bancroft (1999) postulated the existence in the central nervous system of both excitatory and inhibitory systems operating in parallel which provided dual control over sexual response and, consequently, sexual behavior. The inhibitory system of this model was further divided into two independent dimensions: fear of performance failure and threat of performance consequences. Bancroft suggested that the inhibitory system is adaptive in protecting the individual from danger or other negative consequences associated with sexual response.

EARLY TREATMENT CONSIDERATIONS

A thoughtful algorithm for the evaluation and treatment of all forms of erectile dysfunction has been developed by a multidisciplinary panel of experts in family medicine, internal medicine, endocrinology, psychiatry, psychology and urology and is known as the process-of-care (POC) model (Rosen et al., 1998). Four guiding principles direct this model: (1) identification and recognition of erectile dysfunction with its associated concomitant medical and psychological factors; (2) a goal directed, stepwise (with regard to the degree of invasiveness of diagnostic and treatment procedures and the degree of involvement of nonmedical specialists) treatment process for addressing patient and partner needs and preferences; (3) patient and partner education and communication, and (4) clear guidelines for follow-up and referral. This model provides an excellent overview of the evaluation and treatment process. However, several other therapeutic issues deserve further elaboration.

The Therapist's Illusion: Evaluation Is Not Treatment

Although clinicians conceptually separate evaluation and treatment processes, patients do not. For them the cure begins with the first encounter. The patient is, of course, correct; the attentive therapist is aware that the psychotherapeutic relationship and all its transference ramifications are initiated with the first handshake and entry into the consulting room.

Attend to the Therapeutic Relationship before Attending to the Data

The establishment of a respectful, comfortable, and healing relationship with the patient(s) is the primary goal of the evaluation session. Too often the secondary goal of gathering data displaces the more human process of relating to one another. The man and his partner are likely to be anxious and uncomfortable; they are about to share aspects of their intimate life with a stranger.

Talking about sexual matters does not come naturally to most people. The therapist must first set them at ease before progressing into the more difficult material. When couples seem ready to work, one can ask, "What brings you in?" Others may need more soothing, so asking, "How is it for you to come in today and talk with me?" may be helpful. For the very anxious patient, it may be advisable to start by asking," Did you have any trouble finding the office?"

Look for the Early Resistances

Infrequently, even when the presenting problem is sexual, there are first meetings at which sexual issues are not discussed. This is significant and challenges the therapist to assess whether the resistance belongs to the patient or therapist. I still recall my reluctance to ask an elderly European gentleman about his sexual life because he very much reminded me of my father. Unknowingly I was avoiding taking a sexual history. At 15 minutes into the hour this man asked, "So, when are you going to ask me about sex?" He was right. I laughed to myself recognizing the countertransference and was able to proceed.

Patients' reluctance to share sexual material may be due to a number of factors. The old analytic maxim, "resistance before conflict," is good advice. Inquiry should shift from descriptions of their sexual life to understanding what prevents the man or woman from discussing this subject. When the first hour passes without directly addressing the sexual problem, begin the next session by inquiring about the patient's reluctance to talk about sexual matters.

In most ordinary clinical interviews, sociocultural and religious prohibitions against talking about sexual life are encountered. "In our family, such matters were never discussed." "I grew up thinking it was wrong to talk about sex with anyone." Sometimes the gender of the interviewer is the focus of the resistance. "I can't talk about this with a male/female doctor." Acknowledging the patient's discomfort and giving permission and reassurance often overcome resistance stemming from these sources. If the therapist's gender continues to be an unyielding source of resistance, referral should be made to an opposite-sex colleague.

The clinician can also ask the patient what the therapist can do differently to facilitate the discussion. Some patients are well aware of what sets them at ease; others will simply appreciate your willingness to acknowledge and ask about their discomfort. The following vignette demonstrates how cultural ignorance and the patient's resistance can contribute to the avoidance of sexual material in a first hour:

> A middle-aged Arabic woman and her American husband sought consultation about his impotence. She was unable to look at me or discuss her sexual life. Yet, this was an extremely articulate woman, a published author who understood erotic life and demonstrated a wide range of emotion. During our second meeting, I asked why she looked away from me and avoided discussing sexual issues. She explained it was disrespectful to look directly at male authority figures, and that she was unaccustomed to discussing sexual matters with strangers. With much encouragement, she was able to talk about her sexual life, but never once looked at me. While I found the lack of eye contact disconcerting, I respected her need to avoid it, and the evaluation and treatment proceeded with a positive outcome.

Patients' expectations regarding treatment also contribute to resistance. Couples do not know what to expect. Some are afraid that the therapist will physically examine them or watch them engage in sexual behavior. Others may have concerns about the therapist being sexual with them or asking them to engage in sexual behaviors they consider unconventional. The following vignette illustrates one couple's fear:

> Years ago my office was located on the second floor of a five-story psychiatric facility. In addition to a number of outpatient offices, the second floor housed a child inpatient unit. Because the ward was being painted, the furniture had been moved into the outpatient hallways. A hospital bed was placed outside my office, and there were also several other beds randomly distributed throughout the floor. My waiting room was located 20 feet down the hallway in back of a reception area. It was my custom to greet new patients in the waiting room area and walk them back to my office. I did not notice the furniture in the hallway, but they did. They seemed unusually frightened, so I began by asking them how they felt about coming to see me. They coyly asked if I planned to watch them have sex. Puzzled, I asked, "What gave them that impression?" They pointed to the bed outside the door. Their anxiety evaporated after a brief explanation and we all laughed.

The Secret: The Pitfalls from Collusion

A stronger more persistent source of resistance initially stems from patients' wishes not to reveal aspects of their lives that are embarrassing, shameful, or hurtful to themselves or their partner. These secrets from the therapist may have their origins in fragments of traumatic childhood sexual experiences, awareness of unconventional fantasies, extramarital relationships, or conflictual young adult life events that have not been shared with others (suicide of a brother, an abortion, periods of sexual promiscuity, a visit to a prostitute, a homosexual encounter).

Levine (1988) lists three categories of secrets: (1) secrets from oneself, (2) secrets from the partner, and (3) secrets known to both partners but kept from the therapist. Secrets from the self are due to repression or suppression and often emerge during the course of treatment. Some examples are: "I had an inkling that my sexual attractions were to men, but I tried to push this out of my mind and live a straight life" and "I think I really never loved my partner." Secrets from the partner or secrets from the therapist are of a different order and almost always lead to therapeutic impediments (ongoing and past affairs, cross-dressing, child sexual abuse, alcoholism).

Some patients rationalize that these events, feelings, or fantasies are unrelated to the current problem; therefore, they do not need to be shared. Conversely, others are keenly aware of the impact of this secret on their psychological and sexual life but lack sufficient trust, courage, or motivation to address these problematic life dilemmas.

Honesty between patients and therapist is the cornerstone of treatment. Conscious avoidance and withholding of information compromises the therapeutic process. My current policy is not to begin couple treatment if one partner asks me not to talk about a relatively current and important issue (e.g., a 2-year affair that ended 2 months ago). I have less difficulty agreeing to maintain a secret such as "Twenty years ago on an out-of-town business trip I had a one-night affair." My rational is that I do not see a brief remote affair as necessarily relevant and that disclosure of the event to the partner may prove to be more destructive than helpful. Earlier in my career, when I agreed to keep important secrets in an attempt to be "flexible," it often proved to be an error and resulted in unexpected therapeutic failures.

> During the course of my evaluation session with a wife, she revealed an incident of childhood abuse. She begged me not to tell her husband and not to "touch on" this subject in treatment. I agreed to not tell her husband something she did not wish him to know, but I shared my uneasiness about not being able to talk about anything and everything in therapy. She pleaded with me to see them, nevertheless, stating that she did not think her abuse had anything to do with her husband's impotence. My naive initial formulation did not incorporate it either: I saw his dysfunction as a response to traumatic events at work. I decided to see them in conjoint treatment and to avoid the issue of her childhood abuse. The first few conjoint sessions went well. He was beginning to recover his potency, and she was a supportive and helpful partner. In the fourth session, the couple reported that they had avoided any sexual activity during the previous week. I asked, "What do you think this is about?" In an angry, accusatory manner she blurted out, "You promised me we did not have to talk about that and now you are telling him." Before I could say anything, she proceeded to spill the secret and ran out of the session. Although I

attempted to salvage the therapy through phone contacts, the couple refused to return to treatment. When I had asked my question, I had been looking for present-day events that might have disrupted their progress. I incorrectly assumed that because she had no difficulty being sexual with her partner prior to his dysfunction, resumption of sexual life would not lead to a resurgent memory of her abuse. Clearly, the secret was relevant to the success of their therapy.

THE FIRST DECISION: INDIVIDUAL OR COUPLE TREATMENT; ADJUNCTIVE PHARMACOLOGICAL INTERVENTION

The evaluation concludes with the therapist offering the patients his or her treatment recommendations. There are several distinct psychotherapy possibilities: individual therapy for one or both partners, conjoint or couple treatment, separate group psychotherapies for one or both partners, or a mixture of all of these approaches. Given the efficacy and safety of Viagra (Goldstein et al., 1998), or other soon to be released oral agents, one must consider the value of adjunctively adding a pharmacological intervention to facilitate the treatment process.

Treatment recommendations are primarily influenced by a therapist's values and prejudices regarding ideology and treatment modality, as well as more pragmatic considerations such as insurance limitations. Current research data are not sophisticated enough to predict when a given patient with a specific disorder will do best with a particular therapist who engages in a specific form of treatment. In fact, there is significant overlap among practitioners of different orientations who purport to engage in specialized forms of treatment. Many patients, in our experience, are as likely to do well in an individual treatment as they are in a conjoint treatment or with an analytic or behavioral therapist. Long-term outcome data are not available on the role of pharmacological intervention alone, or in combination with specific forms of psychotherapy for men with primarily psychogenic erectile dysfunction.

This does not imply that we should not be thoughtful about offering alternatives to patients as if it really made no difference. Rather, we should recognize the limitations of our knowledge and appreciate that some of what we do is intuitive rather than scientific. Given this caveat, some suggestions for treatment planning follow. These are not intended to be hard-and-fast rules. Ultimately, it is the patient who makes the final decision to accept or reject our proposal.

An additional caveat is that it is often inadvisable for the therapist to switch treatment modalities (i.e., begin individual therapy with the man and then switch to conjoint treatment with the couple). For example, when a primary relationship is formed first between the patient and his therapist, the partner may feel that an alliance exists between them against her. Yet by endeavoring to be sensitive to the partner's feelings, the patient may feel abandoned. Although not a strict rule, it is generally advisable for any one clinician to restrict treatment to one modality with one patient/couple.

I had begun treating Michael, a 45-year-old married college professor, for primary erectile dysfunction. As his potency improved, unresolved interpersonal issues between him and Ruth surfaced. I suggested to Michael that he talk with Ruth about the possibility of conjoint treatment with one of my colleagues. He pooh-poohed my concerns about changing modalities, flattered my therapeutic acumen, and said that he preferred not to see another therapist. He asked me to see Ruth alone first to discuss some of my concerns. I acquiesced and saw Ruth for evaluation when we discussed the pros and cons of my treating the couple, that is, her feeling positively about how I had helped her husband versus her feeling that I might not be able to maintain a therapeutic neutrality because my year-long relationship with Michael. I thought this case might be an exception to my own tenent. Within four sessions Ruth complained that I was taking Michael's side and blaming her for the couple's difficulties. Her feelings reminded her of the jealousy she felt toward her brother for having a special relationship to their father. Ultimately we worked through the boundary/transference issues, but in hindsight this couple would have been better served with a referral for conjoint treatment.

Guidelines for Recommending Treatment

If the erectile dysfunction is lifelong (that is, there has never been a period in the man's life where he has been able to achieve or maintain good quality erections for intercourse), I generally recommend individual therapy. This decision is based on the assumption that lifelong erectile dysfunction is an intrapsychic developmental failure rather than an interpersonal problem. In addition, these men tend to have severe character pathology. Lifelong erectile dysfunction is often the end result of unresolved gender identity, sexual orientation, or paraphilic conflicts. Individual treatment better lends itself to the intensive exploration of early life events and intrapsychic dilemmas. It allows a deeper understanding and working through of the obstacles to establishing a comfortable sexual self. These issues are more difficult to explore and resolve in couple or group treatment. Not only does the presence of others dilute the focus, but patients are often reluctant to share these concerns with others.

However, when a man with lifelong dysfunction has limited psychological reflectiveness, is markedly inarticulate, and/or is estranged from his emotional life (i.e., markedly schizoid, or alexithymic), individual treatment is ill-advised. In these situations, if there is a partner I ask her to join us to help me. She is often aware of pertinent family events and can help the patient talk more quickly about aspects of himself that would remain obscure in individual treatment.

I recommend conjoint treatment for those patients with acquired erectile dysfunction who have viable relationships. Acquired dysfunction suggests that the patient has successfully traversed developmental hurdles to establish a comfortable sexual self. Moreover, the symptom is generally rooted in the present or recent past and is not an outgrowth of early childhood issues. In fact, the dysfunction often represents the couple's shared solution to some aspect of their relationship.

The exceptions to the guideline of "conjoint treatment for acquired dysfunction" are the single man without a partner, the single man with an uncommitted partner, and the couple whose relationship has deteriorated so much that they cannot work productively with one another. Obviously, the man without a partner must be seen in individual treatment. Years ago, some therapists would have demanded that the patient first become involved with a partner and then seek treatment. Although the lack of involvement in a relationship does present clear limitations for therapy, the patient can, nonetheless, benefit. The stickier decision is how to determine whether a partner of a single man is "uncommitted." Meeting with each partner alone is helpful in making this determination. She may articulate her ambivalence about the future of the relationship, indicating that conjoint treatment might be inappropriate. I generally attempt to see dysfunctional couples in a conjoint format first but employ more structure than usual. If this proves unworkable, the therapist can refer one or both for individual treatment.

Sometimes a married men who has no desire to make love to his wife but wishes to be sexual with his lover seeks treatment. These situations present ethical dilemmas for therapists. My comfort level allows me to see these men in individual treatment, but not in conjoint therapy with their lovers or wives.

Some Heuristic Guidelines for When to Recommend an Adjunctive Medical Intervention

The following guidelines are offered in a preliminary fashion. It is hoped that future research will provide empirical support for these guidelines with controlled outcome studies. After a comprehensive evaluation, I would recommend that psychotherapy be augmented by medical intervention in men who have (1) lifelong erectile dysfunction, (2) low sexual confidence and inability to talk with their partner regarding sexual anxieties (e.g., recently divorced men who are dating a new partner), (3) significant medical factors intertwined with psychological conflicts, and (4) past history of psychotherapy for a protracted period of time without significant improvement.

I would not recommend an adjunctive medical intervention to (1) men with recent onset acquired dysfunction with clear precipitants, (2) couples with severe marital discord, (3) young men with significant performance anxiety, and (4) patients who wish to continue treatment without alternative intervention.

THE FOUNDATION AND FRAMEWORK OF PSYCHOTHERAPY

Psychotherapy, like house building, requires a foundation and frame. The foundation is built on the clinician's theoretical base for understanding human behavior and on the strength of the patient–therapist relationship. The frame is formed by the therapeutic contract.

The Therapeutic Contract

The therapeutic contract is a negotiated agreement between the patients and clinician describing fees, frequency of meetings, rules for canceling sessions, anticipated length of treatment, what the patients can expect from the therapist, what the therapist expects from the patient, and, finally, the focus of treatment.

Treatment for sexual problems is generally conducted within a short-term psychotherapy model. The short-term model differs from traditional long-term treatment in the selection of a focus, a higher level of therapist intervention activity, careful patient selection, and special attention to the termination phase of treatment (Mann, 1973; Sifneos, 1972).

The focus is the therapist's initial formulations of the intrapsychic and interpersonal dynamics that contribute to the initiation and maintenance of the erectile dysfunction. Although the focus is offered by the clinician, there must be a mutual agreement to explore the suggested topics. It serves as a starting point for beginning the treatment; it also structures the therapy so that the agreed-on areas are intensively scrutinized. The focus may shift as treatment proceeds, thereby allowing for a broader understanding of the important themes that contribute to the sexual problem. By employing a short-term psychotherapy model, the therapist departs from the traditional stance that all conflicts, especially those from early childhood, require exploration, insight, and resolution. Symptom resolution can often be achieved by working through a conflict in the present, sometimes in only a superficial way. The following vignettes demonstrate the usefulness of choosing a focus:

> A 62-year-old factory worker presented with a 4-year history of erectile dysfunction. He was in excellent health, took no medications, did not smoke or abuse alcohol, and had excellent early morning and masturbatory erections. I asked him what had changed in his life 4 years ago. He launched into an poignant account of his wife's chronic pain secondary to arthritis. He loved his wife dearly and thought that asking her to be sexual would cause her further pain. Together we hypothesized that the symptom (erectile dysfunction) may be serving as his friend to ensure that he would not hurt her. In the first conjoint session, we addressed this issue. His wife acknowledged the severe pain but was tearful and sad when she learned what lay behind his avoidance of sexual contact. She indicated that being sexual, although painful, had great psychological meaning. She highly valued intercourse and missed the closeness.
>
> Alternative coital positions that might reduce pain were reviewed, as was discussion of noncoital pleasuring. I consulted with her physician about pain management before coitus and encouraged them to gradually resume being sexual. With his wife's encouragement and support, his fear of hurting her diminished and his erections became reliable.

Harry provides another illustration of the usefulness of a focus. After being married just 2 years, he found out his wife had been involved in numerous extramarital affairs and divorced her. He said his friends all knew but were reluctant to tell him. Following the divorce he encountered erectile problems with all partners—even those to whom he felt close. We chose to focus on his anger at his wife for her betrayals and his subsequent difficulty in trusting new partners. After 6 months of constantly reworking this theme, Harry regained his potency.

Therapist Activity Level

Short-term psychotherapy requires a higher level of therapist activity than does long-term, insight-oriented treatment. In traditional therapy, the clinician maintains a more receptive, passive therapeutic stance. "Activity" in sex therapy refers not only to the frequency of one's comments but also to the type of intervention offered. Because the short-term model requires a focus, the therapist is active in terms of keeping the patient's attention directed toward the identified conflicts. He or she also gives patients permission to be sexual, provides educational information, dispels myths, offers advice, and prescribes specific sexual exercises (e.g., sensate focus). The therapist is also active in terms of making sure each person can "hear" the other's concerns.

Importance of Empathy

Self psychology (Ornstein & Ornstein, 1984) stresses the therapeutic role of empathy and the result of failures in empathy. As a therapist, I endeavor to "stand inside my patient's shoes" to see how he or she experiences the world. Time after time, patients remark on how important it is for them to be understood. Thus, many of my early comments are clarifications of or reflections on what I think they are experiencing.

In conjoint treatment, I try to understand each partner's unique experience and strive to enable each partner to hear and see, but not necessarily to agree with, his her partner's perspective. I want each person to have a sense of what it feels like to be the other person. This perspective allows partners to recognize differences in feelings and helps them understand why each person has their unique reactions. Patients may try to use the therapist as a judge to rule on issues of fact (i.e., what actually happened). I use these moments to point out that the manner in which a person experiences an event is, for that person, the way it happened.

Engendering Hope

Men/couples are frequently demoralized and hopeless when they come for therapy. The infusion of realistic hope by an "expert" creates a positive therapeutic climate that by itself fosters progress. Couples who are wallowing in sadness and frustration cannot make progress. Follow-up studies support the contention that psychotherapy helps most patients regain their potency (Hawton, Catalan, & Faff, 1992; Kilman & Auerbach, 1979). Even if treatment is unable to completely restore potency, the knowledge patients acquire about themselves and each other may increase their satisfaction with their relationship. And couples can learn to value alternative forms of love making by developing broader sexual scripts where sexual pleasure is given and received. Ideally, in those cases in which intercourse is no longer possible even with medical intervention, couples can continue to exchange physical expressions of love and warmth.

Too Much, Too Soon

Too much affect, argumentativeness, confrontation, or new information early in treatment threatens the therapeutic process. Highly charged early sessions typically result in disruption of treatment. It takes time to forge an empathic bond between therapist and patient that is strong enough to contain and withstand highly charged affect or the revelation of emotionally difficult material.

Therefore, the clinician should cut off "spilling" or overly intense interactions in the early sessions. The therapist can interrupt couples who begin to verbally assault one another in order to modulate the degree of affect by calmly restating and acknowledging their point. This helps patients suppress inappropriately early revelation of highly charged material. Group therapy research (Lieberman, Yalom, & Miles, 1973) supports the fact that negative outcomes are associated with "too much, too soon." Emotionality without some cognitive understanding or framework for hearing these feelings is not beneficial to the therapeutic process. Also, honesty in therapy is sometimes confused with sadism; instead of sharing and promoting intimacy, the intent of "honesty" can be to hurt and drive a wedge between one another.

With quarrelsome couples, my strategy is in part directed to help them recognize the positive aspects of their partner or the relationship. I ask about what they value in their partner, why they fell in love, what motivates them to keep the relationship intact, and so on. Sometimes couples are too far gone, and their unwillingness/inability to acknowledge any positive features presage their uncoupling. Perhaps then treatment can them help them separate in the least destructive manner possible.

The Illusion of Rapid Cure

When I was a youngster, I remember watching a "B" movie in which a patient in psychotherapy suddenly recalls a long-forgotten memory and is cured. I call this powerful fantasy of psychotherapy "Hollywood Freud." The notion of a one-time, dramatic, derepression leading to an instant cure is very misleading.

For most patients healing actually occurs slowly, as a result of a gradual process called "working through." Insight or affect alone is rarely curative. "Working through" is the process of psychologically integrating and assimilating the previously conflictual aspects of oneself into new cognitive and emotional schema. In concrete terms, this process is the ongoing, repetitive discussion of specific issues or themes that ultimately result in the patient's achieving a new and more satisfying perspective.

> Gene is a fast-talking, high energy, 50-year-old, never-married, sports car enthusiast. He has lived in life's fast lane, flying jet planes, gambling, drinking, and palling around with the guys. He is still very attached to his 85-year-old mother, whom he visits daily in a nursing home. Gene says that his mother has never considered any woman he dated good enough for him to marry.
>
> When he recently became engaged to a 48-year-old divorced mother of two, he developed erectile dysfunction. He had not told his mother about his engagement, fearing she would not approve of his fiancee. And, he had doubts about the long-term viability of his proposed marital relationship because his fiancee did not approve of his sports cars, thrice-weekly poker games, or male friends. Nevertheless, Gene said he was ready to settle down and give up his bachelor life.
>
> Psychotherapy focused on whether Gene could really settle down to a conventional lifestyle. Hours were spent working through his attachment to his mother and his lifelong avoidance of long-term relationships. He was also afraid his mother would die if he did not visit her daily or if she found out about his engagement to "this woman." By tediously rehashing these issues, the patient recognized that he was not likely to hasten or prolong his mother' mortality. Gene also began to consider that his mother might be pleased if he finally "settled down." He came to feel less guilty about his mother and less hostile toward his fiancee. Now he is able to decrease the frequency of his visits to his mother and assert himself with his fiancee regarding "his needs to be with the boys." As Gene has began to make these changes, his potency started to return.

The time needed to work through issues depends on the intensity and depth of the conflict. In general, cases of secondary erectile dysfunction, especially those of recent onset, are more amenable to brief treatment than is primary impotence. Sometimes, only one or two sessions prove beneficial.

Cognitive Aspects of Treatment

Cognitive beliefs and expectations are viewed by some clinicians as the primary cause of erectile dysfunction (Ellis, 1980). Whereas patient's beliefs clearly contribute to their dysfunction, I generally do not view them as the sole or primary cause. I give more emphasis to contextual and emotional factors causing dysfunction than cognitive.

That said, it is widely recognized that men socialized in Western culture have assimilated many myths about male sexuality. By maintaining these myths men place unrealistic expectations upon themselves in regard to their sexual performance. Some examples of commonly encountered myths include the following: (1) it is the responsibility of the man to satisfy the woman; (2) size and firmness are necessary determinants of the female partner's satisfaction; (3) a woman's favorite part of sex is intercourse; (4) a man always wants and is always ready to have sex; (5) once a woman learns to like sex, she will become insatiable; (6) with age, all men lose their ability to achieve erections (Cooper, 1978; Schover, 1984; Zilbergeld, 1975, 1993). The myth most often held by partners of impotent men is that the failure to achieve erection indicates a diminution of affection for them or their loss of attractiveness and suggests the man's involvement with another woman.

Rosen, Leiblum, and Spector (1994) list eight forms of cognitive distortion that may interfere with erectile function. These include (1) all-or-nothing thinking (e.g., "I am a complete failure because my erection was not 100% rigid"; (2) overgeneralization (e.g., "If I had trouble getting an erection last night, I won't have one this morning"); (3) disqualifying the positive (e.g., "My partner says I have a good erection because she doesn't want to hurt my feelings"); (4) mind reading (e.g., "I don't need to ask, I know how she felt about last night"), (5) fortune telling (e.g., "I am sure things will go badly tonight"); (6) emotional reasoning (e.g., "Because a man feels something is true, it must be"); (7) categorical imperatives (i.e., shoulds, ought to, and musts dominate the man's cognitive processes); and (8) catastrophizing (e.g., "If I fail tonight my girlfriend will dump me").

Two brief clinical examples illustrate how cognitive factors can compromise erectile functioning. A widower is puzzled to find himself impotent as he ventures out to date just 3 months after his wife's death from a debilitating illness. A middle-age man recounts episode after episode of mutual marital cruelty in his on-again, off-again marriage. In their next breath, these men turn to the therapist asking why they are unable to perform. Both share the belief that the penis is a machine; that is, it should work anytime, anywhere, under any circumstances, and with any partner. For such men, the context in which they make love seems irrelevant. Sadly, many women also share the myth that the penis is a machine.

Therapy helps the man/couple appreciate the importance of the context of love making. The therapist points out what is obvious. For instance, the clinician can suggest that the recently widowed man is still quite psychologically attached to his wife. The symptom is really his "friend" in that it serves two purposes: it reminds him of his old attachment and prevents him from another attachment that he is not yet ready for emotionally. In regard to the man in the embattled relationship, one could simply say, "I don't know how anyone could possibly make love with so much hate surrounding them." Treatment stresses the importance of the context and attempts to help patients understand that lovemaking does not occur in an emotional vacuum.

Alienation from the Self

We often suggest to patients that "the penis is attached to the heart." As corny as this phrase sounds, it conveys the often underappreciated concept that a man's feelings can enhance or interfere with love making. The feelings that reside in the hearts of the men and their partners contribute to the context and influence sexual performance. Context becomes more and more important as a man grows older. Who he is with, how he feels about his partner, the circumstances under which he makes love, the overall quality of his relationship, and the influence of other life events all effect the quality of erection.

The Dysfunction as Friend or Solution

Ego psychology (Blanck & Blanck, 1974) teaches that symptom formation has both an adaptive and a pathological context. A modern way of viewing adaptive context is that the erectile dysfunction is a creative and unique solution for a life dilemma. In accordance with this less pathological perspective, we suggest to the man or couple that the symptom may be his/their friend. Couples seem willing to embrace this explanation for their difficulty because it sounds more positive. Couples come to appreciate that, perhaps unconsciously, they have chosen the least destructive of many possible alternatives; for some, this choice may prevent the behavioral expression of a less acceptable impulse. Two short vignettes provide examples.

> Immediately after his divorce Hans, a 55-year-old European and aristocratic gentleman, had become involved with a 25-year-old unwed mother of a 5-year-old boy. Hans felt punished by the divorce agreement, which required him to sell his condominium as well as give a significant portion of his annual income to his wife. He claimed his wife did not need such a generous settlement as she earned more money from her trust than he made in his vocation. She insisted on the settlement "to make him pay for his freedom." Hans also feared that if he became quickly involved with another woman and remarried he would "live to regret it." Although he described his young friend as supportive and good company, he knew that he could never marry her because of the difference in their ages and backgrounds. However, he did not try to see other women because he was not accustomed to dating several people or having casual sexual liaisons.
>
> I suggested that his erectile dysfunction was a creative solution to the dilemma of not wanting to get too involved and being uncomfortable about sexual behavior with a partner to whom he was not committed. By having erection problems, he prevented himself from either being sexual or becoming attached to another person. His dysfunction slowly got better as we continued to talk about his life crisis.

Another example of symptom as friend occurred in the treatment of a paraphilic man who harbored sadistic fantasies toward women. I suggested that his dysfunction was very useful. It allowed him to relate to his wife emotionally while simultaneously protecting her from his more troubled side. He was referred for psychotherapy but declined the offer.

TRANSFERENCE

"Transference is the experiencing of feelings, drives, attitudes, fantasies, and defenses toward a person in the present which do not befit that person but are a repetition of reactions originating in regard to significant persons of early childhood, unconsciously displaced onto figures in the present" (Greenson, 1967, p. 171). Freud brought this phenomenon to the world's attention in his 1912 paper "The Dynamics of Transference" (Freud, 1912/1957b). Merton Gill's (1982) scholarly thesis, *The Analysis of Transference*, traces the evolution of this concept from its classical roots to more current views of theory and technique.

A person's response to another has multiple origins. In simple terms, transference is one of the many influences that determines how an individual thinks, feels, or behaves. People are generally unaware of how this phenomenon works.

Psychology seeks to make transference paradigms conscious for patients. Transference can be positive or negative. It is the positive transference to the therapist that promotes the healing process. A negative transference fuels expressions of hostile and sadistic feelings toward others.

Therapists occasionally comment about how the room feels full of other people—two sets of parents, four sets of grandparents, brothers, sisters, and previous lovers. In therapy, each partner benefits from the analysis of transference but for different reasons. If we are analyzing a man's transferential responses to his partner, we focus on past and present factors that account for the way in which he experiences her. The insight thus garnered promotes change. In listening to, and particiapting in, the analysis, the woman begins to appreciate how and why he responds to her.

> Larry is a brilliant 42-year-old never-married attorney. As a child, he lived in fear of his father's frequent temper outbursts. His parents' marriage was sterile and his mother turned to him for consolation. She was a gifted musician who encouraged his love of music and literature. Together they often played duets, read books, and maintained a protracted, overly close relationship. The patient developed strong fantasies about wanting to marry his mother, believing that his younger brother was his mother's and his child and feeling that his father intruded on their relationship by coming home from work.
>
> At a literary society to which Larry and his mother belong, he met Jill. She was a talented musician, who was 10 years his senior and had a fiery temper. Initially, they maintained a strictly platonic relationship, based on their mutual interests in music and literature. When the relationship evolved to being sexual, it was marred by Larry's low sexual desire and episodic erectile dysfunction and Jill's angry reaction.

In conjoint treatment, Larry described a pattern of developing platonic relationships with older women whose favor he curried. It also seemed important that these women not be available to him as sexual partners. He thought that he would somehow cause his father to die by being sexual. He knew this idea had no basis in reality but was unable to shake it. Jill's angry outbursts were also transference-based responses to her father, who had ignored her in favor of her sister.

Analysis of the transference demonstrated that Jill was "perfect" for him. He related to her as both the precocious child who wished to please his mother and as the fearful, guilty child who did not have the psychological wherewithal to stand up to father. It became clear to Larry and Jill that the powerful, silent, transferential themes embedded in their relationship were making their sexual relationship problematic.

In individual treatment, transference is traditionally analyzed in terms of the patient's relationship to the therapist. Classically, transference to others has not been interpreted. My position has been that the therapist should actively interpret all transferences, whether to himself or to others. In conjoint treatment, the therapist helps each partner understand the transferential portion of his and her interpersonal responses.

The eroticized or sexualized transference, in which a patient falls in love with and/or becomes sexually attracted to the therapist, poses special problems. It occurs most frequently when a female therapist treats an impotent man in individual psychotherapy. Conjoint treatment dilutes the transference of either partner to the therapist. The eroticized transference requires active setting of limits, interpretation of the erotic and hostile components of the transference, and awareness of one's countertransferential responses. The following case was provided by a former colleague, Dr. Louisa Turner:

During evaluation, a 52 year-old married business consultant with erectile dysfunction and low sexual desire reported a history of several intense, idealized, "obsessive attachments" to blonde women; his wife though was a redhead. These attachments would last for years at a time, and thoughts of these women now filled his days.

In the first therapy hour, he told the therapist that she immediately fit the "light-haired woman" image which made him feel comfortable and emotionally close to her. By the fourth session, the attachment had become sexualized. He spoke of wanting to quit therapy in order to have a sexual relationship with her. He sought to find out personal aspects of the therapist's life, and was unreceptive to any interpretations of his intrusiveness or the defensive nature of the sexual transference.

One of the important themes that emerged much later in treatment concerned his father's promiscuity and encouragement of his young teenage son to follow in his footsteps. His father had told him, "If you don't get her in bed by the fourth date, you're not a man." Together the therapist and patient remembered that it had been in the fourth session that he had sexually approached the therapist.

THE PRESCRIPTION OF BEHAVIORAL TASKS

Insight has traditionally been viewed as the most powerful agent of change in psychotherapy. This idealized perspective is both incorrect and excessively narrow in scope. Insight is useful but not sufficient in overcoming erectile problems. It is the judicious integration of carefully selected behavioral tasks that augments insight to facilitate the resolution of the dysfunction.

Behavioral tasks are employed to (1) overcome performance anxiety (Masters & Johnson, 1970), (2) aid with diagnostic assessment and clarification of underlying dynamics, (3) alter the previously destructive sexual system, (4) confront resistances in each partner, (5) alleviate couple's anxiety about physical intimacy (Kaplan, 1974), (6) dispel myths and educate patients regarding sexual function and anatomy, (7) counteract negative body image concerns (Hartman & Fithian, 1972), and (8) heighten sensuality.

In the early days of sex therapy, clinicians routinely prescribed behavioral tasks at the beginning of treatment. They hoped these exercises would rapidly resolve the sexual dysfunction. Rather than cure, the tasks sometimes precipitated unidentified resistances in one or both partners. This was, in fact, helpful because the astute therapist was able to resolve these resistances to the ongoing treatment process. Currently, therapists are more inclined to delay the prescription of behavioral tasks until after some of the major therapeutic issues have been worked through (e.g., trust).

Behavioral exercises early in treatment are reserved for men whose erectile dysfunction is primarily due to performance anxiety. This conditioning is due to a fear of future failure that stems from previous difficulties achieving or maintaining an adequate erection. After the first failure, some men burden themselves with increasing demands to perform ("I'd better make up for last time") and worry that they will fail again. They no longer abandon themselves to the eroticism of the moment. Their fears cause them to become preoccupied with erection. They begin to observe rather than to participate in the sexual experience. They attempt to "will" an erection rather than abandon themselves to sensation, which greatly diminishes their sexual arousal. Ultimately, they fail again. After several failures, these men tend to avoid sexual situations and feel sapped of their sexual self-confidence.

Sensate Focus I, II, and III

Sensate focus is a behavioral exercise frequently employed to help patients achieve the three requirements necessary for a good sexual life (i.e., willingness, relaxation, and sensuality). Masters and Johnson (1970) developed these structured exercises to heighten sensuality/arousal, while minimizing performance demands.

Sensate focus ensures couples of a successful sexual encounter. The therapist enters into a contract with the couple that requires them to abstain from attempting sexual intercourse during the period that the exercises are prescribed. The therapist also negotiates the frequency with which couples agree to perform the homework tasks during the following week.

In designing sensate focus exercises, the therapist must be both creative and sensitive to both partners' anxieties regarding sexual intimacy. It may be necessary for the clinician to have couples begin the exercises at a rudimentary level, such as holding hands in the dark, in bed, with both partners dressed in pajamas. Others may start by taking a bubble bath and washing each other's backs.

What follows are the instructions for Sensate Focus I, given in Kaplan's (1974) book, *The New Sex Therapy*. These instructions need to be modified to fit the needs of each couple. Also, in the therapy session each couple can negotiate who goes first with each exercise and how many times they will practice the exercises during the week.

The therapist gives instructions, such as the following:

> I'd like you both to get ready for bed: to take your clothes off, shower and relax. I want you (the woman) to lie on your belly. Then you (the man) caress her back as gently and sensitively as you can. Move your hands very slowly. Begin at the back of her neck, caress her ears, and work your way down to her buttocks, legs and feet. Use your hands and/or your lips. Concentrate only on how it feels to touch her body and her skin.
>
> In the meantime, I want you (the woman) to focus your attention on the sensations you feel when he caresses you. Try not to let your mind wander. Don't think about anything else: don't worry about whether he's getting tired or whether he is enjoying it, or anything. Be 'selfish' and just concentrate on your sensations; let yourself feel everything. Communicate with him. He can not possibly know what you are feeling unless you tell him. Let him know where you want to be touched and how and where his caresses feel especially good; let him know if his touch is too light or too heavy, or if he is going too fast. If the experience is unpleasant, tell him so. Don't talk too much or it will interfere with your sensations and his. Try to identify for yourself those areas of your body which are especially sensitive or responsive.
>
> When you feel you have been touched all over, I want you [the woman] to turn over on your back, so that you [the man] can caress the front of her body. Start with her face and neck and go down to her toes. But this first time [Sensate Focus I] do not touch her sexual organs; skip her breasts, nipples, vagina and clitoris. Again, both of you are to concentrate only on what it feels like to caress and to be caressed. Stop if this becomes tedious for either of you.
>
> Now it's your [the man's] turn to receive. I want you [the woman] to do the same to him. Do either of you have any questions about this procedure? (Kaplan, 1974 p. 209)

After couples can comfortably and regularly engage in Sensate Focus I (usually for 2 weeks), they are instructed to begin Sensate Focus II. Now couples are to include breast and genital stimulation as part of the pleasuring exercise but not to the point of orgasm. The aforementioned nondemand characteristics and the need for feedback are reiterated.

After successfully completing Sensate Focus II, couples are moved along to Sensate Focus III, where they are instructed to attempt vaginal containment without active movement by either partner. As the couple develop sexual confidence, intercourse without any prohibition is allowed, if they have not already "broken the rules" and proceeded to enjoy an intercourse experience. Couple's reactions to the exercises are carefully monitored and discussed in therapy.

Murray, a 53-year-old successful insurance agent, and his wife, a 50-year-old nutritional counselor, had been married for 28 years. With the exception of time spent on vacation, Murray had a 7-year history of erectile dysfunction. The frequency of their love making had gradually declined to its current level of once every 4 months. Murray reported considerable performance anxiety, enhanced by his competitive personality style. He summed up his dilemma: "When you have a life full of successes, you don't get much practice at how to deal with inadequacy."

During the first hour, sensate focus exercises were suggested, and instructions given to engage in sensual nongenital touching. They returned in a week, noting how difficult it had been to find time to pleasure one another. Their mutual avoidance was discussed and understood as a means of warding off feelings of inadequacy. Working through the resistance allowed the couple to engage in the exercises three times over the course of the next week. With the pleasuring, Murray began to achieve good, long-lasting erections.

Therapy then progressed to include genital touching, Sensate Focus II. After the first week, they talked about their problem of "silliness." They realized that humor had been used to cope with the dysfunction. Now, however, joking in bed seemed to inhibit sexual closeness. Murray's good erections were maintained, although he was having trouble concentrating on his sensations. Further exploration revealed that he was focusing his attention in a driven, intense manner. To counter this, I redirected him to maintain a relaxed awareness akin to meditation. Murray found this analogy helpful, and the couple felt ready to proceed with vaginal containment. During the following week, they "disobeyed" and moved on to have mutually satisfying intercourse. They feared the recurrence of the old problem, but it did not return, and the remaining two sessions were spent talking about their sexual life. Despite otherwise good communication, they had never been able before to broach this topic with one another.

Other Behavioral Tasks

Other behavioral exercises that are useful in the treatment of erectile dysfunction are aimed at helping the man achieve confidence in maintaining his erection and his ability to regain his erection. This is done by having him purposely become flaccid, only to have him masturbate (or have his partner stimulate him) again to full erection. Some therapists suggest that the woman squeeze the man's penis until he is flaccid. I simply ask patients to stop pleasuring one another. "Quiet vagina" is another exercise used with couples who have significant anxiety about resuming intercourse. In this exercise, the man is on his back with the woman astride him. She gently lowers herself onto his penis and, initially, does not move. Movement is added to the task first by asking the woman to gently and rhythmically move her hips; finally, the man is instructed to thrust. Also, guided explicit fantasy is often helpful for men who have difficulty becoming aroused or for those who are preoccupied with obsessive thoughts of failure.

Relapse Prevention

Relapse prevention is a relatively new concept in psychotherapy. In the past, the patient and therapist reached a mutual decision about when to terminate, worked toward that goal, and ended treatment on a set date. Patients could, of course, recontact their therapist for additional treatment should difficulties arise.

Research from Hawton et al. (1992) demonstrates that at termination, approximately 70% of patients are better. However, 3 months after termination on only 56% of patients maintain their initial gains. Given this phenomenon, McCarthy (1993) suggested that sex therapy treatments incorporate relapse prevention strategies.

Among his useful recommendations are the scheduling of periodic "booster or maintenance" sessions following termination. Patients remark that knowing that they will be seen again in 6 months keeps them on target because they know they will have "to report" on their progress. The follow-up sessions can also be used to work out any "glitches" that have interfered with their progress.

McCarthy (1993) also suggests having patients episodically schedule nondemand pleasuring sessions for noncoital sexual encounters as well as rehearse the coping techniques that they have just experienced for use when mediocre or negative sexual encounters happen. He indicates to patients that when a problem reoccurs they label it a "lapse" to be learned from, as opposed to a relapse to be feared. I often prepare a couple to expect occasional lapses in their erections, stating that it is quite normal for all men sometimes to not have firm erections.

The Role of Adjunctive Medical Interventions

Alternative interventions such as oral medications (Viagra, MUSE [Medicated Urethral System for Erection]), self-injection therapy, and vacuum systems have dramatically changed the role of the mental health clinician (Althof et al., 1991; Goldstein et al., 1998; Padma-Nathan et al., 1997; Turner et al., 1991). Because these medical interventions are safe, efficacious, and reversible, one could argue that patients with psychogenic dysfunction should first be considered for one of these physical interventions. Thus, some prominent urologists have jokingly predicted that sex therapists should contemplate plans for an early retirement.

I believe that the introduction and use of these medical interventions has created a new role for the therapists (Althof, 1999). My notion is rooted in the observation of two unexplained phenomena: (1) at least 85% of the population with erectile dysfunction fail to avail themselves of any treatment; and (2) although the medical treatments have impressive efficacy rates between 44% and 91%, there is an equally impressive discontinuation rate of 20% to 50% (Althof et al., 1989). These treatment dropouts are clearly not due to lack of efficacy or unwanted side effects; they appear to be a multiple determined response, motivated in part by psychological resistance to using a medical intervention and in part by interpersonal issues. Medical therapies address only the end organ; they cannot ameliorate the associated psychological and emotional concerns that can obviate the efficacy of these treatments. Some urologists are so phallocentrically focused on producing an erection that they miss the emotional sequelae associated with erectile dysfunction. It is as if these physicians are saying, "We can get it up, the rest is up to you." In the language of ego psychology, the mental health clinician's revised role is to identify and attenuate resistance to these treatments.

When couples are unable to make us of the impressive interventions, they need our help to overcome unseen intransigent blocks to much or all of their love making. The therapist can help the couple cultivate a romantic ambiance and engage in conversations that will physically and psychologically prepare them to become lovers again. The therapist can also assist them in accepting the changes that have occurred in their lives (e.g., menopause, disability, illness, or other life stressors). Sometimes these resistances need to be worked through prior to beginning a medical intervention. At other times they can be simultaneously addressed. If not confronted, however, these forces can render the best intentioned medical treatment efforts ineffectual.

Not even Viagra, as impressive as it appears, can eliminate the careers of mental health professionals interested in sexual problems. Instead, these interventions may enlarge out therapeutic armamentarium and expand the traditional clinical tasks to include identifying and helping patients/couples overcome their resistances to effectively utilizing new medical treatments. By helping couples surmount these obstacles, we can help them to enjoy once again the satisfaction of a loving sexual relationship.

FINAL THOUGHTS: THERE ARE SOME MEN/COUPLES WHO CANNOT BE HELPED

In spite of our most diligent efforts, it is not possible to help all individuals who present for treatment of erectile dysfunction. For some, talking therapy alone is insufficient to overcome severe early trauma, the aftermath of years of destructive interactions or limited psychological resources in the man or the couple (Levine, 1985).

There are instances in which patients achieve profound psychological gains, yet their potency does not return. Similarly, a couple's relationship may improve but not their sexual life.

> Richard, a reserved 45-year-old author, was urged by his wife, Sidney, to seek treatment for his erectile dysfunction. She was an ambitious, powerful, professional woman who had become increasingly distressed about her husband's failure to seek help for his difficulty. He readily attributed the dysfunction to his rage toward his wife for undermining his authority at home. Three years ago one of his two adolescent sons had begun to have serious school and behavioral problems, compounded by drug abuse. The boy had gotten over his drug problem, but the relationship between Richard and the boy had become strained. At the same time, Sidney's relationship with her son deepened. Richard resented feeling excluded. One of the outcomes of this family crisis was Richard's development of erectile problems. Given the temporal relationship between the sexual symptom and the family crisis, therapy initially focused on the new equilibrium between family members. Although Sidney was able to stop undermining her husband and he was able to develop a better relationship with the boy, Richard's potency did not return.
>
> As treatment increasingly focused on the couples' sexual life, Richard's resistance heightened. He refused to share the content of his sexual fantasies, insisting that it was none of my business and that they were irrelevant to his problem. He began to appear late for treatment hours but denied that his behavior could have any meaning. I sensed that there was something in the content of his sexual fantasies that held the key to understanding his sexual problem. Richard continued to refuse to discuss his fantasy life, stating he would rather be impotent than look at this part of himself. He acknowledged that he did not want to make love to his wife, although he did not want to disrupt their marriage. Sidney felt stymied; she also did not want to disrupt the marriage but did not believe she could tolerate for long a nonsexual relationship. Treatment was soon terminated because Richard decided he did not want to restore his potency or continue discussion about his erectile failures. He was not interested in seeing another therapist or in pursuing medical interventions.

Psychotherapy has its limitations. The therapist cannot help everyone; not everyone wants the problem resolved. Some patients may do better with another therapist, but there are some who will not benefit from any treatment or any therapist. At these times, the therapist should discuss the limitations of his or her method of psychotherapy, as well as any and all other options for the restoration of potency. One might offer referral to another professional who employs different methods or a conjoint medical/psychological intervention. When I have patients who have not regained their potency after what seems like a reasonable period, I initiate a discussion about the benefits and limitations of oral medication, transurethral therapy, self-injection, or the use of an external vacuum pump device. As discussed earlier, patients often need our guidance and support to make better use of these interventions. Viagra will create firm erections in 7 out of 10 men; it will not, however, mend marital discord or resolve intrapsychic conflict.

REFERENCES

Ackerman, M., & Carey, M. (1995). Psychology's role in the assessment of erectile dysfunction: Historical precedents, current knowledge, and methods. *Journal of Consulting and Clinical Psychology, 63,* 862–876.

Althof, S. (1999). New roles for mental health clinicians in the treatment of erectile dysfunction. *Journal of Sex Education and Therapy, 23*(3), 229–231.

Althof, S., & Levine, S. (1997). Psychosexual aspects of erectile dysfunction. In W. Helstrom (Ed.), *Male infertility and sexual dysfunction* (pp. 468–473). New York: Springer-Verlag.

Althof, S., & Seftel, A. (1999). The evaluation and treatment of erectile dysfunction. In J. Oldham & M. Riba (Eds.), *Annual review of psychiatry* (pp. 55–87). Washington, DC: American Psychiatric Press.

Althof, S., Turner, L., Levine, S., Risen, C., Bodner, D., Kursh, E., & Resnick, M. (1991). Long term use of intracavernous therapy in the treatment of erectile dysfunction. *Journal of Sex and Marital Therapy, 17,* 101–112.

Althof, S., Turner, L., Levine, S., Risen, C., Kursh, E., Bodner, D., & Resnick, M. (1989). Why do so many men drop out from auto-injection therapy for impotence? *Journal of Sex and Marital Therapy, 15,* 121–129.

Bancroft, J. (1999). *Central inhibition of sexual response in the male: A theoretical model.* Manuscript submitted for publication.

Barlow, D. (1986). Causes of sexual dysfunction: The role of anxiety and cognitive interference. *Journal of Consulting and Clinical Psychology, 54,* 140–148.

Blanck, G., & Blanck, R. (1974). *Ego psychology: Theory and practice.* New York: Columbia University Press.

Cooper, A. (1978). Treatment of male potency disorders: The present status. In J. LoPiccolo & L. LoPiccolo (Eds.), *Handbook of sex therapy.* New York: Plenum.

Ellis, A. (1980). Treatment of erectile dysfunction. In S. Leiblum & L. Pervin (Eds.), *Principles and practice of sex therapy* (pp. 235–260). New York: Guilford Press.

Freud, S. (1957a). On the universal tendency to debasement in the sphere of love. In J. Strachey (Ed. & Trans.), *The standard edition of the complete psychological works of Sigmund Freud* (Vol. 11, pp. 177–190). London: Hogarth Press. (Original work published 1912)

Freud, S. (1957b). The dynamics of transference. In J. Strachey (Ed. & Trans.), *The standard edition of the complete psychological works of Sigmund Freud* (Vol. 12, pp. 99–108). London: Hogarth Press. (Original work published 1912)

Gagnon, J., Rosen, R., & Leiblum, S. (1982). Cognitive and social aspects of sexual dysfunction: Sexual scripts in sex therapy. *Journal of Sex and Marital Therapy, 8,* 44–56.

Gill, M. (1982). *Analysis of transference: Volume I. Theory and technique.* New York: International Universities Press.

Goldstein, I., Lue, T., Padma-Nathan, H., Rosen R., Steers, W., & Wicker, P. (1998). Oral sildenafil in the treatment of erectile dysfunction. *New England Journal of Medicine, 338,* 1397–1404.

Greenson, R. (1967). *The theory and practice of psychoanalysis: Vol I.* New York: International Universities Press.

Hartman W., & Fithian, M. (1972). *The treatment of the sexual dysfunctions.* Long Beach, CA: Center for Marital and Sexual Studies.

Hawton, K., Catalan, J., & Faff, J. (1992). Sex therapy for erectile dysfunction: Characteristics of couples, treatment outcome, and prognostic factors. *Archives of Sexual Behavior 21,* 161–175.

Kaplan, H. (1974). *The new sex therapy.* New York: Brunner/Mazel.

Kilman, P., & Auerbach, R. (1979). Treatments of premature ejaculation and psychogenic impotence: A critical review of the literature. *Archives of Sexual Behavior, 8,* 81–100.

Levine, S. (1985). The psychological evaluation and therapy of psychogenic impotence. In R. T. Segraves & H. W. Schoenberg (Eds.), *Diagnosis and treatment of erectile disturbances: A guide for clinicians* (pp. 87–104). New York: Plenum.

Levine, S. (1988). *Sex is not simple.* Columbus: Ohio Psychology.

Levine, S. (1992). *Sexual life: A clinician's guide* New York: Plenum.

Lieberman, M., Yalom, I., & Miles, M. (1973). *Encounter groups: First facts.* New York: Basic Books.

LoPiccolo, J. (1992). Postmodern sex therapy for erectile failure. In R. Rosen & S. Leiblum (Eds.), *Erectile disorders: Assessment and treatment* (pp. 171– 197). New York: Guilford Press.

LoPiccolo, J., & LoPiccolo, L. (1978). *Handbook of sex therapy.* New York: Plenum.

Mann, J. (1973). *Time limited psychotherapy.* Cambridge, MA: Harvard University Press.

Masters, W., & Johnson, V. (1966). *Human sexual response.* London: Churchill, Livingstone.

Masters, W., & Johnson, V. (1970). *Human sexual inadequacy.* Boston: Little, Brown.

McCarthy, B. (1993). Relapse prevention strategies and techniques in sex therapy. *Journal of Sex and Marital Therapy, 19,* 142–147.

McCarthy, B., & McCarthy, E. (1984). *Sexual awareness: Sharing sexual pleasure.* New York: Carroll & Graff.

Money, J. (1989). *Lovemaps: Clinical concepts of sexual/erotic health and pathology, paraphilia, and gender transposition in childhood, adolescence and maturity.* New York: Irvington Publishers.

Obler, M. (1973). Systematic desensitization in sexual disorders. *Journal of Behavior Therapy and Experimental Psychiatry, 4,* 93–101.

Ornstein, A., & Ornstein, P. (1984). *Empathy and the therapeutic dialogue.* Paper presented at the 5th Annual Psychotherapy Symposium on Psychotherapy and the Therapeutic Dialogue. Harvard University, Cambridge Hospital, Boston.

Padma-Nathan, H., Hellstrom, W., Kaiser, F., Labasky, R., Lue, T., Noltan. W., Norwood, P., Peterson, C., Shabsigh, R., Tam., P., Place, V., & Gesundheit, N. (1997). Treatment of men with erectile dysfunction with transurethral alprostadil. *New England Journal of Medicine, 336,* 1–7.

Rosen, R., Goldstein, I., Heiman, J., Korenman, S., Lakin, M., Lue, T., Montague, D., Padma-Nathan, H., Sadovsky, R., Segraves, R., & Shabsigh, R. (1998). *A process of care model: Evaluation and treatment of erectile dysfunction.* Piscataway, NJ: Robert Wood Johnson Medical School Center for Continuing Education.

Rosen, R., Leiblum, S., & Spector, I. (1994). Psychologically based treatment for male erectile disorder: A cognitive–interpersonal model. *Journal of Sex and Marital Therapy, 20,* 67–85.

Schnarf, D. (1990). *Constructing the sexual crucible.* New York: Norton.

Schover, L. (1984). *Prime time—Sexual health for men over fifty.* New York: Holt, Rinehart & Winston.

Segraves, R. T. (1989). Male erectile disorder. In American Psychiatric Association Task Force on Treatments of Psychiatric Disorders (Ed.), *Treatments of psychiatric disorders* (Vol. 3, pp. 2218–2329). Washington, DC: American Psychiatric Press.

Sifneos, P. (1972). *Short term psychotherapy and emotional crisis.* Cambridge, MA: Harvard University Press.

Stoller, R. (1975). *Perversion: The erotic form of hatred.* New York: Pantheon.

Turner, L., Althof, S., Levine, S., Bodner, D., Kursh, E., & Resnick, M. (1991). Long term use of vacuum pump devices in the treatment of erectile dysfunction. *Journal of Sex and Marital Therapy, 17,* 81–93.

Vatsayana. (1964). *The kama sutra.* New York: Grove Press.

Zilbergeld, B. (1975). Group treatment of sexual dysfunction in men without partners. *Journal of Sex and Marital Therapy, 1,* 204–214.

Zilbergeld, B. (1993). *The new male sexuality.* New York: Bantam Books.

10

Medical and Psychological Interventions for Erectile Dysfunction
Toward a Combined Treatment Approach

RAYMOND C. ROSEN

Erectile dysfunction (ED) has been the topic of extensive media discussion and scientific interest since the advent of sildenafil. The problem clearly affects a significant proportion of men—at least 20% over the age of 50—and is frequently associated with significant personal or relationship problems. ED has been associated with a wide range of medical and psychological difficulties, including depression, marital discord, and even employment changes. Physical causes include hypertension, diabetes, hyperlipidemia, and side effects associated with prescription or nonprescription drug use. The approval of sildenafil in 1998 had a profound impact on the clinical management of ED, as well as on basic research in male and female sexual response.

This chapter presents an integrated approach to treatment of ED. Current medical and psychological/sex therapy treatment approaches are reviewed in detail, including a consideration of the cost-effectiveness of each. A new process-of-care model or algorithm for clinical decision making is presented in which available treatments are stratified into first-, second-, and third-line therapies according to the cost, degree of medical invasiveness, and acceptability to both partners. According to this new model, oral treatments such as sildenafil and sex therapy are both considered first-line treatment options, which may be used alone or in combination in most cases.

The second part of the chapter presents specific concepts and guidelines for integrating medical and sexual/psychological interventions. At the simplest level, patients need to be educated about the mechanism of action of the drug and the need for concomitant sexual stimulation along with sildenafil use.

Beyond this, many couples also need to address sexual initiation issues, conflicts or resentments in the relationship, loss of sexual desire, and sexual performance difficulties in the partner. Several authors have noted that treatment outcome is much less likely to be successful if these areas are not adequately addressed.

Given the success of sildenafil as first-line therapy for ED, and the likely development of a new class of erectogenic or sexually activating pharmaceutical agents, medical therapies are likely to predominate in this area for the foreseeable future. On the other hand, the availability of these drugs has hardly eliminated or obviated the need for interpersonal or sex therapy interventions. Rather, the availability of sildenafil has highlighted the need for effective integration of these approaches. This chapter provides basic guidelines and case examples toward this end.

Raymond C. Rosen, PhD, is Professor of Psychiatry and Medicine at the University of Medicine and Dentistry of New Jersey–Robert Wood Johnson Medical School. He has published numerous books and articles and has received extensive grant funding for basic and clinical research on sexual disorders. Dr. Rosen is a frequent consultant to the pharmaceutical industry, the Food and Drug Administration, and the National Institutes of Health.

Erectile dysfunction is a common sexual complaint in men which has become the focus of intense public and professional attention since the approval of sildenafil (Viagra) in 1998. In the Massachusetts Male Aging Study (MMAS), a community-based survey of men between the ages of 40 and 70 years (Feldman, Goldstein, Hatzichristou, Krane, & McKinlay, 1994), 52% of respondents reported some degree of erectile difficulty. Complete erectile dysfunction, defined as the total inability to obtain or maintain erections during sexual stimulation, as well as the absence of nocturnal erections, occurred in 10% of respondents. Lesser degrees of mild and moderate ED occurred in 17% and 25%, respectively. In the National Health and Social Life Survey (NHSLS), a nationally representative probability sample of men and women ages 18 to 59 (Laumann, Gagnon, Michael, & Michaels, 1994), 10.4% of men reported being unable to achieve or maintain an erection during the past year (corresponding to approximately the same proportion of men in the MMAS study reporting complete ED). Both studies observed a strong relationship to age. Although the prevalence of mild ED in the MMAS remained constant (17%) between the ages of 40 and 70, there was a doubling in the number of men reporting moderate ED (17 to 34%) and a tripling of complete ED (5 to 15%). If the MMAS data are extrapolated, there are an estimated 18 to 30 million American men who are affected by ED.

Erectile dysfunction is strongly related to both physical and psychological determinants. Among the major predictors of ED observed in the MMAS (Feldman et al., 1994), diabetes mellitus, heart disease, hypertension, and decreased HDL levels were all associated with increased risk for the disorder. Medications for diabetes, hypertension, and cardiovascular disease are other major risk factors. In addition, there is a higher prevalence of ED among men who have undergone radiation or surgery for prostate cancer (Goldstein, Feldman, Deckers, Babyayon, & Krane, 1984, Quinlan, Epstein, Carter, & Walsh, 1991), or who have a lower spinal cord injury (Courtois, McDougal, & Sachs, 1993). The psychological correlates of ED include depression and anger (Feldman et al., 1994; Araujo, Durante, Feldman, Goldstein, & McKinlay, 1998). The NHSLS found a higher rate of erectile difficulties among men who reported poor to fair health, and among men experiencing stress from unemployment or other causes (Laumann et al., 1994). Despite its increasing prevalence among older men, ED is not considered a normal or inevitable part of the aging process. It is rarely (in fewer than 5% of cases) due to aging-related hypogonadism (Korenman et al., 1990; Schiavi, 1990), although the relationship between ED and age-related declines in androgen remains controversial (Zonszein, 1995).

The recent advent of safe and effective oral therapy (Goldstein et al., 1998; Rosen, 1998) has greatly increased the number of patients seeking treatment and has significantly altered the medical and psychological management of the disorder. Historically the province of urologists and mental health professionals, ED is currently managed predominantly in the primary care setting. Recognizing this sudden and dramatic shift in practice patterns, a multidisciplinary panel was convened by the author to develop a new diagnostic and treatment algorithm for ED (Process of Care Consensus Panel, 1999). Figure 10.1 illustrates this process-of-care model. The core elements of the model are (1) a goal-oriented approach to diagnosis and treatment, (2) an emphasis on clinical history taking and a focused physical examination in all cases, (3) specialized testing and referral in predefined situations, (4) a stepwise management approach with ranking of treatment options, and (5) incorporation of patient needs and preferences wherever possible in the decision-making process. The model emphasizes the need for sexual and psychological assessment as part of the evaluation process and places sex therapy on a par with oral medications or vacuum pump devices as potential first-line interventions for ED. Sex therapy is recommended, according to this model, either in isolation or in combination with medical or surgical treatments for ED. A similar diagnostic and treatment model was recently adopted by the First International Consultation on Erectile Dysfunction (World Health Organization, in press).

MEDICAL AND SURGICAL TREATMENTS FOR ERECTILE DYSFUNCTION

Although a comprehensive review of medical and surgical treatments for ED is beyond the scope of this chapter (see, e.g., Carson, Kirby, & Goldstein, 1999), a brief summary of current treatment options may be of value. For the sake of

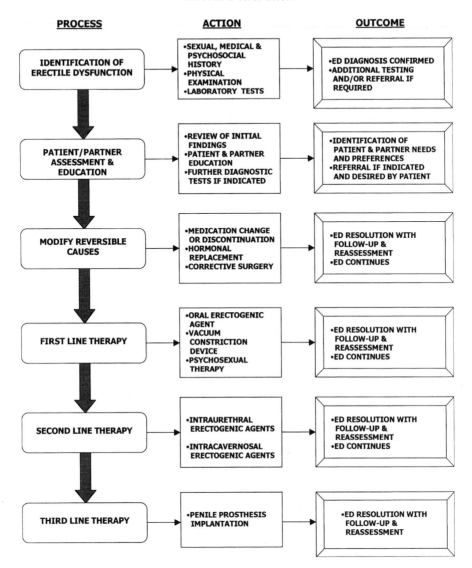

FIGURE 10.1. A process of care model for the clinical management of ED. This model summarizes the essential stages in the initial assessment, case formulation, and step-care treatment approach for the management of ED. Adapted from Process of Care Consensus Panel (1999). Adapted by permission from Nature Publishing Group.

convenience, current medical and surgical treatments can be divided into three major categories: (1) oral pharmacological agents, (2) local (nonsurgical) and mechanical therapies, and (3) surgical interventions. According to the process-of-care model, oral drugs (e.g., sildenafil) should be considered first-line medical therapy, followed by local treatments (intracorporal injections or intraurethral suppositories) or mechanical devices as second-line therapies, and surgical treatments (prostheses, revascularization) as third-line therapies to be used primarily for individuals who fail to respond to either first- or second-line therapy options. Clearly, the majority of men with ED are currently managed with oral drugs, and this trend is likely to continue as new and more effective drugs are developed in the future.

Oral Erectogenic Agents

Phosphodiesterase Type-5 Inhibitors (Sildenafil)

Normal penile erection depends on the relaxation of smooth muscles in the penile corpora (Burnett, 1995; Rajfer, Aronson, Bush, Dorey, & Ignarro, 1992). In response to sexual stimulation, cavernous nerves and endothelial cells release nitric oxide, which stimulates the formation of cyclic guanosine monophosphate (GMP) by guanylate cyclase, which in turn causes vasodilation and relaxation of the coporal smooth muscle tissue. Sildenafil citrate is a selective inhibitor of cyclic GMP-specific phosphodiesterase type-5. By selectively inhibiting cyclic-GMP catabolism in cavernosal smooth muscle cells, sildenafil restores the natural erectile response to sexual stimulation but does not cause erection in the absence of sexual stimulation. Sildenafil is rapidly absorbed, with maximal plasma concentrations occurring within 1 hour after oral administration and a mean terminal half-life of 3 to 5 hours.

The safety and efficacy of sildenafil has been investigated in a large number of controlled clinical trials in males with ED of varying etiologies (see Osterloh et al., 1999, for a recent review). In two large-scale, multicenter trials, sildenafil was administered in doses of 25 mg, 50 mg, and 100 mg, compared to placebo, in either a fixed dose or flexible dose regimen (Goldstein et al., 1998). The majority of patients in both studies were judged to have ED of organic etiology (70%), with fewer patients having psychogenic (11%) or mixed (18%) etiologies. Both studies showed significant dose-related improvements for all measures of erectile function and treatment satisfaction with each of the sildenafil doses compared to placebo. Headache, flushing, and dyspepsia were the most common adverse effects in the dose-escalation study, occurring in 6% to 18% of the men. Other studies have evaluated the safety and efficacy of sildenafil in patients with diabetes, spinal cord injury, and depression.

Based on results of these and other controlled clinical trials, meta-analyses have recently been performed on treatment outcome with sildenafil as a function of age, severity of ED, and type of etiology. Age was not a significant predictor of treatment responsiveness. Patients over the age of 65 show approximately the same ratio of treatment efficacy compared to placebo as patients under the age of 65. Regarding the effects of disease severity on treatment outcome, patients with mild ED showed a slightly higher rate of improvement with sildenafil treatment compared to patients with moderate or severe ED. On the other hand, patients with mild or moderate ED also showed higher rates of response to placebo than did patients with severe ED. If one takes into account the relative placebo response compared to active treatment in each group, there is no evidence of improved treatment outcome as a function of disease severity. In other words, sildenafil is highly effective in older patients (> age 65) and in patients with more severe degrees of ED. Regarding etiology, patients with ED due to psychogenic factors or spinal cord injury were found to have the most positive treatment response (approximately 80% improvement), whereas those with chronic diabetes or radical prostatectomy responded least favorably (< 50%).

Sildenafil's safety has been the topic of much controversy and debate in recent months. Based on adverse events reported in the main clinical trials, the drug has an acceptable overall safety profile. To date, the most frequent adverse events reported were headache, flushing, dyspepsia, rhinitis, and visual disturbances. In the dose escalation and open-label studies, these side effects were observed in less than 20% of patients and rarely resulted in drug discontinuation. Approximately 1 to 2% of patients withdrew from treatment due to drug side effects. Since the approval of sildenafil, increasing concerns have been raised regarding the potential cardiac risks associated with sildenafil use. These risks have recently been reviewed by a consensus panel of the American College of Cardiology (ACC) (ACC/AHAA Expert Consensus, 1999). The major conclusion of this panel was that sildenafil poses no special cardiac risk for the majority of patients. However, the drug is absolutely contraindicated for patients taking nitrates in any form, due to the likely potentiation of hypotensive effects with these drugs. Sildenafil should also be used with caution in patients with a recent history of myocardial infarction or other significant cardiac conditions (e.g., unstable angina and congestive heart failure). Caution was also recommended in patients using multiple antihypertensive agents.

Other PDE-5 inhibitors are currently in development. These drugs may have greater selectivity or potency for the type-5 isoenzyme than does sildenafil, although it is unclear at present whether such differences in pharmacology will have clinical significance. Clinical studies of sildenafil are also under way in women, although it is again unclear what role sildenafil will play in the future treatment of female sexual dysfunction. One conclusion at least can be safely drawn at this time; sildenafil has had a major impact on the office management of male ED (Process of Care Panel, 1999). Clearly, the availability of the drug has led millions of men to seek treatment for their condition who would not otherwise have sought professional help.

Dopamine Agonists

Penile erection is initiated by specific structures and neural networks in the central nervous system. Supraspinal sites that project directly to the spinal cord center for penile erection include the paraventricular nucleus (PVN), the locus cereulus (LC), nucleus paragigantocellularis (NPGi), and the medial pre-optic area (MPOA) of the hypothalamus. Dopamine is a monoaminergic neu-rotransmitter that has localized activity in the PVN and MPOA of the hypo-thalamus. It is excitatory to oxytocinergic pathways that project to the spinal erection generator. Currently only one centrally active agent is in advanced development for the treatment of ED, sublingual apomorphine.

Apomorphine is a dopamine agonist that is active in both D1 and D2 receptors, although it is slightly more selective for the D2 compared to the D1 receptor. Apomorphine is not an opiate but, rather, an aporphine that in rats produces erections in sexual situations. It is a well-known agent that has been available medically since 1869. However, a novel sublingual formulation has been recently developed that appears to be both effective and safe (Heaton, Morales, Adams, Johnston, & El-Rashidy, 1995). Overall it has demonstrated up to 60% efficacy in producing "erections adequate for intercourse" in doses ranging between 2 and 6 mg. The major side effects are nausea, which occurs in up to 20% of patients at the higher doses, and syncope, which occurs in <5% of patients at higher doses. Few if any patients experience syncope at the 2-mg or 4-mg doses. The availability of centrally active erectogenic agents raises new questions and opportunities for both researchers and clinicians. Sublingual apomorphine is currently in advanced stages of clinical testing and is likely to be the second orally active agent approved for the treatment of erectile dysfunction. It has been suggested that due to the central actions of this drug, it may have particular relevance in the treatment of sexual dysfunc-tion in women.

Alpha-1/ Alpha-2 Blockers

The availability of sidenafil has focused attention on the nitric oxide "excita-tory" pathway for initiating corporal smooth muscle relaxation and penile erection. Of equal potential importance is the "inhibitory" contractile path-way that controls corporal smooth muscle contraction and penile detumes-cence. A complete conceptualization of the mechanisms of penile erection in-volves both contractile and relaxatory pathways. Detumescence of the erect penis occurs via adrenergic stimulation which induces (1) contraction of the cavernosal arteries leading to reduced arterial inflow and (2) contraction of the trabecular smooth muscle which causes collapse of the lacunar spaces. Detumescence of the erect penis is mediated primarily by adrenergic nerve ter-minals releasing norepinephrine to alpha-1 and alpha-2 adrenergic receptors on the corporal smooth muscle cell and cavernosal artery. Conversely, local alpha-adrenergic blockers, such as phentolamine mesylate or doxazosin have been shown in both *in vivo* and *in vitro* studies to prevent detumescence, to prolong the duration of erection, and to potentiate the stimulatory effect of smooth muscle relaxation by removing inhibitory responses mediated by the sympathetic nervous system.

Phentolamine mesylate is a combined alpha-1 and alpha-2 adrenergic antagonist, which was originally approved for the treatment of pheochromocytoma-induced hypertension and norephinephrine-related dermal necrosis. Since the early 1980s, the drug has been used in combination with other agents for intracavernosal injection therapy of ED. Recently, a new oral, rapid-release formulation of phentolamine has been developed for treatment of mild or psychogenic erectile dysfunction (Zorgniotti, 1994). Pharmacokinetic studies have shown the drug to be rapidly absorbed (Cmax = 0.25–0.75 hrs) and eliminated, and initial safety and efficacy has been demonstrated in several clinical trials (Becker et al., 1998).

In a recent controlled trial, male patients with mild to moderate ED were randomized to receive oral phentolamine (40 mg or 80 mg) or double-blind placebo over a 4-week treatment period. A mild, dose-dependent effect of treatment on the primary outcome measures was observed. Patients in the 80 mg group were approximately four times as satisfied with the results of treatment as patients in the placebo group, although fewer than 50% of patients overall reported satisfaction with treatment outcome. Results for the 40-mg group were intermediate. Phentolamine was well tolerated by most patients with no serious side effects reported. Mild side effects included nasal congestion, dizziness, and headache in less than 10% of patients. Oral phentolamine has been approved for treatment of ED in relatively few countries (e.g., Mexico and Brazil) at the time of writing. The drug is currently under review with the Food and Drug Administration (FDA).

Local Therapies

According to the process-of-care model, second-line (local) therapies should be selected based on (1) failure, insufficient response, or adverse side effects associated with one or more of the first-line therapies; or (2) patient/partner preferences. These interventions consist of intraurethral administration or intracavernosal injection of alprostadil. Vacuum pump devices can also be included in this category. Although widely used, these treatments are associated with variable efficacy, a high patient discontinuation rate, possible risk of side effects, and moderately high cost.

Intracavernosal Injection Therapy

Prior to the approval of sildenafil, intracavernosal self-injection was the most common medical therapy for erectile dysfunction (Linet & Ogrinc, 1996, Fallon,

1995). The two FDA-approved drugs for intracavernosal injection, alprostadil sterile powder, and alprostadil alfadex are both synthetic formulations of prostaglandin E_1. Injection therapy is effective in most cases of ED, regardless of etiology. It is contraindicated in men with a history of hypersensitivity to the drug employed, in men at risk for priapism (e.g., sickle cell disease and hypercoagulable states), and in men receiving monoamine oxidase inhibitors. The effective therapeutic range is between 1 and 60 micrograms with the majority of responders (85%) requiring less than 20 micrograms. In general, intracavernosal injection therapy with alprostadil is effective in 70% to 80% of patients, although discontinuation rates are high in most studies. Side effects include prolonged erections or priapism, penile pain, and fibrosis with chronic use. In addition to single-agent injection therapy, various combinations of alprostadil, phentolamine, and/or papaverine are widely employed in urological practice (Fallon, 1995).

Intraurethral Alprostadil

Alprostadil (prostaglandin E_1) may be administered intraurethrally in the form of a semisolid pellet inserted by means of a special applicator. To obtain an effective concentration of alprostadil in the corpora cavernosa, 125 to 1,000 micrograms of the drug are delivered by the device to the urethra. In a mixed group of patients with organic ED, 65% of men receiving intraurethral alprostadil responded with a firm erection when tested in the office, and 50% of administrations to that subset resulted in at least one episode of successful intercourse in the home setting (Padma-Nathan et al., 1997). Side effects associated with the intraurethral administration of alprostadil include penile pain and hypotension. Prolonged erections and penile fibrosis are rare (Spivak, Peterson, & Cowley, 1997), although the clinical success rate is low (Fulgham et al., 1998).

Vacuum Constriction Device (VCD) Therapy

VCD therapy is a well-established, noninvasive treatment that has recently been approved by the FDA for over-the-counter distribution (Lewis & Witherington, 1997; Korenman & Viosca, 1992). It provides a useful treatment alternative for patients for whom pharmacological therapies are contraindicated, or who do not desire other interventions. Vacuum constriction devices apply a negative pressure to the flaccid penis, thus drawing venous blood into the penis, which is then retained by the application of an elastic constriction band at the base of the penis. Efficacy rates of 60% to 80% have been reported in most studies. Like intracorporal injection therapy, VCD treatment is associated with a high rate of patient discontinuation. The adverse events occasionally associated with VCD therapy include penile pain, numbness, bruising, and delayed ejaculation (Lewis & Witherington, 1997).

Surgical Treatments

Third-line therapy, according to the process-of-care model, consists of surgical implantation of a penile prosthesis. For select cases of severe, treatment-refractory ED, for patients who fail pharmacological therapy or who prefer a permanent solution for the problem, surgical implantation of a semirigid or inflatable penile prosthesis is available (Lewis, 1995). Various types of surgical prostheses have been described in the literature. The inflatable penile prosthesis provides a more esthetic erection and better concealment than do semirigid prostheses, although there is an increased rate of mechanical failure and complications (5–20%) with the former. Despite the cost, invasiveness and potential medical complications involved, penile implant surgery has been associated with high rates of patient satisfaction in previous studies (Lewis, 1995; Pedersen, 1988). It should be noted, however, that these studies were conducted prior to the advent of newer forms of therapy (e.g., sildenafil).

PSYCHOLOGICAL/SEX THERAPY APPROACHES

Sex therapy approaches for ED have typically emphasized four major components: (1) anxiety reduction and desensitization, (2) cognitive–behavioral interventions, (3) increased sexual stimulation, and (4) interpersonal assertiveness and couple communication training. Recently, attempts have also been made to introduce a systematic relapse prevention training component to the treatment of ED (McCarthy, 1993; Rosen, Leiblum, & Spector, 1994). Although various studies have supported the use of one or more of these interventions in the treatment of psychologically based erectile difficulties, few studies have attempted to isolate the effects of individual treatment components or to evaluate the long-term outcomes associated with psychological treatment (Mohr & Beutler, 1990; Hawton, Catalan, & Fagg, 1992). As noted by the NIH Consensus Panel on Impotence (1993), "Outcome data of psychological and behavioral therapy have not been quantified, and evaluation of the success of specific techniques used in these treatments is poorly documented" (p. 87). In addition, planned comparisons of the effectiveness of psychological treatment with medical or surgical interventions have been entirely lacking, as have studies of the cost-effectiveness or impact of treatment on health-related quality of life (Spilker, 1990).

Men with erectile difficulties (and their partners) are often resistant to psychological interventions due to the potential implication that the problem is "all in his (or her) head," or that the male is purposefully avoiding sexual intimacy. As noted by Zilbergeld (1992), men with ED usually experience both shame and guilt in association with their sexual dysfunction, and organic explanations of the disorder are obviously appealing. For this reason, it is frequently necessary to "bypass" the male's resistance by stressing the value of psychological or sex therapy interventions for the partner relationship. Some men are also more likely to accept psychological treatments, in our experience, when combined with medical or mechanical interventions (Rosen et al., 1994).

Anxiety Reduction and Desensitization

Anxiety-reduction techniques have featured prominently in past and present treatment approaches for ED. For example, the concept of forbidding intercourse and directing the male and his partner in techniques of nondemand body caressing (*in vivo* desensitization) can be traced back to the writings of an 18th-century British physician, Dr. John Hunter (LoPiccolo, 1992). This technique was the forerunner of the "sensate focus" approach subsequently developed by Masters and Johnson (1970), and which served as the foundation of their sex therapy program for ED. Early behavior therapists, such as Wolpe (1958) and Lazarus (1965), similarly emphasized the importance of systematic desensitization in overcoming performance anxiety and inhibitions typically associated with ED. These authors also recommended the use of relaxation techniques and avoidance of intercourse during the early phases of treatment. According to Masters and Johnson (1970), performance anxiety or "spectatoring" is the major causal determinant of psychogenic erectile dysfunction and is best overcome through a program of nongenital, nondemand pleasuring exercises, termed "sensate focus." This approach has been uncritically accepted, for the most part, and has been adopted as the mainstay of sex therapy for erectile dysfunction (Rosen & Leiblum, 1992; Wincze & Carey, 1991).

Based on psychophysiological studies of males with ED compared to nondysfunctional controls, Barlow and associates have suggested that it is not anxiety per se that is responsible for the psychological component of ED, but the associated effects of cognitive distraction (Barlow, Sakheim, & Beck, 1983; Cranston-Cuebas & Barlow, 1990). In fact, laboratory manipulations of both anxiety and performance demand were found to increase sexual arousal in nondysfunctional males, whereas opposite effects were obtained for the dysfunctional subjects. Focusing on arousal, in particular, was found to facilitate performance in normals but to be highly inhibitory in the dysfunctional subjects. Similarly, subjective arousal was rated as significantly lower in dysfunctional subjects, regardless of the actual physiological level of arousal. Finally, attention to nonsexual stimuli (i.e., cognitive distraction) was found to be more disruptive to nondysfunctional compared to dysfunctional men (Cranston-Cuebas & Barlow, 1990). Taken together, these findings suggest that physiological concomitants of anxiety may be far less important than the effects of performance demand or cognitive distraction in males with ED. Unfortunately, no treatment study to date has directly evaluated this hypothesis.

Other clinical difficulties have been noted in the current reliance on relaxation or sensate focus approaches. For example, LoPiccolo (1992) has argued that sensate focus may represent a form of paradoxical intervention. Whereas the therapist assigns sensate focus with the intention of relieving performance anxiety, many patients do not experience a reduction in such anxiety; rather they experience "metaperformance anxiety," or anxiety about not performing despite the injunction not to feel pressure to perform. This effect is illustrated in the self-report of a typical patient receiving sensate focus therapy: "I found myself lying there, thinking, 'I'm now free of pressure to perform. I'm not supposed to get an erection, and we're not allowed to have intercourse even if I do get one. So now that all the pressure is off, why am I not getting an erection? I'm relaxed, I'm enjoying this, so where's the erection?'" (LoPiccolo, 1992, p. 189).

According to this perspective, it is insufficient to assign sensate focus or relaxation exercises in the face of highly internalized performance demands. Rather, the focus of therapy should be on confronting the source of these performance demands via cognitive or psychoeducational interventions (Apfelbaum, 1995; Rosen et al., 1994).

Cognitive–Behavioral Interventions

Cognitive interventions are used increasingly in the psychological treatment of ED. In particular, bibliotherapy and cognitive restructuring techniques are used to overcome sexual ignorance and to challenge the unrealistic sexual expectations that typically accompany ED (e.g., Zilbergeld, 1992; McCarthy, 1988). Men (and their partners) frequently harbor gross misconceptions regarding the basic mechanisms and processes of erectile function and causes of sexual dysfunction. The effects of illness and drugs, aging, and male–female differences in sexual response are additional common areas of ignorance. As noted by Zilbergeld (1992), men frequently subscribe to a "fantasy model of sex" in which male performance is viewed as the cornerstone of every sexual experience, and a firm erection is seen as the sine qua non of a satisfying sexual encounter. Sexual performance difficulties are often interpreted, according to this view, as a loss of masculinity or declining sexual interest in the partner.

Dysfunctional sexual beliefs and expectations are a potentially important focus for treatment. In one study, elderly couples with a history of ED were randomly assigned to either an educational workshop program or a waiting-list control (Goldman & Carroll, 1990). Posttreatment evaluations revealed a significant improvement in sexual knowledge and attitudes in the workshop participants, which was associated with increased sexual frequency and satisfaction. Unfortunately, no long-term follow-up of treatment outcome was provided.

Self-hypnosis and fantasy training procedures have been recommended for developing positive sexual imagery (Brown & Chaves, 1980; Araoz, 1983). In one uncontrolled study, self-hypnosis was reported to be effective in improving sexual performance in approximately 70% of male patients with ED (Araoz, 1983). Unfortunately, no follow-up data was provided nor was any comparison made to other forms of sex therapy intervention. Other authors have recommended that positive imagery training, either with or without mas-turbation, can assist in the development of sexual confidence and control (Rosen et al., 1994; Zilbergeld, 1992). No controlled outcome data have been pro-vided on the use of these approaches to date, however, nor is it apparent which individuals are most likely to benefit from such interventions. In addition, Apfelbaum (1989) has cautioned that whereas sexual fantasies may be used by dysfunctional males to temporarily "bypass" their lack of arousal or interest in the partner, this solution is unlikely to be effective and may lead to a loss of sexual desire when used on a long-term basis.

Sexual Stimulation Techniques

Several authors have noted that ED is most psychologically distressing for couples with limited sexual scripts and few alternatives to intercourse (Zilbergeld, 1992; LoPiccolo, 1992; Gagnon, Rosen, & Leiblum, 1982; Leiblum & Rosen, 1991). In particular, performance demands and fear of failure are increased markedly for individuals or couples who lack alternative means of sexual satisfaction to penile–vaginal intercourse. For these individuals, the male's inability to achieve a firm and lasting erection typically results in a complete cessation of all sexual activity. This, in turn, may lead to diminished sexual desire in one or both partners and increased distance or conflict in the relation-ship (Leiblum & Rosen, 1991). A "vicious cycle" phenomenon frequently en-sues, as the loss of sexual or affectionate interaction is associated with in-creased performance demands and interpersonal distress. In one early study, sexual communication training was found to be superior to sensate focus alone in the treatment of secondary erectile dysfunction (Takefman & Brender, 1984).

LoPiccolo (1992) has emphasized the critical role of the female partner's attitude toward nonintercourse forms of sexual stimulation. According to LoPiccolo (1992), the partner's willingness to be satisfied by manual or oral stimulation may be a critical determinant of treatment outcome in most cases of ED:

> Far more effective than sensate focus in reducing performance anxiety is the patient's knowledge that his partner's sexual gratification does not depend on his having an erection. If the patient can be reassured that his partner finds their love making highly pleasurable, and that she is sexually fulfilled by the orgasms he gives her through manual and oral stimulation, his performance anxiety will be greatly reduced.

From this perspective, treatment is often focused on the sexual receptivity of the partner to nonintercourse forms of stimulation.

Increased genital stimulation may also be necessary for the male partner to achieve adequate erection (McCarthy, 1988; Zilbergeld, 1992), and may augment the effects of sildenafil's use markedly. Among older men, in particular, there is an increasing need for direct, tactile stimulation of the penis, along with a decreasing responsiveness to psychogenic forms of stimulation (Segraves & Segraves, 1992). Thus, the older male may require extended manual or oral stimulation of the penis in order to achieve adequate erection for intercourse. The female partner is frequently unaware of this important physiological change in her partner and may misattribute his lack of arousal to sexual disinterest or a loss of sexual attractiveness to her partner. When informed of the need for change in this area, older couples frequently have difficulty in modifying or adapting their traditional sexual scripts (Leiblum & Segraves, 1989). Many of these couples have minimal experience in foreplay or nonintercourse forms of sexual stimulation (Laumann et al., 1994).

Elsewhere, we have advocated the use of a "sexual scripting" approach to a variety of sexual performance difficulties, including erectile dysfunction (Gagnon et al., 1982; Rosen & Leiblum, 1995; Rosen et al., 1994). Essentially, this approach involves detailed assessment of both the performative, or overt, script between the partners and the ideal or imagined script of each individual partner. Performative scripts can be analyzed according to four major script dimensions: complexity, rigidity, conventionality, and satisfaction. In couples with chronic sexual dysfunctions, including ED, performative scripts typically become increasingly restricted, repetitive, and inflexible, with diminishing sexual satisfaction for either partner. Script restrictions may either precede the onset of a specific sexual problem or may develop as a consequence of the disorder (Leiblum & Rosen, 1991).

Interpersonal and Systemic Interventions

Interpersonal and couples issues play a major role in many, if not most, cases of ED. As noted by Masters and Johnson (1970), "there is no such thing as an uninvolved partner in any marriage in which there is some form of sexual inadequacy" (p. 2). Relationship conflicts may be a primary source of the sexual difficulty or may serve to exacerbate or maintain the male's inability to achieve adequate erections. Although the role of relationship factors is widely acknowledged in the clinical literature on the topic (e.g., Masters & Johnson, 1970; Kaplan, 1974; Leiblum & Rosen, 1991), relatively few studies to date have assessed the relationship between interpersonal distress and treatment outcome for ED. In a British study, sensate focus and graduated sexual stimulation techniques were evaluated in 36 couples presenting for treatment of psychogenic ED (Hawton et al., 1992). A major determinant of treatment outcome in this study was the couples' ratings of marital communication prior to treatment. Couples with higher ratings of marital communication responded more rapidly and with better outcomes to the sex therapy interventions provided.

In addition to the paucity of outcome data, there is a lack of consensus at present regarding the choice of conceptual framework or intervention strategies for overcoming relationship conflicts. Thus, some sex therapists have formulated couples issues from a psychodynamic perspective (e.g., Kaplan, 1974; Scharff, 1988; Levine, 1992); others have provided a cognitive–behavioral perspective (Hawton, Catalan, & Fagg, 1986; Wincze & Carey, 1991); still others have argued for a family systems approach (Verhulst & Heiman, 1979; LoPiccolo, 1992). This lack of agreement concerning theory and practice of couple therapy has impeded efforts to develop more standardized approaches for dealing with couples issues in erectile dysfunction. Rather, this essential aspect of treatment is often based on an eclectic array of techniques and interventions.

In reviewing the current clinical literature, we have identified three major dimensions of couple's conflict that we have most frequently encountered in cases of ED (Leiblum & Rosen, 1991; Rosen et al., 1994). These are (1) status and dominance issues, (2) intimacy and trust, and (3) loss of sexual attraction. Status and dominance issues arise when the balance of power in a relationship is shifted, either because of external factors such as the loss of a job and unemployment or because of internal factors such as depression and loss of self-esteem. Similarly, intimacy or trust difficulties may occur when either partner engages in an extramarital affair, undertakes a new career, or gives birth to a child. In addition, loss of sexual attraction may be associated with weight gain, medical illness or surgery, and abuse of drugs or alcohol. Elsewhere, we have reviewed the multiple factors that may contribute to a loss of "sexual chemistry" between partners in specific cases of ED (Leiblum & Rosen, 1991).

Finally, a number of treatment interventions have been described for single males with chronic erectile difficulties (Reynolds, 1991, 1992; Stravinsky & Greenberg, 1990). Treatment strategies include sexual attitude change, assertiveness training, masturbation exercises, and social skills development. In the only controlled study to date of these interventions, a group treatment format for single men was compared to a waiting-list control (Price, Reynolds, Cohen, Anderson, & Schochet, 1981). Significant improvements in self-esteem and sexual satisfaction were associated with treatment, as well as a nonsignificant trend toward improved erectile function. Previously, sexual surrogate therapy had been used in several centers for treatment of single males (Apfelbaum, 1984; Dauw, 1988). Despite the value of this approach in some cases, the potential risks and uncertain legal status of surrogate therapy have greatly limited its use in recent years (Reynolds, 1991).

Relapse Prevention Training

A major difficulty in the psychological treatment of ED is the high rate of relapse noted in several studies. In one early study, for example, a combined sex and marital therapy approach was evaluated in 16 couples with chronic secondary ED (Levine & Agle, 1978). After 3 months of treatment, 10 of 16 men had recovered erectile function. However, most of these men complained of other sexual difficulties (e.g., hypoactive desire and premature ejaculation), and significant relapse was observed in most patients at 1-year follow-up. A similarly high relapse rate was noted in a subsequent study of rational–emotive therapy for psychogenic erectile failure (Munjack et al., 1984). In this study, male patients and their partners were randomly assigned to either a 6-week treatment program or a waiting-list control. Although significant improvements were noted in the treatment group, these were not maintained at 9-month follow-up.

To facilitate maintenance of treatment gains, McCarthy (1993) has advocated the use of a relapse prevention training (RPT) approach similar to that used in the treatment of addictive disorders (e.g., Marlatt & Gordon, 1985). Among the specific strategies recommended are scheduling of occasional nondemand or noncoital pleasuring sessions, rehearsal of coping responses for dealing with unsatisfactory or negative sexual experiences, increasing the range of affectional or intimate behaviors other than intercourse, and scheduling of periodic therapy follow-up visits. This encourages maintenance of treatment gains and provides opportunities for problem solving of ongoing sexual difficulties or conflicts. In addition to the areas emphasized by McCarthy (1993), we have noted that treatment outcome appears to be strongly linked to the level of confidence or sexual self-efficacy achieved by the end of treatment.

In summary, psychological and interpersonal approaches to treatment have been relatively neglected in the face of increasing "medicalization" of erectile disorder (Bancroft, 1990; Tiefer, 1994). This trend is attributed to the availability of medical therapies and the involvement of a wide variety of physicians in the medical management of the disorder, as well as the reluctance of many males and their partners to consider the emotional or interpersonal antecedents of the problem. Disappointing outcomes associated with psychological intervention are another potential determinant of the shift toward biomedical conceptualization and treatment of the disorder. For many individuals, medical treatments (e.g., sildenafil) may represent a "quick fix" for the disorder, thus avoiding the time-consuming and uncertain outcome of psychological treatment approaches.

COMBINED MEDICAL AND SEX THERAPY APPROACHES

Since the approval of sildenafil, renewed interest has developed in combining medical and sex therapy approaches for ED. Despite the overall effectiveness of sildenafil, the medication is not always completely efficacious or well tolerated (Osterloh et al., 1999). At times, treatment of erectile difficulties with sildenafil only reveals or highlights other sexual problems, such as lack of sexual desire or premature ejaculation. Sexual problems in the partner or other couple's issues may come to light following successful (or unsuccessful) use of sildenafil. Although this concern applies equally in the use of any medical or surgical treatment for ED, in light of the sheer numbers of men taking sildenafil (> 5 million at the time of writing) and the widespread use of the drug, the role of concomitant psychological or interpersonal problems has been highlighted dramatically. Rather than rendering sex therapy obsolete or unnecessary, the approval of sildenafil has led to a redefining of the role and importance of psychological interventions. In particular, a new impetus has emerged for combining medical and sex therapy approaches for ED (Hawton, 1998). Although there are no controlled trials to date evaluating the benefits (and costs) of a combined treatment approach, strong arguments have been made for the potential benefits of combining drug and nondrug approaches to achieve better overall compliance and improved outcomes. There are several specific areas of intervention.

Problems of Initiation

In couples with long-standing ED, initiating or resuming sexual activity may be difficult following an extended period of sexual abstinence. Leiblum (in press) notes that chronic ED typically leads to sexual apathy or avoidance in one or both partners, and that specific interventions may be required to assist the couple in resuming sexual activity. Sexual avoidance in these cases may be related to embarrassment or fear of failure on the part of the male, unrealistic beliefs or expectations, relationship conflicts, and low sexual desire in one or both partners. Many couples make long-term adjustments in their relationships or lifestyles to the absence of sexual activity, and the availability of the drug may not be a sufficient stimulus to overcome the sexual inertia that permeates their relationship. Few physicians assess the sexual relationship beyond the male's ability to achieve satisfactory erection or orgasm, and problems of initiation are unlikely to be addressed in this setting. In a recent follow-up study of patients being treated with sildenafil, Pallas, Levine, Althof, and Risen (1999) reported that about one fourth of their sample were unable to sustain initial improvements with the drug. Many of these individuals appeared to have difficulty in resuming or maintaining an active sexual relationship.

How should problems of initiation be managed clinically? We have previously advocated the use of a "sexual script" approach (Rosen & Leiblum, 1992; Rosen et al., 1994) in treating sexual abstinence or initiation problems in ED generally, and this approach can be readily combined with pharmacological therapy in most cases. At the simplest level, physicians prescribing sildenafil (or other drug therapy) should be encouraged to inquire whether couples have maintained a degree of sexual activity or involvement despite the male's erectile difficulties, and whether any problems are anticipated in resuming sexual activity. Simple encouragement or advice about the importance of sexual stimulation and the need for foreplay may be adequate in some cases, whereas others may require referral for more in-depth couple or sex therapy. After long periods of abstinence, the sexual script is invariably limited to a narrow and restricted range of sexual activity, which the couple typically engage in without interest or enthusiasm. An important focus for therapy in these cases is to explore new options and approaches to love making with the couple, and to encourage a degree of experimentation in their sexual script. The use of sildenafil can be viewed as an opportunity for the male to regain his sexual confidence, which should in turn facilitate a more open and experimental approach to sexual encounters. Partners should similarly be encouraged to adopt a more open-ended and, if possible, playful approach to love making. The use of instructional videos, homework assignments, and open discussion with the couple may all be of value in broadening the sexual script.

Problems of Low Desire

Men with ED frequently have concomitant low desire, either as a cause or as a consequence of their ED. In some cases, the lack of desire may be sufficiently severe to warrant a secondary diagnosis of hypoactive sexual desire disorder (HSDD). In other instances, a generally low level of sexual interest or enthusiasm is evident, even though the full criteria for HSDD diagnosis are not met. Although precise data are not available on the proportion of ED cases that have concomitant HSDD or diminished desire, we would estimate that at least one third of ED cases seen in our clinic in recent years have low desire to a significant degree. Interestingly, this represents a marked discrepancy from the published clinical trial data on sildenafil (Goldstein et al., 1998, Osterloh, Eardley, Carson, & Padma-Nathan, 1998), in which relatively few patients had less than adequate sexual desire. The discrepancy can be explained by the fact that patients needed to be highly motivated to gain entry into the clinical trials, and that they were also recruited on the basis of their being involved in an active sexual relationship. In this sense, conclusions about the effectiveness of sildenafil based on results from clinical trials may significantly overerestimate the efficacy of the drug in individuals or couples with desire disorders. This conclusion is supported by results of the recent follow-up study discussed previously by Pallas et al. (1999).

How should problems of low desire be approached in this context? First, a careful assessment of the previous sexual history of the couple should be conducted, with special attention to each partner's past sexual feelings and desires. As noted by Leiblum (in press), male patients and their partners should be closely questioned about whether sexual activity was something highly valued and then lost or something easily relinquished. For men, sexual intercourse may have long-standing associations with performance anxiety or an overall sense of inadequacy. Such individuals may feel threatened or insecure at the prospect of having to "perform" again sexually. Similarly, female partners frequently have sexual insecurities or dysfunctions of their own, and the loss of erectile ability in the male may be associated with feelings of relief in the female partner. These issues should be identified and openly addressed as early as possible in the therapy process. In some instances, the lack of interest or desire for sex becomes apparent as a form of "resistance" or noncompliance with the prescribed medical therapy (Pallas et al., 1999). If either partner is found to have primary HSDD which predates, or is a major causal factor for, the male's ED, couple or sex therapy should be specifically addressed to this problem. Other chapters in this volume present current interpersonal and cognitive–behavioral approaches to low desire (see Schnarch, Chapter 2, and Pridal & LoPiccolo, Chapter 3). Medical treatments (e.g., sildenafil) can be prescribed in such cases, although the primary focus of treatment should be on the underlying sexual desire disorder.

Other Sexual Dysfunctions

Men with ED or their partners frequently have other sexual dysfunctions, such as premature or retarded ejaculation in the male and arousal or penetration difficulties in the female. Although precise data are lacking on the relative incidence of these problems in couples presenting for treatment of ED, my experience would suggest that at least one in four cases has concomitant sexual problems in one or both partners. Again, a careful assessment is important in determining the history of these problems and their specific relationship to the male's ED. In some instances, ED may develop secondary to premature or retarded ejaculation in the male, or in response to chronic penetration difficulties (i.e., vaginismus and dyspareunia) in the female partner. Treatment of the male's erectile difficulties with sildenafil (or other medical therapy) may only reinitiate or exacerbate these underlying problems. Whenever possible, these problems should be clearly identified and addressed prior to the initiation of medical treatment with sildenafil. In many instances, however, the presence of other sexual problems only becomes apparent in the form of "resistance" or failure of drug therapy (Pallas et al., 1999). At such times, the couple should be referred for more intensive couple or sex therapy.

Some observations are worth noting in regard to specific treatment issues with these problems. Premature ejaculation is likely the most common associated problem in men, although little has been written about the treatment of men with both ED and premature ejaculation (PE). In some instances, we have found that effective restoration of erectile function with sildenafil may sufficiently boost the male's (and his partner's) sexual confidence such that control of ejaculation is similarly improved. Clinical trial data with sildenafil show modest improvements in satisfaction with orgasm following treatment with the drug (Goldstein et al., 1998; Osterloh et al., 1998). However, men with chronic or primary PE were again generally excluded from these trials. Men with chronic or severe PE, in addition to erectile difficulties, are generally not good candidates for treatment with sildenafil, in my experience. Rather some form of pharmacological or sex therapy treatment for PE is recommended either prior to or in conjunction with the use of sildenafil. Commonly used serotonergic drugs, such as clomipramine or paroxetine, are generally effective in restoring ejaculatory control in men, although these drugs may significantly worsen the patient's erectile difficulties and are generally contraindicated for patients with both PE and ED. Sex therapy procedures such as the "stop–start" technique may be preferable for this reason, although no data are available on the effectiveness of combining this approach with sildenafil treatment. Delayed ejaculation is a less common problem in men with ED, although additional sex therapy interventions may again be required for men with both ED and delayed ejaculation (Rosen & Leiblum, 1995).

For women with penetration or lubrication difficulties, these problems should be addressed directly prior to initiation of treatment for the male's ED. In cases of dyspareunia or vaginismus, in particular, a complete medical and sex therapy evaluation for the female partner is recommended at the outset. Male partners of these women frequently develop concomitant erectile difficulties, and both partners may experience pressure to resume intercourse, particularly if the couple is planning to conceive. Depending on the severity of the problem and results of the physical and psychosexual evaluation, medical or sex therapy interventions should be initiated, and the couple should be counseled to avoid attempting intercourse initially. The male may wish to try sildenafil in conjunction with manual (either self- or partner-stimulation) or oral stimulation but should be strongly discouraged from attempting intercourse until sufficient progress has made in treating the sexual dysfunction in the partner. Some women report a recurrence of the penetration problem when the male begins to use sildenafil (or other medical therapy) and intercourse is resumed. Although less debilitating generally than dyspareunia or vaginismus, arousal or lubrication difficulties might also make resumption of intercourse difficult or painful for the female partner. This is particularly common in postmenopausal women not taking hormonal replacement. Again, these problems should be separately addressed prior to the introduction of sildenafil.

Couples or Relationship Problems

Couple or relationship problems are frequently implicated in the development of ED or may arise as a consequence of the problem (Rosen & Leiblum, 1992; Rosen et al., 1994). In either event, couples with severe relationship conflicts or communication difficulties are unlikely to benefit from the use of sildenafil or other isolated medical treatments for ED. Again, these individuals were excluded from the main clinical trials on sildenafil (Osterloh et al., 1998), and information is lacking on the percentage of treatment failures that may be attributed to problems in the relationship. Certainly, this was one of the major reasons for treatment failure identified in the recent Pallas et al. (1999) study, and Leiblum (in press) has similarly commented on the importance of addressing relationship issues in couples preparing to resume sexual activity. Frequent problems that we have encountered here include the possibility that one or the other partner is engaged in an extramarital affair, long-standing anger or resentment over unfulfilled sexual or nonsexual needs, power struggles in the relationship, and a loss of physical or emotional intimacy. Changes in physical appearance (e.g., significant weight gain) and loss of sexual attractiveness are additional factors to be considered.

Good clinical judgment needs to be exercised in advising a couple whether or not to begin using sildenafil (or other medical treatment) prior to or in conjunction with couple therapy for one or more of such problems. There are no clear guidelines or simple "rule of thumb" that can be applied across situations. In each case, a careful assessment should be performed of the type and degree of relationship distress as well as the likely impact on the couple of beginning medical treatment for ED. In some instances, a resumption of sexual activity may lead to reduced tension in the relationship, thereby facilitating more effective communication and problem solving around couples' issues. In other cases, however, attempts at sexual intercourse are likely to dramatically increase underlying conflicts or tensions and should be postponed until significant progress has been made in other areas. Particularly in cases involving extramarital affairs or sexual activity outside of the primary relationship, the introduction of sildenafil (or other medical therapy) should be handled with special care. Unfortunately, due to the increasing prescription of sildenafil by primary care physicians with little experience or knowledge of relationship dynamics, as well as the increasing trend toward Internet prescription of these drugs, this problem is likely to increase significantly in the future.

For couples with less severe relationship problems, physicians or therapists might provide simple guidelines for enhancing relationship satisfaction and for improving communication around sexual issues. For example, couples should be encouraged to communicate directly with one another about their sexual likes and dislikes, preferences, and priorities. Simple suggestions for increasing emotional and physical intimacy can be offered, such as taking more time to talk about personal issues and sharing personal feelings more frequently. Many couples experience a loss of romance along with sexual intimacy, and suggestions can be made for developing a more romantic sexual script (Rosen et al., 1994). Some of these interventions may be offered by the primary care physician in conjunction with prescription of the drug. In the new treatment guidelines for ED (Process of Care Consensus Panel, 1999), we have strongly advised that relationship issues be evaluated in all new cases of ED, and that physicians attempt whenever possible to include partners in the assessment and treatment process. Referral for more specialized couples or sex therapy is advised when indicated.

CASE EXAMPLES

Case 1

John Smith is a 54-year-old accountant, married for 26 years with two children ages 21 and 19, neither of whom is living at home. He presents for treatment complaining of increasing erectile difficulties for the past 6 years. He states: "I can't remember when last I had a good erection. No matter how hard we try, it never gets more than half way. My wife is ready to quit on me!" The patient's medical history is significant for mild hypertension, which is controlled with a low dose of antihypertensive medication (enalapril, 5.0 mg per day). He has been a smoker since his early 20s, but is otherwise in good health. The physical exam and laboratory tests are unremarkable.

Sexual history taking reveals that Mr. Smith has experienced little interest or desire for sex since the early days of his marriage. His early medical history was unremarkable. He began masturbation late (age 15) and had few, albeit successful sexual experiences before marriage. He recalls feeling more physically attracted to his wife prior to their marriage and of the birth of their two children. "During that period (of childbirth and its aftermath), our sex went really downhill. I don't know if it was my problems with erection, or the other way around, but I starting wanting it less, and having it much less often also. It's hard to know which was the chicken, and which was the egg!"

Mrs. Smith generally concurs with her husband's appraisal. She blames part of the problem on the stresses of his family. His mother recently passed through a long bout with cancer and "leaned on him a lot," according to Mrs. Smith. She feels that the loss of his mother has affected him more than he recognizes. She denies difficulty with arousal or orgasm herself and claims to have been approached sexually by other men but not to have acted on any invitations thus far. She feels frustrated and angry at the loss of sexual activity, as well as a great deal of the affectionate exchange that used to characterize their relationship.

During the final session of the evaluation, the Smiths were seen together and a discussion took place about their therapy options. They chose to continue couple therapy at the same time that Mr. Smith requested a trial of sildenafil. It was decided to schedule several sessions of counseling, prior to beginning the medication. Mr. Smith was evaluated for a clinical trial of sildenafil and was accepted.

Sex therapy focused initially on communication issues. It was important for each of them to develop a clearer understanding of the problem and their options. It is important for couples to discuss feelings openly at this phase, if possible, and begin to have more physical exchange. The importance of combining sexual stimulation with the administration of the drug was discussed.

Sildenafil was introduced following the fourth session. This was administered by the clinic urologist in conjunction with a clinical trial. Mr. Smith showed a slight response at 50 mg and improved erections at 100 mg. He reported occasional flushing at this dose. His cardiac history was negative. Additional improvement was reported when the patient was titrated to 100 mg.

The couple were seen intermittently during a 1-year period following. They continued to make steady progress, although other marital issues surfaced. She felt he had been emotionally unavailable for her at many times in the marriage. He resented her criticisms in this and other areas. Couple therapy focused on these issues as well as follow-up of their sexual script and the inclusion of sildenafil.

Comment

Although medication played a major role in the recovery of Mr. Smith's erectile capacity, couple therapy served to open the door on a number of issues for the couple, to prepare them psychologically and practically for the use of the drug, and to continue to improve their relationship once sex was reintroduced. Mr. Smith's desire level increased over the 1-year period, most likely due to a combination of sildenafil's effects and the improvements in other areas. He was strongly encouraged to act more confidently and assertively in the bedroom situation, and therapy sessions focused on reinforcing this attitude.

Case 2

Philip G and Barbara G are both in their early 30s, have been married for 6 years and have no children. She complains that their sexual relationship "is a basket case!" Her husband had been a premature ejaculator since the earliest days of their courtship and had begun to experience episodes of ED in the past year. The couple had previously had seven sessions of sex therapy focused on the stop–start technique. This had worked briefly, but results were not sustained after several months. They were reluctant to return for further sex therapy and felt a lack of emotional connection with their previous therapist.

Mr. G had recently seen a urologist for a consultation. The urologist had focused discussion on the patient's erectile difficulties and had prescribed a trial of sildenafil. Both he and his wife felt reluctant to try sildenafil, partly due to his fear of medication and partly due to the lack of benefit he experienced for his premature ejaculation. A three-session consultation was arranged, focusing on his performance anxiety and altering the couple's sexual script. In particular, the couple were encouraged to experiment with different approaches to foreplay, including nondemand touching and oral sex assignments. This proceeded well over the next 2 months.

In the interim, Mr. G had initiated sex on one occasion after taking half (25 mg) of his usual dose of sildenafil. He felt unusually calm and aroused and at this point requested a brief period of stop–start stimulation with his wife. She agreed, and the couple reported an unusually positive sexual exchange at this point. It culminated in intercourse, with Mr. G being able to last for approximately half an hour. He felt elated.

Comment

This case illustrates the sometimes unplanned or unpredicted course of events that one often encounters in therapy. The clinician can help to establish a more sexually conducive environment for positive sexual risk taking and experimentation. Mr. G had discovered, and the couple had fully optimized, his use of low-dose sildenafil in this context. The previous work on their sexual script and broadening the couple's approach to love making had maximized the "spillover" from drug treatment. The couple were also helped in interpreting these events and in making plans to gradually decrease the need for any medication in the future.

Case 3

George and Martha Y are an unmarried couple in their early 40s. They were referred for treatment of his erectile difficulties of the past several months. Martha had been previously married but divorced after 2 years of marriage. George was single at the time of their meeting, 8 years ago. The couple describe themselves as intellectually compatible but with an almost nonexistent sex life for the past several years. They lived in separate apartments but dated each other exclusively. They both appeared anxious and embarrassed when discussing their problem during the initial visit.

On enquiry, it emerges that Mrs. Y has had problems intermittently with both vaginismus and sexual aversion. Although neither problem is very severe, her sexual difficulties had dominated their sexual relationship. She related an abusive relationship with her first husband and attributed some of her problems in this area to this time. Her partner, George, felt increasingly frustrated and impatient and angry that Martha had refused counseling in the past for this problem. It was only when he begun losing his erection consistently that Martha finally agreed to seek help.

Treatment focused on communication issues and reducing the level of performance demand that both partners experienced. The couple were encouraged to refrain from intercourse and to focus on nondemand touching and Kegel exercises for a period of 6 weeks. Strong emphasis on the wife's having complete control in each of the sessions helped to maintain a low level of anxiety for her. Sensate focus exercises were prescribed.

Four weeks into the treatment, the couple attempted intercourse for the first time since starting treatment. Although Martha felt some anxiety immediately after penetration, she reports telling herself to "relax" and was able to achieve climax soon after. She notes that this is the first time she has climaxed during intercourse for more than 6 months. George experienced no erectile difficulties during the experience.

Comment

Sexual problems or dysfunction in the partners of men with ED is a much neglected topic in the literature. We have seen many cases in which partners presented with low desire, lack of arousal or orgasm, and a variety of penetration problems, either in association or as the primary cause of their husband/partner's ED. This case illustrates one such pattern. In some instances, the preferred approach is to focus directly on the female partner's difficulties and to withhold or delay treatment for the male's problem until sufficient progress has been made. In other instances, it may be possible to work on both problems concurrently. In the present instance, the decision was made to focus initially on the female partner's vaginismus. Only a small degree of success was needed in this area for Mr. Y to recover his erectile function. If his problems had persisted, sildenafil treatment would likely have been introduced.

SUMMARY AND CONCLUSION

Erectile dysfunction is a highly prevalent sexual disorder, with significant effects on mood, quality of life, and interpersonal relationships. Since the approval of sildenafil, millions of men have sought treatment for ED and the drug is now widely used as first-line therapy. Practice patterns in this area have also changed dramatically, as most men now seek treatment from primary care physicians for the disorder. In recognition of these developments, a new process-of-care algorithm for the evaluation and treatment of ED has been developed. This model describes a series of stages in the evaluation and treatment of all cases of ED. Psychological and sex therapy approaches are strongly emphasized in this new model, either in conjunction with or as an alternative to medical therapies. Despite the overall safety and effectiveness of sildenafil, treatment is not always successful as key psychological and interpersonal barriers to treatment have been identified.

This chapter describes current sex therapy approaches for erectile dysfunction. Special emphasis is placed on the combination of pharmacological and nonpharmacological interventions for ED. Among the specific areas to be addressed, problems of initiation, low desire in one or both partners, the presence of other sexual dysfunctions, and couple or relationship problems are frequently encountered. A series of case studies are presented to illustrate the use of combined medical and sex therapy approaches for erectile dysfunction. In each instance, a flexible, individualized treatment approach is likely to produce optimal results. Finally, more research is urgently needed on the costs and benefits of combined medical and sex therapy approaches to erectile dysfunction.

REFERENCES

ACC/AHA Expert Consensus Document: Use of sildenafil (Viagra) in patients with cardiovascular disease. *Circulation* 1999, 99, 168–177.

Apfelbaum, B. (1984). The ego-analytic approach to individual body-work sex therapy: Five case examples. *Journal of Sex Research, 20,* 44–70.

Apfelbaum, B. (1989). Retarded ejaculation: A much misunderstood syndrome. In S. R. Leiblum & R. C. Rosen (Eds.), *Principles and practice of sex therapy: Update for the 1990s* (pp. 168–206). New York: Guilford Press.

Apfelbaum, B. (1995). Masters and Johnson revisited: A case of desire disparity. In R. C. Rosen, S. R. Leiblum (Eds.), *Case studies in sex therapy* (pp. 23–45). New York: Guilford Press.

Araoz, D. L. Hypnosex therapy. *Journal of Clinical Hypnosis, 26,* 37–41.

Araujo, A. B., Durante, R., Feldman, H. A., Goldstein, I., & McKinlay, J. (1998). The relationship between depressive symptoms and male erectile dysfunction: Cross-sectional results from the Massachusetts Male Aging Study. *Psychosomatic Medicine, 60,* 458–465.

Bancroft, J. (1990). Man and his penis: A relationship under threat? *Journal of Psychology and Human Sexuality, 2,* 6–32.

Barlow, D. H., Sakheim, D. K., & Beck, J. G. (1983). Anxiety increases sexual arousal. *Journal of Abnormal Psychology, 92,* 49–54.

Becker, A. J., Stief, C. G., Machtens, S., Schultheiss, D., Hartmann, U., Truss, M. C., & Jonas, U. (1998). Oral phentolamine as treatment for erectile dysfunction. *Journal of Urology, 159,* 1214–1216.

Brown, J. M., & Chaves, J. F. (1980). Hypsosis in the treatment of sexual dysfunction. *Journal of Sex and Marital Therapy, 6,* 63–74.

Burnett, A. L. (1995). The role of nitric oxide in the physiology of erection. *Biology and Reproduction, 52,* 485–489.

Carson, C., Kirby, R., & Goldstein, I. (Eds.). (1999). *Textbook of erectile dysfunction.* Oxford, England: Isis Medical Media.

Courtois, F. J., McDougall, J. C., & Sachs, B. D. (1993). Erectile mechanisms in paraplegia. *Physiological Behavior, 53,* 721–726.

Cranston-Cuebas, M. A., & Barlow, D. H. (1990). Cognitive and affective contributions to sexual functioning. *Annual Review of Sex Research, 1,* 119–161.

Dauw, D. C. (1988). Evaluating the effectiveness of the SECS surrogate-assisted sex therapy model. *Journal of Sex Research, 24,* 269–275.

Fallon, B. (1995). Intracavernous injection therapy for male erectile dysfunction. *Urological Clinics of North America, 22,* 833–845.

Feldman, H. A., Goldstein, I., Hatzichristou, D. G., Krane, R. T., & McKinlay, J. B. (1994). Impotence and its medical and psychosocial correlates: results of the Massachusetts Male Aging Study. *Journal of Urology, 151,* 54–61.

Fulgham, P. F., Cochran, J. S., Denman, J. L., Feagins, B. A., Gross, M. B., Kadesky, K. T., & Roehrboom, C. S. (1998). Disappointing results with transurethral alprostadil in men with erectile dysfunction. (erectile dysfunction) in a urology practice setting. *Journal of Urology, 59,* 237.

Gagnon, J. H., Rosen, R. C., & Leiblum, S. R. (1982). Cognitive and social aspects of sexual dysfunction: Sexual scripts in sex therapy. *Journal of Sex and Marital Therapy, 8,* 44–56.

Goldman, A., & Carroll, J. L. (1990). Educational intervention as an adjunct to treatment of erectile dysfunction in older couples. *Journal of Sex and Marital Therapy, 16,* 127–141.

Goldstein, I., Feldman, M. I., Deckers, P. J., Babayan, R. K., & Krane, R. J. (1984). Radiation-associated impotence. A clinical study of its mechanism. *Journal of the American Medical Association, 251,* 903–910.

Goldstein, I., Lue, T. F., Padma-Nathan, H., Rosen, R. C., Steers, W. D., & Wicker, P. A. (1998). Oral Sildenafil in the treatment of erectile dysfunction. *New England Journal of Medicine, 338,* 1397–1404.

Hawton, K. (1998). Integration of treatments for male erectile dysfunction. *Lancet, 351,* 7–8.

Hawton, K., Catalan, J., & Fagg, J. (1986). Long-term outcome of sex therapy. *Behaviour Research and Therapy, 24,* 665–675.

Hawton, K., Catalan, J., & Fagg, J. (1992). Sex therapy for erectile dysfunction: Characteristics of couples, treatment outcome, and prognostic factors. *Archives of Sexual Behavior, 21,* 161–176.

Heaton, J. P., Morales, A., Adams, M. A., Johnston, B., & El-Rashidy, R. (1995). Recovery of erectile function by the oral administration of apomorphine. *Urology, 45,* 200–206.

Kaplan, H. S. (1974). *The new sex therapy.* New York: Brunner/Mazel.

Korenman, S. G., Morley, J. E., Mooradian, A. D., Davis, S. S., Kaiser, F. E., Silver, A. J., Viosca, S. P., & Garza, D. (1990). Secondary hypogonadism in older men: Its relationship to impotence. *Journal of Clinical Endrocrinology and Metabolism, 71,* 963–969.

Korenman, S. G., & Viosca, S. P. (1992). Use of a vacuum tumescence device in the management of impotence in men with a history of penile implant or severe pelvic disease. *Journal of the American Geriatric Society, 40,* 61–64.

Laumann, E. O., Gagnon, J. H., Michael, R. T., & Michaels, S. (1994). *The social organization of sexuality: Sexuality practices in the United States.* Chicago: University of Chicago Press.

Lazarus, A. A. (1965). The treatment of a sexually inadequate man. In L. P. Ullmann & L. Drasner (Eds.), *Case studies in behavior modification* (pp. 243–260). New York: Holt, Rinehart and Winston.

Leiblum, S. R. (in press). After Viagra: Making the transition from sexual abstinence to sexual intimacy. *American Journal of Psychiatry.*

Leiblum, S. R., & Rosen, R. C. (1991). Couples therapy for erectile disorders: Conceptual and clinical considerations. *Journal of Sex and Marital Therapy, 4,* 147–159.

Leiblum, S. R., & Segraves, R. T. (1989). Sex therapy with aging adults. In S. R. Leiblum & R. C. Rosen (Eds.), *Principles and practice of sex therapy: Update for the 1990s,* (2nd ed., pp. 352–381). New York: Guilford Press.

Levine, S. B. (1922). Intrapsychic and intrapersonal aspects of impotence: Psychogenic erectile dysfunction. In R. C. Rosen & S. R. Leiblum (Eds.), *Erectile disorders: Assessment and treatment* (pp. 198–225). New York: Guilford Press.

Levine, S. B., & Agle, D. (1978). The effectiveness of sex therapy for chronic secondary psychological impotence. *Journal of Sex and Marital Therapy, 4,* 235–258.

Lewis, R. W. (1995). Long-term results of penile prosthetic implants. *Urologic Clinics of North America, 22,* 847–856.

Lewis, R. W., & Witherington, R. (1997). External vacuum therapy for erectile dysfunction: Use and results. *World Journal of Urology, 15,* 78–82.

Linet, O. I., Ogrinc, F. G., for the Alprostadil Study Group. (1996). Efficacy and safety of intracavernosal alprostadil in men with erectile dysfunction. *New England Journal of Medicine, 334,* 873–877.

LoPiccolo, J. (1992). Postmodern sex therapy for erectile failure. In R. C. Rosen & S. R. Leiblum (Eds.), *Erectile disorders: Assessment and treatment* (pp. 171–197). New York: Guilford Press.

Marlatt, G. A., & Gordon, J. R. (1985). *Relapse prevention: Maintenance strategies in the treatment of addictive behaviors.* New York: Guilford Press.

Masters, W. H., & Johnson, V. E. (1970). *Human sexual inadequacy.* Boston: Little, Brown.

McCarthy, B. W. (1988). *Male sexual awareness.* New York: Carroll and Graf.

McCarthy, B. W. (1993). Relapse prevention strategies and techniques in sex therapy. *Journal of Sex and Marital Therapy, 19,* 142–147.

Mohr, D. C., & Beutler, L. E. (1990). Erectile dysfunction: A review of diagnostic and treatment procedures. *Clinical Psychology Review, 10,* 123–150.

Munjack, D. J., Schlaks, A., Sanchez, V. C., Usigli, R., Zulueta, A., & Leonard, M. (1984). Rational-emotive therapy in the treatment of erectile failure: An initial study. *Journal of Sex and Marital Therapy, 10,* 170–175.

NIH Consensus Panel on Impotence. (1993). Impotence. *Journal of the American Medical Association, 270,* 83–90.

Osterloh, I., Eardley, I., Carson, C. C, & Padma-Nathan, H. (1999). Sildenafil: A selective phosphodiesterase 5 inhibitor for the treatment of erectile dysfunction. In C. C. Carson, R. S. Kirby, and I. Goldstein (Eds.), *Textbook of Erectile Dysfunction* (pp. 285–308). Oxford, England: Isis Medical Media.

Padma-Nathan, H., Hellstrom, W. J., Kaiser, F. E., Labasky, R. F., Lue, T. F., Norwood, P. L., & Teiner, P. Y. (1997). Treatment of men with erectile dysfunction with transurethral alprostadil. *New England Journal of Medicine, 157,* 792A.

Pallas, J., Levine, S., Althof, S., & Risen, C. (1999, March 5). *A prospective study of the use of Viagra in a mental health professionals' practice.* Unpublished paper presented at the Society for Sex Therapy and Research, Boston, MA.

Pedersen, B. (1988). Evaluation of patients and partners 1 to 4 years after penile prosthesis surgery. *Journal of Urology, 139,* 956–958.

Price, S. C., Reynolds, B. S., Cohen, B. D., Anderson, A. J., & Schochet, B. V. (1981). Group treatment of erectile dysfunction for men without partners: A controlled evaluation. *Archives of Sexual Behavior, 10,* 253–268.

Process of Care Consensus Panel. (1999). The process of care model for evaluation and treatment of erectile dysfunction. *International Journal of Impotence Research, 11,* 59–74.

Quinlan, D. M., Epstein, J. I., Carter, B. S., & Walsh, P. C. (1991). Sexual function following radical prostatectomy: Influence of preservation of neurovascular bundles. *Journal of Urology, 145,* 998–1002.

Rajfer, J., Aronson, W. J., Bush, P. A., Dorey, F. J., & Ignarro, L. J. (1992). Nitric oxide as a mediator of relaxation of the corpus cavernosum in response to nonadrenergic, noncholinergic neurotransmission. *New England Journal of Medicine, 326,* 90–94.

Reynolds, B. (1991). Psychological treatment of erectile dysfunction in men without partners: Outcome results and a new direction. *Journal of Sex and Marital Therapy, 17,* 136–146.

Reynolds, B. (1992). An audiotape adjunct in the treatment of sexual dysfunction in men without partners. *Journal of Sex Education and Therapy, 18,* 35–41.

Rosen, R. C. (1998). Sildenafil: Medical advance or media event? *The Lancet, 351,* 1599–1600

Rosen, R. C., & Leiblum, S. R. (1992). Erectile disorders: An overview of historical trends and clinical perspectives. In R. C. Rosen & S. R. Leiblum (Eds.), *Erectile disorders: Assessment and treatment* (pp. 3–26). New York Guilford Press.

Rosen, R. C. & Leiblum, S. R. (1995). Treatment of sexual dysfunction: An integrated approach. *Journal of Consulting and Clinical Psychology, 63,* 877–890.

Rosen, R. C., Leiblum, S. R., & Spector, I. (1994). Psychologically-based treatment for male erectile disorder: A cognitive-interpersonal model. *Journal of Sex and Marital Therapy, 20,* 67–85.

Scharff, D. E. (1988). An object relations approach to inhibited sexual desire. In S. R. Leiblum & R. C. Rosen (Eds.), *Sexual desire disorders* (pp. 45–74. New York: Guilford Press.

Schiavi, R. (1990). Sexuality and aging in men. *Annual Review of Sex Research, 1,* 227–250.

Segraves, R. T., & Segraves, K. B. (1992). Aging and drug effects on male sexuality. In R. C. Rosen & S. R. Leiblum (Eds.), *Erectile disorders: Assessment and treatment* (pp. 96–138). New York: Guilford Press.

Spilker, B. (1990). *Quality of life assessments in clinical trials.* New York: Raven Press.

Spivak, A. P., Peterson, C. A., & Cowley, C. (1997). Long-term safety profile of transurethral aplprostadil for the treatment of erectile dysfunction. *Journal of Urology, 157,* 792A.

Stravynski, A., & Greenberg, D. (1990). The treatment of sexual dysfunction in single men. *Sexual and Marital Therapy, 5,* 115–122.

Takefman, J., & Brender, W. (1984). An analysis of the effectiveness of two components in the treatment of erectile dysfunction. *Archives of Sexual Behavior, 13,* 321–340.

Tiefer, L. (1994). Three crises facing sexology. *Archives of Sexual Behavior, 23,* 361–374.

Verhulst, J., & Heiman, J. R. (1979). An interactional approach to sexual dysfunction. *American Journal of Family Therapy, 7,* 19–36.

Wincze, J. P., & Carey, M. P. (1991). *Sexual dysfunction: A guide for assessment and treatment.* New York: Guilford Press.

Wolpe, J. (1958). *Psychotherapy by reciprocal inhibition.* Stanford, CA: 1958; Stanford University Press.

World Health Organization. (in press). *First international consultation on erectile dysfunction.* Geneva: WHO Press.

Zilbergeld, B. (1992). *The new male sexuality.* New York: Bantam Books.

Zonszein, J. (1995). Diagnosis and management of endocrine disorders of erectile dysfunction. *Urology Clinics of North America, 22,* 789–802.

Zorgniotti, A. W. (1994). Experience with buccal phentolamine mesylate for impotence. *International Journal of Impotence Research, 6,* 37–41.

11

Premature Ejaculation

DEREK C. POLONSKY

According to recent surveys, premature ejaculation (PE) is perhaps the most common male sexual complaint. Yet, there is little agreement regarding the definition of the disorder, the etiology or developmental determinants, and even the treatment of the disorder. The defining characteristic of PE is the fact that the male feels as though he has little or no control over when ejaculation occurs, which typically leads to feelings of shame and inadequacy. This was not always the case, however. In fact, Dr. Polonsky notes that some authors have suggested that PE did not become a "problem" worthy of treatment until several decades ago, when the duration *of intercourse became an important goal, in part spurred on by the increased focus on sexual pleasure for both partners rather than reproductive viability.*

Despite a variety of treatment approaches, outcomes are uncertain and relapse is not uncommon. For this reason, Polonsky postulates that it is essential to understand the meaning *of sexuality to the male, as well as his ability to be comfortable in an intimate relationship, and the role the premature ejaculation may play in the dyadic relationship. There may be a variety of psychological factors or reasons why the man has difficulty in gaining mastery over when he ejaculates.*

Current approaches to the treatment of PE include a variety of behavioral and pharmacological treatments, each of which has shown varying degrees of efficacy. Polonsky suggests that there are four basic types of PE: simple, simple plus relational, complicated, and complicated plus relational. The author provides provocative and cogent illustrations of each. He notes that the "simple" or straightforward cases can make the therapist "look good" because, in some of these cases, support and coaching are all that are necessary for a successful outcome. Cases in which relational issues are implicated are generally more challenging, because the partner may sabotage treatment due to her own is-

305

sues. Indeed, there are almost always reciprocal and complicated interpersonal dynamics, which are important to assess and manage for successful outcome.

Complicated cases may involve intensive individual therapy focused on nonsexual issues prior to focusing on ejaculatory control itself. Moreover, straightforward instructions do not always work, and successful outcome frequently depends on a degree of therapist ingenuity and creativity. Finally, more complicated individual and relational issues require a skillful blend of intrapsychic, interpersonal, and directive behavioral interventions.

In this important new chapter, Polonsky's skill as a sensitive and empathic therapist is evident. In his case illustrations, he reveals the complexities involved in treating what at first blush appears to be a simple behavioral problem. He notes that postulating a "single" cause of PE is shortsighted or naïve, as there is no agreed-on physical cause and no generalizable psychological issue or underlying conflict. Men with PE are not always hypersensitive to stimulation but are typically rather anxious about the disorder or other aspects of sexual functioning. Adjunctive medication to improve ejaculatory latency seems helpful in some cases, although it is important to assist the client psychologically to develop a better sense of his own sexual confidence or control.

Derek C. Polonsky, MD, is a clinical instructor in psychiatry at Harvard Medical School. He is a psychiatrist and sex therapist with extensive experience in the field of sex and marital therapy.

When Supreme Court Justice Potter Stewart was asked about the definition of pornography, he said, "I don't know how to define it, but I know what it is when I see it." A review of the literature on premature ejaculation parallels the comment of Justice Stewart. The definitions are elaborate and complicated, yet we have come to know and understand PE as a problem that many men suffer with quietly; not being able to control to their satisfaction when they have an orgasm, and feeling an unremitting sense of shame and humiliation that is reinforced by each sexual encounter.

DEFINITION

DSM-IV (American Psychiatric Association, 1994, defines premature ejaculation (302.75) as follows:

  A. Persistent or recurrent ejaculation with minimal sexual stimulation before, on, or shortly after penetration and before the person wishes it. The clinician must take into account factors that affect duration of the excitement phase, such as age, novelty of the sexual partner or situation, and recent frequency of sexual activity.

B. The disturbance causes marked distress or interpersonal difficulty.

C. The premature ejaculation is not due exclusively to the direct effects of a substance (e.g. withdrawal from opioids). (p. 511)

As noted in A, ejaculation occurs before the individual wishes it. The individual has an awareness that orgasm occurs suddenly and often takes him by surprise. The ability to decide when one wishes to ejaculate is missed. This often (though not always) has an impact on the individual's partner, resulting in B; the relationship is burdened by the lack of ejaculatory control with spiraling consequences. The individual feels a reinforced sense of shame, dread, humiliation, and inadequacy with painful consequences. Sex is not seen as a shared activity to be embraced and viewed as a source of reciprocal pleasure and enhancement; rather, it becomes an ordeal to be endured, with the outcome preordained. The partner initially may be confused and may feel responsible, but the more usual response in a partner who has some sexual sophistication is to feel frustrated, impatient, and angry. This in turn is perceived by the individual, which only intensifies his anxiety and distress and distorts even further the nature of the sexual experience.

Kinsey, Pomeroy, and Martin (1948) found that 75% of men ejaculated within 2 minutes. His account is one of the first attempts to document the specific sexual activities of the American male. However, he made no attempt to examine either individual or partner satisfaction.

Semans (1955) described the problem of PE in a paper remarkable for the time in which it was written and for his emphasis on considering both partners in the treatment:

> In patients with premature ejaculation the reflex mechanism is abnormally rapid, and penile stimulation ends in ejaculation before the maximum response is experienced by the wife. Premature ejaculation is very undesirable for the husband since it may lead to actual sexual impotence following repeated episodes. The wife also reacts unfavorably, describing a feeling of nervous tension after coitus instead of the feeling of relaxation obtained normally. (p. 353)

Grenier and Byers (1995) choose to use the term "rapid" ejaculation, feeling that there is less pejorative connotation. They described "ejaculatory latency" as "the length of time between intromission and ejaculation." They found that there was only weak correlation between ejaculatory latency and perceived ejaculatory control; what this means is that men with similar ejaculatory latency may view their sexual functioning as either satisfactory or problematic, which further points to difficulties in definition.

Masters and Johnson (1970) diagnosed PE when the male would have an orgasm before his partner more than 50% of the time. This definition is problematic because it did not take into account the now known fact that approximately 30 to 40% of women do not have an orgasm with intercourse, nor did it allow for the numbers of women who are slow to have an orgasm. Rapid orgasm is defined as a "problem" in men, but it is seen as an "attribute" in women, who, in addition, may have the capacity for multiple orgasms. The gender difference is that men have a refractory period during which time there is usually a loss of erection and a time during which another orgasm is not possible. In addition, during the "resolution" phase for men, the subjective experiences of sexual tension and excitement abates, and even if the penis remains firm, the partner usually senses a diminished sexual passion to which she responds.

Birch (1998) highlights the confusion and complexity in the definitions. He points out that for men who have infrequent sexual activity, they may have difficulty with control. He raises important factors such as the rapidity and continuity of thrusting and also the different positions of intercourse as important factors in ejaculatory control. Zilbergeld (1992) asked men who felt they had good ejaculatory control what made the difference and found that they were able to pay more attention to their level of arousal and would use techniques such as withdrawing and slowing thrusting. Many men still labor under the fantasized view of intercourse in which "real" men will be able to thrust vigorously for long periods: the "engineer's view of sex," which involves a penis as hard as a rock, moving in the cylindrical vagina like a piston of a high-performance engine, generating friction and heat that would make any woman melt. Anything short of that would be mediocre and unacceptable.

Metz, Pryor, Nesvacil, Abuzzahab, and Koznar (1997) pointed out additional factors that make precise definition of PE difficult. They make a connection to the partner's orgasm (and therefore ease or difficulty in attaining it), examine the duration between insertion and ejaculation, and consider the number of thrusts during the period of ejaculatory latency.

Adding to the complexity of definition is the observation that for some men, PE is situational. They may find that with some partners their control is impaired and that external pressures (concerns about job, finances, family, etc.) may have an impact on their control. The dynamics of the couple's relationship may be an important component of the ejaculatory control, where unconscious factors are expressed in the arena of sexual functioning.

INCIDENCE

PE is the most common sexual problem for men. Almost all men ejaculate rapidly in their first-partner sexual experiences but with time are able to teach themselves how to achieve control that is gratifying and satisfactory. However, ejaculatory control is elusive for many men, and their sexual experience becomes defined by it. The figures vary by author, with the range being between 30% and 75%. As indicated previously, obtaining an accurate figure of incidence is complicated by the lack of agreement as to definition. Many men who have PE may develop a secondary erectile disorder and may therefore present to the clinician with a different chief complaint.

ETIOLOGY

There have been many attempts to explain the cause or causes of PE. These have included a belief that unconscious conflicts are expressed by coming rapidly, that interpersonal struggles are manifested by PE, that there is a biological difference in the bulocavernosus reflex, that there is a difference in the sensitivity of the skin of the penis, and that PE actually represents the norm, given that animals have a very short ejaculatory latency.

Psychoanalytic Perspective

For many years, it was believed that sexual difficulties were reflective of unresolved unconscious conflicts that could only be addressed with psychoanalysis. Given the fact that little change occurred during the course of these long therapies, it is remarkable that they continued to be recommended. One may reflect on the double burden for so many men, who in addition to viewing themselves as failures in bed also viewed themselves as failures on the couch. The view was held that PE was indicative of an individual who was angry and withholding. Helen Singer Kaplan (1973) believed that PE was an expression of unconscious hatred of women, and that coming quickly both "soiled" the woman and deprived her of satisfaction. She later revised this view and came to believe that there was no reliable and consistent psychological constellation that could explain the phenomenon. Another view has been that PE is an expression of castration anxiety. The vagina is seen as frightening and dangerous, and the PE serves to "get the penis out of there" as rapidly as possible.

Interpersonal Perspective

Levine (1992) writes:

> One of the principles of the sexual equilibrium is that the sexual fate of one person is tied to the capacities and attitudes of the partner. The search for a control strategy is not a calm pursuit for most men. Desperation can quickly set in. The partner may calm or exacerbate his concerns about how he ought to be able to perform during intercourse. Unless the woman is particularly calming, the man begins to search for mental tricks to delay ejaculation. (p. 96)

Levine points to the interactions that may be experienced but not verbalized. A man may bring fear and uncertainty to a sexual encounter; he may be worried about having come rapidly in past love-making attempts. His partner may be reassuring and supportive, and he may be able to allow her to have an impact on his worry with improvement of his control. She may be kind and patient and yet he may be so focused on his inner distress that he is unable to be affected by the reassurance, and thus the problem continues or gets worse. (A less formal way of describing this is, "My mind is made up, don't confuse me with facts. Regardless of what you tell me, I know that you are disappointed or disapproving, and I will react accordingly.") The impact of the unconscious distortions, collusions, and mutual projections are powerful and have been illustrated well by Dicks (1964), Main (1961), and Framo (1982). Interpersonal conflict may be expressed by various sexual symptoms. PE may be an identifying complaint for some couples, yet skill and care need to be used in untangling the strands that make up the fabric of the relationship.

Biological Differences

An intriguing question has been whether there is a definable difference in the nervous system of men who ejaculate rapidly. Are they somehow "wired" differently, so that their ejaculatory latency is less. Is this analogous to different physical characteristics that define people; some are short, others are tall ? Assalian (1994) states that men with PE have "a constitutionally hypersensitive sympathetic nervous system which prevents them from differentiating between ejaculation and its inevitability" (p. 3). Metz et al. (1997) undertook a psychophysiological review of PE. In studies of the bulbocavernous reflex it was found that there are some differences between men with PE and those whose control is not of concern. These findings are interesting, but an important question is left unanswered. If these men were to undergo a course of "training" to help them attain better control, would the measured differences in the bulbocavernous reflex change? It is logical that the physiology of men who ejaculate rapidly might show some difference, but is it the cause or a physiological indicator that measures in the laboratory what the man already knows behaviorally?

Many men describe feeling "too excited" and therefore unable to control ejaculation. It was natural to wonder whether there was a heightened sensitivity of the skin of the penis in these men. In fact, some of the suggested treatments (which *do not* work) were designed to diminish the sensitivity of the penis. Putting on several condoms and using an anesthetic jelly were attempts to address this. Rowland, Stefan, Haensel, Blom, & Koosslob (1993) studied penile sensitivity in men with PE and erectile dysfunction (ED). They state that "subjective threshold to vibrotactile stimulation of the penis in men with PE does not differ from that of sexually functional men" (p. 195). They found that men who had symptoms of PE and ED actually had decreased sensitivity relative to controls and men with PE. They conclude "the findings from the PE and ED group, which clearly indicate that PE can occur in men with *decreased* penile sensitivity, argue strongly for a role for central (cognitive) factors in the mediation of ejaculation latency" (p. 196).

Premature Ejaculation Is "the Norm"

Hong (1984) reviewed the ejaculatory latency in animals and describes the survival quality of ejaculating rapidly. In his view, being able to mount the partner and ejaculate rapidly was protective. During intercourse, he proposed, the animal was vulnerable to attack. "The fact that many primates ejaculate almost immediately after intromission suggests the hypothesis that swift intercourse is a normal pattern and may have evolutionary survival value" (p. 111). Hong goes on to state that "the duration of intercourse did not become a major clinical issue until the past 2 decades or so. In fact special efforts have been made to find literature on premature ejaculation prior to the 20th century, but none was successful" (p. 119). Hong points out an interesting change in our societal values as he writes:

> [A]s long as sex was considered primarily as the means of reproduction, pleasure was left out of the equation of female sexuality, particularly in the male-dominated societies in the west. This began to change around the 1960s. The mass availability of reliable contraceptives and women's heightened awareness of their individuality have rendered procreation a markedly lower priority and simultaneously dampened the double standard in regard to sexual fulfillment.

What Hong does emphasize is that evolution endowed man with greater dexterity.

> Therefore, it might be more in tune with nature to make men aware of this unique dexterity that has contributed so much to their humanness than to condition their ejaculatory response artificially by the various means that have been prescribed in popular sex manuals. The tender touch, the passionate caress, the gentle rub, the titillating probe, and all those other infinite maneuvers that humans, as the most sophisticate bipedal primate, are best equipped to do, can be much more satisfying to women than simply a longer time span between intromission and ejaculation. (p. 120)

OUTCOMES OF THERAPY

Semans (1955) description of premature ejaculation and his outlining a treatment is interesting and historically important. He emphasized the need to evaluate the presence of psychological issues (either individual or couples) and recommended treatment by a psychiatrist when that is found. He insisted on having the wife be an integral part of the treatment, both asking for her ideas of the cause and offering his own explanations, and he was clear about the need for reciprocity between the couple and for the husband to make sure that he provided pleasurable caressing of his wife's clitoris. He presented eight men whom he had treated and described follow-ups of 15 months with sustained changes.

Masters and Johnson (1970) embraced his approach and felt that success-ful treatment of premature ejaculation was almost guaranteed. In fact, they believed that within 15 years, PE would not longer be a problem seen by clini-cians. However, a review of the long-term outcome of the treatment of PE is discouraging. Three years after treatment has ended, almost all men studied have returned to their pretreatment ejaculatory latencies. The fact is stated repeatedly, but there appears to be no retrospective study to examine what has happened. McCarthy (1989) has often stressed the need for "relapse preven-tion strategies." LoPiccolo (1997) described a "postmodern" sex therapy in which the clinician must address the *need* for individuals or couples to hold on to a sexual symptom. There have been many examples in clinical practice where an individual states a wish to cure a presenting complaint and yet resists pow-erfully any movement for change. Levine (1992) reminds us that "we used to assume that the anorgasmic wives of premature ejaculators were victims of their husband's dysfunctions. Now we are more cognizant of the possibility that the woman and the man are equally uncomfortable about sexual experi-ences. The correct diagnostic focus is on the sexual equilibrium rather than on the man or the woman" (p. 102). The meaning of the lack of long-term cure is therefore complicated. Rather than seeing this as a failure of therapeutic ap-proach, it is essential to understand the meaning to the individual of his sexu-ality; the ability to be involved in a close, attached relationship; the means by which a sexual symptom in one partner may mask sexual discomfort in the other and finally the way in which a sexual symptom may offer a means for regulating the intensity of a couple's closeness or distance. Anecdotally, clini-cians are beginning to notice that the "cure" that Viagra has produced is not always met with enthusiasm, which may parallel a discomfort with an ability for more prolonged intercourse.

CURRENT THERAPEUTIC APPROACHES

Whereas the optimism of Masters and Johnson has faded in the light of current follow-up data, there are several approaches that clinicians may use with men who would like to develop better ejaculatory control. Masters and Johnson felt that treatment needed to take place in the context of "the couple," but often one might be asked to help a man who is not in a committed relationship because of the anxiety associated with his PE. The clinician has at this time a variety of approaches that can be used to help an individual.

Behavioral/Supportive Approach

In this situation, the man usually presents on his own with the complaint. A thorough psychiatric history needs to be obtained which includes an under-standing of the dynamics in the family of origin and an appreciation of the individual's sexual development and his capacity for engaging in and maintaining relationships in depth. One needs to assess the individual's masturbation practices and identify conflicts or discomfort with the activity. I have found it useful then to provide the individual with a series of specific instructions which I encourage him to practice on a regular basis (see Appendix). The objective is to provide an opportunity for developing some self-confidence and mastery at the same time increasing an understanding of the person's experience in relationships. Often, the therapist has to provide support and practical guidance with establishing a relationship with a partner, offer suggestions for how to "script" the sexuality, and literally "walk" the individual through the process. The "script" that many men follow is one that is tailor-made for increasing anxiety and isolation and almost guarantees that the ejaculatory control will be poor. It is often based on the unrealistic portrayal of sexuality in movies, where there is a seamless progression through intensifying states of sexual arousal and breathless nonverbal passion, usually with the male directing the pace and at all times knowing exactly what will please his partner. It is a daunting task for the man with poor ejaculatory control to manage on his own. The therapist can provide a model for slowing things down, for getting to know and trust a new partner, and for telling the partner early on that he has concerns about his sexual performance. In the absence of changing the script, the more usual pattern is for the man to feel alone with his struggle to "hold off" and for his partner to feel confused about what has happened. When the partner has had sexual experiences that were different, she might be able to recognize the issue as residing with her partner. But often the woman may wonder about her own abilities and feel she has somehow failed to be a good sexual partner, and the spiral of self-doubt and anxiety begins for both.

Behavioral/Relational Approach

The couple will come in together and will usually identify the PE as "the problem." The history-taking sequence is modified to encompass an understanding of the history of the relationship, the evolution of the couple's sexuality, the perception each has about the "problem," and initially some education on the part of the therapist about the nature and incidence of PE. It is useful to meet with each partner alone at least once to better understand family-of-origin themes and to be more expansive in learning about the individual's sexual relationships. The "behavioral" approach involves a combination of suggestions (see Appendix) and a focus on the interaction between the partners. The clinical illustrations elaborate on the techniques.

Medication

The search for magic potions that will enhance sexual prowess and ability has been one of man's enduring pursuits. Herds of rhinos have been decimated to that end. In the last decade, though, science has begun to produce some measurable results, culminating in 1998 with the release of Viagra.

The SSRI (selective serotonin reuptake inhibitors) antidepressants have a noticeable effect on sexual functioning. One side effect was initially described as "difficulty in having an orgasm," both for men and for women. This side effect became intriguing and resulted in a number of studies to see whether the side effect might be helpful with men who suffered with PE.

Althof (1995) investigated the effect of 50 mg of clomipramine (Anafranil) in a double-blind crossover trial. They found a dramatic increase (500%) in the ejaculatory latency to about 7 minutes. When the medication was discontinued, the latency returned to baseline. Importantly, three of the five women reported experiencing an orgasm during intercourse, which was directly related to the increased control. Strassberg et al. (1999) studied the effects of clomipramine in a double-blind, placebo-controlled crossover design study. The sample included 23 subjects with PE. While the average reported orgasmic latency increased from less than 1 minute to 3.5 minutes, "the beneficial effects of the drug were not uniform across clinical subjects." When the effect on the individuals was observed, seven reported an orgasmic latency of 5 minutes, two reported a latency of at least 2 minutes, and the remaining subjects reported "modest or nonexistent" change.

In another study by Althof, a group of eight men were given paroxetene (Paxil) and nine were given placebo. In the men taking the paroxetene, the ejaculatory latency increased to 7–10 minutes and they described increased libido. (This is not surprising and is probably associated with increased confidence associated with not worrying that they would come quickly. Anecdotally, there have been similar reports in men treated for ED with sildenafil (Viagra). In Althof's study, the men reported increased ejaculatory latency, increased sexual satisfaction, and heightened partner satisfaction. Althof suggests that clomipramine could be the first line of treatment, with 50 mg being given about 2 hours before intercourse is planned.

All of the SSRIs have been found to increase the ejaculatory latency, and the choice of drug is often determined by physician's experience with a particular SSRI and the individual's reaction to it. Some are experienced as more sedating; others produce gastrointestinal side effects. The doses are as follows: fluoxetene (Prozac) 20 mg per day; sertraline (Zoloft) up to 200 mg per day, and paroxetene 40 mg per day.

Viagra (Sildenafil)

The emergence of sildenafil represents a dramatic development in the treatment of erectile difficulties. At this time there have been no studies to look at its effect on ejaculatory control, but there are some clinical reports that some men have noticed improved ejaculatory control. This bears further study. Are these men feeling more confident and therefore less anxious in a sexual situation? Are they less worried about rapid ejaculation because of the ability to get another erection more easily. Do they feel less worried that they will lose an erection and therefore able to focus more on the enjoyment of the experience rather than "rushing it before they lose it"?

THE TREATMENT OF PREMATURE EJACULATION

In reviewing the histories and treatments of the men I have seen with PE over the past 25 years, a number of patterns have emerged. The clinical illustrations are arranged to reflect 4 different presentations. Although there is obviously overlap, the attempt is to distinguish some of the characteristics that are seen in practice and to highlight the ways in which the treatment may vary.

Clinical Presentations

1. *"Simple" premature ejaculation.* The individual appears to have identified a wish for better control and has demonstrated an ability to engage in relationships that reflect mutuality and reciprocity. Therapy is
   sought out individually to help with mastery.
2. *"Simple" plus "relational."* This represents a variant of 1. The individual is in a relationship and the partner participates in the treatment.
   The PE is usually the identified complaint, but the couple seeks help to
   better manage the control of ejaculation and to improve "communication skills" between them.
3. *"Complicated."* The men in this group have complicated psychological issues that affect profoundly their ability to manage relationships.
   In addition, they suffer with PE and are hampered in their ability to
   involve a partner in a collaborative way.
4. *"Complicated" and "relational."* These couples are a challenge to the
   skills and creativity of the therapist. They each have complicated psychological difficulties, usually have severe conflicts around intimacy,
   and have had difficulty in integrating their feelings about sex.

Simple Premature Ejaculation

This is the situation that makes the therapist look good. The usual presentation is a young man in his 20s who has noticed that his ability to control
orgasm is not what he would like. Sex is enjoyable, and he is on the way to
developing attachments with significant others. He may figure out on his own
how to gain better control. If he is lucky, he will have a partner who has some
experience and can encourage and support his developing sexual abilities. The
less fortunate men may have struggled over time without success to gain better

control, and PE ultimately becomes the defining character of his sexuality, associated with shame, pain, and humiliation.

The effect of supportive, encouraging coaching for young men who are at the beginning of their sexual development is impressive. Open, direct, adult-to-adult discussions of sexuality are an infrequent occurrence. It is unusual for young men to feel comfortable revealing their worries to their peers. They are all in a situation in which they are feeling unsure of themselves and are often burdened by the exaggerated descriptions of sexual athleticism to which they are exposed. Zilbergeld (1992) has addressed this concern masterfully in *The New Male Sexuality,* where he describes the attributes of the "perfect penis"— hard as steel, always ready, and able to last forever. Sex education in the schools has been under siege, and the programs may deal with biology, contraception, relational issues and AIDS prevention but usually not with issues of sexual satisfaction or dysfunction. I was curious about early masturbation practices given the easy arousability and short refractory period of adolescents. I found that many of the men I have seen with PE, when asked, revealed that the focus in their masturbating was on getting to their orgasm rapidly. This was a wonderful, intense, exciting experience, and given that they could have another erection relatively soon, they tended to try to achieve the experience as soon as practicable. Invariably, no one had ever talked with them about the value of learning and training as it related to the gradual buildup of pleasurable feelings in the penis or the value of watching and noticing the sensations in different parts of the penis; the increased sensitivity of the glans, the difference between sensations at the tip versus the deeper kind of feeling at the base of the penis and in the pelvis. Observing a group of 10-year-old boys playing a game one might notice how they are often hurried and eager to get to a prescribed goal. Noticing how they actually get there is often irrelevant. (The jokes about men's refusal to ask for directions is a reflection of this characteristic.) It is remarkable to watch later adolescent boys spending hours in training for a particular sport, learning to do drills that help them master the game and become proficient at the sport. When it comes to sex, all too often one is provided with no instruction manual, and many are literally thrown into an unknown, somewhat scary situation having to fend for themselves. Added to this is the expectation that one should know what is pleasing and exciting to one's partner without needing to ask; this makes for a situation that at best is Bewildering and for many is fraught with worry and the potential for self-doubt and disappointment. Levine (1992) and Metz et al. (1997) also refer to early masturbatory patterns as they relate to "learning" and ejaculatory control. Their view is similar to the "hurried back seat" scene proposed by Masters and Johnson (1970). Masters and Johnson proposed that the early sexual experiences of many young men were characterized by the absence of privacy, the fear of being discovered, and the need to get it over quickly, all effective training to rapid ejaculation.

It is enormously helpful to spend a lot of time talking with young men about expectations. Spelling out the unspoken demands relieves worries and misapprehensions: *"you ought to be getting laid often"; "you ought to have only one thing on your mind"; "you should do what comes naturally"; "you ought to know what your partner wants without asking."* I have found it helpful to emphasize the value of getting to know a partner before jumping into a sexual situation, pointing out that if we do not know who we are with, and we are feeling shaky about our ability, the burden will only increase exponentially. Revealing to the partner doubt or that one has a problem of coming quickly puts in place one of the foundation blocks of trust in a relationship that will lead to greater comfort.

I have seen many single young men who were not in committed relationships and whose focus on PE made them worry about trying to form a closer attachment that involved sex. The suggestion that "when you are in a relationship, come back for help with your partner" was not reassuring. Instead, treatment was designed to focus on developing some mastery on their own. In the "simple" situation, the directions are followed religiously; there is an unspoken supportive "parental" transference with the therapist; improvements are evident to the individual, and the therapist additionally provides a helpful role as the individual begins to start a relationship with a partner. Coaching and support continue, and guidance about talking directly with the partner is given. The role of the therapist may include becoming the permissive encouraging parent who is saying, "You own your sexual feelings; they feel good, you can develop mastery and you can feel great sharing these feelings with someone else—and I am supportive of your doing this." When I was a resident in training, I was told that this "transference cure" was infantilizing and undermined the work of therapy. However, it is precisely what these young men need.

Simple Plus Relational

In using this description, I am simplifying a more complicated issue. I mean to indicate that the ejaculatory control seems as if it should be simple to change; the man is motivated and interested, has had some good sexual experiences, and with some coaching and training could be expected to gain control. The relational aspect has to do with the reactions of the partner and the way in which he deals with that. Levine (1992) describes the possible "function" of the early ejaculation as a way in which the wife may avoid an awareness of her own discomfort with arousal, excitement, and sexual expressiveness. Couples often engage in an unconscious collusion whereby conflicts or difficulties in one partner provide an emotionally protective function for the other. If the therapist's approach is simply to achieve better ejaculatory control, the importance of the unconscious agreements may be missed, and the treatment will invariably founder.

Zilbergeld (1995) has written about the role of the angry or hostile spouse in the treatment of sexual problems. To the degree that anger increases anxiety, when it is expressed in the context of the sexual problem, a formidable barrier has been created to being able to tolerate the anxiety involved in becoming more competent sexually. Premature ejaculation is not unique in the sexual dysfunctions in that anxiety invariably makes the situation worse. For change to take place, a level of safety, trust, and patient collaboration is desirable.

Clinical Illustration

Anne and Paul were in their early 30s. Paul, an accomplished professional, was tall and handsome and had always struggled with ejaculatory control. Anne was a musician who was attractive and clearly paid attention to her clothing and appearance, always wearing a brilliant red lipstick. Although she was engaging and funny, I often felt uneasy with her, sensing that there was a veiled hostility lurking not far beneath the surface. She was angry with Paul and had little restraint in expressing it. In the past, she had other sexual partners who did not have this "problem" and it was becoming tiresome for her. Paul was quiet and often deferential and took on the "badge of dishonor" that Levine (1992) has referred to. Although his appearance was impressive, and he was effective in his career, with Anne he appeared to be reduced in size, seeming small, reserved, and tentative. Anne was interested in sex and wanted to have active, vigorous intercourse that would allow her passion to rise in intensity. She was continually disappointed when Paul would come quickly. The issue became an entrenched power struggle. Anne was willing to talk about "sensate focus" and "pleasuring," but it was clear that she wanted results. The desired result was to be able to have prolonged vaginal intercourse. She had little patience for Paul's "poor" control. Paul focused on his "inadequacy" and was filled with a sense of shame. From Anne's vantage point, she had been sensitive and understanding in the past, hoping that the situation would improve, but now she had had it.

Doing exercises together was burdensome. Anne felt bored and unaroused by the activity and was resentful at having to do it. Exploring her anger was difficult, although I encouraged her to moderate it. If I suggested that Anne's anger might intensify Paul's worry, she would in turn get angry with me and feel that I, as the male therapist, was not sensitive to what she had to suffer with.

The treatment was slow, with slight gains being made in terms of Paul's control. However I was constantly aware of the precarious balance in the relationship. Anne's position was "understandable" intellectually; she had sexual experiences with men who were able to last much longer. She felt this was good for her, and she felt deprived in not having that with Paul. Power issues were dominant in the therapy and turned to discussing a "deal" between the two. Paul wanted to have another child (which Anne did not want) and Anne wanted to spend a year abroad studying music. They worked out a compromise which allowed both and resulted in their stopping therapy. I believe that

Paul would have been a good candidate for clomipramine but he was reluctant to take medication.

I have described this illustration as "simple–relational" because I believe that Paul had the capacity to develop better control but the dynamics of the relationship overshadowed his ability to pay attention to his pleasure and comfort. I did not have the opportunity to explore thoroughly his reluctance to try medication.

It seems almost quaint to reflect on our ideas of unidimensional sexual difficulties, that is, that one partner would present with a clearly identifiable sexual symptom that was amenable to a specific, well-defined treatment. Our understanding of the reciprocal and complicated dynamics that exist with couples is more sophisticated, and the unconscious collusions and distortions that serve some unidentified function exert considerable power (Dicks, 1964; Main, 1966). Although the psychological need for the shared problems may not be immediately apparent, their effects on a couple's interaction are powerful.

Complicated

Clinical Illustration

Howard was a man in his mid-40s who was urged by his wife's therapist to seek treatment. He felt intrinsically that therapy was "bad" and that one ought to be able to figure out solutions on one's own. The therapist described a man who was terrified of being sexual because of complaints of back pain and his conviction that sex would make this worse. As a teenager, he had been masturbating in his bed when a spring broke through the mattress and protruded into his back, causing considerable pain. He was quite frightened by this occurrence and began to worry that he had caused bodily damage. He believed that his sexual feelings and masturbating had caused the problem. This early event provided the crystal around which a delusional-like state developed that served to isolate him from taking any pleasure in his penis. It became clear that on the occasions when he would have intercourse with his wife, he would ejaculate almost immediately, and this experience only increased an already powerful feeling of self-hatred. I learned from Howard that his father was a distant, intellectual man who would engage in strange rituals which involved a repetitive loud clearing of his throat while rocking back and forth in a chair grunting loudly. Howard had no recollections of warmth and connection with his father, and as one might have expected, no discussion about body parts, let alone sex. As a child, Howard was left very much to fend for himself, with little positive male role modeling from his father. The mattress incident served to be the focal point which fostered an identification with this strange elusive father.

The puzzle was how to engage Howard. I wanted to interest him in the concept that his body might be a source of pleasure for him. I said:

"You know it sounds to me like your father was really quite strange; he would engage in this bizarre behavior, was somewhat removed and unrelated to the rest of the family, and I could imagine that it was very hard for a young boy to feel that this is someone from whom one might learn things. As boys begin to go through puberty , there are tremendous changes in their bodies, a growth spurt, and then strong sexual feelings related to the increasing hormones. Just as you dare to get in touch with some of the good feelings associated with this development, the mattress spring bursts through, terrifies you, and you were convinced that you had done something terrible. Your father was not there as a supportive source of information, and I imagine that you were frightened and felt very alone"

For the first several meetings, I did much of the talking, trying to provide for Howard a road map that he could use to begin to orient himself emotionally This included talks about his son who was 11, which provided an opportunity to talk about sexuality in a developing boy.

Howard described his shame in coming so quickly, and his knowledge that it left his wife Myrna quite unsatisfied. I intuitively felt that I should meet with him alone for a period before inviting him to bring his wife. I wanted to encourage his taking pleasure in his own sexual feelings in a more positive way before adding the intensity of sexuality with his wife. I asked him about masturbation (thinking that I could suggest some exercises that would heighten his awareness) and he seemed horrified by the idea. It was as if he expected that another spring would come bursting forth from the mattress, this time doing even more damage that the first. I suggested that he needed some help to get to know his penis, that they *"needed to introduce themselves to each other."* The disconnection from his body was long-standing, and some unusual measures were in order. Talking about this in a more cerebral way would not have been helpful.

Howard was intrigued and began to ask more question about sexual physiology and welcomed my sharing information with him. He was very apprehensive about masturbating and asked that his wife join our meetings.

She was appreciative of his asking her to be a part of the therapy and was kind and sympathetic. He had shared with her much of our conversations, and she confirmed the father's strange demeanor. We talked about ejaculatory control and had an open, relaxed talk about sexual physiology and people's reactions to coming quickly. In talking about masturbating, I often use the story about the young boy who was found masturbating by a parent who says, "Don't do that, you'll go blind!" to which the boy replies, "Can't I do it until I need glasses." This story lightens the atmosphere, relieves the tension, and allows me to model talking openly and matter of factly about sex. The relief that couples seem to feel is easy to see.

Weekly meetings were too intense for Howard. He needed to be able to maintain control and distance that respected his defensive style. I had suggested the couple's viewing the videotape *You Can Last Longer* (Dunn & Polonsky, 1992) together. The wife was interested in the behavioral approach, and was willing to try the exercises. About a month later, she described giving Howard a "hand job" and talked about how it was enjoyable for her to look at and hold his penis. She was surprised, though, that it took him a long time to come this way, and she suggested that he guide her with his hand and show her what he found arousing. He was surprised to notice that this made him much more aroused, and with the collaboration, he was able to have an orgasm.

The treatment has moved very slowly This is a man in his mid-40s who has been disconnected from his penis and pleasurable body investment for most of his life. I have continued to provide a model of an adult who is encouraging and informing with a sense of humor about an activity that can produce the pleasure that he deserves.

With complicated multiproblem relationships the therapist often flies by the seat of his other pants. The straightforward instructions do not work, and one has to integrate several styles, combined with considerable patience.

Complicated and Relational

Clinical Illustration

I received a request for a consultation from a colleague. She had been seeing a couple in their early 60s for several months. The relationship had become very turbulent, with frequent blowups, often resulting in the wife's banishing the husband from the house for days at a time. The reason for the consultation was that the husband had a sudden onset of PE. Throughout the marriage, ejaculatory control had never been an issue.

Mr. O was a refined, 60-year-old professional man who was noticeably uncomfortable with my direct and explicit sexual questioning. I could find no evidence in the history of urinary infection, prostatic inflammation, or infection. Mr. O described having very little ejaculatory control at this time, coming almost instantly after entering his wife's vagina. It was clear that the marital strife was considerable. There was a great deal of tension, revolving primarily around the wife's frustration with his emotional reticence and his struggling to develop an emotional vocabulary that he had not had for most of his life. Initially I gave him information about ejaculatory control, talked specifically about ways to enhance it and also suggested the videotape (Dunn & Polonsky, 1992) Although we had scheduled another appointment, he canceled this. I heard from my colleague that Mr. O had been very embarrassed by the directness of my discussions. She continued to work with the couple, and there was a gradual shift in the turbulence and a dialogue began in their therapy.

About a year later Mr. O called me requesting to come in with his wife. She genuinely wanted to help him improve their sexual relationship and was open and forthcoming with my questions. She had a sense of humor and we talked about their sexual patterns. We talked about ways they could broaden their repertoire to include sensual touching.

As this progressed I asked them about oral sex. Mrs. O said that she was squeamish about both performing and receiving it. I explained that often people do have mixed feelings about it and said that for many the association with "those parts being associated with elimination" lessens the appeal. I chose consciously to anticipate the reservations and to bring them up knowing that I had an opportunity to cover material I knew they would not bring up on their own.

Mr. O stated that he believed that intercourse was the only way to give her satisfaction and that if he ejaculated quickly he was letting her down. This provided an opportunity for her to "reality test" for him and let him know that it was their enjoying each other and feeling close that was really important.

My impression was that the meeting had gone well. The wife was open and eager to try things, and he seemed to be more comfortable than before. They canceled the next meeting, and said they would call to reschedule. I again spoke with my colleague who told me that Mr. O found the direct sexual discussions almost too much to bear. As much as he struggled to feel that it was acceptable, he felt that there was something "unseemly" about talking this way with another person.

A few months later, my colleague told me that they had been viewing the videotape together. They had used the model of my meeting with them to continue talking about how to improve their sexual relationship and continued to make gains in their talking with each other. Mr. O's ejaculatory control improved enormously.

Discussion. It is clear that the primary problem was not PE. There had been long-standing relational difficulties which they were addressing with a skilled and compassionate therapist. Nevertheless, the PE was disturbing and uncomfortable, and Mr. O wanted some help directed to the specific symptom. What was striking was how much I did not know of Mr. O's discomfort in talking with me, and how I totally misread the couple meeting. It was one of those meetings in which I felt I was doing "brilliant" therapy, giving information, picking up on cues, and engaging with the couple in a warm and humorous way, and yet I had no idea that Mr. O was "dying a thousand deaths" with the frankness of the discussion. (His compliance with me mirrored what was an issue in the marriage in that the wife complained that she never knew what he was thinking.) However, my impact on him and the couple was enormously helpful. They took from me what they needed and then used their resources to make gains on their own.

Clinical Illustration

The inventive therapist uses the presenting symptom as the introduction to the couple, and then brings his or her unique approach to disentangle what is going on and to tailor a treatment approach that both addresses the manifest concern of the couple as well as the "hidden" issues that need to be addressed before the symptom can be dropped.

A couple in their mid-40s stated specifically that they wanted a sexually focused therapy to deal with the husband's long-standing PE. They were not interested in explorative type therapy—"been there, done that" (they had each seen an individual therapist and had also done some couple therapy).

Regardless of one's dynamic formulation, it is often useful to meet a couple on their terms. By using a sexual approach when that is requested, a clinician can engage a couple and the dynamic issues will soon present themselves. I talked about a behavioral approach and made suggestions for them to do assigned touching exercises (sensate focus). They were delighted with the directions and the structure, felt enormous relief, and did the exercises regularly. They were eager to move on to the next phase and I added "breasts and genitals" with the suggestion that the aim was to learn something about each other in terms of touch and feeling that was new. Progress continued unabated and I suggested penile stimulation including the "squeeze." They found this very rewarding and the husband felt free of worry and anxiety about delaying orgasm. Within a few weeks he felt that he had developed much better control and was more aware of what he could do to delay ejaculation. I thought that they were ready to move to next stage. This was many years ago when I was more wedded to using the terminology from Masters and Johnson. I talked about bridging and attempting "vaginal *containment*." (I now feel that this sounds more like the Three Mile Island nuclear disaster rather than anything that might suggest sexual arousal.) I reassured them that couples often feel anxious as they moved to the next stage. When I greeted them in my waiting room the following week, it was clear that this had not been a good week. They came into the office lamenting that it had been a terrible. The husband had not been able to get an erection, and it all started when I mentioned the idea of (in his words) "vaginal *entrapment!!*" Both described having a dream after the "failure." In the husband's dream, he came into the kitchen wanting to feed his daughter's bird. He opened the cage and put his hand in. The bird flapped its wings frantically and fell dead on the bottom of the cage, shriveled up. The husband was terrified. The wife's dream also took place in the kitchen. She entered the kitchen and found that one of the children had switched on the food processor without its safety lid and was about to put her hand into the bowl, at which point she awoke in a sweat. These two dreams provided the focus to delve into the enormous problems relating to anger in each of their families. Both sets of parents were controlling, intrusive, and devaluing. The wife's parents were more overt, and the couple often felt powerless to resist the assaults. We spent many months going over different experiences each had with their parents and ways they could each respond, resulting in each feeling less victimized. In their past therapies, none of the family issues had been addressed. After about 6 months, I raised the sexual issue again and wondered whether they wanted to return to the behavioral program. They each smiled and said that they had been practicing on their own and that ejaculatory control was no longer a problem.

This illustration highlights the interplay of intrapsychic, interpersonal, and directed approaches. It required using all for the treatment to be effective. The husband needed some help in mastering better ejaculatory control, but an understanding of the role of the anger in both families of origin was a crucial part of the improvement. If the family-of-origin issues had remained unexpressed, the practical suggestions relating to orgasm control would have been ineffective. In the sexual arena vulnerability and trust are central concerns for many. The sexual symptoms may be identified by the couple as needing to be fixed, obscuring deep-seated worries about aggression, closeness, and its consequences.

DISCUSSION

It is nearly 50 years since Semans (1955) first presented a novel treatment for PE. Although the solution was behavioral, he was quite clear that the wife was an integral part of any treatment. Not only did he value her understanding and description of the problem, but he emphasized the need for the husband to learn to stimulate her to orgasm by means other than intercourse. It is important to be reminded of the intricate bond between two people in their sexual intimacy.

As indicated in this chapter, PE is defined in different ways, and at the outset of an evaluation, the therapist has to try to clarify the patient's definition, the partner's definition, how each is affected, and the perceived goal of treatment. For many, the perception of what constitutes desirable sex is shaped by images in the media, in which nonverbal genital sex is often overvalued. The myth of the sexual athlete is embraced by magazines and soap operas and has resulted in many believing that the sexual ideal is intercourse that is prolonged, vigorous, and consuming. Playfulness and mutual discovery are often ignored. If men and their partners have become focused on achieving this goal and the man ejaculates rapidly, the pursuit of "control" becomes a task in which the couple becomes mired, and failures are usually the outcome. What is needed is some intervention from a benign authority—an experienced partner, a trusted friend, or more usually a good therapist. Helping an individual and his partner expand the range of their sensual/sexual repertoire to move beyond an exclusive genital focus involves skill and understanding.

The man with PE suffers in many ways. He often feels incompetent and alone. He feels an intense shame that he may not reveal to his partner, and it is unusual to share it with friends. Therapy provides support, information, and the hope for change and mastery. The partner of a man with PE may similarly feel alone and confused. She may not understand what is happening and may feel that she is somehow deficient. She may have had different sexual experiences and still feel confused about what is happening with her partner. She may feel angry and resentful, assuming that he is selfish and uninterested in her pleasure and satisfaction. Therapy provides a place for information, explanation, and change.

The unconscious cues in a relationship are expressed in many ways. The sharing of a sexual symptom to hide conflicts around closeness, pleasure, and competence needs to be considered. When there is resistance to change, the therapist may be confounded as to cause and attempts to identify the contributing factors in one or both partners. The impact of a critical partner has to be assessed in any treatment. Treating the symptom without looking at the feared repercussions of not "being cured" probably accounts for some of the poor long-term outcomes.

In considering etiology, the results of many studies have pointed out that finding a discrete cause is an elusive venture. It is a relief to realize that there is no generalizable psychological issue involved for men with PE. They do not hate women or dread castration. Many are profoundly affected emotionally by what they view as a disability, and the impact of this concept of themselves affects how they behave in a relationship. The therapist has a central role in helping to bring an awareness of the man's emotional withdrawal as having more "negative" impact than his lack of control. Struggling on his own to hang on for dear life does not make for a pleasurable connection with a partner.

Studies looking at the hypersensitivity theory of the penile skin have revealed that men with PE are if anything less sensitive. I believe that we may have confused hypersensitivy with anxiety. Men who are anxious about ejaculating rapidly may have to formulate an explanation to save face. "I was so excited—I came fast!" Other studies looking at the physiology of the bulbocavernous reflex have indicated that there are some differences in the nerve potentials in men with rapid ejaculation as compared with those who have better control. As indicated earlier, there has been no study to examine whether there is a measurable change if the men have undergone a series of training exercises.

The use of medication has been explored, and the results in terms of ejaculatory latency measurements have been impressive. Clompramine and the SSRIs have had a significant, measurable impact on ejaculatory control. Men need to be told of this option, and the therapist should discuss the pros and cons. I indicate my reservations about using some medications long term in therapeutic doses for their side effects but feel that an informed decision for the individual needs to be made. Tiefer (1994) articulates the need for careful reflection when she writes:

> [W]here are we going with all this medicalization? In the last few years we have seen the explosive development of devices, drugs, and surgical procedures to treat erectile dysfunction. Watching this explosion first hand I wonder whether our time and resources are actually being used in the best way to improve couples' sexual satisfaction. It certainly seem a one-sided development, sometimes grossly inattentive to the quality of the couples' sexual interaction and experiences. (p. 7)

As the field of sexual therapy has grown, new approaches to sexual problems have been devised and promoted. They are initially embraced with enthusiasm and hopefulness, but usually a more sober reality tempers the euphoria and we again confront the inherent complexities that unfold in the sexual drama. More commonly, therapists struggle with the "difficult cases" that defy all our interventions. The therapist is challenged to listen to the patient at many levels, paying attention to the individual's psyche, looking at the fabric of the family's relational styles, and shaping the nature of his experiences in close relationships. One needs to understand the dynamics of the couple and how they express their wishes and desires—what is perceived and what is misperceived. The meaning of sexuality and closeness for the couple should be understood and not assumed. Levine (1988) has aptly captured the varieties of meaning with the title of his book: *Sex Is Not Simple*. It means different things to people. A sexual symptom may be the squeaky wheel that gets attention.

For some, a whole range of sensual and sexual feelings is embraced, and rapid ejaculation may be seen as a minor inconvenience; the enjoyment of reciprocal excitement and pleasure and the sense of well-being about one's self and partner may provide a gratifying shared closeness. The couple may not feel that they had a sexual problem.

All too often men and their partners are quick to diagnose themselves in negative, self-blaming ways with great suffering to both partners. Meaning may be ascribed to coming early that has no bearing on reality. Premature ejaculation is only one of the many sexual symptoms around which the distress of an individual or couple may be focused. A man with ejaculatory problems may be with a partner who has some (unidentified) sexual constriction. If the partner has trouble with closeness or difficulty with arousal or orgasm herself, the PE may mask those difficulties and provide the "obvious" problem that the couple defines. Similarly, a woman may have vaginismus, and given this obvious serious nature of the problem, her partner's sexual anxieties remain hidden.

Although medications have been found to increase ejaculatory latency, there is often a benefit to first trying an approach that focuses on learning and mastery. While there are generalized conclusions that long-term results for treating PE are poor, much of the research does not adequately address issues relating to therapist style and approach, patient–therapist match, and therapist's gender and age. For some men, seeing a man may be preferable when the support of a male would be helpful. For others, having a woman therapist who is accepting and encouraging may be an important factor in giving up some preconceived ideas of what women want or expect. In considering outcome, one has to look beyond the implication that the "squeeze technique" failed. How the instructions are presented by the therapist may be an important component in the lack of success. Is the therapist able to form a relationship with the patient that allows him to feel safe and understood? The clinician may inadvertently hamper the therapy with statements such as "this is very easy to cure," communicating a sense of his own mastery while minimizing the perceived incompetence on the part of the patient. The instructions need to be given in great detail (see Appendix). In my experience, some of the men who would be considered "treatment failures" were given unclear and vague directions. What actually transpires in a therapist's office is often not clearly revealed and is an important element in any outcome measure that is hard to evaluate.

The "noncompliant" individual is a special challenge. I have seen many men who simply do not practice the exercises that I believe will result in better control. They all have excuses, and I believe that the PE has become a defense that they are unwilling to give up. Trying to understand what this is requires time and patience. In these instances the sexual symptom is identified by the individual as the reason for treatment, with the assumption that a cure is desired. The reluctance to practice exercises that in themselves are quite easy provides an opportunity to point out the paradox and help engage the patient in a more explorative therapy.

Finally, McCarthy (1989) has often emphasized the need for "relapse prevention." Patients need to be reminded and encouraged to continue doing the exercises. Follow-up meetings reinforce this message. The therapist needs to be active in calling the patient if he has heard from him for a while. The negative internalized view of himself as a sexual being has been long standing, and the unconscious hold on that is compelling. Consistent (although infrequent) contact with the therapist who can ally with the competent effective part of the individual is important in preventing a relapse to older patterns. The therapist who has an understanding of some of the maladaptive relational patterns may be able to clarify how nonsexual events have resulted in a regression to earlier symptomatic behavior.

SUMMARY

1. Premature ejaculation is the most common sexual complaint for men.
2. The definition is difficult but usually centers on the fact that orgasm occurs before a man wishes it.
3. Etiology is not clear.
4. Treatment approaches now include an integrating of individual and couple dynamics; cognitive and behavioral approaches, and more recently the introduction of various medications.
5. Strategies to prevent relapse have been recommended.

APPENDIX: EXERCISES FOR LEARNING CONTROL

I have a series of exercises that will help you better know your sexual responses and with practice I believe will help you develop ways of having more control over when you come. By practicing these exercises, you will become more familiar with the different sensations you experience in your penis and will develop an awareness of what you might do. There are some general statements that I'd like you to know.

1. This is a very common issue for men. Roughly 30% of men say that they are not satisfied with their ability to control orgasm. Men are convinced that everyone else lasts just fine.

2. Often the focus becomes "am I going to last"—and there is a change aware from enjoyment and pleasure to one of business and performance, where one will be judged and criticized.

3. Men often think their problem is that they become too excited too quickly and that they need to distract themselves in some way. (Think of a baseball game, do a mathematical calculation.) I believe the issue is learning to STAY at the high level of arousal; learning what you can do keep a balance between coming and being very aroused.

4. Many partners are convinced that the man is selfish—interested only in his getting off and not caring about her being left high and dry. Frankly, most men feel shame and a sense of defeat rather than a self-congratulatory high. In addition, for many men who come very soon, the subjective experience is that their orgasm is not very intense.

5. Talking with your partner about your worries and learning something about your partner's wishes and worries will lessen considerably the pressure you feel around control.

6. The reverse holds true; that is, if you don't talk about your concerns, and march forward trying to cover it up, the pressure will only mount, and anxiety usually makes every aspect of sex more difficult and less enjoyable.

7. It is important to know something about your partner's sexual interests and needs. Guys often have the idea that "real men" can thrust vigorously and continuously for long periods—the more rapid and longer, the better for the woman. Most women will not confirm this perception.

8. Practice and frequency are absolutely crucial. Almost all men will have less control over when they come if they have not had an orgasm for a while.

The suggestions I am going to give you may sound a little mechanical, but they are designed to help you learn to anticipate what will bring you closer to orgasm and also what you can do to delay it.

Phase 1

Masturbate in your usual way until you feel that an orgasm is approaching. Try to pay attention to the feelings in your penis that tell you that you are close to coming. You may feel a heightened tingling at the tip of your penis, or a sense of fullness in your groin. At that point, stop masturbating and squeeze your penis firmly between your thumb and forefinger, either at the base (front to back) or at the junction of the shaft and the head until the feeling that you're going to come subsides.

Using the second hand of a watch, wait 1 minute, and then repeat the previous step, masturbating until you feel the point at which coming is imminent. Time how long it takes for you to get to this point.

Stop the masturbating, and squeeze again. Wait 1 minute—and repeat this two more times.

With the fourth time, continue the masturbating, focusing your attention on the sensations in your penis and groin and continue through allowing yourself to have an orgasm.

Try to do this Phase 1 step 3 times a week for 2 weeks. You will probably notice that the time taken after you wait the minute begins to increase, giving you a way of confirming that something is changing for you.

Phase 2

With regular practice, you will notice that you have begun to learn what you need to do to decide when you will have an orgasm. It may be slowing the rhythm of your masturbating; it may be recognizing earlier the level of arousal and excitement; it may be noticing sooner when you should stop the stimulation.

With this next phase, I want you to begin to try to keep the arousal constant at a high level. If "10" means you are going to come, then the aim is to try to keep yourself at 7.5 to 8. Begin with your usual pattern of masturbating, paying attention to the level of arousal. Try to gauge in your mind as you are focusing on your penis and groin what your level is. As you begin to approach "6" or "7," slow the rhythm of your masturbating so that you maintain a constant level of arousal. There will be the heightened tingle you feel in your penis accompanied by an increasing pressure in your erection. Slow the rhythm, but try to keep the level of arousal constant. For those of you who like a mechanical model to make things clearer, think about driving a stick shift car, and imagine being stationary on a hill. Your left foot is on the clutch, your right foot on the accelerator. By balancing the two, you can keep the car from either moving forward or rolling back. That is what you want to learn to do. It may happen when you are doing this that the first few times you do not gauge your arousal accurately, and you may suddenly go from 7 to 10. Don't worry about that. Try to reflect on what your sensations were, and the next time you do this phase, go a little slower but continue to pay attention to trying to keep the level of arousal high and constant.

After you have done this a few times, you will find that you will be able to keep yourself at a constant high state of arousal, and when you are at that point for 10 or 15 minutes, there will be a change in your "excitability." You will notice that it is easier to keep the arousal high and not to come. The goal in this phase is to be able to keep yourself at the highest level of arousal you can maintain for 15 minutes and then let yourself go with the flow and come. You will notice that the intensity of your orgasm will be terrific.

Phase 2(a)

Continue practicing as previously. Ideally you should do it no less than three times per week. Frequency is a major component in learning control. Compare this to the kind of training athletes do to master a particular skill in their game. They will practice over and over—the repetition being a key until the process becomes somewhat automatic, and their body instinctively has learned to do something it did not do before.

During this phase, I want to introduce you to the pubococcygeus muscle. This is the muscle that you contract if you want to stop urinating midstream. During the previous exercise, I want you to see what happens if you contract the muscle forcefully—notice whether you feel closer to coming or whether it helps you delay coming. Then relax the muscle and see what effect it has. Then practice a slow, gradual contraction of the muscle. You can practice getting control of this muscle almost anywhere and anytime. Doing so gets you more aware of the sensations in your groin. For some men, the contraction may stave off orgasm; for others it may hurry it. For still others, the gradual, partial contraction may create an ability to hold off coming allowing you more of a role in deciding when.

Phase 3

The only difference here is the addition of a lubricant. (KY Jelly, Astroglide, Lubriderm—NOT Petroleum Jelly). The lubricant simulates more the sensation of your penis being in someone's vagina, which is more stimulating than "dry" masturbation. Repeat the exercises you have been doing, and pay attention to how this feels different.

NOTE: Whether you practice Phases 1 through 3 alone or with your partner is a matter of personal preference. Some men like to be able to develop some mastery on their own, feeling a total freedom from any kind of performance pressure. Others choose to involve a partner immediately. Be guided by what makes you most comfortable.

Phase 4: Bringing a Partner into the Picture

If you are in a long-term relationship, the two of you probably have agreed that you would like a change in your sexual relationship. The exercises just discussed will have prepared you for the next phase. If you are just starting a new relationship, I encourage you to get to know the person you are with before you enter into a sexual relationship. It really makes a difference to have a sense of trust and comfort and to feel that you can be open in a relationship. Although it would appear that to reveal sexual concerns is unmanly, to keep a sexual problem a secret places a huge load on your shoulders that will increase anxiety and likely make control of your orgasm difficult. Further, it will be hard for you to focus on playfulness and enjoyment and not be governed by a worry about performance.

After you have practiced Phases 1 through 3 (whether alone or with a partner) you will be ready to put your penis into your partner's vagina. Remember that you will probably both be a little anxious at moving to this new level, and you may even have less control and come quite quickly. This is not unusual. You might find that for the first time, it will be helpful for you to lie on your back and have your partner straddle your body. Let her hold your penis, and guide it to the opening of her vagina. Initially just keep your penis at the opening to her vagina, and concentrate on what that feels like. If you feel like you are going to come, have her move it away. The object of this phase is to try to get your penis into her vagina and simply pay attention to what that feels like without moving or thrusting. Think about what you have learned in the previous exercises, and try to get your focus on what you are feeling in your penis and groin. You may find that squeezing your penis at the base (front to back) between your thumb and forefinger will diminish any urge to ejaculate. Once you feel that you are in control, your partner may begin to move slowly, in a way that parallels what you did when you were using a hand to stimulated your penis. Pay attention to the level of arousal here—trying to keep yourself at a 7.5 and guiding your partner's movements. After getting close to coming three or four times, allow your orgasm to build and focus on the sensations. After you have had an orgasm, ask your partner what she would like you to do. It may be that she does not wish for any stimulation at that time; it may be that "returning the favor" is what would feel good. Talking with each other about expectations and what feels pleasurable relieves one of the need for reading minds. Telling each other how you like to be stimulated, what feels good, and what does not paves the way for feeling confident that there are ways to provide each other with exciting and enjoyable sexual feelings that are not exclusively dependent on sexual intercourse.

Practice and frequency are the single most effective things you can do to continue to develop more effective control over when you have an orgasm. It is important to remember that there will be times when you again come very quickly, and where you might simply not be able to control your orgasm. Try to recall the times you felt good about and remind yourself that the gains you have made are real. By dwelling on the "failure" you may withdraw emotionally from your partner, which has much more impact than coming quickly.

ADDITIONAL COMMENTS

I don't have a strong conviction for "squeeze' versus "stop–start." Frankly, I like the squeeze simply because the individual has some specific activity to do. (Not unlike the suggestion to husbands whose wives were in active labor to go and "boil water and get newspaper," I don't believe it did anything, but it may have bound some anxiety for the husband and made him feel useful). It may in the short run be helpful in that it does provide a little distraction, that is the squeeze provides a sensation that is different from the experience of increased penile pleasure.

I have found the suggestion regarding the second hand of a watch useful for several reasons. Men often do better with specific instructions they can follow; when told to wait "a minute", for many, 20 seconds seems like a long time. I want to make sure that they allow sufficient time to elapse so that they have gotten down to a lower level of arousal. Finally, timing how long it takes to get to the point of *ejaculatory inevitability* provides concrete evidence of change which is often reinforcing.

Levine (1992) is the only source I have found who has confirmed the change associated with staying at high levels of arousal: *"The best way to increase the capac-*

*ity to sustain a high level of arousal without ejaculation is to experience sexual inten-
sity. The nervous system accommodates to stimulation by raising the threshold for the
ejaculatory reflex"* (p. 98)

REFERENCES

Althof, S. E. (1995). Pharmacologic treatment of rapid ejaculation. *Psychiatric Clinics of North
America, 18,* 85–94.

American Psychiatric Association. (1994). *Diagnostic and statistical manual of mental disorders*
(4th ed.). Washington, DC: Author.

Assalian, P. (1994). Premature ejaculation—Is it really psychogenic? *Journal of Sex Education
and Therapy, 20,* 1–4.

Birch, R. W. (1998). *Male sexual endurance.* Columbus, OH: PEC.

Dicks, H. V. (1964). Concepts of marital diagnosis of therapy as developed at the Tavistock
Family Psychiatric Clinic, London. In E. M. Nash, L. Jessner, & D. W. W. Abse (Eds.), *Mar-
riage counseling in medical practice* (pp. 255–275). Chapel Hill, NC: University of North
Carolina Press.

Dunn, M. & Polonsky, D. C. (1992). *You can last longer.* [videotape]. Chapel Hill, NC: The
Sinclair Institute.

Framo, J. L. (1982). *Explorations in marital and family therapy.* New York: Springer.

Grenier, G., & Byers, S. (1995). Rapid ejaculation: A review of conceptual etiological and treatment issues. *Archives of Sexual Behavior, 24,* 447–472.

Hong, J. (1984). Survival of the fastest: On the origins of premature ejaculation. *Journal of Sex
Research, 20,* 109–112.

Kaplan, H. S. (1974). *The new sex therapy.* New York: Bunner/Mazel.

Kinsey, A. C., Pomeroy, W. B., & Martin, C. E. (1948). *Sexual behavior in the human male.*
Philadelphia: Saunders.

Levine, S. B. (1988). *Sex is not simple.* Columbus, OH: Ohio Psychology.

Levine, S. B. (1992). *Helping men to control ejaculation: Sexual life—A clinician's guide.* New
York: Plenum.

LoPiccolo, J. (1997). *Postmodern sex therapy.* Annual meeting of SSTAR, Chicago.

Main, T. F. (1966). Mutual projection in marriage. *Comprehensive Psychiatry, 7,* 432.

Masters, W. H., & Johnson, V. E. (1970). *Human sexual inadequacy.* Boston: Little, Brown.

McCarthy, B. W. (1989). Cognitive-behavioral strategies and techniques in the treatment of early
ejaculation. In S. R. Leiblum & R. C. Rosen (Eds.), *Principles and practice of sex therapy—
Update for the 1990s* (2nd ed., pp. 141–167). New York: Guilford Press.

Metz, M. E., Prior, J. L., Nesvacil, L. J., Abuzzchab, F., & Koznar, J. (1997, Spring). Premature
ejaculation: A psychophysiological review. *Journal of Sex and Marital Therapy, 23,* 3–23.

Rosen, R. C. (1995). A case of premature ejaculation: Too little, too late? In R. C. Rosen & S. R.
Leiblum (Eds.), *Case studies in sex therapy* (pp. 279–294). New York: Guilford Press.

Rowland, D. L., Stefan, M., Haensel, J., Blom, H. M., & Koosslob, A. (1993, Fall). Penile sensitivity in men with premature ejaculation and erectile dysfunction. *Journal of Sex and Marital
Therapy, 19,* 189–197.

Semans, J. H. (1955). Premature ejaculation: A new approach. *Southern Medical Journal, 49,*
353–358.

Tiefer, L. (1994). Might premature ejaculation be organic?: The perfect penis takes a giant step
forward. *Journal of Sex Education and Therapy, 20,* 7–8.

Zilbergeld, B. (1992). *The new male sexuality.* New York: Bantam Books.

Zilbergeld, B. (1995). The critical and demanding partner in sex therapy. In R. C. Rosen & S. R.
Leiblum (Eds.), *Case studies in sex therapy* (pp. 311–330). New York: Guilford Press.

IV

SPECIAL POPULATIONS

12

Therapy with Sexual Minorities

MARGARET NICHOLS

As Margaret Nichols observes, there has been a sea change in the attitudes of the gay community toward bisexuality and other sexual lifestyles previously considered "fringe." The self-designated "queer" community now includes among its members transgendered individuals and some who practice behaviors considered fetishistic or "kinky." Nichols suggests that it behooves straight clinicians to recognize and understand these alternative lifestyles because they often come to be adapted or adopted by more traditional couples. If sex therapists are to be effective with clients outside the "mainstream," they must understand the lifestyles of individuals who function within sexual minorities.

She notes that there has been a breaking down of traditional gender roles within both the straight and gay community so that now it is increasingly viable for transgendered, as well as gay and bisexual, individuals to evolve a unique and blended gender role without surgery or full commitment to being either male or female. Furthermore, what is viewed as "safe sex" within the queer community has changed as both political forces and medical treatments for AIDS have evolved over the last 30 years.

Nichols believes that sex therapy with "queer" clients is not significantly different from sex therapy with traditional heterosexual clients except insofar as issues of sexual identity, alternative lifestyles, and "kinky" sexual practices may become the focus of treatment. For example, nonmonogamous sex often becomes a topic of discussion and the therapist may have to face his or her own scruples about facilitating relationship choices that may feel uncomfortable. Nichols presents case vignettes in which agreed-on deception is part of the couple contract, as well as nonmonogamous sex for one partner in a lesbian relationship. In fact, the whole issue of what constitutes sexual pathology may need to be reassessed when working with sexual minorities. Nichols writes that she and her colleagues have "put aside" preconceived concepts of "nor-

mal" and "pathological" sexuality and simply ask themselves, "Is it consensual?" and "Is anyone clearly being damaged here?" If the answer to these questions are "yes" and "no," respectively, we consider the sexual practices nonpathological.

In her conclusion, Nichols observes that certain attitudes and behaviors are necessary for working with sexual minority clients, including a genuine attitude of nonjudgmentalism and preconceptions about what constitutes sexual "normality." Therapists must be willing to admit ignorance and to allow themselves to be taught by their clients. Indeed, this is a necessary attitude for us to adopt when working with any client.

Margaret Nichols, PhD, is Director of the Institute for Personal Growth/ Institute for Behavioral Solutions, twin organizations in Highland Park and Jersey City, New Jersey. Dr. Nichols's specialties in sex therapy include issues of the gay/lesbian/bisexual community, AIDS, and other members of the social "sexual fringe."

All psychotherapy is bound by history and geography, and perhaps none is more constrained by these forces than counseling done with members of special subgroups of the culture at large. The therapist must interpret the client's personal experience through the lens of a social context that is different from and perhaps alien to his or her own. He or she must be an anthropologist and sociologist as well as a psychologist/therapist.

Many sex therapists are already accustomed to receiving referrals of lesbian and gay clients, and previous editions of this book included chapters designed to familiarize counselors with gay issues (Leiblum & Pervin, 1980; Leiblum & Rosen, 1989). However, as we enter the millennium, there is an increasing tendency for the gay and lesbian community to include within its boundaries bisexuals, transgendered people, and people who practice forbidden sex acts, especially the many varieties of dominant/submissive sex: those individuals whom the mainstream of society considers "the garbage heap of sex-and-gender trash" (Califia, 1997, p. 256). Thus the updated version of this chapter reflects the growth and changes what many now call the "queer" community—a title change that emphasizes the nonmainstream element of all its members. Although this chapter primarily describes sexual minorities within a large urban/suburban setting, it is still relevant to more rural or mid-American locations. Eventually, New York and West Coast urban cultural phenomena trickle out to the rest of the United States, at least within this community. And even individuals who do not consider themselves to be "members" of a sexual minority community cannot help but be influenced by its mores.

It is important to note that some gay people will take exception to my inclusion of bisexuals, transgenderists, and kinky-sex aficionados as members of "their" community. But I would argue that the affinity of these other sexual minorities for the lesbian and gay culture is not accidental. Whereas breaking barriers of sexual orientation and gender roles does not necessarily mean that other taboos will be overcome, it does make such a result more likely. Moreover, there is considerable overlap of these different sexual minorities. In the last week, for example, I have done an intake on a lesbian couple who, as an aside, mentioned their extensive sadomasochistic experience, which includes public sex with multiple partners; talked to a colleague about a self-identified lesbian and a gay man who have become romantically/sexually involved; and supervised a staff therapist working with a male-to-female lesbian transsexual.

There are problems inherent even in arriving at common definitions of sexual minorities, because the phenomena we are attempting to define are so variable and complex. Let us take sexual preference as an example. We tend to think of sexual orientation as (1) a single phenomenon in which identity, behavior, and attractions are all consistent; (2) dichotomous (you're either gay or straight) or at most tripartite (gay, bi, het); (3) unrelated to gender identity; and (4) stable throughout one's lifetime. In fact, it seems that none of these things is true. Desire, behavior, and self-identification are not consistent within an individual; for example, many people experience at least occasional same-sex desire, but fewer demonstrate behavior and fewer still consider themselves to be gay (Laumann, Gagnon, Michael, & Michaels, 1994). As Kinsey pointed out more than 50 years ago, same-sex attractions exist along a continuum, and we superimpose discrete categories upon this continuum. The categories themselves are arbitrary and artificial and vary with factors such as historical time period or who is applying the label. For example, probably most individuals with primary same-sex attraction and secondary heterosexual desire self-label as "gay" if they are over 35 and "bisexual" if they are under 25. Sexual orientation and gender identity seem to have more than a passing acquaintance, as any self-identified "butch" lesbian can explain (Nestle, 1992). And although sexual identity is indeed stable and fixed for many, some individuals seem to have more fluid and changing orientation (McWhirter, Sanders, & Reinisch, 1990): The switch from lesbian to bisexual is so common that a Boston bisexual women's group calls itself the "Hasbians." For the most part, when terms such as "gay" or "bisexual" are used here they refer to one's self-identification, but they may describe behavior or desire when discussing cases in which clients themselves are confused about their orientation.

This chapter is written from what Morin (1995) calls the "paradoxical perspective" of sex. Derived in part from the work of sexologist Robert Stoller (1985) and philosopher Georges Bataille (1962), this paradigm eschews the pathology model as simplistic, thinly veiled moralism and the "new sex therapy" approach as overly mechanistic and medical. In this model, sexuality is a set of phenomena that are powerful, complex, multidetermined, and multifunctional. Sex is part hardwiring and part early environmental imprinting, with perhaps a few modifications along the way. But the "environmental influences" are nothing so simple as Oedipal complexes or even role models: They have their root in psychological attempts to deal with the terror and powerlessness inherent in childhood, among other things. Thus, sex is *by design* hostile, dangerous, shame and anxiety evoking, objectifying, and frightening as well as joyful, intimate, and sweet. The paradoxical view takes little for granted, including the two-gender system, the assumption of the "heterosexual imperative," and romantic views such as the belief that monogamy and high sex drive are compatible.

From the paradoxical point of view, the "queer" community is particularly interesting because of its sheer diversity and inventiveness. Extremes of sex and gender behavior can be observed in quite psychologically healthy, indeed brilliant, individuals. The community, particularly that which is concentrated in urban centers, validates and seems to encourage pushing the envelope of tradition. An illustration is the case of Martin, a 38-year-old academician, prestigious in his field and in many ways quite mainstream. When I first saw Martin in my office, he was married with two young children and a house in a quiet suburban community. After attaining tenure and approaching midlife, Martin took stock of his life and for the first time since early adolescence started acting on his homoerotic desires. Over a period of 3 years he finally, painfully extricated himself from his marriage while negotiating joint custody of his daughter and son, and he ultimately partnered with another man with children. But Martin changed in other ways as well. He began to explore leather bars and dominant/submissive sexuality and played with what is sometimes called "gender bending" or "gender fuck" (Califia, 1994): a muscle tee shirt with a strand of pearls. He challenged his traditional concepts of relationship, negotiating with his partner a version of an "open relationship," sometimes called "modified monogamy" (Shernoff, 1999). In many ways, once Martin broke the gay taboo he was free to question many more of his beliefs and turned his brilliance to inventing an authentic and original life. In the queer community all stereotypes and beliefs about sex and gender are both confirmed and disconfirmed. The male tendency to split lust and love and pursue the former relentlessly is evidenced at its extreme, but gay men also write and speak openly about sex, including group sex and anonymous sex, as a spiritual experience. Some lesbians consider themselves "butches" or "femmes," but the "butch" may be the caretaker or she may be, as it is sometimes quipped, "butch in the streets and femme in the sheets." There are male-to-female transgendered lesbians and support groups for gay male semen donors used by some lesbians desiring children. There are several lesbian-produced, lesbian-oriented porn magazines thriving for over a decade, an annual anthology of "best lesbian/bi women's written erotica," lesbian topless bars, and a lesbian sadomasochistic club sponsoring group "play parties" in every major urban center in the country.

From the paradoxical paradigm, the queer community has much to teach the mainstream. So this chapter has two goals: to help heterosexual sex therapists become better service providers for their sexual minority clients and to give a glimpse of the rich information to be gleaned from a community that is a living laboratory for fearless sex and gender experiments.

PSYCHOLOGICAL ISSUES AND THE GAY COMMUNITY

Just as treatment of mainstream clients depends on social trends and developments (e.g., the treatment of erectile dysfunction changed radically with the development of Viagra), the issues sexual minority clients bring to therapy depend on their subcultural context. This section ties together history with psychological issues.

Psychotherapists working with sexual minorities should be aware that the very existence of these minorities is a recent cultural phenomenon. For example, the form assumed by homosexuality in the last half century is somewhat unique. Throughout most of history, same-sex behavior was just that—acts, not "essential" nature. By contrast, in most Western industrialized nations today, homosexuality not only connotes a preferred sexual partner but also represents an identity, a lifestyle, and a subculture (Boswell, 1980). Sexual minorities can be compared to racial or ethnic minorities, but this comparison is only partially accurate. Because sexual preferences are not usually passed from one generation to the next, gays and other subgroups cannot count on family-of-origin networks to help buttress them against prejudice or hostility from the mainstream culture. Moreover, gayness, unlike skin color but like many other aspects of sexuality, can be hidden, and thus individual gay people have the option of "passing" for straight with all the psychological issues attendant to that choice. In this regard, many gays could be compared to, for example, Jews who change their names and try to assimilate, or light-skinned blacks who "pass" for whites.

1969: The Beginnings of an Open Community

In its current visible form, the existence of the "gay community" can be dated from the 1969 "Stonewall Rebellion," a protest in Greenwich Village that marked the start of the "Gay Liberation Movement." Before the 1970s, there was a nearly universal consensus among Americans that homosexuality was an illness, a sin, or both. Gay people themselves shared this belief. Even the most self-accepting homosexuals saw themselves as inferior to the heterosexual mainstream. Before Stonewall, the political efforts of homosexual groups centered on convincing society that homosexuality was a congenital disability for which the homosexual was blameless. Homosexuals never considered "coming out of the closet"; gay people did their best to "pass" for straight and suppress or at least hide their gay feelings. Moreover, it could be dangerous to act on one's gay attractions. Homosexuals could be jailed or committed to psychiatric institutions. Police raids on gay bars and other social gatherings were frequent, and those caught in the police net were ruined by the publicity attendant to the crackdowns (Katz, 1976).

Stonewall and Gay Liberation signaled a radical cultural change that began with the view homosexuals had of themselves. The liberation movement helped gays affirm the soundness and positive aspects of their orientation: "Gay is good" became a rallying cry just as "black is beautiful" had been in the 1960s. In urban areas of the country, gay people "came out" and built communities that could support them as families of origin often could not. Shame was replaced by pride. Most significantly, during the 1970s, gay men and lesbians "came out"—went public with their orientation—in ways that made it impossible for many Americans to dismiss homosexuality as something "out there" that happened to "others." Before Stonewall, information about homosexuality was scarce, and what did exist was uniformly negative. By the end of the 1970s, most Americans had been exposed to some version of the "gay and proud" theme, if only via watching gay people on television talk shows. Many had experienced a friend or family member "coming out" to them. Because of these cultural changes, gay people who were adolescents after 1970 usually seem more comfortable with their orientation and less psychologically scarred by their experiences than those born before the mid-1950s.

Gay men and lesbians developed their communities in quite different ways. Gay men clustered in large urban centers where they developed an almost quintessentially male culture, complete with hypermasculine appearance—short hair and mustaches, Levis, and work boots. Many gay men viewed the freedom to have sex as a cornerstone of gayness. Even in the prosexual atmosphere of the 1970s, gay men had more sexual opportunities than did anyone else—they could act on the traditional male fantasy (lots of sex, little commitment), unfettered by the traditional female fantasy (lots of intimacy and commitment) with which heterosexuals still had to contend.

When Bell and Weinberg (1978) published their study of gay men and lesbians in the San Francisco area, many people were shocked to learn that some gay men had had 500 to 1,000 different sexual partners during adulthood. But, in fact, accumulating so many different partners was not too difficult for a gay man living in San Francisco in the 1970s. With the abundance of bathhouses and "back rooms" where sex might occur in "orgy" style, one man could have several different partners in one night. It would be a mistake to characterize this behavior as pathological, although certainly some few men did become compulsive sexual "addicts." Nor was this behavior a flight from intimacy. As McWhirter and Mattison (1984) point out in their groundbreaking book on gay couples, most gay men eventually formed committed partnerships that often lasted for long periods, a finding corroborated by Blumstein and Schwartz's (1983) study comparing gay, lesbian, and heterosexual couples. But gay men tended to couple in a manner distinctly geared to their lifestyles: Most had mutually consensual nonmonogamous relationships.

Another aspect of gay male sexuality as it evolved in the 1970s was the development of "high-tech sex." Not only did gay men have more sex than anyone else, they also experimented with forms of sexuality previously associated only with fetishists. For example, Jay and Young (1979) report that 37% of gay men had experiences with sadomasochistic practices, 23% with "water sports" (urination), and 22% with "fist fucking" (insertion of hand into partner's anus, etc.). Sex therapists inexperienced with the gay male community often equate these practices with fetishism, but they lack the rigidity of what is ordinarily considered a fetish. Gay male sexuality in the 1970s pushed sexual boundaries and included a wide range of sometimes rather exotic sexual techniques.

At the same time that gay men were building a community emphasizing sexual experimentation, novelty, and diversity, lesbians were building communities based on feminist principles. For many gay women, feminism became the foundation of their orientation. Many lesbians seemed to see men—including gay men—as oppressive, and if they acted politically, they were apt to do so in feminist or lesbian-only organizations rather than in a "gay rights" context (Stein, 1993). Often lesbians were interested in "reclaiming" areas of life—spirituality, history, family structure, the arts—that had been male dominated and that had ignored women's needs and voices. Not only was sex *not* the focus of lesbianism, it was actually quite a problematic issue.

In the 1970s (and to a lesser extent in the present) feminist interest in sexuality often focused on the sexual exploitation of women. Rape, incest, and pornography occupied center stage; women's sexual pleasure was less discussed or explored. Within the lesbian community this perspective resulted in the promulgation of sometimes absurd standards of "politically correct" sex. Anything associated with stereotypical heterosexual sex was viewed automatically as "patriarchal," even when practiced by two women. Thus, many lesbians came to define as "politically incorrect" such behaviors as the attraction to or desire to wear "feminine" clothing or makeup, any sexual act that involved a more "active" and more "passive" partner, "rough" sex, fantasies involving domination/ submission or overpowerment, and sometimes even the desire to penetrate a partner or be penetrated oneself.

This attitude toward sex proved stifling for many women. To make matters worse, whereas gay men usually defined their orientation as a visceral sexual attraction over which they had no control, lesbians tended to define their orientation as a political or relationship choice and not necessarily an indication of where their exclusive or even strongest sexual attraction lay. Thus, some self-defined lesbians were in essence bisexual women who, for various reasons, choose not to act on their heterosexual sexual attractions. A great many of these women felt ashamed of their heterosexual fantasies or attractions, just as a primarily heterosexual person might feel frightened by his or her homosexual fantasies and attractions (Nichols, 1988, 1990).

Clearly, gay male and lesbian lifestyles, behaviors, identities, and values evolved differently following the early gay liberation and feminist movements. But this changed radically in the 1980s because of two phenomena: the divergence of lesbianism from feminism and the AIDS epidemic.

The 1980s: The Impact of HIV

In the United States, AIDS was first noticed in the gay male community. As early as 1981, when the Centers for Disease Control called it GRID (Gay Related Immune Deficiency Syndrome), gay activists were debating the implications of this disease for the gay male community. At first, many gay men resisted the idea that HIV was communicated sexually; it was even believed that the "sexual communicability" concept was a government plot to undermine the gay male community (Shilts, 1987).

Within the gay community there was virulent debate about such things as shutting down gay bathhouses, a central source of multiple anonymous sexual encounters for gay men. As the death toll mounted, gay men became increasingly frightened and the community became more sexually conservative. Within a few years, the kind of sexual activity that had previously seemed "liberating" and "life affirming" became a potential death sentence. As a consequence, in the 1980s incidence of casual and anonymous sex among gay men dropped precipitously as venues of public sex one by one closed down. Sexual practices changed: Anal sex became rare, oral sex was done with caution or condoms, and mutual masturbation gained primacy.

In part, AIDS had a profoundly negative impact on how gay men viewed their sexuality. Many gay men came to view penises and ejaculate as "toxic" or dangerous. Inhibited sexual desire and sexual aversion, problems once rarely encountered among gay men, became more widespread. A few men found themselves unable to stop unsafe sex practices, and the concept of "sex addiction" was discussed for the first time in the gay male community. The heterosexual community seemed to place blame on gay men for AIDS ("You deserve this disease because you caused it by your sinful promiscuous behavior"), and, not surprisingly, some gay men blamed themselves as well. An entire generation of young gay men had never experienced a time that sex was not deadly. But most gay men responded to the challenge of AIDS with ingenious safer sex scripts. Thousands of men participated in safe-sex workshops designed by their peers. AIDS prevention emphasized eroticizing safe sex as well as basics of transmission. New video and print pornography was produced to provide visual images of "hot" safe sex.

The gay male sexual norms developed in the 1970s were modified but not destroyed in the 1980s. Although the number of monogamous couples increased, a substantial number of male relationships remained nonexclusive. Bathhouses and back rooms were shut down for a time, but other private clubs emerged in which safe sex was the norm. For example, "jack off" (J.O.) clubs proliferated, as did other private sex clubs where penetration was not allowed. Telephone sex became more widespread. Gay men greatly modified their sexual and relationship behavior but never completely mimicked the heterosexual norm.

Meanwhile, lesbians became *more* interested in sex. During the 1980s the lesbian community fostered a sex radical movement that continues to grow and that is unparalleled by heterosexual women. The sex radicals included both lesbian and bisexual women and did much more than promote the joys of sex. They engaged in, described, and advertised sex that included activities considered outside the boundaries of "normal" female sexuality: rough sex, "dirty" sex, role-polarized sex, "promiscuity," anonymous sex, sex without love, and sadomasochistic sex.

By the mid-1980s, some women were producing pornographic magazines for lesbians and lesbian video porn that included scenes with dildoes, vaginal "fist fucking," and bondage and submission. Other lesbians created support organizations for women who enjoyed unusual or kinky sex. These groups met to demonstrate sexual techniques and to hold sex parties that ranged from "jill-off" events (modeled after "jack-off" clubs) to public forums for group sadomasochistic activities.

As the feminist influence within the lesbian community waned in the 1980s, many gay women shed the antimale attitudes that had helped contribute to lesbians and gay men forming, for the most part, separate communities. In addition, lesbians responded to illness in their gay male brothers in noteworthy ways: In some areas of the country, lesbians actually formed a greater part of the community caregiving system for people with AIDs than did gay men. This brought lesbians and gay men into intimate contact. The so-called lesbian baby boom that started toward the end of the 1980s also helped to break down barriers: As many lesbians began to raise little boys, they bonded with gay men in order to provide role models and "uncles" for their children.

During the 1980s and early 1990s a "bisexual pride" movement began within the gay community. Most people view bisexuality with suspicion. Frequently, gays and lesbians see the bisexual as a gay person who is too afraid to "come out." Sometimes this has been the case: The gay community abounds with stories of men and women who use the bisexual label to avoid facing their homosexual attractions. But in recent years the scientific discourse about bisexuality has increased (Klein & Wolf, 1985), as has the publication of personal testimonials (Hutchins & Kaahumanu, 1991). As knowledge increases and prejudice softens, more bisexuals feel comfortable being open about their orientation. Although bisexuality is stigmatized within both the gay and heterosexual community, most self-identified bisexuals now consider themselves part of the gay community and feel more tolerance from gays and lesbians than from heterosexuals Moreover, by the end of the 1990s acceptance had increased enough so that most gay organizations now identify themselves as "gay, lesbian, and bisexual."

In addition, the 1990s saw the inclusion of transgendered people, particularly those with bisexual or gay sexual attractions, within the gay community. The traditional categories of "transsexual" versus "transvestite" seem to have largely been abandoned in favor of an array of gender/orientation variations that ranges from postoperative transsexuals who self-define as homosexual to "he/shes"—men who retain their penises but dress as females and take hormones to increase breast size and change secondary sex characteristics.

The last trend that emerged in the 1980s was the change in the style of gay political action. Many gay people believed that the U.S. government engaged in deliberate nonresponse to HIV and thus passively encouraged the devastation of an entire generation of gay men. Enraged and cynical, some AIDS ac-

tivists eschewed orderly marches and legislative reform in favor of more mili-
tant tactics, akin to the tactics used in the anti-Vietnam movement. ACT UP,
one such group, specialized in clever and highly newsworthy civil disobedience
actions and enjoyed widespread support during its existence. With ACT UP,
gay politics came full circle from the pre-Stonewall days, when homosexuals
asked nicely for tolerance for their "disability." Now, gays used in-your-face
tactics to show their rage against a power structure perceived as willfully allowing gay men to die.

The 1990s and Beyond: The Emergence of the Queer Nation

In the community that came to describe itself as "lesbian, gay, bisexual, and
transgendered," the last decade of the century was characterized by increasing
social acceptance, continued breakdown of sex and gender categories, expanding
diversity of lifestyle, and a "role reversal" in sexual attitudes of men and women.

For any gay person born in the baby-boom generation or before, the ac-
culturation of homosexuals into the heterosexual community seems to have
proceeded at warp speed. Within only 30 years, same-sex lifestyle and identity
became visible instead of hidden and tolerated (if not accepted) by most Americans. It has become possible for even those whose career is in the public eye—
congresspeople, entertainment celebrities—to increasingly "come out." Corporate America, quick to seize on opportunity, has addressed major ad
campaigns to gays, especially gay men, whose household income is the highest
of any group in the country. By the turn of the century, Ikea Furniture had run
television ads featuring same-sex couples, Absolut Vodka is a staple ad of all
gay magazines, and Ellen de Generes "came out" on prime-time TV. In some
ways, the lesbian and gay lifestyle has lost its "edge" and become assimilated.
But this is only superficially true. In fact, the community has greatly expanded
its diversity.

The number of self-identified bisexuals appears to be increasing, and some
of this increase comes from the ranks of those who previously identified as gay
(Nichols, 1994). This appears to be particularly common within the lesbian
community—for example, a support group of bisexual women in the North-
east calls itself the "Hasbians." The increase in self-acknowledged bisexuality
has gone hand in hand with increased tolerance from the gay community:

> For a long time, I was afraid to say I was bisexual, because it was largely regarded
> as a term for a lesbian who didn't want to "fess up" and I knew women who were
> like this and who used the term this way. I've only started calling myself "bisexual"
> in the last five years because the term seems to have lost the "closed lesbian"
> connotation. (Beemyn & Eliason, 1996, p. 73)

At the Institute for Personal Growth (IPG), the agency I founded and direct, which has worked intensively with a gay population since 1979, the populations of clients has increasingly included bisexual women who previously

identified as lesbian but still consider themselves part of the gay community. Alison, for example, came to IPG in 1981 with her partner of 10 years for couple counseling. At that time, both Alison and Marcia, her lover, were lesbian–feminist activists raising a son, Brian, to whom Marcia had given birth in a previous heterosexual marriage. In 1997 Alison returned for help grieving the loss of her relationship with Joseph, with whom she had connected after breaking up with Marcia. Alison continued to act as a parent to Brian—she helped pay for his college education and had recently bought him a car. She identified as bisexual and held a position as treasurer for a large New York City support group for lesbian/bisexual women interested in sadomasochistic sex.

Because prejudice against bisexuality has waned within the community, men and women "coming out" now seem to have less conflict self-labeling as bisexual. Cindy, a student at a nearby university, identified herself as a "lesbian bisexual" when she first sought treatment for depression. Most of her sexual and romantic partners were female, but she sometimes had casual sex with men—usually bisexual men—and on one occasion felt she had fallen in love with a man. Unlike her counterparts from earlier decades, Cindy had no anxiety about her identity, did not fear exclusion from her community, and did not see her behavior or feelings as contradictory. Martin, the man mentioned earlier, could easily acknowledge his attractions to women and inherent bisexuality despite taking on a gay male identity. Even a decade earlier this would have been difficult; a man in a similar situation might feel pressured to hide his attraction to his former wife.

Similarly, gender categories are breaking down and becoming more ambiguous, and the categories of "homosexual" and "transgendered" overlap more and more. In the lesbian community, a subgroup of women label themselves as "butch" or "femme" (Nestle, 1992). "Radical Fairies" is a group of gay men who see cross-dressing in political terms. Once again, many younger lesbians and gays take gender ambiguity—sometimes called "gender fuck" or "gender bending"—for granted: "My gender identity is as fluid as the rest of me . . . I am a 24-year old woman who also identifies as a teenage boy" (Bernstein & Silberman, 1996, p. 221).

Some transsexuals now challenge the two-gender model as well. Kate Bornstein (1994), a male-to-female lesbian transsexual, considers herself a third gender, not a "woman trapped in a male body." Her stance is radical: "One answer to the question 'Who is a transsexual?' might well be, 'Anyone who admits it.' A more political answer might be, 'Anyone whose performance of gender calls into question the construct of gender itself'" (p. 121).

The breakdowns of gender are evident in interesting ways. Peter, a transgendered client recently seen at IPG, was helped in therapy to recognize that his gender identity seemed to be changing in unpredictable ways over time, and he learned to resist the temptation to push himself into a bad fit with either gender category. At the time he left therapy, he dressed as a woman a substantial part of the time, had recognized attractions to men as well as to women, and felt that for the moment he did not want to go further with sex hormones or surgery, although he left that option open for the future. Claire, a postoperative male-to-female transsexual, also recognized her attractions to women after surgery and when she left therapy was partnered with another bisexual (genetic) female. Daniel, a bisexual man in a nonmonogamous marriage to a bisexual woman, came for treatment with questions about gender identity. Eventually Daniel recognized that his "gender-switch" needs were circumscribed: He enjoyed cross-dressing within the privacy of his home and enjoyed sex with men, but not with women, while cross-dressed. Another client, Genevieve, found the butch–femme movement a godsend. Her attractions were only to feminine women, and for years she had "felt like a man" and agonized about sex reassignment surgery. Joining a "butch support group" helped her validate her internal experience; she found she no longer felt a need for anatomical change

An unusually striking example of gender attitude shifts is the case of Lisa, who first sought therapy at IPG in the early 1980s. At the age of 22 Lisa identified as a "radical/separatist/lesbian/feminist," and sought help in controlling her rage at men, which was getting in the way of employment. In 1997, IPG received a call from Lee—who identified himself as the former Lisa and was now a transsexual male who had undergone double mastectomy but still retained female genitals.

In the 1990s many lesbians and gay men made more "traditional" life choices. There was a large increase in the number of gay men raising children, primarily through adoption or co-parenting with lesbians, and a growing trend for gay men to create communities in small towns, where the lifestyle is more couple and family oriented and less sexual (Signorile, 1997). The proliferation of parenting options available to infertile heterosexuals has also filtered to the gay community. For example, Richard, a single gay man in his early 40s, recently became the father of a boy carried by a surrogate mother with Richard's sperm and an egg donated by a close female friend with children of her own.

The phenomenon of lesbians choosing motherhood has become so common that younger women "coming out" seem to see motherhood as an option to nearly the same degree as do heterosexual women. Lesbian and bisexual women climb the corporate ladder—they are sometimes called "execudykes"; they spend money on clothes and makeup and balance home and career in much the same way as do heterosexual women except that, unlike heterosexual women, they have partners who tend to share housework and childrearing equally. Both lesbians and gay men are united in a strong movement to obtain the right to legally marry.

Within the lesbian community, the 1990s has marked the emergence of an ethos of diversity and respect for individual difference that stands in sharp contrast to earlier years in which "personal is political" seemed to mean "there is only one correct way to live." Thus the explosion of lesbians choosing motherhood has been matched by an explosion of lesbians choosing lusty sexual expression.

In San Francisco today, the hottest lesbian club hosts a once-a-week splash that unabashedly features go-go dancers on pedastals and patrons clad in leather miniskirts. Across town sixty or seventy women gather to discuss the legal ins and outs of donor insemination, foster adoption programs, power of attorney contracts, and parenting. . . . There are many other signs of lesbian life . . . but few seem to capture the spirit of the moment so completely as femmes strutting around in their lipstick and high heels and the prospective mothers worrying about the quality of the school system. (Stein, 1993, p. xi)

Lesbian sexual styles are developing quite differently from what main-stream culture has come to think of as "women's sexuality," usually translated as romantic, gentle, sensual sexual expression. The emerging lesbian sexual scene has been influenced more by gay men than by heterosexual women. With organizations with names such as Lesbian Sex Mafia, bars named Clit Club, magazines named *On Our Backs, Bad Attitude,* and *Cunt,* lesbians

are moving beyond the realm of Sisterhood into the world of the nasty, the sexy, and the tasty. We are pushing the boundaries of what is acceptable lesbianism. We use the word "fuck" like the boys used to, we wear lipstick, we lust openly and pridefully . . . fuck, suck, clit, cunt. These are the words of our sex, and these are the words of our empowerment. (Stein, 1993, pp. 48, 88)

As the lesbian community seems to have become more respectful of individual sexual freedom, the gay male community is engaged in bitter controversy about sex. By the end of the first decade of HIV, the rate of new infection in the gay male population had dropped to nearly zero. While new infection rates continue to be low, in recent years the 1970s style hedonistic lifestyle reemerged among urban middle-class gay males in the form of a series of huge all-night dance parties, held at varying locations and thus called "the circuit." Ironically, these parties are sometimes fund raisers for AIDS organizations. They are distinguished by enormous amounts of both drugs and sex. Symbolic of the controversy about circuit parties was the announcement in 1999 by the New York City Gay Men's Health Crisis, the world's largest HIV service organization, that it would no longer hold its annual "Morning Party" fund raiser on the Fire Island Pines, because in recent years it had been the site of several drug overdoses and numerous alleged incidents of unsafe sex.

Even more controversial than circuit parties is the recent phenomenon in urban gay male communities that is called "barebacking"—the reemergence of anal sex without the use of condoms. What is unusual is that there are public advocates of barebacking and a vigorous public discourse (Gendin, 1999; Scarce, 1999). Barebackers and their supporters regard the promoters of safe sex, from the Centers for Disease Control to AIDS prevention workers in the gay community, as "condom nazis" whose messages are erotophobic and hypocritical. They point out that many safe-sex edicts are rational on the surface but moralistic in essence (Browning, 1994). For example, three commonly cited sex safe "rules" are (1) reduce the overall number of your sexual partners; (2) avoid anal sex, especially anal sex without a condom, under all circumstances; and (3) eliminate "fisting" (anal penetration by the hand) and "rimming" (analingus) entirely.

In fact, none of these activities are necessary to reduce the risk of HIV infection. Since the mid-1980s, most HIV sexual transmission, even among gay men, has taken place between steady sex partners, so the admonition to reduce numbers of partners is misleading an unnecessary. Although passive anal sex is almost certainly the most common route of sexual transmission of HIV, passive vaginal sex is also a common route and yet heterosexuals were never warned to "avoid vaginal sex." Moreover, the "never without a condom" rule is unnecessary between two monogamous partners with the same HIV status. Finally, "fisting" and "rimming" are most definitely not routes of transmission of HIV; their inclusion as "unsafe acts" is barely veiled moral repugnancy.

Proponents of barebacking feel, with some justification, that HIV ushered in an era in which sex-negative, homophobic attitudes became validated. They take a harm-reduction view of prevention, reasoning that no sex is entirely "safe" from various risks. They value sex as part of gay male identity; some see sex as a path to spiritual union. The public champions of barebacking advocate certain rules for containing risk and providing information needed to make responsible, consensual decisions. For example, most barebacking parties follow one of two scripts: Either they are limited only to HIV-positive men or they require HIV-positive men to identify themselves publicly and only bareback in the anal receptive position, which carries less transmission risk than does anal insertive.

The emergence of barebacking may in part stem from changes in the treatment of HIV. In the mid-1990s new medications—protease inhibitors in combination with older drugs—transformed HIV from an always fatal illness to one that for many is instead a lifetime disability. The impact of this development has been too enormous to describe fully here, but two trends stand out. A large number of men who had literally prepared for death—cashed in their life insurance to viatical companies, made no preparations for the future, refrained from establishing intimate relationships—suddenly became nearly well. With this reprieve came unexpected psychological and practical difficulties that have been labeled the "Lazarus syndrome" (Ragaza, 1999).

A recent couple therapy case at IPG exemplifies this phenomenon. Victor and Howard were an HIV-discordant couple who had been together for 5 years when the new medications came on the market. Howard, the HIV-infected partner, responded dramatically to these drugs. Both men were forced to look closely at a relationship that both had assumed would end within a few more years. As a consequence of the "Lazarus syndrome," the couple broke up. Victor, the HIV-negative partner, had felt obligated to remain with Howard to take care of him while he died, and Howard was afraid to die alone. Once death was no longer an imminent possibility, both men realized that they did not have enough in common to sustain a relationship that might last decades.

The emergence of AIDS in the 1980s and the transformation of the disease from a certain death sentence to a long-term illness 15 years later has created sharply defined generational differences within the gay and lesbian community. While the baby-boom generation of gays and lesbians has lost unprecedented numbers of peers to early death, and the generation of gay men under 35 never knew a time when sex was "safe," the youngest members of the gay community have never known a gay person who died of AIDS.

Some fear that these rapid changes may result in a higher rate of seroconversion among young gay men. This week a young lesbian cried in my office because her 27-year-old gay male brother had just tested seropositive for HIV—after testing negative 4 months ago. The brother contracted HIV from a male sex partner who lied about his serostatus. Ten years ago few gay men would have considered having anal-receptive unprotected sex with anyone but a long-term, committed lover—and then they took the test and were given results together.

The rapid and dramatic changes in the gay community in the last 30 years of the 20th century have produced a phenomenon familiar to heterosexuals: a generation gap. Nonheterosexual men and women born after 1970 "came out," for the most part, during or after the development of AIDS activism. They often differentiate themselves sharply from older gays by calling themselves "queer," just as young black urban men use the term "nigga" in part to defuse the power of an epithet of bigotry and in part to distinguish themselves from their community elders.

> The term "queer" emphasizes the blurring of identities . . . the queer movement/community was founded on principles of inclusivity and flexibility. (Beemyn & Eliason, 1996, p. 170)

> The word "queer" breaks down boundaries among microcommunities (lesbians, gay men, bisexuals, transgendered people, fags, dykes, perverts) and gives us a united queer community. . . . (Bernstein & Silberman, 1996, xviii)

"Generation Q" feels alienated from older gays and lesbians. Myers-Parelli, a young lesbian, discusses her coming out to her parents.

> When a lesbian comes out, the books read, parents are supposed to faint/cry/scream/disown you/deny/argue. But all mine said was "So?" If my coming out was not following the course that other lesbians had charted, I wondered, then how much of the rest of my life would their experiences apply to? (Bernstein & Silberman, 1996, p. 213)

ISSUES AND CASES IN SEX THERAPY

Sex therapy with "queer" clients is not so different from sex therapy with straight clients except insofar as issues of sexual identity, alternative lifestyles, and more "kinky" sexual practices may become the focus of treatment. Case vignettes are be offered to highlight the kinds of problems and issues that arise in work with these diverse and intriguing clients.

At IPG we find it useful to ask questions in the assessment phase of treatment that are not asked of heterosexual clients (see Appendix). These questions yield valuable information about, for example, the degree to which the individual may feel confusion or self-hatred about his or her sexuality and whether there may be elements of his or her gender or sexual identity that may be ego-dystonic. Gay men who were "sissy" boys often have been deeply damaged by the reactions of others to them in childhood; both lesbians and gay men may be troubled if their fantasies and/or attractions do not match their self-labeling.

There are some sexual problems that therapists are more or less likely to see in the lesbian and gay male population than among heterosexual clients. Vaginismus and dyspareunia are almost never complaints for lesbians; women who experience these difficulties tend to avoid penetrative sex. Delayed ejaculation does not trouble gay men as frequently as straight men: Many gay men include in their repertoires an acceptance of masturbation as a way to "end" a sexual encounter. Aversion to oral sex, on the other hand, is a common complaint. Especially since HIV made anal sex taboo for many gay males, oral sex is often as important a sexual act for gay men and women as vaginal penetration is for heterosexuals.

Therapists who work with gay, lesbian, and heterosexual couples are often struck by the absence of gender-specific roles among gay and lesbian couples. Even in couples in which the partners seem role stereotyped in physical appearance, these apparent roles rarely hold up in actual behavior. The partner who looks masculine may be the one who enjoys children and keeping house, whereas the woman who loves lipstick and high heels may also be the one who does household plumbing repairs. Most important, it is rare to find one member of a gay or lesbian couple totally financially dependent on the other, and it is less common for a gay or lesbian household to contain children. Thus, gay couples obviously are less likely to stay together because one person is financially dependent on the other or "for the sake of the kids." These differences make the power dynamics in gay couples somewhat different and, interestingly, make the quality of their sexual/intimate relationship assume a higher priority than in more traditional heterosexual marriages.

However, even if roles in same-sex relationships tend to be a bit more variable and fluid, roles in the bedroom may be rigidified. This problem is a bit easier to deal with in same-sex couples. For one thing, same-sex partners are not dealing with opposing sexual role expectations (e.g., male must initiate, female must be submissive) as are heterosexual partners. Gay men and lesbians tend to have a more varied sexual repertoire than do heterosexuals; penetration is not the main focus of sexual activity for either men or women. Lesbians, and especially gay men, often have a knowledge of sexual technique that may surpass that of the therapist, and because there is nothing in gay sex comparable to the heterosexual emphasis on vaginal intercourse, they may be more willing to experiment with new sexual approaches.

Nonmonogamy

Gay male couples (and some lesbian couples) often have sexually nonexclusive relationships (Shernoff, 1999). Both men and women in gay relationships sometimes request help in conducting nonmonogamous relationships within the context of a primary commitment to one partner. In these cases most nongay therapists have to examine their own beliefs about nonmonogamy. Most people, including sex therapists, are raised to regard nonmonogamy as sinful or destructive and are reluctant to acknowledge that sexual openness can work quite well for many couples provided that conflicts arising from jealousy and other issues are adequately anticipated and addressed.

The therapist can help the couple construct "rules of conduct" for nonmonogamy that will minimize pain and strife, and when nonmonogamy works it often actually enhances the sexual relationship of the primary partners.

Case 1

With the aid of a counselor, Joe and Harold, monogamous partners for 2 years, negotiated a transition to nonmonogamy that began with joint expeditions to "jack off" parties, moved to "three-ways," and eventually permitted both Joe and Harold to have independent sexual contacts provided that these contacts were "one-night stands." Sally and Jessica were in conflict because Sally felt unable to commit to monogamy, and Jessica was doubtful about her ability to handle her jealousy. In therapy, the two women negotiated an agreement in which Sally was permitted outside affairs as long as Jessica never knew about them; that is, Sally could not see women who were mutual acquaintances and had to conduct her affairs so that Jessica would not find out.

Nonmonogamy tends to be more common among gay male couples and also tends to be more successful. In large part, this is because gay men (like their heterosexual counterparts) can often separate sex and love quite easily and are satisfied with extramarital encounters that are purely sexual. By contrast, lesbians (like most women) fuse sex and love and tend to want not casual sexual encounters but "affairs" that are potentially more threatening to the primary relationship.

Just as nonmonogamy is a common issue for many gay male couples, lesbian couples often suffer from fusion or the existence of such intense closeness and intimacy that the individual identities of the two women become completely submerged in the couple (Nichols, 1990, 1988). Fusion is often an underlying cause of inhibited sexual desire in lesbian couples, the most frequent sexual complaint among gay women. Female couples tend to have less frequent sex than either heterosexuals or gay men (Blumstein & Schwartz, 1983). Often this is not a problem, and many lesbian couples eventually cease having sex or have it rather rarely—a few times per year, for example. But when one women has a lusty sexual appetite, problems arise.

The sex therapist sometimes has access to special resources less available in the heterosexual world. Among gay men, paying for sex is so acceptable that quasi-surrogates are easily available. And lesbian erotica is so much more varied and abundant than that available to heterosexual women that a sex therapist can easily recommend a wide range of videos, magazines, and books with specific sexual variations—butch–femme sex, for example, or any of a wide variety of sadomasochistic (S/M) practices.

Identity and "Coming Out" Problems

The number of individuals seeking treatment because they are confused about their sexual orientation or because they wish to change orientation has declined dramatically in the last several decades. Consequently, the *meaning* of identity confusion is different now. In the past, an individual with same-sex attractions could be expected to experience a sometimes prolonged period of internal struggle and conflict before embracing a gay or lesbian identity (Nichols, 1995, 1990). Now, many self-identified lesbians, gays, and bisexuals "come out" to themselves and others with a minimum of fear, shame, or self-hatred. The degree to which gays and bisexuals experience "internalized homophobia" has also diminished dramatically. When clients present with severe sexual orientation confusion or self-hatred related to sexual identity, it is often symptomatic of deeper pathology.

Case 2

When Herb, a 44-year old white male computer programmer, came to our practice complaining of severe depression, his first words were, "I'm not entirely sure I'm heterosexual." Herb still lives with his aging parents and has never lived independently except for his undergraduate college years. He has had one sexual experience with a woman, which was practically coerced by the woman, and none with males. He masturbates two or three times a week and his masturbation fantasies are entirely homosexual. Herb is conscious of sexual attractions to males, which he describes as "an unnatural preoccupation with the male body." He admires women but has no experience of being sexually aroused by a woman. He "cannot imagine" being gay, despite the fact that his mother and several friends have gone out of their way to express acceptance of homosexuality and despite working in a corporation that has had an explicit policy of gay nondiscrimination for many years and has recently introduced domestic partner benefits.

Twenty years ago Herb's story was commonplace. In 2000 it is highly unusual. Therefore, we considered Herb's struggle with sexual identity symptomatic of a deeper, entrenched problem and diagnosed him with avoidant personality disorder. Our treatment goal is the same as it would have been with this presenting problem 20 years ago: to help him accept his gay orientation. However, we expect Herb's process to be longer and more difficult and assume that a lack of social skills and entrenched problems with intimacy will affect the course of treatment.

Herb's situation also reflects the continued existence of homophobia in the treatment biases of some heterosexual therapists. Before coming to IPG, Herb spent 15 years in therapy with two different heterosexual male therapists. Neither one made sexual orientation a focus of treatment, despite Herb's report that he gave the same information to these previous therapists that he gave to us. One of them avoided discussion of sexual identity completely; the other told Herb that he "did not have enough sexual experience" to determine his sexual orientation. These therapists may have colluded with Herb's avoidant behavior in a way that left Herb isolated and fearful of what would happen to him when his parents die—a realistic concern.

Case 3

The case of June is a less serious example of how the meaning of sexual identity confusion has changed over the last several decades.

June came for help in 1996, when she was 22. Like Herb, June still lived with her parents and had limited sexual experience. However, unlike Herb, June did not masturbate at all, much less masturbate to homosexual fantasy. This is not uncommon among gay women, just as women, no matter what their sexual orientation, tend to have diminished sexuality as compared to men in all areas.

The only clue to her sexuality lay in her "friendships" with other women. Several of these relationships followed the same pattern: June became so intensely involved that her life revolved around the friendship, and she became broken-hearted when the "friend" eventually became involved in a love relationship with someone else. Most recently, these "friendships" had been with self-identified lesbians.

During the course of therapy June admitted to herself that her attractions had been romantic. She was given "homework" to learn to masturbate, and in the course of learning to pleasure herself she was asked to read books of women's sexual fantasies in order to discover what turned her on. Not surprisingly, she found the lesbian fantasies most erotic. It was difficult to determine why June's sexuality had been apparently repressed for so long. She came from a politically liberal, not particularly religious family and had always lived in the New York metropolitan area, where she had abundant exposure to gay lifestyles. She was not aware of homophobic feelings and attitudes and not particularly fearful of losing family or friends if she "came out."

As treatment continued it appeared that June's "repression" was more connected to issues of independence, intimacy, and lack of social skills than to "internalized homophobia." June had great difficulty with the idea of breaking from her parents to become an autonomous adult. She was also afraid of rejection and lacked assertive abilities. Thus, even when she was more certain she "might be gay," she found it almost impossible to make her attractions obvious to the object of her desire. Although, with prodding, she joined some gay groups and developed a network of lesbian acquaintances, her relationships with women never went beyond friendship. In fact, the only shift in her object choice was that as her same-sex desires became more obvious to her, she tended to develop infatuations with lesbians already in relationships. She became the "third wheel" of these relationships, the friend who tagged along with the couple when they allowed it. June left treatment without having a sexual experience, let alone a relationship. She was, however, much clearer about her barriers to intimacy. "I'm just the kind of person who has to move slowly," she said as treatment ended. "Maybe in a few years I'll be in a relationship." In a case such as this, June's identity confusion was akin to a red herring, masking deeper problems.

Because the mainstream culture is more accepting of homosexuality, gay lifestyles are much more visible than they were only a few short years ago: the existence of openly gay celebrities such as Ellen de Generes and, yes, Melissa Etheridge was unthinkable to previous generations. Therefore, it is more common for young people to question their identity even if they are *not* gay. As recently as 20 years ago a therapist could assume that a reasonably healthy client exhibiting sexual identity confusion was very likely to be gay or at least strongly bisexual. This is no longer true.

Case 4

Tony came to therapy during his undergraduate years because in high school he had had sexual contact with a male teacher over an extended period. Tony was ashamed of this relationship and had kept it hidden from his male friends and his girlfriends. Although Tony himself raised the question whether he might be gay, his relationship with the teacher appeared to have more to do with a need for male nurturing than with sexuality. Tony was always the recipient of touching or oral sex in these encounters, and although he became aroused to orgasm, he seemed to do so in spite of the same-sex nature of the encounters rather than because of it. He reported no same-sex fantasies, attractions, or behaviors either before or after his relationship with the older man.

Tony's attitude toward his sexual identity was striking in that he seemed comparatively undisturbed by the prospect of being gay or bisexual. "I'd rather be straight," he said. "But if I am gay, I want to find out now so I don't waste my life pretending to be something I am not."

After 8 months of treatment Tony was able to let go of the disturbing feelings and memories associated with the past. He told his girlfriend, his mother, and eventually even some male friends about his experience. For a time he attended meetings of a support group for men who had been sexually abused as children. We both concluded that Tony probably was not "repressing his true feelings." Occasionally things are what they seem to be on the surface.

Sometimes the new openness about sexual orientation, especially on college campuses, creates new kinds of "coming out" problems.

Case 5

Claire was a young college student who saw me intermittently over a period of 3 years as part of treatment for her recurrent depressive disorder. When Claire was a psychology undergraduate student, she was an "out" activist for gay and women's causes and experienced few reprisals for her openness from other students or faculty. After college Claire decided to get some field experience before continuing graduate work to become a psychotherapist, so she obtained a job as an aide on the adolescent unit of a nearby private psychiatric hospital. She was shocked to discover that her openness met with virulent disapproval from staff social workers. Claire was "out" to the adolescents in her care, and as a result several of them revealed their homosexuality to her. Her openness was labeled "inappropriate" by her superiors and she was faulted for "disrupting the treatment process" of the teens on her unit. Eventually, she was unjustly accused of being sexually provocative with a young female patient and was fired. Our work then was to repair the damage done to her self-confidence and her trust of others, and, sadly, to help her develop a less idealistic vision of the world. Fortunately, she will be attending Smith College for graduate work, situated in the "lesbian capital of the world."

Case 6

Irene saw me briefly for counseling during the summer break between her freshman and sophomore years at a large Ivy League university. Her problem was ironic: In her first year away, she had confirmed for herself the lesbian identity she had felt emerging in her high school years. There was tremendous support for her identity development at the college she attended. Moreover, her parents, who had raised Irene in a bohemian neighborhood of a large city, were entirely accepting of alternative lifestyles. In fact, her mother had told her years earlier that she suspected Irene might be gay and that if this were true, the mother would do all she could to help her. But Irene found herself unable to "come out" to her parents, and this filled her with self-recrimination. Therapy helped her to understand that her reluctance to "come out" had little to do with internalized homophobia and lots to do with needing a way to separate from her liberal but overprotective parents.

Bisexuality, Nonmonogamy, Sadomasochism, and "Sexual Fringe" Issues

In the last decade sexual minority issues even more taboo than homosexuality have come bursting out of the closet. It is worth mentioning a few representative cases because sex therapists are more likely than other practitioners to encounter clients who occupy relatively unpopulated positions on the sexual landscape. In many of these situations the presenting problems have nothing to do with the unusual sex behavior. On the contrary, just as 20 years ago many gay clients sought out gay-affirmative therapists so that they *wouldn't* have to talk about their sexual orientation, so today other sexual minorities may seek out sex therapists, especially those known to work with the gay community, in order to find a professional who will not be shocked or repulsed by their lifestyle. When working with these clients, it is important that the therapist put aside preconceived concepts of "normal" and "pathological" sexuality. At IPG our rules for "pathology" are simple. We ask ourselves, "Is it consensual?" and "Is anyone clearly being damaged here?" If the answers to these questions are "yes" and "no," respectively, we consider the sexual practices nonpathological.

Case 7

Michael and Jenny are a suburban professional couple that at first glance appear conservative, even a little bland. She is an internist and he is an executive in the finance industry; together they are raising two little girls. They were referred to IPG for marriage counseling by friends in the S/M community.

For the most part, Jenny and Mike needed help with problems common to many committed, long-term partnerships, with some notable exceptions. The couple was part of the polyamory subculture, a movement comparable to the experiments with "open relationship" in the 1970s. The polyamory community has emerged in large part on the Internet, through bulletin boards and newsgroups. Polyamorists who meet and correspond with each other "on line" may eventually extend this to meeting "in the flesh."

Polyamorists have a vision of establishing extended families and small communities in which multiple committed romantic and sexual partnerships are the norm. For example, Mike and Jenny have a third man, Jim, who lives with them, serves as an "uncle" to their children, is a sexual partner of Jenny, and is Mike's best friend. All three are involved as family members and sexual partners of another polamorous trio in a nearby state. Jim and Mike have outside sexual partners as well.

When Mike and Jenny first entered couple counseling, Jim was their only "extra" partner. Mike had complaints about sex with Jenny, who was at that time his only sexual partner. His predominant sexual "script" involved physical beatings, with him as either giver of or recipient of pain. Jenny's sexual tastes were more traditional, and it was nearly impossible for her to comply with Mike's wishes. What made treatment difficult was that even though Mike greatly desired to actualize his primary script, he was capable of becoming erotically aroused by virtually any sexual activity, and for a long time he refused to believe that he was unique. Therefore, he personalized Jenny's difficulties as covert attempts to control and punish him.

One therapeutic intervention was to have Mike "interview" his friends in the polyamory community until he realized that most of them had sexual repertoires far more limited than his. Once he accepted that he might never have the sexual relationship with Jenny that he desired and mourned the loss of this fantasy, he turned his energy to active pursuit of partners who could participate in his scripts. He was successful. More recently, Mike has become close with a bisexual man. Mike very much wants to have sex with this man, primarily because he feels it would enhance the relationship. Although Mike is at most only incidentally attracted to men, he feels he can develop the ability to enjoy male–male sex because his sexuality is so flexible. Treatment interventions have included bibliotherapy and helping Mike identify ways he might find a "tutor" in the gay male community.

Case 8

Another atypical couple was Daniel, mentioned earlier as the bisexual man with gender issues, and his bisexual wife, Kate. Both self-identified as bisexual from adolescence. For the first 10 years of their marriage they were monogamous. However, they practiced monogamy not because they held it as a moral value but simply because they felt their relationship needed a lot of stability before they could "open" the relationship without damage. Daniel is probably a "Kinsey 4 or 5": more gay than straight. However, he is deeply in love with Kate and feels no conflict about giving up the possibility of a primary relationship with a man. Kate is most likely a Kinsey 2: mostly straight.

Soon past the 10-year mark in their marriage, Kate and Daniel came to IPG for help negotiating the change in the relationship. At IPG, our experience with couple counseling for gay men gave us substantial expertise with the phenomenon of nonexclusive relationships. With our help, Daniel and Kate decided that it would be less threatening for them to "open" the relationship by incorporating extra people into their couple sex rather than by having separate sexual liaisons. They located their first outside sexual contact, a bisexual man, at a support group for bisexuals. Daniel, Kate, and Luis met for sex and friendly companionship several times and the couple negotiated feelings of jealousy, exclusion, and insecurity that arose very well. However, Kate was unhappy because she wanted same-sex contact herself. They located other couples who desired this kind of sexual contact by, once again, accessing the Internet, which is a golden resource for those on the sexual "fringe." Here, however, they discovered that most "bisexual couples" were in fact heterosexual men with bisexual women, and Daniel became frustrated. After a year or so or experimentation, they finally began to locate couples where both partners were bisexual and, to their delight, found two such couples who were not only good sexual partners but good friends as well.

Desire Discrepancy and Other Sexual Script Issues

As noted earlier, the most common sexual problem that lesbians bring to treatment is desire discrepancy/inhibited sexual desire. Treatment is complicated by a number of factors. One factor that stands out as characteristic of lesbian couples is that the woman who desires sex more is usually not contented with being pleasured by her mate. She often insists that her partner be "turned on" and even have orgasm. In part this is because women have a hard time being selfish about sex. A lesbian might have a very hard time enjoying receiving pleasure without reciprocating, because she believes this is morally wrong. This makes one potential solution to discrepant desire—that the less sexual partner give but not receive pleasure at times—more difficult for the therapist to negotiate.

Compared to men, women sometimes seem to have dramatically sharp drops in sexual desire after the limerance period of a relationship wears off. When this happens to only one woman in a lesbian couple, her more desirous partner tends to feel rejected, not only because she equates decreased desire with decreased love but also because she believes "love conquers all." In other words, if the less sexual partner "really wanted to," she could feel more desire. The less sexual partner, on the other hand, may believe that high sexual desire is "objectifying" and a bit crude and may feel her lover's interest in sex is inappropriate.

Case 9

Reggie is a lesbian in her mid-30s with a strong sex drive. She and Betty had great sex for the first 6 months of their relationship. As is all too typical of lesbian couples, they moved in together and pledged undying love after 3 months. By the time Betty's interest in sex had dropped precipitously, Reggie had made plans to accompany Betty to China to bring home the daughter Betty was adopting as a single mother.

After 9 months together, the difference in sexual desire between the two women was vast; Betty probably would have been content with sex four times per year and Reggie would have liked four times per week. Had their lives been less entangled they might have parted when this became clear. Instead, with so much at stake, the couple entered sex therapy. Reggie took Betty's lack of interest very personally, and in turn Betty could not understand how sex could be so important to Reggie that she might leave a relationship because of it. In the midst of couple counseling with a lesbian therapist who seemed to subtly reinforce Betty's position, Reggie came to IPG for help. We validated her need to have sex play a strong role in her relationships, essentially helping her overcome her guilt at leaving a "marriage" entered into far too hastily.

The case of Reggie and Betty highlights another issue new to the gay and lesbian community: how to handle separations when children are involved. In this case, Betty had initiated adoption as a single parent long before meeting Reggie, and neither woman assumed that Reggie would be an equal co-parent. In fact, since the separation Reggie has attempted to stay involved with Molly, the little girl Betty adopted, with Betty's blessing. But when two women or two men have a child together, the picture is complicated and difficult. In most states, same-sex partners have neither rights nor responsibilities as co-parents. They are not expected to pay child support after separation, nor are their rights to visitation recognized. An angry and vengeful parent can often terminate the ex-lover's relationship with their child with complete legality. Fortunately, Betty and Reggie have engineered an amicable separation and Betty has her daughter's best interests at heart.

Case 10

The case of Walter and Bob, by contrast, is an example of a better working out of discrepant desire. The difference in sex drive between Walter and Bob was probably about the same as that for Reggie and Betty. But other aspects of their situation were dissimilar. Neither man believed the other was "wrong": each accepted the situation for what it was—a difference between them with no personal meaning. The discrepancy, however, had been apparent from the beginning of their relationship. Bob never showed high sexual desire, even at the height of romance. Walter, however, was pragmatic. He had had plenty of lovers in the past who were great in bed and made terrible partners, so he appreciated Bob's maturity and capacity for nonsexual intimacy. Compared to Reggie, Walter did not romanticize sex at all, nor did he believe Bob capable of extraordinary change. Further, Walter was older and had had extensive sexual experience. He did not experience the lack of earth-shattering sex in his relationship with Bob as a sadness or deprivation. Finally, both men were able to work out some compromises in which Bob "helped" Walter masturbate to orgasm when he himself was not "in the mood."

Case 11

Aurora and Shelley's sexual problems are somewhat typical of the queer community. These women began sex therapy because Shelley seemed to have lost nearly all her interest in sex with Aurora. After several months of treatment, Shelley finally admitted that she had consuming fantasies of S/M sex and felt compelled to "try it," although she had not acted on her desires up until this point. Because S/M sexual activity is so public and, by now, so generally accepted within the lesbian community, Shelley knew she could easily get support for her interests and opportunity to actualize her fantasies. Aurora, on the other hand, was an incest survivor who was horrified at the thought of sex that involved dominance and submission. Ultimately, the women separated, and Shelley became active in what is sometimes called the "leatherdyke" community.

Sex Addiction in the Millennium

Although the concept of sex addiction is fraught with opportunity for moralistic and sex-negative abuse, sometimes one works with individuals for whom no other model seems appropriate.

Case 12

Billy came for help when he felt he was destroying his relationship with Roger and endangering his own health. Before the HIV epidemic, Billy had had a "golden showers" fetish. His sex life had revolved around public scenes in the backrooms of gay bars in which scores of men urinated on him. Because this sexual activity actually carried little risk of HIV transmission, Billy had never become infected, but the AIDS epidemic resulted in the closing down of the backroom settings where Billy's sexuality had played out. Forced to change his sexual script, he began to have sex in public parks and bathrooms, acting as a "bottom" in oral sex (i.e., the person who gives oral sex and might swallow semen).

Billy became involved with Roger in 1989 and for a while he gave up public sex. But when Roger and Billy became more intimate and eventually lived together in a marriage-like arrangement, Billy found he lost interest in sex with Roger. He discovered that his desire was fully dependent on an element of risk, danger, and anonymity. He was no longer capable of play-acting dangerous sexual scenes with Roger as the two had done early in the relationship. "I can't have that kind of sex with my 'wife,'" he complained, sounding eerily like a heterosexual man. "And I'm not interested in sweet, close sex."

Billy eventually joined Sex Addicts Anonymous in desperation. For several years he was completely asexual, as even masturbation aroused almost uncontrollable urges in him to "act out." Fortunately, Roger was able to take "the long view." Roger had himself had a great deal of sex in the pre-AIDS era and was willing to sacrifice partner sex for an otherwise extraordinarily loving and intimate relationship. Even years later, Billy could only occasionally be sexual with Roger.

Case 13

Byron was addicted to the World Wide Web, but in his case his "addiction" may have been a step forward. When Byron entered treatment he was an anachronism. Well into his 50s, Byron had "come out" in the bad old days of complete shame and secrecy, and his history included flight into the priesthood to escape his sexual urges, disillusionment with the priesthood when he discovered the extent of homosexual activity within the monastery walls, and suicide attempts and hospitalizations.

Byron had never had a steady lover and rarely had sex; he was isolated and self-hating. Then he discovered the Internet. Byron invented a persona for himself of a 20-something "hunk." He scanned a picture of a young man taken from a pornographic magazine into his computer profile and corresponded with dozens of admiring cybersuitors. He because cybersexually active and his mood brightened considerably. He had some anxious moments when his suitors pressed to meet him in "3-D," or real life, but he always managed to elude this attempts at face-to-face meetings. Despite the obvious fact that his suitors were falling in love with a fictitious Byron, Byron seemed to derive satisfaction and self-esteem from these interactions. It was as though he was experiencing an adolescence he had never had a chance to explore. Byron's addiction seemed benign, and when he left treatment he had no desire to expand his sexual relationships to the flesh.

CONCLUSION

Although work within the queer community challenges the therapist to learn things not usually taught in graduate school, the clinician benefits from this work perhaps more than the client. For example, after several years of working with members of the S/M, or "leather," community, I noticed that S/M partners often had unusually good communication with each other about their sexual likes and dislikes, and I began to teach my non-S/M clients communication skills I learned from the "leather" population.

Certain attitudes and behaviors are useful in working with sexual minority clients. First, one must erase all preconceptions about "normal" and "abnormal" sex. The therapist must be open to all possibilities of erotic variation and be willing to suspend judgment. The IPG criteria may be helpful: Lack of consensuality and clear destructiveness are the only definite characteristics of "pathological" sex.

The therapist must also remember that work with this population requires suspending preconceived notions of gender and relationships as well as biases about sexual acts. Many clients who live on the sexual "fringe" desperately need to have their lifestyle validated by an "authority figure." This validation is surely a major aspect of the therapeutic experience for most clients who are socially stigmatized.

Counselors must also stay current with developments in the queer community. A subscription to a gay magazine, trips to a local gay bookstore, or periodic searches at websites like, for example, amazon.com are helpful, as continuing education courses about the sexual fringe are difficult to find.

The therapist who works with the queer community must not be afraid to admit not knowing. It is often useful to ask clients themselves for information; they feel flattered and more empowered in their own treatment.

Although this chapter of necessity emphasizes *differences*, it is useful to remember that we are all more alike than we are different. Colorful and unusual differences in behavior and style may be prominent in minority clients; nevertheless, most therapeutic interventions will not vary that much from interventions used in a more mainstream population.

APPENDIX: SEXUAL ORIENTATION/ GENDER IDENTITY QUESTIONNAIRE

1. Which of the following best describe how you think of yourself? (check all that apply)

   _____ bisexual   _____ transvestite, heterosexual
   _____ possibly gay/lesbian   _____ transvestite, gay or bisexual
   _____ definitely gay/lesbian   _____ transexual, hetersexual
   _____ heterosexual   _____ transsexual, gay or bisexual
   _____ unsure   _____ do not label myself

2. At what age did you first feel "different" regarding your gender or sexuality?
   _____ years old
   Please describe what made you feel different: _____
   _____

3. Did you/do you spend part of your life denying your feelings or identity to yourself? _____ no _____ yes. If yes, describe: _____
   _____
   _____

4. Which of the following statements best describes your feelings about your sexuality and/or identity?
   ___ I am confused and unsure about my sexuality and/or identity.
   ___ I am trying to change and be like "normal" people.
   ___ I feel I cannot change, but I wish I could.
   ___ I accept my sexuality/identity and do not think much about it.
   ___ I feel fine about it.
   ___ I am glad I'm different.

5. If you feel sure of who you are (i.e., do not feel uncertain of your sexual orientation or gender identity) when did you "come out" to yourself? _____
   _____

   What were the circumstances? _____
   _____

6. Have you ever tried to change your identity or orientation? _____ no _____ yes

Have you ever been suicidal over it? ___ no ___ yes. If yes to either, please describe: _____

_____

7. When you were young, were you a "tomboy" girl or a "sissy" boy?
   ___ no ___ yes. If yes, how did you, your family, and peers react?

   _____

   _____

8. How old were you when you first started to masturbate? ____ years
   If you have fantasies while you masturbate, please describe:

   _____

9. Please describe your first sexual experiences with another person (include your age and partner's age): _____

   _____

10. How many different opposite-sex partners have you had? _____
    Briefly describe these experiences:

    _____

    _____

11. How many different same-sex partners have you had? _____
    Briefly describe these experiences:

    _____

    _____

12. Have you had exposure to other people who are/might be "like you" (e.g., the gay community, the transgendered community, the bisexual community)
    ___ no ___ yes. If yes, please describe: _____

    _____

13. Have you read any books or articles about "people like you"?
    ___ no ___ yes. If yes, please describe:

    _____

    _____

14. Have you ever sought help or advice from someone else (counselor, minister, etc.) about your identity/sexuality?
    ___ no ___ yes. If yes, who and what advice did you get?

    _____

    _____

15. Who knows about your sexuality/identity?
    ___ some of my friends (which ones? _____)
    ___ most/all of my friends
    ___ my lover/partner/spouse
    ___ parents
    ___ other family
    ___ employer other (describe: _____)

16. The scales below represent points along a continuum of sexual orientation (i.e., whether you are attracted to men or women). On these scales "0" represents exclusively heterosexual and "6" represents exclusively homosexual. Please circle the appropriate number for each question below:

a. Think of all the sexual experiences you have ever had, whether they were pleasurable or unpleasurable. Simply on the basis of number of heterosexual versus homosexual experiences, where do you fit on the scale below?

0	1	2	3	4	5	6
Exclusively			Equally			Exclusively
heterosexual			heterosexual			homosexual
			& homosexual			

b. Now think of your total pleasurable sexual experiences. Where do you fit on the scale below?

0	1	2	3	4	5	6
Exclusively			Equally			Exclusively
heterosexual			heterosexual			homosexual
			& homosexual			

c. Think of all the sexual attractions and fantasies you have ever had in your life, whether or not you acted on them. Where do you fall on the scale below on the basis of sexual attractions and fantasies?

0	1	2	3	4	5	6
Exclusively			Equally			Exclusively
heterosexual			heterosexual			homosexual
			& homosexual			

d. Now think of all the romantic/love relationships you have ever had. Where do you fall on the scale?

0	1	2	3	4	5	6
Exclusively			Equally			Exclusively
heterosexual			heterosexual			homosexual
			& homosexual			

e. Now think of your sexual behavior in the past year only. Rate yourself on the scale.

0	1	2	3	4	5	6
Exclusively			Equally			Exclusively
heterosexual			heterosexual			homosexual
			& homosexual			

f. Think of your sexual fantasies and attractions in the past year only. Rate yourself on the scale.

0	1	2	3	4	5	6
Exclusively heterosexual			Equally heterosexual & homosexual			Exclusively homosexual

g. Think of the romantic/love relationships you have had in the past year. Rate yourself on the scale.

0	1	2	3	4	5	6
Exclusively heterosexual			Equally heterosexual & homosexual			Exclusively homosexual

h. Overall in your opinion, how would you rate yourself on this scale?

0	1	2	3	4	5	6
Exclusively heterosexual			Equally heterosexual & homosexual			Exclusively homosexual

Why? _____

PLEASE COMPLETE THE FOLLOWING QUESTIONS ONLY IF YOU ARE/THINK YOU MIGHT BE TRANSSEXUAL OR TRANSVESTITE.

1. Have you ever felt/do you feel you were not "really" the gender you were born as?_____ no _____ yes. If yes, please describe including age you first felt this:

_____
_____

2. Have you ever/do you dress in clothing of the opposite sex?
_____ no _____ yes. If yes, please describe how and when this started and your current cross-dressing activities:

_____
_____

3. Do you have a persona of the opposite sex? _____ no _____ yes. If yes, what is her/his name, how and when does s/he emerge, who knows of this persona?

_____
_____

4. Have you ever taken hormones to change your body? _____ no _____ yes.
If yes, please describe: _____

_____

5. Are you considering gender reassignment surgery? _____ no _____ yes
   Explain: _____

REFERENCES

Bataille, G. (1962). *Erotism: Death and sensuality.* San Francisco: City Lights Press.

Beemyn, B., & Eliason, M. (1996). *Queer studies: A lesbian, gay, bisexual and transgender anthology.* New York: New York University Press.

Bell, A., & Weinberg, M. (1978). *Homosexualities: A study of diversity among men and women.* New York: Simon & Schuster.

Bernstein, R., & Silberman, S. (Eds.). (1996). *Generation Q.* Los Angeles: Alyson.

Blumstein, P., & Schwartz, P. (1983). *American couples.* New York: William Morrow.

Bornstein, K. (1994). *Gender outlaw: On men, women, and the rest of us.* New York: Routledge Press.

Browning, F. (1994). *The culture of desire.* New York: Vintage Books.

Califia, P. (1994). *Public sex: The culture of radical sex.* Pittsburgh, PA: Cleis Press.

Califia, P. (1997). *Sex changes: The politics of transgenderism.* San Francisco: Cleis Press.

Gendin, S. (1999, February). They shoot bare backers, don't they? *POZ Magazine,* pp. 15–21.

Hutchins, L. & Kaahumanu, L. (1991). *Bi any other name: Bisexual people speak out.* Boston: Alyson.

Jay, K., & Young, A. (1979). *The gay report.* New York: Summit Books.

Katz, J. (1976). *Gay American history.* New York: Crowell.

Klein, F., & Wolf, T. (1985). *Two lives to lead: Bisexuality in men and women.* New York: Harrington Park Press.

Laumann, E., Gagnon, J., Michael, R., & Michaels, S. (1994). *The social organization of sexuality: Sexual practices in the United States.* Chicago: University of Chicago Press.

Leiblum, S., & Pervin, L. (Eds.). (1980). *Principles and practice of sex therapy.* New York: Guilford Press.

Leiblum, S. & Rosen, R. (Eds.). (1989). *Principles and practice of sex therapy* (2nd ed.): *Update for the 1990s.* New York: Guilford Press.

McWhirter, D., & Mattison, A. (1984). *The male couple.* Englewood Cliffs, NJ: Prentice Hall.

McWhirter, D., Sanders, S., & Reinisch, J. (Eds.). (1990). *Homosexuality/heterosexuality: Concepts of sexual orientation.* London: Oxford University Press.

Morin, J. (1995). *The erotic mind.* New York: HarperCollins.

Nestle, J. (Ed.). (1992). *The persistent desire: A femme–butch reader.* Boston: Alyson.

Nichols, M. (1988). Low sexual desire in lesbian couples. In S. Leiblum & R. Rosen (Eds.), *Sexual desire disorders* (pp. 387–412). New York: Guilford Press.

Nichols, M. (1990). Lesbian relationships: Implications for the study of sexuality and gender. In D. McWhirter, S. Sanders, & J. Reinisch (Eds.), *Homosexuality/heterosexuality: Concepts of sexual orientation* (pp. 351–363) London: Oxford University Press.

Nichols, M. (1994). Therapy with bisexual women: Working on the edge of emerging cultural and personal identities. In M. P. Mirkin (Ed.), *Women in context: Toward a feminist reconstruction of psychotherapy* (pp. 149–169). New York: Guilford Press.

Nichols, M. (1995). Sexual desire disorder in a lesbian–feminist couple: The intersection of therapy and politics. In R. C. Rosen & S. R. Leiblum (Eds.), *Case studies in sex therapy* (pp. 161–175). New York: Guilford Press.

Ragaza, A. (1999, April). Back to life, back to reality. *POZ Magazine,* pp. 38–39.

Scarce, M. (1999, February). A ride on the wild side. *POZ Magazine,* pp. 24–29.

Shernoff, M. (1999, March/April). When are open relationships a therapeutic option? *Family Therapy Networker,* 63–71.

Shilts, R. (1987). *And the band played on.* New York: St. Martin's Press.

Signorile, M. (1997). *Life outside.* New York: HarperCollins.

Stein, A. (Ed.). (1993). *Sister, sexperts, and queers: Beyond the lesbian nation.* New York: Penguin Books.

Stoller, R. (1985). *Observing the erotic imagination.* New Haven: Yale University Press.

13

Assessment and Treatment of Gender Dysphoria

RICHARD A. CARROLL

The topic of gender dysphoria is given special coverage for the first time in this edition of Principles and Practice of Sex Therapy, *although throughout history there have been many individuals who experience gender dissatisfaction or incongruence. Most sex therapists encounter patients struggling with the increasingly fluid issues of gender identity—the inner sense of maleness or femaleness. The variety of ways of expressing one's gender identity is increasingly complex and varied for many individuals, and there is greater acceptance in society generally. Nonetheless, gender dysphoria is a source of considerable anxiety and distress for those who have difficulty in adapting to a largely bigendered world.*

As Richard A. Carroll points out in this chapter, gender dyphoria usually originates in childhood and tends to be quite persistent through adulthood for most individuals. It is essential for the clinician to obtain a comprehensive and detailed developmental history when working with gender-dysphoric clients. Whether first seen as children, adolescents, or adults, individuals with gender identity conflict can benefit significantly from empathic and respectful counseling.

The author identifies several challenges facing clinicians in this area. The clinician serves neither exclusively as a gatekeeper nor as an advocate of surgical gender change but should focus on reducing the client's psychological distress and arriving at a workable resolution of the conflict. As Carroll notes, therapeutic outcomes and solutions vary greatly from one individual to another.

This chapter also presents the current Standards of Care for Gender Dys-

phoria, established by the Harry Benjamin International Gender Dysphoria Association and provides a capsule overview of the common presentations of gender dysphoria: female-to-male, androphilic male-to-female, and autogynephilic male-to-female types.

Finally, Carroll provides solid guidelines and suggestions for working with these fascinating although often deeply troubled individuals. Presenting composite case examples, he illustrates the typical course of therapy and highly varied outcomes of treatment.

Richard A. Carroll, PhD, is a clinical psychologist who specializes in the treatment of gender-dysphoric individuals at Northwestern University Medical School where he is an Assistant Professor in the Department of Psychiatry and Codirector of the Center for Sexual Health. A member of the Harry Benjamin International Gender Dysphoria Association, he is well versed in the issues and dilemmas of men and women experiencing gender dysphoria and provides a sensitive and thoughtful overview of this important and often neglected topic.

The topic of gender dysphoria has recently gained a great deal of attention in the field of mental health and society at large. After an initial period of fascination with the phenomenon of sex change in the 1960s and 1970s, professional and public interest almost disappeared. Beginning in the early 1990s, a new attitude toward transgendered phenomena has developed. This has been due, in part, to the increasing acceptance of homosexuality as a nonpathological variant of normal sexuality and in part to the emergence of a transgendered community, representing a wide range of individuals who have blended masculinity and femininity in various ways. The clinician is now confronted with an often bewildering array of individuals with transgendered experiences, including transsexuals, transvestites, she-males, third sex, two spirit, drag queens and kings, and cross-dressers.

It is difficult to establish the prevalence of gender identity disorder in the adult population given the negative judgments attached to it. The best estimate comes from a study conducted in the Netherlands, which found that about 1 in 11,000 men and 1 in 30,000 women seek treatment for gender identity disorder at a specialized clinic (Bakker, van Kesteren, Gooren, & Bezemer, 1993). However, these numbers are likely to be a significant underestimation of the number of adults who experience some form of gender dysphoria, because the majority of such individuals do not seek treatment. For the purposes of this overview, I focus on those individuals who come to clinicians for help with their gender dysphoria.

The problem most likely to be presented by transgendered individuals is gender dysphoria, which is defined as unhappiness with one's given gender. The fourth edition of *Diagnostic and Statistical Manual of Mental Disorders*

(DSM-IV; American Psychiatric Association, 1994) defines the criteria for gender identity disorder as (1) unhappiness with one's given gender, and (2) the desire to take on the identity of the other gender. This replaces the old diagnosis of transsexualism, though the label "transsexual" is still commonly used to refer to an individual who desires a full gender change. Some individuals, however, may experience gender dysphoria but have not developed the desire to change their gender. Gender dysphoria, then, refers to a broader category of experiences. The phrase "transgendered experience" is currently used to refer to the many different ways individuals may experience a gender identity outside the simple categories of male or female. This is the preferred label within the transgendered community today. It should be remembered that there are many individuals who have blended genders in some way who never seek treatment and who may be very comfortable with their atypical gender identity or gender role.

The phenomenon of gender dysphoria has existed throughout recorded history. Ancient and current mythologies abound with descriptions of individuals who, for various reasons, take on the body or role of the other gender (Bullough & Bullough, 1993). A prominent example, taken from Greek mythology is that of Tiresias, who spent part of his life as a man and part as a woman. Tiresias, because of his unique experience, was considered a wise seer; which is a theme often associated with the transgender experience. Bullough and Bullough (1993) cite a wide variety of historical accounts, of cross-dressing, male and female impersonation, and gender change. These include Catholic saints, French nobility, political figures, and famous artists. They suggest that throughout Western history, women have taken on male roles primarily for the purpose of gaining the benefits of being male in male-dominated societies, but that men have taken on female roles (especially cross-dressing) primarily for purposes of sexual excitement and entertainment. In other cultures, niches have been defined for transgendered individuals that do not carry the intensely disapproving judgments typically seen in Western culture (e.g., the berdache of Native American cultures and the hjira of India, who are integrated into society as members of a third gender) (Denny, 1997).

The history of attitudes to transgendered persons in Western culture has generally been quite negative up until recent times. The *Malleus Maleficarum*, which was the DSM of the 15th- and 16th-century Inquisition, stated that dressing or taking on the persona of the other gender was evidence of witchcraft and the treatment of choice was decidedly intrusive (e.g., burning at the stake). Demonization gave way to medicalization of transgender behavior beginning in the 19th century. The prevailing attitude, however, showed little improvement at first. Richard von Kraft-Ebing, one of the first modern sexologists, in his major work, *Psychopathia Sexualis* (von Kraft-Ebing, 1906/1933), defined transgendered behavior as perversion, usually due to overindulgence in sex or masturbation. Later sexologists, such as Havelock Ellis and Magnus Hirschfeld, have attempted to bring a more scientific and humane approach to understanding these phenomena (Bullough & Bullough, 1993).

GENDER IDENTITY DISORDER
IN CHILDHOOD AND ADOLESCENCE

Although this chapter focuses on gender dysphoria in adults, some attention must be paid to gender identity problems in children and adolescents. Readers interested in this topic should consult an excellent overview of the topic by Zucker and Bradley (1995). The diagnosis of gender identity disorder is essentially the same in children, adolescents, and adults (i.e., a discomfort with one's given gender and a desire to become the other gender). However, the phenomena are strikingly different in several ways. First, the prevalence of gender dysphoria appears to be much higher in children than in adults. For example, on the Child Behavior Checklist, a measure of childhood behavior (Achenbach & Edelbrock, 1981), about 1 to 2% of mothers of a male, nonclinical norm group reported of their sons "wishes to be of the opposite sex" and about 3 to 4% of mothers of a female norm group reported that their daughters expressed a wish to be a boy (cited in Zucker & Bradley, 1995). Gender dysphoria in children, therefore, does not appear to be the relatively rare phenomenon that it is in adults.

This leads one to wonder what happens to the many children who express a desire to be the other gender in childhood but do not grow up to be an adult transsexual. In a seminal study, Green (1987) followed up on the lives of 44 boys who had been brought to a child mental health clinic because they had expressed a desire to become a girl. Surprisingly, only one (2%) of the original group of female-identified boys manifested significant gender dysphoria as an adolescent or young adult. However, 75% manifested a homosexual orientation. It became clear, then, that the vast majority of gender-dysphoric children do not grow up to become gender-dysphoric adults, though why this lack of continuity occurs is unclear. It also highlights an important connection between early cross-gender identification and adult homosexuality.

A related question is whether children simply grow out of their gender dysphoria or whether early intervention actually prevents them from developing adult gender identity disorder. A wide variety of interventions have attempted to treat childhood gender identity disturbance, including behavioral, psychodynamic, group, and family treatments. Zucker and Bradley (1995) conclude, "A sizable number of children and their families achieve a great deal of change. In these cases, the gender identity disorder resolves fully, and nothing in the children's behavior or fantasy suggests that gender identity issues remain problematic" (p. 282). The Harry Benjamin International Gender Dysphoria (HBIGDA) Standards of Care (HBIGDA, 1998) state that hormonal or surgical interventions should not be done to children in order to effect a gender reassignment; but rather, psychological treatment should be offered to assist the child's and the family adjustment.

Zucker and Bradley (1995) also found that children (both males and females, ages 6–11) with gender identity disorder are more likely to demonstrate mental health problems than are matched controls, primarily in the area of internalizing symptomatology (e.g., depression or anxiety). What remains unclear is whether this associated psychopathology is the result of, the cause of, or unrelated to the gender identity disturbance. It does strongly suggest, however, that these children need and will benefit from psychological interventions, whether or not these interventions are focused on their gender dysphoria.

Gender identity problems in adolescence are not so readily resolved or outgrown. Gender identity disorders during this period, especially later adolescence, resemble adult forms of gender dysphoria more than childhood forms. During adolescence, clinicians also begin to see a different phenomenon, which is transvestism (i.e., sexual arousal to the act of cross-dressing). This, as will be seen, corresponds to one form of adult gender dysphoria. Zucker and Bradley (1995) found that these transvestic adolescents had high levels of behavioral disturbance, especially conduct disorder, attention-deficit disorder, and overanxious disorder.

A current debate in the field of gender disorders is whether adolescents who show clear-cut evidence of a persistent cross-gender identification should be given the option of pursuing physical gender reassignment or whether they should be given psychological treatment to resolve the gender identity problem. The recent HBIGDA Standards of Care (HBIGDA, 1998) strongly recommend against hormonal or surgical interventions before the age of 18. However, there is a recent move to give puberty-delaying hormones to adolescent boys who wish to become girls in order to give them time to come to a resolution of their gender dysphoria before the physical effects of puberty become pronounced (Cohen-Kettenis & van Goozen, 1995).

THE ROLE OF THE CLINICIAN IN THE TREATMENT OF GENDER DYSPHORIA

Before exploring the assessment and treatment of individuals seeking help for their gender dysphoria, it is important to consider the role of the clinician in working with transgendered individuals. Prior to the development of gender reassignment as an intervention for gender dysphoria, the therapist's only option was to help patients accept their given genders. For many years clinicians viewed the transgendered phenomena as a form of psychotic disorder and recommended psychoanalysis or psychotherapy as the treatment of choice (Meyer, 1979).

As evidence began to accumulate that gender reassignment could relieve the suffering of transsexuals, therapists were thrust into the role of gatekeeper to these desired interventions. This was often due to physician's reluctance to provide medical treatment to individuals who were considered unstable or disturbed. It was also due to physician's fear of malpractice suits if the patient was unhappy with the surgical results. Therefore, approval for medical treatment from mental health professionals was seen as an important legal and clinical safeguard for medical care providers. This role was subsequently built into all versions of the HBIGDA Standards of Care (HBIGDA, 1998).

This presents the mental health professional with a challenge. Unlike most patients, the transgendered person seeking treatment is often motivated to present in a psychologically healthy manner in order to obtain approval for surgery and/or hormonal treatment. The clinician must seek to uncover the extent of the patient's mental distress, both related and unrelated to the gender dysphoria.

To establish a productive clinical alliance, clinicians are advised to clarify their role with the patient from the outset. This can be done by clearly acknowledging the dual roles of attempting to help patients resolve their distress as well as helping assess the appropriateness of medical interventions. Currently, most professionals who work with gender dysphoria patients believe that it is the patient's right to resolve their gender dilemma without undue influence from the clinician, who now acts as a consultant with expertise in gender dysphoria. Clinicians must provide careful recommendations as to what they think will be most helpful in dealing with the gender dysphoria and any other psychological issues that may exist. Clinicians must also describe their responsibility to judge the suitability of individuals for hormonal or surgical intervention, which may involve refusing to write a letter of approval for such treatment.

Often patients are frustrated by the recommendation of engaging in therapy before any medical treatment begins. They may be angered initially by what they see as an unnecessary obstacle to their desired goal (i.e., a quick gender transition). In most cases, however, a supportive attitude and reference to the HBIGDA Standards of Care will allow the patient to accept the recommendations and to use therapy productively. On a few occasions, even after a course of psychological treatment, the therapist may feel that the patient is too unstable or confused to proceed with medical treatment. This situation is difficult for patient and clinician alike, but it must be accepted as part of the responsibility of professionals who work with gender-dysphoric patients.

The HBIGDA Standards of Care summarize the 10 tasks of the mental health professional:

1. to accurately diagnose the individual's gender dysphoria;
2. to accurately diagnose any comorbid psychiatric conditions and see to their appropriate treatment;
3. to counsel the individual about the range of treatment options and their implications;
4. to engage in psychotherapy;
5. to ascertain eligibility and readiness for hormone and surgical therapy;
6. to make formal recommendations to medical and surgical colleagues;
7. to document their patient's relevant history in a letter of recommendation;
8. to be a colleague on a team of professionals with interest in the gender identity disorders;
9. to educate family member, employers, and institutions about gender identity disorders;
10. to be available for follow-up of previously seen gender patients. (HBIGDA, 1998, p. 22)

Due to the difficulties in work with transgendered patients noted previously, clinicians who work with these individuals should have both general knowledge of psychopathology and special training in gender disorders. The Standards of Care specify that a clinician should have: (1) a master's degree in a mental health field, (2) competence in sexual disorders (not just gender disorders), (3) competence in psychotherapy, and (4) continuing education in gender disorders. It is strongly recommended that mental health professionals who wish to work with gender dysphoria become members of the Harry Benjamin International Gender Dysphoria Association or, at least, have a thorough knowledge of its Standards of Care.

ASSESSMENT OF GENDER DYSPHORIA

Gender and Sexual History

The goal of assessment is similar to the goal for any other patient: to understand the presenting problem (gender dysphoria) in the context of the person's life and to make recommendations as to appropriate treatment. What is different about the assessment of gender patients, however, is the need to focus specifically on understanding both gender history and sexual history. Taking a gender history involves exploring the various manifestations of gender identity over time. This includes such questions as:

1. Type of play as a child (gender conforming vs. nonconforming);
2. Dress or desired dress as a child;
3. Gender identity as a child, adolescent and adult (looking for changes over time);
4. Reactions from family, friends, peers, and others to the child's gender behavior;
5. Feeling about one's body and reactions to puberty;
6. Onset of gender dysphoria;
7. History of cross-dressing;
8. Other cross-gender experiences as an adult (e.g., passing in public as other gender);
9. Attempts to adopt a cross-gender role (e.g., name change, electrolysis),
10. Contact with transgender groups or individuals; and
11. Goals for gender transition.

In addition to this information, a careful sexual history is necessary, including:

1. First sexual experience;
2. Sexual abuse or trauma;

3. Earliest sexual fantasies and masturbation patterns;
4. Any experience of sexual arousal associated with cross-dressing;
5. Number and pattern of sexual experiences with both genders;
6. Nature of any significant romantic/sexual relationships (including marriage);
7. Content of current sexual fantasies (especially the genders of those involved);
8. Current and desired sexual script;
9. History of sexual problems; and
10. Presence of paraphilias (especially domination or masochistic fantasies).

Attempts to accurately assess the transgendered individual begin with an awareness of the heterogeneity of the phenomenon itself. For many years, the mental health field has struggled to understand and categorize this complex problem, most notably by attempting to define "true" or "primary" transsexualism and attempting to distinguish it from "secondary" forms of the disorder (Levine & Lothstein, 1981). Behind this often lay an assumption that there is one clear manifestation of transsexualism, with a single consistent etiology. It was widely felt that only the "true transsexual" was appropriate for gender reassignment. Years of clinical observation and research, however, have suggested that there are varying presentations of gender dysphoria and that one can no longer identify one, among the many forms of transgendered experience, as "true." Others later suggested that cross-gender experiences constitute more of a continuum than a discrete phenomenon (Blanchard, 1985; Docter & Fleming, 1992). It has recently been suggested that transgender experiences constitute a multidimensional matrix, which includes at least four dimensions, including (1) the body, (2) the social role, (3) sexuality, and (4) gender identity (Carroll, 1999).

COMMON PRESENTATIONS OF GENDER DYSPHORIA

There are three primary forms of gender dysphoria as seen in the clinician's office. A brief description of these typical presentations follows.

The Female-to-Male Gender Dysphoric

Female-to-male gender dysphoria patients present strikingly consistent histories. These individuals were almost always identified as masculine in appearance or behavior beginning early in childhood, often as young as 3 years of age. They enjoyed rough-and-tumble games and sports. They preferred the company of boys to girls. They hated to be put into dresses or other "girlish" clothes. They usually verbalized their wish to grow up to be a male. In adolescence, they reacted with disgust to the physical changes associated with puberty. Their sexual attraction was to females and they developed crushes on girls or women even in childhood. They may have tried to fit in socially by dating boys, but this was ultimately frustrating. They have almost never experienced sexual attraction to males. In adolescence or young adulthood, they often tried a lesbian solution to their dilemma, but this failed because they did not want women to be attracted to them as women; rather, they wanted women to be attracted to them as males. They may have been able to develop relationships with female partners who are attracted to their masculinity and support their desire to transition to male. Often these female partners are women who do not see themselves as lesbian but, rather, view themselves as heterosexual, though they have had bad experiences in relationships with men. At some point in adulthood, female-to-male patients became aware of the possibility of gender reassignment and sought treatment.

The Male-to-Female Gender Dysphoric: The Androphilic Type

Unlike female-to-male transgendered individuals, there are two distinct types of men who desire to become women: (1) androphilic and (2) autogynephilic. The androphilic (attracted to males) type, also known as the homosexual type, is the classic picture of the transsexual, in that this individual was the person described in the early literature on transsexualism. This form of gender dysphoria is in many ways the reverse of the female-to-male pattern.

These boys were almost always viewed as effeminate, pretty, and gentle from birth. They avoided rough games, sports, and masculine play. They liked to dress up as girls from a young age, but this was never associated with sexual arousal. They cross-dressed in order to adopt the identity of girls or women. They often had a particularly strong bond with their mothers. There may have been some encouragement from others for their effeminate behavior, dress, or looks, but not usually. From a young age, they were attracted to males. They almost never experienced sexual attraction to females. They usually experienced harassment from others, including family or peers due to their effeminacy. In adolescence they came out as homosexual and developed homosexual relationships. They may have been involved in prostitution or in a drag queen lifestyle. In young adulthood they became frustrated with gay relationships because they wanted to be with heterosexual men who were attracted to them as women. In early adulthood they decided that they had to make a full transition to female.

The Male-to-Female Gender Dysphoric: The Autogynephilic Type

The second form of male-to-female gender dysphoria is remarkably different from that described previously. This form has also been called the heterosexual or transvestic form of male-to-female transsexualism. In the past this person was usually labeled a transvestite or "secondary" transsexual and was not considered appropriate for surgery. Currently, however, professionals understand that this person may also benefit from gender reassignment. In fact, the majority of men seeking treatment for gender dysphoria are of this type.

To understand this form of gender dysphoria, one must understand the phenomenon of autogynephilia. The term refers to the experience of sexual arousal (philia) to the fantasy of oneself (auto) as being a female (gyne). Blanchard (1989) and colleagues have convincingly demonstrated that it is this sexual arousal pattern that underlies most cross-dressing in men, many of whom become gender dysphoric. Most men who receive a DSM-IV diagnosis of transvestic fetishism will manifest autogynephilia as a prominent form of sexual arousal.

The typical early history of autogynephilic gender dysphorics is not unusual. They are not considered effeminate as boys but, rather, are often seen as masculine. They frequently report that they began dressing in female clothing, usually their mother's or sister's clothes, before the onset of puberty. They will describe this experience as pleasurable or comforting but not sexual. With the onset of puberty, these cross-dressing experiences become sexually exciting and usually become the predominant source of sexual excitement. As adolescents, they will also typically develop sexual attractions to girls and women. They will note, however, that, in addition to be sexually attracted to girls or women, they imagine having feminine bodies or looking like women. They usually date females during adolescence and young adulthood. During this time, they also struggle with their transvestism and make attempts to stop it by purging their female wardrobes. To suppress their feminine identification, they often force themselves into stereotypical masculine behavior or roles (e.g., weightlifting, aggressive behavior, or joining the military). Over time, however, their urge to cross-dress and their fantasies of becoming female became stronger. They often manifest depression and/or substance abuse as a result of the internal gender identity conflicts. Eventually they feel that they must follow their desire to become female and seek treatment. This may not be until middle age. Sometimes, they have resisted the urge to become female due to fears of losing their wife, children, or job. When they present for treatment, they are often desperate to make a quick change and may be impulsive in their efforts to change gender.

As noted earlier, the assessment of gender-dysphoric individuals has to include a broader assessment of their psychological functioning. Given the potential attempt to appear well adjusted, psychological testing is useful in assessing underlying personality and psychopathology.

The literature regarding the associated psychopathology of gender dysphorics has changed over time. Early on, most of the clinical literature suggested that gender dysphorics usually manifest severe personality disorders (Lothstein, 1984). More recent studies have indicated that most transgendered individuals do not typically exhibit significant elevations in psychopathology (Brown, Wise, & Costa, 1995). The question remains whether this change in the literature reflects an improvement in research quality, an overcoming of clinical biases, or a change in the population of gender dysphorics presenting for treatment.

ETIOLOGY

The etiology of transgendered experiences remains uncertain and there is little research that can claim to support one explanation over another. Part of the difficulty is that etiological theories have to account for such diverse phenomena as cross-dressing, androphilic and autogynephilic male-to-female gender dysphoria, drag queens, and gynephilic female-to-male gender dysphoria. Various etiologies, however, have been postulated.

Biological models have been suggested, but no significant differences between gender dysphorics and normal populations have been consistently found on measures of hormone levels or genetic inheritance. However, higher incidences of temporal lobe abnormalities have been found in transgendered individuals (Hoenig, 1985). A recent study of the brains of male-to-female transsexuals found that a small region of the brain that is associated with sexual behavior in rats (the bed nucleus of the stria terminialis) is "female-sized" rather than "male-sized" (Zhou, Hofman, Gooren, & Swaab, 1997). It is unclear, however, whether this is due to the use of hormones or due to some difference prior to medical treatment.

Based on animal models of sexuality–hormone relationships and studies of various intersex conditions (e.g., congenital adrenal hyperplasia or hermaphroditism) hypotheses have been generated regarding the possible impact of the fetal hormonal environment in the development of gender disorders. There is not yet, however, any convincing research to support these theories. It should also be noted that the vast majority of gender dysphorics do not have any genetic or intersex abnormalities.

Some authors, including Harry Benjamin (1966) and John Money (1984) suggested that transsexualism might be due to a "gender fixation," similar to imprinting in birds. They argued that at some critical phase of development, the child locked on to the other gender parent and cross-gender identification occurred. This theory, however, has not been well articulated and it appears unlikely that such a biologically rooted imprinting process occurs in humans.

For many years, psychoanalytic theories have argued for a psychological origin. One version argues that it is due to a symbiosis that exists between the child and the other-gender parent (Stoller, 1985). Another psychodynamic theory postulates that gender dysphoria is a psychotic disorder created by severe intrapsychic conflict (Meyer, 1979). More recent theorists have drawn on object relations and self psychology theory to develop new models of gender disorder that suggest that the gender-dysphoric boy develops an all-good image of the mother, which becomes merged with his self-image and becomes split off (Beitel, 1985).

Behavioral theorists have applied learning theory to gender disorders and have speculated that gender identity follows from gender role behavior, which, they argue, is shaped by external contingencies. The socialization of gender categories and behavior in children has been shown to begin at birth. Behavioral theory hypothesizes that in order for gender dysphoria to develop, cross-gender behavior and identity must be reinforced and gender congruent behavior must be punished (Rekers, 1985). Some support for this comes from Green's (1987) work, in which he found, in almost all the cases observed, that as the feminine behavior of the young boy developed, the principal caregiver made no attempt to discourage it. Empirical support, however, for this theory has not been forthcoming for adults manifesting gender dysphoria. Given the difficulties of retrospective research, it would be difficult to find such support.

TREATMENT OF GENDER DYSPHORIA

If the core dilemma for the transgendered person is the incongruity between his or her internal sense of gender identity and his or her external role or physical presentation, then two treatment options become obvious. One can either (1) change the identity to match the body or (2) change the body to match the identity. Clinicians, and transgendered individuals themselves, are finding that these options do not represent the variety of resolutions to cross-gender experience. It is becoming clear that there are many successful outcomes for individuals who present in a clinical setting with unhappiness with their biological gender. The treatment of gender dysphoria now depends primarily on the patient's desired outcome.

POSSIBLE RESOLUTIONS TO GENDER DYSPHORIA

There are many possible resolutions to the gender-dysphoric dilemma due to the many combinations of physical changes, lifestyle choices, sexual orientations, and ways of manifesting the transgendered part of oneself. Physically, patients may undergo any number of medical interventions to create changes in the body, including hormonal treatment, genital surgery, electrolysis, breast surgery, or other cosmetic surgery. The person may decide to live in the other gender role part time or full time. In terms of sexuality, individuals may prefer sex as a woman or as a man with a female, male, both or neither. Their sexuality may or may not include cross-dressing. Individuals may view themselves as male, female, both, a third gender, a transsexual, a transvestite, or a transgendered person.

The most common outcomes of treatment for gender dysphoria may be summarized as follows: (1) an unresolved outcome, (2) acceptance of biological gender and role, (3) engaging in a cross-gender role on an intermittent or part-time basis, or (4) adopting the other gender role full time (i.e., gender reassignment). Each of these options has several possible variations as well.

Treatment Dropout

The least understand outcome is that of patients who leave treatment after an evaluation or period of mental health intervention. The proportion of these apparent dropouts can be quite high, often on the order of 50%. Due to a lack of clinical or research follow-up, we have no way of knowing what the ultimate outcome of their gender dysphoria might be. Patients who leave organized gender identity programs often do so because they are not willing or not able to engage in a structured long-term program of psychological and medical treatment. Some are angered by the recommendation for psychological treatment, feeling that they know what they want and do not need therapy. Others appear unable to accept the delay or possible denial of medical treatment. Some treatment dropouts leave to find an easier path to their goal of quick gender reassignment, such as black market hormones or surgery done without regard for the HBIGDA Standards of Care. Patients may also leave treatment because they are unable to afford services.

Yet another reason for treatment dropout may be the patient's underlying ambivalence about pursuing a resolution to their gender dysphoria. Even though they have made the initial effort to seek help, they may experience considerable doubt about their identity, and rather than explore these issues in therapy, they may seek to reduce their distress by avoiding the exploration of their internal gender conflicts. Patients may also leave treatment because they are unable to overcome the obstacles created by their marriage, children, job, or other external circumstance. Interestingly, some patients return to treatment years after an initial contact. A return to treatment may be the result of a change in the individual's life, such as a divorce, children leaving home, change in job or home, or death of a parent. Another problem stems from the fact that many gender-dysphoric patients are also depressed (Lothstein, 1984). After years of struggling with their gender conflict, as well as with the gender role expectations in their social world, they may experience a pervasive sense of hopelessness and powerlessness.

Whatever the reason, there are many patients who come to treatment for help with gender dysphoria whom mental health professionals apparently are unable to help or who are unable to use what professionals have to offer. A complete understanding of the outcomes of treatment for gender-dysphoria must take such individuals into consideration. Future empirical research with gender-dysphoric individuals should more carefully explore this population of treatment dropouts.

Acceptance of Given Gender

The second treatment outcome with gender-dysphoric individuals is the patient's acceptance of his or her original gender and a reduction in his or her gender dysphoria. Mental health professionals for many years have desired such an outcome for their patients. There have been a number of case reports from both the behavioral and psychodynamic perspectives that suggest that patients may resolve their gender dysphoria psychologically (i.e., by removing the desire to be the other gender) (see, e.g., Barlow, Abel, & Blanchard, 1979; Lothstein & Levine, 1981). However, these claims have not been supported by controlled group studies. It appears now that the majority of adults with gender dysphoria cannot, or will not, completely accept their given gender through psychological treatment.

One population, in which the acceptance of natal gender and the cessation of cross-gender behavior appears to be a possibility is a subgroup of male autogynephilic transsexuals (Carroll & Donahey, 1994; see also Case 3). These individuals present to clinicians with a desire to end their cross-dressing, though they also experience varying degrees of gender dysphoria, with at least occasional desires to become female. The most common motivation for giving up cross-dressing is the fear of losing their marriages, families, or other valued parts of their lives. Some of these individuals have been able to abandon cross-dressing completely and experience a decrease in, or cessation of, gender dysphoria by approaching their transvestism from the perspective of a paraphilia and using standard behavioral interventions (e.g., covert sensitization or stimulus control techniques), psychotherapy, and couple therapy.

Part-Time Cross-Gender Behavior

The most common resolution to cross-gender feelings for men is living part time as female in the form of episodic cross-dressing. Most of these men do not seek psychotherapy for their gender dysphoria. The majority of these men are heterosexual, often married, usually vocationally stable or successful. The cross-dressing is, or was, usually associated with sexual arousal. Psychological evaluations of cross-dressers suggest that they are not more psychologically disturbed than is the normal population (Docter, 1988).

Others have addressed the same issue of diversity in cross-gender identification for females. Devor (1989) has suggested the term "gender blending" to describe the diverse ways that women may incorporate masculine and feminine aspects of self through the physical body, gender identity, gender role, sexual practices, and sexual orientation.

Recent research with nonclinical populations suggest that many cross-gendered individuals, especially cross-dressers, may be entirely satisfied by adopting the dress and/or role of the other gender on a part-time basis (e.g., cross-dressers) or by adopting only selective aspects of the other gender on a full-time basis (e.g., masculine females).

Gender Reassignment

The fourth possible resolution to gender dysphoria is to make a full transition to the desired gender. The HBIGDA Standards of Care (HBIGDA, 1998) present clear guidelines as to the process of gender reassignment. These include the following:

1. A psychological evaluation performed by a gender disorder specialist focusing on both mental health and gender identity;
2. A 3-month period (minimum) of psychotherapy or a 3-month period (minimum) of living as the desired gender (the real-life experience);
3. Evaluation for, and continued use of, appropriate hormones;
4. A period of 1 year (minimum) of living full time as the desired gender (the real-life experience) and continuous use of hormones;
5. An evaluation by a second gender disorder specialist supporting the person's readiness for gender surgery;
6. Gender reassignment surgery (genital, breast, or other surgery designed to change primary gender characteristics); and
7. Follow-up care.

The Standards of Care present these steps in greater detail and should be consulted by anyone working with gender disorders. It should be emphasized that these guidelines are minimal standards. In fact, most established programs require longer periods of hormones, real-life experience, and therapy than the minimum periods defined by the Standards of Care.

The most essential aspect of the gender reassignment process is the "real-life experience," or the "real-life test." This involves the person living and working at all times in the desired gender role. It also includes making legal name and gender changes. It is the most important aspect of gender transition because it requires that the gender-dysphoric individual try on the gender role that he or she wishes to adopt and determine whether it fulfills his or her needs. It is used to reduce the chances that a person will regret irreversible gender surgery. For a few individuals, the real-life experience makes it clear that the desired gender role does not provide what they had hoped and they abandon their pursuit of gender reassignment. Evidence of a successful real-life experience comes from examining the person's vocational, social, and psychological adjustment. Corroborating evidence is usually sought from significant others in the patient's life.

The Standards of Care outline the role of the clinician with regard to the gender reassignment process. They do not, however, elaborate on the complexities of therapy with these patients. Besides assessment and approval for medical treatment, the central task of the clinician is to provide psychological treatment before any medical interventions occur. Over the years, the Standards of Care have relied less and less on therapy. For example, the original Standards of Care required a period of 6 months of regular therapy for all patients who sought gender reassignment. In the most recent version, psychotherapy is not required at all but is strongly recommended, and it is left to the evaluating clinician to determine whether it is necessary.

Psychotherapy with gender-dysphoric patients can be both challenging and rewarding. As noted previously, many patients have great difficulty with the recommendation for therapy, though they may come to value it over time. Few patients are as appreciative as those who have been able to find a sense of psychological well-being, usually for the first time in their lives, through this process.

There are four main goals of psychotherapy with the gender-dysphoric patient:

1. Helping patients to understand themselves and their life situation, including a broader understanding of their personality, sexuality, and relationships. An historical perspective is useful in this process and helps patients to understand the development of their gender identity as well as other aspects of their life. Though one cannot usually identify the "cause" of the person's gender dysphoria, it is beneficial to patients to have a clear picture of their own life story.

2. An exploration of the options available for the resolution of gender dysphoria. This exploration includes consideration of options that the patient may have not seriously considered. For example, many patients have not thought about living part time as the other gender and taking hormones but living most of the time in their original gender and not pursuing surgery. The patient must evaluate the benefits and costs, advantages, and disadvantages of the various options. For example, few male-to-female patients have considered the fact that as a woman, they are likely to make less money or to be harassed by men. Likewise, few female-to-male patients realize that once they start taking hormones they are likely to develop male-pattern baldness.

A valuable aid in this process is guiding the patient to sources of information for transgendered individuals. A valuable resource is the International Foundation for Gender Education (P.O. Box 229, Waltham, MA 02254-0229, or www.ifge.org). The clinician working with transgendered patients should become educated about local support groups. Patients typically find the opportunity to talk with other gender-dysphoric individuals very helpful. The Internet and online group discussions serve this function as well.

3. Addressing psychological difficulties in the person's life other than the gender identity issue. Most individuals who seek treatment for gender dysphoria have experienced considerable distress in their lives, usually as a result of their gender conflict. This has manifested itself typically as a depression, but it may also be expressed through acting-out behavior or substance abuse. The gender problem also typically interferes with the development of peer, family, and intimate relationships. Confusion and conflicts regarding sexual orientation are also common. Although the gender patient need not be a paragon of mental health, research indicates that patients with attendant mental health difficulties fare more poorly through the course of gender reassignment.

A related issue is whether a gender-dysphoric patient with a significant mental health problem, such as schizophrenia, bipolar disorder, or severe personality disorder, should be allowed to pursue gender reassignment surgery.

None of these mental disorders necessarily rules out gender reassignment, but it is the responsibility of the mental health professional to help the patient receive appropriate treatment for these other conditions before pursuing medical intervention. An actively psychotic person should not undergo surgery.

4. Therapy with gender patients should focus the person's life goals through development of a carefully delineated plan. This plan should address the following issues:

    a. When and how the patient will make a full transition to the other gender role.

    b. How he or she will make the gender change at work (e.g., whether to stay on the same job or to quit and start a new job after the transition).

    c. When and how to reveal his or her intentions to family and friends.

    d. When and where to obtain hormonal and/or surgical treatment.

    e. If not pursuing full-time transition, when he or she will present as one gender or the other.

When problems occur in treatment, it is usually because the patient did not anticipate the obstacles he or she would encounter. For example, some gender-dysphoric patients begin to present themselves in androgynous or gender-confused ways (e.g., a male wearing two earrings, makeup, and female shirts) at their workplace which may then trigger negative reactions or dismissal. Another common mistake for transitioning gender patients is to come out too quickly or to be too confrontational in their approach with others. If the clinician is sufficiently aware of these real obstacles and the patient is able to anticipate them, serious problems may be avoided.

OUTCOME OF GENDER REASSIGNMENT

Gender reassignment (sex change) has been the most carefully studied outcome for gender dysphoria. More than 75 empirical studies of the outcome of gender reassignment surgery have been published (see Pfäfflin & Junge, 1998). The quality of this research, however, is relatively weak (Abramowitz, 1986; Green & Fleming, 1990; Snaith, Tarsh, & Reid, 1993) and includes the following limitations:

1. The lack of any, or appropriate, control groups for comparison;
2. High levels of subject attrition;
3. Selection biases in terms of subject recruitment (e.g., high- or low-functioning individuals);
4. Lack of randomized treatment groups;
5. Limited information on subject's mental health history, diagnosis, and previous treatment;

6. Lack of specificity or consistency in the surgical and/or hormonal interventions;
7. Lack of longitudinal data or follow-up evaluations of sufficient duration;
8. Combining subjects with vastly different time periods since surgery;
9. Evaluations by the clinicians who approved or conducted the gender reassignment process;
10. Lack of validated or standardized assessment instruments and the prevalence of ad hoc questionnaires;
11. Mixing of various patient subgroups into heterogeneous subject samples (e.g., males and females, heterosexual and homosexuals); and
12. Diverse definitions of outcome success or failure.

Fortunately, despite these methodological shortcomings, there is a great deal of consistency in the findings of various studies. For the most part, gender reassignment results in improvement or a satisfactory outcome in two-thirds (Abramowitz, 1986) to 90% of patients (Green & Fleming, 1990). This appears to be true with both male and female transsexuals, with a variety of surgical, hormonal, and psychological interventions, and when outcome is measured at widely varying points in time. Most studies define success as improvement in social, psychological, or vocational function and/or satisfaction with the outcome. The domains that have shown the greatest improvement are self-satisfaction, interpersonal interaction, and psychological health, whereas the areas of economic success typically show less improvement. The areas of satisfaction with cosmetic results were often inconsistent, due perhaps to significant changes in technique and/or expectations over the years. The impact on sexual functioning is unclear. The overall evidence of positive outcomes for the gender reassignment process is a striking conclusion.

Every review of gender reassignment outcome must carefully consider the "casualties" or "failures" involved. Casualties have been defined as regretting surgery, a psychotic episode, suicide, or hospitalization. Using these criteria, the rate of poor outcomes appears to be 8% of subjects (Abramowitz, 1986; Pauly, 1981). It is questionable, however, as to whether problems following reassignment can be viewed strictly as outcomes of the process. It may be possible that an individual with a history of depression or psychiatric hospitalizations would continue to experience these problems postoperatively but still be considered better off after reassignment. A better definition of failure would be the situation in which the individual experienced significant regret about the change and/or manifested some clear decline in one or more areas of functioning.

A review of the outcome literature by Pfäfflin (1992) suggests that the incidence of regrets about gender reassignment surgery is quite low. For female-to-male transsexuals the incidence was less than 1%. For male-to-female individuals, the rate was less than 2%. The review also suggested that poor differential diagnosis, failure to go through a trial period of living as the desired gender, and poor surgical results were the primary reasons for postoperative regrets. Those who began to cross-dress later in life and those with serious psychological difficulties before gender reassignment are more likely to regret surgery (Kuiper & Cohen-Kettenis, 1998).

The evidence suggests that postoperative transsexuals have a greater risk of suicide than does a nonclinical population. About 2% of male-to-female transsexuals and 0.5% of female-to-male transsexuals attempt suicide. It is unclear, however, whether this should be viewed as an effect of reassignment surgery or the manifestation of preexisting psychological difficulties. It is also true that there is a higher than normal rate of suicide among gender dysphorics who do not go through gender reassignment surgery.

Overall, gender reassignment surgery is associated with successful outcomes. The relevant questions then become: For whom does it work?; What works best? What are the predictors of a positive outcome?

Good Candidates

Most of the research on outcomes has examined male-to-female transsexuals and female-to-male transsexuals separately. A number of studies have compared the outcomes between the two groups (Bodlund & Kullgren, 1995; Sørensen, 1981a, 1981b; Wålinder & Thuwe, 1975). The consensus derived from the literature at this point clearly suggests that female-to-male transsexuals manifest a more favorable psychosocial outcome following gender reassignment than do male-to-female transexuals.

Kuiper and Cohen-Kettenis (1995) suggested that this might be due several factors, including better social acceptance of these individuals, greater ease for female-to-males in passing as their desired gender, and greater burdens for male-to-females, such as marriage and childrearing. Clinical observations frequently suggest that female-to-male transsexuals, as a group, present as mentally healthier and more stable than do male-to-females. They also appear to be more cooperative with treatment.

Other research has compared the outcome among male-to-female transsexuals between those classified as autogynephilic versus androphilic. These studies found that significantly more autogynephilic transsexuals regretted reassignment surgery than did androphilic transsexuals. The reasons for the differences between these two groups remain uncertain.

Several studies have found that those individuals with character pathology, negative self-image, poor judgment, a history of serious depression, an "overreactive temperament," or other serious psychological disorders show a significantly poorer response to gender reassignment, are more likely to regret reassignment surgery, and are more likely to attempt suicide following reassignment (Abramowitz, 1986; Bodlund & Kullgren, 1995; Botzer & Vehrs, 1995; Green & Fleming, 1990).

The impact of age as a predictor of response to gender reassignment is unclear. Some authors (Lindemalm, Körlin, & Uddenberg, 1987; Wålinder, Lundstrum, & Thuwe, 1978) found that older patients did not respond as well to reassignment as did younger patients. However, in a recent follow-up study of postoperative male-to-female transsexuals, Schroder and Carroll (1999) did not find a relationship between age at surgery and outcome.

Although most established programs have refused gender reassignment to adolescents, there is some evidence that the standard process of psychotherapy, hormonal treatment, real-life experiment, and surgical reassignment may benefit older adolescents as well (Cohen-Kettenis & van Goozen, 1995).

Botzer and Vehrs (1995) found that greater satisfaction with reassignment surgery was also associated with a better work history, family and other social support, and realistic expectations. Schroder and Carroll (1999) found that the individuals who reported high levels of current stress reported less satisfaction with the psychosocial outcome of reassignment surgery.

Effective Treatment

A large-scale review of male-to-female postoperative transsexuals focused on factors contributing to favorable outcomes of gender surgery (Botzer & Vehrs, 1995). The authors found that patients reported more satisfaction when they had undergone at least a 1-year period of living in the desired gender role before surgery and that the longer the period is, the better the outcome. A break in the real-life trial of living as female was associated with a poorer outcome. Not surprisingly, better psychosocial outcomes for gender reassignment have consistently been found to be related to good surgical outcomes (Fleming, MacGowan, Robinson, Spitz, & Salt, 1982; Ross & Need, 1989; Schroder & Carroll, 1999). Consistent administration of hormones has also been associated with better postoperative satisfaction (Wålinder et al., 1978). Realistic expectations of surgery were also predictive of better outcome in this large follow-up study. There is, therefore, significant empirical support for the use of the HBIGDA Standards of Care.

CASES OF TREATMENT OF GENDER DYSPHORIA

In the cases described next, the gender of the pronouns used is based on the gender identity that the person ultimately adopted, in order to make the reports clearer. In clinical work with gender dysphoria patients, it is customary to refer the patient's gender based on the way in which he or she presents.

Case 1

Ms. A was a 45-year-old, white male who had presented with a desire to have genital gender reassignment surgery. Her presenting problem was that all her life she had wanted to be a woman. She had been married for 15 years and had two daughters. She was working as a steelworker and had been steadily employed for 22 years.

Ms. A came from a working-class background. She was the third of three sons. Her parents were both immigrants from Italy and her father had worked in the steel mills all her life. She denied that they had ever expressed either an overt or covert wish for her to be a girl. She reported that her father had been very masculine and a hard worker. She had a distant but not conflictual relationship with him. Ms. A noted, however, that she had never been the son he wanted her to be. She described her mother as negative and uncaring. She never felt close to her mother, though she had tried to improve the relationship over time.

In childhood, Ms. A was not at all effeminate; rather she was an active and rough boy. She was involved with sports and not interested in female games or girls her own age. At age 6 or 7, she began to occasionally put on her mother's clothes. She reported that this felt pleasurable, but she did not have sexual arousal during this activity. She was ashamed of this behavior and kept it hidden from her family.

Ms. A reported that beginning with adolescence, the cross-dressing became sexually stimulating, and it was also emotionally satisfying to imagine herself as a woman. Her cross-dressing consisted of putting on her mothers' clothes, applying makeup, and looking at herself in the mirror. She would usually sexually stimulate herself. Her cross-dressing had continued up to the present, usually once or twice a week. On four occasions she purged herself of her collection of female clothes, makeup, and accessories (e.g., wigs) because she felt disgusted with the behavior. This was also prompted on two occasions by her girlfriend or wife finding her clothes, becoming upset, and threatening to leave. Over time, however, she would begin to cross-dress again and rebuild a female wardrobe.

Her sexual attraction during adolescence and young adulthood was primarily toward women. She rarely dated girls in high school. She first had sex at the urging of her female partner. She did not have any serious relationships with women before meeting her wife. She also began to have fantasies during the cross-dressing that were of herself, as female, being with a man but not sexually involved. They would, instead, be having a romantic dinner and kissing. Men's bodies were not sexually appealing to her, but, rather, the fantasy of being with a man made her feel more like a woman.

Beginning at the age of 15, Ms. A occasionally went out in public dressed as a woman. She was anxious while doing this and tended to do it at night and remain in her car, so that others would not be able to perceive her as male. In her mid-20s, she became aware of transsexualism and the gender reassignment process. She then developed a desire to make the transition to female but did not seek out treatment due to conflicts about these urges.

Ms. A met her wife at the age of 18. She was attracted to her because she was pretty, feminine, and caring. The coupled dated for a year before marrying. Ms. A hoped that the marriage would eliminate her desire to become female and the urge to cross-dress. She enjoyed the sexual relationship and initially found that she was less interested in cross-dressing. She never relinquished her autogynephilic fantasies. After a year, however, her desire to cross-dress grew stronger again and she began to go out occasionally as female. She admitted to her wife that she had a strong need to cross-dress. After some distress and conflict, her wife accepted this behavior and allowed Ms. A to cross-dress at home. Eventually, her wife would also go shopping with Ms. A for female clothes. She refused, however, to make love with Ms. A when she was dressed as a woman. During this period, Ms. A continued to work and live as a male. Shortly before the start of treatment, Ms. A revealed her cross-dressing and gender dysphoria to her daughters, because she felt that they should know her real self.

Ms. A described the year prior to seeking treatment as extremely difficult. Her struggle with her desire to become female, while wanting to hold on to her marriage and her family, became more intense. She became depressed and started to abuse alcohol. She also began to go out at night as female and approach unknown women and ask them how to become more feminine. This activity was also sexually exciting.

Ms. A sought treatment due to her growing unhappiness. At the start of treatment, she was insistent on obtaining gender surgery but was naive about the process. As part of the initial evaluation, she was seen for several sessions alone and once with her wife. Her wife was supportive of Ms. A, including her desire to come out as female. The initial evaluation also revealed that Ms. A was chronically depressed and abused alcohol. In spite of these difficulties, Ms. A was functioning well in her work and social roles. As a male, she had risen through the ranks of her company and had been president of her softball league for many years. She also had good relationships with her daughters.

According to the HBIGDA Standards of Care and given the presence of depression and alcohol abuse, it was recommended that Ms. A engage in psychological treatment for a minimum of 1 year before any hormonal or surgical intervention. She was not pleased with this recommendation but accepted it. She resisted the view that she needed time to consider her pursuit of gender reassignment. Couple and family therapy were also recommended to Ms. A to address the inevitable issues that the gender dilemma created in the family.

Despite her early resistance, Ms. A began to use the therapy productively by thinking through her future options and mapping out a plan for transition. She also was able to listen to the therapist's suggestions on how to address these issues with her daughters. She began to address her problems with depression and alcohol. Couple sessions explored her wife's feelings about the future and helped them to come to a decision to divorce but to remain involved with their daughters. Their daughters responded well to the family sessions and agreed that Ms. A was happier when able to live as a woman.

After 1 year of therapy, Ms. A started on female hormones and began the process of coming out as female. Coworkers accepted the change and she was even reelected president of her softball league, though she had to switch to a mixed-gender team. Her parents and siblings, however, remained adamantly opposed to the change and stopped socializing with her. Ms. A and her wife divorced but lived in adjoining apartments so that they could remain close to each other and their daughters. Her daughters remained supportive, though they endured some harassment at school when their father's gender transition became public. Ms. A also began to date men sporadically. These relationships did not last very long and never extended beyond kissing. The relationships were with men who knew of her gender transition and had known her as a man. Ms. A remained frustrated with these romantic experiences. Over time, her depression lifted and did not return. She also significantly curtailed her drinking. She lost considerable weight and even stopped smoking, all because she felt she now had a reason to want to be healthy.

After two years of feminizing hormones, living full time as a woman, and continued therapy, Ms. A felt ready for genital surgery. According to HBIGDA guidelines, she received a second evaluation from another psychologist, who also approved surgery. Her surgery went well and despite some minor complications, Ms. A was pleased with the cosmetic results.

A follow-up 1 year after surgery found that Ms. A was doing well. She had remained in her job, though she had experienced some pressure from her employer to leave and had to threaten a lawsuit to protect her job. She continued to live next door to her ex-wife and daughters, who now called her Aunt A. She had lost some of her old friends, mostly male, and had gained some new ones, mostly female. Her biggest frustration was difficulty in establishing a romantic relationship with a man. She had dated several, but they had backed away when she wanted the relationship to become more serious and/or sexual. Overall, she felt strongly that the gender reassignment was the best thing that had ever happened to her.

Comments

This case is quite typical of the autogynephilic transsexual in that there is a history of early cross-gender identification but not effeminate behavior in childhood. Cross-dressing is associated with sexual arousal during adolescence and young adulthood. In addition to the autogynephilia, there is a sexual attraction to females. There is a pattern of attempting to stop the cross-dressing and purging the female wardrobe. Gender dysphoria and the wish for gender reassignment become more pronounced with age.

The course of treatment is also similar to most in that it began with initial resistance to therapy but then developed into a productive process. The outcome is characteristic in that Ms. A experienced a significant improvement in psychological well-being but had difficulties in finding and establishing satisfying romantic or sexual relationships.

What is atypical with Ms. A is the consistent support of her wife and daughters. In most cases, male-to-female transsexuals lose their relationships with their wives and become estranged from their children. This case shows that with appropriate intervention the families of transsexuals need not be harmed by the gender transition. In sum, Ms. A's story demonstrates that for many gender patients, carefully evaluated and treated appropriately, gender reassignment is a successful resolution to gender dysphoria.

Case 2

Mr. B presented as a 21-year-old, white female and a senior at a large state college. He reported that he was confused about his sexual identity and felt he did not fit into the role of being a woman. Initially, he was not pursuing a gender transition but, rather, wanted to alleviate thoughts of himself as a male. He had sought psychological treatment at school but felt angry that the counselor had told him that he was just going through a stage and did not address his gender identity confusion. His parents, likewise, told him that he was just immature and that having sex with a man would cure him of his gender dysphoria.

Mr. B was born and raised in an upper-middle-class section of a small city. He had one older sister. He described his mother as very loving, very feminine, but also stubborn, square, and closed-minded. As a child he was close to his mother, but over time he felt that his mother was unhappy that he was not his mother's "little girl." He described his father as masculine and smart. He was not very affectionate, but he was more easygoing than her mother. In childhood he felt closer to his father and they would often do things together. He described his older sister as intelligent and feminine. He felt that his sister was the parent's favorite child in the family.

Mr. B described his childhood as uncomfortable because he was always worried about things. He noted that he was a tomboy and always preferred to play sports with the boys. He hated being forced to be with girls in grade school. He became distraught at puberty when he developed breasts and started menstruation. He became more alienated from the family during adolescence. Despite this unhappiness, he tried to date boys in order to fit into the social cliques at school. He was, however, never sexually or romantically attracted to boys. Concurrently, he was suppressing his sexual and emotional attraction to girls and women.

A separate interview with Mr. B's parents indicated that they thought the problem was his attitude. They felt he was trying to cling to childhood by rejecting his given gender role. They described Mr. B as a delightful child, free-spirited and extroverted. They did admit that when asked at age 3 what he wanted to be when he grew up, he answered, "A boy." They noted that at puberty he became more withdrawn and hostile. They believed this was due to his problems with relationships.

In college, Mr. B went through a period of alcohol abuse and depression.

Having more freedom was confusing to him. His family had been very strict and protective. His gender dysphoria and attraction to women intensified, but he still avoided initiating sexual relationships with women because he felt lesbian sex was disgusting. His excessive drinking was an escape from his gender conflicts. He did, however, give up his pretense of dating men and he began to adopt a more masculine appearance. His parents became more concerned about him but resisted taking him to a psychologist, for which he was resentful. He eventually sought therapy on his own but found that it did not help. His school counselor then referred him to a gender dysphoria program.

The initial evaluation identified long-standing gender dysphoria, as well as chronic depression and alcohol abuse. Psychological testing indicated that while attempting to maintain an outwardly pleasant demeanor, he was experiencing considerable anger and hopelessness. A period of 1 year of psychotherapy, with occasional family therapy sessions, was recommended. His parents reluctantly agreed to the plan. Mr. B was cooperative throughout therapy. Once he realized that he was not going to be pushed to give up his masculine identification, he became more trusting. He used psychotherapy to explore his gender conflicts, his low self-esteem, his confusion about relationships and sexuality, and his future goals. He stopped drinking and began to focus on his schoolwork. He established a romantic and sexual relationship with a bisexual woman who was attracted to his masculine demeanor. His appearance continued to evolve to a more androgynous look. He had not, however, gone out as male in public due to his fear of being caught as a woman dressed as a man.

The occasional family sessions were difficult because his parents were upset with his apparent movement toward gender transition. They insisted that he hide this from the extended family and their friends. Family therapy focused on educating them about gender dysphoria and helping them to cope with the changes in Mr. B.

After 1 year of therapy, Mr. B was functioning well in school, had a stable relationship with a woman, and was no longer depressed. He had decided to pursue a full gender transition to male and was ready to begin hormonal treatment. After taking hormones for several months, he became more comfortable going out publicly as man, but only at night and in distant towns. Therapy began to focus more on his plans for making a gender transition and his relationships with his girlfriend. It also addressed ways to help his family understand and accept his gender identity. After another year of treatment, Mr. B moved to another state, where he started working as a man. He had had all his school records and identification papers changed to his male name and gender.

Several years later, Mr. B returned for a follow-up evaluation for breast surgery and hysterectomy. He was doing well at his job, where no one knew of his past. He was engaged to be married to his former girlfriend. He was seen for a second opinion by another psychologist, who also approved him for gender surgery, which involved bilateral mastectomy and a hysterectomy. He also had surgery to create a male chest. He was very pleased with the cosmetic results. At the time he reiterated his desire to have genital surgery but was unable to afford the cost. He was frustrated but determined to save the necessary funds.

Another 4 years later Mr. B called again to say that he had saved enough money for the female-to-male genital surgery. He was again reevaluated and found ready for genital surgery. This involved phalloplasty, which is the creation of a penis out of a flap of tissue taken from the forearm and attached to the nerve and vascular systems of the pelvic region. Despite some early complications, the surgical results were very good. At a 1-year follow-up, Mr. B was able to have intercourse with his neophallus, which had sexual sensation, though he was not able to achieve orgasm through intercourse. He had broken up with his fiancée and had developed a new relationship with a heterosexual woman who knew of his previous gender. He felt as though he had accomplished all the goals he had set for himself regarding his gender identity, except marriage and children. He hoped that in time he would have these as well. His main disappointment had been his parent's inability to accept his new identity and their continued estrangement from him.

Comments

Mr. B's history is typical of female-to-male transsexuals in most respects, especially the early masculine identification, attraction to women, and rejection of a lesbian orientation. The presence of a period of depression and alcohol abuse is also common. His story is somewhat different than most in that he pursued treatment at a relatively early age and was able to afford phalloplastic surgery. The outcome, however, was typical (i.e., great satisfaction with the gender transition.)

Case 3

The third case is that of a 40-year-old, white man who was married with four children. Mr. C was a colonel in the Army. He presented with a request for help in controlling his cross-dressing activities. His wife had recently discovered that he was cross-dressing and was threatening to divorce him and take their children away. She had discovered his cross-dressing once before, at which time he underwent a brief period of treatment and stopped the behavior for 6 months. He had continued it since then for 4 years without his wife's knowledge. At the time of the initial evaluation he was highly motivated to control the cross-dressing, due primarily to fear of losing his family. He was also concerned that he would be discovered by his superiors and dishonorably discharged. He reported being ashamed of the behavior, which made him feel less than a man.

At age 6, Mr. C began to cross-dress in the clothes of his younger sister. Cross-dressing became sexually arousing at puberty at age 11. When he was 9, his younger sister died in a car accident. He reported that for several years after her death, he consciously wished to take her place and continued to cross-dress in her clothes. He fantasized that he could be his mother's little girl. During childhood and adolescence, he cross-dressed about once a month. He also developed more typical sexual attraction toward females. From ages 12 to 14 he experienced infatuations with several male peers, though he had never had any sexual experience with males and had not had homosexual urges since that time. He stopped cross-dressing for 7 years when he first went into the Army but started again shortly after getting married at age 24. Since that time, he had gone through cycles of increasing time and effort in his cross-dressing, followed by purging himself of his feminine attire, stopping for several months, and then slowing beginning it again.

Mr. C's cross-dressing involved secretly taking his female clothing and accessories, such as a wig and makeup, on out-of-town trips. While away, he would spend 2 to 3 hours preparing himself in order to achieve an illusion of himself as a female. He would go out in public with the hope of receiving attention as a woman. The whole process was sexually arousing and would culminate with masturbation after returning to his room, using the image of himself as a woman out in public. He would also engage in frequent masturbation to these fantasies when he was not able to cross-dress. He described the cross-dressing and passing as a female as intensely exciting. Mr. C also reported that beginning about 1 year before the evaluation, he had begun to think more frequently about gender reassignment.

The patient was the middle of seven children. He described his father as very violent, alcoholic, and extremely strict. He routinely physically abused the patient and his siblings, with the exception of the sister who died. He described his mother as timid, insecure, and unaffectionate. She was seriously depressed and completely unavailable to the patient for several years before and after his sister's death.

Treatment first focused on helping Mr. C and his wife through the crisis, brought on by rediscovery of the transvestic behavior. Mr. C's wife was also significantly depressed at this point and she was referred for individual treatment. Once the couple was more stable, the options for the resolution of the problem were explored. It was suggested that he could try to stop the behavior or she could try to accept the behavior with limits. Both insisted that they wanted to completely stop the transvestic behavior. The treatment then consisted of a combination of behavioral interventions to inhibit the behavior, psychotherapy to explore underlying psychological issues, and intermittent couple therapy sessions to deal with marital issues. Covert sensitization was used to give Mr. C a way to inhibit the urge to cross-dress by imagining aversive consequences to his behavior. For example, he was asked to write out a scenario in which he was caught while cross-dressing and thrown in jail, humiliated in front of his neighbors, divorced by his wife, cut off from contact with his children, and dishonorably discharged from the Army.

The behavioral treatment quickly succeeded in eliminating the behavior, though the impulse continued at a reduced frequency. Psychotherapy focused on exploring the possible origins to his cross-dressing, including the comfort he received by cross-dressing, even before his sister's death, as an escape from his father's abusiveness and his mother's emotional absence. The couple sessions provided reassurance to his wife that he was able to control the behavior and a focus on strengthening their sexual and emotional intimacy.

He remained in regular treatment for 6 months and treatment continued through intermittent follow-up visits. Several years later, he reported an absence of any cross-dressing impulses or behavior other than occasional sexual dreams of cross-dressing. He also reported a complete absence of desires to become a woman.

Comments

This case is similar to that of other paraphilias except that the sexual impulse is for cross-dressing and the sexual fantasy is the image of being a woman. What is interesting about this case is the patient's increasing desire to become a female. In spite of this, treating the autogynephilia as a paraphilia resulted in suppression of both the cross-dressing behavior and the autogynephilic fantasy. What remains striking is how similar Ms. A and Mr. C were, yet how they pursued different goals and ended up with different outcomes. It remains unclear as to why some individuals with autogynephilia choose to make a gender transition (Ms. A) whereas others attempt to eradicate their cross-dressing and desire to become female (Mr. C).

REFERENCES

Abramowitz, S. I. (1986). Psychosocial outcomes of sex reassignment surgery. *Journal of Consulting and Clinical Psychology, 54*, 183–189.

Achenbach, T. M., & Edelbrock, C. S. (1981). Behavioral problems and Competencies reported by the parents of normal and disturbed children aged four through sixteen. *Monographs of the Society for Research in Child Development, 46*(1, Serial No. 188).

American Psychiatric Association. (1994*). Diagnostic and statistical manual of mental disorders* (4th ed.). Washington, DC: Author.

Bakker, A., van Kesteren, P. J., Gooren, L. J. G., & Bezemer, P. D. (1993). The prevalence of transsexualism in the Netherlands. *Acta Psychiatrica Scandinavica, 87*, 237–238.

Barlow, D. H., Abel, G. G., & Blanchard, E. B. (1979). Gender identity change in transsexuals: Follow-up and replication. *Archives of General Psychiatry, 36*, 1001–1007.

Beitel, A. (1985). The spectrum of gender identity disturbances: An intrapsychic model. In B. W. Steiner (Ed.), *Gender dysphoria: Development, research, management* (pp. 189–206). New York: Plenum.

Benjamin, H. (1966). *The transsexual phenomenon.* New York: Julian Press.

Blanchard, R. (1985). Research methods for the typological study of gender disorders in males. In B. W. Steiner (Ed.), *Gender dysphoria: Development, research, management* (pp. 227–257). New York: Plenum.

Blanchard, R. (1989). The concept of autogynephilia and the typology of male gender dysphoria. *Journal of Nervous and Mental Disorders, 177*, 616–623.

Bodlund, O., & Kullgren, G. (1995). *Transsexualism: General outcome and prognostic factors.* Paper presented at the XIVth International Symposium on Gender Dysphoria, Kloster Irsee, Germany.

Botzer, M. C., & Vehrs, B. (1995). *Psychosocial and treatment factors contributing to favorable outcomes of gender reassignment surgery.* Paper presented at the XIVth International Symposium on Gender Dysphoria, Kloster Irsee, Germany.

Brown, G., Wise, T., & Costa, P. (1995). *Personality characteristics and sexual functioning of 188 American transgendered men: Comparison of patients with nonpatients.* Paper presented at the XIVth International Symposium on Gender Dysphoria, Kloster Irsee, Germany.

Bullough, V., & Bullough, B. (1993). *Cross dressing sex, and gender.* Philadelphia: University of Pennsylvania Press.

Carroll, R. A. (1999). Outcomes of treatment for gender dysphoria. *Journal of Sex Education and Therapy, 24*(3), 128–136.

Carroll, R. A., & Donahey, K. (1994). *Autogynephilia: Three treatments, three outcomes.* Paper presented at the annual meeting of the Society for Sex Therapy and Research, Atlanta.

Cohen-Kettenis, P., & van Goozen, S. (1995). *Post-operative functioning in adolescent transsexuals.* Paper presented at the XIVth International Symposium on Gender Dysphoria, Kloster Irsee, Germany.

Denny, D. (1997) Transgender: Some historical, cross-cultural, and Contemporary models and methods of coping and treatment. In B. Bullough, V. Bullough, & J. Elias (Ed.), *Gender blending* (pp. 33–47). New York: Prometheus Books.

Devor, H. (1989). *Gender blending.* Bloomington: University of Indiana Press.

Docter, R. F. (1988). *Transvestites and transsexuals: Toward a theory of cross-gender behavior.* New York: Plenum.

Docter, R. F., & Fleming, J. S. (1992). Dimensions of transvestism and transsexualism: The validation and factorial structure of the Cross-Gender Questionnaire. In W. O. Bockting & E. Coleman (Ed.), *Gender dysphoria: Interdisciplinary approaches in clinical management* (pp. 15–37). Binghamton, NY: Haworth Press.

Fleming, M., MacGowan, B. R., Robinson, L., Spitz, J., & Salt, P. (1982). The body image of the post-operative female-to-male transsexual. *Journal of Consulting and Clinical Psychology, 50*, 461–462.

Green, R. (1987). *The "sissy boy syndrome" and the development of homosexuality.* New Haven, CT: Yale University Press.

Green, R., & Fleming, D. T. (1990). Transsexual surgery follow-up: Status in the 1990s. *Annual Review of Sex Research, 1*, 163–174.

Harry Benjamin International Gender Dysphoria Association. (1998). *The standards of care of gender identity disorders (5th version).* Dusseldorf: Symposion.

Hoenig, J. (1985). Etiology of transsexualism. In B. W. Steiner (Ed.), *Gender dysphoria: Development, research and management* (pp. 33–74). New York: Plenum.

Kuiper, A. J., & Cohen-Kettenis, P. T. (1995). *Factors influencing post-operative "regret" in transsexuals.* Paper presented at the XIVth International Symposium on Gender Dysphoria, Kloster Irsee, Germany.

Kuiper, A. J., & Cohen-Kettenis, P. T. (1998). Gender role reversal among postoperative transsexuals. *International Journal of Transgenderism, 2.* (http://www.symposion.com/ijt/).

Levine, S., & Lothstein, L. (1981). Transsexualism or the gender dysphoria syndromes. *Journal of Sex and Marital Therapy, 7*, 85–113.

Lindemalm, G., Körlin, D., & Uddenberg, N. (1987). Prognostic factors vs. outcome in male-to-female transsexualism: A follow-up study of 13 cases. *Acta Psychiatrica Scandinavica, 75*, 268–274.

Lothstein, L. M. (1984). Psychological testing with transsexuals: A 30-year review. *Journal of Personality Assessment, 48*, 500–507.

Lothstein, L. M., & Levine, S. B. (1981). Expressive psychotherapy with gender dysphoric patients. *Archives of General Psychiatry, 38*, 924–929.

Meyer, J. M. (1979). The theory of gender identity disorders. *Journal of the American Psycho-analytic Association, 30,* 381–418.

Money, J. M. (1994). The concept of gender identity disorder in childhood and adolescence after 39 years. *Journal of Sex and Marital Therapy, 20,* 163–177.

Pauly, I. B. (1981). Outcome of sex reassignment surgery for transsexuals. *Australian and New Zealand Journal of Psychiatry, 15,* 45–51.

Pfäfflin, F. (1992). Regrets after sex reassignment surgery. In W. O. Bockting & E. Coleman (Ed.), *Gender dysphoria: Interdisciplinary approaches in clinical management.* Binghamton, NY: Haworth Press.

Pfäfflin, F., & Junge, A. (1998). Thirty years of international follow-up studies after SRS: A comprehensive review, 1961–1991. Symposion Electronic Books: (http://www.symposion.com/ijt/books/index:htm#Sex Reassignment)

Rekers, G. S. (1985) Gender identity problems. In P. A. Bornstein & A. E. Kazdin (Eds.), *Handbook of clinical behavior therapy with children* (pp. 658–699). Homewood, IL: Dorsey Press.

Ross, M., & Need, J. (1989). Effects of adequacy of gender reassignment surgery on psychological adjustment: A follow-up of fourteen male-to-female patients. *Archives of Sexual Behavior, 18,* 145–153.

Schroder, M., & Carroll, R. (1999). Sexological outcomes of gender reassignment surgery. *Journal of Sex Education and Therapy, 24*(3), 137–146.

Snaith, P., Tarsh, M. J., & Reid, R. (1993). Sex reassignment surgery: A study of 141 Dutch transsexuals. *British Journal of Psychiatry, 162,* 681–685.

Sørensen, T. (1981a). A follow-up study of operative transsexual males. *Acta Psychiatrica Scandinavica, 63,* 486–503.

Sørensen, T. (1981b). A follow-up study of operative transsexual females. *Acta Psychiatrica Scandinavica, 64,* 50–64.

Stoller, R. J. (1985). *Presentations of gender.* New Haven, CT: Yale University Press.

von Krofft-Ebing (1933). *Psychopathia sexualis, with special reference to the antipathic sexual instinct: A medico-forensic study.* (F. J. Rebman, Trans.). New York: Physicians and Surgeons. (Original work published 1906)

Wålinder, J., Lundström, B., & Thuwe, I. (1978). Prognostic factors in the assessment of male transsexuals for sex reassignment. *British Journal of Psychiatry, 132,* 16–20.

Wålinder, J., & Thuwe, I. (1975). *A social–psychiatric follow-up study of 24 sex-reassignment transsexuals.* Gotheborg, Sweden: Scandinavian University Books.

Zhou, J. N., Hofman, M. A., Gooren, L. J., & Swaab, D. F. (1997). A sex Difference in the Human brain and its relation to transsexuality. *Nature, 378,* 68–70.

Zucker, K. J, & Bradley, S. J. (1995). *Gender identity disorder and psychosexual problems in children and adolescents.* New York: Guilford Press.

14

Sexual Problems in Chronic Illness

LESLIE R. SCHOVER

Despite the fact that sexual problems are frequently associated with chronic illness, physicians and practitioners have tended to avoid the sexual concerns or problems of individuals suffering from major illnesses. In part, this avoidance is due to time pressures, but it is also frequently related to discomfort, reluctance, or ignorance on the part of the clinician regarding available assessment or treatments options.

In her updated chapter, Leslie R. Schover discusses the specific ways in which chronic illness typically compromises sexual function. Lack of desire or arousal is often associated with the diagnosis or treatment of diseases such as cancer and AIDS or diseases related to central nervous system function. Chemotherapy, radiation, and various pharmacological treatments often reduce sexual desire and arousal as well.

Psychological factors, as well as medical–organic issues, are often implicated in diminished sexual interest or arousal. Depression, loss of self-esteem, changes in physical appearance, and assorted body image or performance fears can also reduce the willingness to be involved sexually in individuals with chronic illnesses. Intermittent or chronic pain problems are another common source of diminished sexual desire.

Sex therapy with the medically ill client poses special challenges for the clinician and can call for creative approaches to individual problems. For example, Schover points out that sexual counseling for these individuals may occur in a medical center or hospital milieu, where constraints on privacy and other communication barriers exist. Nevertheless, the resourceful clinician is likely to find practical solutions to the problems.

The author considers a variety of assessment approaches, although she stresses the particular role of the clinical interview. She provides an inventory of specific questions to ask when conducting the initial interview. Finally, she emphasizes that there is much to be gained from even a few sessions of sexual counseling. Treatment goals may be modest but even a few simple suggestions may make a major difference to the patient and his or her partner.

Schover emphasizes the rewards as well as the challenges of providing sexual counseling for patients coping with major illness. She concludes her current chapter by affirming the importance of sexual intimacy and pleasure in the face of physical disease.

Leslie R. Schover, PhD, is Associate Professor of Behavioral Science at the University of Texas, M. D. Anderson Cancer Center in Houston, Texas. She is a nationally recognized author on the topic of sexuality and illness and has published widely. She is the author of Sexuality and Fertility after Cancer.

Men and women with a chronic illness are at heightened risk for having sexual problems. Chronic illness is a risk factor both because of the physiological changes from a disease or its treatment and because of the psychological impact. Decreased frequencies of sex as well as high rates of sexual dysfunction have been documented in patients with cardiovascular disease, cancer, neurological disease, diabetes, end-stage renal disease, chronic obstructive pulmonary disease, and chronic pain (Schover & Jensen, 1988).

Although sexual function is clearly an aspect of health-related quality of life, many popular scales measuring quality of life omit direct questions about sexual issues or include them only as supplementary measures (Cella, 1996; Ware, 1993). What is the importance of sexuality to the men and women themselves? Typically, sexuality does rate as a salient issue. For example, in studies of men facing possible loss of erections because of treatment for prostate cancer, about a third to a half consider the sexual dysfunction to be an important problem (Fowler, Barry, Lu-Yao, Wasson, & Bin, 1996; Gaylis, Friedel, & Armas, 1998; Karakiewicz, Aprikian, Bazinet, & Elhilali, 1997). The incredible response to the debut of sildenafil (Viagra) provides another indication that sexual function is precious to couples (Schover, 1998). When people are quite debilitated or close to death, sexual function may not be so crucial, but intimate relationships remain a source of warmth and pleasure. In a classic survey of terminally ill cancer patients, although sexual intercourse was not a high priority, the intimacy of touch was rated as very important (Lieber, Plumb, Gerstenzang, & Holland, 1976).

BARRIERS TO IDENTIFYING THE PROBLEMS

Studies on a variety of chronically ill populations concur that physicians often fail to discuss sexual concerns and patients would like more information. This is true for cardiovascular disease (Steinke & Patteron-Midgley, 1996), particularly in women (Brezinka & Kittel, 1996); for recipients of organ transplants

(Hart et al., 1997); for patients undergoing cancer surgery (Burton & Parker, 1997); for men newly diagnosed with prostate cancer (Crawford et al., 1997); for patients having joint replacement (Spica & Schwab, 1996); or for those with rheumatic disease (Dale, 1996).

The need to assess risk factors for the human immunodeficiency virus (HIV) should lend urgency to incorporating sexual assessment into routine medical evaluations. A recent research project tested this assumption by having actors pose in primary care visits with physicians or nurses as real, heterosexual patients at high risk for HIV. Questions about condom use, sexual orientation, and number of past partners were asked by health care providers only 9% to 63% of the time, and actual patient education on reducing sexual risk behaviors was provided even less frequently (Carney & Ward, 1998). The lack of physician assessment is probably even more prevalent for sexual dysfunction associated with chronic illness. In the early 1980s, a study of more than 1,000 medical outpatients in the Veterans Administration found that about a third of men had erection problems, yet hardly any of these dysfunctions had previously been noted in the medical record (Slag et al., 1983).

In the 1970s, it was fashionable to include human sexuality modules in medical student training. The focus was less on didactic material than on emotional aspects of sexuality. An intensive week or weekend course often involved showing erotic films in the hopes that students' anxiety and guilt about sexuality would be reduced. Panels of speakers with alternate sexual lifestyles were also frequently included. These courses tended to preach to the converted. Because they were typically optional rather than required, the more liberal students took them and the conservative students stayed away or reacted with defensiveness. Not surprisingly, many medical schools began to reduce the time allotted to sexuality to just a few hours in the behavioral sciences module. The gap between the ideal and the typical in teaching sexuality to medical students has probably widened in recent years (Leiblum, 1995).

The American Medical Association has been aware of the lack of physician training in assessing and treating sexual problems and has developed a special sexuality educational workshop for continuing medical education (American Medical Association, 1997). With the advent of managed care, however, time pressures on physicians are increasing. The chance is slim that any issue will be addressed other than the patient's presenting complaint. A recent survey of more than 4,000 outpatient visits to family physicians revealed that the average time with a physician was 10 minutes (Stange et al., 1998). This period included history taking, the physical examination, giving feedback, planning treatment, and answering the patient's questions. If a patient reported recent emotional distress, only 18% received a diagnosis of depression or anxiety on visiting their family physician, and the visit length only increased from a mean of 10 minutes to 12.8 minutes (Callahan et al., 1998). Even for patients who are smokers, only 32% of those seen for a tobacco-related illness were given advice to stop smoking by family physicians, and the duration of that advice was typically less than 1.5 minutes (Jaen, Crabtree, Zyzanski, Goodwin, & Stange, 1998). Under these conditions, asking about sexuality is a low priority.

Other barriers to health care providers' assessing sexual problems in patients with chronic illness include discomfort in discussing sexuality, lack of knowledge about the sexual consequences of an illness or its treatment, or ignorance about the types of treatments available for sexual problems. Some physicians (typically young ones) believe that people over age 50 should not be sexually active. Now we must add to the list the penalties in managed care organizations for physicians who refer too many patients for specialty care.

Not surprisingly, sexual problems are typically only identified when patients bring up the topic, and then often not with the physician him- or herself but with an allied care provider such as a nurse, physical therapist, or social worker. Indeed, most of the articles cited previously on sexuality and various chronic medical conditions come from the professional literature of allied care providers. Because few sexual problems are identified in health care settings, few referrals to specialists are made, whether the expertise required is that of a mental health professional trained in sex therapy or of a urologist or gynecologist.

Although surveys of patients typically find that a majority would like their health care providers to ask about sexual issues, a much smaller minority of patients ever actively raise the topic or seek help from a specialist. Well-educated and affluent patients may search the Internet for information on getting help for a sexual problem. Patients who attend support groups sometimes exchange information about sexual problems (Crawford et al., 1997). Patients are often hungry for information provided in a self-help format, particularly disease-specific booklets about sexual issues provided free of charge by nonprofit organizations such as the National Arthritis Foundation, the Multiple Sclerosis Society, or the American Cancer Society (see, e.g., Schover, 1995a, 1995b). They are less apt to spend money to buy a self-help book, although a few are available (Carlton, 1997; Schover, 1997).

Thus patient barriers to asking for help with sexual problems associated with chronic illness include embarrassment in raising the issue with health care providers, lack of knowledge about what is normal after an illness or with aging, lack of knowledge about treatments available, feeling it is stigmatizing to seek sexual counseling, doubting whether a specialist will have a worthwhile medical treatment to offer, and finding out that insurance may not cover treatment of sexual dysfunctions (particularly if treatment will fall under mental health coverage).

Because of the barriers, both to patient and physician recognition of sexual problems, it is difficult to design successful treatment programs in medical settings. Many sex therapists may see an occasional patient with a chronic illness in a private practice office. A few health psychologists working directly in inpatient or outpatient medical centers may be able to integrate sexual assessment and counseling into the framework of more general psychological services for a particular population of patients. Definite patterns do exist, however, in the types of sexual problems that are common.

COMMON SEXUAL PROBLEMS
RELATED TO CHRONIC ILLNESS

Although the whole spectrum of sexual dysfunctions can be seen in chronically ill populations, some problems are especially common. A clinician should be alert for multiple sexual dysfunctions across the phases of the response cycle. For example, a young woman who has had a bone marrow transplant for advanced breast cancer may experience loss of desire for sex. When she attempts to have sexual activity, touch no longer feels very erotic, and because of premature ovarian failure, she has vaginal dryness and dyspareunia. Under these conditions, it becomes difficult for her to reach orgasm. Although some of the sexual dysfunctions may be transient and improve with a change in the patient's medical status, others can be long-term changes.

Low Sexual Desire

Low sexual desire is one of the most typical complaints in men or women with a chronic illness. Although lack of interest in sex sometimes predates the onset of a disease, the more usual picture is a global decrease in desire associated with diagnosis or treatment of a medical problem. Some of the general aspects of having a serious illness often contribute: anxiety about the future, fatigue, chronic pain, or loss of the sense of physical well-being. Direct physiological causes of low desire include abnormal hormone levels. In men, low testosterone may be seen with emaciation or extreme physical stress (e.g., in advanced cases AIDS) (Schurmeyer, Muller, von zur Muhlen, & Schmidt, 1997). Men on hormonal therapy to reduce circulating androgens to treat advanced prostate cancer also typically experience a global loss of interest in sex (Schover, 1993). In premenopausal women, sudden loss of ovarian androgens (e.g., after bilateral oophorectomy or as a result of cancer chemotherapy) may reduce desire for sex (Sherwin, 1998). The more gradual decrease in circulating androgens after natural menopause does not appear to be coupled with lower desire in aging women, however (Cawood & Bancroft, 1996; Dennerstein, Dudley, Hopper, & Burger, 1997).

Loss of desire can occur with damage to the central nervous system as well, for example, in generalized dementia or with some specific brain lesions (Hawton, 1984; Neau et al., 1998). In men or women, elevations of the hormone prolactin related to a pituitary tumor, end-stage renal disease, or medications such as opiate pain relievers or phenothiazines can reduce desire for sex (Schover & Jensen, 1988). Other medications may reduce desire for sex because they act as central nervous system depressants or interfere with the hypothalamic–pituitary–gonadal hormone axis (Segraves, 1988).

Psychological factors also play an important role in reducing sexual desire during a chronic illness. The incidence of depression may increase in medical populations, particularly as physical debilitation worsens (Massie & Popkin, 1998). A man or woman may feel more comfortable asking for help for a loss of sexual desire than with acknowledging a general state of depression. Clinicians need to screen carefully for other signs of depression when low desire is the presenting complaint.

> Herbert, a 45-year-old carpenter, was evaluated for sexual dysfunction. He had several episodes of losing erections around the time he was diagnosed with scleroderma, a progressive autoimmune disease of the connective tissue. He was told he might have only 5 to 10 years to live because his heart was enlarged, and his lungs were becoming fibrotic as part of the illness. Not only was he experiencing shortness of breath, but he was losing the hand dexterity he needed for his work because of loss of flexibility in his skin and joints.
>
> Herbert had lost all desire for sex, so that he and his wife had not even attempted love making for several months. On further questioning, the clinician discovered that Herbert was depressed in mood, had lost 10 pounds because of poor appetite, was awakening each morning at 3 or 4 A.M., and was feeling absent-minded and indecisive. He became tearful during the session when discussing his failures to fulfill his sexual and occupational roles.

Loss of self-esteem related to illness is another factor that can decrease sexual desire. Men often base their self-worth on traditional male roles of wage earner and sexual performer. If an illness threatens to interfere with job skills or erections, it is experienced as an assault against masculine role performance (Liss-Levinson, 1982). Men also tend to withdraw emotionally and sexually if they feel ashamed by illness-related dependency.

The conventional wisdom is that women focus more on changes in physical appearance, whereas men are devastated by changed sexual performance. Yet, procedures such as mastectomy appear to have only minor impact on women's sexual desire and activity (Schover et al., 1995). Conserving the breast by substituting lumpectomy and radiation for mastectomy or having breast reconstruction enhances women's perceptions of being attractive but has little impact on sexual behavior or satisfaction. An element of self-image that appears to have more influence on women's desire for sex is the sexual self-schema (Andersen & Cyranowski, 1995). A carefully designed questionnaire demonstrated that women's view of themselves as sexual could be divided into three factors: two positive scales measuring romantic/passionate feelings and openness to experiencing a variety of sexual behaviors, and a negative factor including embarrassment or sexual inhibition. In women after treatment for gynecological cancer, a negative score on sexual self-schema accounted for a significant proportion of the variance in sexual responsiveness (Andersen, Woods, & Copeland, 1997). In cohorts of older women with chronic illnesses, concern about staying sexually active and functional appears quite a bit less than in comparable groups of men (Althof, Coffman, & Levine, 1984; Schreiner-Engle, Schiavi, Vietorisz, & Smith, 1987). This gender difference may diminish, however, as women who came of age later in the century reach menopause with higher expectations about sexuality as an aspect of quality of life.

An illness may evoke specific fears about sexual activity (Schover & Jensen, 1988). Patients or partners sometimes worry that cancer could be sexually transmitted. After a heart attack or stroke, a common fear is that sex could provoke another cardiovascular crisis. Guilt about such past sexual behavior as an affair, premarital sex, sex with a prostitute, or an abortion can trigger a fear that a disease is the punishment for sin. Because our society generally labels sex as unclean, many patients have a vague notion that intercourse is unhealthy and could interfere with medical treatment. Some even use a kind of religious "bargaining," vowing to give up sex altogether if only they can get well or survive longer.

Finally, loss of desire for sex may reflect decreased intimacy for a couple in which one spouse is ill. The illness often reduces private time for relaxing, talking, or exchanging affection because both spouses are scrambling to take care of children, finances, and daily life tasks. One spouse may assume a caretaker role and then have a difficult time switching gears to being an erotic partner. The person who is ill may become increasingly self-centered and angry at the world, shutting out even his or her spouse or partner.

Erectile Dysfunction

Difficulty in achieving or maintaining erections is the most common sexual presenting complaint in men with a chronic illness. The hormonal, vascular, and neurological mechanisms of erection are all vulnerable to damage. The well-known Massachusetts Male Aging Study (Feldman, Goldstein, Hatzichristou, Krane, & McKinlay, 1994) showed that in addition to increasing with age, the prevalence of erectile dysfunction was higher in men with heart disease, hypertension, diabetes, and their associated medications. Cigarette smoking and high cholesterol also were risk factors for impaired erections. Men treated for prostate cancer with radiation therapy, radical prostate surgery, or hormonal therapy also have high rates of erection problems (Fossa et al., 1997; Schover, 1993; Talcott et al., 1998). Other cancer treatments, especially for pelvic tumors, also commonly cause erectile dysfunction (Schover, Montague, & Lakin, 1997). Additional chronic illnesses with high rates of erectile dysfunction include end-stage renal disease, multiple sclerosis, and central nervous system disorders (Schover & Jensen, 1988).

Although the majority of erection problems in men with chronic illness have an organic basis, a smaller group of men has psychogenic erectile dysfunction, often related to fears of failure, that causes performance anxiety during sex, distracting thoughts about changed bodily appearance, or feeling humiliated by physical dependency on the partner. Psychological factors that contribute to decreased desire for sex can also create anxiety that impairs erections. The clinician should be alert for signs of a psychogenic dysfunction, including preserved nocturnal erections, satisfactory erections during masturbation or erotic stimulation, better function with a particular partner, or a sudden onset of the problem that does not coincide with any new physical factor.

> Todd was a 42-year-old man diagnosed with Type I diabetes at age 14. During the last 2 years of a stormy marriage, he began to have trouble with erections. After he found out that his wife was having an affair with her boss at work, he was unable to function with her at all sexually. They divorced and Todd was treated with medication for a series of panic attacks. A year later, he was able to taper off of his medication and had begun dating again. His first tries at sexual activity with a new partner ended in failure when he lost his erection, but his girlfriend continued to be supportive and caring. Within several weeks his erections normalized without any medical intervention.

Female Arousal-Phase Dysfunctions

In women, too, the arousal phase is often disrupted by illness, so that vaginal expansion and lubrication are not adequate for comfortable intercourse. Erotic stimulation may also be experienced as annoying or neutral instead of pleasurable. Many of these arousal-phase problems are seen in women who become prematurely menopausal because of an illness—for example, women whose ovaries are damaged by cancer chemotherapy or pelvic radiotherapy or who have surgery to remove both ovaries. Women with cardiovascular disease or diabetes may also experience more vaginal atrophy at menopause (Schreiner-Engel et al., 1987), perhaps because of impaired genital blood flow. Radiation therapy that includes the vagina in the target field can also cause the mucosa to become thin and the vaginal barrel to shrink and lose elasticity (Schover, Fife, & Gershenson, 1989). Many women can reverse the vaginal effects of menopause by taking estrogen, but women who have had breast cancer are usually cautioned not to use estrogen replacement for fear of stimulating growth in any remaining malignant cells (Colditz, 1997). Problems with vaginal lubrication are also common even in premenopausal women with multiple sclerosis (Hulter & Lundberg, 1995) or spinal cord injury, presumably because the peripheral autonomic nervous system does not respond to central nervous system sexual arousal.

Women who lack desire for sex or who are distracted by fears of dyspareunia may also have difficulty becoming subjectively and physiologically aroused if they try to engage in sex. Another emotional factor that can inhibit arousal is a reminder during love making of a physical defect. For example, some women after a mastectomy no longer enjoy the caressing of their remaining breast.

Male Orgasmic Dysfunction

For both men and women, orgasm is a more robust part of the sexual response than arousal. With chronic illness, orgasm-phase dysfunctions are less common than impairments of the excitement phase. Few physical conditions other than central nervous system damage from a stroke, brain tumor, or spinal cord injury or neurological disease such as multiple sclerosis actually prevent men from reaching orgasm. Although only 14% of men attain the sensation of orgasm after spinal cord injury (Yalla, 1982), men continue to have orgasms after amputation of the penis for cancer or after radical pelvic cancer surgery that removes the semen-producing glands—the prostate and seminal vesicles (Schover, 1987). The sensory nerves that control the muscular contractions of ejaculation as well as the sensation of orgasmic pleasure are protected near the sidewall of the pelvis so that they are rarely damaged. Premature ejaculation also seems unrelated to chronic illness (Schover & Jensen, 1988).

A number of conditions can decrease the intensity of orgasmic pleasure, however (Schover, 1997; Schover & Jensen, 1988). Men who reach orgasm without a firm erection (e.g., after organic damage to the erection reflex) may complain that their orgasmic sensation is lessened. "Dry" orgasms that occur without ejaculation of semen (e.g., after a transurethral prostatectomy, radical prostatectomy, or cystectomy, or after other surgeries that damage the nerves regulating the emission phase of male orgasm) are sometimes rated as less intense than normal.

Some psychotropic medications, especially the phenothiazines or the serotonin selective reuptake inhibitor (SSRI) antidepressants, make it difficult to reach orgasm or impair orgasmic sensation (Segraves & Segraves, 1992; Segraves, 1998). Even high doses of alcohol can interfere with orgasm.

Occasionally men with a chronic illness develop orgasm-phase problems because of psychological factors. One common scenario is that a man with organically impaired erections simply gives up on sex, not even experimenting with masturbation or penile stimulation from a partner to see whether orgasm could occur without a firm erection. Men with infertility sometimes develop problems ejaculating that occur only at the wife's midcycle phase when the couple is advised to have intercourse to try to conceive a child.

Female Orgasmic Dysfunction

Surveys about sexual function in groups of medical patients often focus on ease of reaching orgasm as a measure of women's sexual satisfaction. Orgasm is certainly one important dimension of female sexuality, but problems in achieving orgasm in chronically ill populations are typically secondary to decreased sexual desire and arousability. If a woman does not feel like having sex and has trouble enjoying erotic stimulation, it is unlikely that she will reach orgasm. For example, in women with diabetes, reports of trouble reaching orgasm vary widely from study to study and have no clear correlation with complications of the disease (Spector, Leiblum, Carey, & Rosen, 1993). Women with multiple sclerosis certainly do experience a higher than usual rate of difficulty with orgasm, however (Hulter & Lundberg, 1995). Women with spinal cord injuries may be unable to reach orgasm or may report unusual experiences, such as having a sensation of orgasm at the anatomical area where sensation begins to be present or swelling of the lips and pleasurable sensations in that region at orgasm (Whipple & Komisaruk, 1997). A case series reviewed by Schover, Evans, and von Eschenbach (1987), of cancer patients who sought sexual counseling in a cancer center, revealed a high frequency of orgasm-phase sexual problems before cancer diagnosis similar to that reported in healthy women in the community. New problems with orgasm were less common after cancer treatment compared to new diagnoses of low desire or dyspareunia.

In women, as well as in men, antidepressant medications can delay or prevent orgasm, especially the SSRIs (Segraves, 1998). A change of dose or type of medication may be able to restore better orgasms while preserving good efficacy against depression.

Like men, women can undergo loss of portions of the genital tissue or pelvic organs and still retain a normal capacity for orgasm. Despite reports that hysterectomy for benign disease could impair orgasms, or at least coital orgasms, several studies have found that women typically retain unchanged orgasmic capacity after removal of the uterus (Alexander et al., 1996; Helstrom, Lundberg, Sorbom, & Backstrom, 1993; Virtanen et al., 1993). After surgery for gynecological cancer (e.g., example partial or radical vulvectomy), women's sexual satisfaction and ability to reach orgasm correlate more strongly with their relationship satisfaction than with the extent of tissue removed (Weijmar Schultz, van de Wiel, Bouma, Janssens, & Littlewood, 1990).

Women with chronic illness may have trouble reaching orgasm because of lack of sexual desire or arousal. Dyspareunia, chronic nongenital pain, nausea, fatigue, or anxiety about physical attractiveness also may interfere with experiencing sexual pleasure and thus with reaching orgasm.

Chronic Pain

Men or women can have sexual problems related to chronic pain. Low back pain or arthritis can impair range of motion or make vigorous movement difficult during sexual activity (Schover & Jensen, 1988). Pain can produce fatigue or depression, reducing sexual desire. Genital pain is a common sexual problem for women with gynecological cancer (Schover et al., 1987). Any syndrome associated with postmenopausal vaginal atrophy can also produce dyspareunia. Men sometimes develop pain with ejaculation or syndromes of prostatic, testicular, or penile pain. The causes for these symptoms are often multifactorial, with a strong role for chronic anxiety and pelvic floor muscle tension (Kursh & Schover, 1997), although acute prostatitis or penile curvature associated with Peyronie's disease are some of the more common medical factors seen. Opiate pain medications can also interfere with sexual function by depressing the central nervous system or by elevating the pituitary hormone, prolactin.

Overview of Diagnostic Issues

To summarize, all the sexual dysfunction may be seen as a consequence of chronic illness, but for men and women, sexual desire and arousal appear to be more vulnerable to disruption than orgasm. Many patients have multiple sexual problems that involve more than one phase of the sexual response cycle. Depression, chronic pain, and iatrogenic effects of medications or surgical therapies frequently complicate an already intricate pattern of emotional and organic factors. The next section describes a plan for assessing these multidimensional problems to arrive at a comprehensive treatment plan.

ASSESSMENT TECHNIQUES

The most important tool for assessing a sexual problem is the clinical interview (Schover & Jensen, 1988). If the patient has a committed relationship, it is usually preferable to see both partners jointly. Occasionally, one partner may request an initial individual session because of anxiety about discussing sexual issues in the other partner's presence. Such requests should certainly be honored. Scheduling a conjoint interview, however, communicates the message that sexuality is a couple issue, setting the stage for treatment. If time permits, or if the clinician feels that some issues are not being discussed frankly, a few minutes can be spent alone with each partner at the end of the session.

Screening questionnaires on sexuality can be a useful tool in identifying those patients who are particularly distressed over sexual issues within a larger population, in better defining sexual problems for research purposes, or to provide repeated measures of sexual function over time. If only a brief, general assessment of sexual function is desired, several questionnaires that measure quality of life in chronically ill patients have a sexuality section. These include the Psychosocial Adjustment to Illness Scale (PAIS; Derogatis, 1983), the Cancer Rehabilitation and Evaluation System (CARES; Ganz, Schag, Lee, & Sim, 1992), or some versions of the Functional Assessment of Cancer Therapy (FACT; Cella, 1996).

Some newer instruments are also available that can specify sexual function in detail, including problems in the realms of desire, arousal, orgasm, pain, and dissatisfaction. For men, the International Index of Erectile Function (IIEF; Rosen et al., 1997) is a well-validated measure that has even been used cross-culturally. Although no one instrument for women has attained the same level of psychometric validity, several alternative questionnaires are available (Derogatis & Conklin-Powers, 1998). Derogatis and colleagues have also developed male and female versions of a structured interview on sexual function that can also be administered in a self-report format (Derogatis, 1997). Because of limitations on patients' stamina and patience, the clinician should have a clear rationale for adding a detailed sexuality questionnaire to the assessment. Either having the questionnaire should save time in the interview or the information it provides should be important for purposes of research or program evaluation.

Some special issues arise when evaluating patients in a medical hospital or clinic setting. The majority of patients referred to the sex therapist have never seen a mental health professional. They may view psychotherapy as stigmatizing or fear that the referral means that their problems are viewed as psychogenic. The complexities of managed care insurance for mental health services may also be new and confusing to them. To make patients comfortable, the clinician may want to start by discussing the purpose of the evaluation, explaining that sexual problems are common after a chronic illness and that the interview is designed to find out how the patient (and partner) have coped with these problems. The goal will be to decide whether some counseling can be of help, perhaps in addition to medical treatments for the sexual dysfunction.

Another patient concern may be confidentiality. Sexual information is very private, yet in a hospital setting the medical chart is accessible to many, including clerks, nurses, and the patients themselves. It is important to keep chart notes brief, limiting them to a thumbnail sketch of the history, a diagnosis, and a treatment plan. More detailed information can be kept in a private file if allowed. Occasionally, interviews must also be conducted in a hospital room with another patient in the neighboring bed and staff walking in and out. If there is no reasonable alternative, such as a more private interview area on the hospital floor, or waiting for the opportunity to see the patient after hospital discharge, the clinician should check whether the patient wants to proceed with the interview. Sometimes leaving a television or radio on can provide some masking background noise.

Given the short hospital stays provided under managed care, much of the sexual counseling of people with chronic illness has shifted to the outpatient setting. While in the hospital, patients are typically acutely ill and unable to focus on quality-of-life issues. Furthermore, mental health services provided in the hospital are sometimes unable to be billed separately from the general fee that will be paid for a specific inpatient diagnosis or procedure.

Many patients are referred for sexual assessment and counseling by the physician who provides primary care. Referring health professionals vary in their wish for information about the assessment. Some see the referral as a way to avoid dealing with an unsettling topic. Others are interested and want to discuss the details of the case. Because sexuality is such a private area, the sex therapist should go the extra mile to ask the patient's permission to share the assessment report with the referring physician or mental health professional. Sometimes information gained in the assessment could have an impact on medical care, for example, when the clinician finds out that the patient is chemically dependent or is not complying with a medical treatment.

Whether practicing in a medical setting or in a private office, the sex therapist who treats chronically ill patients should develop a network of medical specialists who can collaborate in assessing and treating sexual problems. A urologist or internist who specializes in male sexual dysfunction is a very important colleague, as is a gynecologist with the patience and expertise to assess factors in dyspareunia and to prescribe appropriate hormonal replacement. Other sexual problems may require input from an endocrinologist, internist, diabetologist, oncologist, enterostomal therapist, physical therapist, or other specialist.

The Assessment Interview

Because many patients who seek sexual counseling are anxious about seeing a mental health professional for the first time, the interview should start with some reassurance and relationship building. A comfortable strategy is to begin by reviewing background information from the medical chart, such as the patient's age, occupation, years of marriage or other relationships, number of children, and medical history. Then the clinician can move to more emotionally laden topics such as the way that the patient coped with her or his medical condition and the degree of social and emotional support available in the patient's environment. It is helpful to ask about lifestyle factors, including preventive medical checkups, diet, exercise, smoking, and other substance use.

The clinician can then turn to the marital relationship or, for an unmarried patient, to a history of intimate dating relationships and previous marriages. Despite a cultural "myth" that illness in one partner often leads to divorce, couples in happy marriages often say that an illness has brought them closer (Schover & Jensen, 1988; Schover, 1997). It is the minority of relationships that are already fragile and conflicted that are at risk to disintegrate during the stress of an illness. To assess this dimension, the interviewer can focus on relationship strengths. Couples do well when partners can communicate caring openly, share other feelings (especially fear and sadness), temporarily switch some of their marital roles as the illness demands, negotiate to resolve disagreements, and share fairly equal needs for intimacy. Table 14.1 suggests questions that assess these areas. For unmarried patients, the interviewer can focus on whether dating or social relationships meet similar criteria.

A discussion of relationships evolves easily into a specific discussion of sexuality. A nonthreatening way to bring up the topic is to ask about sexual

TABLE 14.1. Assessing Relationship Strengths

Strengths	Questions to ask
Ability to show caring	How easily does each partner reach out with an affectionate gesture, compliment, or loving comment? How do each of you show caring to the other? Has expression of caring changed since the illness began? . . . since the sexual problem began?
Ability to share emotions	How do you let your partner know if you feel . . . (angry, frightened, depressed)? How openly do you show your positive feelings? How much have you discussed this illness with each other? How much have you discussed the sexual problem?
Role flexibility	If your illness prevents you from managing your usual jobs in the family, can your mate take over? How do each of you feel about switching roles, such as child care, household chores, or financial management?
Ability to negotiate about disagreements	How do you make family decisions? If you and your partner disagree, how does the issue get resolved? Are there particular issues that cause chronic tension? How has the illness affected conflict between you?
Similar needs for intimacy	Do the two of you usually agree about the amount of time you like to spend together? Are you similar in how much you like to talk to each other? How has the illness affected each of your needs for togetherness versus time alone?

skills that can help a couple stay sexually active despite the debilitation of a chronic illness. Table 14.2 outlines an assessment strategy for this topic, including how sex is initiated, the quality of sexual communication, whether the patient focuses too much on performance, the patient's comfort with a variety of stimulation, and issues of body image.

Of course, as in assessing any sexual dysfunction (Wincze & Carey, 1991), it is also crucial to ask about all aspects of sexual function, including desire for sex, ability to get physically and subjectively aroused, capacity to reach orgasm with varying types of stimulation, any pain during sexual activity, and overall sexual satisfaction (Schover & Jensen, 1988). In patients with a chronic illness, the clinician needs to be especially alert to the impact of organic factors such as aging, menopause, or cardiovascular risks on sexual function. As assessing sexual dysfunction is discussed in detail in other chapters in this volume, this chapter does not elaborate on the topic.

Several other special issues can complicate sexual issues in patients with

TABLE 14.2. Assessing Sexual Skills

Skill	Questions to ask
Flexibility in initiating sex	Who usually gets things started when you make love? Has there been a change in sexual initiation since the sexual problems began?
Clear sexual communication	If you would like a particular kind of touch during sex, how do you let your partner know (verbal, nonverbal, no cue at all)? How much have the two of you discussed this sexual problem? Have you been able to change your sexual routine to accommodate to your illness? . . . to the problem?
Focus on pleasure rather than performance	How would you define pleasurable sex? What aspects of sex are most important to each of you? Can you enjoy a sexual experience even if it includes some technical problems?
Comfort with noncoital orgasms	Do you ever help your partner reach orgasm through manual or oral caressing rather than during intercourse? If your illness or sexual problem makes intercourse difficult, will you sometimes use other lovemaking techniques to have orgasms together?
Agreement on the variety of sexual behavior	Do the two of you sometimes disagree about experimenting sexually, for example, trying oral sex, a new position for intercourse, or a new place to have sex?
Feeling sexually attractive despite physical changes	How do you feel about your own sexual attractiveness? How do you think your partner sees you? Has your illness or the sexual problem changed how attractive you feel?

an illness. For young couples, fertility may be an even more salient concern than is sexual dysfunction. Clinicians should become familiar with causes of infertility related to chronic diseases such as cancer and end-stage renal disease and with the emotional impact of infertility treatment (Leiblum, 1997; Schover, 1997). An illness can also bring an extramarital affair to light, or affect a partner's commitment to a marriage. Sometimes the healthier spouse begins an affair as a way of punishing a partner for becoming ill or to cope with separation anxiety (see the case of Leonard and Kim, presented later in this chapter). In other instances one partner abandons an affair when the illness is diagnosed and undergoes the stress of secretly mourning the loss. Unmarried patients often have marginal social support for coping with an illness. A sexual dysfunction may prevent a single man or woman even from looking for a new dating partner once he or she is feeling better physically, thereby increasing social isolation.

TREATMENT TECHNIQUES

At the end of the assessment interview, the clinician should present the patient with a proposed treatment plan, including the goals of treatment, techniques that would be used, and an estimate of the length of time treatment might take. It is important to emphasize that sex therapy necessitates that patients take an active role, trying out new behaviors at home and discussing them in session. Patients in medical settings often expect professionals to prescribe a pill or perform a procedure that will cure their problem; thus they need to be prepared for a more consultative relationship with the clinician. Many patients seen in medical settings want reassurance that their sexual problem is not unusual, along with an explanation of its causes. They may also wish to have some suggestions for overcoming the problem or a referral for medical treatment.

Brief Sexual Counseling

It is the exceptional patient who expects or wants to engage in a full course of formal sex therapy. For example, in 384 evaluations of cancer patients referred to a sexual rehabilitation service, 73% were seen only once or twice (Schover et al., 1987). This trend to brief interventions has only been strengthened by the trend for lessened mental health insurance coverage in recent years.

Nevertheless, a great deal of good can often be accomplished in just a few sessions. Table 14.3 lists the elements of brief sexual counseling for patients with a chronic illness (Schover & Jensen, 1988). The most salient role of the sex therapist is to provide education about the reasons for the sexual problems, to encourage the patient or couple to view themselves as capable of changing their sex life to make it more enjoyable, and to integrate this type of counseling with available medical treatments for sexual problems, such as methods to improve erections or to decrease dyspareunia.

Intensive Sex Therapy

For those patients or couples who are open to more intensive treatment, the techniques of sex therapy can easily be applied to a patient whose dysfunction is related to a chronic illness (Schover & Jensen, 1988). Although the entire spectrum of sexual dysfunctions may be seen, some special issues arise in medi-

TABLE 14.3. **Elements of Brief Sexual Counseling**

Counseling element	Clinical techniques
Sex education	Use models and diagrams to teach patients about genital anatomy and the sexual response cycle. Educate patients about the impact of their particular disease or treatment on sexual function. Make sure patients understand the sexual changes with normal aging in men and women. Provide any disease-specific patient education materials that are available.
Attitude change	Challenge maladaptive beliefs (e.g., sex is unhealthy; sex should always be spontaneous; intercourse is the only *normal* type of sex; cancer is contagious through sex; strenuous sex can cause heart attacks or strokes). Promote positive cognitions about sex (e.g., sex is part of a good quality of life; I don't need perfect erections to enjoy sex; being sexually active will not affect my health).
Suggestions on resuming sex comfortably	Teach patients the sensate focus exercises as a way to resume sex in a stepwise manner. Encourage expressing affection outside the bedroom. Encourage open communication about changes in sexual pleasure or preferences. Suggest substituting noncoital caressing for intercourse.
Ideas on overcoming physical handicaps	Use knowledge from other allied health professionals (physical therapists, enterostomal therapists, palliative care specialists) to educate patients on coping with ostomies, limb prostheses, finding comfortable positions for lovemaking; try a vibrator to compensate for reduced genital sensation, or find times for sex when fatigue and pain can be minimized.
Decreasing marital conflict that is illness-related	Encourage the partner with an illness to stay as independent as possible, minimizing the caretaker role for the healthy partner. Intervene in problem solving about role flexibility and time management. Minimize emotional interference in the relationship from extended family conflict.

cal settings. Although it has been traditional to have one sex therapy session weekly, giving behavioral homework in between (Wincze & Carey, 1991), medical patients may live a distance away from the treatment center, so that a few may want to stay in town for several days at a time, having daily appointments with the clinician in order to complete a treatment program.

More commonly, appointments are stretched out over long periods, so that 2 or 3 months pass in between them. It is difficult to keep effective treatment momentum on this type of schedule. Patients forget the details of their experience with a behavioral assignment, even if the clinician asks them to keep diaries. If a homework session is not successful, it is important for the clinician to be able to troubleshoot soon afterward, so that the couple does not become overly discouraged. Options to cope with long-distance treatment may include scheduling telephone contacts in between face-to-face sessions or referring the patient to a sex therapist closer to home. In the future, teleconferencing techniques may be an excellent tool to facilitate long-distance psychotherapy sessions, as they allow for both visual and verbal contact.

Including the Partner

In a sex therapy clinic, it is relatively easy to structure treatment as couple therapy. People often expect that sex therapy will include both partners. In a medical setting, the ill patient is more clearly labeled as the one with the problem. Thus the clinician may encounter more resistance to involving the partner. If the sexual dysfunction also has a physiological component, the patient may have trouble understanding why couple therapy would be necessary. Sometimes the partner is not physically available at the medical center, because he or she is at home taking care of children, work, and household tasks during the patient's hospitalization. It is important to emphasize that sexuality, except for masturbation, takes place between partners. Coping with changes in sexual function and general health is a task in which both should also ideally participate.

As wellness programs and patient education become more integral to medical care, most hospitals are facilitating partner involvement in health care by inviting spouses to participate in seminars or support groups relevant to a chronic illness (e.g., cardiac rehabilitation classes, diabetes education seminars, or prostate cancer support groups). The sex therapist can participate in such programs, giving talks or workshops about the importance of relationships and sexuality as one aspect of quality of life. Not only does this provide an important service for patients and their partners, but it is often a way to encourage patients to seek counseling on an individual or couple basis.

Goals of Sex Therapy

When sexual dysfunction is purely psychogenic, the goal of sex therapy is typically to reverse the symptom. When a problem has a multifactorial basis, however, treatment goals may be more modest. For example, a couple that discontinued all sexual activity after a wife's stroke may be happy to resume some gentle lovemaking, even if the frequency never approaches its previous levels and the wife is rarely orgasmic. Some couples are content to vary their sexual routine by learning to bring each other to orgasm through noncoital stimulation if an organic erection problem has made intercourse impossible. They may feel it is not worthwhile to pursue treatments such as Viagra (sildenafil) or penile injection therapy, which that could restore firm erections. It is important to discuss realistic goals with the patient or couple before beginning sex therapy so that all parties share a common definition of success.

CASE STUDY

Leonard was only 50 when his heart disease became so severe that he was put on the waiting list for a cardiac transplant. The owner of a small manufacturing company, he had been married for 6 years to his second wife, Kim, a 42-year-old real estate agent. His children from his first marriage were adults, but the couple was raising Kim's daughter, age 13. Leonard was originally seen by the physician in our sexual dysfunction clinic for erectile dysfunction. As Leonard's cardiac function deteriorated and he was put on more medications, he had increasing difficulty maintaining firm erections. Shortness of breath and mild chest pain during sex would distract and scare him, contributing to the erection problem. He still woke with erections, but they were not as firm as they had been several years before. A Rigiscan test monitoring erections during his sleep revealed that they were marginal both in rigidity and duration. He was prescribed Caverject penile injections, which worked quite well. He and Kim were referred for sex therapy, however, because she had lost interest in sex, to her husband's dismay.

In the initial interview it was obvious that Leonard and Kim were committed to each other. They described themselves as best friends, sharing many leisure interests and having done a good job of sharing parenting in their blended family. Kim's exhusband had been an alcoholic who physically abused her. She had left the marriage when her daughter was just a toddler and was proud of herself for living independently as a single parent in the years before she met Leonard. Leonard's ex-wife had left him for another man, but their marriage had grown distant for years before that event.

When Leonard and Kim met, they felt a strong attraction to each other and had a passionate and pleasurable sex life. They had used a variety of types of sexual caressing and were able to tell each other verbally what each enjoyed. They had never acted out sexual fantasies or done anything unconventional, but both found their sex life satisfying. Kim was sensitive to any position that made her feel coerced or held down during sex because of marital rape experiences in her first marriage, but Leonard soon learned to avoid triggering her anxiety.

Leonard's diagnosis of cardiac failure came at an especially stressful time for Kim, because she and her brother had just put their mother in a nursing home with dementia. Kim and her mother had always been close, but the mother was a critical and driven person who often made Kim feel guilty and inadequate. Kim's brother was very much the favored child in the family. Every time Kim visited her mother, the elderly lady would blame Kim for moving her into the nursing home, and Kim would come home reduced to tears.

Because of the seriousness of his illness, Leonard and Kim had discussed what would happen financially if he died. He was in the midst of trying to sell his business, hoping that he would receive a solid amount of money that would enable the couple to live in comfort for the rest of their lives or would provide enough income for Kim and her daughter if the worst happened. If Leonard's health condition became generally known, however, or if he died before making a good deal, the business might need to be sold for a much lesser amount. This stress was adding to the couple's distress.

Kim said that she felt exhausted and depressed, which did not help her desire for sex. Furthermore, she disliked Leonard's using the penile injections. She felt that the erections he got were "artificial," and that he no longer was really aroused by their sexual caressing. Kim had gained 20 pounds in the past year and was feeling very unattractive, even though Leonard tried to reassure her. The clinician asked Kim if she thought that avoiding sex might be connected to her fears that Leonard would die. Perhaps it was hard to allow herself to feel emotionally close and vulnerable to Leonard. Kim denied such feelings and said her major concern was wanting sex to be "natural."

The clinician suggested that the couple try a series of sensate focus exercises, without Leonard using Caverject, and without any expectation that his erections would be firm enough to allow intercourse to take place. The goal, instead, would be to feel relaxed and close to each other. She asked the couple to return in 2 weeks to talk abut their initial experience. At their next appointment, both appeared more relaxed. They felt the sensate focus experiences had restored some of their sense of intimacy and gotten them out of a performance mode. Leonard still was focusing on intercourse, however, and asked Kim whether she would reconsider trying sex with the Caverject. On questioning from the clinician, Leonard admitted that he saw Kim as young and attractive and feared she would stay with him out of pity rather than love as he became increasingly disabled. He felt that being able to perform intercourse with a hard erection was essential to fulfilling Kim's sexual needs. Although she denied that intercourse was so important to her, Leonard had trouble accepting her statements. The clinician suggested that the couple try vaginal penetration with a partial erection as part of the sensate focus exercises but that they should just try to enjoy the sensations they felt, returning in a few moments to using manual and oral caressing to bring each other to orgasm. Leonard had already discovered that he could reach orgasm with his wife's stimulation without having a full erection.

Leonard and Kim did not return for 4 months but for a good reason. A matching donor heart was found for Leonard and he had his transplant. His surgery and recovery proceeded smoothly, and the couple sent the clinician a Christmas card with a note saying they planned to return once life settled down. They also mentioned that Leonard had successfully sold his business.

Then the clinician received an emergency call from Leonard. He asked for an urgent appointment because he had just found out that Kim was having an extramarital affair with a man who was one of her real estate customers.

Leonard was agitated and tearful during his visit. During his prolonged recovery from surgery, he had felt very dependent on Kim. At first, Leonard felt panic when Kim left him alone in the house (e.g., to go to the grocery store). He was afraid his heart would stop and he would die alone. He knew his anxiety was burdening Kim, and so he tried to hide his feelings and encouraged her to go back to work. Kim, who had always had a strong need for autonomy, agreed to resume her normal schedule. Leonard tried to occupy himself by getting a new computer and making an investment plan for the money from the sale of his business, but he felt rather lost and lonely without a daily job. His friends were all still working full time. He went to the couple's swim and tennis club to use the pool but found himself frustrated that he could not yet get back to playing his weekly tennis games. He even tried visiting Kim's mother in the nursing home but quickly grew impatient with his mother-in-law's abusive tirades. He and Kim had not resumed sexual activity since surgery, despite several tries on Leonard's part to initiate some touching. Kim was always too tired or distracted.

Leonard grew suspicious when Kim started working longer hours than usual. She told him she wanted to make a couple of large commissions to put away money for her daughter's college fund. She seemed unusually happy, however, and even had her hair restyled. One evening when Kim said she had an open house, Leonard deliberately drove past the address and saw that the place was dark. The next day he followed his wife to work and parked in a neighboring lot. His patience was rewarded when she left the office at lunch and drove to a motel. He stayed long enough to see her go to a room, where she was joined by a man.

That evening, Leonard confronted Kim, who broke down in tears and confessed she had just started having an affair with the husband in a couple who had recently bought a house through her. The couple talked all night. Kim told Leonard that she wanted to stay married to him and that the affair had been a terrible mistake. In front of Leonard, she called her lover and told him their affair was over. Leonard got on the phone and threatened angrily to tell the man's wife about the affair if he found that the two were still seeing each other. He kept pressing Kim for details of the sexual encounters, and whenever she gave him any information, he pounced on it angrily, wanting more: "How many times did you come when you had intercourse?" he demanded. "What position did he use?" "Was it better than it used to be with us?" Kim refused to answer any more questions and finally said she thought it would be better if she and her daughter moved out of the house.

The clinician used crisis intervention with Leonard, letting him tell all the details of his story but helping him focus on his immediate goal, which was to get Kim into counseling and stop her from moving out. In Leonard's presence, the clinician called Kim, who said she wanted to stay in the marriage and was willing to come in the next day with Leonard. Over several sessions, the clinician helped Leonard and Kim explore what had happened. Kim said she had been feeling lonely and resentful during Leonard's illness. She was taking care of everyone else—Leonard, her angry mother, her teenage daughter—and felt she received little recognition. Leonard's wish for sex often felt like further demands that she service him rather than concern for her needs, as he professed. She had also had some nightmares and flashbacks about the violence during her first marriage. She tried to prepare herself for Leonard's death—so much so that when his transplant succeeded, she found herself feeling trapped and resentful. These feelings made her feel even more guilty and upset with herself. When her real estate client flirted with her and showered her with compliments, she bloomed like a flower after a rainstorm in the desert.

Leonard understood his wife intellectually, but emotionally he kept obsessing that she had chosen another man because her sexual needs were unsatisfied. Leonard's attempts to initiate sex, his constant pressure on Kim to tell him more sexual details of the affair, and his expectation that she would report several times a day on her exact schedule and whereabouts caused a number of flareups between them. The clinician reiterated that Leonard's vigilance could not prevent Kim from continuing the affair if that was her goal. Leonard needed to accept that Kim wanted to stay married to him and work with her to put the affair in the past. Leonard agreed to have Kim schedule two evenings a week when she would be out of the house and would not account to him for her activities. Questions about the sexual part of the affair were agreed to be off limits. For her part, Kim did her best to make Leonard feel loved. She gave him compliments and affection and scheduled special activities together. As he felt better physically, they took walks together and played tennis doubles. She took the initiative to put candles in their bedroom and exchange massages with scented body lotion. One night she even suggested they make love using Caverject and was surprised to find that she could forget about the source of the erection and just enjoy it. Leonard decided to set up a small consulting business rather than to stay completely retired. The couple's focus gradually shifted from coping with illness and impending death to designing a mutual, foreseeable future. Although the pain of the affair would not disappear, it receded into the background and both partners could speak with pride about their accomplishment in coping with a life-threatening illness and becoming survivors together.

CONCLUSIONS

Sex therapy with chronically ill patients present special challenges. The clinician may have to work within a hospital setting where sex therapy is a novelty, juggling treatment to accommodate patients' reduced energy levels and disrupted daily life routines. Most patients need brief sexual counseling rather than formal sex therapy. The goals of treatment may also be limited by the physiological impact of the disease or its therapies on sexual function. Nevertheless, the potential rewards are great because helping medical patients regain sexual pleasure is a victory in the face of sadness and a confirmation of the will to live and be intimate with others.

REFERENCES

Alexander, D. A., Naji, A. A., Pinion, S. B., Mollison, J., Kitchener, H. C., Parkin, D. E., Abramovich, D. R., & Russell, I. T. (1996). Randomized trial comparing hysterectomy with endometrial ablation for dysfunctional uterine bleeding: Psychiatric and psychosocial aspects. *British Medical Journal, 312*(7026), 280–284.

Althof, S. E., Coffman, C. B., & Levine, S. B. (1984). The effects of coronary bypass surgery on female sexual, psychological, and vocational adaptation. *Journal of Sex and Marital Therapy, 10,* 176–184.

American Medical Association. (1997). *Talking to patients about sex: Skills training for physicians* (312-464-5083). Chicago: AMA Office of Women's and Minority Health.

Andersen, B. L., & Cyranowski, J. M. (1995). Women's sexuality: Behaviors, responses, and individual differences. *Journal of Consulting and Clinical Psychology, 63,* 891–906.

Andersen, B. L., Woods, X. A., & Copeland, L. J. (1997). Sexual self-schema and sexual morbidity among gynecologic cancer survivors. *Journal of Consulting and clinical Psychology, 65,* 221–229.

Brezinka, V., & Kittel, F. (1996). Psychosocial factors of coronary heart disease in women: A review. *Social Science and Medicine, 42,* 1351–1365.

Burton, M. V., & Parker, R. W. (1997). Psychological aspects of cancer surgery: Surgeons' attitudes and opinions. *Psycho-Oncology, 6,* 47–64.

Callahan, E. J., Jaen, C. R., Crabtree, B. F., Zyzanski, S. J., Goodwin, M. A., & Stange, K. C. (1998). The impact of recent emotional distress and diagnosis of depression or anxiety on the physician–patient encounter in family practice. *Journal of Family Practice, 46,* 410–418.

Carlton, L. (1997). *In sickness and in health: Sex, love, and chronic illness.* New York: Dell Books.

Carney, P. A., & Ward, D. H. (1998). Using unannounced standardized patients to assess the HIV preventive practices of family nurse practitioners and family physicians. *The Nurse Practitioner, 23,* 56–58, 63, 67–68.

Cawood, E. H., & Bancroft, J. (1996). Steroid hormones, the menopause, sexuality and well-being of women. *Psychological Medicine, 26,* 925–936.

Cella, D. F. (1996). Quality of life outcomes: Measurement and validation. *Oncology, 10*(Suppl. 11), 233–246.

Colditz, G. A. (1997). Estrogen replacement therapy for breast cancer patients. *Oncology, 11,* 1491–1494, 1497–1498, 1501.

Crawford, E. D., Bennett, C. L., Stone, N. N., Knight, S. J., DeAntoni, E., Sharp, L., Garnick, M. B., & Porterfield, H. A. (1997). Comparison of perspectives on prostate cancer: Analyses of survey data. *Urology, 50,* 366–372.

Dale, K. G. (1996). Intimacy and rheumatic diseases. *Rehabilitation Nursing, 21,* 38–40.

Dennerstein, L., Dudley, E. C., Hopper, J. L., & Burger, H. (1997). Sexuality, hormones and the menopausal transition. *Maturitas, 26,* 83–93.

Derogatis, L. R. (1983). *Psychosocial Adjustment to Illness Scale (PAIS and PAIS-SR): Administration, scoring and procedures manual—I.* Baltimore: Clinical Psychometric Research.

Derogatis, L. R. (1997). The Derogatis Interview for Sexual Functioning (DISF/DISF-SR): An introductory report. *Journal of Sex and Marital Therapy, 23,* 291–304.

Derogatis, L. R., & Conklin-Powers, B. (1998). Psychological assessment measures of female sexual functioning in clinical trials. *International Journal of Impotence Research, 10*(Suppl. 2), S111–S116.

Feldman, H. A., Goldstein, I., Hatzichristou, D. G., Krane, R. J., & McKinlay, J. B. (1994). Impotence and its medical and psychosocial correlates: Results of the Massachusetts Male Aging Study. *Journal of Urology, 151,* 54–61.

Fossa, S. D., Woehre, H., Kurth, K. H., Hetherington, J., Bakke, H., Tustad, D. A., & Skanvik, R. (1997). Influence of urological morbidity on quality of life in patients with prostate cancer. *European Journal of Urology, 31*(Suppl. 3), 3–8.

Fowler, F. J. Jr., Barry, M. J., Lu-Yao, G., Wasson, J. H., & Bin, L. (1996). Outcomes of external-beam radiation therapy for prostate cancer: A study of medicare beneficiaries in three surveillance, epidemiology, and end results areas. *Journal of Clinical Oncology, 14*, 2258–2265.

Ganz, P. A., Schag, C. F., Lee, J. J., & Sim, M. S. (1992). The CARES: A generic measure of health-related quality of life for patients with cancer. *Quality of Life Research, 1*, 19–29.

Gaylis, F. D., Friedel, W. E., & Armas, O. A. (1998). Radical retropubic prostatectomy outcomes at a community hospital. *Journal of Urology, 159*, 167–171.

Hart, L. K., Milde, F. K., Zehr, P. S., Cox, D. M., Tarara, D. T., & Fearing, M. O. (1997). Survey of sexual concerns among organ transplant recipients. *Journal of Transplant Coordination, 7*, 82–87.

Hawton, K. (1984). Sexual adjustment of men who have had strokes. *Journal of Psychosomatic Research, 21*, 243–249.

Helstrom, L., Lundberg, P. O., Sorbom, D., & Backstrom, T. (1993). Sexuality after hysterectomy: A factor analysis of women's sexual lives before and after subtotal hysterectomy. *Obstetrics and Gynecology, 81*, 357–362.

Hulter, B. M., & Lundberg, P. O. (1995). Sexual function in women with advanced multiple sclerosis. *Journal of Neurology, Neurosurgery and Psychiatry, 59*, 83–86.

Jaen, C. R., Crabtree, B. F., Zyzanski, S. J., Goodwin, M. A., & Stange, K. C. (1998). Making time for tobacco cessation counseling. *Journal of Family Practice, 46*, 425–428.

Karakiewicz, P. L., Aprikian, A. G., Bazinet, M., & Elhilali, M. M. (1997). Patient attitudes regarding treatment-related erectile dysfunction at the time of early detection of prostate cancer. *Urology, 50*, 7704–709.

Kursh, E. D., & Schover, L. R. (1997). The dilemma of chronic genital pain. *American Urological Association Updates* [Lesson 37], *16*, 290–296.

Leiblum, S. R. (1995). Teaching human sexuality to medical students: A unique challenge. *Trends in Health Care, Law and Ethics, 10*, 41–44.

Leiblum, S. R. (Ed.). (1997). *Infertility: Psychological issues and counseling strategies.* New York: Wiley.

Lieber, L., Plumb, M. M., Gerstenzang, M. L., & Holland, J. (1976). The communication of affection between cancer patients and their spouses *Psychosomatic Medicine, 38*, 379–389.

Liss-Levinson, W. S. (1982). Clinical observations on the emotional responses of males to cancer. *Psychotherapy: Theory, Research, and Practice, 19*, 325–330.

Massie, M. J., & Popkin, M. K. (1998). Depressive disorders. In J. C. Holland (Ed.), *Psychooncology* (pp. 518–540). New York: Oxford University Press.

Neau, J. P., Ingrand, P., Moruille-Brachet, C., Rosier, M. P., Couderq, C., Alvarez, A., & Gil, R. (1998). Functional recovery and social outcome after cerebral infarction in young adults. *Cerebrovascular Diseases, 8*, 296–302.

Rosen, R. C., Riley, A., Wagner, G., Osterloh, I. A., Kirkpatrick, J., & Mishra, A. (1997). The International Index of Erectile Function (IIEF): A multidimensional scale for assessment of erectile dysfunction. *Urology, 49*, 822–830.

Schover, L. R. (1987). Sexuality and fertility in urologic cancer patients. *Cancer, 60*, 553–558.

Schover, L. R. (1993). Sexual rehabilitation after treatment for prostate cancer. *Cancer, 71*(Suppl. 1), 1024–1030.

Schover, L. R. (1995a). *Sexuality and cancer: For the man who has cancer and his partner* [4658-PS]. Atlanta, GA: American Cancer Society.

Schover, L. R. (1995b). *Sexuality and cancer: For the woman who has cancer and her partner* [4657-PS]. Atlanta, GA: American Cancer Society.

Schover, L. R. (1997). *Sexuality and fertility after cancer.* New York: Wiley.

Schover, L. R. (1998). Editorial: Some perspective on Viagramania. *Cleveland Clinic Medical Journal, 65*, 331–332.

Schover, L. R., Evans, R. B., & von Eschenbach, A. C. (1987). Sexual rehabilitation in a cancer center: Diagnosis and outcome in 384 consultations. *Archives of Sexual Behavior, 16*, 445–461.

Schover, L. R., Fife, M., & Gershenson, D. M. (1989). Sexual function and treatment for early stage cervical cancer. *Cancer, 63*, 204–212.

Schover, L. R., & Jensen, S. B. (1988). *Sexuality and chronic illness: A comprehensive approach.* New York: Guilford Press.

Schover, L. R., Montague, D. K., & Lakin, M. (1997). Supportive care and the quality of life of the cancer patient: Sexual problems. In V. T. DeVita, S. Hellman, & S. A. Rosenberg (Eds.), *Cancer: Principles practice of oncology* (5th ed., pp. 2857–2872). Philadelphia: Lippincott.

Schover, L. R., Yetman, R. J., Tuason, L. J., Meisler, E., Esselstyn, C. B., Hermann, R. E., Grundfest-Broniatowski, S., & Dowden, R. V. (1995). Comparison of partial mastectomy with breast reconstruction on psychosocial adjustment, body image, and sexuality. *Cancer, 75*, 54–64.

Schreiner-Engel, P., Schiavi, R. C., Vietorisz, D., & Smith, H. (1987). The differential impact of diabetes type on female sexuality. *Journal of Psychosomatic Research, 31*, 23–33.

Schurmeyer, T. H., Muller, V., von zur Muhlen, A., & Schmidt, R. D. (1997). Endocrine testicular function in HIV infected outpatients. *European Journal of Medical Research, 2*, 275–281.

Segraves, R. T. (1988). Drugs and desire. In S. R. Leiblum & R. C. Rosen (Eds.), *Sexual desire disorders* (pp. 313–347). New York: Guilford Press.

Segraves, R. T. (1998). Antidepressant-induced sexual dysfunction. *Journal of Clinical Psychiatry, 59*(Suppl. 4), 48–54.

Segraves, R. T., & Segraves, K. B. (1992). Aging and drug effects on male sexuality. In R. C. Rosen & S. R. Leiblum (Eds.), *Erectile disorders: Assessment and treatment* (pp. 96–138). New York: Guilford Press.

Sherwin, B. B. (1998). Use of combined estrogen-androgen preparations in the postmenopause: Evidence from clinical studies. *International Journal of Fertility, 43*, 98–103.

Slag, M. F., Morley, J. E., Elson, M. K., Trence, D. L., Nelson, C. J., Nelson, A. E., Kinlaw, W. B., Beyer, H. S., Nuttall, F. Q., & Shafer, R. B. (1983). Impotence in medical clinic outpatients. *Journal of the American Medical Association, 249*, 1736–1740.

Spector, I. P., Leiblum, S. R., Carey, M. P., & Rosen, R. C. (1993). Diabetes and female sexual function: A critical review. *Annals of Behavioral Medicine, 15*, 257–264.

Spica, M. M., & Schwab, M. D. (1996). Sexual expression after total joint replacement. *Orthopaedic Nursing, 15*, 41–44.

Stange, K. C., Zyzanski, S. J., Jaen, C. F., Callahan, E. J., Kelly, R. B., Gillanders, W. R., Shank, J. C., Chao, J. Medalie, J. H., Miller, W. L., Crabtree, B. F., Flocke, S. A., Gilchrist, V. J., Langa, D. M., & Goodwin, M. A. (1998). Illuminating the "black box": A description of 4454 patient visits to 138 family physicians. *Journal of Family Practice, 46*, 377–389.

Steinke, E., & Patterson-Midgley, P. (1996). Sexual counseling following acute myocardial infarction. *Clinical Nursing Research, 5*, 462–472.

Talcott, J. A., Rieker, P., Clark, J. A., Propert, K. J., Weeks, J. C., Beard, C. J., Wishnow, K. I., Kaplan, I., Loughlin, K. R., Richie, J. P., & Kantoff, P. W. (1998). Patient-reported symptoms after primary therapy for early prostate cancer: Results of a prospective cohort study. *Journal of Clinical Oncology, 16*, 275–0283.

Virtanen, H., Makinen, J., Tenho, T., Kiilholma, P., Pitkanen, Y., & Hirvonen, T. (1993). Effects of abdominal hysterectomy on urinary and sexual symptoms. *British Journal of Urology, 72*, 868–872.

Ware, J. E. (1993). *SF-36 Health Survey: Manual and interpretation guide.* Boston: The Health Institute.

Weijmar Schultz, W. C , van de Wiel, H. B., Bouma, J., Janssens, J., & Littlewood, J. (1990). Psychosexual functioning after the treatment of cancer of the vulva: A longitudinal study. *Cancer, 66*, 402–407.

Whipple, B., & Komisaruk, B. R. (1997). Sexuality and women with complete spinal cord injury. *Spinal Cord, 35*, 136–138.

Wincze, J. P., & Carey, M. P. (1991). *Sexual dysfunction: A guide for assessment and treatment.* New York: Guilford Press.

Yalla, S. V. (1982). Sexual dysfunction in the paraplegic and quadriplegic. In A. H. Bennett (Ed.), *Management of male impotence* (pp. 182–191). Baltimore: Williams & Wilkins.

15

Sex Therapy with Aging Adults

SANDRA R. LEIBLUM
R. TAYLOR SEGRAVES

We are all getting older, like it or not. The changes in sexual interest and function that accompany aging, as well as the sexual concerns of aging adults, are a topic that is both personally and professionally relevant. In this chapter, the sexuality of older adults is reviewed from a normative perspective and the special issues that accompany sexual counseling in this population are described.

Most survey studies of older adults find that they remain interested in an active and varied sex life, although sexual frequency and activity do tend to decline with aging. There are wide individual differences, however, and Leiblum and Segraves remind readers that it is important not to stereotype older adults as disengaged and sexually disinterested.

The most salient marker of aging in women is the menopause, occurring at around age 50. Most women notice changes in their physical appearance as well as in their sexual response. Lack of lubrication and diminished sexual desire are common complaints among both heterosexual and homosexual women. Hormone replacement of both estrogen and androgen can prove helpful in reducing vaginal atrophy and in increasing sexual interest and sensitivity. For women who are reluctant to take hormones, changes in the sexual script and over-the-counter lubricants may help as well.

The changes in men with aging are not dissimilar to the changes occurring in women, but they occur more gradually. Most notably, erectile performance declines and for some men, there is less penile sensitivity. The force and frequency of desire for sexual release decrease in older men. Vasoactive agents are a viable treatment for many men, but it is important to determine the interest and desire of his female partner prior to initiating pharmacological interventions.

Sometimes the biggest problem for older men and women is the lack of, or loss of, a partner. Grief about both physical and psychological losses may need to comprise part of the therapy with this population. Many chronic diseases and the use of varied medications inhibit or interfere with the sexual response of older adults, but psychological factors are often implicated as well. It is a mistake to prematurely conclude that organic factors are the primary culprits in the sexual complaints of either older men or older women without taking a thorough sexual history of both partners in a couple.

Sandra Leiblum and R. Taylor Segraves remind readers that with the increase in life expectancy and the ever-growing population of healthy older adults, sexual intimacy is an important quality-of-life issue. Nevertheless, a plethora of both pharmacological and therapeutic options for conducting sex therapy with aging adults now exist. The results can be gratifying for both the clinician and the patient.

Sandra R. Leiblum, PhD, is Professor of Psychiatry and Director of the Center for Sexual and Marital Health at the University of Medicine and Dentistry of New Jersey–Robert Wood Johnson Medical School in Piscataway, New Jersey. She has long been interested in the physical and psychological changes associated with menopause and its aftermath and has conducted considerable research in this area.

R. Taylor Segraves, MD, PhD, is Professor of Psychiatry at Case Western Reserve University, Chair, Department of Psychiatry at MetroHealth Medical Center, and Editor-in-Chief of Journal of Sex and Marital Therapy. *He has published widely in the area of medical and psychological evaluation of erectile disorders.*

Despite the preponderance of youthful images in the advertising media, we are an aging population. The percentage of Americans 65 years and older has more than tripled during this past century—it is estimated that the population of those 65 and older is already 35 million. More notable is the fact that the population of those over 85 is the fastest-growing age group in the country (Rowe & Kahn, 1998). Currently, the life expectancies for men and women are 76 and 80, respectively, and surveys suggest that many middle-aged folks hope to live to be 100.

Nevertheless, despite their increasing presence (and power) and the ever-growing number of articles on successful aging, older adults are often victims of negative stereotypes that associate aging with images of fragility, incompetence, and disengagement. Young adults, in particular, continue to believe that older adults are sad, sick, and asexual, with little energy or enthusiasm for social or intellectual pursuits.

Most young people find it difficult, if not impossible, to imagine their parents and grandparents as sexually interested and active. Nevertheless, although the frequency of sexual activity tends to fall with increasing age, interest in physical and social exchange continues. Moreover, according to the recent large-scale MacArthur Foundation Research Study on Successful Aging, social connectedness is highly correlated with longevity (Rowe & Kahn, 1998). It is well documented that married men live longer, healthier, and more productively than do single men; happily married women gain a 1-year increase in life expectancy as compared to divorced women; and happily married men tend to live 2 years longer than divorced or single men (Rowe & Kahn, 1998). In fact, the suicide rate for divorced men and widowers is markedly higher than for married men. Not only does loneliness appear to speed demise, but older men are used to having women take care of their health, nourishment, and scheduling, and without a woman present to do this, many feel lost.

Even before the introduction of sildenafil as an impressively effective treatment of erectile dysfunction in older men, many senior adults were sexually lively and active (Comfort, 1976; Renshaw, 1988). In his large-scale Consumer Union survey of 4, 246 adults over the age of 50, Brecher (1984) found that the majority of both married husbands and wives considered the sexual side of their marriages important. The vast majority of respondents were still having sexual intercourse, and those who were sexually active were more likely to report happy marriages than were those who were not (although the happily married couple were probably more likely to be sexually active!). More than three-quarters of the men and women who responded to this survey rated their enjoyment of sex as high. In fact, there was a positive association between satisfaction with one's sexual life and marital satisfaction. Conversely, low enjoyment of marital sex was an important predictor of marital unhappiness.

Other studies report similar findings. The most current survey by the National Council on Aging and the American Association for Retired Persons (*Healthy Sexuality and Vital Aging,* 1999) found that in a survey of 1,000 men and women over the age of 50, 60% were satisfied with their sex lives. A full 61% reported that sex was as good or better than when they were young, and 70% had sex at least once a week.

Of those older individuals in this survey who said their sex life was bland to nonexistent, 34% mostly reported problems with illness, loss of a partner, medication, or treatments such as dialysis or chemotherapy that robbed them of energy and enthusiasm for sexual activity.

Even when sexual performance is not Olympic, men report enjoying sexual exchange (Schiavi, 1992). Women, too, express a continued desire for physical intimacy, even though their interest in active genital exchange may diminish over time.

Nevertheless, there is a reduction in sexual frequency for both men and women with aging. In the largest recent large-scale study of the sexual behavior of more than 3,000 U.S. adults ages 18 to 59, 36% of men ages 25 to 29 reported having coitus two to three times a week in the last year as compared to only 17% of men ages 55 to 59 (Laumann, Gagnon, Michael, & Michaels, 1994). Among women, 37% of respondents reported coitus two to three times a week at ages 25 to 29 versus 5% at ages 55 to 59. There was a similar decline in masturbation frequency with approximately 10% of females reporting once-weekly masturbation at ages 25 to 29 as compared to 2.4% at ages 55 to 59.

Among men, 33% of respondents ages 25 to 29 reported weekly masturbation compared to only 10% of men ages 55 to 59. Sexual frequency declines, although it is important to note that there are large individual variations, with some adults engaging in frequent masturbation and partner-related activities across their entire life span and others showing little interest from the start of their sexual life.

Older couples report much the same sexual complaints as younger couples (Brecher, 1984). Problems with sexual desire discrepancy, arousal difficulties, erectile failure, anorgasmia, early or delayed ejaculation, pain with intercourse, script incompatibility, and problematic sexual communication and technique are common. Despite prevailing preconceptions, few of the couples in Brecher's survey said that they wanted less variety in their sexual lives. In fact, many of the husbands and some of the wives indicated that they would enjoy greater sexual experimentation in their marriage. Research suggests that if sex was a source of pleasure and gratification during early and middle adulthood, it will probably continue to be an important source of life satisfaction as one grows older.

On the other hand, it must be acknowledged that there remain many elderly couples who grew up in a post-Victorian society and in fundamental and traditional households in which sexually proscriptive values and beliefs persist. For these individuals, sex is sanctioned primarily for procreation; sexual behaviors other than intercourse, such as oral–genital sex, are considered unnatural; sexual relations outside marriage are forbidden; and masturbation is sinful. For such individuals, the opportunity to "retire" from an active sexual life may be ardently anticipated and easily accepted. An example of this point of view is expressed in this letter to *Time* magazine, posted after the introduction of Viagra to American society:

> I can't understand all the fuss about sexual erection (May 4, 1998), which for many seems the most important thing in life. We have been given a certain amount of sexual intercourse in a life-time and there is no point in trying to force nature for more. This modern attitude is the product of a sick and decadent society that refuses to accept the limitations inherent to our human nature. For my part, I have sired six children and after this performance, I am not ashamed to admit that I am impotent and proud of it. (Letter to the editor of *Time* magazine, printed in June 1998)

It should be noted that this attitude, although ardently expressed, is not widely typical of either aging men or aging women.

It is not only heterosexual couples who report changes in their sexual life with aging; homosexual men and women do so as well. Nonetheless, most of the stereotypes concerning older gay men and women are unjustified. For example, societal stereotypes portray older gay men as isolated, lonely, sexless, fearful, and depressed. They are sometimes depicted as sexually predatory toward younger gay men who reject their company and exclude them from the youthful gay culture.

These portraits are inaccurate. Older gay men are not necessarily more lonely than younger gay men. In fact, many are less worried about exposure of their homosexuality with increasing age. However, as with heterosexual men, there is a decrease in sexual frequency with advancing age, and more homosexual men tend to be living alone. Weinberg (1970) has reported no differences in unhappiness or depression as a function of age among gay men.

Similarly, among lesbians, the myth of social isolation and sexual disinterest is unsupported. Many older gay women have close friends and social support. In large cities, there are some organizations, regrettably only a few, that provide social support and services for elderly gays and lesbians—places where they can be surrounded by their peers and assisted by counselors. In New York City, there is SAGE (Senior Action in a Gay Environment) and in San Francisco, there is GLOBE (Gay and Lesbian Outreach to Elders).

For the most part, lovers of both gay men and gay women tend to be within a decade of their own age (Pope & Schultz, 1990), and interest in and desire for some form of physical intimacy is characteristic of most older homosexual men and women (Wahler & Gabbay, 1997). Overall, sexual counseling with aging adults—gay or straight—may well become a growth industry in the new millennium.

OBSERVATIONS ABOUT SEX AND AGING

When working with an elderly population, therapists must be careful to confront and rectify their own biased beliefs. For instance, it is often assumed that older men and women tend to be inflexible and rigid, unwilling, or incapable of new learning. Although this may be true for some older individuals (perhaps the man quoted previously), others are quite amenable to suggestions for change. Many have undergone a considerable though "quiet" sexual revolution over the passing years. As one 76-year-old bride confided to her therapist, "I never did anything fancy in my first marriage, but if *you* recommended it, I would be willing to try almost anything now!"

In fact, the myth asserting "you can't teach an old dog new tricks" is patently false. Older people are using computers, cruising the Internet, entering "chat" rooms, and embarking on new careers after retirement. Many are grateful for suggestions about books and videotapes that will supplement their sexual education and many are enthusiastic about trying new sexual positions or techniques.

Some research suggests that sexual preferences do change with aging as a function of changes in sexual physiology and marital status. For example, Turner and Adams (1988), in a study looking at the sexual practices of a group of 60- to 85-year-old men and women, found that many respondents reported a greater interest in petting and masturbation and less interest in coitus as they grew older. This appears to be changing, though, with the advent of vasoactive drugs and other pharmacological preparations that facilitate arousal and erection. Already we are seeing many older men eager to experiment more creatively with their more reliable erections (which sometimes poses problems for their older wives).

One of the most significant aspects of growing old for both gay and straight individuals is the loss of a partner and the necessity of developing new relationships. It is not surprising that many newly "single" older adults experience the worries characteristic of their grandchildren. Concerns about personal desirability, attractiveness, and sex appeal are often real and significant issues. How to meet eligible partners can be a source of considerable preoccupation. Some older adults are worried about the risks of acquiring sexually transmitted diseases. One 72-year-old man called a clinic wanting to know whether it was likely he had "contracted AIDS" because he recently had casual sex with a woman he had met at a singles dance. And, in fact, the Centers for Disease Control reports that about 10% of individuals who are infected with HIV are over the age of 60. Another 70-year-old woman reported being offended by her gynecologist. She explained that she had asked her doctor, "How do you keep from getting herpes?" and he just laughed and told her "not to worry." She felt humiliated and insulted because it was a genuine concern and a reasonable question. It is important to treat the concerns of older adults—whether realistic or not—with respect.

As will be stated repeatedly throughout this chapter, many older adults are unaware of the normal age-related changes in sexual response that accompany aging and are perplexed or put off by changes in their own or their partner's sexual response. One long-married woman, for example, complained to her therapist that "nothing happens when I walk around naked. He doesn't even get an erection!" She failed to appreciate that visual stimulation alone was insufficiently arousing to her aging mate and that more direct manual or oral stimulation was necessary to supply the additional arousal "boost" needed to achieve erections.

Explicit information about changes in sexual physiology with aging can help eliminate erroneous expectations and can permit modification in long-standing sexual practices that may have become counterproductive. Couples can be counseled, for example, not to delay sexual exchange until late at night when fatigue or sleepiness may be great but, rather, to schedule their sexual encounters during the afternoon or early evening—times of greater energy and alertness.

FEMALE SEXUAL RESPONSE AND AGING

In many respects, the sexual complaints of older women mirror those of younger women—lack of, or diminished sexual desire, difficulty becoming sexually aroused either physically or psychologically, difficulty achieving orgasm, and pain or discomfort with sexual exchange, especially intercourse (Leiblum & Segraves, 1989). In addition to these problems, women may mourn or regret changes in their body—its size, shape, and firmness may differ significantly from the good "ole" days. They may complain, as well, about the changing body of their partner, the reduction in, or loss of, passion and attention given to emotional and sexual intimacy, and changes in sexual urgency or intensity. Menopause, surgery, and various losses—psychological and physical—can exacerbate these complaints.

On the other hand, there are many older women who are enjoying sex for the first time in their lives with passion and abandonment because of a new and appreciative partner, an increase in personal self-confidence, or the shedding, at last, of old inhibitions and habits. There are some normal age-related changes that are quite ubiquitous, however. Androgen levels decrease with age, beginning in the mid-20s. By the 50s, circulating levels of testosterone are about half the amount they were in earlier decades. Since testosterone is the major sex steroid responsible for stimulating sexual appetite, this decrease has repercussions for many older women. "Androgen deficiency" appears to be associated with a reduction of sexual motivation, as well as reduced genital and breast sensitivity. More significantly, too little bioavailable testosterone is associated with a diminished sense of well-being and excessive fatigue (Davis, 2000).

Changes in sex steroids, estrogen and testosterone, contribute to changes in the anatomy and physiology of the genitals as well. Specifically, as the walls of the vagina become thinner and more friable, the incidence of painful intercourse increases. Atrophy of the Bartholin glands and a decrease in the number of maturity of vaginal cells can cause an increased latency of lubrication with sexual stimulation. Lack of lubrication contributes to painful intercourse or dysareunia, which can lead to marital friction if the women begins to avoid sexual intimacy. Vaginal secretions change in both quantity and quality. These vaginal atrophy changes lead to an increased susceptibility to vaginal infections, which also diminishes sexual enthusiasm and genital comfort. Finally, stress incontinence is associated with reduced estrogen supplies and is yet another contribution to diminished sexual comfort for some older women.

The Menopause and Sexuality

The menopause, occurring around age 50, represents a clear marker of aging for many women. About this time, if not before, women will begin to notice changes in their appearance. Wrinkles, loss of breast and abdominal elasticity, senile or sagging skin and facial features, and gray hair (or hair loss, including that in the pubic area) may be noted and will lead women to either run to their plastic surgeons or calmly observe the marks of a life fully lived. Weight gain is common, due to slower basal body metabolism, and at times, seems inexorable, irrespective of diet or exercise. Some women note an increase in weight gain with hormone replacement. Further, women's body shape changes at midlife, from more gynecoid "pear-shaped" to android "apple-shaped" with weight accumulating around the waist (Vliet, 1995).

The termination of menstruation, a process intimately associated with declining estrogen levels, is such a salient reminder of the aging process that both women and their partners have, historically, tended to attribute any complaints, physical or psychological, occurring around this time as caused by "the changes." Nevertheless, cross-cultural and anthropological studies suggest that the meaning of this event varies considerably across cultures (Avis, 1996; Locke, 1998). In non-Western cultures, where menopause eliminates the constraints and prohibitions placed on menstruating women, aging is a positive experience and women may be esteemed as "crones," repositories of wisdom and history.

Even the expected biological changes with menopause are somewhat culturally determined. For instance, reporting of hot flashes and night sweats is significantly lower in Japanese women, who also have a lower incidence of heart disease, breast cancer, and osteoporosis. Although some of these differences are due to dietary differences, some of them may be mediated through the influence of culturally determined lifestyle practices (Locke, 1998). In our own Western society, with its premium on youth and sexual attractiveness, menopause may take on a different meaning. Even so, research suggests that women consistently feel relief over the cessation of menses and do not agree that they become less sexually attractive subsequent to menopause (Avis, 1996). In fact, many postmenopausal women have a more positive view of menopause than do younger, premenopausal women.

Nevertheless, many, but by no means all, women report sexual problems that either began, or were exacerbated, by menopause. These include vaginal dryness, loss or diminution of sexual desire, difficulty becoming sexually aroused, loss of clitoral sensation, fewer orgasms, and decreased sexual frequency. Dyspareunia is the most common sexual complaint of older women seeking gynecological (painful intercourse) consultation (Bachmann, Leiblum, & Grill, 1989).

Surgical Menopause and Sexual Response

Whereas the majority of women experience menopausal changes over a protracted period of time, beginning in the mid-30s, 35–40% of women are catapulted into early menopause by undergoing hysterectomy with bilateral oophorectomy. In fact, hysterectomy continues to be the second most commonly performed surgical procedure in the United States, affecting about one-third of American women (Rako, 1996). Even women who keep their ovaries following a hysterectomy will enter menopause about 4 years sooner than those with a natural menopause (Levine, 1998). Blood flow to the ovaries is reduced following hysterectomy which may account for an earlier menopause. Moreover, when both ovaries are removed and both estrogen and androgen supplies are quickly withdrawn, women may experience a range of menopausal symptoms, including a noticeable loss of desire. Women who have undergone chemotherapy may also experience a "chemical menopause" with the same symptoms as women who have had their ovaries removed (Kaplan, 1992).

Perhaps more significant than the physical changes accompanying hysterectomy are the psychological sequelae. For some women (and their partners) the operation constitutes a genuine life crisis. It leads them to examine their feelings about their uterus and ovaries and may stir up deeply held beliefs about their sense of womanliness. To the extent that a woman views her uterus as symbolic of her womanhood, she may become depressed following a hysterectomy. She may also worry about postoperative pain with intercourse. Indirectly, the operation sometimes leads to sexual problems because the woman feels less confident about her body image and sexual desirability.

However, for some women, the operation provides a welcome relief from physically uncomfortable symptoms and abnormal bleeding. When performed to relieve pain, abnormal bleeding, or dysmenorrhea, hysterectomy may result in improved sexual activity. In fact, a 1999 study evaluating 1,299 women undergoing hysterectomy for benign disease found a significant increase in libido and frequency of sexual relations along with decreased dyspareunia and anorgasmia (Rhodes, Kjerulff; Laugenberg, & Guzinski, 1999). Recent research, however, suggests that women who are most adversely affected by hysterectomies are those with a lifelong history of depression (Garth, Cooper, & Day, 1982; Avis, Brambilla, McKinlay, & Vass, 1994).

Clinical Example

A 55-year-old insurance salesman consulted his internist because of concerns about his decreased libido. Following an endocrine evaluation, he was referred for a psychological consultation. He reported having coitus three to four times a week without difficulty. However, he complained of a lack of sexual desire. "It's like looking at a dessert tray in a fancy restaurant when you're full. You notice that the pastries are beautiful. You just don't want to eat them!"

The patient was evasive concerning his emotional relationship with his wife, and so a conjoint session was arranged. His wife, an attractive manager of a small restaurant, reported sadly that her husband had "lost interest in her." She did not think he was having an affair. Tears came into her eyes as she related that the changes seemed to coincide with her hysterectomy. As she continued to speak, it became apparent that she felt unattractive and doubtful about her femininity. She indicated that she and her husband rarely talked intimately anymore. When she would discuss painful feelings or personal worries, her husband would immediately interrupt her and try to "solve" her problem.

As the couple talked together in the session, it became clear that following his wife's hysterectomy, the husband had increased his frequency of sexual initiations in order to reassure his wife of her continued appeal for him. This had backfired because she intuited that his overtures exceeded his genuine ardor. Once he was able to admit that he was proposing sex in the absence of desire, he and his wife were able to have a more honest conversation about his reactions to her hysterectomy and her worries and fears about the "losses associated with aging." This resulted in renewed feelings of intimacy and connection and a more realistic schedule of sex.

Desire and Arousal Problems

Second to dyspareunia, desire problems are the most common sexual problem of older women. A recent Australian study, which involved telephone interviews with over 2,000 women ages 45 to 55, reported that 31% of women experienced a decline in sexual interest (Dennerstein et al., 1994). The decline in interest was associated with menopause rather than with age.

The majority of studies investigating sexual desire in older women report similar findings—a reduction in sexual fantasy or thoughts as well as a reduction in coital frequency. The age-related decrease in sexual desire is due to a variety of factors including the age, health, sexual desire, and sexual difficulties of both the woman and her partner, relationship satisfaction, the woman's past level of sexual satisfaction, sexual comfort and sexual interest, the number of medications affecting sexual response that either she or her partner is taking, and, certainly, the effects of the hormonal changes associated with menopause. Moreover, a number of popular antidepressant medications can diminish desire.

Changes in sexual arousal are also due to many factors in addition to the hormonal changes associated with menopause. Recently, Goldstein et al. (1998) have demonstrated that arousal difficulties in older women may be exacerbated or caused by atherosclerotic vascular disease, which results in delayed vaginal engorgement, diminished vaginal lubrication, pain or discomfort with intercourse, and decreased vaginal and clitoral sensations and orgasm. The use of vasoactive drugs is currently being evaluated by many pharmaceutical companies as a means of enhancing sexual arousal in women, much as they do in men with erectile problems. It is likely that in the next decade a host of medications will be available to women that will facilitate smooth muscle relaxation and increased blood flow to the female genitals.

It should be noted, however, that several studies have found that many postmenopausal women report little or no changes in *subjective sexual arousal* (Morrell, Dixen, Carter, & Davidson, 1984; Myers & Morokoff, 1985). Whereas there is clearly less vaginal lubrication during sexual arousal in women not taking estrogen replacement, the psychological experience of sexual excitement does not appear to be significantly correlated with physiological measures of arousal, and many women continue to report considerable subjective arousal when shown erotic material.

Orgasmic Responsiveness

Some women experience changes in their orgasm with aging, notably changes in the duration of orgasm, the ease and reliability of orgasm, and the number of uterine and vaginal contractions that accompany orgasm. Women who have lost their uterus and/or ovaries may have more difficulty becoming sexually aroused and orgasmic because the uterus may contribute to arousal and orgasmic contractions. On the other hand, the clitoris—which is far larger than typically believed—can be quite effective in providing erotic sensations and the ability to remain multiply orgasmic continues. Further, Kinsey, Pomeroy, Martin, and Gebhard (1953) reported that women under 60 noted no change in the frequency of orgasm achieved through activities that were not dependent on their male partners, such as masturbation. Moreover, some women report increases in orgasmic responsivity associated with the absence of worry or concerns about contraception and pregnancy.

Hormones and Sexuality

Many of the anatomic changes associated with aging are due to estrogen deficiency. As noted earlier, estrogen plays a significant role in skin elasticity and thickness. It helps prevent heart disease by reducing cholesterol levels and increasing blood vessel suppleness. Estrogen loss clearly affects bone density, resulting in hip fractures for over 65,000 American women every year. The age-related reduction in vaginal lubrication is associated with declining estrogen levels, which is effectively reversed with hormone replacement.

Estrogen, though, does not appear to affect libido, except perhaps indirectly, via sleep disruptions and fatigue due to hot flashes or cold sweats during the night. Estrogen replacement results in improvement in vasomotor symptoms, vaginal dryness, and general well-being. Oral estrogen therapy improves sexual satisfaction in women who suffer from atrophic vaginitis, which may be causing their dyspareunia, but women without coital dyspareunia appear to benefit little from estrogen replacement (Davis & Burger, 1996).

The hormone of desire appears to be androgen, and there is increasing evidence that androgens play a major role in female sexuality. Androgen deprivation after menopause contributes to a decline in sexual interest for many women (Rako, 1996; Davis, 1998).

Moreover, a decline in testosterone has been observed in premenopausal women also as they grow older. As noted earlier, the levels of free testosterone in women in their 40s are approximately 50% lower than those of women in their 20s (Davis & Burger, 1996). The decline in total circulating androgens appears to result from both ovarian failure and the age-related decline in adrenal androgen and preandrogen production. Sexual complaints in women with reduced levels of androgen typically center on reduced (or absent) libido, but complaints of lessened feelings of well-being and loss of energy are common as well (Rako, 1996; Davis & Burger, 1996).

Sherwin's (1998) recent review of the use of combined estrogen–androgen preparations for postmenopausal women concludes that such combined preparations "enhance energy level, well-being, and sexual desire/interest to levels over and above those that may be induced by estrogen alone" (Sherwin, 1998, p. 102). However, she notes that when other life stresses, physical illnesses, or long-standing sexual dysfunctions exist, combined estrogen–androgen replacement therapy alone will not reverse the problem. Moreover, for women for whom hirsutism is a problem, androgen therapy is contraindicated. Finally, the use of testosterone replacement remains controversial for women undergoing spontaneous menopause and for women who are not yet perimenopausal (Davis, 1998).

Clinical Example

Arlene, an obese, attractive, well-groomed, and energetic 56-year-old African American woman requested sex therapy because of her total lack of sexual desire. She reported that she had once enjoyed an active and uninhibited sexual life, even to the point of calling her husband at work and saying, "Come home! I'm so horny, I can die!" However, there was a rapid and dramatic loss of sexual interest 3 years earlier, at age 53. "It was like a door closing," she declared. "It was the last thing on my list of things that interested me." Whereas formerly sex had been a high-priority activity, now it was avoided.

In taking a sexual history, Arlene reported that she began to miss periods beginning at age 51, but her last menstrual period occurred at age 54. She was put on estrogen–progesterone therapy because of "wild hot flashes" which disturbed her sleep and because she was worried about developing osteoporosis like her mother.

The hormone replacement alleviated vaginal dryness—"I can lubricate easily." The physical sensations of arousal were present, but she said, "I can't get emotionally aroused—I didn't see any point in having sex since it wasn't any fun anymore."

Compounding the problem and exacerbating it was her long-standing dissatisfaction with her husband. She had always railed against his general obsessive style and the amount of time he spent at the office, but now he was also having difficulty maintaining his erections during intercourse. Things had come to a head 18 months ago when he accepted a job 90 minutes from home, which resulted in his being away from home 2 to 3 days each week. She was furious that he lacked the initiative to search for a job closer to home and that, when he was home, he was too tired to spend leisure time with her.

The combination of her marital dissatisfaction, her husband's erectile difficulties, and her own lack of desire led to a total cessation of physical intimacy. Although her menopausal changes appeared to contribute to the problems, they were not the sole cause of her lack of libido and, furthermore, testosterone therapy was contraindicated because of her general hirsuitism, which required an hour of electrolysis weekly.

Conjoint sexual therapy was undertaken, which led to significant improvement. During the sessions, Arlene made it clear that she might be willing to "reenter the sexual arena"—despite her lack of desire—if her husband would show "good faith" by returning from work at a reasonable time and joining her on "fun" excursions. He was sufficiently motivated by the promise of physical intimacy that he kept his side of the bargain and even initiated several social activities. Whereas formerly friends and neighbors had asked if she was separated, never seeing her accompanied by her husband, she once again felt like a "married woman" and took pleasure in their companionship. These changes, modest though they appeared to be, resulted in greater receptivity on Arlene's part.

She agreed to only playful touching at first—hand holding, "patty cake hand slapping," writing "messages" on each other's backs, clothed, and then, naked. She began to spontaneously initiate hugs and kisses, which he eagerly reciprocated.

It was suggested at this point in the therapy that he might want to consider experimenting with the use of Viagra on his own—during masturbation—to see whether he noted improvement in his erectile response. Arlene was enthusiastic about this, even saying that she wanted to be present to observe.

By the 12th session, Arlene and her husband had begun massage and more consistent physical exchange. While Arlene still reports only a modest level of desire, she is receptive to her husband in ways she had not been for several years.

Psychological and Interpersonal Issues Affecting Sexuality in Aging Women

As is evident in the case example, over and above the physical and hormonal changes accompanying aging in women are the psychological and interpersonal issues. Many women continue to be constrained by long-standing sexual inhibitions, the aftermath of sexual abuse or victimization, fears of being considered unattractive or "invisible," and unsatisfactory relationships. For single, divorced, or widowed women, a major problem is the lack of reliable opportunity for sexual encounters. Lesbian women, too, have difficulty finding partners who are both interested in and comfortable with sexual exchange as they age. Finally, both heterosexual and homosexual women bemoan the lack of passion and lust that may characterize their current sexual life, as compared to the memories of past romantic and sexual escapades. Unfortunately, in long partnered couples, predictability often replaces spontaneity and sexual encounters may have become routine and perfunctory. Sex therapy in these situations must focus on ways of resolving the intrapsychic issues, reviving the couple relationship and rewriting the sexual script. On a more positive note, some older women are reporting outstanding sex lives, as they relinquish old inhibitions and experience greater feelings of entitlement, as well as a more active approach to ensuring sexual satisfaction. Therapists can assist in this process by suggesting alternatives to coitus, affirming the woman's right to sexual pleasure, and encouraging an active approach to the quest for physical intimacy.

SEXUAL CHANGES IN THE AGING MALE

Substantial changes in sexual performance occur with aging in the male. Although these changes are pronounced, they occur gradually, allowing the man and his partner time to adapt to a shifting pattern of responsiveness. Studies of various parameters of sexual behavior have indicated a gradual decline in sexual activity after age 50, with a more precipitous decline after 70 (Kinsey, Pomeroy, & Martin, 1948; Schiavi, 1999). It is important to stress, however, that age alone does not preclude coitus in healthy males. Some males will remain sexually active into their 80s and 90s albeit at a lower frequency than in their 40s and 50s. Moreover, there is considerable individual variability in the effects of age on sexual behavior. Whereas most 70-year-old men may have intercourse once a week or less, others will report coitus three times a week or more. One cannot assume that advanced age alone accounts for diminished activity.

Nevertheless, a decline in sexual function in aging men is a reliable finding (Kinsey et al., 1948; Pfeiffer, Verwoerdt, & Davis, 1972). Population-based studies in both the United States and abroad support age-related changes in sexual activity and response (Marsiglio & Donnelly, 1991; Kivela, Pahlaka, & Honkakoski, 1986; Boyle, 1999; Mulligan & Moss, 1991; Lendorf, Jancker, & Rosenkilde, 1994; Michaels, Laumann, & Gagnon, 1994).

A number of studies have examined the relationship of disease to erectile dysfunction and aging (Mulligan, Retchin, Chinchilla, & Bettinger, 1988; Diokno, Brown, & Herzog, 1990). The most comprehensive study to date is the Massachusetts Male Aging Study (Feldman, Goldstein, Hatzichristou, Krane, & McKinlay, 1994; Goldstein & Hatzichristou, 1994). A cross-sectional community-based sample completed a sexual function questionnaire. Self-reported total erectile failure increased from 5% at age 40 to 15% at age 70. Risk factors for erectile dysfunction included diabetes, heart disease, hypertension, low concentration of high-density lipoprotein, and the use of cardiovascular drugs as well as a number of psychological factors.

Scandinavian population-based studies reveal similar findings. Helgason et al. (1996) studied a random sample of Swedish men ages 50 to 80 and found a decline in potency and coital frequency with aging. In the 70- to 80-year-old age group, 49% reported erectile potency and 46% reported an orgasm at least once a month as compared with a potency rate of 97% for men 50 to 59 and an orgasm rate of at least once a month for 97% of men. Clearly, with aging, both erections and ejaculations occur less reliably and with diminished frequency.

Clinical Significance of Changes in Sexual Behavior with Aging

Regrettably, a number of men and their partners fall prey to the psychosocial trap of expecting constancy of sexual performance across the life span and try to "force" a sexual response characteristic of their youth. For example, whereas a young male may achieve a full erection in seconds, an older man may require minutes to achieve the same response. Preejaculatory fluid emission may be decreased or absent, and the aging male may experience less ejaculatory demand. Ejaculation is typically less forceful and the seminal fluid volume is decreased. The refractory period may extend to days rather than minutes. Some men experience changes in penile sensitivity (Rowland, 1998) and decreased frequency of nocturnal erections (Schiavi & Schreiner-Engel, 1988) with aging. The amplitude and latency of somatosensory evoked potentials from the area of the genitals may also change with increased age (Benelmans et al., 1999). These sensory changes could influence sexual function by interfering with reflex mechanisms mediating erections and ejaculations and by diminishing pleasurable sensations (Schiavi, 1999). The force and frequency of desire for sexual release decrease with age. When a parallel reduction in sexual interest does not coexist in the partner, the path is open for misunderstanding, disappointment, and withdrawal. It is for this reason that Masters and Johnson (1977) have emphasized that the older male and his partner should be aware of these changes so that they do not engender unnecessary and avoidable psychological sexual dysfunction.

The clinical significance of decreased genital responsiveness to sexual stimuli with aging is complex. On the one hand, one can label this decreased responsiveness as erectile unreliability and a natural aspect of aging or, alternatively, as partial impotence, a syndrome requiring treatment. As most individuals are adverse to declining physical function with aging, many men seek treatment to reverse this complaint. In certain instances, one observes older men repeatedly attempting to have coitus at a frequency they enjoyed in their youth. Treatment of such men may be difficult, particularly if they are using sexual activity as a way of denying aging rather than as a source of pleasure. In these cases, the man may still be dissatisfied even if treatment succeeds in increasing his erectile performance.

How does one draw the line between normal aging and disease? Clinicians wish to restore quality of life when the intervention carries minimal risk. Vasoactive agents which enhance erectile responsiveness are a logical option for many aging men. Third-party payers may have a different view of the value of restoring the quality of life from providers or consumers of health care.

Clinical Example

To reemphasize the point that the rate of decline in sexual function in males is highly variable, one of the authors was recently called to consult on a 70-year-old woman who had made a suicide gesture. The story quickly unfolded that her 71-year-old husband was having an affair with a 60-year-old neighbor. Domestic harmony was restored following a family conference in which the 45-year-old son insisted that his father be more responsible.

Hormonal Changes with Aging

Sex hormone production in the disease-free male remains relatively stable until the fifth decade, when a gradual decline in androgen production begins in many men (Bancroft, 1983). As androgen continues to decline over the next few decades, pituitary-stimulating hormones may demonstrate elevation although serum androgen levels remain within normal limits. The elevation of pituitary-stimulating hormones represents the relative inability of the aging testes to efficiently produce androgens. Many investigators have suspected that the decline in circulating androgen is responsible for the decrease in libido with aging in men. This is a reasonable hypothesis as sexual desire is clearly diminished in clinically hypogonadal men and restored by replacement testosterone. Schiavi and coworkers (Schiavi, Schreiner-Engel, Mandele, Schanzer, & Cohen, 1990; Schiavi, 1999) carefully investigated endocrinological variables and aging in a sample of 45- to 75-year-old-men. They concluded that bioavailable testosterone was unrelated to erectile function, although it may be related to libido.

Bancroft (1983) has suggested that part of the decline in libido with aging may be related to changes in receptor sensitivity to circulating androgens. As part of the comprehensive workup with men complaining of loss of desire, clinicians should routinely evaluate serum androgen levels and prolactin levels, although many men will describe erectile dysfunction rather than decreased libido. In human males, androgen production appears more closely associated with libido than with erectile capacity. However, clinically, it may be difficult to reliably distinguish between the two complaints. Some men may develop psychogenic erectile problems while attempting coitus in the absence of sexual desire. It is important to note that androgen therapy is not indicated for men with a complaint of erectile failure who have normal libido.

Hypogonadism and hyperprolactinemia are treatable causes of low libido. Hyperprolactinemia may indicate the presence of pituitary adenomas or may be secondary to drug influences on the pituitary. The mechanism mediating the relationship between diminished libido and elevated prolactin is unclear. In the presence of low bioavailable testosterone, one would want to assess luteinizing hormone (LH) levels. Low to normal LH levels are suggestive of pituitary or hypothalamic defects whereas high LH levels suggest testicular failure. Hyperprolactinemia is usually associated with low testosterone levels and may also present as low libido associated with decreased erectile function. The major point is that in the age of safe vasoactive agents, one does not want to proceed directly to vasoactive drug therapy and overlook other treatable causes of sexual dysfunction. Vasoactive therapy *does not* appear to be useful in men with a primary complaint of decreased sexual interest.

Clinical Example

A 65-year-old man with a history of recurrent major depressive disorder related that he had minimal desire for sexual activity. The patient was euthymic at the time of evaluation. He reported early-morning erections and the ability to have coitus with his spouse although he had no wish to do so. He denied masturbation. Although he felt "fond" of his wife, he was completely lacking in sexual interest for both her and other women, even though he might find them attractive. Their attractiveness was described more as an aesthetic experience than a sexual turn-on. He reported no sexual fantasies.

An extensive endocrine evaluation was conducted and all his levels fell within normal limits. His lack of sexual desire persisted in spite of numerous changes of antidepressant drugs to find a drug that would have minimal impact on libido. Sildenafil was prescribed in the hope that enhancing erectile function might rekindle desire because libido and arousal are intertwined in normal sexual functioning. However, the patient reported minimal effects of sildenafil on his erections and no effect on his sex drive.

Similar disappointing findings have been noted by other clinicians who have attempted to enhance sexual drive by prescribing sildenafil to enhance erections.

Disease and Changes in Sexual Behavior

With increasing age, men are more susceptible to disease. Many of these diseases may directly or indirectly affect sexual activity (Melman & Gingell, 1999).

Diseases with direct effects on sexual function include diseases associated with peripheral neuropathies such as diabetes mellitus, alcoholic neuropathy, and multiple sclerosis (see Tables 15.1 and 15.2) (Segraves, 1998). Indirect causes of sexual dysfunction include any chronic disease that causes general malaise or pain. Many surgical and medical procedures may interfere with the autonomic nerve supply to the genitals. These procedures include anterior resection of the rectum, radical retropubic postatectomy, retroperitoneal lymphadenectomy, radical transvesical prostectomy, abdominoperitoneal resection, and aortoiliac and aortofemoral surgery. Pelvic radiation for prostate cancer can also cause nerve damage and result in erectile failure. Many of the agents used in cancer chemotherapy are also neurotoxic. Other causes of sexual dysfunction include vascular disease affecting either the small vessels of the penis or the arteries feeding the small vessels. Sexual dysfunction has also been noted in patients with brain injury, particularly to the temporal lobes and dorsal septal region (Segraves & Rahman, 1998).

TABLE 15.1. Organic Etiologies of Erectile Disorders

Urethral rupure	Aortoiliac surgery
Spinal cord injury	Arteriosclerosis
Retroperitoneal resection	Diabetes mellitus
Radical prostatectomy	Multiple sclerosis
Proctocolectomy	Laminectomy
Pelvic radiation	Pelvic fracture

Many pharmacological agents have been reported to be associated with sexual dysfunction. As men grow older, they are more likely to be taking multiple pharmacological agents. Hypotensive agents have been reported to be associated with erectile, libido, and ejaculatory problems. Current evidence suggests that diuretics such as hydrochlorothiazide, chlorthalidone, and spironolactone may be associated with erectile dysfunction. Antihypertensive agents with central antiadrenergic effects may cause sexual dysfunction. These drugs include methyldopa and reserpine. Beta-blockers are another group of agents that may interfere with erectile function. Sexual dysfunction may be less common with beta-blockers such as pindolol, metoprolol, and nadolol than with propranolol. It is notable that erectile failure has been reported with the use of timolol eye drops. Ejaculatory problems are common with guanethedine, bethanidine, labetalol, and nifedipine. Drugs associated with sexual side effects are tested in Tables 15.3 and 15.4. The angiotension-converting enzyme inhibitors such as captopril, lisinopril, and enalapril appear to have fewer sexual side effects than many of the other hypotensive agents.

Other drugs that have been reported to cause sexual side effects include cimetidine, an H2 antagonist. Ranitidine appears less likely to cause this side effect. Decreased libido appears to be associated with antiepileptic drugs and digoxin.

Psychiatric drugs may also be a cause of sexual dysfunction (Segraves & Segraves, 1993a, 1993b). The antipsychotic drugs such as haloperidol, thioridazine, fluphenazine, amoxapine, and chlorpromazine appear to be associated with erectile dysfunction (Aizenberg, Zemishlany, Dorfman-Etrog, & Weizman, 1995). The newer antipsychotics such as olanzapine and risperidone appear to have a lower incidence of sexual dysfunction than do the older antipsychotics (Montejo et al., 1998). Lithium carbonate may be associated with an adverse impact on sexual functioning in a minority of patients (Segraves, 1998). The antidepressant drugs may be associated with ejaculatory problems, decreased libido, erectile problems, and, less commonly, pain with ejaculation. Antidepressants with a decreased likelihood of causing sexual dysfunction include bupropion (Segraves et al., 1998), nefazodone (Feiger, Kiev, & Shrivastava, 1996), mirtazapine (Boyarsky, 1998), and fluvoxamine (Waldinger, Hengeveld, Zwinderman, & Olivier, 1998).

Clearly, one wants to screen for cases of possible drug-induced sexual dysfunction which can be easily resolved by discontinuing the drug or substituting a different agent. Antidotes for antidepressant-induced sexual dysfunc-

TABLE 15.2. Organic Causes of Ejaculatory Disorders

Diabetes mellitus	Proctocolectomy
Multiple sclerosis	Cerebral vascular accident
Cord injury	Cystectomy
Sympathectomy	Aortoiliac surgery
Tabes dorsalis	

TABLE 15.3. Drugs Associated with Decreased Libido

Methyldopa	Lithium	Cimetidine
Methazolamide	Digoxin	Amitriptyline
Paroxetine	Haloperidol	Alprazolam
Sertraline	Fluphenazine	Chlorthalidone
Phenelzine	Fluoxetine	Chlorpromazine
Imipramine	Hydrochlorothiazide	Pridone
Spironolactone	Protriptyline	Clofibrate
Thiorodazine	Amoxapine	Cimetidine
Clonidine	Thiothixine	Clomipramine

tion including sildenafil have been reported and certain antidepressants are less likely to cause sexual dysfunction than others. The same is true of antipsychotic and antihypertensive medications. In general, one would prefer to change agents rather than add another agent to offset the side effect of the first agent.

Assessment of Sexual Function

In the aging male, it is likely that organic factors are at least partially responsible either alone or together with psychogenic factors for causing sexual complaints. Clues as to multiple etiologies must be pursued. One wants to first identify easily reversible causes of sexual dysfunction. A sexual history and physical examination will provide the basis for further evaluation and give the clinician information to formulate general hypotheses about etiology. Suggested routine laboratory tests include serum testosterone, complete blood count, prostrate specific antigen, and basic serum chemistries (Kirby, 1999). It is important that the interview not be overly structured in order to facilitate the spontaneous flow of information from the patient. The history should establish the nature of the complaint, its course over time and situations, a description of typical sexual behavior for the patient, and an overview of the relationship with the partner. Where possible, one would like to include the partner in the evaluation. Unfortunately, this is not always possible. The basic interview should establish whether the problem is mainly one of libido, arousal, or orgasm.

TABLE 15.4. Drugs Associated with Ejaculatory Difficulties

Alprazolam	Imipramine	Thioridazine
Amoxapine	Fluphenazine	Thiothixine
Chlordiazepoxide	Doxepin	Tranylcypromine
Sertraline	Desipramine	Venlafaxine
Paroxetine	Clorprothixine	Citalopram
Clomipramine	Bethanidine	Haloperidol
Fluvoxamine	Naproxen	
Fluoxetine	Nortriptyline	

Decreased sexual desire is one of the most common complaints of patients in sex therapy settings. The first thing that one needs to establish is whether the problem is situation specific or generalized. This distinction is based on the assumption that most organic etiologies to diminished libido will be present in all sexual situations (i.e., generalized). If the problem is generalized, one first searches for reversible causes of decreased libido such as major depression and generalized anxiety disorder. One also would want to exclude drug-induced libido disturbances as well as endocrinopathies.

Situational diminished libido is most likely secondary to marital or interpersonal discord. With aging, the strength of desire tends to be less robust and more easily disrupted by minor irritations that might not have interrupted desire in a younger male. One searches for causes of interpersonal disputes and possible solutions.

Clinical Example

A 90-year-old professor and his 80-year-old wife requested a consultation. The professor complained of diminished desire since assuming emeritus status and setting up his office at home. His wife would begin house cleaning as he was writing a new textbook. The sound of the vacuum cleaner would interrupt his concentration, and he would be annoyed all day. The clinician was able to encourage the retired professor to apply for a space in the university library where he could write without interruption. He then had a decrease in his irritation at his wife and resumed coitus on a once-a-month basis,

Arousal disorders are also common in aging men. If the problem is situational, one looks for reversible interpersonal problems. If the problem is generalized, one searches again for reversible organic etiologies such as major depression and endocrinopathies. Clearly, it is important not to treat erectile dysfunction secondary to major depression with oral vasoactive agents without also treating depression which is a life-threatening disease. Similarly, one would not want to miss a prolactineoma.

Difficulties with orgasm in males are most often organically based. One of the most easily reversible causes of male anorgasmia are drug-induced problems.

Treatment of Sexual Dysfunction in the Older Male

The introduction of successful oral vasoactive substances for the treatment of erectile dysfunction has had a major impact on the treatment of men with erectile problems (Goldstein et al., 1998). Sildenafil, an inhibitor of cyclic guanosine monophosphate, increases the erectile response to sexual stimulation. A pivotal multicenter trial reported that 69% of men with erectile problems of moderate severity from multiple causes responded to this agent with a return of function. As primary care physicians become more comfortable prescribing this agent, the advent of sildenafil will undoubtedly have a major impact on the types of patients referred to mental health professionals. Whereas many older couples respond with pleasure to the return of erectile function, this result is not universal. One case report (Wise, 1999) discusses instances of marital discord precipitated by sildenafil therapy. Noting the high divorce rate in dropouts from sex therapy, intracavernosal injection therapy, and vacuum erection device therapy, one of the authors speculated about his observation: It is possible that the dropouts included a number of patients who realized that a rigid erection was not the solution for the problem for which they sought therapy. Many individuals in dysfunctional relationships will tend to minimize the relationship problems and point to a sexual complaint as the primary problem (Segraves & Segraves, 1998).

Similarly, the rapid reversal of sexual dysfunction in one partner will create problems if the other partner does not wish to resume sexual relations. Many men may complain of erectile failure, but a more careful history by a seasoned clinician will reveal that the major problem is hypoactive sexual desire rather than erectile failure. It is too early to be certain of the types and frequency of difficulties that will be precipitated by the unilateral resolution of a sexual problem. Clearly, restoration of sexual function will not resolve interpersonal difficulties or diminished desire for sexual activity.

Clinical Examples

The following two cases highlight quite different responses to sildenafil treatment. One patient, a 72-year-old widower and retired real estate developer was prescribed sertraline for a major depressive disorder. His depression resolved on 100 mg sertraline and he became interested in dating again at which point he noticed erectile problems for the first time in his life. Attempts to switch to a different antidepressant were unsuccessful. His health insurance covered six sildenafil tablets a month. The sildenafil restored his ability to have erections and he praises it as one of the miracles of the modern world.

Another patient, a 65-year-old divorced man who runs a major construction firm, requested help for dealing with a major depression. Bupropion helped lift his depression. However, as his depression resolved, he mentioned that he had intermittent erectile difficulties with his current partner that preceded his depressive episode. Questioning revealed that his partner desired marriage and her mention of marriage appeared to precede his bouts of intermittent erectile problems.

This patient's first marriage and separation had been extremely traumatic for him, as he had found his first wife in bed with his best friend. She then ridiculed him in front of the friend, saying that she would never have had an affair if her husband was a real man. He subsequently suffered intermittent erectile problems as he began dating other women. The patient did not want a conjoint session as his partner might misinterpret this as commitment. The patient appeared to have a deep respect and love for his partner but to be afraid of a repeat of the first marriage. Attempts to point this out to him were met with disbelief. He then saw a television program about sildenafil and requested a prescription for the drug, which was provided.

At the next session, he reported that he had a firm erection on sildenafil but absolutely no desire to use it. This revelation helped to highlight his ambivalence about intimacy with his partner and his fear of being reinjured. Although he acknowledged this ambivalence and fear, he continued to refuse to involve his partner in therapy and to deflect all attempts on her part to discuss their relationship and possible marriage. As of the time that this chapter was written, he continues to date the same woman with no plans of ever remarrying. Her discussion of marriage still provokes intermittent bouts of erectile failure.

SEX THERAPY WITH ELDERLY ADULTS

A generation gap often exists in attitudes toward sexual behavior. Many beliefs held by younger mental health professionals may seem alien to older men. For example, the vast majority of aging males firmly believe that all sexual expression must involve penile vaginal penetration and attempts to convince them otherwise is likely to be unsuccessful (though worth the effort). Similarly, many such men may find the concept that the interpersonal relationship might influence their ability to have an erection an alien concept. Education of such patients about natural consequences of aging may help over time.

Most patients will not volunteer information about their sex lives but will usually respond to questioning by a professional. Hawton (1985) gives an excellent discussion of conducting a sexual interview which applies to individuals of all ages. He emphasizes the need to choose language that is comfortable and understood by the patient, starting with open questions to elicit further information followed by direct questions to establish the specific details of the problem; interviewing both members of the relationship when possible, and taking a careful history of illness and medications. He emphasizes the importance of the clinician's formulating the problem in terms of major factors and presenting this formulation to the couple to make certain that they understand and agree with the formulation.

Many studies have shown that illness in the male frequently ends coital activity in elderly couples. The loss of conventional forms of sexual expression may require new adaptations by the couple. Some may make this adaptation successfully whereas others do not.

It is important once again to emphasize that sexual problems in the elderly are not exclusively organic in etiology and may have emotional origins. Often a careful history and formulation of the current problem combined with the patient's understanding of the problem serve as a useful springboard for discussion and education about both changes in sexual response with aging and the role of psychological factors in sexual performance. Hesitancy in discussing sexual behavior does not necessarily imply inhibition in the bedroom.

Often, sexual difficulties in the elderly can be resolved by simple advice. Arthritic conditions that inhibit sexual expression may be bypassed by changing positions or using pillows, taking warm bathes prior to sex, and changing the time that anti-inflammatory medications are taken.

Occasionally, one encounters an aging male with lifelong premature ejaculation. In these instances both older men as well as younger men respond satisfactorily to the use of serotonergic antidepressants such as paroxetine or clomipramine.

SUMMARY

Both men and women are living longer and healthier. Most want and expect continued physical intimacy as they grow older. Sexual intimacy offers tremendous symbolic gratification as well as physical pleasure. The advent of safe, easily administered vasoactive agents has changed the type of sex therapy desired by older couples. In some instances, the availability of a possible return of function for one member of a couple may create friction in the relationship. In other instances, it helps restore a valued intimacy. It is the clinician's job to evaluate and determine the best means of intervention. Never before has there been such a plethora of pharmacological and therapeutic options for conducting sex therapy with aging adults.

REFERENCES

Aizenberg D., Zemishlany Z., Dorfman-Etrog, P., & Weizman, A. (1995). Sexual dysfunction in schizophrenic patients. *Journal of Clinical Psychopharmacology, 56,* 461–463.

Avis, N. (1996). Women's perceptions of the menopause. *European Menopause Journal, 3,* 80–84.

Avis, N., Brambilla, D., McKinlay, S., & Vass, K. (1994). A longitudinal analysis of the relation between depression and menopause: Results from the Massachusetts Women's Health Study. *Annals of Epidemiology, 4,* 214–220.

Bachmann, G., Leiblum, S., & Grill, J. (1989). Sexuality in sexagenarian women. *Maturitas, 13,* 45–50.

Bancroft, J. (1983). *Human sexuality and its problems.* Edinburgh: Churchill Livingstone.

Benelmans, B. L. H., Meuleman, E. J. H., Amber, B. W. M., Doesburgm, W. H., Kerrebroek, P. E. V., & Debruyne, F. M. J. (1991). Penile sessory disorders in erectile dysfunction: Results of a comprehensive neuro-urophysiological diagnostic evaluation in 123 patients. *Journal of Urology, 146,* 777–782.

Boyarsky, B. K. (1998). *Mirtazapine and sexual side effects.* Paper presented at the annual meeting of the American Psychiatric Association, Toronto.

Boyle, P. (1999). Epidemiology of erectile dysfunction. In C. C. Carson, R. S. Kirby, & I. Goldstein (Eds.), *Textbook of erectile dysfunction* (pp. 15–24). Oxford: Isis.

Brecher, E. (1984). *Love, sex and aging: A Consumer's Union Survey.* Boston: Little, Brown.

Comfort, A. (1976). *A good age.* New York: Simon & Schuster.

Davis, S. (1998). The clinical use of androgens in female sexual disorders. *Journal of Sex and Marital Therapy, 24,* 153–164.

Davis, S. (2000, January 28). *Natural hormonal changes and loss of sexual desire.* Paper presented at the Second Taskforce on Female Sexuality.

Davis, S., & Burger, H. (1996). Androgens and the postmenopausal woman. *Journal of Clinical Endocrinology and Metabolism, 81,* 2759–2763.

Diokno, A. C., Brown, M. B., & Herzog, A. R. (1990). Sexual function in the elderly. *Archives of Sexual Behavior, 150,* 197–200.

Feiger, A., Kiev, A., Shrivastava, R. K. (1996). Nefazodone versus sertraline in outpatients with major depression, focus on efficacy, tolerability, and effects on sexual function and satisfaction. *Journal of Clinical Psychiatry, 57*(Suppl. 2) 53–62.

Feldman, H., Goldstein, I., Hatzichritou, D., Krane, R., & McKinlay, J. (1994). Impotence and its medical and psychological correlates: Results of the Massachusetts Male Aging Study. *Journal of Urology, 151,* 54–61.

Garth, D., Cooper, P., & Day, A. (1982). Hysterectomy and psychiatric disorder: I. Levels of psychiatric morbidity before and after hysterectomy. *British Journal of Psychiatry, 140,* 335–342.

Goldstein, I., Lue, T. F., Padma-Natham, H., Rosen, R., Steers, W. D., Wicker, P. A. (1998) Oral sildenafil in the treatment of erectile dysfunction. *New England Journal of Medicine, 338,* 1397–1404.

Goldstein, I., & Hatzichristou, D. G. (1994). Epidemiology of impotence. In A. H. Benett (Ed.), *Impotence: Diagnosis and management of erectile dysfunction* (pp. 1–17). Philadelphia: Saunders.

Hawton, K. (1985). *Sex therapy: A practical guide.* Oxford: Oxford University Press.

Healthy sexuality and vital aging. (1999). Washington, DC: American Association for Retired Persons.

Helgason, A. R., Adollfson, J., Dickkman, P,. Arver, S., Frederickson, M., Gothberg, M., & Steinbeck, G. (1996). Sexual desire, erection, orgasm, and ejacualtory function and their importance to elderly men in a population based study. *Age and Aging, 25,* 285–291.

Kaplan, H. S. (1992). A neglected issue: The sexual side-effects of current treatments for breast cancer. *Journal of Sex and Marital Therapy, 18,* 3–19.

Kinsey, A. C., Pomeroy, W. B., & Martin, C. R. (1948). *Sexual behavior in the human male.* Philadelphia: Saunders.

Kinsey, A. C., Pomeroy, W. B., Martin, C. R., & Gebhard, P. H. (1953). *Sexual behavior in the human female.* Philadelphia: Saunders.

Kirby, R. S. (1999). Basic assessment of the patient with erectile dysfunction. In C. C. Carson, R. S. Kirby, & I. Goldstein (Eds.), *Textbook of erectile dysfunction* (pp. 195–206). Oxford: Isis.

Kivela, S. L., Pahkala, K., & Honkakoski, A. (1986). Sexual desire, intercourse, and related factors among elderly Finns. *Nordisk Sexologi, 4,* 18–27.

Laumann, E., Gagnon, J., Michael, R., & Michaels, S. (1994). *The social organization of sexuality.* Chicago: University of Chicago Press.

Leiblum, S., & Segraves, R. T. (1989). Sex therapy with aging adults. In S. R. Leiblum & R. C. Rosen (Eds.), *Principles and practice of sex therapy* (2nd ed.): *Update for the 1990s* (pp. 352–381). New York: Guilford Press.

Lendorf, A., Juncker, L., Rosenkilde, P. (1994) Frequency of erectile dysfunction in a Danish subpopulation. *Nordisk Sexologi, 12,* 118–124.

Levine, S. (1998). *Sexuality in mid-life.* New York: Plenum Press.

Locke, M. (1998). Menopause: Lessons from anthropology. *Psychomatic Medicine, 60,* 410–419.

Marsiglio, W., & Donnelly, D. (1991). Sexual relations in later life: A national survey of married persons. *Journal of Gerontology, 46,* 338–344.

Masters, W., & Johnson, V. (1977). Sex after 65. *Reflections, 12,* 31–43.

Melman, A., & Gingell, J. C. (1999). The epidemiology and pathology of erectile dysfunction. *Journal of Urology, 161,* 5–11.

Michaels, S. Laumann, E., & Gagnon, J. (1994). *The social organization of sexuality: Sexual practices in the United States.* Chicago: University of Chicago Press

Montejo, A L., Llorca, G., Izquierdo, J. A., Lesesma, J. A., Iglesia, S. S. & Daniel, E. (1998). *New antipsychotic induced sexual dysfunction, comparative incidence with risperidone and olanzapine.* Paper presented at the annual meeting of the American Psychiatric Association, Toronto.

Morrell, M., Dixen, J., Carter, S., & Davidson, J. (1984). The influence of age and cycling status on sexual arousability in women. *American Journal of Obstetrics and Gynecology, 148,* 66–71.

Mulligan, T., & Moss, C. R. (1991). Sexuality and aging in male veterans: A cross-sectional study of interest, ability and activity. *Archives of Sexual Behavior, 20,* 17–25.

Mulligan, T., Retchin, S. M., Chinchilli, V., & Bettinger, C. (1988) The role of aging and chronic disease in sexual dysfunction. *Journal of the American Geriatric Society, 36,* 520–552.

Myers, L., & Morokoff, P. (1985). *Physiological and subjective sexual arousal in pre- and post-menopausal women.* Paper presented at the annual meeting of the American Psychological Association.

Pfeiffer, E., Voerwoerdt, A., & Davis, G. C. (1972). Sexual behavior in middle life. *American Journal of Psychiatry, 128,* 82–87.

Pope, M., & Schultz, R. (1990). Sexual attitudes and behavior in midlife and aging homosexual males. *Journal of Homosexuality, 20*(3–4), 169–177.

Rako, S. (1996). *The hormone of desire: The truth about sexuality, menopause, and testosterone.* New York: Harmony Books.

Renshaw, T. (1988). Sexuality in the later years. *Geriatric Sexual Counselling Mediguide to Aging, 3*(1), 1–6.

Rhodes, J., Kjerluff, K., Laugenberg, P., & Guzinski, G. (1999). Hysterectomy and sexual functioning. *Journal of the American Medical Association, 282,* 1934–1941.

Rowe, J., & Kahn, R. (1998). *Successful aging.* New York: Pantheon Books.

Rowland, D. L. (1998). Penile sensitivity in men: A composite of recent findings. *Urology, 52,* 1101–1105.

Schiavi, R. C. (1992). Normal aging and the evaluation of sexual dysfunction. *Psychiatric Medicine, 10,* 217–225.

Schiavi, R. C. (1999). *Aging and male sexuality.* Cambridge: Cambridge University Press.

Schiavi, R. C., & Schreiner-Engel, P. (1988). Nocturnal penile tumescence in healthy aging men. *Journal of Gerontology, 43,* M146–M150.

Schiavi, R. C., Schreiner-Engel, P. Mandeli, I. Schanzer, H., & Cohen, E. (1990). Healthy aging and male sexual function. *American Journal of Psychiatry, 147,* 766–771.

Segraves, R. T. (1998). Antidepressant-induced sexual dysfunction. *Journal of Clinical Psychiatry, 59*(Suppl. 4), 48–54.

Segraves, R. C., Kavoussi, R, Batey, S., Hughes, A., Ascher, J., & Donahue, R. (1988). *Evaluation of the sexual side effects of bupropion SR and sertraline in depressed outpatients.* Poster presented at New Clinical Drug Evaluation Unit, Boca Raton, FL.

Segraves, R. T., & Rahman, M. I. (1998). Sexual disorders. In L. S. Goldman, T. N. Wise, & D. S. Brody (Eds.), *Psychiatry for primary care physicians* (pp. 197–216). Chicago: American Medical Association.

Segraves, R. T., & Segraves, K. B. (1993a). Aging and drug effects on male sexuality. In R. C. Rosen & S. R. Leiblum (Eds.), *Erectile disorders: Assessment and treatment* (pp. 96–138). New York: Guilford Press.

Segraves, R. T., & Segraves, K. B. (1993b). Medical aspects of orgasm disorders. In W. O'Donahue & W. Geer (Eds.), *Handbook of sexual dysfunction: Asessment and treatment* (pp. 225–252). Boston: Allyn & Bacon.

Segraves, R. T., & Seagraves, K. B. (1998). Pharmacotherapy for sexual disorders: Advantages and pitfalls. *Sex and Marital Therapy, 13,* 259–309.

Sherwin, B. (1998). The role of combined estrogen–androgen preparations in the postmenopause: Evidence from clinical studies. *International Journal of Fertility, 43,* 98–103.

Turner, B., & Adams, C. (1988). Reported change in preferred sexual activity over the adult years. *Journal of Sex Research, 25,* 289–303.

Vliet, E. (1995). *Screaming to be heard: Hormonal connections women suspect and doctors ignore.* New York: Evans.

Wahler, J., & Gabbay, S. (1997). Gay male aging: A review of the literature. *Journal of Gay and Lesbian Social Services, 6*(3), 1–20.

Waldinger, M. D., Hengeveld, M.W., Zwinderman, A., & Olivier, B. (1998). Effect of SSRI antidepressants on ejaculation: A double-blind, randomized, placebo-controlled study with fluoxetine, fluvoxamine, paroxetine, and sertraline. *Journal of Clinical Psychopharmacology, 18,* 274–281.

Weinberg, M. (1970). The male homosexual: Age related variations in social and psychological characteristics. *Social Problems, 17,* 527–538.

Wise, T. N. (1999). Psychosocial side effects of sildenafil therapy for erectile dysfunction. *Journal of Sex and Marital Therapy, 25,* 145–150.

16

Assessment and Treatment of Atypical Sexual Behavior

JOHN P. WINCZE

Atypical sexual behavior presents a special challenge for the clinician. Usually, in the clinical setting such behavior appears as intransigent, provocative, and perplexing. Although many theories have been advanced to account for the development of atypical sexual behavior, none is wholly convincing. John P. Wincze embraces a cognitive-behavioral perspective, which includes both learning factors and the role of biological predisposition. Certainly, reinforcement and repetition, whether during sexual fantasies or masturbation, play a role in strengthening the relevant associations.

Contributing to the difficulty in treating these individuals is the typical ambivalence of the patient. These individuals frequently seek treatment only at the initiation of someone else, such as a spouse, family member, or law enforcement officer. Extinction of the behavior may represent an actual loss for the patient. Many patients rationalize their behavior, typically claiming that their paraphilia is essentially harmless. Wincze notes that weak or ambivalent motivation for change is a poor prognostic sign.

Assessment of the patient presenting with atypical sexual behavior is not very different from assessment of any patient presenting for psychotherapy. Asking patients to keep a log of their sexual acting out is helpful, as well as interviews with relevant family members. Psychophysiological assessment may be included as well, particularly in cases of forensic evaluation. Risk assessment and dangerousness of the behavior both to the patient and to others is important to assess when considering treatment interventions.

Wincze proposes that patients be advised to "purge" themselves of all sexually stimulating material, including videos, Internet materials, and fetishistic clothing—a proposal that often meets with strong patient resistance. Cog-

nitive interventions include the mental suppression of pivotal thoughts and confronting faulty cognitions that underplay the seriousness of the acting out. Victim empathy may form part of the therapy, as well as consideration of a relapse prevention program. Finally, it is necessary to attend to comorbid difficulties, such as anxiety and depression, if treatment is to be successful.

John P. Wincze, PhD, is Professor of Psychology and Psychiatry at Brown University in Rhode Island and Adjunct Professor of Psychology at Boston University. He is an authority in the treatment of individuals with both paraphiliac and nonparaphiliac sexual behavior.

Abnormal psychology and human sexuality textbooks usually point out the difficulty in defining sexual behavior that is referred to as "deviant" or "bizarre" (Barlow & Durand, 1998; Crooks & Baur, 1993; Halgin & Whitbourne, 1997). Such behaviors are dependent on the laws, the culture, and the time period of a given society. The most common term for these behaviors is "atypical," which underscores a nonjudgmental departure from the norm. Inherent in such sexual behavior is the assumption of statistical infrequency compared to what most people do. But, what most people do sexually is not precisely known because personal sexual behavior, for the most part, is secretive and not commonly discussed.

As clinicians, we are more likely to treat individuals whose sexual behavior has brought them into contact with the law or has troubled their spouse, family, or neighbors. The actual prevalence of such behaviors is unknown as it is quite likely that individuals with similar behaviors who have not troubled others would not seek help. With some sexual behaviors that are solitary, such as cross-dressing, it is especially difficult to determine prevalence because there is often no offended party to complain and bring pressure on the individual and the legal or mental health systems.

Atypical sexual behaviors are generally excesses and not deficits because sexual deficits (e.g., erectile dysfunction and vaginismus) are classified as sexual dysfunctions. The term "atypical sexual behavior" encompasses paraphilias and paraphilia-related disorders as well as sexual behaviors that do not satisfy criteria for paraphilia classification because they are less intense and episodic.

The most prevalent paraphiliac behaviors in order of most common to least are exhibitionism, voyeurism, pedophilia, transvestism, masochism, sadism, and paraphilia—not otherwise specified (Kafka, 1997a). In the classification of paraphilia-related disorders, the most commonly reported prevalences in rank order are compulsive masturbation, compulsive use of pornography, promiscuity, and phone sex (Kafka, 1997a). We have every reason to believe that the use of the computer for sexual purposes can be added to the list and may be the most prevalent paraphilia-related disorder because it allows and accesses all of the previously named categories (Cooper, Scherer, Boies, & Gordon, 1999). Recent figures on Web site use would verify this contention; for example, the five most visited sexually oriented Web sites had roughly 9 million visitors (hits) in April 1998 (Goldberg, 1998). Leiblum (1997) and Young and Rogers (1998) point to the potential harmful effects of social isolation and depression as a result of Internet sexual addiction.

The fourth edition of *Diagnostic and Statistical Manual of Mental Disorders* (DSM-IV; American Psychiatric Association, 1994) defines paraphilia as follows: "The essential features of paraphilia are recurrent, intense sexual arousing fantasies, sexual urges, or behaviors generally involving 1) nonhuman objects, 2) the suffering or humiliation of oneself or one's partner, or 3) children or other nonconsenting persons, that occur over a period of at least 6 months (Criterion A). . . . The behavior, sexual urges, or fantasies cause clinically significant distress or impairment in social, occupational, or other important areas of functioning (Criterion B)" (pp. 522–523). The term "paraphilia-related disorders" may be defined as "intensely sexually arousing fantasies, urges, and sexual activities that are culturally sanctioned aspects of normative sexual arousal and behavior" (Kafka, 1997a, p. 506).

Some sexual behaviors in North American society such as oral sex and homosexuality have in the past been considered abnormal or atypical (Crooks & Baur, 1993) but currently are not so defined. Clinicians today are witnessing the emergence of potentially new classifications. Clients complain about spending inordinate amounts of time on the computer (some, more than 10 hours a day) or of arranging sexual contacts that lead to risky experiences. The awareness that the use of the Internet for sexual satisfaction is problematic often comes following discovery by a partner or the police or after interference with one's job.

Another rather recent sexual problem is phone sex. Some clients have spent more than $1,500 a month on a consistent basis seeking erotic and sexually explicit conversations with anonymous men or women. One recent client was blackmailed following a phone sex call he made. He received a return call from a man claiming to be the parent of a minor who asked for money and threatened disclosure. Although the client sought only adult contact and had never deliberately called a minor, he nonetheless paid several thousand dollars to the blackmailer to avoid embarrassment.

Regardless of the nature or frequency of the atypical sexual behavior, there are common elements in the clinical presentation, assessment, and treatment of such behaviors. This chapter focuses on helping the clinician to theoretically conceptualize atypical sexual behavior and to acquire helpful assessment and treatment strategies.

WHY ATYPICAL BEHAVIORS DEVELOP

Information about atypical sexual behavior comes entirely from retrospective studies. Such studies provide information about common ingredients in the backgrounds of individuals with atypical sexual behaviors, but little information about cause exists. Most human sexuality textbooks and abnormal psychology textbooks agree that atypical sexual behaviors develop early in child-hood (Crooks & Baur, 1993; Barlow & Durand, 1998). The development of a pattern of atypical sexual behavior may be influenced by both learning experi-ences and biological predisposition. Abel (personal communication, February, 1995) theorizes that atypical sexual behavior develops through four stages. The first stage occurs when a child is exposed to sexualized stimulation either directly (actual physical contact) or indirectly (observing, hearing). The sec-ond stage involves a cognitive rehearsal of what was experienced with imag-ined consequences (positive or negative). The third stage involves actually try-ing out or experimenting with the behavior and directly experiencing positive or negative consequences. Finally (and depending on prior behavioral conse-quences), the behavior may be repeated and varied or shaped into different manifestations which will lead to greater reinforcement. This model is useful as it also explains why some individuals may develop an atypical behavior while others experiencing the same event may not. It all depends historically on how reinforcing or punishing a sexualized behavior was to an individual. For example, one of my patients recounted how as a child he cross-dressed in his sister's underwear only to be discovered by his sister and beaten up. He never again cross-dressed. It is, of course, pure speculation as to whether these events really foretold his future, but it is interesting that although my patient never developed cross-dressing, he did develop other paraphiliac behaviors.

Is there a biological difference in an individual who develops paraphiliac or atypical sexual behavior? Although there are no specific biological markers of atypical sexual behavior, Janssen (1997) and Bancroft (1998) discuss a pos-sible neurophysiological basis for sexual inhibition and sexual-risk-taking. According to this theoretical model, sexual risk taking behavior may be more likely manifested in individuals who possess a neurophysiological trait of low inhibition proneness. It is an easy transition to speculate that this trait may also be operating in individuals who express atypical sexual behavior because such behavior by definition carries risk (breaking the law, violating rights of others, or going against social mores).

Money (Money & Lamacz, 1989) has postulated an integrated theory of biological and psychosocial factors. Atypical sexual behavior is conceptual-ized by Money as "love maps" that have gone astray. Love maps develop early in childhood and are formulated through early sexualized learning experiences that are then indelibly etched in a person's brain. It is further speculated that hormonal factors may influence a child's susceptibility.

Regardless of the etiology of atypical sexual behavior, it is clear that such behaviors are maintained because they are highly reinforcing to an individual. The antecedent thoughts and preparatory behaviors can result in literally hours of anticipatory pleasure. In addition to the physical and psychological plea-sure associated with such behaviors, these behaviors can also reduce anxiety, mollify depression, satisfy anger and revenge, or simply fill uncomfortable idle time. These maintenance factors are extremely important to consider when formulating a treatment strategy.

PATIENT MOTIVATION AND THERAPY

Patients experiencing atypical sexual behavior often present to therapy with mixed motivation. More often than not, the law, a victim, a neighbor or a family member has threatened or cajoled a patient into therapy. Few patients enter therapy on their own accord without an external motivator. However, even those who request therapy independently are usually ambivalent because "giving up" the atypical behavior is "giving up" a powerful source of pleasure and/or a reliable psychological crutch. Relinquishing such behavior sometimes results in depression and suicidal thoughts. Therapists must be aware of this mixed motivation and deal with it thoroughly and explicitly with each patient.

Most patients do not view their behavior as causing harm, which further diminishes their motivation to change. Most atypical behaviors are either "victimless (cross-dressing, fur fetish, enemas) or take place with an unsuspecting or seemingly cooperative victim (voyeurism, most child molestation). Such acts are consequently easily justified in a patient's mind as completely harmless or causing minimal (acceptable) levels of harm. A patient's motivational level must be a foremost consideration when approaching the initial assessment of the problem and formulating a treatment plan. Weak or ambivalent motivation will result in treatment failure.

ASSESSMENT

The initial assessment of a patient presenting with atypical sexual behavior can best proceed by taking into consideration the motivational issues outlined earlier. In addition to assuming ambivalence about change, it is useful to recognize that most patients are also experiencing shame and embarrassment as well as rejection by the therapist (Schwartz & Masters, 1983). Reassuring patients that (1) you deal with such behaviors, (2) effective treatment strategies exist, and (3) such behaviors although unusual are not uncommon will serve to build rapport and help patients to speak comfortably about their problems.

For patients who are not well motivated for treatment, discussions should begin with a focus on how their behavior may be affecting their lives in terms of time wasted, money spent, and energy expended over time. Such discussions usually help patients realistically understand the consequences and ramifications of their behavior.

Once such areas are reviewed with a patient, the following content areas should be covered in order:

1. *Demographics*: family of origin, education, work, current living situation, current support system, current marriage or partnership if any.
2. *Atypical sexual problem behavior*: detailed description of atypical sexual behavior for which treatment is sought.
3. *Psychosexual history*: earliest sexual memories, experiences, and mes-

sages to the present time in chronological order. Include possible gender dysphoria and other atypical sexual behaviors and fantasies.

4. *Mental health*: current psychosocial stressors, self esteem and mental health history, substance abuse history, social skill and sexual skill deficits.

5. *Medical*: history of medical, surgical and pharmacological treatment.

It may take two to four sessions to complete this assessment. At the end of the first session, patients should begin to record a log of their sexual-acting-out behavior (Figure 16.1). The log can serve two purposes: (1) It provides additional assessment information, which can serve as a measure of progress, and (2) it provides a therapeutic intervention by interrupting the automatic thought process that accompanies most atypical sexual behavior. Patients should be cautioned not to put their name on the log (which is usually a pocket-size notebook) in case it is lost or discovered. Behavioral psychologists tend to want as much data as possible, but the patient's motivation and compliance must be taken into consideration. The recording task should not be made too complex or too burdensome. The clinician should simply ask patients to record the date and brief description of the sexual-acting-out behavior. Some patients may prefer to use behavior codes to protect their anonymity. The log should continue throughout the duration of the treatment program.

In addition to the assessment interviews and behavioral log, assessment information may also be obtained from a partner or family member (if available) and from sexual questionnaires. The involvement of a supportive significant other is usually predictive of a favorable treatment outcome because it helps a patient with accountability (no secrets) and early identification of behavioral chains leading to sexual acting out. The supportive person also can assist the patient in distraction and identification of alternative behaviors that will interfere with the sexual-acting-out chain. It is important for the therapist to explain to this person that his or her role is *support* and not police work. Detailed quizzing and snooping usually create anger, divisiveness, and a breakdown of positive motivation.

Questionnaires may be helpful supplemental ways of acquiring assessment information. The Derogatis Sexual Functioning Inventory (DSFI; Derogatis

Date	Urge	Act	Comment
2/1/99	X		Angry at wife
2/1/99		X	Saw sexy woman at exercise
2/2/99	O	O	
2/3/99	X		Wake up with erection

FIGURE 16.1. Sample format for behavioral log.

& Melisaratos, 1979) is useful as a general measure of many different aspects of sexual identity, attitude, self-confidence, and functioning. For a more specific assessment of the atypical behavior, the Abel Questionnaire for Men (Abel, 1996) is useful. This questionnaire covers all possible paraphiliac behavior and may elicit responses not forthcoming in an interview. The entire Abel screen includes exposing a patient to a series of slides of males and females and asking the patient to rate the slides on a Likert scaling of attractiveness. The time looking at each slide is surreptitiously recorded and serves as a measure of sexual interest.

There are many other paper-and-pencil scales and questionnaires that are often used as adjuncts to the assessment process. A comprehensive listing of such materials has been published by Prentky and Edmunds (1997) and is offered as a resource guide for practitioners.

A final assessment tool for consideration is the use of the penile strain gauge for men (Barlow, Becker, Leitenberg , & Agras, 1970; Bancroft, Jones, & Pullan, 1966). This psychophysiological methodology is commonly used in research on male sexual arousal but also in clinical settings especially in forensic evaluations of child sex offenders and rapists (Simon & Schouten, 1991; Quinsey, Chaplin, & Upfold, 1984). Simon and Schouten (1991), in a review of the literature on the use of penile plethysmography, point out methodological concerns and, thus, like all assessment tools, penile plethysmography should be used only in conjunction with other sources of assessment information. Following a comprehensive assessment, a treatment program can be outlined.

TREATMENT

Reducing Dangerousness

The first consideration in formulating a treatment strategy is the reduction of dangerousness (in terms of risk to the patient [suicide] and dangerousness to potential victims). Because depression and suicide are real possibilities in individuals undergoing treatment for atypical sexual behaviors, the initial focus should be on this issue. For individuals who present risk, treatment with cognitive–behavioral strategies, pharmacology, and even hospitalization should be considered. The other initial focus of treatment should be on risk to potential victims. In cases of rapists and child molesters, potential known victims must be warned and the patient should be isolated from high-risk situations. For example, a child-molesting teacher should take a leave of absence from his or her job. For male offenders who present a danger to others, pharmacological intervention should be started as quickly as possible. Pharmacological agents such as Lupron or Depo Provera are generally effective in reducing both sexual desire and high frequencies of sexual-acting-out behaviors in men (Berlin, 1989; Bradford & Pawlak, 1993). Collaboration with an endocrinologist is desirable when working with testosterone-lowering agents. Another pharmacological approach is the use of selective serotonin reuptake inhibitors (SSRIs) such as sertraline (Zoloft) or fluoxetine (Prozac) to suppress sexual desire (Bradford, 1995; Kafka, 1997b; Kruesi, Fine, Valladares, Phillips, & Rapoport, 1992). These medications are familiar to most clinicians, but they are less reliable in their impact on sexual functioning and are not available in depot preparations lending more easily to noncompliance. In some cases, however, in which depressive states lead to sexual acting out, the SSRIs may have the advantage of reducing these triggers.

Suppression of Behavior

Once risk and danger are assessed and under control, psychotherapy strategies may be implemented. In most cases, suppression of the atypical behavior will be an initial focus. In addition to pharmacological approaches to suppression, which were discussed earlier, other behavioral procedures are often used.

Purging of all sexually stimulating material (videos, magazines, clothing) is desired at the beginning of therapy. By reducing the presence of sexually evoking stimuli, sexual acting out is reduced. This process may be met with a great deal of resistance and emotionality by some patients and may cause anxiety and depression. I have had some patients take weeks before being able to throw everything out. Some patients prefer to purge in stages, first by boxing objects and sealing the boxes with duct tape and then throwing the boxes out one at a time. Resistance emerges because of the money invested in the objects and feelings of loss and of insecurity. Discussions addressing this process and the possible negative reaction should be part of the therapy program.

Cognitive procedures are also commonly used to reduce and control the atypical sexual behavior. These procedures include (1) specific attempts at suppression and (2) identifying and challenging faulty cognitions.

Because sexual fantasies and thoughts precede behavior, recognizing these sexual cognitions and suppressing them may be helpful in controlling sexual acting out. However, as Johnston, Ward, and Hudson (1997) point out, mental suppression techniques such as thought stopping may increase sexual thoughts in some individuals. Furthermore, mental suppression should include replacing unwanted but desired sexual thoughts with more acceptable thoughts in order to increase the effectiveness of this technique. Thus, it may not be helpful to instruct a cross-dresser to use thought stopping (subvocalization of the word "stop") upon thinking of cross-dressing unless you also instruct him to follow the thought stopping with a positive and engaging thought (such as snorkeling, traveling, or planning an evening with a desired partner). The rationale behind this two-step process is that in order to control the reinforcement inherent in the sexual thought, an individual must replace such thoughts with nonsexual reinforcement, otherwise thoughts will quickly return to the sexual arena. The reinforcement of the nonsexual thought will thus be added to the overall motivation of wanting to control the sexual acting out. Taken together, cognitive–behavioral procedures that address faulty cognitions and address mental suppression are effective in a comprehensive treatment approach to controlling atypical sexual behavior.

In addition to thought suppression, it is important to identify and alter cognitions that facilitate sexual acting out (Johnston et al., 1997). Because sexual arousal is so rewarding, it is likely that individuals with atypical sexual behavior have developed self statements which support their actions. Examples of such statements are as follows:

1. Statements that underplay or deny the impact of their behavior: "Women like it when I expose my penis to them." "It excites women even if they don't show it."
2. Statements that deny any ability to control their behavior: "She was wearing a short skirt and I couldn't stop myself."

Therapy involves identifying, monitoring, and challenging such statements through discussions, thought logs, readings, and role playing.

Because cognitions often distort the true impact of a person's atypical sexual behavior on a victim, specific efforts are often made to sensitize the patient to the victim's feelings. This victim empathy training may include specific discussions about victimization, readings of women's reactions to uninvited sexual behavior, and a realistic review of the patient's own experiences. I have found, for example, that patients selectively focus on victims' ambiguous reaction or joking reaction as positive and neglect to remember the times at which negative reactions were obvious.

The use of aversive stimulation such as electric shock, negative images, or nausea-inducing drugs have all been used to suppress atypical sexual behavior. There has been controversy around the use of these procedures. Nonetheless, for selective cases, a therapist may find some form of aversion therapy helpful as an adjunct to a comprehensive therapy program. For example, Maletzky (1980) reported on the beneficial use of smell aversion (odor of rotting meat or valuric acid) which pairs nausea with sexual urges as part of an overall treatment program. Many clinicians may find aversion therapy techniques cumbersome, however, and objectionable, and consequently they have never enjoyed widespread use.

Maintenance and Control

Because atypical sexual behavior patterns are usually long standing and highly reinforcing, they are resistant to change. Suppression techniques are helpful in inducing change, but in order to maintain changes, other therapeutic strategies must be implemented. Relapse prevention (Laws, 1989) is a treatment strategy designed to identify high-risk stimuli and situations, develop alternative "safe" strategies to avoid and respond to sexual stimulation, and develop and identify a support system. A relapse prevention program for sexual acting out usually involves having the patient fill out a relapse prevention form containing various statements such as:

"Patterns of sexual behavior I want to change."
"Common feelings before each sexual incident."
"Things I am stressed about before I act out."
"Aspects of my lifestyle which present a danger for relapse."
"Self statements which are cues to relapse."
"My plan for dealing with danger of relapse."

Once the patient fills out the form (usually at home), the form is then reviewed with the therapist and usually modified as needed and expanded. This then serves as a guide for staying on track and the patient is asked to review his program every week.

In addition to the relapse prevention program, specific efforts are usually necessary to develop behaviors to replace the atypical sexual behavior. If an individual spends 5 to 10 hours a day cross-dressing or watching pornographic videos and then stops the behavior, what will the individual now do with those hours? It is not unusual for such individuals to have poor skills in structuring idle time. Therapy often focuses on building up compensatory behaviors to fill idle time, including social activities, hobbies, recreational activities, and partner interactions. Learning or improving organizational skills and committing to daily schedules is an important part of the overall therapy program.

Treatment of Comorbid Problems

One final component of most therapy programs dealing with atypical sexual behaviors is to treat anxiety and/or depression, which are often comorbid with the sexual behavior. It is common for such dysphoric states to be triggers for sexual acting out. Sex often provides a temporary relief for the anxiety or depression, thus further reinforcing the value of the sexual behavior to the individual. Cognitive–behavioral therapy for the anxiety and depression along with pharmacological interventions should be considered as part of an overall treatment strategy.

Summary of Treatment Strategies

1. Increase motivation to engage in therapy by challenging faulty cognitions and providing information on the realistic impact of atypical behavior.
2. Assess and treat dangerousness to self and to others.
   a. *Possible suicide risk*. Options include pharmacology, behavioral contracts, and hospitalization.

    b. *Possible risk to others.* Options include warning victims and changing jobs or activities, pharmacology, and contacting child protection agency or the police.
3. Atypical sexual behavior suppression. Options include:
    a. Purging all stimulus items in environment.
    b. Cognitive suppression and cognitive restructuring.
    c. Changing patterns of behavior to reduce exposure to risk.
    d. Pharmacology: antiandrogen, SSRIs (Lupron, Depo Provera, Prozac, Zoloft).
    e. Victim sensitivity: awareness of true impact on victim short and long term.
    f. Aversion therapy.
4. Maintenance of control over atypical sexual behavior.
    a. Relapse prevention program which identifies risk, develops alternative responses to risk, and identifies supportive resources.
    b. Development of new nonsexual activities to occupy time void.
5. Treatment of comorbid problems.

CASE EXAMPLES

Atypical sexual behaviors can occur in individuals from all walks of life, all educational and socioeconomic backgrounds, and all intellectual levels. Among the hundreds of cases I have treated over the years are individuals from the most influential and successful strata of our society and individuals who are the most destitute. Diversity in the backgrounds of individuals manifesting atypical sexual behaviors is enormous and the specific expression of the atypical behavior is quite varied. Even within a specific category of atypical sexual behavior, such as exhibitionism, an incredible amount of diversity exists (Van de Loo, 1987).

Because of diversity, there are no typical cases, and, thus, it is challenging to select cases that are representative of patients presenting with atypical sexual behavior problems. The two cases that are presented are certainly unique in their own ways but do illustrate some commonly used treatment strategies. Both cases are also common in the long-term nature of therapy and in the need for long-term follow-up to maintain therapy gains. Finally, both cases are representative of the types of cases therapists are likely to encounter today.

Case 1. Successful Outcome: Voyeurism/Frottage/Sexual Assault

Background

Edward began keeping lists of girls in the seventh grade. At first, the lists were only the names of the pretty girls in his school, but as time went on, he added descriptions of each girl's clothing and body shape. He would masturbate daily to fantasies of the girls on his list. As time went on, he began to think of ways to actually connect with each girl on his list. At some point, he discovered that looking up a girl's skirt or touching her breasts would satisfy his connection with a girl. Although risky, he found this sexually exciting and spent hours, when he was in high school, planning just how he would connect with a girl. At times, he would wait in a stairwell and position himself so he could look up a girl's skirt and at other times he would position himself to touch a girl's breast in a crowded hallway or elevator. This latter behavior brought assault charges and a 4-year probation that included therapy.

Ed came from a loving middle-class family, but he was somewhat odd in appearance and very awkward socially. This awkwardness made him unpopular and rejected by his peers. At the time of his arrest, he was living at home after failing his first year of college. By this time, his voyeuristic and frotteuristic behavior had extended to public places such as malls and bus stops. His arrest occurred in a mall after he touched a woman's breasts in an elevator. Although his arrest was humiliating and embarrassing, he revealed that his biggest problem in court was restraining himself from looking up the skirt of the female prosecutor. Fortunately for him, he did control himself in court and received no jail time and was remanded to therapy.

Assessment and Clinical Formulation

Ed was open and contrite throughout the assessment process. Although he felt terrible that his behavior upset a woman, he conceptualized his sexualized behavior as a harmless game. He did acknowledge, however, that he was spending at least 3 or 4 hours a day going to public places in order to look up women's skirts. His typical behavior included going to malls and staring at women, then selecting one and following her until he had an opportunity to look up her skirt or touch her. After completing this act, he would masturbate in a men's room, and later that day, he would put the incident on his list. During the assessment he provided his list, which verified an almost daily frequency of his sexual acting out. In addition, Ed completed the DSFI (Derogatis & Melisaratos, 1979), which showed him to be naive and sexually inexperienced. In fact, he reported during the interviews that he had never had a date with a girl and he felt anxious and awkward around girls.

The lists he composed of his sexual exploits served as stimulus material for masturbation. Other sources of erotic stimulation for him were pornographic videos and computer pornography.

In addition to the problems of sexual acting out and social skills deficits, Ed was mildly depressed. His affect was very bland and he reported being depressed most of the time, although he denied any suicidal ideation. His appetite was not suppressed and he had no trouble sleeping.

Following three assessment interviews and a review of the DSFI and a review of his behavioral list, the following areas were identified for treatment:

1. Control of voyeuristic and frotteuristic behavior and discontinuance of keeping lists of women.
2. Improve social skills including assertion.
3. Control depression.
4. Improve use of free time by developing hobbies or interests.

Ed agreed that all these areas were important for treatment. Because he was having daily urges to act out sexually, treatment began with a focus on control of this behavior. A psychiatric consult was also initiated to explore the possibility of a pharmacological intervention for his depression.

Treatment

Sexual Acting Out. Ed was asked to immediately purge his environment of all stimulus material. He complied with this request and disposed of pornographic videos and all lists of females names and "contacts." In addition, he contracted to use his computer only when other family members were in the house and to avoid all pornographic sites. He also completed a relapse prevention questionnaire which helped him to (1) identify high-risk situations and stimuli, (2) identify seemingly unimportant decisions which led to risk behavior, (3) identify strategies for early intervention when there is initial awareness of risk, and (4) identify a list of resources and support people to help him and disclose his problem to.

Ed also agreed to follow specific "rules of conduct" in public, such as never looking at a woman for longer than 3 seconds and only going to a mall or public institution if there is a specific and prescribed reason to do so.

Because Ed did not have a supportive partner, his father was involved in his treatment in a limited way. Ed's father was made aware of the general guidelines and periodically reminded Ed of his therapy program, but Ed did not feel comfortable disclosing to his father those occasions on which he was struggling with his urges.

A final component of Ed's program for controlling his atypical sexual behavior was victim sensitivity training. Ed held a number of cognitive distortions related to his behavior, of which the most important was that what he was doing was harmless. Discussions focused on a more realistic appraisal of not only the true impact on female victims but also the true impact on him in terms of self-perception, wasted time, and wasted energy. Ed, like many sex offenders, held the belief that a victim's silence meant enjoyment.

Depression. A psychiatric consult agreed that Ed could benefit from antidepressant medication and Paxil (paroxetine) 20 mg was prescribed. In addition, cognitive restructuring to challenge negative self statements, catastrophizing, and all-or-none thinking was initiated.

Social Skills Training, Assertion Training, and Activity Building. The final areas of focus for Ed's comprehensive therapy program were on building social skills and a more productive use of unstructured time. Of course, it was important to build in alternative behaviors that would help maintain treatment gains. Social skills training and assertiveness training helped Ed to approach and converse with females. Ed was also given assignments to explore a new activity every week and to consider returning to college. His dropout from college was primarily because of feelings of loneliness and not due to academic deficiencies.

Treatment Outcome and Commentary

Ed was compliant throughout treatment and, like many court-referred patients, showed dramatic changes early in therapy. He purged all erotic stimuli including his lists, he completed the relapse prevention questionnaire and discussed it in detail in therapy, he complied with the medication prescribed, and he was responsive to discussion about victim sensitivity. In spite of his motivation to change and compliance with therapy, Ed continued to be bothered by strong urges to look up women's skirts whenever he was in public. For the most part, he was able to control his urges but occasionally he would relapse and look up a woman's skirt. His response to each relapse was anger at himself and panic feelings. Following each incident, he would call to arrange an urgent therapy session which usually occurred within a week of the incident. The urgent sessions were spent carefully reviewing all behavioral and cognitive antecedents of his relapse. In a sense, these sessions were reminders and fine tuning for overall control. Unanticipated situations and emotions were often the focus of discussion.

In all, Ed spent about 5 years in therapy. The first 6 months of therapy involved a schedule of weekly sessions which were then faded to monthly sessions over the next 6 months. Monthly sessions continued for another 6 months and then quarterly booster sessions were established for the next 2½ years; then sessions were further spaced to twice yearly. Since the beginning of therapy, Ed never again surreptitiously touched a woman's breasts. His relapses all involved looking up women's skirts. He had no relapses in the last 3½ years of therapy. Ed also returned to college and successfully passed all his courses. He also joined a coed bowling league and enjoyed some social activities.

This case incorporated all the treatment components previously outlined with the exception of keeping behavioral records. For most cases, keeping behavioral records of sexual urges serves as a reminder of patterns of behavior and helps to pinpoint stimulus antecedents. This procedure would have been counterproductive for Ed because the lists of his atypical sexual behavior were stimulus material for his sexual acting out. Therapists treating individuals with atypical sexual behavior should always be aware of the possibility that the treatment may create a problem. For example, therapists running group treatment programs for individuals with problems of sexual acting out (e.g., child molesters) should be aware that some individuals may be sexually stimulated by recounting their own experiences of molesting children or hearing the stories of others.

Case 2. Partially Successful Outcome: Cross-Dressing/Internet Sexual Encounters/Pornographic Stimulation from Videos, Magazines, and Phone Sex

Background

Vinney and Mary came to therapy following an incident in which she observed Vinney dressed in women's clothing. Mary was aware that Vinney fantasized about cross-dressing because they had discussed their sexual fantasies with each other before they were married. What disturbed her at the time of entering therapy was that she had returned home early with their 5-year-old son from a preschool meeting and found Vinney cross-dressed. Both she and their son saw Vinney fully dressed as a woman, with makeup.

Vinney and Mary had been married for 4 years at the time of this "incident." Vinney was 28 and Mary was 36 and each worked in a middle-management position. Mary was liberal minded and prided herself on her acceptance of other people's sexual practices. She was aware that Vinney enjoyed fantasies of cross-dressing and on several occasions allowed Vinney to be cross-dressed when they had sexual relations. She had no idea, however, as to the extent of the cross-dressing and the extent of his use of pornography and his use of the Internet. The Internet actually posed the greatest problem because it was used not only for pornographic stimulation but also for to "chats" with women for sexual stimulation and arrangements for sexual liaisons with women.

In his job, he often traveled, and through the Internet he would arrange sexual encounters with women in every city to which he traveled. He would take his laptop computer with him when he traveled and continued making new arrangements for sexual encounters while traveling.

Internet activity for sexual purposes occurred at work and at home, and he estimated that he averaged about 2 hours a day on the Internet at work and 4 hours a day at home. On some days, he spent as much as 4 hours of work time and 8 hours of at home time on the Internet "chatting" about sex or viewing pornographic Web sites.

In his employment, he had a private office with no one monitoring his work. This situation allowed him the freedom to explore his sexual interests on the Internet and even allowed him to cross-dress at work.

Vinney came from a family he described as dysfunctional and disorganized. His father was emotionally and physically uninvolved in the family and often expressed misogynistic views. Vinney's mother "did everything" for his father and similarly showed little affection to Vinney and his younger brother. Vinney reported being totally unsupervised growing up and never had to account for his behavior.

Vinney began cross-dressing in his mother's underwear at age 12, and as a teenager, he also remembered stealing women's underwear from the homes of his friends. By the time he was 18, he was cross-dressing on almost a daily basis. He also remembered frequently viewing his father's pornographic magazines, which were easily available in his home.

Mary was an only child and reported that her mother was overly nurturing, and similar to Vinney's mother, Mary's mother catered to her father. Her parents eventually experienced marital problems and inappropriately discussed their sexual problems with her when she was only 11 years old. It is no surprise that Mary equated sex with love and had numerous sexual encounters with boys as a teenager. As an adult, she could now look back and understand that she was victimized and used, but she carried this profile into her marriage with Vinney.

Assessment and Clinical Formulation

Vinney and Mary were initially interviewed separately to allow each to freely discuss his or her conceptualization of the problem and to identify treatment goals. Although both were upset over the "incident," Vinney downplayed the potential impact of having his son view him cross-dressed. He did not see cross-dressing in general as a problem, and he did not see his use of the Internet or of pornography as a problem.

Vinney revealed that he frequently had sex with women whom he had met on the Internet. Mary was unaware of his infidelity. Vinney rationalized, however, that he did not consider his behavior as infidelity because his sexual encounters with other women did not include intercourse. Bondage and domination culminating in masturbation and oral sex were all part of the typical venue.

For Mary, the image of her husband cross-dressed in her son's presence was profound and damaging. She viewed the experience traumatically and as a result questioned her marriage and her own behavior. She was willing to stay in the marriage but only if Vinney rid the house of all pornographic magazines and videotapes and completely controlled his cross-dressing. She also began to identify the deficits in their marriage and in their sexual relationship. Specifically, she was feeling victimized and was feeling that her own needs were not even being addressed by Vinney let alone being met. She was viewing Vinney as another child and not as an equal partner.

Additional individual sessions were scheduled with Vinney in an attempt to explore the more global impact his behavior was having on his work, his marriage, his son, and his use of time. Although he could appreciate the negative impact on an intellectual level, the thought of giving up his sexual pleasures was depressing and stressful. He did agree to work on the marriage but initially was resistant to controlling his use of pornography and the Internet. In spite of its danger and superficiality, he justified his use of the Internet as a way of relieving boredom, reducing anxiety, and making friends. As part of the assessment process, he kept a log of his cross-dressing and Internet behavior. The log underscored the great amount of time and energy he devoted to sexual interests. In addition, Mary strongly expressed to Vinney the negative impact that his behavior was having on her. Even though she was not aware of the extent of his use of the Internet and his sexual liaisons with women, she was aware that his cross-dressing and use of pornography were upsetting and alienating to her . She clearly articulated that sex with Vinney made her feel used and not loved. Further, she imposed a ban on all sexual relations with Vinney until his behavior could make her feel loved.

The net effect of Mary's sexual ban and Vinney's awareness of the extent and pervasiveness of his sexual acting out was to bring to Vinney a level of motivation to control his behavior unlike any he had ever previously experienced. Thus, following four sessions alone with Vinney, one session alone with Mary, and two couple therapy sessions, a treatment strategy was developed.

Control of Vinney's sexual acting out was identified as the most important goal of therapy. The assessment process brought home to Vinney the negative impact that his sexual behavior was having on all aspects of his life. Therapy had to be structured to control his sexual acting out (i.e., cross-dressing), use of pornography, and use of the Internet—including meeting women for sexual relations. The control strategy included identifying high-risk antecedents to sexual acting out and developing thought patterns to challenge rather than support his sexual-acting-out behavior. Speaking generally, cognitive restructuring is the crucial linchpin of the control strategy. Unless a patient genuinely supports the changes he is working on, lasting change will not occur.

A change in Mary's attitude emerged and crystalized during the assessment process. In the past, she had deferred, forgiven, and accepted Vinney. The assessment process seemed to empower her to consider herself and her role as protectorate of her child. Although she accepted the role of supporting Vinney in his efforts to change, she made it clear that her feelings toward Vinney were in limbo and that she could not promise that she would still be in the marriage even if Vinney changed. Thus, relationship issues were also identified as a focus of therapy.

Because Vinney had spent such a large percentage of his time preparing for and engaging in sexual activities, therapy also had to address building in rewarding and competing behaviors. This included efforts on an interpersonal level as well as a solitary level. Vinney was encouraged to become more involved with his son and he was encouraged to develop other interests to occupy his time more constructively. He followed through on both of these suggestions and became involved as a coach for his son's soccer team and began reading novels. Both of these efforts were rewarding for him.

Treatment Outcome and Commentary

Individually tailored treatment strategies were devised for each atypical sexual behavior. Surprisingly, cross-dressing and the use of pornography videos and magazines were easily controlled by purging and self-monitoring.

In spite of the volume of clothing and tapes, Vinney complied easily with the purging process with only miminal anxiety and depression. He was pleased to rid his house of these items although his financial investment and years of collecting were considerable.

The greater challenge for Vinney was to control his use of the computer. Vinney took the following steps to control his use of the Internet:

1. He cut down on his business travels and confined his travel only to essential trips. Further, he discussed his travel plans ahead of time with Mary and purposely left his laptop computer home whenever he traveled.

2. Vinney removed all messages from his computer bulletin board and contacted all people on his regularly used chat lines indicating that he was no longer available.

3. Finally, he moved the household computer to a more central and open location in his house so that computer use was not secretive (I have had some patients give up their computer password and have their wife establish a new password which only she knew. In this fashion, logging on would always be with a partner's awareness because it could only occur when a partner was in the household).

Taking such steps greatly reduced Vinney's overall "problematic" computer use. At home, there were virtually no further incidents, and Vinney and Mary independently reported that Vinney was no longer on the computer for long periods and independent checks by Mary never resulted in unexpectedly finding Vinney viewing pornographic images or "chatting." The workplace proved more difficult for Vinney because his computer behavior was totally unmonitored. After 1 year of therapy, Vinney had eliminated his computer use at home but was still occasionally viewing pornography and "chatting" at work. He acknowledged the danger and acknowledged that there should be no computer use for sex. However, because his job required his constant computer use, it was all too easy for him to "slip up."

Through Mary's eyes, Vinney had greatly changed and was controlling his behavior. He was more available to her and generally their communication and activities together were pleasant and never problematic. After 2 years of therapy, however, Mary was still unable to resume sexual activities with Vinney and chose to live in the same household but as "brother and sister." She was not sure whether her attitude would ever change. Vinney, to his credit, maintained overall control of his atypical sexual behavior in spite of the lack of a sexual relationship with Mary. He progressively became more understanding of the negative impact that his sexual behavior had had on his overall development as a person and on his interpersonal relationships.

Therapy was faded to twice yearly after 2 years and was maintained for an additional 3 years. At the last follow-up, Vinney had still maintained control of his atypical sexual behavior and he and Mary were happily living a celibate although affectionate relationship.

CONCLUSION: OUTCOME ISSUES IN THE TREATMENT OF ATYPICAL SEXUAL BEHAVIOR

Both cases reflect the complexity of issues presented to therapists treating atypical sexual behaviors. Group therapy for some forms of atypical sexual behavior (child molestation) has some limited value, but the predisposing, precipitating, and maintaining factors for most cases are so individualistic that prolonged individual therapy is most often required. In addition to the complexity involved in developing a treatment program to control the sexual behavior, there is also a need to consider treating comorbid conditions such as depression, anxiety, and substance abuse that so often present in such cases (Goodman, 1993; Kafka, 1997b).

The components of therapy for the two cases involved cognitive–behavioral procedures combined with stimulus control procedures (purging the environment of stimulus material) to achieve suppression of the atypical behavior. Aversion therapy procedures such as covert sensitization (Cautela, 1967; Barlow, 1993) were not used in these cases although they have met with some success in appropriately chosen cases. Following the initial assessment in both cases, it was determined that targeting the suppression of the atypical behavior was the highest priority. Whereas both cases required challenges to cognitions that were supportive of maintaining the atypical sexual behavior, case 2 required a more prolonged attack in this area in preparation for behavioral suppression strategies.

Neither case presented with conditions that warranted a pharmacological intervention of testosterone suppression. My guidelines for using such a strategy occur when the following two conditions are present:

1. *High-frequency and highly compulsive behavior over at least a 6-month period of time with accompanying obsessive thoughts and inability to stop the behavior.* (Both cases partially met this criterion although, case one demonstrated ability to immediately control his behavior when instructed to do so.)
2. *Danger to self or to others.* Danger to self means physical danger as in autoerotic aphyxiation and danger to others means psychological or physical harm to an unconsenting victim as in child molestation or sexual assault. (Case 1 met this condition but case 2 did not.)

Because the conditions for pharmacological suppression were not present, the cognitive strategies were implemented. In conjunction with these suppression procedures, relapse prevention (Laws, 1989) procedures were also implemented to help both patients maintain gains. It was easy in case 1 to identify, isolate, and control high-risk stimulus conditions, but in case 2, the use of the computer was the major part of Vinney's job and, therefore, could not be avoided. Although a number of precautions were discussed and built into Vinney's overall strategy designed to control his misuse of the computer, he was still confronted with a daily exposure to easy access to pornographic stimulation. One hundred percent control was never achieved although the overall percentage of wasted time was greatly reduced.

Both cases also benefited from helping each patient to develop rewarding activities that filled the void once the time associated with preparing for and performing the atypical behavior was reduced. This is a key element to treatment strategies in most cases, because this wasted time is usually easy to identify and quite considerable. Therapists have to help patients take responsibility to find rewarding activities. In patients who feel limited in their ability to find a rewarding activity, a reinforcement sampling procedure (Ayllon & Azrin, 1968) may be helpful. In this strategy, patients are asked to try out one new activity a week regardless of what they feel a priori about the activity.

Finally, both cases benefited from addressing collateral problems. In case 1, depression and social skills were identified as treatment targets; in case 2, marital stress was targeted. Without treatment of comorbid problems, long-term success could not be assured. Depression, worry, stress, anger, and conflict are so often used as a rationale for sexual acting out that identification and reduction of these dysphoric states is essential to maintain gains.

The treatment outcome for individuals suffering from paraphiliac disorders who undergo comprehensive treatment programs is generally optimistic (Barlow & Durand, 1998). Maletzky (1991) has reported a highly successful program that has treated more than 5,000 sex offenders. Similarily Abel (1989) and Marshall, Jones, Ward, Johnston, and Barbaree (1991) have reported favorable treatment results. Maletzky's (1991) program is an intensive program of about 3 or 4 months. Generally, treatment programs of 6 months or less can achieve favorable control over the atypical sexual behavior, but maintenance of gains is usually best achieved by quarterly to yearly "booster" sessions. Therapist and patient must keep in mind that thoughts and urges related to atypical sexual behavior will not disappear through treatment. There is always a need to recognize vulnerability and keep a prevention program in place.

REFERENCES

Abel, G. G. (1989). Behavioral treatment of child molesters. In A. J. Stunkard & A. Baum (Eds.), *Perspectives in behavioral medicine: Eating, sleeping, and sex* (pp. 223–242). Hillsdale, NJ: Erlbaum.

Abel, G. (1996). *Abel Questionnaire for Men.* Distributed by Abel Screening, Inc., Atlanta, GA.

American Psychiatric Association. (1994). *Diagnostic and statistical manual of mental disorders* (4th ed.). Washington, DC: Author.

Ayllon, T., & Azrin, N. (1968). *The token economy: A motivated system for therapy and rehabilitation.* New York: Appleton-Century-Croft.

Bancroft, J. (1998, May). *Individual differences in sexual risk taking—A psycho–socio–biological theoretical approach.* Paper presented at Kinsey Institute Conference, "The Theory of Sex Research," Bloomington, IN.

Bancroft, J. H., Jones, G. H., & Pullan, B. R. (1966). A simple transducer for measuring penile erections, with comments on its use in the treatment of sexual disorcers. *Behaviour Research and Therapy, 4,* 239–241.

Barlow, D. H. (1993) Covert sensitization for paraphilia. In J. R. Coutela & A. J. Kearney (Eds.), *Covert conditioning casebook* (pp. 187–198). Pacific Grove, CA: Brooks/Cole.

Barlow, D. H., Becker, R., Leitenberg, H., & Agras, W. S. (1970). A mechanical strain gauge for recording penile circumference change. *Journal of Applied Behavior Analysis, 3,* 73–76.

Barlow, D. H., & Durand, M. V. (1998). *Abnormal psychology: An integrative approach* (2nd ed.). Boston: Brooks/Cole.

Berlin, F. (1989). The paraphilias and Depo-Provera: Some medical, ethical and legal considerations. *Bulletin of the American Academy of Psychiatry and the Law, 17,* 233–239.

Bradford, J. M. (1995). *An open pilot study of sertraline in the treatment of outpatients with pedophilia.* Paper presented at the annual meeting of the American Psychiatric Association, Miami, FL.

Bradford, J., & Pawlak, A. (1993). Double-blind placebo crossover study of Cyproterone Acetate in the treatment of the paraphilias. *Archives of Sexual Behavior, 22,* 383–402.

Cautela, J. R. (1967). Covert sensitization. *Psychological Reports, 20,* 459–468.

Cooper, A., Scherer, C. R., Boies, S. C., & Gordon, B. L. (1999). Sexuality on the Internet: From sexual exploration to pathological expression. *Professional Psychology Research and Practice, 30,* 1–24.

Crooks, R., & Baur, K. (1993). *Our sexuality* (5th ed.) Redwood City, CA: Benjamin/Cummings.

Derogatis, L., & Melisaratos, N. (1979). The DSFI: A multidimensional measure of sexual functioning. *Journal of Sex and Marital Therapy, 5,* 244–281.

Goldberg, A. (1998). *Monthly users report on adult sexually oriented sites for April, 1998.* Washington, DC: Relevant Knowledge.

Goodman, A. (1993). Diagnosis and treatment of sexual addiction. *Journal of Sex and Marital Therapy, 19,* 225–251.

Halgin, R. P., & Whitbourne, S. K. (1997). *Abnormal psychology: The human experience of psychological disorders.* Guilford, CT: Brown & Benchmark.

Janssen, E. (1997). *Inhibitory mechanisms and sexual response.* Paper presented at 23rd Conference of the International Academy of Sex Research, Baton Rouge, LA.

Johnston, L., Ward, T., & Hudson, S. (1997) Deviant sexual thoughts: Mental control and the treatment of sex offenders. *Journal of Sex Research, 34,* 121–130.

Kafka, M. (1997a). Hypersexual desire in males: An operational definition and clinical implications for males with paraphilias and paraphilia-related disorders. *Archives of Sexual Behavior, 26,* 505–526.

Kafka, M. (1997b) A monoamine hypothesis for the pathophysiology of paraphiliac disorders. *Archives of Sexual Behavior, 26,* 343–358.

Kruesi, M. J., Fine, S., Valladares, L., Phillips, R., & Rapoport, J. L. (1992). Paraphilias: A double-blind crossover comparison of clomipramine versus desipramine. *Archives of Sexual Behavior, 21,* 587–593.

Laws, D. R. (Ed.). (1989). *Relapse prevention with sex offenders.* New York: Guilford Press.

Leiblum, S. R. (1997). Sex and the Net: Clinical implications. *Journal of Sex Education and Therapy, 22,* 21–28.

Maletzky, B. M. (1980). Assisted covert sensitization. In D. J. Cox & R. J. Daitzman (Eds.), *Exhibitionism: Description, assessment, and treatment.* New York: Garland.

Maletzky, B. M. (1991). *Treating the sexual offender.* Newbury Park, CA: Sage.

Marshall, W. L., Jones, R., Ward, T., Johnston, P., & Barbaree, H. E. (1991). Treatment outcome with sex offenders. *Clinical Psychology Review, 11,* 465–485.

Money, J., & Lamacz, M. (1990). *Vandalized love maps.* Buffalo, NY: Prometheus Press.

Prentky, R., & Edmunds, S. B. (1997). *Assessing sexual abuse: A resource guide for practitioners.* Burlington, VT: Safer Society Press.

Quinsey, V., Chaplin, T., & Upfold, D. (1984). Sexual arousal to nonsexual violence and sadomasochistic themes among rapists and non-sex-offenders. *Journal of Consulting and Clinical Psychology, 52,* 651–657.

Schwartz, M., & Masters, W. (1983). Conceptual factors in the treatment of paraphilias: A preliminary report. *Journal of Sex and Marital Therapy, 9,* 3–18.

Simon, W. T., & Schouten, P. G. (1991). Plethysmography in the assessment and treatment of sexual deviance: An overview. *Archives of Sexual Behavior, 20,* 75–91.

Van de Loo, E. (1987). *Genital exposing behaviour in adult human males.* Leiden, Netherlands: Rijksoniversiteit.

Young, K. S., & Rogers, R. C. (1998). The relationship between depression and internet addiction. *Cyber Psychology and Behavior, 1,* 25–28.

17

The Paraphilia-Related Disorders
Nonparaphilic Hypersexuality and Sexual Compulsivity/Addiction

MARTIN P. KAFKA

Historically, hypersexuality has been regarded as both an addiction and an impulse control disorder. The sexual addiction model regards high-frequency sexual behavior as a form of self-soothing or self-medicating and includes both paraphilic and nonparaphilic types of sexual behavior. The recommended treatment among those embracing the addiction model is the 12-Step approach, with sex being regarded as the "drug of choice."

Many clinicians consider both paraphilic and nonparaphilic compulsive sexual behavior as mediated by anxiety reduction, rather than by sexual desire per se. Treatment recommendations from a sexual compulsivity perspective emphasize both medical and psychotherapeutic approaches, along with the use of specific medications (e.g., selective serotonin reuptake inhibitors) as needed.

In his chapter, Martin P. Kafka provides a new and useful model for conceptualizing, assessing, and treating nonparaphilic sexual behavior problems. Kafka believes that such behaviors, like the core paraphilias, are primarily dysregulations of sexual arousal and desire. The results include a high frequency of sexual behavior, loss of control over sexual impulses, and considerable time spent in sexual fantasies and activities, leading to negative personal and psychosocial consequences over time.

Kafka defines paraphilia-related disorders as recurrent, intense sexually arousing fantasies, urges, or behaviors involving essentially normative aspects of sexual expression, which increase in frequency or intensity to the extent that they significantly interfere with the sexual relationship with a partner.

Such behaviors as compulsive masturbation, uncontrolled promiscuity, depen-
dence on pornography (including Internet pornography), or telephone sex are
all included in the category of paraphilia-related disorders.

The author observes an important similarity with the paraphilias in that
more males than females display these disorders, they typically show a waxing
and waning over time (which often increases with stress), and they are experi-
enced usually by the patient as obligatory and insistent. In particular, Kafka
recommends that clinicians assess Axis I diagnoses in detail as many men and
women with this disorder experience comorbid mood disorders (e.g., dysthy-
mic disorder, major depression), anxiety disorder, substance abuse, and other
impulse disorders such as attention-deficit/hyperactivity disorder. In addition,
the relationship must be evaluated because the paraphilia-related behavior usu-
ally has adverse consequences on intimacy with a partner. Moreover, the strength
of the partner relationship can be materially important in determining the out-
come of treatment.

In terms of treatment, Kafka suggests that therapy be directed toward
gaining control over the patient's hypersexual behavior, along with a focus on
current life issues. Developmental factors must generally be considered also,
because they may be contributing to the current sexual behavior. Group therapy
can be helpful for some individuals, in addition to cognitive-behavioral therapy,
which aims to identify the essential cognitive distortions and beliefs that pro-
vide a rationalization for the patient's acting out. Finally psychopharmaco-
logical treatments may be needed in some cases, such as serotonin reuptake
inhibitors, psychostimulants, and even orally administered antiandrogens.

Dr. Kafka provides a comprehensive and useful multidimensional model
for understanding, evaluating, and treating these challenging and potentially
self-destructive disorders.

Martin P. Kafka, MD, is Clinical Assistant Professor of Psychiatry at
Harvard Medical School and Senior Attending Psychiatrist at McLean Hospi-
tal in Belmont, Massachusetts. He is a recognized expert in the characteriza-
tion of paraphilias and paraphilia-related disorders, and the development of
new treatment models in this area.

HISTORICAL OVERVIEW OF CLINICAL NONPARAPHILIC HYPERSEXUALITY DISORDERS

Hypersexuality disorders, the disinhibited or exaggerated expressions of human
sexual arousal and appetitive behavior, were clinically documented by the late
19th-century Western European pioneer sexologists Richard von Krafft-Ebbing
(1886), Havelock Ellis (1905), and Magnus Hirshfeld (1948). These investigators each described a panoply of socially deviant sexual behaviors (i.e.,
paraphilias) as well as clinical examples of males and females whose nonparaphilic sexual appetite appeared insatiable. The clinical examples of such

appetitive behaviors described by these investigators were precursors to the 20th-century characterization of protracted promiscuity as Don Juanism (Stoller, 1975) or satyriasis (Allen, 1969) in males and nymphomania (Ellis & Sagarin, 1965) in females. These aforementioned European investigators also described compulsive masturbation as common behavior in their clinical samples.

Despite these earlier characterizations, empirical studies that define the boundaries of nonparaphilic hypersexual behavior disorders are scant. It is historically noteworthy that especially during the late 19th and early 20th centuries, masturbation was not a culturally accepted expression of normative sexual behavior and compulsive masturbation, in particular, was considered a cause of "moral degeneration" or neurasthenia. Indeed, the history of masturbation as a precursor of mental (Hare, 1962) as well as physical illnesses is retrospectively described as late as 1948 (Kinsey, Pomeroy, & Martin, 1948a).

In organized American psychiatry, the second edition of *Diagnostic and Statistical Manual of Mental Disorders* (DSM-II; American Psychiatric Association, 1968) recognized sexual deviations as personality disorders but there was no mention of nonparaphilic hypersexuality disorders. By 1980, DSM-III (American Psychiatric Association, 1980) subclassified paraphilic disorders as distinct pathologies (sexual disorders) and Don Juanism and nymphomania were included as psychosexual disorders not otherwise specified. The marginalization of nonparaphilic hypersexuality has continued in more recent American Psychiatric Association diagnostic manuals primarily because a lack of empirical research has hampered the characterization of specific nonparaphilic behaviors as diagnostic entities.

CONTEMPORARY CLINICAL CONCEPTUALIZATIONS OF NONPARAPHILIC HYPERSEXUALITY DISORDERS

Medical progress associated with the discovery, production, and distribution of oral contraceptive agents was one of the sociocultural factors associated with the liberalization of sexual attitudes and behavior during the so-called sexual revolution in the United States and Western Europe. During the late 1960s, 1970s, and early 1980s, these social changes contributed to a deemphasis of hypersexual behavior as a pathology and its reconceptualization as a variant of normative sexual expression (Levine & Troiden, 1988; Rinehart & McCabe, 1997). This position was further enhanced by the depathologization of homosexuality in the United States and, among some male homosexuals, the destigmatization of promiscuity. These same social conditions, however, have also been associated with a higher divorce rate during those same decades and to a resurgence of sexually transmitted diseases, including some with devastating emotional consequences (e.g., herpes genitalis, and gonorrhea), as well as substantial morbidity and mortality (e.g., cervical carcinoma, hepatitis B, and human immunodeficiency virus HIV/AIDS) (Holmes, Mardk, Sparling, & Weisner, 1990). The sobering effect of these serious illnesses, more prevalent among humans with multiple sexual partners, has contributed to a reevaluation of contemporary sexual mores.

In 1978, Orford suggested that excessive appetitive and consummatory behaviors, including promiscuous hypersexuality, could become an addiction-like behavioral syndrome despite the absence of an exogenous substance of abuse (Orford, 1978, 1985). Since the 1983 publication of Carnes's descriptive book *Out of the Shadows: Understanding Sexual Addiction*, the clinical concept of sexual addiction has become widely popularized (Carnes, 1989, 1990, 1991). This clinical term has been especially embraced in the popular press and has resonated to persons suffering from either repetitive paraphilic or nonparaphilic hypersexual behaviors associated with volitional impairment and significant psychosocial consequences.

During the same year as the publication of Carnes's conceptual book describing sexual addiction, Quadland suggested the term "sexual compulsivity" to describe volitional impairment associated with nonparaphilic hypersexual behavior (Quadland, 1983, 1985). Since 1986, "sexual compulsivity" as a clinical descriptor for both paraphilic and nonparaphilic sexual behavior disorders has been clinically promulgated by Coleman (1986, 1987, 1992) and the term has been adopted by other clinical investigators as well (Anthony & Hollander, 1993; Black 1998; Black, Kehrberg, Flumerfelt, & Schlosser, 1997; Travin, 1995). Although these two differing conceptualizations initially led to a "debate" between the their respective advocates (Coleman, 1986), more recently clinicians have integrated the two theoretical positions by combining descriptive terms as sexual compulsivity/addiction or vice versa (Shaffer, 1994).

Before discussing the distinctions between the sexual addiction and compulsivity models, it is important to clarify what these models of hypersexual behaviors share:

1. Both frameworks assert that a group of nonparaphilic as well as paraphilic sexual behaviors can be associated with significant psychosocial impairment and psychiatric comorbidity.
2. Although both "positions" have different terms used to characterize the specific nonparaphilic sexual behaviors that met criteria for sexual addiction or compulsivity, there is mention of sexual promiscuity, compulsive masturbation, pornography dependence, phone sex dependence, and hypersexuality within a stable relationship (that contributes to the destabilization of that relationship) as expressions of sexual compulsivity/addiction.
3. Advocates of these conceptualizations suggest that both familial environment and developmental factors play a role in development of sexual addiction/compulsivity.
4. Both models specifically suggest that nonparaphilic (and paraphilic) sexual disorders characterized by compulsivity or addiction are inherently recidivistic because they are conditioned responses to dysphoric affective states, especially anxiety, depression, and shame.

5. It is generally agreed upon that nonparaphilic sexual compulsivity/addiction is more prevalent in males.

6. Both theoretical positions give credence to the conceptualization of a "love addiction" or repetitive pathological "crushes" on unattainable partners.

7. Both models acknowledge a neurobiological substrate or genetically mediated vulnerability as a prominent component of the etiology of sexual compulsivity/addiction.

8. The concept of sexual behavior as addiction/compulsivity is clinically popular because it personally resonates to persons who appear unable to control the intensity of their sexual arousal and appetitive behaviors.

9. Sexual addiction/compulsivity is conceptualized as a condition that can be substantially mitigated by certain psychological treatments.

The addiction and compulsivity models characterizing nonparaphilic hypersexual disorders do have some important differences both in theory and practice. The addiction model as applied to sexual behavior has birthed a proliferation of self-help groups based on the Alcoholics Anonymous 12-Step approach conceptually modified to identify sexual behavior as the "drug of choice" (Carnes, 1983, 1989). These support groups, now nationwide, were already providing presumably therapeutic benefits to more than 20,000 adults by 1990 (Dolan, 1990) the same year that a "Sexual Addiction Hotline" was averaging 300–500 calls/month inquiring for specialized sexual addiction treatment services (*Psychiatric Times,* 1990).

The sexual addiction model suggests that repetitive sexual risk-taking behavior accompanied by orgasmic release represents "a pathological relationship with a mood altering behavior" (Carnes, 1990) or a " form of self -medication for sleep, anxiety, pain and family and life problems" (Carnes, 1991, p. 23). Although the sexual "high" produces short-term relief/euphoria, subsequent dysphoric affects such as guilt, shame, remorse, and depression become negative reinforcement contingencies as the addiction cycle progresses (Goodman, 1997). In several important aspects, there is a phenomenological overlap between sex as "addiction" and the definition of impulsivity offered by the contemporary DSM-IV (American Psychiatric Association, 1994, p. 609).

Carnes's elaborated typology for such behaviors encompassed both paraphilic and nonparaphilic sexual behaviors, suggested a "rigid" family developmental pathology that predisposes to sexual addiction, established 12-Step groups and individual psychotherapy as a primary methods of therapy, and provided data derived from a 25-item assessment inventory, the Sexual Addiction Screening Test (Carnes, 1983, 1989, 1991). Carnes also provided sexual behavior data from 932 subjects and additional developmental-, behavioral-, and treatment-related data in a convenience sample survey of 289 male and female sex addicts in *Don't Call It Love: Recovery from Sexual Addiction* (Carnes, 1991). The conceptual framework of a behavioral addiction model as applied to sexual behavior has been thoughtfully elaborated by Irons and

Schneider (1997) and Goodman (1997), although their writings include little new empirical data.

Coleman suggested that both paraphilic and nonparaphilic compulsive sexual behaviors were mediated by anxiety reduction, not sexual desire per se, and these disorders were clinically related to obsessive–compulsive disorder (OCD) (Coleman, 1990, 1992). He reported a 10-question screening assessment tool but no accompanying empirical data regarding its utility (Coleman, 1992, 1995). While the behavioral addiction model for sexual behavior emphasized 12-Step program and individual or conjoint psychotherapy as a primary treatment modalities, the sexual compulsivity model incorporated a medical/psychotherapeutic approach to nonparaphilic hypersexual behaviors that included the prescriptive use of selective serotonin reuptake inhibitors, and medications with demonstrated efficacy for OCD, as well as individual and marital psychotherapies (Assalian & Ravart, 1993; Coleman, 1992, 1995; Travin, 1995). The use of 12-Step addiction group therapy is not advocated in Coleman's model of compulsive sexual behavior, just as the prescription of psychopharmacological agents for the mitigation of sexual addiction was not formally embraced by Carnes although these medications are commonly prescribed in sexual addiction treatment centers (Coleman, 1990; Schneider & Irons, 1997).

AN ALTERNATIVE NOSOLOGY FOR NONPARAPHILIC SEXUAL COMPULSIVITY/ADDICTION: PARAPHILIA-RELATED DISORDERS

Both aforementioned descriptive models for nonparaphilic hypersexual disorders as well as DSM-III, DSM-III-R and DSM-IV implicit characterization of paraphilias (and nonparaphilic hypersexuality disorders) as disorders of impulse control (American Psychiatric Association, 1980, 1987, 1994) are nosologically imprecise because these descriptive models try to conform the disinhibition of an endogenously derived appetitive behavior into a framework that "fits" into other available diagnostic categories that describe nonappetitive behaviors associated with impaired impulse control.

I have suggested that like paraphilias, nonparaphilic sexual disorders are first and foremost dysregulations or disinhibitions of human sexual arousal and desire (Kafka, 1991, 1997a, 1997b). The hallmark of this disinhibition that gives it the status of a clinical condition is the volitional impairment; the amount of time consumed by nonrelational sexual fantasies, urges, and activities and adverse personal and psychosocial consequences that accompany sexual disinhibition.

When Alfred Kinsey reported on the sexual behavior of U.S. males in 1948 (Kinsey et al., 1948b), he developed the construct of "total sexual outlet" (TSO) to describe sexual appetitive behavior in both males and females. He defined TSO as the total number of orgasms achieved in a given period (e.g., 1 week) regardless of which sexual behaviors contributed to TSO (Kinsey et al., 1948b). For example, if, over a measured year, a man masturbated on the average twice a week and had partnered sexual intercourse once a week, his average TSO is three times a week for that year. Kinsey reported that in comparison to females, males were more likely to sustain a higher TSO, in part because men were more likely to masturbate whether they were in a partnered relationship or not. Although there was no clear-cut defining "line" that separated men with a "high sex drive," Kinsey and associates noted that only 7.6 % of males in his study reported a consistent TSO/week of 7 or more for at least 5 years' duration after age 15. In that group, the predominant sexual behavior contributing to TSO was masturbation, regardless of marital status. In more recent surveys, it has been reported that only 3–5% of high school or college age males (n = 1,077) acknowledge at least daily masturbation for a year's duration (Atwood & Gagnon, 1987). In the most contemporary and technically sophisticated survey of American males, Laumann, Gagnon, Michael, and Michaels (1994) reported that only 3.1% of surveyed males (n = 1320) masturbated daily or more than once a day; that is, they had a TSO of ≥ 7 for at least 1 year from masturbation alone (S. Michaels, personal communication, October 18, 1995). In contrast, in a study of 100 outpatient males consecutively evaluated for the treatment of paraphilias or paraphilia-related disorders, 72% of these men reported prolonged periods of a "high sex drive" characterized as a TSO ≥ 7 for at least 6 consecutive months after age 15. Fifty-seven percent of that sample maintained a TSO ≥ 7 for at least 5 years. In that group of males, masturbation was the primary outlet for TSO over the lifetime in both paraphilic and nonparaphilic hypersexual groups, regardless of marital or relational status. In addition, the average amount of time per day consumed by both groups with problematic sexual fantasies, urges, and activities was 1 to 2 hours at the time of seeking treatment (mean age of 37 years) (Kafka, 1997a). These data have been basically replicated in a second group of 120 males with paraphilias (PAs) and nonparaphilic hypersexual behavior disorders (currently unpublished observations by this author). Thus, the great majority of males seeking treatment with me could be characterized as "hypersexual" in comparison with available normative data sets. In contrast to the sexual dysfunction hypoactive sexual desire disorder, a condition characterized by a paucity of sexual fantasies, urges, and activities, hypersexual disorders, both paraphilic and nonparaphilic subtypes, are defined by behavioral excesses of fantasies, urges, and overt sexual behaviors.

I have suggested using the term "paraphilia-related disorder" (PRD; Kafka, 1993, 1994a, 1995a; Kafka & Hennen, 1999) to characterize specific nonparaphilic hypersexual conditions. The advantage of this descriptive term is that it does not speculatively characterize only the form of the behavioral enactment of nonparaphilic hypersexuality (as an impulsivity, compulsivity, or addiction) but, rather, acknowledges that such behaviors, albeit not socially deviant, share many of the same clinical characteristics as the family of paraphilic disorders (see discussion later).

In accordance with DSM nosology, PRDs, like PAs (American Psychiatric Association, 1994), endure for at least 6 months, are manifested by intense and sexually arousing sexual fantasies, urges, and activities and produce personal distress or significant psychosocial impairment (Kafka, 1994a, 1995a; Kafka & Hennen, 1999). The major distinction between PAs and PRDs, then, is the designation of the former behaviors as socially deviant in comparison with the latter.

Table 17.1 presents an operational definition for PRDs (Kafka, 1994a, 1995a; Kafka & Prentky, 1992a) in conformity with DSM-IV sexual disorders criteria.

In support of this diagnostic designation, the distinction between "normal" and "deviant" sexual behavior has been subject to social, religious, and scientific traditions (Marmor, 1971). For example, both masturbation and homosexuality were considered socially deviant sexual behaviors within the past century in both Western Europe and the United States. These behaviors, especially homosexuality, are still considered socially deviant (i.e., paraphilic) in some non-Western cultures. On the other hand, homosexual pedophilia, a contemporary paraphilia, was a culturally permissible behavior at the height of ancient Greek culture (Greenberg, 1988). These aforementioned examples are offered to suggest that it may be possible for certain contemporary, culturally accepted sexual activities to become "paraphilic-like" (i.e., repetitive, intrusive, and accompanied by impairment in reciprocal affectionate sexual relationships) even though these behaviors are not currently considered markedly socially anomalous.

In males, and presumably in females, PRDs share many of the common clinical characteristics of paraphilic disorders. First, although the male:female prevalence ratio of PRDs, estimated at 5:1 (Black et al., 1997; Carnes & Delmonico, 1996; Schneider & Schneider, 1996) is not as high as the estimated ratio for paraphilias (20:1) (American Psychiatric Association, 1987, 1994), PRDs are nonetheless predominantly male disorders. Second, clinical populations of PAs and PRDs both report the onset of intensified or unconventional sexual arousal during adolescence (Abel, Mittelman, & Becker, 1985; Black, 1997; Kafka, 1997a). Third, several empirical studies have reported that per-

---

TABLE 17.1. Paraphilia-Related Disorders

A. Over a period of at least 6 months, recurrent, intense sexually arousing fantasies, sexual urges, or behaviors involving culturally normative aspects of sexual expression which increase in frequency or intensity so as to significantly interfere with the expression of the capacity for reciprocal, affectionate activity.

B. These fantasies, sexual urges or behaviors cause clinically significant distress or impairment in social, occupational, or other important areas of functioning.

C. These fantasies, urges, or activities do not occur exclusively during an episode of another primary Axis I psychiatric condition (e.g., bipolar disorder), psychoactive substance abuse (e.g., alcohol, cocaine, and amphetamine), or a general medical condition (e.g., brain injury, dementia, and prescription drug use).

sons presenting for clinical treatment for PAs (Abel, Becker, Cunningham-Rathner, Mittlebaum, & Rouleau, 1988; Buhrich & Beaumont, 1981; Freund, Sher, & Hickes, 1983; Rooth, 1973) or PRDs (Carnes, 1983, 1989, 1991) more commonly self-report the presence of multiple rather than a single hypersexual outlet over the course of a lifetime. These studies suggests that there is a general diathesis or vulnerability for PAs and/or PRDs. Fourth, although many studies of paraphilic sex offenders do not systematically assess PRDs, nevertheless PRDs may be common among paraphilic males (Anthony & Hollander, 1993; Black et al., 1997; Breitner, 1973; Gagné, 1981; Kafka & Hennen, 1999; Levine, Risen, & Althof, 1990; Prentky, Burgess, & Rokous, 1989; Travin, 1995). Fifth, men and women with PRDs as well as PAs describe their sexual behavior as obligatory, repetitive, and stereotyped at times. In addition, sexually arousing fantasies, urges and behaviors can be time-consuming; for example, those with PAs and PRDs usually spend several hours a day on such behaviors when symptomatic (Black et al., 1997; Carnes, 1983; Kafka, 1997a). Sixth, analogous to paraphilic arousal (American Psychiatric Association, 1994), PRDs may wax and wane, be either ego-syntonic or ego-dystonic, and are more likely to occur or intensify during periods of "stress" (Black et al., 1997). Seventh, as previously described, males with PAs as well as PRDs are equally likely to self-report periods of persistently heightened sexual behaviors leading to orgasm in comparison to population norms. Finally, as is the case for PA disorders as well, many persons with PRDs may withdraw from sexual encounters with a partner and prefer engaging in unconventional sexual activities, which become more sexually arousing than "vanilla sex." This may promote extramarital encounters, reliance on masturbation for sexual activity, and /or pair-bond dysfunction.

WHAT ARE THE COMMON CONTEMPORARY PARAPHILIA-RELATED DISORDERS AND HOW MIGHT THEY BE RELATED TO PARAPHILIAS?

The lack of a consensus nosology among investigators for describing specific PRDs is one of the primary factors that has hampered the scientific scrutiny of these behaviors. Table 17.2 lists the PRDs most commonly diagnosed in my clinical database of nearly 500 male or female outpatients seeking evaluation and treatment for either PAs, PRDs, or, most commonly, an admixture of PA/PRD disorders. Although other investigators use different terminology, these conditions are generally clinically consistent across investigators. In a representative sample of more than 200 consecutively evaluated males from that database (Kafka & Hennen, 1999), the most prevalent PRDs were compulsive masturbation (sample prevalence, 70%), protracted heterosexual and/or homosexual promiscuity (51%), pornography dependence (50%), telephone sex dependence (24%), and severe sexual desire incompatibility (12%). In that sample, 86% of the PA group reported at least one lifetime PRD, most commonly compulsive masturbation. The frequency distribution of these disorders in females is less thoroughly studied, although compulsive masturbation, protracted promiscuity (including prostitution), severe sexual desire incompatibility, and the PA sexual masochism have been reported. Carnes, Coleman, and others describe pathological "crushes," "obsessional fixations," or "love addictions" (Carnes, 1991; Coleman, 1992; Kasl, 1989; Schaef, 1989) as predominant female expressions of sexual compulsivity/addiction. There is currently, however, a substantial lack of empirical data on these conditions. For example, it is not evident that these are primarily genital/sexual behavior disorders or, perhaps, attachment disorders or obsessional symptoms not primarily mediated by sexual arousal or appetitive behavior. More data are required before these conditions can be definitively considered as sexual disorders if we maintain the DSM-III, DSM-III-R and DSM-IV nosology that limits sexual disorders to primary disturbances of genital/sexual behavior and desire.

TABLE 17.2. Paraphilia-Related Disorders: Nonparaphilic Hypersexuality

Paraphilia-related disorder	Objective for sexual arousal
Compulsive masturbation	Masturbation is a primary sexual outlet even during a stable intimate relationship, most commonly at least once per day
Protracted promiscuity (heterosexual subtype, homosexual subtype, bisexual subtype)	A "persistent pattern of sexual conquests involving a succession of people who exist only as things to be used" (American Psychiatric Association, 1980); can include one-night stands, use of prostitutes, massage parlors, "cruising," brief or protracted repetitive sex affairs, serial polygamy, escort services, etc.
Pornography dependence	A persistent, repetitive pattern of dependence on visual pornographic materials (e.g., magazines, videos, Internet pornography)
Telephone sex dependence	A persistent, repetitive dependence on telephone sex that is time-consuming and associated with significant cost
Cybersex	An ego-dystonic, time-consuming dependence on Internet and Internet-related sexually oriented chat-rooms, message boards, etc, primarily for sexual arousal and activity (Cooper 1999)
Severe sexual desire incompatibility	An ongoing romantic affiliation in which excessive sexual desire in one partner produces sexual demands on the other partner (who does not suffer from hypoactive sexual desire) that markedly interfere with the capacity to sustain that relationship
Paraphilia-related disorder not otherwise specified?	May include prostitution, sexual harassment (Lybarger, 1997; Shults, 1995); time-consuming and distracting sexual fantasizing experienced as ego-dystonic but not always accompanied by explicit genital/sexual behavior, pathological crushes or "love addiction," nonpsychotic erotomania

THE CLINICAL AND DIAGNOSTIC ASSESSMENT
OF PARAPHILIA-RELATED DISORDERS

General Principles

Several principles are of particular relevance in the evaluation and treatment of PRDs. First, paraphilic and PRD behaviors are secretive because they engender considerably more shame, guilt, and blame than do other sexual disorders. Indeed, these sexuality disorders are arguably the most shame/guilt-inducing contemporary psychiatric conditions. Sometimes it may take years before a person with these conditions acknowledges them to a professional or is "caught" engaging in an unconventional sexual behavior by a spouse or significant other. Thus, the first principle for the evaluation of PRDs (or PAs) is to ask specific clinically relevant questions and to inquire without a spouse or significant other present. In this regard, I always inform patients that when I ask them personal questions about sexual behavior, it is because sexual disorders are highly misunderstood by the lay public and are, in fact, readily treatable conditions. I suggest that the failure to address and diagnose these conditions during the early part of evaluation/treatment can lead to misdiagnosis, costly and unproductive psychotherapy, and an incomplete understanding of the causes of a person's suffering. This helps to establish a rationale for self-disclosure early in the process of evaluation or treatment of both PAs or PRDs.

Table 17.3 includes diagnostic screening questions that are relevant to elicit either PAs or PRDs. If a person answers yes to one or more of these questions, I would recommend asking specifically about the presence of PAs and PRDs.

TABLE 17.3. Screening Questions for the Diagnosis of Paraphilia-Related Disorders

1. Have you ever had persistent, repetitive trouble controlling your sexual behavior? (Carnes, 1989; Coleman, 1992; Kafka,1997a)

2. Has your sexual behavior ever caused you significant personal distress or caused significant personal consequences to you such as loss of a relationship, legal problems, job-related problems, or medical problems including a sexually transmitted disease or unwanted pregnancy? (Carnes, 1989; Coleman, 1992; Kafka, 1997a)

3. Have you ever had repetitive sexual activities that you felt needed to be kept secret or that you felt very ashamed of? (Carnes, 1989; Coleman, 1992)

4. Have you ever been troubled by feeling that you spend too much time engaging in sexual fantasy, masturbation or other sexual behavior? (Carnes, 1989; Coleman, 1992; Kafka, 1997a)

5. Have you ever felt that you have a high sex drive? For example, if we include both partnered sex and masturbation, have you ever been sexual seven or more times a week during at least a 6-month period since adolescence? When was that? Did it last longer than 6 months? (Kafka, 1997a)

Developmental Factors

Family psychopathology has been suggested to play a role in the developmental pathway to PRDs (Anderson & Coleman, 1990; Carnes, 1983, 1991;
Coleman, 1995). Reports of physical and sexual abuse in persons suffering
PRDs vary from 19% (n = 63 male PRDs; Kafka & Hennen, 1999) to approximately 80% (n = 289 male/female sex addicts including paraphiliacs; Carnes,
1991). These marked discrepancies are likely due to differences in both sample
ascertainment and composition. Careful, controlled studies of family milieu
and developmental variables are needed. It is certainly possible that specific
developmental trauma or conditions such as sexual abuse, preadolescent exposure to sexually explicit behavior, early exposure to pornography, covert or
overt sexualization by a parent or peer, preadolescent or early adolescent sexual
experience, or overly restrictive prohibitions regarding the normalcy of both
sexual and affectionate expression could be risk factors that have an impact on
a vulnerable child or adolescent. In addition, factors such as a lack of a current
intimate partner or a significant current intimacy dysfunction will exacerbate
the clinical course of a PRD.

The Importance of Assessing Axis I Comorbidity

In the few studies that systematically evaluated Axis I diagnoses in "sexually
compulsive" males and females (Black et al., 1997) or PRDs (Kafka & Prentky,
1994, 1998), one of the major findings is that most subjects with these disorders have multiple lifetime comorbid mood, anxiety, psychoactive substance
abuse, and/or other impulse disorder diagnoses. For example, Black reported,
in 36 male and female respondents to an advertisement for "compulsive sexual
behavior," a lifetime prevalence of any psychoactive substance abuse (64%,
primarily alcohol abuse), any anxiety disorder (50%, especially phobic disorders), any mood disorder (39%, major depression and dysthymia), and an
unspecified but significant total incidence of impulse control disorders, including compulsive buying. Kafka and Prentky (1994, 1998), in two outpatient
males samples, reported that the typical male with PRDs without PAs (combined sample n = 44) had multiple lifetime Axis I disorders including any mood
disorder (61–65%, especially dysthymic disorder), any psychoactive substance
abuse (39–47%, especially alcohol abuse), any anxiety disorder (43–46%, especially social phobia), attention-deficit/hyperactivity disorder (17%), and any
impulse control disorder (7–17%), especially the atypical impulse control disorder reckless driving. It is of clinical interest that in both these studies, males
with PRDS did not significantly differ from males with PAs in the lifetime
prevalence of mood, anxiety, psychoactive substance abuse, or impulse control
disorders. In the second study, however (Kafka & Prentky, 1998), the addition
of the retrospective assessment of attention-deficit/hyperactivity disorder did
statistically distinguish the paraphilic (prevalence of attention-deficit/hyperac-
tivity disorder 50%) from the PRD group. Although I could not find a system-

atic study of Axis I disorders in the sexual addiction literature, it is noteworthy that several authors have reported "depression" (Blanchard, 1990; Turner, 1990) and other impulse control disorders or behavioral addictions (Carnes, 1991; Carnes & Delmonico, 1996) in recovering sex addicts.

The clinical implications of these reports are significant for several reasons. First, these findings strongly suggest that any person, male or female, who seeks evaluation for a nonsexual psychiatric condition should be systematically queried (see Table 17.3) regarding their sexual behavior. Second, dysthymic disorder and attention-deficit/hyperactivity disorder in adults are not conditions that are routinely assessed by many clinicians. The appropriate assessment of these conditions requires retrospective as well as current symptom ascertainment. In addition, many persons with current psychoactive substance abuse may deny the severity of their use of these substances. Thus, the concurrent presence of these clinically significant and common comorbid psychiatric conditions may be undetected and then untreated. Third, comorbid psychiatric conditions may be risk factors that substantially contribute to the onset, severity, and social deviance of hypersexual behaviors, including PRDs (Kafka & Prentky, 1998). For example, depressive disorders predispose to impulsivity or risk taking as an action-oriented response to dysphoric affect, a response repertoire more prevalent in depressed males in comparison to females (Nolen-Hoeksema, 1990). Thrill-seeking behavior correlated with onset of depression, especially in men in comparison to women, and in younger men in comparison to older men (Fishbain, Fletcher, & Aldrich, 1987; Parker & Brown, 1979). These findings are consistent with the self-medication or sexual addiction/impulse disorder model of PRDs. In addition, depressive conditions can be associated with increased sexual appetitive behavior (Mathew, Largen, & Claghorn, 1979; Mathew & Weinman, 1982; Nofzinger et al., 1993). Alternatively, anxiety, depressive, impulsivity, and PRDs could share a common pathophysiology. For example, perturbations of brain serotonin are associated with depressive disorders (Meltzer, 1990; Risch & Nemeroff, 1992), anxiety disorders (van Praag, Kahn, & Asmes, 1987), and impulse control disorders (Coccaro, 1989) in humans as well as hypersexual behavior in male mammals (Ferguson et al., 1970; Sheard, 1969; Tagliamonte, Tagliamonte, Gessa, & Brodie, 1969). Attention-deficit/hyperactivity disorder is also associated with risk-taking behavior, antisocial impulsivity (Barkley, Guevreman, Anestopoulos, DuPaul, & Shelton, 1993; Mannuza, Klein, Bessler, Malloy, & LaPadula, 1993; Murphy & Barkley, 1996), and perhaps disinhibited sexual behavior in adults (Comings, 1994). Last, as discussed later in this chapter, the effective psychological and/or psychopharmacological treatment or comorbid Axis I disorders can substantially ameliorate both PRDs as well as PAs.

Comorbidity with Other Sexual Disorders

The comorbidity of PAs with PRDs has already been mentioned. In my study of 206 consecutively evaluated outpatient males with either PAs or PRDs, 86%

of the paraphilic sample (especially men with multiple PAs) had a least one lifetime PRD, most commonly compulsive masturbation or pornography dependence. In addition, both PA and PRD males and females commonly report reduced sexual arousal to "conventional" partnered sex, especially when the initial infatuation phase of an relationship has passed. In these circumstances, patients with PRDs or PAs may present to psychotherapists and sex therapists with apparent hypoactive sexual desire disorder, acquired and situational subtypes. In addition, diminished sexual arousal in a current relational context could present as female arousal disorder, male erectile disorder, and, perhaps, sexual aversion. Thus, it is imperative to take a full sexual history of patients who present with these sexual dysfunctions as a primary complaint to rule out the presence of paraphilic or nonparaphilic hypersexuality disorders.

I have examined several patients referred for current hypoactive sexual desire disorder, acquired subtype, and sexual aversion who had a prior history of hypersexual behaviors for many years preceding loss of desire. In this regard, it is intriguing that Nutter and Condron (1985) reported that males with hypoactive sexual desire disorder self-reported more frequent current masturbation (but less frequent sexual intercourse) than did a control group of normal males. It is possible, then, that like eating disorders and sleep disorders, the dysregulation of sexual desire and appetitive behavior can be clinically associated with marked variations of sexual desire and arousal over the life-span.

Case Example

Sally is a 45-year-old premenopausal married housewife who was referred by her therapist for an evaluation for "sexual anorexia." Despite describing a happy marriage with a caring supportive husband, over the past 4 years Sally had noticed an insidious waning of her interest in sexual relations with him. At the time of the evaluation, she described feeling a physical discomfort about being touched in any affectionate manner. She felt "frightened . . . uncomfortable . . . repulsed" by sexual contact. She had no sexual interest in other men as well. Her marked lack of interest and anxious discomfort regarding sexual activities distressed both her and her spouse. Prior to the onset of sexual dysfunction, Sally described a "normal" sexual appetite with her spouse during most of their marriage.

From adolescence until her late 20s, however, Sally had been "a sex addict out of control." She described multiple brief affairs and "one-night stands" with approximately 100 different males during those years. As a consequence of protracted promiscuity, she had one abortion and had contracted gonorrhea. She attributed her recovery from protracted promiscuity to individual intensive psychotherapy, a woman's psychotherapy group, and abstinence from alcohol and marijuana.

Axis I nonsexual disorders included:

Dysthymic disorder, early onset subtype
Attention-deficit/hyperactivity disorder, combined subtype
Psychoactive substance abuse, alcohol and marijuana, in remission

Axis I sexual disorders diagnoses included:

Sexual disorder not otherwise specified: the PRD protracted promiscuity,
    heterosexual subtype, in remission
Hypoactive sexual desire, generalized, acquired subtype
Sexual aversion disorder

Sally's current sexual dysfunctions were successfully treated with a combination of supportive psychotherapy, sensate focus exercises with her spouse, a selective serotonin reuptake inhibitor (SSRI), and a psychostimulant. The antidepressant diminished her anxiety and discomfort about sexual arousal and the addition of the psychostimulant helped her to be less distracted during sexual relations with her spouse. Then, with the addition of sensate focus exercises and supportive management over a 4-month period, Sally reported a return of sexual arousal and activity with her husband that has persisted during the ensuing 2 years.

The Pair-Bond

Although there is no compelling data that contemporary relationship dysfunction is a primary etiological factor for PRDs, the presence of a meaningful pair-bond can have profound effects on the clinical course and outcome of treatment. Like PAs (Marshall, 1989), PRDs have been described as intimacy dysfunctions by many clinicians (Carnes, 1991; Coleman, 1995; Schneider & Schneider, 1991, 1996). At least some significant others, characterized as "codependents," suffer from low self-esteem, depression, overdependent behavior, "enabling behaviors" (e.g., protecting the identified patient from the brunt of the consequences of his or her behavior), and comorbid impulse control disorders (Schneider & Schneider, 1991) prior to the disclosure or discovery of a PRD in their partner.

Certainly, the sudden personal disclosure or unexpected discovery of a nonparaphilic (or paraphilic) disorder in a partner during a stable pair-bonded relationship can have devastating consequences because mutual trust has been severely breached by a betrayal. It is clinically helpful, whenever possible, to include the significant other during the assessment process and/or early treatment phases to assess the impact of disclosure on the pair-bond and to attempt to contain the relationship crisis that invariably follows disclosure. It may be helpful to send the affected partner for individual or group therapy if conjoint treatment is not feasible. In particular, when protracted sexual promiscuity is an identified PRD, assessment for sexually transmitted diseases should be prescribed for the identified patient and, if indicated, the significant other, especially if identified problematic behaviors included "unprotected sex." There may be certain clinical situations, however, in which the identified patient is unwilling to include the significant other. For example, the latter person may still be unaware of the sexual disorder or may be too emotionally unstable to tolerate disclosure, or imminent disclosure would almost certainly be followed by divorce or its equivalent.

The assessment of the current pair-bond should include an assessment of the strength of the commitment of the couple, the impact of the current disclosure, and the possible defensive role of the PRDs in maintaining a power/control struggle in the context of the relationship as well as the impact of the PRD in producing or exacerbating an intimacy dysfunction.

The process and negotiation of the extent and timing of disclosure of nonparaphilic hypersexual behaviors in an intimate partnership should be subject to joint negotiation (Schneider & Schneider, 1996). Both Schneider (Schneider & Schneider, 1991) and Corley (Corley, Schneider, & Irons, 1998) reported that the honesty that follows full disclosure is most likely to lead to the best marital outcome and that the reestablishment of trust may take years. In their study, most partners (75%) identified in a survey of 82 health professional couples threatened to leave the relationship but did not do so, and only 8% divorced after disclosure (Corley et al., 1998). Disclosure was reported as not usually a one-time event but a process that balanced what the partner wanted to know with what the identified patient was willing to disclose. Whereas 60% of the hypersexual sample studied reported that full disclosure was most helpful, about a quarter of the sample reported that full disclosure was not helpful. Although the relapse risk, as defined by at least one recurrence, increased to around 50% over 5 years, neither the process of disclosure nor threats by the partner to leave were significantly associated with relapse in that study. Although these studies are encouraging, they are drawn from convenience samples of highly educated upper-middle-class professionals and may not be representative of the full spectrum of responses from couples of differing socioeconomic status.

The quality of current sexual intimacy and interpersonal communication of the pair-bond can profoundly influence treatment outcome as well. The lack of a current partner; the presence of sexual dysfunction in the partner, especially hypoactive sexual desire disorder or sexual aversion disorder; or an asexual partnership, are factors associated with the continued expression of PRDs, albeit, usually at a substantially lowered frequency after successful treatment.

Case Example

Tim was a 30-year-old married male salesman who was referred for evaluation while he was receiving concurrent individual psychotherapy and aversive conditioning (ammonia aversion). Tim was still having a problem with continued use of visual pornography, including videos and Internet pornography. This problem had significantly disrupted his marriage of 7 years when his wife discovered a large video collection in his closet. Since that discovery, his wife had become much less interested in sexual relations and their marital communication was characterized by episodic verbal arguments without adequate resolution. The lack of sexual relations appeared to be a justification for Tim to continue to use pornography, which continued to aggravate marital relations in a vicious cycle. Tim had masturbated one to two times a day nearly every day since age 14 and had enjoyed his intensified sexuality.

Tim came from a family that included a father who kept pornography around the house and a brother who also had used pornography extensively since adolescence. Although Tim reported no overt physical or sexual abuse in his family, he was distant from his father. Tim reported no experiences of physical or sexual abuse.

Tim's lifetime Axis I diagnoses included:

Axis I: Major depression, single episode, in remission
Sexual disorder not otherwise specified: the PRDs compulsive masturbation and pornography dependence

Despite treatment with a variety of antidepressants, marital therapy, and aversive conditioning, Tim continued a low level use of pornography. The combination of treatments given to Tim helped him to feel less guilty about his use of pornography so he continued to use pornography on occasion, especially when he felt disconnected from his wife or was alone by himself. Marital dysfunction persisted without resolution. Overall, his use of pornography was no longer considered "compulsive" or "out of control" by him and it was no longer associated with feeling anxious or depressed.

TREATMENT MODALITIES FOR PARAPHILIA-RELATED DISORDERS

Psychodynamic Psychotherapy

At present, there is no compelling empirically derived data to suggest that individual psychodynamic therapy as the primary or solitary treatment modality is effective for either PAs (Person, 1989) or PRDs. Psychodynamic psychotherapy, however, can help to synthesize the role of developmental antecedents; reduce current anxiety, depression, guilt, and shame; and improve social adjustment. As is commonly the case for the treatment of PAs, multimodal treatment approaches, using behavioral, psychodynamic, group, psychoeducational, and pharmacological treatments, are commonly prescribed and tailored to the specific needs of the patient or couple. The informed individual psychotherapist, regardless of theoretical persuasion, may function as the mental health professional to select and integrate different therapeutic interventions, akin to the model of "primary care therapist" advocated by Khantzian (1986) for the recovering substance abuser. In the sexual addiction literature, the most commonly prescribed combination of therapies associated with successful outcome are 12-Step group therapy (see later) and individual psychotherapy with a clinician familiar with PRDs (Carnes, 1991; Corley et al., 1998; Schneider & Schneider, 1991; Swisher, 1995). This outcome literature, however, is based on skewed samples collected by surveys of self-selected 12-Step attendees.

I would suggest that any psychological treatment(s) administered to a person with nonparaphilic hypersexuality disorders should contain attention to several of the following domains as listed in Table 17.4.

Case Example

Philip was a 32-year-old married college professor who was referred by his marital therapist. He had recently abruptly "confessed" to his wife that he had been unable to control repetitive promiscuous heterosexual behavior at the university where he was tenured. Almost all affairs were brief, primarily sexual in nature, and without the development of other aspects of intimacy. He had felt so much shame and guilt about his behavior that he felt compelled to acknowledge his problem and hope for forgiveness from her. Inasmuch as there had been both significant sexual problems and volatile arguments prior to this disclosure, the impact of this disclosure on his spouse led to outrage and then emotional withdrawal from him. Philip presented for treatment as acutely depressed with suicidal ideation but no plan.

Philip acknowledged that he had been promiscuous both before and during his marriage and also reported a problem with compulsive masturbation. He also reported regularly achieving orgasm 7 to 14 times a week, usually by at least daily masturbation, since early adolescence. He denied any paraphilic arousal or behavior. Prior to telling his wife about his nonparaphilic hypersexual behavior, he estimated that such behavior easily consumed at least 1 hour a day from sexual fantasies, urges, and activities. Despite the current crisis, he continued to masturbate "to control anxiety" during the early phase of evaluation and he struggled to control sexualizing fantasies of other women.

Philip reported no physical or sexual abuse during his childhood although he experienced both his parents as narcissistic, distant, and unfairly critical of him. On the other hand, both his older sister and brother were idealized by them and the three sibs were frequently unfairly compared and contrasted. Despite substantial academic prominence, Philip felt persistent low self-esteem and inner emptiness since childhood, which he attributed to this developmental family configuration.

Philip met lifetime Axis I diagnostic criteria for:
Adjustment disorder with mixed anxiety and depressed mood
Sexual disorder not otherwise specified: the PRDs, including protracted
promiscuity, heterosexual subtype, and compulsive masturbation

TABLE 17.4. Selected Pertinent Psychological or Behavioral Domains to Be Addressed during the Evaluation and Treatment of Paraphilia-Related Disorders

Gaining control over hypersexual symptomatology

- Psychoeducation about what we know and don't know about these conditions and their Axis I and developmental comorbidity
- Discussion of the range of available therapeutic strategies and selective referral to cognitive and behavior therapies, support groups, marital therapy, and/or pharmacotherapy
- Collaborative limit setting to establish a "bottom line" to hypersexual behavior toward which the patient can work
- Negotiating the use of phone blocks, discarding PRD paraphernalia such as pornography, canceling subscriptions for pornography, holding or discontinuing credit cards, and using an Internet censor with password controlled by partner, family member, or therapist
- Facilitating decisions about self-disclosure/trust in revealing the details of hypersexual activities to a significant other, involvement of partner if indicated
- Psychotherapeutic interventions that specifically target current sexual symptoms in preference to early developmental conflicts

Here-and-now issues

- Destigmatization: discussing the paradigm shift from "badness" to "illness" to diminish blame, shame, and guilt
- Clarification of thoughts, affects, behaviors, and common precipitating stressors that might precede hypersexual behaviors
- Developing alternative response strategies for managing dysphoric affects that precede both covert and overt problematic sexual behaviors
- Maintenance of interpersonal boundaries to reduce stressors: assertiveness training, social skills training, relaxation/meditation, recognition, and modulation of stressful affects
- If involved in a 12-Step group program: establishing a sponsor, monitoring attendance and a bottom line, encouraging and reviewing progress with the 12-Step methodology
- Consideration of 6–12 months of celibacy as a personal growth experience
- Psychoeducation regarding a "healthy" sexual relationship: how to develop and maintain intimacy, how to remain single but not be depressed/lonely, what is healthy sexuality
- Mourning a lifestyle of hypersexual behaviors: the role of suffering, pleasure, and escape from painful affects
- If referred for pharmacotherapy: monitor changes in sexual arousal and impulse control, assess concurrent depressive/anxious symptoms, collaboration with other treaters

Developmental factors (issues preferably managed after symptom stabilization)

- Coming to terms with family dysfunction, identification of the role of psychiatric illness in family members
- Events that may have shaped early sexual behaviors including physical/sexual abuse/neglect, premature sexualization in relationships
- The development and elaboration of the "false self" to compartmentalize non-paraphilic hypersexuality and manage painful affects
- Possible psychodynamic or behavioral contexts for the meaning and perpetuation of sexual symptom formation
- Assessing the developmental effects of Axis I comorbid diagnoses

Philip and his wife were referred to couple therapy. Eventually, his wife became increasingly detached from him and filed for divorce within 1 year after her husband had revealed his history of recurrent infidelity.

Philip was involved in crisis intervention and then individual psychotherapy with me. He did not want to attend any self-help groups because of a fear of public recognition, but he was interested in pharmacological therapy because he continued to masturbate compulsively during the early phase of treatment. He was stabilized on an SSRI titrated to a dose that helped to reduce persistent sexualizing of his female students and associated compulsive masturbation. He also reported feeling less low-grade chronic anxiety and depression after pharmacotherapy. This anxiety and depression had been part of his "personality" for so long that he had not recognized it in prior psychotherapies.

Early during the treatment, Philip needed help to identify affects associated with risk-taking promiscuous behavior. Psychological issues addressed in psychotherapy centered around Philip's difficulty in identifying both emotional stressors and pertinent affects and expressing his needs without expecting criticism and rejection from others. He had become a proficient interpersonal conflict avoider and defensively was drawn to be a caretaker for others but without establishing interpersonal boundaries that respected his needs. This was identified as a "false self" pattern of defensiveness. Anger was a prominent affect that he had either avoided or suppressed. This same pattern was evident in his marriage but proved more difficult to modify there because he felt so guilty and remorseful about his sexual behaviors and the effects of those behaviors on his spouse. Philip almost had a relapse of nonparaphilic hypersexuality when he began to spend more time with an attractive student. Fortunately, he was able to recognize the pattern of his grooming behavior before he enacted sexual behavior. This "slip" or "lapse" provided more psychotherapeutic material containing the aforementioned themes.

Unfortunately, Philip prematurely and abruptly terminated his psychotherapy when he began to establish a new romantic relationship soon after his divorce. Although he was no longer hypersexual, issues related to maintaining interpersonal boundaries, identifying dysphoric affects, and managing an intimate relationship were not adequately resolved prior to the termination of treatment.

Group Psychotherapies

Men with PRDs have been treated with therapist-led group psychotherapy. Quadland (1985) reported favorable outcome in 30 gay/bisexual men enrolled in a semistructured 20-week group therapy program with a goal of controlling protracted promiscuity. Earle and Crow (1989) and Turner (1990) report the use of outpatient group psychotherapy for "sexual addicts," but no outcome was included. A model for an outpatient group therapy for the husband and wife of bisexual men has been published as well (Wolf, 1987).

Since the formation of Alcoholics Anonymous and the articulation of the 12-Step recovery program, self-help groups based in 12-Step methodology have been formed for many forms of impulsive/addictive behaviors, including drugs, sex, food, gambling, kleptomania, and others. These programs can have a profound effect on the process of recovery, especially if the program is zealously adhered to. For example, 12-Step recovery programs commonly require daily attendance at a 12-Step meeting for the first 3 months of recovery from alcoholism (Galanter, Talbott, & Gallegos, 1990), and outcome from bulimia nervosa (Malenbaum, Herzog, & Eisenthal, 1988) was associated with five or more 12-Step meetings a week for at least 3 years.

There are now several different 12-Step programs for recovering "sex addicts," some of which are distinguished by geographic location or differing philosophies as to what constitutes " recovery," "abstinence," and "bottom line" in the context of normalizing sexual behaviors (Salmon, 1995). Naditch (Naditch & Barton,1990) and Carnes (1991) noted a positive long-term outcome associated with 12-Step sexual addiction programs in conjunction with individual psychotherapy in a retrospective survey of men and women recovering from both nonviolent paraphilias and PRDs.

The self-help fellowships for treatment of PRDs can offer several important advantages (Salmon, 1995). First, these groups have become increasingly prevalent in many parts of the country; thus they are generally readily accessible especially in metropolitan areas. Second, there is no financial burden associated with this form of treatment. Third, these groups are helpful in lessening the shame, secrecy, stigmatization, and blame that accompany nonparaphilic hypersexuality. Fourth, there can be a sense of "healing community," which includes fellowship, spiritual values, association with other persons in recovery, self-help support groups for the "co-addict," and the provision of a sponsor relationship that can include daily check-in phone calls and crisis management. Fifth, in many respects, the program offered by zealous adherence to the 12-Step recovery model for PRDs bears some resemblance to a cognitive–behavioral therapy-based relapse prevention program, a model of psychological treatment prevalent for the treatment of sex offender paraphiliacs (Carnes, 1991; Laws, 1989).

On the other hand, 12-Step programs such as Sex and Love Addicts Anonymous, Sexaholics Anonymous, and Sexually Compulsives Anonymous, require an intensive evening/weekend time commitment, a sponsor, the regional availability of appropriate groups, and, most important, a person who is willing to work in an intensive recovery program over a several-years period.

Case Example

William was a 40-year-old exclusively homosexual male who described himself as "living two lives." While he maintained a distinguished professional career as a physician, he reported that he was unable to stop himself from going to movie theaters where pornographic films were prominently displayed while men engaged in sexual activities, including unprotected anal sex. He reported no other lifetime paraphilic behavior or PRDs but acknowledged a sexual outlet of 8 to 10 orgasms a week during the past decade, including sex with more than 300 males. Prior to seeking treatment, William reported that he spent approximately 4 hours a day engaged in nonparaphilic hypersexual fantasies, urges, and activities. William had one partner whom he dated consistently for several years, although he continued to be promiscuous during that partnership as well.

William reported attending religious schools through his teenage years and had a long history of social anxiety and reticence. Although there was no apparent physical or sexual abuse, he had more emotional connection to his mother, a nurturing but depressed woman who died when he was in his early 20s. In fact, his relationship with his father was very conflicted because, especially after father lost his spouse, father developed a chronic depression and was consistently both demanding and hostile–rejecting of his son. In part because of his religious training, William harbored intense fears that he would be humiliated and rejected by both his father and his peers if he were to openly acknowledge his homosexuality. Thus, he had remained basically "in the closet" regarding his sexual orientation prior to seeking treatment.

William met lifetime Axis I diagnostic criteria for:

Major depression, recurrent, nonpsychotic
Dysthymic disorder, early onset subtype
Social phobia
Alcohol abuse, in remission
Sexual disorder, not otherwise specified: the PRD protracted
    promiscuity, homosexual subtype

William was relieved to be able to finally confide with me about his hidden life for the first time. After several appointments and the development of a therapeutic alliance, I suggested that one of his current problems was that he had not fully acknowledged his homosexuality to peers. I suggested strongly that he begin to attend local 12-Step support groups where he could maintain anonymity but meet other gay males in a nonsexual context. Eventually I was able to give him the phone number of another patient who had expressed an interest in helping hypersexual males to connect to the 12-Step sexual recovery program. Because William had faithfully attended Alcoholics Anonymous for many years prior to his current treatment, he accepted help to get to the first meeting and then began to attend regularly on his own. Over the first 2 years of treatment, William attended three to five meetings a week, "worked the program," obtained a sponsor, and eventually led workshops for gay males.

At the same time, he continued in weekly psychotherapy with me for 1 year and than met with me biweekly for at least another year. Themes relevant to his psychotherapy included identifying the relationship between his personal history of chronic low self-esteem, social reticence, and chronic depression. He began to feel less self-hate when he recognized that all his first-degree relatives suffered from depressive disorders. Inasmuch as his hypersexual behavior rapidly diminished once his sought treatment, we focused on precipitants to his sexual promiscuity, including a hostile–dependent relationship with his father, some work dissatisfaction, and his social isolation. William had to learn to let go of the expectation that his father would ever express love and acceptance of him and he was eventually able to do so. I advised against any dating or sexual activity and he was able to comply with this treatment suggestion as well during the first 2 years of treatment.

Recently, William has began to date age-appropriate peers without a serious relapse of protracted promiscuity.

Cognitive–Behavioral Therapies

Relapse prevention is an integrated cognitive–behavioral and group therapy treatment approach that was originally evolved from a theoretical understanding of and treatment for addictive disorders such as alcohol abuse, nicotine dependence, and compulsive overeating (Marlatt & Gordon, 1980). Several different techniques can (1) identify and modify cognitive distortions and beliefs that rationalize hypersexual behavior, (2) sensitize the patient to recognize and then anticipate high-risk situations, (3) identify specific behavioral/affective/cognitive precursors to relapse, and (4) help to implement extensive behavior rehearsal of new comprehensive problem-solving techniques as well as social and sexual skills training.

The relapse prevention model and accompanying cognitive–behavioral and social learning techniques are now becoming commonly employed in specialized sex offender treatment programs in the United States and Canada (Marques, Day, Nelson, & West, 1994). To my knowledge, there are no published data on this comprehensive approach to the treatment of PRDs. Given the aforementioned similarities between PAs and PRDs, systematic and controlled clinical trials of relapse prevention group and individual therapy would be a definite contribution to the treatment literature.

Case Example

Tom was a 39-year-old married businessman who was referred for pharmacological assessment because of persistent dependence on phone sex, video pornography, and compulsive masturbation despite relapse prevention sex offender group therapy and individual psychodynamic psychotherapy. Tom had been arrested for exhibitionism 2 years before as well and was on probation. In an attempt to control his urges to expose himself, he had made a behavioral contract with his wife that he would immediately tell her if he had urges to expose himself or if he had done so. He had agreed to take a lie detector test any time she requested it. He had a signed agreement with his wife that he would live separately from her if his exhibitionism relapsed. He reported that this behavioral contracting intervention was helpful in assisting him to refrain from exposing himself, but it had not affected his nonparaphilic hypersexuality disorders. He also still had recurrent urges to expose himself as well. He reported that his hypersexual fantasies, urges, and activities distracted him for 1 to 2 hours a day although he currently denied a high frequency of genital/sexual behavior. During adolescence and in his early 20s, Tom had masturbated at least once a day but never considered it a problem.

Despite pharmacological treatment with a prior psychiatrist using different SSRIs, Tom had not experienced periods of sustained remission of depression, nonparaphilic hypersexual behavior, and urges to expose himself to women that lasted more than 4 to 6 months. During relapse periods, he had used behavioral and relapse prevention techniques to maintain control over paraphilic urges, but he was unable to control PRDs.

Tom denied any overt physical or sexual abuse, although as a child he felt closer to his father than his mother. His mother was described as a chronically depressed woman who was socially withdrawn and interpersonally critical of him during his formative years. Three of his four adult siblings suffered from depression or alcoholism. As a child, Tom reported that he was considered a 'lazy" student despite high intelligence, had temper tantrums at home, and was easily bored by classroom assignments and homework.

A careful psychiatric assessment revealed the following Axis I lifetime diagnoses:

Dysthymic disorder, early onset subtype
Attention-deficit/hyperactivity disorder, inattentive subtype
Obsessive–compulsive disorder
Psychoactive substance abuse, alcohol, in remission
Exhibitionism, partial remission
Sexual disorder not otherwise specified: the PRDs phone sex dependence
    and pornography dependence

Tom continued in group therapy and maintained the behavioral contract with his wife. Tom was restarted on SSRIs that had worked best for his condition. Because the diagnosis of attention-deficit disorders had not previously been ascertained by other clinicians, after the optimal dose of antidepressant was achieved, a psychostimulant was added. At that point, Tom reported a marked decrease in "distracting" sexual fantasies, improved concentrating, and diminished depression and irritability. He spontaneously stopped his episodic use of phone sex and pornography. He has remained in remission of both paraphilic behaviors and PRDs for 1 year to date. When he had residual sexual urges, he was able to use relapse prevention techniques to better effect after pharmacological stabilization. For example, he could more readily identify stress-related affects and was able to effectively use relaxation exercises to relieve stress and self-managed increased sexual ideation. He responded to stressors by planning alternative activities, speaking with his wife, or calling group members.

Behavior Therapy Techniques

Behavior therapy techniques are used frequently in treatment centers specialized in the assessment and treatment of sexually aggressive paraphiliacs. These techniques appear to be applicable to both nonviolent PAs and PRDs as well. Aversive techniques, for example, can be applied to a wide range of human behaviors, including sexual behaviors, when accompanied by the voluntary consent and understanding of the patient. Maletzky (1991) provides the most current and practical compendium of current theory and technique for the use of behavior therapy conditioning techniques applied to sexually aggressive paraphiliacs and nonviolent paraphiliacs as well as selected cases examples of PRDs.

McConaghy (McConaghy & Armstrong, 1985) reported that imaginal desensitization was as effective as covert sensitization in reducing compulsive sexual behaviors in a group of 20 men with PAs and PRDs (promiscuity) at both 1-month and 1-year follow-up.

Olfactory aversion was designed to reduce unconventional sexual arousal with aversive smells, such as ammonia (Colson, 1972). The advantage of olfactory aversion is the immediacy of a powerful noxious odor that can be rapidly introduced during the practiced repetition of specific sexually arousing fantasies. Ammonia aversion uses encapsulated ammonia ampules that are portable and can be broken and inhaled both in conjunction with behavioral homework and in *in vivo* practice in situations that trigger sexual urges. As is the case for any conditioning therapy, aversion therapy requires persistent and repetitive practice to specific self-identified precursor situations that are sexually arousing.

Case Example

David was a successful 35-year-old divorced businessman who sought help for repeated visits to escort services and massages parlors as well as periods of extensive phone sex and pornography dependence. He decided to seek help when his second wife found his credit card receipts from escort services he used while he was on a business trip. When his wife threatened marital separation, David panicked and sought treatment.

David acknowledged a history of a high sex drive since age 15 and was usually sexual 7 to 10 times a week. He estimated that problematic sexual fantasies, urges, and activities consumed 1 to 2 hours a day prior to seeking treatment. He reported compulsive masturbation with pornography dependence beginning during adolescence. During his first marriage, his use of escort services (prostitutes) and pornography was eventually discovered by his wife and was a major factor that led to divorce. He had never acquired a venereal disease so he viewed his promiscuous behavior as "low risk." He had developed a penchant for phone sex services as well, at times costing him over $100 a week.

David described a caring mother who suffered from depressive nervous breakdowns and was hospitalized during his early childhood. Father was characterized as a distant loner who worked long hours and contributed little to childrearing. One older brother had a history of alcohol abuse. There was no history of physical or sexual abuse, early trauma, or premature sexualization in his family. Despite being a bright student, David described himself as chronically depressed and began to abuse drugs and alcohol during adolescence. He graduated from college and established a successful small business despite continued drug and alcohol use. He became abstinent of drugs and alcohol after his divorce.

David had received extensive individual psychotherapy with several prior competent mental health professionals and cursorily had attended Alcoholics Anonymous during his early sobriety. When he came for help now, he did not want extensive psychotherapy or 12-Step groups.

David met Axis I lifetime diagnoses for:

Dysthymic disorder, early-onset subtype
Major depression, nonpsychotic, recurrent
Social phobia, in remission
Psychoactive substance abuse, alcohol, marijuana, cocaine, in remission
Sexual disorder not otherwise specified: the PRDs including compulsive
    masturbation, dependence on pornography, phone sex dependence,
    protracted promiscuity, heterosexual subtype

Initially, I met with David and his wife to assess her perspective on his behavior. After she felt acknowledged in her distress and was provided with an explanation that these behaviors were associated with her spouse's depressive condition, she withdrew her threat to leave David and became more supportive. She had previously encouraged David to seek counseling for depressive behaviors, but he had resisted.

David met intermittently with me over a 2-year period, at first for pharmacological treatment. David did have a positive response to an SSRI in high doses. His interest in phone sex, pornography, and compulsive masturbation was markedly diminished. Later in the treatment, when he developed some tolerance to the therapeutic effect, I added a psychostimulant. David felt more resilient with this combination and his urges to visit prostitutes diminished again. He reported good communication and a healthy sexual interest with his wife. Despite this, David occasionally still visited prostitutes, especially when traveling without his wife. Over time, he began to feel anxious and guilty about his continued occasional use of escort services. He no longer felt depressed, however, and reported that his promiscuity, in contrast to his previous history, seemed unrelated to his mood state.

We discussed the possible use of behavior therapy techniques for his residual sexual symptom. By that time, he and his wife were trying to have children, so I instructed him daily to vividly imagine, and then write down in exquisite details, the consequences to his marriage if his hidden sexual life were again discovered by his wife. In addition, he was instructed to practice daily imagining becoming sexually aroused by a prostitute and then use ammonia smelling salt capsules when he felt any arousal. The combination of the smell aversion and vividly imagined aversive consequences (covert aversion) had a profound effect on David's residual promiscuity and he ceased calling escort services. He stated he realized how much he stood to lose as a result of "choosing" sexual pleasure when he was alone. I believe these techniques helped to markedly reduce the compartmentalization of affects that were previously associated with his continued ability to minimize potentially devastating consequences for episodic and discrete episodes of promiscuous behavior.

Psychopharmacology

As is the case for the previously mentioned psychological treatment modalities as well, published data supporting a pharmacological approach for the amelioration of nonparaphilic hypersexuality disorders are scant but encouraging. A persuasive rationale for the use of psychopharmacological agents for these conditions can be based on several lines of clinical evidence. First, there is the aforementioned association between specific Axis I disorders such as chronic mood and anxiety disorders and attention-deficit/hyperactivity disorder and the possible shared pathophysiology between these conditions and nonparaphilic hypersexuality disorders (see section on Axis I comorbidity). Second, there is the rationale that both increased sexual arousal and disinhibited sexual appetitive behaviors may be mitigated by pharmacological agents that enhance central (i.e., brain) serotonin (Kafka, 1997b). Third, there are case reports and case series supporting the use of SSRIs for PRDs even in the absence of significant depressive or obsessive–compulsive disorder comorbidity (Kafka, 1991, 1994b, 1995b; Kafka & Prentky, 1992b). Fourth, there is a developing scientific literature on the indications for and use of serotonergic (Greenberg & Bradford, 1997) and antiandrogenic medications (Prentky, 1997) for the paraphilic disorders. Fifth, at least in my clinical experience with the pharmacological treatment of over 100 males with PRDs who have failed a panoply of psychological treatments, the use of SSRIs, psychostimulants (Kafka & Hennen, 2000), and an orally administered antiandrogen—medroxyprogesterone, alone or in various combinations—can have profound effects in ameliorating nonparaphilic as well as paraphilic hypersexuality disorders in nonpsychotic males. We do not currently have sufficient outcome data to determine whether these agents need to be prescribed for the "short term" (e.g., 1 year) while other psychological therapies are ongoing or whether pharmacological therapy requires longer-term prescription for the successful management of nonparaphilic hypersexuality disorders.

In my clinical experience, psychopharmacological treatment for PRDs should not only be reserved for situations in which other therapeutic endeavors have either failed or been only partially successful. Instead, the careful diagnosis of chronic psychiatric disorders that have been empirically demonstrated to have a genetic/biological component should be followed by a discussion of all available treatment modalities, both psychological and biological. In addition, any patient with a persistently high weekly TSO or hypersexual disorders that could severely disrupt or endanger a stable pair-bond should be evaluated for pharmacotherapy as well as psychotherapy and group therapy.

CONCLUSION: THE DIAGNOSIS AND TREATMENT OF NONPARAPHILIC HYPERSEXUALITY DISORDERS

In contrast to other disturbances of human sexuality, the status of PRDs remains controversial because we lack sufficient empirical studies of these behaviors and their treatment outcome. As a result, these serious conditions are only cursorily addressed in most textbooks and academic courses teaching about human sexuality disorders. Despite the lack of empirical information regarding nonparaphilic hypersexuality disorders, there is certainly clinical lore that they are prevalent conditions that may remain "hidden" from spouses and family members. The current social policy of "don't ask, don't tell" regarding the status of homosexuals in the U.S. military also applies to our patients. It is imperative to form a trusting and collaborative therapeutic alliance and offer hope and effective treatment modalities to persons impaired by these conditions. As demonstrated by the case examples in this chapter, the successful treatment of these conditions commonly requires more than one type of mental health intervention. As clinicians, then, it behooves us to sustain collegial relationships with a collaborative network of resources and specialized clinicians who may share differing competencies but can work collaboratively.

The healing and recovery period that is necessary when PRDs disrupt the pair-bond should be measured in years, not months. Marriages and other intimate partnerships need time to heal from betrayal and to reestablish a trusting bond, even if problematic sexual behavior ceases early in treatment. In most cases, especially during the first few years of treatment, we need to speak about "effective treatment" or "control" rather than "cure" as an outcome measure. In kind, we can analogously think of the successful amelioration of other chronic medical conditions such as psychoactive substance abuse, obsessive–compulsive disorder, diabetes mellitus, atherosclerotic vascular disease, and hypertension in similar terms.

REFERENCES

Abel, G. G., Becker, J. V., Cunningham-Rathner, J., Mittelman, M., & Rouleau, J. L. (1988). Multiple paraphilic diagnoses among sex offenders. *Bulletin of the American Academy of Psychiatry and the Law, 16,* 153–168.

Abel, G. G., Mittleman, M., & Becker, J. V. (1985). Sex offenders: Results of assessment and recommendations for treatment. In H. H. Ben-Aron, S. Hucker, & C. D. Webster (Eds.), *Clinical criminology: Assessment and treatment of criminal behavior* (pp.191–205). Toronto: M&M Graphics.

Allen, C. (1969). *A textbook of psychosexual disorders.* London: Oxford University Press.

American Psychiatric Association. (1968). *Diagnostic and statistical manual of mental disorders* (2nd ed.). Washington DC: Author.

American Psychiatric Association. (1980). *Diagnostic and statistical manual of mental disorders* (3rd ed.). Washington D.C: Author.

American Psychiatric Association. (1987). *Diagnostic and statistical manual of mental disorders* (3rd ed., rev.). Washington, DC: Author.

American Psychiatric Association. (1994). *Diagnostic and statistical manual of mental disorders* (4th ed.). Washington DC: Author.

Anderson, N., & Coleman, E. (1990). Childhood abuse and family sexual attitudes in sexually compulsive males: A comparison of three clinical groups. *American Journal of Preventative Psychiatry and Neurology, 3,* 8–15.

Anthony, D. T. & Hollander, E. (1993). Sexual compulsions. In E. Hollander (Ed.), *Obsessive–compulsive-related disorders* (pp. 139–150). Washington, DC: American Psychiatric Press.

Assalian, P., & Ravart, M. (1993). Compulsive sexual behavior: Etiology, clinical manifestations and pharmacological treatment. *Canadian Journal of Human Sexuality, 2,* 221–226.

Atwood, J. D., & Gagnon, J. (1987). Masturbatory behavior in college youth. *Journal of Sex Education and Therapy, 13,* 35–42.

Barkley, R. A., Guevremont, D. C., Anastopoulos, A. D., DuPaul, G. J., & Shelton, T. L. (1993). Driving-related risks and outcomes of attention deficit hyperactivity disorder in adolescents and young adults. *Pediatrics, 92,* 212–218.

Black, D. W. (1998). Compulsive sexual behavior: A review. *Journal of Practical Psychiatry and Behavior, 4,* 217–229.

Black, D. W., Kehrberg, L. L. D., Flumerfelt, D. L., & Schlosser, S. S. (1997). Characteristics of 36 subjects reporting compulsive sexual behavior. *American Journal of Psychiatry, 154,* 243–249.

Blanchard, G. (1990). Differential diagnosis of sex offenders: Distinguishing characteristics of the sex addict? *American Journal of Preventative Psychiatry and Neurology, 2,* 45–47.

Breitner, I. E. (1973). Psychiatric problems of promiscuity. *Southern Medical Journal, 66,* 334–336.

Buhrich, N., & Beaumont, N. (1981). Comparison of transvestism in Australia and America. *Archives of Sexual Behavior, 10,* 269–279.

Carnes, P. (1983). *Out of the shadows: Understanding sexual addiction.* Minneapolis: CompCare.

Carnes, P. (1989). *Contrary to love: Helping the sexual addict.* Minneapolis: CompCare.

Carnes, P. (1990). Sexual addiction. In A. Horton, B. L. Johnston, & L. M. Roundy (Eds.), *The incest perpetrator: A family member no one wants to treat* (pp. 126–143). Newbury Park, CA: Sage.

Carnes, P. (1991). *Don't call it love: Recovery from sexual addiction.* New York: Bantam Books.

Carnes, P., & Delmonico, D. (1996). Childhood abuse and multiple addictions: Research findings in a sample of self-identified sexual addicts. *Sexual Addiction and Compulsivity, 3,* 258–268.

Coccaro, E. F. (1989). Central serotonin and impulsive aggression. *British Journal of Psychiatry, 155*(Suppl. 8), 52–62.

Coleman, E. (1986, July). Sexual compulsion vs. sexual addiction: The debate continues. *SIECUS Report,* pp. 7–11.

Coleman, E. (1987). Sexual compulsivity: Definition, etiology, and treatment considerations. *Journal of Chemical Dependency Treatment, 1,* 189–204.

Coleman, E. (1990). The obsessive–compulsive model for describing compulsive sexual behavior. *American Journal of Preventative Psychiatry and Neurology, 2,* 9–14.

Coleman, E. (1992). Is your patient suffering from compulsive sexual behavior? *Psychiatric Annals, 22,* 320–325.

Coleman, E. (1995). Treatment of compulsive sexual behavior. In R. C. Rosen & S. R. Leiblum (Eds.), *Case studies in sex therapy* (pp. 333–349). New York: Guilford Press.

Colson, C. E. (1972). Olfactory aversion for homosexual behavior. *Journal of Behavior Therapy and Experimental Psychiatry, 3,* 185–187.

Comings, D. (1994). Role of genetic factors in human sexual behavior based on studies of Tourette syndrome and ADHD probands and their relatives. *American Journal of Medical Genetics, 54,* 227–241.

Cooper, A., Putnam, D. E., & Planchon, L. A. (1999). Online sexual compulsivity: Getting tangled in the net. *Sexual Addiction and Compulsivity, 6,* 79–104

Corley, M. D., Schneider, J., & Irons, R. (1998). *Sexual misconduct in physicians: The importance of and process for disclosure to physician's spouse and family.* Paper presented at the International Conference on Physician Health, Victoria, British Columbia.

Dolan, B. (1990, June 4). Do people get hooked on sex? *Time Magazine,* p. 72.

Earle, R., & Crow, G. (1989). *Lonely all the time: Understanding and overcoming sexual addiction.* New York: Pocket Books.

Ellis, A., & Sagarin, E. (1965). *Nymphomania: A study of oversexed women.* London: Ortolan.

Ellis, H. (1905). *Studies in the psychology of sex* (Vols. 1, 2). New York: Random House.

Ferguson, J., Henriksen, S., Cohen, H., Mitchell, G., Barchas, J., & Dement, W. (1970). "Hypersexuality" and behavioral changes in cats caused by administration of p-chlorophenylalanine. *Science, 168,* 499–501.

Fishbain, D., Fletcher, J., & Aldrich, T. (1987). Russian roulette deaths and their relationship to risk taking behavior: a controlled study. *American Journal of Psychiatry, 144,* 563–567.

Freund, K., Sher, H., & Hucker, S. (1983). The courtship disorders. *Archives of Sexual Behavior,* 12: 369–379.

Gagné, P. (1981). Treatment of sex offenders with medroxyprogesterone acetate. *American Journal of Psychiatry, 138,* 644–646.

Galanter, M., Talbott, D., & Gallegos, K. (1990). Combined Alcoholics Anonymous and professional care for addicted physicians. *American Journal of Psychiatry, 147,* 64–68.

Goodman, A. (1997). Sexual addiction. In J. H. Lowensohn, P. Ruiz, R. B. Millman, & J. G. Langrod (Eds.), *Substance abuse: A comprehensive textbook* (3rd ed., pp. 340–354). Baltimore: Williams & Wilkins.

Greenberg, D. F. (1988). *The construction of homosexuality.* Chicago: University of Chicago Press.

Greenberg, D. M., & Bradford, J. M. W. (1997). Treatment of the paraphilic disorders: a review of the role of the selective serotonin reuptake inhibitors. *Sexual Abuse: Journal of Treatment and Research, 9,* 349–360.

Hare, E. H. (1962). Masturbatory insanity: The history of an idea. *Journal of Mental Science, 108,* 1–25.

Hirshfeld, M. (1948). Hypereroticism. *Sexual anomalies: The origins, nature and treatment of sexual disorders* (pp. 86–100). New York: Emerson Books.

Holmes, K. K., Mardh, P., Sparling, P. F., & Weisner, P. J. (1990). *Sexually transmitted diseases.* New York: McGraw-Hill

Irons, R. R., & Schneider, J. P. (1997). Addictive sexual disorders. In N. S. Miller (Ed.), *The principles and practice of addictions in psychiatry* (pp. 441–457). Philadephia: Saunders.

Kafka, M. P. (1991). Successful antidepressant treatment of nonparaphilic sexual addictions and paraphilias in men. *Journal of Clinical Psychiatry, 52,* 60–65.

Kafka, M. P. (1993). Update on paraphilia and paraphilia-related disorders. *Currents in Affective Disorders, 12,* 5–13.

Kafka, M. P. (1994a). Paraphilia-related disorders: Common, neglected, and misunderstood. *Harvard Review of Psychiatry, 2,* 39–40.

Kafka, M. P. (1994b). Sertraline pharmacotherapy for paraphilias and paraphilia-related disorders; an open trial. *Annals of Clinical Psychiatry, 6,* 189–195.

Kafka, M. P. (1995a). Sexual impulsivity. In E. Hollander & D. J. Stein (Eds.), *Impulsivity and aggression* (pp. 201–228). Chichester, UK: Wiley.

Kafka, M. P. (1995b). Current concepts in the drug treatment of paraphilias and paraphilia-related disorders. *C.N.S. Drugs, 3,* 9–21.

Kafka, M. P. (1997a). Hypersexual desire in males: An operational definition and clinical implications for men with paraphilias and paraphilia-related disorders. *Archives of Sexual Behavior, 26,* 505–526.

Kafka, M. P. (1997b). A monoamine hypothesis for the pathophysiology of paraphilic disorders. *Archives of Sexual Behavior, 26,* 337–352.

Kafka, M. P., & Hennen, J. (1999). The paraphilia-related disorders: An empirical investigation of nonparaphilic hypersexuality disorders in 206 outpatient males. *Journal of Sex and Marital Therapy, 25,* 305–320.

Kafka, M. P., & Hennen, J. (2000). Psychostimulant augmentation during treatment with selective serotonin reuptake inhibitors in males with paraphilias and paraphilia-related disorders: A case series. *Journal of Clinical Psychiatry.*

Kafka, M. P., & Prentky, R. (1992a). A comparative study of nonparaphilic sexual addictions and paraphilias in men. *Journal of Clinical Psychiatry, 53,* 345–350.

Kafka, M. P., & Prentky, R. (1992b). Fluoxetine treatment of nonparaphilic sexual addictions and paraphilias in men. *Journal of Clinical Psychiatry, 52,* 351–358.

Kafka, M. P., & Prentky, R. A. (1994). Preliminary observations of DSM III-R Axis I comorbidity in men with paraphilias and paraphilia-related disorders. *Journal of Clinical Psychiatry, 55,* 481–487.

Kafka, M. P., & Prentky, R. A. (1998). Attention deficit hyperactivity disorder in males with paraphilias and paraphilia-related disorders: A comorbidity study. *Journal of Clinical Psychiatry, 59,* 388–396.

Kasl, C. (1989). *Women, sex and addiction.* New York: Harper & Row.

Khantzian, E. J. (1986). A contemporary psychodynamic approach to drug abuse treatment. *American Journal of Drug and Alcohol Abuse, 12,* 213–222.

Kinsey, A. C., Pomeroy, W. B., & Martin, C. E. (1948a). *Sexual behavior in the human male.* Philadelphia: Saunders.

Kinsey, A. C., Pomeroy, W. B., & Martin, C. E. (1948b). Total sexual outlet. In A. C. Kinsey, W. B. Pomeroy, & C. E. Martin, *Sexual behavior in the human male* (pp.193–217). Philadelphia: Saunders.

Krafft-Ebbing, R. (1886). *Psychopathia sexualis* (1965, in English). New York: Putnam & Sons.

Laumann, E. O., Gagnon, J. H., Michael, R. T., & Michaels, S. (1994). *The social organization of sexuality: Sexual practices in the United States.* Chicago: University of Chicago Press.

Laws, D. R. (Ed.). (1989). *Relapse prevention with sex offenders.* New York: Guilford Press.

Levine, M. P., & Troiden, R. R. (1988). The myth of sexual compulsivity. *Journal of Sex Research, 25,* 347–363.

Levine, S. B., Risen, C. B., & Althof, S. E. (1990). Essay on the diagnosis and nature of paraphilia. *Journal of Sex and Marital Therapy, 16,* 89–102.

Lybarger, J. S. (1997). Sexual addiction: A hidden factor in sexual harassment. *Sexual Addiction and Compulsivity, 4,* 77–89.

Malenbaum, R., Herzog, D., & Eisenthal, S. (1988). Overeaters Anonymous: Impact on bulimia. *International Journal of Eating Disorders, 7,* 139–143.

Maletzky, B. M. (1991). *Treating the sexual offender.* Newbury Park, CA: Sage.

Mannuza, S., Klein, R. G., Bessler, A., Malloy, P., & LaPadula, M. (1993). Adult outcome of hyperactive boys: Educational achievement, occupational rank, and psychiatric status. *Archives of General Psychiatry, 50,* 565–576.

Marlatt, G. A., & Gordon, J. R. (1980). Determinants of relapse: implications for the maintenance of behavior change. In P. O. Davison & S. M. Davison (Eds.), *Behavioral medicine: Changing health lifestyles* (pp. 410–452). New York: Bruner Mazel.

Marmor, J. (1971). "Normal" and "deviant" sexual behavior. *Journal of the American Medical Association, 217,* 165–170.

Marques, J. K., Day, D. M., Nelson, C., & West, M. (1994). Effects of cognitive-behavioral treatment on sex offender recidivism: Preliminary results of a longitudinal study. *Criminal Justice and Behavior, 21,* 28–54.

Marshall, W. L. (1989). Intimacy, loneliness, and sexual offenders. *Behaviour Research and Therapy, 27,* 491–503.

Mathew, R. J., Largen, J. L., & Claghorn, J. L. (1979). Biological symptoms of depression. *Psychosomatic Medicine, 41,* 439–443.

Mathew, R. J. & Weinman, M. L. (1982). Sexual dysfunctions in depression. *Archives of Sexual Behavior, 11,* 323–328.

McConaghy, N., & Armstrong, M. S. (1985). Expectancy, covert sensitization and imaginal desensitization in compulsive sexuality. *Acta Psychiatrica Scandinavica, 72,* 176–187.

Meltzer, H. (1990). Role of serotonin in depression. In P. M. Whitaker & S. J. Peroutka (Eds.), *The neuropharmacology of serotonin* (pp. 486–500). New York: New York Academy of Sciences.

Murphy, K. & Barkley, R. A. (1996). Attention deficit hyperactivity disorder in adults: comorbidities and adaptive impairments. *Comprehensive Psychiatry, 37,* 393–401.

Naditch, M. P., & Barton, S. A. N. (1990). Outcome study of an inpatient sexual dependence program. *American Journal of Preventative Psychiatry and Neurology, 2,* 27–32

Nofzinger, E. A., Thase, M. E., Reynolds, C. F., Frank, E., Jennings, J. R., Garamoni, G. L., Fasiczka, A. L., & Kupfer, D. J. (1993). Sexual function in depressed men: Assessment by self-report, behavioral and nocturnal penile tumescence measures before and after treatment with cognitive therapy. *Archives of General Psychiatry, 50,* 24–30.

Nolen-Hoeksema, S. (1990). *Sex differences in depression.* Stanford, CA: Stanford University Press.

Nutter, D. E., & Condron, M. K. (1985). Sexual fantasy and activity patterns of males with inhibited sexual desire and males with erectile dysfunction versus normal controls. *Journal of Sex and Marital Therapy, 11,* 91–98.

Orford, J. (1978). Hypersexuality: Implications for a theory of dependence. *British Journal of Addiction, 73,* 299–310.

Orford, J. (1985). Excessive sexuality. In J. Orford (Ed.), *Excessive appetites: A psychological view of the addictions* (pp. 91–106). Chichester, UK: Wiley.

Parker, G., & Brown, L. (1979). Repetoire of responses to potential precipitants of depression. *Australia and New Zealand Journal of Psychiatry, 13,* 327–333.

Person, E. S. (1989). Paraphilias and gender identity disorders. In R. Michels (Ed.), *Psychiatry* (pp. 1–18). Philadelphia: Lippincott.

Prentky, R. A. (1997). Arousal reduction in sexual offenders: a review of antiandrogenic interventions. *Sexual Abuse: A Journal of Research and Treatment, 9,* 335–348.

Prentky, R. A., Burgess, A. W., & Rokous, F. (1989). The presumptive role of fantasy in serial sexual homicide. *American Journal of Psychiatry, 146,* 887–891.

Psychiatric Times. (1990). National "Sexual Addiction" hotline refers callers. p. 17.

Quadland, M. (1983). Overcoming sexual compulsivity. *NY Native,* pp. 7–20.

Quadland, M. C. (1985). Compulsive sexual behavior; definition of a problem and an approach to treatment. *Journal of Sex and Marital Therapy, 11,* 121–132.

Rinehart, N. J., & McCabe, M. P. (1997). Hypersexuality: Psychopathology or normal variant of sexuality. *Journal of Sex and Marital Therapy, 12,* 45–60.

Risch, S. C., & Nemeroff, C. B. (1992). Neurochemical alterations of serotonergic neuronal systems in depression. *Journal of Clinical Psychiatry, 53*(Suppl.), 3–7.

Rooth, G. (1973). Exhibitionism, sexual violence and paedophilia. *British Journal of Psychiatry, 122,* 705–710.

Salmon, R. F. (1995). Therapist's guide to 12-step meetings for sexual dependencies. *Sexual Compulsivity and Addiction, 2,* 193–213.

Schaef, A. W. (1989). *Escape from intimacy.* San Francisco: Harper & Row.

Schneider, J. P., & Irons, R. (1997). Treatment of gambling, eating and sex addictions. In N. S. Miller, M. S. Gold, & D. S. Smith (Eds.), *Manual of therapeutics for addictions* (pp. 225–234). Chichester, UK: Wiley.

Schneider, J. P., & Schneider, B. (1991). *Sex, lies and forgiveness: Couples speak out on the healing from sexual addiction.* Center City, MN: Hazelden Educational Materials.

Schneider, J., & Schneider, B. (1996). Couple recovery from sexual addiction/coaddiction: Results of a survey of 88 marriages. *Sexual Addiction and Compulsivity, 3,* 111–126.

Shaffer, H. (1994). Considering two models of excessive sexual behavior: Addiction and obsessive compulsive disorder. *Journal of Sexual Addiction and Compulsivity, 1,* 6–18.

Sheard, M. H. (1969). The effects of p-chlorophenylalanine on behavior in rats: Relation to brain serotonin and 5-hydroxyindole acetic acid. *Brain Research, 15,* 524–528.

Shults, C. (1995). Sexual harassment as sexual addiction. *Journal of Sexual Addiction and Compulsivity, 2,* 128–141.

Stoller, R. J. (1975). *Perversion: The erotic form of hatred.* New York: Pantheon Books.

Swisher, S. (1995). Therapeutic interventions recommended for treatment of sexual addiction/compulsivity. *Sexual Addiction and Compulsivity, 2,* 31–39.

Tagliamonte, A., Tagliamonte, P., Gessa, G. L., & Brodie, B. B. (1969). Compulsive sexual activity induced by p-chlorophenylalanine in normal and pinealectomized rats. *Science, 166,* 1433–1435.

Travin, S. (1995). Compulsive sexual behaviors. In S. Levine (Ed.), *Psychiatric clinics of North America: Clinical sexuality* (pp. 155–169). Philadelphia: Saunders.

Turner, M. (1990). Long-term outpatient group therapy as a modality for treating sexual addiction. *American Journal of Preventative Psychiatry and Neurology, 2,* 23–26.

van Praag, H. M., Kahn, R. S., & Asnis, G. M. (1987). Denosologization of biological psychiatry or the specificity of 5-HT disturbances in psychiatric disorders. *Journal of Affective Disorders, 13,* 1–8.

Wolf, T. J. (1987). Group psychotherapy for bisexual men and their wives. *Journal of Homosexuality, 14,* 191–199.

Index